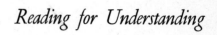

Reading for Understanding

Reading for Understanding

Fiction Drama Poetry

Caroline Shrodes SAN FRANCISCO STATE COLLEGE

Justine Van Gundy SAN FRANCISCO STATE COLLEGE

Joel Dorius SAN FRANCISCO STATE COLLEGE

The Macmillan Company, *New York*

First Printing

Library of Congress catalog card number: 68–11432

The Macmillan Company, New York

Collier-Macmillan Canada, Ltd., Toronto, Ontario

Printed in the United States of America

ACKNOWLEDGMENTS

Chatto & Windus, Ltd. Anton Chekhov, "The Bet" from Selected Tales of Tchekhov, Vol. 2 (1962). Also by courtesy of David Garnett.

Coward-McCann, Inc. Edward Albee, The Zoo Story by Edward Albee from The Zoo Story, The Sandbox and The Death of Bessie Smith, by Edward Albee; Copyright © 1960 by Edward Albee. Note: This play is the sole property of the author and is fully protected by copyright. It may not be acted by professionals or by amateurs without written consent. Public reading and or radio and television broadcasts are likewise forbidden. All inquiries concerning rights should be addressed to the author's agent, The William Morris Agency, 1750 Broadway, New York, N.Y. 10019.

J. M. Dent & Sons Ltd. Joseph Conrad, "The Secret Sharer" is published by courtesy of the publisher and the Trustees of the Joseph Conrad Estate. Dylan Thomas, "The Force That Through the Green Fuse Drives the Flower" and "A Refusal to Mourn the Death, by Fire, of a Child in London" are published by courtesy of the publisher and the Trustees for the Copyrights of the late Dylan Thomas.

Doubleday & Company, Inc. Vladimir Nabokov, "That in Aleppo Once . . . ," copyright 1943 by The Atlantic Monthly Company, from the book Nabokov's Dozen by Vladimir Nabokov. Reprinted by permission of Doubleday & Company, Inc. Theodore Force That Through the Green Fuse Drives the Flower" and "A Refusal to Mourn Knew a Woman," copyright 1954 by Theodore Roethke, "In a Dark Time," Copy-

vi

Preface

THIS ANTHOLOGY offers the beginning student of literature a selection of short stories, novellas, plays, and poems chosen for their literary excellence, range in structure and tone, and universality of theme. Although the editors wish to make the student aware of the organic growth of each art form by maintaining a balance between early writing and more recent developments, inevitably the historical range varies from one genre to another. The selections have been made with the hope of reaching both those students who already read literature with enjoyment and understanding and those who have yet to be awakened to its significance and its relevance to their own experience.

Variety in theme as well as form has been one principle of choice. College students today seem increasingly unresponsive to approaches either to life or to art that strike them as oversimplified. Accordingly, we have chosen relatively complex works whose themes have concerned men of many times and places—themes of identity and alienation, illusion and reality, love and hate, doubt and belief, art and life. A major consideration has been to help the student to perceive relationships between form and content. As he becomes familiar with the formal elements of each genre, he learns methods of analysis and interpretation that will help him in his independent reading and prepare him for advanced courses in literature.

Although the short story lacks the long history and has not undergone the mutations of the other art forms, the selections we include vary considerably in structure, theme, and tone. Preponderantly American, the fiction includes work by many of the great masters of the short story. We have avoided the simple narrative of action on the assumption that students are familiar with it and do not need the help of the instructor in interpretation. In most of the stories, which range from Hawthorne to Flannery O'Connor, external action is subordinate to movement in man's interior world.

Drama on the highest level is the rarest of the major literary genres. For this form we have selected plays, three of them in translation, from a few of the great periods of dramatic history. There are examples from Greek and Shakespearian tragedy, the social drama of Ibsen, the impressionism of Chekhov, the tragic irony of Yeats, and the contemporary theater of the absurd. Although the tragic vision of life pervades most of our selections, there is a considerable variety in dramatic form and tone. The richness and suggestiveness of these plays depend upon the skill and power of the playwright in employing dramatic conventions to convey a heightened image of life.

Poetry is the one form in which work of the highest order has been produced in English continually during the last four hundred years. Our selections offer the student an opportunity to trace the development of this form and to study it both extensively and intensively. The inclusion of forty-three poets provides a wide range of content, form, and style. At the same time, since a poet's craft, themes, and range are not fully reflected in isolated examples, we have usually included several poems from each writer so that they may illuminate each other. The poetry ranges from Wyatt in the mid-sixteenth century to Thom Gunn in the mid-twentieth. The principal criteria for the selection of poems have been literary quality, suitability for discussion, and representativeness.

We have not hesitated to omit many poems frequently anthologized and to include others which should be accessible to lively if untrained readers of poetry. Although there are many meditative poems, these are also notable for their lyric power. The range is wide—from the ironic tone of Donne and the satiric of Pope to the heroic of Yeats, from the pastoral and elegiac of Spenser and Milton to the urban and critical of Eliot and Auden, from the religious affirmation of Herbert or Hopkins to the pessimism of Roethke or Lowell.

Two features of the poetry section—the concentration upon one form, the sonnet, and one poet, Yeats—should make this volume especially useful. Since the sonnet is the shortest form in English for which brilliant examples can be found throughout most literary periods in the last four hundred years, it lends itself to intensive and comparative study. The group of nineteen poems by William Butler Yeats, moving from the relatively accessible to the admittedly difficult, provides an exceptional opportunity to study a major poet in depth. In addition we include Yeat's adaptation of *Oedipus Rex* and his play, *The Words Upon the Window-Pane*.

Since many of the students who use this volume will have little background in the reading of poetry, we have thought it advisable to gloss the poems, especially those before Wordsworth, more fully than is usually the practice in introductory texts. Brief biographical notes at the end of the book enable the student to identify each author in time and place and provide a convenient listing of a few of his major works.

Because of the single-column page design of this book, prose passages in

Antony and Cleopatra occupy fewer lines than in the O. J. Campbell text of the play, which, with its notes, is used here. As a result, in some of these passages the numbering of the lines does not always represent the actual number of lines in the passage, but where that is so, lines glossed in the footnotes have been numbered separately to avoid any difficulty in locating references.

A supplementary manual has been designed for the convenience of the instructor. The editorial commentaries provide a close reading of many of the selections and suggest the ways in which form shapes and expresses meaning. The questions which follow the commentaries are suggestive of the kinds of dialogue in which the instructor may wish to engage his students. We hope that these editorial materials may help students read with heightened understanding and enjoyment.

C. S.
J. VG.
J. D.

Contents

Fiction

Drama

Poetry

* Sonnets

* Sonnets

* Sonnets

* Sonnets

* Sonnets

Fiction

Nathaniel Hawthorne 1804–1864

The Birthmark

IN THE latter part of the last century there lived a man of science, an eminent proficient in every branch of natural philosophy, who not long before our story opens had made experience of a spiritual affinity more attractive than any chemical one. He had left his laboratory to the care of an assistant, cleared his fine countenance from the furnace smoke, washed the stain of acids from his fingers, and persuaded a beautiful woman to become his wife. In those days when the comparatively recent discovery of electricity and other kindred mysteries of Nature seemed to open paths into the region of miracle, it was not unusual for the love of science to rival the love of woman in its depth and absorbing energy. The higher intellect, the imagination, the spirit, and even the heart might all find their congenial aliment in pursuits which, as some of their ardent votaries believed, would ascend from one step of powerful intelligence to another, until the philosopher should lay his hand on the secret of creative force and perhaps make new worlds for himself. We know not whether Aylmer possessed this degree of faith in man's ultimate control over Nature. He had devoted himself, however, too unreservedly to scientific studies ever to be weaned from them by any second passion. His love for his young wife might prove the stronger of the two; but it could only be by inter-twining itself with his love of science, and uniting the strength of the latter to his own.

Such a union accordingly took place, and was attended with truly re-markable consequences and a deeply impressive moral. One day, very soon after their marriage, Aylmer sat gazing at his wife with a trouble in his countenance that grew stronger until he spoke.

"Georgiana," said he, "has it never occurred to you that the mark upon your cheek might be removed?"

"No, indeed," said she, smiling; but perceiving the seriousness of his manner, she blushed deeply. "To tell you the truth it has been so often called a charm that I was simple enough to imagine it might be so."

"Ah, upon another face perhaps it might," replied her husband; "but

3

never on yours. No, dearest Georgiana, you came so nearly perfect from the hand of Nature that this slightest possible defect, which we hesitate whether to term a defect or a beauty, shocks me, as being the visible mark of earthly imperfection."

"Shocks you, my husband!" cried Georgiana, deeply hurt; at first reddening with momentary anger, but then bursting into tears. "Then why did you take me from my mother's side? You cannot love what shocks you!"

To explain this conversation it must be mentioned that in the centre of Georgiana's left cheek there was a singular mark, deeply interwoven, as it were, with the texture and substance of her face. In the usual state of her complexion—a healthy though delicate bloom—the mark wore a tint of deeper crimson, which imperfectly defined its shape amid the surrounding rosiness. When she blushed it gradually became more indistinct, and finally vanished amid the triumphant rush of blood that bathed the whole cheek with its brilliant glow. But if any shifting motion caused her to turn pale there was the mark again, a crimson stain upon the snow, in what Aylmer sometimes deemed an almost fearful distinctness. Its shape bore not a little similarity to the human hand, though of the smallest pygmy size. Georgiana's lovers were wont to say that some fairy at her birth hour had laid her tiny hand upon the infant's cheek, and left this impress there in token of the magic endowments that were to give her such sway over all hearts. Many a desperate swain would have risked life for the privilege of pressing his lips to the mysterious hand. It must not be concealed, however, that the impression wrought by this fairy sign manual varied exceedingly, according to the difference of temperament in the beholders. Some fastidious persons—but they were exclusively of her own sex—affirmed that the bloody hand, as they chose to call it, quite destroyed the effect of Georgiana's beauty, and rendered her countenance even hideous. But it would be as reasonable to say that one of those small blue stains which sometimes occur in the purest statuary marble would convert the Eve of Powers to a monster. Masculine observers, if the birthmark did not heighten their admiration, contented themselves with wishing it away, that the world might possess one living specimen of ideal loveliness without the semblance of a flaw. After his marriage—for he thought little or nothing of the matter before—Aylmer discovered that this was the case with himself.

Had she been less beautiful—if Envy's self could have found aught else to sneer at—he might have felt his affection heightened by the prettiness of this mimic hand, now vaguely portrayed, now lost, now stealing forth again and glimmering to and fro with every pulse of emotion that throbbed within her heart; but seeing her otherwise so perfect, he found this one defect grow more and more intolerable with every moment of their united lives. It was the fatal flaw of humanity which Nature, in one shape or another, stamps ineffaceably on all her productions, either to imply that they are temporary and finite, or that their perfection must be wrought by toil and pain. The crimson hand expressed the ineludible gripe in which mortality clutches the highest and purest of earthly mould, degrading them into kindred with the lowest, and even with the very brutes, like whom their visible frames return to dust. In this manner, selecting it as the symbol of his wife's liability to sin, sorrow, decay, and death, Aylmer's sombre imagination was not long in rendering the birthmark a frightful object, causing him more trouble and horror than ever Georgiana's beauty, whether of soul or sense, had given him delight.

At all the seasons which should have been their happiest, he invariably and without intending it, nay, in spite of a purpose to the contrary, reverted to this one disastrous topic. Trifling as it at first appeared, it so connected itself with innumerable trains of thought and modes of feeling that it became the central point of all. With the morning twilight Aylmer opened his eyes upon his wife's face and recognized the symbol of imperfection; and when they sat together at the evening hearth his eyes wandered stealthily to her cheek, and beheld, flickering with the blaze of the wood fire, the spectral hand that wrote mortality where he would fain have worshipped. Georgiana soon learned to shudder at his gaze. It needed but a glance with the peculiar expression that his face often wore to change the roses of her cheek into a deathlike paleness, amid which the crimson hand was brought strongly out, like a bas-relief of ruby on the whitest marble.

Late one night when the lights were growing dim, so as hardly to betray the stain on the poor wife's cheek, she herself, for the first time, voluntarily took up the subject.

"Do you remember, my dear Aylmer," said she, with a feeble attempt at a smile, "have you any recollection of a dream last night about this odious hand?"

"None! none whatever!" replied Aylmer, starting; but then he added, in a dry, cold tone, affected for the sake of concealing the real depth of his emotion, "I might well dream of it; for before I fell asleep it had taken a pretty firm hold of my fancy."

"And you did dream of it?" continued Georgiana, hastily; for she dreaded lest a gush of tears should interrupt what she had to say. "A terrible dream! I wonder that you can forget it. Is it possible to forget this one expression?—'It is in her heart now; we must have it out!' Reflect, my husband; for by all means I would have you recall that dream."

The mind is in a sad state when Sleep, the all-involving, cannot confine her spectres within the dim region of her sway, but suffers them to break forth, affrighting this actual life with secrets that perchance belong to a deeper one. Aylmer now remembered his dream. He had fancied himself with his servant Aminadab, attempting an operation for the removal of the birthmark; but the deeper went the knife, the deeper sank the hand, until at length its tiny grasp appeared to have caught hold of Georgiana's heart;

whence, however, her husband was inexorably resolved to cut or wrench it away.

When the dream had shaped itself perfectly in his memory, Aylmer sat in his wife's presence with a guilty feeling. Truth often finds its way to the mind close muffled in robes of sleep, and then speaks with uncompromising directness of matters in regard to which we practise an unconscious self-deception during our waking moments. Until now he had not been aware of the tyrannizing influence acquired by one idea over his mind, and of the lengths which he might find in his heart to go for the sake of giving himself peace.

"Aylmer," resumed Georgiana, solemnly, "I know not what may be the cost to both of us to rid me of this fatal birthmark. Perhaps its removal may cause cureless deformity; or it may be the stain goes as deep as life itself. Again: do we know that there is a possibility, on any terms, of unclasping the firm gripe of this little hand which was laid upon me before I came into the world?"

"Dearest Georgiana, I have spent much thought upon the subject," hastily interrupted Aylmer. "I am convinced of the perfect practicability of its removal."

"If there be the remotest possibility of it," continued Georgiana, "let the attempt be made at whatever risk. Danger is nothing to me; for life, while this hateful mark makes me the object of your horror and disgust—life is a burden which I would fling down with joy. Either remove this dreadful hand, or take my wretched life! You have deep science. All the world bears witness of it. You have achieved great wonders. Cannot you remove this little, little mark, which I cover with the tips of two small fingers? Is this beyond your power, for the sake of your own peace, and to save your poor wife from madness?"

"Noblest, dearest, tenderest wife," cried Aylmer, rapturously, "doubt not my power. I have already given this matter the deepest thought—thought which might almost have enlightened me to create a being less perfect than yourself. Georgiana, you have led me deeper than ever into the heart of science. I feel myself fully competent to render this dear cheek as faultless as its fellow; and then, most beloved, what will be my triumph when I shall have corrected what Nature left imperfect in her fairest work! Even Pygmalion, when his sculptured woman assumed life, felt not greater ecstasy than mine will be."

"It is resolved, then," said Georgiana, faintly smiling. "And, Aylmer, spare me not, though you should find the birthmark take refuge in my heart at last."

Her husband tenderly kissed her cheek—her right cheek—not that which bore the impress of the crimson hand.

The next day Aylmer apprised his wife of a plan that he had formed whereby he might have opportunity for the intense thought and constant watchfulness which the proposed operation would require; while Georgiana, likewise, would enjoy the perfect repose essential to its success. They were to seclude themselves in the extensive apartments occupied by Aylmer as a laboratory, and where, during his toilsome youth, he had made discoveries in the elemental powers of Nature that had roused the admiration of all the learned societies in Europe. Seated calmly in this laboratory, the pale philosopher had investigated the secrets of the highest cloud region and of the profoundest mines; he had satisfied himself of the causes that kindled and kept alive the fires of the volcano; and had explained the mystery of fountains, and how it is that they gush forth, some so bright and pure, and others with such rich medicinal virtues, from the dark bosom of the earth. Here, too, at an earlier period, he had studied the wonders of the human frame, and attempted to fathom the very process by which Nature assimilates all her precious influences from earth and air, and from the spiritual world, to create and foster man, her masterpiece. The latter pursuit, however, Aylmer had long laid aside in unwilling recognition of the truth—against which all seekers sooner or later stumble—that our great creative Mother, while she amuses us with apparently working in the broadest sunshine, is yet severely careful to keep her own secrets, and, in spite of her pretended openness, shows us nothing but results. She permits us, indeed, to mar, but seldom to mend, and, like a jealous patentee, on no account to make. Now, however, Aylmer resumed these half-forgotten investigations; not, of course, with such hopes or wishes as first suggested them; but because they involved much physiological truth and lay in the path of his proposed scheme for the treatment of Georgiana.

As he led her over the threshold of the laboratory, Georgiana was cold and tremulous. Aylmer looked cheerfully into her face, with intent to reassure her, but was so startled with the intense glow of the birthmark upon the whiteness of her cheek that he could not restrain a strong convulsive shudder. His wife fainted.

"Aminadab! Aminadab!" shouted Aylmer, stamping violently on the floor.

Forthwith there issued from an inner apartment a man of low stature, but bulky frame, with shaggy hair hanging about his visage, which was grimed with the vapors of the furnace. This personage had been Aylmer's underworker during his whole scientific career, and was admirably fitted for that office by his great mechanical readiness, and the skill with which, while incapable of comprehending a single principle, he executed all the details of his master's experiments. With his vast strength, his shaggy hair, his smoky aspect, and the indescribable earthiness that incrusted him, he seemed to represent man's physical nature; while Aylmer's slender figure, and pale, intellectual face, were no less apt a type of the spiritual element.

"Throw open the door of the boudoir, Aminadab," said Aylmer, "and burn a pastil."

"Yes, master," answered Aminadab, looking intently at the lifeless form of Georgiana; and then he muttered to himself, "If she were my wife, I'd never part with that birthmark."

When Georgiana recovered consciousness she found herself breathing an atmosphere of penetrating fragrance, the gentle potency of which had recalled her from her deathlike faintness. The scene around her looked like enchantment. Aylmer had converted those smoky, dingy, sombre rooms, where he had spent his brightest years in recondite pursuits, into a series of beautiful apartments not unfit to be the secluded abode of a lovely woman. The walls were hung with gorgeous curtains, which imparted the combination of grandeur and grace that no other species of adornment can achieve; and as they fell from the ceiling to the floor, their rich and ponderous folds, concealing all angles and straight lines, appeared to shut in the scene from infinite space. For aught Georgiana knew, it might be a pavilion among the clouds. And Aylmer, excluding the sunshine, which would have interfered with his chemical processes, had supplied its place with perfumed lamps, emitting flames of various hue, but all uniting in a soft, impurpled radiance. He now knelt by his wife's side, watching her earnestly, but without alarm; for he was confident in his science, and felt that he could draw a magic circle round her within which no evil might intrude.

"Where am I? Ah, I remember," said Georgiana, faintly; and she placed her hand over her cheek to hide the terrible mark from her husband's eyes.

"Fear not, dearest!" exclaimed he. "Do not shrink from me! Believe me, Georgiana, I even rejoice in this single imperfection, since it will be such a rapture to remove it."

"Oh, spare me!" sadly replied his wife. "Pray do not look at it again. I never can forget that convulsive shudder."

In order to soothe Georgiana, and, as it were, to release her mind from the burden of actual things, Aylmer now put in practice some of the light and playful secrets which science had taught him among its profounder lore. Airy figures, absolutely bodiless ideas, and forms of unsubstantial beauty came and danced before her, imprinting their momentary footsteps on beams of light. Though she had some indistinct idea of the method of these optical phenomena, still the illusion was almost perfect enough to warrant the belief that her husband possessed sway over the spiritual world. Then again, when she felt a wish to look forth from her seclusion, immediately, as if her thoughts were answered, the procession of external existence flitted across a screen. The scenery and the figures of actual life were perfectly represented, but with that bewitching, yet indescribable difference which always makes a picture, an image, or a shadow so much more attractive than the original. When wearied of this, Aylmer bade her cast her eyes upon a vessel containing a quantity of earth. She did so, with little interest at first; but was soon startled to perceive the germ of a plant shooting upward from the soil. Then came the slender stalk; the leaves gradually unfolded themselves; and amid them was a perfect and lovely flower.

"It is magical!" cried Georgiana. "I dare not touch it."

"Nay, pluck it," answered Aylmer—"pluck it, and inhale its brief perfume while you may. The flower will wither in a few moments and leave nothing save its brown seed vessels; but thence may be perpetuated a race as ephemeral as itself."

But Georgiana had no sooner touched the flower than the whole plant suffered a blight, its leaves turning coal-black as if by the agency of fire.

"There was too powerful a stimulus," said Aylmer, thoughtfully.

To make up for this abortive experiment, he proposed to take her portrait by a scientific process of his own invention. It was to be effected by rays of light striking upon a polished plate of metal. Georgiana assented; but, on looking at the result, was affrighted to find the features of the portrait blurred and indefinable; while the minute figure of a hand appeared where the cheek should have been. Aylmer snatched the metallic plate and threw it into a jar of corrosive acid.

Soon, however, he forgot these mortifying failures. In the intervals of study and chemical experiment he came to her flushed and exhausted, but seemed invigorated by her presence, and spoke in glowing language of the resources of his art. He gave a history of the long dynasty of the alchemists, who spent so many ages in quest of the universal solvent by which the golden principle might be elicted from all things vile and base. Aylmer appeared to believe that, by the plainest scientific logic, it was altogether within the limits of possibility to discover this long-sought medium; "but," he added, "a philosopher who should go deep enough to acquire the power would attain too lofty a wisdom to stoop to the exercise of it." Not less singular were his opinions in regard to the elixir vitæ. He more than intimated that it was at his option to concoct a liquid that should prolong life for years, perhaps interminably; but that it would produce a discord in Nature which all the world, and chiefly the quaffer of the immortal nostrum, would find cause to curse.

"Aylmer, are you in earnest?" asked Georgiana, looking at him with amazement and fear. "It is terrible to possess such power, or even to dream of possessing it."

"Oh, do not tremble, my love," said her husband. "I would not wrong either you or myself by working such inharmonious effects upon our lives; but I would have you consider how trifling, in comparison, is the skill requisite to remove this little hand."

At the mention of the birthmark, Georgiana, as usual, shrank as if a redhot iron had touched her cheek.

Again Aylmer applied himself to his labors. She could hear his voice in the distant furnace room giving directions to Aminadab, whose harsh, uncouth, misshapen tones were audible in response, more like the grunt or growl of a brute than human speech. After hours of absence, Aylmer reappeared and proposed that she should now examine his cabinet of chemical products and natural treasures of the earth. Among the former he showed her a small vial, in which, he remarked, was contained a gentle yet most powerful fragrance, capable of impregnating all the breezes that blow across a kingdom. They were of inestimable value, the contents of that little vial; and, as he said so, he threw some of the perfume into the air and filled the room with piercing and invigorating delight.

"And what is this?" asked Georgiana, pointing to a small crystal globe containing a gold-colored liquid. "It is so beautiful to the eye that I could imagine it the elixir of life."

"In one sense it is," replied Aylmer; "or, rather, the elixir of immortality. It is the most precious poison that ever was concocted in this world. By its aid I could apportion the lifetime of any mortal at whom you might point your finger. The strength of the dose would determine whether he were to linger out years, or drop dead in the midst of a breath. No king on his guarded throne could keep his life if I, in my private station, should deem that the welfare of millions justified me in depriving him of it."

"Why do you keep such a terrific drug?" inquired Georgiana in horror.

"Do not mistrust me, dearest," said her husband, smiling; "its virtuous potency is yet greater than its harmful one. But see! here is a powerful cosmetic. With a few drops of this in a vase of water, freckles may be washed away as easily as the hands are cleansed. A stronger infusion would take the blood out of the cheek, and leave the rosiest beauty a pale ghost."

"Is it with this lotion that you intend to bathe my cheek?" asked Georgiana, anxiously.

"Oh, no," hastily replied her husband; "this is merely superficial. Your case demands a remedy that shall go deeper."

In his interviews with Georgiana, Aylmer generally made minute inquiries as to her sensations and whether the confinement of the rooms and the temperature of the atmosphere agreed with her. These questions had such a particular drift that Georgiana began to conjecture that she was already subjected to certain physical influences, either breathed in with the fragrant air or taken with her food. She fancied likewise, but it might be altogether fancy, that there was a stirring up of her system—a strange, indefinite sensation creeping through her veins, and tingling, half painfully, half pleasurably, at her heart. Still, whenever she dared to look into the mirror, there she beheld herself pale as a white rose and with the crimson birthmark stamped upon her cheek. Not even Aylmer now hated it so much as she.

To dispel the tedium of the hours which her husband found it necessary to devote to the processes of combination and analysis, Georgiana turned over the volumes of his scientific library. In many dark old tomes she met with chapters full of romance and poetry. They were the works of philosophers of the middle ages, such as Albertus Magnus, Cornelius Agrippa, Paracelsus, and the famous friar who created the prophetic Brazen Head. All these antique naturalists stood in advance of their centuries, yet were imbued with some of their credulity, and therefore were believed, and perhaps imagined themselves to have acquired from the investigation of Nature a power above Nature, and from physics a sway over the spiritual world. Hardly less curious and imaginative were the early volumes of the Transactions of the Royal Society, in which the members, knowing little of the limits of natural possibility, were continually recording wonders or proposing methods whereby wonders might be wrought.

But to Georgiana the most engrossing volume was a large folio from her husband's own hand, in which he had recorded every experiment of his scientific career, its original aim, the methods adopted for its development, and its final success or failure, with the circumstances to which either event was attributable. The book, in truth, was both the history and emblem of his ardent, ambitious, imaginative, yet practical and laborious life. He handled physical details as if there were nothing beyond them; yet spiritualized them all, and redeemed himself from materialism by his strong and eager aspiration towards the infinite. In his grasp the veriest clod of earth assumed a soul. Georgiana, as she read, reverenced Aylmer and loved him more profoundly than ever, but with a less entire dependence on his judgment than heretofore. Much as he had accomplished, she could not but observe that his most splendid successes were almost invariably failures, if compared with the ideal at which he aimed. His brightest diamonds were the merest pebbles, and felt to be so by himself, in comparison with the inestimable gems which lay hidden beyond his reach. The volume, rich with achievements that had won renown for its author, was yet as melancholy a record as ever mortal hand had penned. It was the sad confession and continual exemplification of the shortcomings of the composite man, the spirit burdened with clay and working in matter, and of the despair that assails the higher nature at finding itself so miserably thwarted by the earthly part. Perhaps every man of genius in whatever sphere might recognize the image of his own experience in Aylmer's journal.

So deeply did these reflections affect Georgiana that she laid her face upon the open volume and burst into tears. In this situation she was found by her husband.

"It is dangerous to read in a sorcerer's books," said he with a smile, though his countenance was uneasy and displeased. "Georgiana, there are pages in that volume which I can scarcely glance over and keep my senses. Take heed lest it prove as detrimental to you."

"It has made me worship you more than ever," said she.

"Ah, wait for this one success," rejoined he, "then worship me if you will. I shall deem myself hardly unworthy of it. But come, I have sought you for the luxury of your voice. Sing to me, dearest."

So she poured out the liquid music of her voice to quench the thirst of his spirit. He then took his leave with a boyish exuberance of gayety, assuring her that her seclusion would endure but a little longer, and that the result was already certain. Scarcely had he departed when Georgiana felt irresistibly impelled to follow him. She had forgotten to inform Aylmer of a symptom which for two or three hours past had begun to excite her attention. It was a sensation in the fatal birthmark, not painful, but which induced a restlessness throughout her system. Hastening after her husband, she intruded for the first time into the laboratory.

The first thing that struck her eye was the furnace, that hot and feverish worker, with the intense glow of its fire, which by the quantities of soot clustered above it seemed to have been burning for ages. There was a distilling apparatus in full operation. Around the room were retorts, tubes, cylinders, crucibles, and other apparatus of chemical research. An electrical machine stood ready for immediate use. The atmosphere felt oppressively close, and was tainted with gaseous odors which had been tormented forth by the processes of science. The severe and homely simplicity of the apartment, with its naked walls and brick pavement, looked strange, accustomed as Georgiana had become to the fantastic elegance of her boudoir. But what chiefly, indeed almost solely, drew her attention, was the aspect of Aylmer himself.

He was pale as death, anxious and absorbed, and hung over the furnace as if it depended upon his utmost watchfulness whether the liquid which it was distilling should be the draught of immortal happiness or misery. How different from the sanguine and joyous mien that he had assumed for Georgiana's encouragement!

"Carefully now, Aminadab; carefully, thou human machine; carefully, thou man of clay!" muttered Aylmer, more to himself than his assistant. "Now, if there be a thought too much or too little, it is all over."

"Ho! ho!" mumbled Aminadab. "Look, master! look!"

Aylmer raised his eyes hastily, and at first reddened, then grew paler than ever, on beholding Geogiana. He rushed towards her and seized her arm with a gripe that left the print of his fingers upon it.

"Why do you come hither? Have you no trust in your husband?" cried he, impetuously. "Would you throw the blight of that fatal birthmark over my labors? It is not well done. Go, prying woman, go!"

"Nay, Aylmer," said Georgiana with the firmness of which she possessed no stinted endowment, "it is not you that have a right to complain. You mistrust your wife; you have concealed the anxiety with which you watch the development of this experiment. Think not so unworthily of me, my husband. Tell me all the risk we run, and fear not that I shall shrink; for my share in it is far less than your own."

"No, no, Georgiana!" said Aylmer, impatiently; "it must not be."

"I submit," replied she calmly. "And, Aylmer, I shall quaff whatever draught you bring me; but it will be on the same principle that would induce me to take a dose of poison if offered by your hand."

"My noble wife," said Aylmer, deeply moved, "I knew not the height and depth of your nature until now. Nothing shall be concealed. Know, then, that this crimson hand, superficial as it seems, has clutched its grasp into your being with a strength of which I had no previous conception. I have already administered agents powerful enough to do aught except to change your entire physical system. Only one thing remains to be tried. If that fail us we are ruined."

"Why did you hesitate to tell me this?" asked she.

"Because, Georgiana," said Aylmer, in a low voice, "there is danger."

"Danger? There is but one danger—that this horrible stigma shall be left upon my cheek!" cried Georgiana. "Remove it, remove it, whatever be the cost, or we shall both go mad!"

"Heaven knows your words are too true," said Aylmer, sadly. "And now, dearest, return to your boudoir. In a little while all will be tested."

He conducted her back and took leave of her with a solemn tenderness which spoke far more than his words how much was now at stake. After his departure Georgiana became rapt in musings. She considered the character of Aylmer, and did it completer justice than at any previous moment. Her heart exulted, while it trembled, at his honorable love—so pure and lofty that it would accept nothing less than perfection nor miserably make itself contented with an earthlier nature than he had dreamed of. She felt how much more precious was such a sentiment than the meaner kind which would have borne with the imperfection for her sake, and have been guilty of treason to holy love by degrading its perfect idea to the level of the actual; and with her whole spirit she prayed that, for a single moment, she might satisfy his highest and deepest conception. Longer than one moment she well knew it could not be; for his spirit was ever on the march, ever ascending, and each instant required something that was beyond the scope of the instant before.

The sound of her husband's footsteps aroused her. He bore a crystal goblet containing a liquor colorless as water, but bright enough to be the draught of immortality. Aylmer was pale; but it seemed rather the consequence of a highly wrought state of mind and tension of spirit than of fear or doubt.

"The concoction of the draught has been perfect," said he, in answer to Georgiana's look. "Unless all my science have deceived me, it cannot fail."

"Save on your account, my dearest Aylmer," observed his wife, "'I might wish to put off this birthmark of mortality by relinquishing mortality itself in preference to any other mode. Life is but a sad possession to those who have attained precisely the degree of moral advancement at which I stand. Were I weaker and blinder it might be happiness. Were I stronger, it might be endured hopefully. But, being what I find myself, methinks I am of all mortals the most fit to die."

"You are fit for heaven without tasting death!" replied her husband. "But why do we speak of dying? The draught cannot fail. Behold its effect upon this plant."

On the window seat there stood a geranium diseased with yellow blotches, which had overspread all its leaves. Aylmer poured a small quantity of the liquid upon the soil in which it grew. In a little time, when the roots of the plant had taken up the moisture, the unsightly blotches began to be extinguished in a living verdure.

"There needed no proof," said Georgiana, quietly. "Give me the goblet. I joyfully stake all upon your word."

"Drink, then, thou lofty creature!" exclaimed Aylmer, with fervid admiration. "There is no taint of imperfection on thy spirit. Thy sensible frame, too, shall soon be all perfect."

She quaffed the liquid and returned the goblet to his hand.

"It is grateful," said she with a placid smile. "Methinks it is like water from a heavenly fountain; for it contains I know not what of unobtrusive fragrance and deliciousness. It allays a feverish thirst that had parched me for many days. Now, dearest, let me sleep. My earthly senses are closing over my spirit like the leaves around the heart of a rose at sunset."

She spoke the last words with a gentle reluctance, as if it required almost more energy than she could command to pronounce the faint and lingering syllables. Scarcely had they loitered through her lips ere she was lost in slumber. Aylmer sat by her side, watching her aspect with the emotions proper to a man the whole value of whose existence was involved in the process now to be tested. Mingled with this mood, however, was the philosophic investigation characteristic of the man of science. Not the minutest symptom escaped him. A heightened flush of the cheek, a slight irregularity of breath, a quiver of the eyelid, a hardly perceptible tremor through the frame—such were the details which, as the moments passed, he wrote down in his folio volume. Intense thought had set its stamp upon every previous page of that volume, but the thoughts of years were all concentrated upon the last.

While thus employed, he failed not to gaze often at the fatal hand, and not without a shudder. Yet once, by a strange and unaccountable impulse, he pressed it with his lips. His spirit recoiled, however, in the very act; and Georgiana, out of the midst of her deep sleep, moved uneasily and mur mured as if in remonstrance. Again Aylmer resumed his watch. Nor was it without avail. The crimson hand, which at first had been strongly visible upon the marble paleness of Georgiana's cheek, now grew more faintly outlined. She remained not less pale than ever; but the birthmark, with every breath that came and went, lost somewhat of its former distinctness. Its presence had been awful; its departure was more awful still. Watch the stain of the rainbow fading out the sky, and you will know how that mysterious symbol passed away.

"By heaven! it is well-nigh gone!" said Aylmer to himself, in almost irrepressible ecstasy. "I can scarcely trace it now. Success! success! And now it is like the faintest rose color. The lightest flush of blood across her cheek would overcome it. But she is so pale!"

He drew aside the window curtain and suffered the light of natural day to fall into the room and rest upon her cheek. At the same time he heard a gross, hoarse chuckle, which he had long known as his servant Aminadab's expression of delight.

"Ah, clod; ah, earthly mass!" cried Aylmer, laughing in a sort of frenzy, "you have served me well! Matter and spirit—earth and heaven—have both done their part in this! Laugh, thing of the senses! You have earned the right to laugh."

These exclamations broke Georgiana's sleep. She slowly unclosed her eyes and gazed into the mirror which her husband had arranged for that purpose. A faint smile flitted over her lips when she recognized how barely perceptible was now that crimson hand which had once blazed forth with such disastrous brilliancy as to scare away all their happiness. But then her eyes sought Aylmer's face with a trouble and anxiety that he could by no means account for.

"My poor Aylmer!" murmured she.

"Poor? Nay, richest, happiest, most favored!" exclaimed he. "My peerless bride, it is successful! You are perfect!"

"My poor Aylmer," she repeated, with a more than human tenderness, "you have aimed loftily; you have done nobly. Do not repent that with so high and pure a feeling, you have rejected the best the earth could offer. Aylmer, dearest Aylmer, I am dying!"

Alas! it was too true! The fatal hand had grappled with the mystery of life, and was the bond by which an angelic spirit kept itself in union with a mortal frame. As the last crimson tint of the birthmark—that sole token of human imperfection—faded from her cheek, the parting breath of the now perfect woman passed into the atmosphere, and her soul, lingering a moment near her husband, took its heavenward flight. Then a hoarse, chuckling laugh was heard again! Thus ever does the gross fatality of earth exult in its invariable triumph over the immortal essence which, in this dim sphere of half development, demands the completeness of a higher state. Yet, had Alymer reached a profounder wisdom, he need not thus have flung away the happiness which would have woven his mortal life of the selfsame texture with the celestial. The momentary circumstance was too strong for him; he failed to look beyond the shadowy scope of time, and, living once for all in eternity, to find the perfect future in the present.

Henry James 1843–1916

The Beast in the Jungle

I

W H A T determined the speech that startled him in the course of their encounter scarcely matters, being probably but some words spoken by himself quite without intention—spoken as they lingered and slowly moved together after their renewal of acquaintance. He had been conveyed by friends, an hour or two before, to the house at which she was staying; the party of visitors at the other house, of whom he was one, and thanks to whom it was his theory, as always, that he was lost in the crowd, had been invited over to luncheon. There had been after luncheon much dispersal, all in the interest of the original motive, a view of Weatherend itself and the fine things, intrinsic features, pictures, heirlooms, treasures of all the arts, that made the place almost famous; and the great rooms were so numerous that guests could wander at their will, hang back from the principal group, and, in cases where they took such matters with the least seriousness, give themselves up to mysterious appreciations and measurements. There were persons to be observed, singly or in couples, bending toward objects in out-of-the-way corners with their hands on their knees and their heads nodding quite as with the emphasis of an excited sense of smell. When they were two they either mingled their sounds of ecstasy or melted into silences of even deeper import, so that there were aspects of the occasion that gave it for Marcher much the air of the "look round," previous to a sale highly advertised, that excites or quenches, as may be, the dream of acquisition. The dream of acquisition at Weatherend would have had to be wild indeed, and John Marcher found himself, among such suggestions, disconcerted almost equally by the presence of those who knew too much and by that of those who knew nothing. The great rooms caused so much poetry and history to press upon him that he needed to wander apart to feel in a proper relation with them, though his doing so was not, as happened, like the gloating of some of his companions, to be compared to the movements of a dog sniffing a cupboard. It had an issue promptly enough in a direction that was not to have been calculated.

It led, in short, in the course of the October afternoon, to his closer meeting with May Bartram, whose face, a reminder, yet not quite a remembrance, as they sat, much separated, at a very long table, had begun merely by troubling him rather pleasantly. It affected him as the sequel of something of which he had lost the beginning. He knew it, and for the time quite welcomed it, as a continuation, but didn't know what it continued, which was an interest, or an amusement, the greater as he was also somehow aware—yet without a direct sign from her—that the young woman herself had not lost the thread. She had not lost it, but she wouldn't give it back to him, he saw, without some putting forth of his hand for it; and he not only saw that, but saw several things more, things odd enough in the light of the fact that at the moment some accident of grouping brought them face to face he was still merely fumbling with the idea that any contact between them in the past would have had no importance. If it had had no importance he scarcely knew why his actual impression of her should so seem to have so much; the answer to which, however, was that in such a life as they all appeared to be leading for the moment one could but take things as they came. He was satisfied, without in the least being able to say why, that this young lady might roughly have ranked in the house as a poor relation; satisfied also that she was not there on a brief visit, but was more or less a part of the establishment —almost a working, a remunerated part. Didn't she enjoy at periods a protection that she paid for by helping, among other services, to show the place and explain it, deal with the tiresome people, answer questions about the dates of the buildings, the styles of the furniture, the authorship of the pictures, the favourite haunts of the ghost? It wasn't that she looked as if you could have given her shillings—it was impossible to look less so. Yet when she finally drifted toward him, distinctly handsome, though ever so much older—older than when he had seen her before—it might have been as an effect of her guessing that he had, within the couple of hours, devoted more imagination to her than to all the others put together, and had thereby penetrated to a kind of truth that the others were too stupid for. She *was* there on harder terms than anyone; she was there as a consequence of things suffered, in one way and another, in the interval of years; and she remembered him very much as she was remembered— only a good deal better.

By the time they at last thus came to speech they were alone in one of the rooms—remarkable for a fine portrait over the chimney-place—out of which their friends had passed, and the charm of it was that even before they had spoken they had practically arranged with each other to stay behind for talk. The charm, happily, was in other things too; it was partly in there being scarce a spot at Weatherend without something to stay behind for. It was in the way the autumn day looked into the high windows as it waned; in the way the red light, breaking at the close from under a low, sombre sky, reached out in a long shaft and played over old wainscots, old tapestry, old gold, old colour. It was most of all perhaps in the way she came to him as if, since she had been turned on to deal with the simpler sort, he might, should he choose to keep the whole thing down, just take her mild attention for a part of her general business. As soon as he heard her voice, however, the gap was filled up and the missing link supplied; the slight irony he divined in her attitude lost its advantage. He almost jumped at it to get there before her. "I met you years and years ago in Rome. I remember all about it." She confessed to disappointment— she had been so sure he didn't; and to prove how well he did he began to pour forth the particular recollections that popped up as he called for them. Her face and her voice, all at his service now, worked the miracle— the impression operating like the torch of a lamplighter who touches into flame, one by one, a long row of gas jets. Marcher flattered himself that the illumination was brilliant, yet he was really still more pleased on her showing him, with amusement, that in his haste to make everything right he had got most things rather wrong. It hadn't been at Rome—it had been at Naples; and it hadn't been seven years before—it had been more nearly ten. She hadn't been either with her uncle and aunt, but with her mother and her brother; in addition to which it was not with the Pembles that *he* had been, but with the Boyers, coming down in their company from Rome—a point on which she insisted, a little to his confusion, and as to which she had her evidence in hand. The Boyers she had known, but she didn't know the Pembles, though she had heard of them, and it was the people he was with who had made them acquainted. The incident of the thunderstorm that had raged round them with such violence as to drive them for refuge into an excavation—this incident had not occurred at the Palace of the Cæsars, but at Pompeii, on an occasion when they had been present there at an important find.

He accepted her amendments, he enjoyed her corrections, though the moral of them was, she pointed out, that he *really* didn't remember the least thing about her; and he only felt it as a drawback that when all was made conformable to the truth there didn't appear much of anything left. They lingered together still, she neglecting her office—for from the moment he was so clever she had no proper right to him—and both neglecting the house, just waiting as to see if a memory or two more wouldn't again breathe upon them. It had not taken them many minutes, after all, to put down on the table, like the cards of a pack, those that constituted their respective hands; only what came out was that the pack was unfortunately not perfect—that the past, invoked, invited, encouraged, could give them, naturally, no more than it had. It had made them meet—her at twenty, him at twenty-five; but nothing was so strange, they seemed to say to each other, as that, while so occupied, it hadn't done a little more for them. They looked at each other as with the feeling of an occasion missed; the present one would have been so much better if the other, in the far distance, in the foreign land, hadn't been so stupidly meagre. There weren't apparently, all counted, more than a dozen little old things that had succeeded in coming to pass between them; trivialities of youth, simplicities of freshness, stupidities of ignorance, small possible germs, but too deeply buried—too deeply (didn't it seem?) to sprout after so many years. Marcher said to himself that he ought to have rendered her some service —saved her from a capsized boat in the Bay, or at least recovered her dressing-bag, filched from her cab, in the streets of Naples, by a lazzarone with a stiletto. Or it would have been nice if he could have been taken with fever, alone, at his hotel, and she could have come to look after him, to write to his people, to drive him out in convalescence. *Then* they would be in possession of the something or other that their actual show seemed to lack. It yet somehow presented itself, this show, as too good to be spoiled; so that they were reduced for a few minutes more to wondering a little helplessly why—since they seemed to know a certain number of the same people—their reunion had been so long averted. They didn't use that name for it, but their delay from minute to minute to join the others was a kind of confession that they didn't quite want it to be a failure. Their attempted supposition of reasons for their not having met but showed how little they knew of each other. There came in fact a moment when Marcher felt a positive pang. It was vain to pretend she was an old friend, for all the communities were wanting, in spite of which it was as an old friend that he saw she would have suited him. He had new ones enough—was surrounded with them, for instance, at that hour at the other house; as a new one he probably wouldn't have so much as noticed her. He would have liked to invent something, get her to make-believe with him that some passage of a romantic or critical kind *had* originally occurred. He was really almost reaching out in imagination—as against time—for something that would do, and saying to himself that if it didn't come this new incident would simply and rather awkwardly close. They would separate, and now for no second or for no third chance. They would have tried and not succeeded. Then it was, just at the turn, as he afterwards made it out to himself, that, everything else failing, she herself decided to take up the case and, as it were, save the situation. He felt as soon as she spoke that she had been consciously keeping back what she said and hoping to get on without it; a scruple in her that immensely touched him when, by the end of three or four minutes more, he was able to measure it. What she brought out, at any rate, quite cleared the air and supplied the link—the link it was such a mystery he should frivolously have managed to lose.

"You know you told me something that I've never forgotten and that again and again has made me think of you since; it was that tremendously hot day when we went to Sorrento, across the bay, for the breeze. What I allude to was what you said to me, on the way back, as we sat, under the awning of the boat, enjoying the cool. Have you forgotten?"

He had forgotten, and he was even more surprised than ashamed. But the great thing was that he saw it was no vulgar reminder of any "sweet" speech. The vanity of women had long memories, but she was making no claim on him of a compliment or a mistake. With another woman, a totally different one, he might have feared the recall possibly even of some imbecile "offer." So, in having to say that he had indeed forgotten, he was conscious rather of a loss than of a gain; he already saw an interest in the matter of her reference. "I try to think—but I give it up. Yet I remember the Sorrento day."

"I'm not very sure you do," May Bartram after a moment said; "and I'm not very sure I ought to want you to. It's dreadful to bring a person back, at any time, to what he was ten years before. If you've lived away from it," she smiled, "so much the better."

"Ah, if *you* haven't why should I?" he asked.

"Lived away, you mean, from what I myself was?"

"From what *I* was. I was of course an ass," Marcher went on; "but I would rather know from you just the sort of ass I was than—from the moment you have something in your mind—not know anything."

Still, however, she hesitated. "But if you've completely ceased to be that sort—?"

"Why, I can then just so all the more bear to know. Besides, perhaps I haven't."

"Perhaps. Yet if you haven't," she added, "I should suppose you would remember. Not indeed that *I* in the least connect with my impression the invidious name you use. If I had only thought you foolish," she explained, "the thing I speak of wouldn't so have remained with me. It was about yourself." She waited, as if it might come to him; but as, only meeting her eyes in wonder, he gave no sign, she burnt her ships. "Has it ever happened?"

Then it was that, while he continued to stare, a light broke for him and the blood slowly came to his face, which began to burn with recognition. "Do you mean I told you—?" But he faltered, lest what came to him shouldn't be right, lest he should only give himself away.

"It was something about yourself that it was natural one shouldn't forget—that is if one remembered you at all. That's why I ask you," she smiled, "if the thing you then spoke of has ever come to pass?"

Oh, then he saw, but he was lost in wonder and found himself embarrassed. This, he also saw, made her sorry for him, as if her allusions had been a mistake. It took him but a moment, however, to feel that it had not been, much as it had been a surprise. After the first little shock of it her knowledge on the contrary began, even if rather strangely, to taste sweet to him. She was the only other person in the world then who would have it, and she had had it all these years, while the fact of his having so breathed his secret had unaccountably faded from him. No wonder they couldn't have met as if nothing had happened. "I judge," he finally said, "that I know what you mean. Only I had strangely enough lost the consciousness of having taken you so far into my confidence."

"Is it because you've taken so many others as well?"

"I've taken nobody. Not a creature since then."

"So that I'm the only person who knows?"

"The only person in the world."

"Well," she quickly replied, "I myself have never spoken. I've never, never repeated of you what you told me." She looked at him so that he perfectly believed her. Their eyes met over it in such a way that he was without a doubt. "And I never will."

She spoke with an earnestness that, as if almost excessive, put him at ease about her possible derision. Somehow the whole question was a new luxury to him—that is, from the moment she was in possession. If she didn't take the ironic view she clearly took the sympathetic, and that was what he had had, in all the long time, from no one whomsoever. What he felt was that he couldn't at present have begun to tell her and yet could profit perhaps exquisitely by the accident of having done so of old. "Please don't then. We're just right as it is."

"Oh, I am," she laughed, "if you are!" To which she added: "Then you do still feel in the same way?"

It was impossible to him not to take to himself that she was really interested, and it all kept coming as a sort of revelation. He had thought of himself so long as abominably alone, and, lo, he wasn't alone a bit. He hadn't been, it appeared, for an hour—since those moments on the Sorrento boat. It was *she* who had been, he seemed to see as he looked at her—she who had been made so by the graceless fact of his lapse of fidelity. To tell her what he had told her—what had it been but to ask something of her? something that she had given, in her charity, without his having, by a remembrance, by a return of the spirit, failing another encounter, so much as thanked her. What he had asked of her had been simply at first not to laugh at him. She had beautifully not done so for ten years, and she was not doing so now. So he had endless gratitude to make up. Only for that he must see just how he had figured to her. "What, exactly, was the account I gave—?"

"Of the way you did feel? Well, it was very simple. You said you had had from your earliest time, as the deepest thing within you, the sense of being kept for something rare and strange, possibly prodigious and terrible, that was sooner or later to happen to you, that you had in your bones the foreboding and the conviction of, and that would perhaps overwhelm you."

"Do you call that very simple?" John Marcher asked.

She thought a moment. "It was perhaps because I seemed, as you spoke, to understand it."

"You do understand it?" he eagerly asked.

Again she kept her kind eyes on him. "You still have the belief?"

"Oh!" he exclaimed helplessly. There was too much to say.

"Whatever it is to be," she clearly made out, "it hasn't yet come."

He shook his head in complete surrender now. "It hasn't yet come. Only, you know, it isn't anything I'm to *do*, to achieve in the world, to be distinguished or admired for. I'm not such an ass as *that*. It would be much better, no doubt, if I were."

"It's to be something you're merely to suffer?"

"Well, say to wait for—to have to meet, to face, to see suddenly break out in my life; possibly destroying all further consciousness, possibly annihilating me; possibly, on the other hand, only altering everything, striking at the root of all my world and leaving me to the consequences, however they shape themselves."

She took this in, but the light in her eyes continued for him not to be that of mockery. "Isn't what you describe perhaps but the expectation—or, at any rate, the sense of danger, familiar to so many people—of falling in love?"

John Marcher thought. "Did you ask me that before?"

"No—I wasn't so free-and-easy then. But it's what strikes me now."

"Of course," he said after a moment, "it strikes you. Of course it strikes *me*. Of course what's in store for me may be no more than that. The only thing is," he went on, "that I think that if it had been that, I should by this time know."

"Do you mean because you've *been* in love?" And then as he but looked at her in silence: "You've been in love, and it hasn't meant such a cataclysm, hasn't proved the great affair?"

"Here I am, you see. It hasn't been overwhelming."

"Then it hasn't been love," said May Bartram.

"Well, I at least thought it was. I took it for that—I've taken it till now. It was agreeable, it was delightful, it was miserable," he explained. "But it wasn't strange. It wasn't what *my* affair's to be.

"You want something all to yourself—something that nobody else knows or *has* known?"

"It isn't a question of what I 'want'—God knows I don't want anything. It's only a question of the apprehension that haunts me—that I live with day by day."

He said this so lucidly and consistently that, visibly, it further imposed itself. If she had not been interested before she would have been interested now. "Is it a sense of coming violence?"

Evidently now too, again, he liked to talk of it. "I don't think of it as—when it does come—necessarily violent. I only think of it as natural and as of course, above all, unmistakable. I think of it simply as *the* thing. *The* thing will of itself appear natural."

"Then how will it appear strange?"

Marcher bethought himself. "It won't—to *me*."

"To whom then?"

"Well," he replied, smiling at last, "say to you."

"Oh then, I'm to be present?"

"Why, you *are* present—since you know."

"I see." She turned it over. "But I mean at the catastrophe."

At this, for a minute, their lightness gave way to their gravity; it was as if the long look they exchanged held them together. "It will only depend on yourself—if you'll watch with me."

"Are you afraid?" she asked.

"Don't leave me *now*," he went on.

"Are you afraid?" she repeated.

"Do you think me simply out of my mind?" he pursued instead of answering. "Do I merely strike you as a harmless lunatic?"

"No," said May Bartram. "I understand you. I believe you."

"You mean you feel how my obsession—poor old thing!—may correspond to some possible reality?"

"To some possible reality."

"Then you *will* watch with me?"

She hesitated, then for the third time put her question. "Are you afraid?"

"Did I tell you I was—at Naples?"

"No, you said nothing about it."

"Then I don't know. And I should *like* to know," said John Marcher. "You'll tell me yourself whether you think so. If you'll watch with me you'll see."

"Very good then." They had been moving by this time across the room, and at the door, before passing out, they paused as if for the full wind-up of their understanding. "I'll watch with you," said May Bartram.

II

The fact that she "knew"—knew and yet neither chaffed him nor betrayed him—had in a short time begun to constitute between them a sensible bond, which became more marked when, within the year that followed their afternoon at Weatherend, the opportunities for meeting multiplied. The event that thus promoted these occasions was the death of the ancient lady, her great-aunt, under whose wing, since losing her mother, she had to such an extent found shelter, and who, though but the widowed mother of the new successor to the property, had succeeded —thanks to a high tone and a high temper—in not forfeiting the supreme position at the great house. The deposition of this personage arrived but with her death, which, followed by many changes, made in particular a difference for the young woman in whom Marcher's expert attention had recognised from the first a dependent with a pride that might ache though it didn't bristle. Nothing for a long time had made him easier than the thought that the aching must have been much soothed by Miss Bartram's now finding herself able to set up a small home in London. She had acquired property, to an amount that made that luxury just possible, under her aunt's extremely complicated will, and when the whole matter began to be straightened out, which indeed took time, she let him know that the happy issue was at last in view. He had seen her again before that day, both because she had more than once accompanied the ancient lady to town and because he had paid another visit to the friends who so conveniently made of Weatherend one of the charms of their own hospitality. These friends had taken him back there; he had achieved there again with Miss Bartram some quiet detachment; and he had in London succeeded in persuading her to more than one brief absence from her aunt. They went together, on these latter occasions, to the National Gallery and the South Kensington Museum, where, among vivid reminders, they talked of Italy at large—not now attempting to recover, as at first, the taste of their youth and their ignorance. That recovery, the first day at Weatherend, had served its purpose well, had given them quite enough; so that they were, to Marcher's sense, no longer hovering about the head-waters of their stream, but had felt their boat pushed sharply off and down the current.

They were literally afloat together; for our gentleman this was marked, quite as marked as that the fortunate cause of it was just the buried treasure of her knowledge. He had with his own hands dug up this little hoard, brought to light—that is to within reach of the dim day constituted by their discretions and privacies—the object of value the hiding-place of which he had, after putting it into the ground himself, so strangely, so long forgotten. The exquisite luck of having again just stumbled on the spot made him indifferent to any other question; he would doubtless have devoted more time to the odd accident of his lapse of memory if he had not been moved to devote so much to the sweetness, the comfort, as he felt, for the future, that this accident itself had helped to keep fresh. It had never entered into his plan that anyone should "know," and mainly for the reason that it was not in him to tell anyone. That would have been impossible, since nothing but the amusement of a cold world would have waited on it. Since, however, a mysterious fate had opened his mouth in youth, in spite of him, he would count that a compensation and profit by it to the utmost. That the right person *should* know tempered the asperity of his secret more even than his shyness had permitted him to imagine; and May Bartram was clearly right, because—well, because there she was. Her knowledge simply settled it; he would have been sure enough by this time had she been wrong. There was that in his situation, no doubt, that disposed him too much to see her as a mere confidant, taking all her light for him from the fact—the fact only—of her interest in his predicament, from her mercy, sympathy, seriousness, her consent not to regard him as the funniest of the funny. Aware, in fine, that her price for him was just in her giving him this constant sense of his being admirably spared, he was careful to remember that she had, after all, also a life of her own, with things that might happen to *her*, things that in friendship one should likewise take account of. Something fairly remarkable came to pass with him, for that matter, in this connection—something represented by a certain passage of his consciousness, in the suddenest way, from one extreme to the other.

He had thought himself, so long as nobody knew, the most disinterested person in the world, carrying his concentrated burden, his perpetual suspense, ever so quietly, holding his tongue about it, giving others no glimpse of it nor of its effect upon his life, asking of them no allowance and only making on his side all those that were asked. He had disturbed nobody with the queerness of having to know a haunted man, though he had had moments of rather special temptation on hearing people say that they were "unsettled." If they were as unsettled as he was—he who had never been settled for an hour in his life—they would know what it meant. Yet it wasn't, all the same, for him to make them, and he listened to them civilly enough. This was why he had such good—though possibly such rather colourless—manners; this was why, above all, he could regard himself, in a greedy world, as decently—as, in fact, perhaps even a little sublimely—unselfish. Our point is accordingly that he valued this character quite sufficiently to measure his present danger of letting it lapse, against which he promised himself to be much on his guard. He was quite ready, none the less, to be selfish just a little, since, surely, no more charming occasion for it had come to him. "Just a little," in a word, was just as much as Miss Bartram, taking one day with another, would let him. He never would be in the least coercive, and he would keep well before him the lines on which consideration for her—the very highest—ought to proceed. He would thoroughly establish the heads under which her affairs, her requirements, her peculiarities—he went so far as to give them the latitude of that name—would come into their intercourse. All this naturally was a sign of how much he took the intercourse itself for granted. There was nothing more to be done about *that*. It simply existed; had sprung into being with her first penetrating question to him in the autumn light there at Weatherend. The real form it should have taken on the basis that stood out large was the form of their marrying. But the devil in this was that the very basis itself put marrying out of the question. His conviction, his apprehension, his obsession, in short, was not a condition he could invite a woman to share; and that consequence of it was precisely what was the matter with him. Something or other lay in wait for him, amid the twists and the turns of the months and the years, like a crouching beast in the jungle. It signified little whether the crouching beast were destined to slay him or to be slain. The definite point was the inevitable spring of the creature; and the definite lesson from that was that a man of feeling didn't cause himself to be accompanied by a lady on a tiger-hunt. Such was the image under which he had ended by figuring his life.

They had at first, none the less, in the scattered hours spent together, made no allusion to that view of it; which was a sign he was handsomely ready to give that he didn't expect, that he in fact didn't care always to be talking about it. Such a feature in one's outlook was really a hump on one's back. The difference it made every minute of the day existed quite independently of discussion. One discussed, of course, *like* a hunchback, for there was always, if nothing else, the hunchback face. That remained, and she was watching him; but people watched best, as a general thing, in silence, so that such would be predominantly the manner of their vigil. Yet he didn't want, at the same time, to be solemn; solemn was what he imagined he too much tended to be with other people. The thing to be, with the one person who knew, was easy and natural—to make the reference rather than be seeming to avoid it, to avoid it rather than be seeming to make it, and to keep it, in any case, familiar, facetious even, rather than pedantic and portentous. Some such consideration as the latter was doubtless in his mind, for instance, when he wrote pleasantly to Miss Bartram that perhaps the great thing he had so long felt as in the lap of the gods was no more than this circumstance, which touched him so nearly, of her acquiring a house in London. It was the first allusion they had yet again made, needing any other hitherto so little; but when she replied, after having given him the news, that she was by no means satisfied with such a trifle, as the climax to so special a suspense, she almost set him wondering if she hadn't even a larger conception of singularity for him than he had for himself. He was at all events destined to become aware little by little, as time went by, that she was all the while looking at his life, judging it, measuring it, in the light of the things she knew, which grew to be at last, with the consecration of the years, never mentioned between them save as "the real truth" about him.

That had always been his own form of reference to it, but she adopted the form so quietly that, looking back at the end of a period, he knew there was no moment at which it was traceable that she had, as he might say, got inside his condition, or exchanged the attitude of beautifully indulging for that of still more beautifully believing him.

It was always open to him to accuse her of seeing him but as the most harmless of maniacs, and this, in the long run—since it covered so much ground—was his easiest description of their friendship. He had a screw loose for her, but she liked him in spite of it, and was practically, against the rest of the world, his kind, wise keeper, unremunerated, but fairly amused and, in the absence of other near ties, not disreputably occupied. The rest of the world of course thought him queer, but she, she only, knew how, and above all why, queer; which was precisely what enabled her to dispose the concealing veil in the right folds. She took his gaiety from him —since it had to pass with them for gaiety—as she took everything else; but she certainly so far justified by her unerring touch his finer sense of the degree to which he had ended by convincing her. *She* at least never spoke of the secret of his life except as "the real truth about you," and she had in fact a wonderful way of making it seem, as such, the secret of her own life too. That was in fine how he so constantly felt her as allowing for him; he couldn't on the whole call it anything else. He allowed for himself, but she, exactly, allowed still more; partly because, better placed for a sight of the matter, she traced his unhappy perversion through portions of its course into which he could scarce follow it. He knew how he felt, but, besides knowing that, she knew how he *looked* as well; he knew each of the things of importance he was insidiously kept from doing, but she could add up the amount they made, understand how much, with a lighter weight on his spirit, he might have done, and thereby establish how, clever as he was, he fell short. Above all she was in the secret of the difference between the forms he went through—those of his little office under Government, those of caring for his modest patrimony, for his library, for his garden in the country, for the people in London whose invitations he accepted and repaid—and the detachment that reigned beneath them and that made of all behaviour, all that could in the least be called behaviour, a long act of dissimulation. What it had come to was that he wore a mask painted with the social simper, out of the eye-holes of which there looked eyes of an expression not in the least matching the other features. This the stupid world, even after years, had never more than half discovered. It was only May Bartram who had, and she achieved, by an art indescribable, the feat of at once—or perhaps it was only alternately—meeting the eyes from in front and mingling her own vision, as from over his shoulder, with their peep through the apertures.

So, while they grew older together, she did watch with him, and so she let this association give shape and colour to her own existence. Beneath *her* forms as well detachment had learned to sit, and behaviour had become for her, in the social sense, a false account of herself. There was but one account of her that would have been true all the while, and that she could give, directly, to nobody, least of all to John Marcher. Her whole attitude was a virtual statement, but the perception of that only seemed destined to take its place for him as one of the many things necessarily crowded out of his consciousness. If she had, moreover, like himself, to make sacrifices to their real truth, it was to be granted that her compensation might have affected her as more prompt and more natural. They had long periods, in this London time, during which, when they were together, a stranger might have listened to them without in the least pricking up his ears; on the other hand, the real truth was equally liable at any moment to rise to the surface, and the auditor would then have wondered indeed what they were talking about. They had from an early time made up their mind that society was, luckily, unintelligent, and the margin that this gave them had fairly become one of their commonplaces. Yet there were still moments when the situation turned almost fresh— usually under the effect of some expression drawn from herself. Her expressions doubtless repeated themselves, but her intervals were generous. "What saves us, you know, is that we answer so completely to so usual an appearance: that of the man and woman whose friendship has become such a daily habit, or almost, as to be at last indispensable." That, for instance, was a remark she had frequently enough had occasion to make, though she had given it at different times different developments. What we are especially concerned with is the turn it happened to take from her one afternoon when he had come to see her in honour of her birthday. This anniversary had fallen on a Sunday, at a season of thick fog and general outward gloom; but he had brought her his customary offering, having known her now long enough to have established a hundred little customs. It was one of his proofs to himself, the present he made her on her birthday, that he had not sunk into real selfishness. It was mostly nothing more than a small trinket, but it was always fine of its kind, and he was regularly careful to pay for it more than he thought he could afford. "Our habit saves you, at least, don't you see? because it makes you, after all, for the vulgar, indistinguishable from other men. What's the most inveterate mark of men in general? Why, the capacity to spend endless time with dull women—to spend it, I won't say without being bored, but without minding that they are, without being driven off at a tangent by it; which comes to the same thing. I'm your dull woman, a part of the daily bread for which you pray at church. That covers your tracks more than anything."

"And what covers yours?" asked Marcher, whom his dull woman could mostly to this extent amuse. "I see of course what you mean by your saving me, in one way and another, so far as other people are concerned—I've seen it all along. Only, what is it that saves *you?* I often think, you know, of that."

She looked as if she sometimes thought of that too, but in rather a different way. "Where other people, you mean, are concerned?"

"Well, you're really so in with me, you know—as a sort of result of my being so in with yourself. I mean of my having such an immense regard for you, being so tremendously grateful for all you've done for me. I sometimes ask myself if it's quite fair. Fair I mean to have so involved and—since one may say it—interested you. I almost feel as if you hadn't really had time to do anything else."

"Anything else but be interested?" she asked. "Ah, what else does one ever want to be? If I've been 'watching' with you, as we long ago agreed that I was to do, watching is always in itself an absorption."

"Oh, certainly," John Marcher said, "if you hadn't had your curiosity—! Only, doesn't it sometimes come to you, as time goes on, that your curiosity is not being particularly repaid?"

May Bartram had a pause. "Do you ask that, by any chance, because you feel at all that yours isn't? I mean because you have to wait so long."

Oh, he understood what she meant. "For the thing to happen that never does happen? For the beast to jump out? No, I'm just where I was about it. It isn't a matter as to which I can *choose*, I can decide for a change. It isn't one as to which there *can* be a change. It's in the lap of the gods. One's in the hands of one's law—there one is. As to the form the law will take, the way it will operate, that's its own affair."

"Yes," Miss Bartram replied; "of course one's fate is coming, of course it *has* come, in its own form and its own way, all the while. Only, you know, the form and the way in your case were to have been—well, something so exceptional and, as one may say, so particularly *your* own."

Something in this made him look at her with suspicion. "You say 'were to *have* been,' as if in your heart you had begun to doubt."

"Oh!" she vaguely protested.

"As if you believed," he went on, "that nothing will now take place."

She shook her head slowly, but rather inscrutably. "You're far from my thought."

He continued to look at her. "What then is the matter with you?"

"Well," she said after another wait, "the matter with me is simply that I'm more sure than ever my curiosity, as you call it, will be but too well repaid."

They were frankly grave now; he had got up from his seat; had turned once more about the little drawing-room to which, year after year, he brought his inevitable topic; in which he had, as he might have said, tasted their intimate community with every sauce, where every object was as familiar to him as the things of his own house and the very carpets were worn with his fitful walk very much as the desks in old counting-houses are worn by the elbows of generations of clerks. The generations of his nervous moods had been at work there, and the place was the written history of his whole middle life. Under the impression of what his friend had just said he knew himself, for some reason, more aware of these things, which made him, after a moment, stop again before her. "Is it, possibly, that you've grown afraid?"

"Afraid?" He thought, as she repeated the word, that his question had made her, a little, change colour; so that, lest he should have touched on a truth, he explained very kindly. "You remember that that was what you asked *me* long ago—that first day at Weatherend."

"Oh yes, and you told me you didn't know—that I was to see for myself. We've said little about it since, even in so long a time."

"Precisely," Marcher interposed— "quite as if it were too delicate a matter for us to make free with. Quite as if we might find, on pressure, that I *am* afraid. For then," he said, "we shouldn't, should we? quite know what to do."

She had for the time no answer to this question. "There have been days when I thought you were. Only, of course," she added, "there have been days when we have thought almost anything."

"Everything. Oh!" Marcher softly groaned as with a gasp, half spent, at the face, more uncovered just then than it had been for a long while, of the imagination always with them. It had always had its incalculable moments of glaring out, quite as with the very eyes of the very Beast, and, used as he was to them, they could still draw from him the tribute of a sigh that rose from the depths of his being. All that they had thought, first and last, rolled over him; the past seemed to have been reduced to mere barren speculation. This in fact was what the place had just struck him as so full of—the simplification of everything but the state of suspense. That remained only by seeming to hang in the void surrounding it. Even his original fear, if fear it had been, had lost itself in the desert. "I judge, however," he continued, "that you see I'm not afraid now."

"What I see is, as I make it out, that you've achieved something almost unprecedented in the way of getting used to danger. Living with it so long and so closely, you've lost your sense of it; you know it's there, but you're indifferent and you cease even, as of old, to have to whistle in the dark. Considering what the danger is," May Bartram wound up, "I'm bound to say that I don't think your attitude could well be surpassed."

John Marcher faintly smiled. "It's heroic?"

"Certainly—call it that."

He considered. "I *am*, then, a man of courage?"

"That's what you were to show me."

He still, however, wondered. "But doesn't the man of courage know what he's afraid of—or *not* afraid of? I don't know *that*, you see. I don't focus it. I can't name it. I only know I'm exposed."

"Yes, but exposed—how shall I say?—so directly. So intimately. That's surely enough."

"Enough to make you feel, then—at what we may call the end of our watch—that I'm not afraid?"

"You're not afraid. But it isn't," she said, "the end of our watch. That is, it isn't the end of yours. You've everything still to see."

"Then why haven't *you*?" he asked. He had had, all along, to-day, the sense of her keeping something back, and he still had it. As this was his first impression of that, it made a kind of date. The case was the more marked as she didn't at first answer; which in turn made him go on. "You know something I don't." Then his voice, for that of a man of courage, trembled a little. "You know what's to happen." Her silence, with the face she showed, was almost a confession—it made him sure. "You know, and you're afraid to tell me. It's so bad that you're afraid I'll find out."

All this might be true, for she did look as if, unexpectedly to her, he had crossed some mystic line that she had secretly drawn round her. Yet she might, after all, not have worried; and the real upshot was that he himself, at all events, needn't. "You'll never find out."

III

It was all to have made, none the less, as I have said, a date; as came out in the fact that again and again, even after long intervals, other things that passed between them wore, in relation to this hour, but the character of recalls and results. Its immediate effect had been indeed rather to lighten insistence—almost to provoke a reaction; as if their topic had dropped by its own weight and as if moreover, for that matter, Marcher had been visited by one of his occasional warnings against egotism. He had kept up, he felt, and very decently on the whole, his consciousness of the importance of not being selfish, and it was true that he had never sinned in that direction without promptly enough trying to press the scales the other way. He often repaired his fault, the season permitting, by inviting his friend to accompany him to the opera; and it not infrequently thus happened that, to show he didn't wish her to have but one sort of food for her mind, he was the cause of her appearing there with him a dozen nights in the month. It even happened that, seeing her home at such times, he occasionally went in with her to finish, as he called it, the evening, and, the better to make his point, sat down to the frugal but always careful little supper that awaited his pleasure. His point was made, he thought, by his not eternally insisting with her on himself; made for instance, at such hours, when it befell that, her piano at hand and each of them familiar with it, they went over passages of the opera together. It chanced to be on one of these occasions, however, that he reminded her of her not having answered a certain question he had put to her during the talk that had taken place between them on her last birthday. "What is it that saves *you?*"—saved her, he meant, from that appearance of variation from the usual human type. If he had practically escaped remark, as she pretended, by doing, in the most important particular, what most men do—find the answer to life in patching up an alliance of a sort with a woman no better than himself—how had she escaped it, and how could the alliance, such as it was, since they must suppose it had been more or less noticed, have failed to make her rather positively talked about?

"I never said," May Bartram replied, "that it hadn't made me talked about."

"Ah well then, you're not 'saved.' "

"It has not been a question for me. If you've had your woman, I've had," she said, "my man."

"And you mean that makes you all right?"

She hesitated. "I don't know why it shouldn't make me—humanly, which is what we're speaking of—as right as it makes you."

"I see," Marcher returned. " 'Humanly,' no doubt, as showing that you're living for something. Not, that is, just for me and my secret."

May Bartram smiled. "I don't pretend it exactly shows that I'm not living for you. It's my intimacy with you that's in question."

He laughed as he saw what she meant. "Yes, but since, as you say, I'm only, so far as people make out, ordinary, you're—aren't you?—no more than ordinary either. You help me to pass for a man like another. So if I *am*, as I understand you, you're not compromised. Is that it?"

She had another hesitation, but she spoke clearly enough. "That's it. It's all that concerns me—to help you to pass for a man like another."

He was careful to acknowledge the remark handsomely. "How kind, how beautiful, you are to me! How shall I ever repay you?"

She had her last grave pause, as if there might be a choice of ways. But she chose. "By going on as you are."

It was into this going on as he was that they relapsed, and really for so long a time that the day inevitably came for a further sounding of their depths. It was as if these depths, constantly bridged over by a structure that was firm enough in spite of its lightness and of its occasional oscillation in the somewhat vertiginous air, invited on occasion, in the interest of their nerves, a dropping of the plummet and a measurement of the abyss. A difference had been made moreover, once for all, by the fact that she had, all the while, not appeared to feel the need of rebutting his charge of an idea within her that she didn't dare to express, uttered just before one of the fullest of their later discussions ended. It had come up for him then that she "knew" something and that what she knew was bad—too bad to tell him. When he had spoken of it as visibly so bad that she was afraid he might find it out, her reply had left the matter too equivocal to be let alone and yet, for Marcher's special sensibility, almost too formidable again to touch. He circled about it at a distance that alternately narrowed and widened and that yet was not much affected by the consciousness in him that there was nothing she could "know," after all, any better than he did. She had no source of knowledge that he hadn't equally—except of course that she might have finer nerves. That was what women had where they were interested; they made out things, where people were concerned, that the people often couldn't have made out for themselves. Their nerves, their sensibility, their imagination, were conductors and revealers, and the beauty of May Bartram was in particular that she had given herself so to his case. He felt in these days what, oddly enough, he had never felt before, the growth of a dread of losing her by some catastrophe—some catastrophe that yet wouldn't at all be *the* catastrophe: partly because she had, almost of a sudden, begun to strike him as useful to him as never yet, and partly by reason of an appearance of uncertainty in her health, coincident and equally new. It was characteristic of the inner detachment he had hitherto so successfully cultivated and to which our whole account of him is a reference, it was characteristic that his complications, such as they were, had never yet seemed so as at this crisis to thicken about him, even to the point of making him ask himself if he were, by any chance, of a truth, within sight or sound, within touch or reach, within the immediate jurisdiction of the thing that waited.

When the day came, as come it had to, that his friend confessed to him her fear of a deep disorder in her blood, he felt somehow the shadow of a change and the chill of a shock. He immediately began to imagine aggravations and disasters, and above all to think of her peril as the direct menace for himself of personal privation. This indeed gave him one of those partial recoveries of equanimity that were agreeable to him—it showed him that what was still first in his mind was the loss she herself might suffer. "What if she should have to die before knowing, before seeing——?" It would have been brutal, in the early stages of her trouble, to put that question to her; but it had immediately sounded for him to his own concern, and the possibility was what most made him sorry for her. If she did "know," moreover, in the sense of her having had some—what should he think?—mystical, irresistible light, this would make the matter not better, but worse, inasmuch as her original adoption of his own curiosity had quite become the basis of her life. She had been living to see what would *be* to be seen, and it would be cruel to her to have to give up before the accomplishment of the vision. These reflections, as I say, refreshed his generosity; yet, make them as he might, he saw himself, with the lapse of the period, more and more disconcerted. It lapsed for him with a strange, steady sweep, and the oddest oddity was that it gave him, independently of the threat of such inconvenience, almost the only positive surprise his career, if career it could be called, had yet offered him. She kept the house as she had never done; he had to go to her to see her—she could meet him nowhere now, though there was scarce a corner of their loved old London in which she had not in the past, at one time or another, done so; and he found her always seated by her fire in the deep, old-fashioned chair she was less and less able to leave. He had been struck one day, after an absence exceeding his usual measure, with her suddenly looking much older to him than he had ever thought of her being; then he recognised that the suddenness was all on his side—he had just been suddenly struck. She looked older because inevitably, after so many years, she *was* old, or almost; which was of course true in still greater measure of her companion. If she was old, or almost, John Marcher assuredly was, and yet it was her showing of the lesson, not his own, that brought the truth home to him. His surprises bègan here; when once they had begun they multipled; they came rather with a rush: it was as if, in the oddest way in the world, they had all been kept back, sown in a thick cluster, for the late afternoon of life, the time at which, for people in general, the unexpected has died out.

One of them was that he should have caught himself—for he *had* so done—*really* wondering if the great accident would take form now as nothing more than his being condemned to see this charming woman, this admirable friend, pass away from him. He had never so unreservedly qualified her as while confronted in thought with such a possibility; in spite of which there was small doubt for him that as an answer to his long riddle the mere effacement of even so fine a feature of his situation would be an abject anticlimax. It would represent, as connected with his past attitude, a drop of dignity under the shadow of which his existence could only become the most grotesque of failures. He had been far from holding it a failure—long as he had waited for the appearance that was to make it a success. He had waited for a quite other thing, not for such a one as that. The breath of his good faith came short, however, as he recognised how long he had waited, or how long, at least, his companion had. That she, at all events, might be recorded as having waited in vain—this affected him sharply, and all the more because of his at first having done little more than amuse himself with the idea. It grew more grave as the gravity of her condition grew, and the state of mind it produced in him, which he ended by watching, himself, as if it had been some definite disfigurement of his outer person, may pass for another of his surprises. This conjoined itself still with another, the really stupefying consciousness of a question that he would have allowed to shape itself had he dared. What did everything mean—what, that is, did *she* mean, she and her vain waiting and her probable death and the soundless admonition of it all—unless that, at this time of day, it was simply, it was overwhelmingly too late? He had never, at any stage of his queer consciousness, admitted the whisper of such a correction; he had never, till within these last few months, been so false to his conviction as not to hold that what was to come to him had time, whether *he* struck himself as having it or not. That at last, at last, he certainly hadn't it, to speak of, or had it but in the scantiest measure— such, soon enough, as things went with him, became the inference with which his old obsession had to reckon: and this it was not helped to do by the more and more confirmed appearance that the great vagueness casting the long shadow in which he had lived had, to attest itself, almost no margin left. Since it was in Time that he was to have met his fate, so it was in Time that his fate was to have acted; and as he waked up to the sense of no longer being young, which was exactly the sense of being stale, just as that, in turn, was the sense of being weak, he waked up to another matter beside. It all hung together; they were subject, he and the great vagueness, to an equal and indivisible law. When the possibilities themselves had, accordingly, turned stale, when the secret of the gods had grown faint, had perhaps even quite evaporated, that, and that only, was failure. It wouldn't have been failure to be bankrupt, dishonoured, pilloried, hanged; it was failure not to be anything. And so, in the dark valley into which his path had taken its unlooked-for twist, he wondered not a little as he groped. He didn't care what awful crash might overtake him, with what ignominy or what monstrosity he might yet be associated —since he wasn't, after all, too utterly old to suffer—if it would only be decently porportionate to the posture he had kept, all his life, in the promised presence of it. He had but one desire left—that he shouldn't have been "sold."

IV

Then it was that one afternoon, while the spring of the year was young and new, she met, all in her own way, his frankest betrayal of these alarms. He had gone in late to see her, but evening had not settled, and she was presented to him in that long, fresh light of waning April days which affects us often with a sadness sharper than the greyest hours of autumn. The week had been warm, the spring was supposed to have begun early, and May Bartram sat, for the first time in the year, without a fire, a fact that, to Marcher's sense, gave the scene of which she formed part a smooth and ultimate look, an air of knowing, in its immaculate order and its cold, meaningless cheer, that it would never see a fire again. Her own aspect—

he could scarce have said why—intensified this note. Almost as white as wax, with the marks and signs in her face as numerous and as fine as if they had been etched by a needle, with soft white draperies relieved by a faded green scarf, the delicate tone of which had been consecrated by the years, she was the picture of a serene, exquisite, but impenetrable sphinx, whose head, or indeed all whose person, might have been powdered with silver. She was a sphinx, yet with her white petals and green fronds she might have been a lily too—only an artificial lily, wonderfully imitated and constantly kept, without dust or stain, though not exempt from a slight droop and a complexity of faint creases, under some clear glass bell. The perfection of household care, of high polish and finish, always reigned in her rooms, but they especially looked to Marcher at present as if everything had been wound up, tucked in, put away, so that she might sit with folded hands and with nothing more to do. She was "out of it," to his vision; her work was over; she communicated with him as across some gulf, or from some island of rest that she had already reached, and it made him feel strangely abandoned. Was it—or, rather, wasn't it—that if for so long she had been watching with him the answer to their question had swum into her ken and taken on its name, so that her occupation was verily gone? He had as much as charged her with this in saying to her, many months before, that she even then knew something she was keeping from him. It was a point he had never since ventured to press, vaguely fearing, as he did, that it might become a difference, perhaps a disagreement, between them. He had in short, in this later time, turned nervous, which was what, in all the other years, he had never been; and the oddity was that his nervousness should have waited till he had begun to doubt, should have held off so long as he was sure. There was something, it seemed to him, that the wrong word would bring down on his head, something that would so at least put an end to his suspense. But he wanted not to speak the wrong word; that would make everything ugly. He wanted the knowledge he lacked to drop on him, if drop it could, by its own august weight. If she was to forsake him it was surely for her to take leave. This was why he didn't ask her again, directly, what she knew; but it was also why, approaching the matter from another side, he said to her in the course of his visit: "What do you regard as the very worst that, at this time of day, *can* happen to me?"

He had asked her that in the past often enough; they had, with the odd, irregular rhythm of their intensities and avoidances, exchanged ideas about it and then had seen the ideas washed away by cool intervals, washed like figures traced in sea-sand. It had ever been the mark of their talk that the oldest allusions in it required but a little dismissal and reaction to come out again, sounding for the hour as new. She could thus at present meet his inquiry quite freshly and patiently. "Oh, yes, I've repeatedly thought, only it always seemed to me of old that I couldn't quite make up my mind. I thought of dreadful things, between which it was difficult to choose; and so must you have done."

"Rather! I feel now as if I had scarce done anything else. I appear to myself to have spent my life in thinking of nothing *but* dreadful things. A great many of them I've at different times named to you, but there were others I couldn't name."

"They were too, too dreadful?"

"Too, too dreadful—some of them."

She looked at him a minute, and there came to him as he met it an inconsequent sense that her eyes, when one got their full clearness, were still as beautiful as they had been in youth, only beautiful with a strange, cold light—a light that somehow was a part of the effect, if it wasn't rather a part of the cause, of the pale, hard sweetness of the season and the hour. "And yet," she said at last, "there are horrors we have mentioned."

It deepened the strangeness to see her, as such a figure in such a picture, talk of "horrors," but she was to do, in a few minutes, something stranger yet—though even of this he was to take the full measure but afterwards—and the note of it was already in the air. It was, for the matter of that, one of the signs that her eyes were having again such a high flicker of their prime. He had to admit, however, what she said. "Oh yes, there were times when we did go far." He caught himself in the act, speaking as if it all were over. Well, he wished it were; and the consummation depended, for him, clearly, more and more on his companion.

But she had now a soft smile. "Oh, far——!"

It was oddly ironic. "Do you mean you're prepared to go further?"

She was frail and ancient and charming as she continued to look at him, yet it was rather as if she had lost the thread. "Do you consider that we went so far?"

"Why, I thought it the point you were just making—that we *had* looked most things in the face."

"Including each other?" She still smiled. "But you're quite right. We've had together great imaginations, often great fears; but some of them have been unspoken."

"Then the worst—we haven't faced that. I *could* face it, I believe, if I knew what you think it. I feel," he explained, "as if I had lost my power to conceive such things." And he wondered if he looked as blank as he sounded. "It's spent."

"Then why do you assume," she asked, "that mine isn't?"

"Because you've given me signs to the contrary. It isn't a question for you of conceiving, imagining, comparing. It isn't a question now of choosing." At last he came out with it. "You know something that I don't. You've showed me that before."

These last words affected her, he could see in a moment, remarkably, and she spoke with firmness. "I've shown you, my dear, nothing."

He shook his head. "You can't hide it."

"Oh, oh!" May Bartram murmured over what she couldn't hide. It was almost a smothered groan.

"You admitted it months ago, when I spoke of it to you as of something you were afraid I would find out. Your answer was that I couldn't, that I wouldn't, and I don't pretend I have. But you had something therefore in mind, and I see now that it must have been, that it still is, the possibility that, of all possibilities, has settled itself for you as the worse. This," he went on, "is why I appeal to you. I'm only afraid of ignorance now—I'm not afraid of knowledge." And then as for a while she said nothing: "What makes me sure is that I see in your face and feel here, in this air and amid these appearances, that you're out of it. You've done. You've had your experience. You leave me to my fate."

Well, she listened, motionless and white in her chair, as if she had in fact a decision to make, so that her whole manner was a virtual confession, though still with a small, fine, inner stiffness, an imperfect surrender. "It *would* be the worst," she finally let herself say. "I mean the thing that I've never said."

It hushed him a moment. "More monstrous than all the monstrosities we've named?"

"More monstrous. Isn't that what you sufficiently express," she asked, "in calling it the worst?"

Marcher thought. "Assuredly—if you mean, as I do, something that includes all the loss and all the shame that are thinkable."

"It would if it *should* happen," said May Bartram. "What we're speaking of, remember, is only my idea."

"It's your belief," Marcher returned. "That's enough for me. I feel your beliefs are right. Therefore if, having this one, you give me no more light on it, you abandon me."

"No, no!" she repeated. "I'm with you—don't you see?—still." And as if to make it more vivid to him she rose from her chair—a movement she seldom made in these days—and showed herself, all draped and all soft, in her fairness and slimness. "I haven't forsaken you."

It was really, in its effort against weakness, a generous assurance, and had the success of the impulse not, happily, been great, it would have touched him to pain more than to pleasure. But the cold charm in her eyes had spread, as she hovered before him, to all the rest of her person, so that it was, for the minute, almost like a recovery of youth. He couldn't pity her for that; he could only take her as she showed—as capable still of helping him. It was as if, at the same time, her light might at any instant go out; wherefore he must make the most of it. There passed before him with intensity the three or four things he wanted most to know; but the question that came of itself to his lips really covered the others. "Then tell me if I shall consciously suffer."

She promptly shook her head. "Never!"

It confirmed the authority he imputed to her, and it produced on him an extraordinary effect. "Well, what's better than that? Do you call that the worst?"

"You think nothing is better?" she asked.

She seemed to mean something so special that he again sharply wondered, though still with the dawn of a prospect of relief. "Why not, if one doesn't *know?*" After which, as their eyes, over his question, met in a silence, the dawn deepened and something to his purpose came, prodigiously, out of her very face. His own, as he took it in, suddenly flushed to the forehead, and he gasped with the force of a perception to which, on the instant, everything fitted. The sound of his gasp filled the air; then he became articulate. "I see—if I don't suffer!"

In her own look, however, was doubt. "You see what?"

"Why, what you mean—what you've always meant."

She again shook her head. "What I mean isn't what I've always meant. It's different."

"It's something new?"

She hesitated. "Something new. It's not what you think. I see what you think."

His divination drew breath then; only her correction might be wrong. "It isn't that I *am* a donkey?" he asked between faintness and grimness. "It isn't that it's all a mistake?"

"A mistake?" she pityingly echoed. *That* possibility, for her, he saw, would be monstrous; and if she guaranteed him the immunity from pain it would accordingly not be what she had in mind. "Oh, no," she declared; "it's nothing of that sort. You've been right."

Yet he couldn't help asking himself if she weren't, thus pressed, speaking but to save him. It seemed to him he should be most lost if his history should prove all a platitude. "Are you telling me the truth, so that I sha'n't have been a bigger idiot than I can bear to know? I *haven't* lived with a vain imagination, in the most besotted illusion? I haven't waited but to see the door shut in my face?"

She shook her head again. "However the case stands *that* isn't the truth. Whatever the reality, it *is* a reality. The door isn't shut. The door's open," said May Bartram.

"Then something's to come?"

She waited once again, always with her cold, sweet eyes on him. "It's never too late." She had, with her gliding step, diminished the distance between them, and she stood nearer to him, close to him, a minute, as if still full of the unspoken. Her movement might have been for some finer emphasis of what she was at once hesitating and deciding to say. He had been standing by the chimney-piece, fireless and sparely adorned, a small, perfect old French clock and two morsels of rosy Dresden constituting all its furniture; and her hand grasped the shelf while she kept him waiting, grasped it a little as for support and encouragement. She only kept him waiting, however; that is, he only waited. It had become suddenly, from her movement and attitude, beautiful and vivid to him that she had something more to give him; her wasted face delicately shone with it, and it glittered, almost as with the white lustre of silver, in her expression. She was right, incontestably, for what he saw in her face was the truth, and strangely, without consequence, while their talk of it as dreadful was still in the air, she appeared to present it as inordinately soft. This, prompting bewilderment, made him but gape the more gratefully for her revelation, so that they continued for some minutes silent, her face shining at him, her contact imponderably pressing, and his stare all kind, but all expectant. The end, none the less, was that what he had expected failed to sound. Something else took place instead, which seemed to consist at first in the mere closing of her eyes. She gave way at the same instant to a slow, fine shudder, and though he remained staring—though he stared, in fact, but the harder—she turned off and regained her chair. It was the end of what she had been intending, but it left him thinking only of that.

"Well, you don't say——?"

She had touched in her passage a bell near the chimney and had sunk back, strangely pale. "I'm afraid I'm too ill."

"Too ill to tell me?" It sprang up sharp to him, and almost to his lips, the fear that she would die without giving him light. He checked himself in time from so expressing his question, but she answered as if she had heard the words.

"Don't you know—now?"

" 'Now'——?" She had spoken as if something that had made a difference had come up within the moment. But her maid, quickly obedient to her bell, was already with them. "I know nothing." And he was afterwards to say to himself that he must have spoken with odious impatience, such an impatience as to show that, supremely disconcerted, he washed his hands of the whole question.

"Oh!" said May Bartram.

"Are you in pain?" he asked, as the woman went to her.

"No," said May Bartram.

Her maid, who had put an arm round her as if to take her to her room, fixed on him eyes that appealingly contradicted her; in spite of which, however, he showed once more his mystification. "What then has happened?"

She was once more, with her companion's help, on her feet, and, feeling withdrawal imposed on him, he had found, blankly, his hat and gloves and had reached the door. Yet he waited for her answer. "What *was* to," she said.

V

He came back the next day, but she was then unable to see him, and as it was literally the first time this had occurred in the long stretch of their acquaintance he turned away, defeated and sore, almost angry—or feeling at least that such a break in their custom was really the beginning of the end—and wandered alone with his thoughts, especially with one of them that he was unable to keep down. She was dying, and he would lose her; she was dying, and his life would end. He stopped in the park, into which he had passed, and stared before him at his recurrent doubt. Away from her the doubt pressed again; in her presence he had believed her, but as he felt his forlornness he threw himself into the explanation that, nearest at hand, had most of a miserable warmth for him and least of a cold torment. She had deceived him to save him—to put him off with something in which he should be able to rest. What could the thing that was to happen to him be, after all, but just this thing that had begun to happen? Her dying, her death, his consequent solitude—*that* was what he had figured as the beast in the jungle, that was what had been in the lap of the gods. He had had her word for it as he left her; for what else, on earth, could she have meant? It wasn't a thing of a monstrous order; not a fate rare and distinguished; not a stroke of fortune that overwhelmed and immortalised; it had only the stamp of the common doom. But poor Marcher, at this hour, judged the common doom sufficient. It would serve his turn, and even as the consummation of infinite waiting he would bend his pride to accept it. He sat down on a bench in the twilight. He hadn't been a fool. Something had *been*, as she had said, to come. Before he rose indeed it had quite struck him that the final fact really matched with the long avenue through which he had had to reach it. As sharing his suspense, and as giving herself all, giving her life, to bring it to an end, she had come with him every step of the way. He had lived by her aid, and to leave her behind would be cruelly, damnably to miss her. What could be more overwhelming than that?

Well, he was to know within the week, for though she kept him a while at bay, left him restless and wretched during a series of days on each of which he asked about her only again to have to turn away, she ended his trial by receiving him where she had always received him. Yet she had been brought out at some hazard into the presence of so many of the things that were, consciously, vainly, half their past, and there was scant service left in the gentleness of her mere desire, all too visible, to check his obsession and wind up his long trouble. That was clearly what she wanted; the one thing more, for her own peace, while she could still put out her hand. He was so affected by her state that once seated by her chair, he was moved to let everything go; it was she herself therefore who brought him back, took up again, before she dismissed him, her last word of the other time. She showed how she wished to leave their affair in order. "I'm not sure you understood. You've nothing to wait for more. It *has* come."

Oh, how he looked at her! "Really?"

"Really."

"The thing that, as you said, *was* to?"

"The thing that we began in your youth to watch for."

Face to face with her once more he believed her; it was a claim to which he had so abjectly little to oppose. "You mean that it has come as a positive, definite occurrence, with a name and a date?"

"Positive. Definite. I don't know about the 'name,' but, oh, with a date!"

He found himself again too helplessly at sea. "But come in the night—come and passed me by?"

May Bartram had her strange, faint smile. "Oh no, it hasn't passed you by!"

"But if I haven't been aware of it, and it hasn't touched me——?"

"Ah, your not being aware of it," and she seemed to hesitate an instant to deal with this—"your not being aware of it is the strangeness *in* the strangeness. It's the wonder *of* the wonder." She spoke as with the softness almost of a sick child, yet now at last, at the end of all, with the perfect straightness of a sybil. She visibly knew that she knew, and the effect on him was of something co-ordinate, in its high character, with the law that had ruled him. It was the true voice of the law; so on her lips would the law itself have sounded. "It *has* touched you," she went on. "It has done its office. It has made you all its own."

"So utterly without my knowing it?"

"So utterly without your knowing it." His hand, as he leaned to her, was on the arm of her chair, and, dimly smiling always now, she placed her own on it. "It's enough if *I* know it."

"Oh!" he confusedly sounded, as she herself of late so often had done.

"What I long ago said is true. You'll never know now, and I think you ought to be content. You've *had* it," said May Bartram.

"But had what?"

"Why, what was to have marked you out. The proof of your law. It has acted. I'm too glad," she then gravely added, "to have been able to see what it's *not*."

He continued to attach his eyes to her, and with the sense that it was all beyond him, and that *she* was too, he would still have sharply challenged her, had he not felt it an abuse of her weakness to do more than take devoutly what she gave him, take it as hushed as to a revelation. If he did speak, it was out of the foreknowledge of his loneliness to come. "If you're glad of what it's 'not,' it might then have been worse?"

She turned her eyes away, she looked straight before her; with which, after a moment: "Well, you know our fears."

He wondered. "It's something then we never feared?"

On this, slowly, she turned to him. "Did we ever dream, with all our dreams, that we should sit and talk of it thus?"

He tried for a little to make out if they had; but it was as if their dreams, numberless enough, were in solution in some thick, cold mist, in which thought lost itself. "It might have been that we couldn't talk?"

"Well"—she did her best for him—"not from this side. This, you see," she said, "is the *other* side."

"I think," poor Marcher returned, "that all sides are the same to me." Then, however, as she softly shook her head in correction: "We mightn't, as it were, have got across——?"

"To where we are—no. We're *here*"—she made her weak emphasis.

"And much good does it do us!" was her friend's frank comment.

"It does us the good it can. It does us the good that *it* isn't here. It's past. It's behind," said May Bartram. "Before—" but her voice dropped.

He had got up, not to tire her, but it was hard to combat his yearning. She after all told him nothing but that his light had failed—which he knew well enough without her. "Before—?" he blankly echoed.

"Before, you see, it was always to *come*. That kept it present."

"Oh, I don't care what comes now! Besides," Marcher added, "it seems to me I liked it better present, as you say, than I can like it absent with *your* absence."

"Oh, mine!"—and her pale hands made light of it.

"With the absence of everything." He had a dreadful sense of standing there before her for—so far as anything but this proved, this bottomless drop was concerned—the last time of their life. It rested on him with a weight he felt he could scare bear, and this weight it apparently was that still pressed out what remained in him of speakable protest. "I believe you; but I can't begin to pretend I understand. *Nothing*, for me, is past; nothing *will* pass until I pass myself, which I pray my stars may be as soon as possible. Say, however," he added, "that I've eaten my cake, as you contend, to the last crumb—how can the thing I've never felt at all be the thing I was marked out to feel?"

She met him, perhaps, less directly, but she met him unperturbed. "You take your 'feelings' for granted. You were to suffer your fate. That was not necessarily to know it."

"How in the world—when what is such knowledge but suffering?"

She looked up at him a while, in silence. "No—you don't understand."
"I suffer," said John Marcher.

"Don't, don't!"

"How can I help at least *that?*"

"*Don't!*" May Bartram repeated.

She spoke it in a tone so special, in spite of her weakness, that he stared an instant—stared as if some light, hitherto hidden, had shimmered across his vision. Darkness again closed over it, but the gleam had already become for him an idea. "Because I haven't the right——"

"Don't *know*—when you needn't," she mercifully urged. "You needn't—for we shouldn't."

"Shouldn't?" If he could but know what she meant!

"No—it's too much."

"Too much?" he still asked—but with a mystification that was the next moment, of a sudden, to give way. Her words, if they meant something, affected him in this light—the light also of her wasted face—as meaning *all*, and the sense of what knowledge had been for herself came over him with a rush which broke through into a question. "Is it of that, then, you're dying?"

She but watched him, gravely at first, as if to see, with this, where he was, and she might have seen something, or feared something, that moved her sympathy. "I would live for you still—if I could." Her eyes closed for a little, as if, withdrawn into herself, she were, for a last time, trying. "But I can't!" she said as she raised them again to take leave of him.

She couldn't indeed, as but too promptly and sharply appeared, and he had no vision of her after this that was anything but darkness and doom. They had parted forever in that strange talk; access to her chamber of pain, rigidly guarded, was almost wholly forbidden him; he was feeling now moreover, in the face of doctors, nurses, the two or three relatives attracted doubtless by the presumption of what she had to "leave," how few were the rights, as they were called in such cases, that he had to put forward, and how odd it might even seem that their intimacy shouldn't have given him more of them. The stupidest fourth cousin had more, even though she had been nothing in such a person's life. She had been a feature of features in *his*, for what else was it to have been so indispensable? Strange beyond saying were the ways of existence, baffling for him the anomaly of his lack, as he felt it to be, of producible claim. A woman might have been, as it were, everything to him, and it might yet present him in no connection that anyone appeared obliged to recognise. If this was the case in these closing weeks it was the case more sharply on the occasion of the last offices rendered, in the great grey London cemetery, to what had been mortal, to what had been precious, in his friend. The concourse at her grave was not numerous, but he saw himself treated as scarce more nearly concerned with it than if there had been a thousand others. He was in short from this moment face to face with the fact that he was to profit extraordinarily little by the interest May Bartram had taken in him. He couldn't quite have said what he expected, but he had somehow not expected this approach to a double privation. Not only had her interest failed him, but he seemed to feel himself unattended—and for a reason he couldn't sound—by the distinction, the dignity, the propriety, if nothing else, of the man markedly bereaved. It was as if, in the view of society, he had not *been* markedly bereaved, as if there still failed some sign or proof of it, and as if, none the less, his character could never be affirmed, nor the deficiency ever made up. There were moments, as the weeks went by, when he would have liked, by some almost aggressive act, to take his stand on the intimacy of his loss, in order that it *might* be questioned and his retort, to the relief of his spirit, so recorded; but the moments of an irritation more helpless followed fast on these, the moments during which, turning things over with a good conscience but with a bare horizon, he found himself wondering if he oughtn't to have begun, so to speak, further back.

He found himself wondering indeed at many things, and this last speculation had others to keep it company. What could he have done, after all, in her lifetime, without giving them both, as it were, away? He couldn't have made it known she was watching him, for that would have published the superstition of the Beast. This was what closed his mouth now—now that the Jungle had been threshed to vacancy and that the Beast had stolen away. It sounded too foolish and too flat; the difference for him in this particular, the extinction in his life of the element of suspense, was such in fact as to surprise. He could scarce have said what the effect resembled; the abrupt cessation, the positive prohibition, of music perhaps, more than anything else, in some place all adjusted and all accustomed to sonority and to attention. If he could at any rate have conceived lifting the veil from his image at some moment of the past (what had he done, after all, if not lift it to *her?*) so to do this to-day, to talk to people at large of the Jungle cleared and confide to them that he now felt it as safe, would have been not only to see them listen as to a goodwife's tale, but really to hear himself tell one. What it presently came to in truth was that poor Marcher waded through his beaten grass, where no life stirred, where no breath sounded, where no evil eye seemed to gleam from a possible lair, very much as if vaguely looking for the Beast, and still more as if missing it. He walked about in an existence that had grown strangely more spacious, and, stopping fitfully in places where the undergrowth of life struck him as closer, asked himself yearningly, wondered secretly and sorely, if it would have lurked here or there. It would have at all events *sprung*; what was at least complete was his belief in the truth itself of the assurance given him. The change from his old

sense to his new was absolute and final: what was to happen *had* so
absolutely and finally happened that he was as little able to know a fear
for his future as to know a hope; so absent in short was any question of
anything still to come. He was to live entirely with the other question,
that of his unidentified past, that of his having to see his fortune im-
penetrably muffled and masked.

The torment of this vision became then his occupation; he couldn't perhaps have consented to live but for the possibility of guessing. She had told
him, his friend, not to guess; she had forbidden him, so far as he might, to
know, and she had even in a sort denied the power in him to learn: which
were so many things, precisely, to deprive him of rest. It wasn't that he
wanted, he argued for fairness, that anything that had happened to him
should happen over again; it was only that he shouldn't, as an anticlimax,
have been taken sleeping so sound as not to be able to win back by an
effort of thought the lost stuff of consciousness. He declared to himself at
moments that he would either win it back or have done with consciousness
for ever; he made this idea his one motive, in fine, made it so much his
passion that none other, to compare with it, seemed ever to have touched
him. The lost stuff of consciousness became thus for him as a strayed
or stolen child to an unappeasable father; he hunted it up and down very
much as if he were knocking at doors and inquiring of the police. This
was the spirit in which, inevitably, he set himself to travel; he started
on a journey that was to be as long as he could make it; it danced before
him that, as the other side of the globe couldn't possibly have less to say
to him, it might, by a possibility of suggestion, have more. Before he
quitted London, however, he made a pilgrimage to May Bartram's grave,
took his way to it through the endless avenues of the grim suburban
necropolis, sought it out in the wilderness of tombs, and, though he had
come but for the renewal of the act of farewell, found himself, when he
had at last stood by it, beguiled into long intensities. He stood for an
hour, powerless to turn away and yet powerless to penetrate the darkness
of death; fixing with his eyes her inscribed name and date, beating his
forehead against the fact of the secret they kept, drawing his breath,
while he waited as if, in pity of him, some sense would rise from the stones.
He kneeled on the stones, however, in vain; they kept what they concealed;
and if the face of the tomb did become a face for him it was because
her two names were like a pair of eyes that didn't know him. He gave
them a last long look, but no palest light broke.

VI

He stayed away, after this, for a year; he visited the depths of Asia,
spending himself on scenes of romantic interest, of superlative sanctity;
but what was present to him everywhere was that for a man who had

known what *he* had known the world was vulgar and vain. The state of mind in which he had lived for so many years shone out to him, in reflection, as a light that coloured and refined, a light beside which the glow of the East was garish, cheap and thin. The terrible truth was that he had lost—with everything else—a distinction as well; the things he saw couldn't help being common when he had become common to look at them. He was simply now one of them himself—he was in the dust, without a peg for the sense of difference; and there were hours when, before the temples of gods and the sepulchres of kings, his spirit turned, for nobleness of association, to the barely discriminated slab in the London suburb. That had become for him, and more intensely with time and distance, his one witness of a past glory. It was all that was left to him for proof or pride, yet the past glories of Pharaohs were nothing to him as he thought of it. Small wonder then that he came back to it on the morrow of his return. He was drawn there this time as irresistibly as the other, yet with a confidence, almost, that was doubtless the effect of the many months that had elapsed. He had lived, in spite of himself, into his change of feeling, and in wandering over the earth had wandered, as might be said, from the circumference to the centre of his desert. He had settled to his safety and accepted perforce his extinction; figuring to himself, with some colour, in the likeness of certain little old men he remembered to have seen, of whom, all meagre and wizened as they might look, it was related that they had in their time fought twenty duels or been loved by ten princesses. They indeed had been wondrous for others, while he was but wondrous for himself; which, however, was exactly the cause of his haste to renew the wonder by getting back, as he might put it, into his own presence. That had quickened his steps and checked his delay. If his visit was prompt it was because he had been separated so long from the part of himself that alone he now valued.

It is accordingly not false to say that he reached his goal with a certain elation, and stood there again with a certain assurance. The creature beneath the sod *knew* of his rare experience, so that, strangely now, the place had lost for him its mere blankness of expression. It met him in mildness—not, as before, in mockery; it wore for him the air of conscious greeting that we find, after absence, in things that have closely belonged to us and which seem to confess of themselves to the connection. The plot of ground, the graven tablet, the tended flowers affected him so as belonging to him that he quite felt for the hour like a contented landlord reviewing a piece of property. Whatever had happened—well, had happened. He had not come back this time with the vanity of that question, his former worrying, "What *what?*" now practically so spent. Yet he would, none the less, never again so cut himself off from the spot; he would come back to it every month, for if he did nothing else by its aid he at least held up his head. It thus grew for him, in the oddest way, a positive resource; he carried out his idea of periodical returns, which took their place at last among the most inveterate of his habits. What it all amounted to, oddly enough, was that, in his now so simplified world, this garden of death gave him the few square feet of earth on which he could still most live. It was as if, being nothing anywhere else for anyone, nothing even for himself, he were just everything here, and if not for a crowd of witnesses, or indeed for any witness but John Marcher, then by clear right of the register that he could scan like an open page. The open page was the tomb of his friend, and *there* were the facts of the past, there the truth of his life, there the backward reaches in which he could lose himself. He did this, from time to time, with such effect that he seemed to wander through the old years with his hand in the arm of a companion who was, in the most extraordinary manner, his other, his younger self; and to wander, which was more extraordinary yet, round and round a third presence—not wandering she, but stationary, still, whose eyes, turning with his revolution, never ceased to follow him, and whose seat was his point, so to speak, of orientation. Thus in short he settled to live—feeding only on the sense that he once *had* lived, and dependent on it not only for a support but for an identity.

It sufficed him, in its way, for months, and the year elapsed; it would doubtless even have carried him further but for an accident, superficially slight, which moved him, in a quite other direction, with a force beyond any of his impressions of Egypt or of India. It was a thing of the merest chance—the turn, as he afterwards felt, of a hair, though he was indeed to live to believe that if light hadn't come to him in this particular fashion it would still have come in another. He was to live to believe this, I say, though he was not to live, I may not less definitely mention, to do much else. We allow him at any rate the benefit of the conviction, struggling up for him at the end, that, whatever might have happened or not happened, he would have come round of himself to the light. The incident of an autumn day had put the match to the train laid from of old by his misery. With the light before him he knew that even of late his ache had only been smothered. It was strangely drugged, but it throbbed; at the touch it began to bleed. And the touch, in the event, was the face of a fellow-mortal. This face, one grey afternoon when the leaves were thick in the alleys, looked into Marcher's own, at the cemetery, with an expression like the cut of a blade. He felt it, that is, so deep down that he winced at the steady thrust. The person who so mutely assaulted him was a figure he had noticed, on reaching his own goal, absorbed by a grave a short distance away, a grave apparently fresh, so that the emotion of the visitor would probably match it for frankness. This fact alone forbade further attention, though during the time he stayed he remained vaguely conscious of his neighbour, a middle-aged man apparently, in mourning, whose bowed back, among the clustered monuments and mortuary yews, was constantly presented. Marcher's theory that these were elements in contact with which he himself revived, had suffered, on this occasion, it may be granted, a sensible though inscrutable check. The autumn day was dire for him as none had recently been, and he rested with a heaviness he had not yet known on the low tone table that bore May Bartram's name. He rested without power to move, as if some spring in him, some spell vouchsafed, had suddenly been broken forever. If he could have done that moment as he wanted he would simply have stretched himself on the slab that was ready to take him, treating it as a place prepared to receive his last sleep. What in all the wide world had he now to keep awake for? He stared before him with the question, and it was then that, as one of the cemetery walks passed near him, he caught the shock of the face.

His neighbour at the other grave had withdrawn, as he himself, with force in him to move, would have done by now, and was advancing along the path on his way to one of the gates. This brought him near, and his pace was slow, so that—and all the more as there was a kind of hunger in his look—the two men were for a minute directly confronted. Marcher felt him on the spot as one of the deeply stricken—a perception so sharp that nothing else in the picture lived for it, neither his dress, his age, nor his presumable character and class; nothing lived but the deep ravage of the features that he showed. He *showed* them—that was the point; he was moved, as he passed, by some impulse that was either a signal for sympathy or, more possibly, a challenge to another sorrow. He might already have been aware of our friend, might, at some previous hour, have noticed in him the smooth habit of the scene, with which the state of his own senses so scantly consorted, and might thereby have been stirred as by a kind of overt discord. What Marcher was at all events conscious of was, in the first place, that the image of scarred passion presented to him was conscious too—of something that profaned the air; and, in the second, that, roused, startled, shocked, he was yet the next moment looking after it, as it went, with envy. The most extraordinary thing that had happened to him—though he had given that name to other matters as well—took place, after his immediate vague stare, as a consequence of this impression. The stranger passed, but the raw glare of his grief remained, making our friend wonder in pity what wrong, what wound it expressed, what injury not to be healed. What had the man *had* to make him, by the loss of it, so bleed and yet live?

Something—and this reached him with a pang—that *he,* John Marcher, hadn't; the proof of which was precisely John Marcher's arid end. No passion had ever touched him, for this was what passion meant; he had survived and maundered and pined, but where had been *his* deep ravage?

The extraordinary thing we speak of was the sudden rush of the result of this question. The sight that had just met his eyes named to him, as in letters of quick flame, something he had utterly, insanely missed, and what he had missed; made these things a train of fire, made them mark themselves in an anguish of inward throbs. He had seen *outside* of his life, not learned it within, the way a woman was mourned when she had been loved for herself; such was the force of his conviction of the meaning of the stranger's face, which still flared for him like a smoky torch. It had not come to him, the knowledge, on the wings of experience; it had brushed him, jostled him, upset him, with the disrespect of chance, the insolence of an accident. Now that the illumination had begun, however, it blazed to the zenith, and what he presently stood there gazing at was the sounded void of his life. He gazed, he drew breath, in pain; he turned in his dismay, and, turning, he had before him in sharper incision than ever the open page of his story. The name on the table smote him as the passage of his neighbour had done, and what it said to him, full in the face, was that *she* was what he had missed. This was the awful thought, the answer to all the past, the vision at the dread clearness of which he turned as cold as the stone beneath him. Everything fell together, confessed, explained, overwhelmed; leaving him most of all stupefied at the blindness he had cherished. The fate he had been marked for he had met with a vengeance—he had emptied the cup to the lees; he had been the man of his time, *the* man, to whom nothing on earth was to have happened. That was the rare stroke—that was his visitation. So he saw it, as we say, in pale horror, while the pieces fitted and fitted. So *she* had seen it, while he didn't, and so she served at this hour to drive the truth home. It was the truth, vivid and monstrous, that all the while he had waited the wait was itself his portion. This the companion of his vigil had at a given moment perceived, and she had then offered him the chance to baffle his doom. One's doom, however, was never baffled, and on the day she had told him that his own had come down she had seen him but stupidly stare at the escape she offered him.

The escape would have been to love her; then, *then* he would have lived. *She* had lived—who could say now with what passion?—since she had loved him for himself; whereas he had never thought of her (ah, how it hugely glared at him!) but in the chill of his egotism and the light of her use. Her spoken words came back to him, and the chain stretched and stretched. The beast had lurked indeed, and the beast, at its hour, had sprung; it had sprung in that twilight of the cold April when, pale, ill, wasted, but all beautiful, and perhaps even then recoverable, she had risen from her chair to stand before him and let him imaginably guess. It had sprung as he didn't guess; it had sprung as she hopelessly turned from him, and the mark, by the time he left her, had fallen where it *was* to fall. He had justified his fear and achieved his fate; he had failed, with the last exactitude, of all he was to fail of; and a moan now rose to his lips as he remembered she had prayed he mightn't know. This horror of waking—*this* was knowledge, knowledge under the breath of which the very tears in his eyes seemed to freeze. Through them, none the less, he tried to fix it and hold it; he kept it there before him so that he might feel the pain. That at least, belated and bitter, had something of the taste of life. But the bitterness suddenly sickened him, and it was as if, horribly, he saw, in the truth, in the cruelty of his image, what had been appointed and done. He saw the Jungle of his life and saw the lurking Beast; then, while he looked, perceived it, as by a stir of the air, rise, huge and hideous, for the leap that was to settle him. His eyes darkened—it was close; and, instinctively turning, in his hallucination, to avoid it, he flung himself, on his face, on the tomb.

Joseph Conrad 1857–1924

The Secret Sharer

I

On my right hand there were lines of fishing-stakes resembling a mysterious system of half-submerged bamboo fences, incomprehensible in its division of the domain of tropical fishes, and crazy of aspect as if abandoned forever by some nomad tribe of fishermen now gone to the other end of the ocean; for there was no sign of human habitation as far as the eye could reach. To the left a group of barren islets, suggesting ruins of stone walls, towers, and blockhouses, had its foundations set in a blue sea that itself looked solid, so still and stable did it lie below my feet; even the track of light from the westering sun shone smoothly, without that animated glitter which tells of an imperceptible ripple. And when I turned my head to take a parting glance at the tug which had just left us anchored outside the bar, I saw the straight line of the flat shore joined to the stable sea, edge to edge, with a perfect and unmarked closeness, in one leveled floor half brown, half blue under the enormous dome of the sky. Corresponding in their insignificance to the islets of the sea, two small clumps of trees, one on each side of the only fault in the impeccable joint, marked the mouth of the river Meinam we had just left on the first preparatory stage of our homeward journey; and, far back on the inland level, a larger and loftier mass, the grove surrounding the great Paknam pagoda, was the only thing on which the eye could rest from the vain task of exploring the monotonous sweep of the horizon. Here and there gleams as of a few scattered pieces of silver marked the windings of the great river; and on the nearest of them, just within the bar, the tug steaming right into the land became lost to my sight, hull and funnel and masts, as though the impassive earth had swallowed her up without an effort, without a tremor. My eye followed the light cloud of her smoke, now here, now there, above the plain, according to the devious curves of the stream, but always fainter and farther away, till I lost it at last behind the miter-shaped hill of the great pagoda. And then I was left alone with my ship, anchored at the head of the Gulf of Siam.

She floated at the starting-point of a long journey, very still in an

53

immense stillness, the shadows of her spars flung far to the eastward by the setting sun. At that moment I was alone on her decks. There was not a sound in her—and around us nothing moved, nothing lived, not a canoe on the water, not a bird in the air, not a cloud in the sky. In this breathless pause at the threshold of a long passage we seemed to be measuring our fitness for a long and arduous enterprise, the appointed task of both our existences to be carried out, far from all human eyes, with only sky and sea for spectators and for judges.

There must have been some glare in the air to interfere with one's sight, because it was only just before the sun left us that my roaming eyes made out beyond the highest ridge of the principal islet of the group something which did away with the solemnity of perfect solitude. The tide of darkness flowed on swiftly; and with tropical suddenness a swarm of stars came out above the shadowy earth, while I lingered yet, my hand resting lightly on my ship's rail as if on the shoulder of a trusted friend. But, with all that multitude of celestial bodies staring down at one, the comfort of quiet communion with her was gone for good. And there were also disturbing sounds by this time—voices, footsteps forward; the steward flitted along the maindeck, a busily ministering spirit; a hand-bell tinkled urgently under the poop-deck. . . .

I found my two officers waiting for me near the supper table, in the lighted cuddy. We sat down at once, and as I helped the chief mate, I said:

"Are you aware that there is a ship anchored inside the islands? I saw her mastheads above the ridge as the sun went down."

He raised sharply his simple face, overcharged by a terrible growth of whisker, and emitted his usual ejaculations: "Bless my soul, sir! You don't say so!"

My second mate was a round-cheeked, silent young man, grave beyond his years, I thought; but as our eyes happened to meet I detected a slight quiver on his lips. I looked down at once. It was not my part to encourage sneering on board my ship. It must be said, too, that I knew very little of my officers. In consequence of certain events of no particular significance, except to myself, I had been appointed to the command only a fortnight before. Neither did I know much of the hands forward. All these people had been together for eighteen months or so, and my position was that of the only stranger on board. I mention this because it has some bearing on what is to follow. But what I felt most was my being a stranger to the ship; and if all the truth must be told, I was somewhat of a stranger to myself. The youngest man on board (barring the second mate), and untried as yet by a position of the fullest responsibility, I was willing to take the adequacy of the others for granted. They had simply to be equal to their tasks; but I wondered how far I should turn out faithful to that ideal conception of one's own personality every man sets up for himself secretly.

Meantime the chief mate, with an almost visible effect of collaboration on the part of his round eyes and frightful whiskers, was trying to evolve a theory of the anchored ship. His dominant trait was to take all things into earnest consideration. He was of a painstaking turn of mind. As he used to say, he "liked to account to himself" for practically everything that came in his way, down to a miserable scorpion he had found in his cabin a week before. The why and the wherefore of that scorpion—how it got on board and came to select his room rather than the pantry (which was a dark place and more what a scorpion would be partial to), and how on earth it managed to drown itself in the inkwell of his writing-desk—had exercised him infinitely. The ship within the islands was much more easily accounted for; and just as we were about to rise from table he made his pronouncement. She was, he doubted not, a ship from home lately arrived. Probably she drew too much water to cross the bar except at the top of spring tides. Therefore she went into that natural harbor to wait for a few days in preference to remaining in an open roadstead.

"That's so," confirmed the second mate, suddenly, in his slightly hoarse voice. "She draws over twenty feet. She's the Liverpool ship *Sephora* with a cargo of coal. Hundred and twenty-three days from Cardiff."

We looked at him in surprise.

"The tugboat skipper told me when he came on board for your letters, sir," explained the young man. "He expects to take her up the river the day after tomorrow."

After thus overwhelming us with the extent of his information he slipped out of the cabin. The mate observed regretfully that he "could not account for that young fellow's whims." What prevented him telling us all about it at once, he wanted to know.

I detained him as he was making a move. For the last two days the crew had had plenty of hard work, and the night before they had very little sleep. I felt painfully that I—a stranger—was doing something unusual when I directed him to let all hands turn in without setting an anchor-watch. I proposed to keep on deck myself till one o'clock or thereabouts. I would get the second mate to relieve me at that hour.

"He will turn out the cook and the steward at four," I concluded, "and then give you a call. Of course at the slightest sign of any sort of wind we'll have the hands up and make a start at once."

He concealed his astonishment. "Very well, sir." Outside the cuddy he put his head in the second mate's door to inform him of my unheard-of caprice to take a five hours' anchor-watch on myself. I heard the other raise his voice incredulously—"What? The Captain himself?" Then a few more murmurs, a door closed, then another. A few moments later I went on deck.

My strangeness, which had made me sleepless, had prompted that unconventional arrangement, as if I had expected in those solitary hours of the night to get on terms with the ship of which I knew nothing, manned by men of whom I knew very little more. Fast alongside a wharf, littered like any ship in port with a tangle of unrelated things, invaded by unrelated shore people, I had hardly seen her yet properly. Now, as she lay cleared for sea, the stretch of her main-deck seemed to me very fine under the stars. Very fine, very roomy for her size, and very inviting, I descended the poop and paced the waist, my mind picturing to myself the coming passage through the Malay Archipelago, down the Indian Ocean, and up the Atlantic. All its phases were familiar enough to me, very characteristic, all the alternatives which were likely to face me on the high seas—everything! . . . except the novel responsiblity of command. But I took heart from the reasonable thought that the ship was like other ships, the men like other men, and that the sea was not likely to keep any special surprises expressly for my discomfiture.

Arrived at that comforting conclusion, I bethought myself of a cigar and went below to get it. All was still down there. Everybody at the after end of the ship was sleeping profoundly. I came out again on the quarter-deck, agreeably at ease in my sleeping-suit on that warm breathless night, barefooted, a glowing cigar in my teeth, and, going forward, I was met by the profound silence of the fore end of the ship. Only as I passed the door of the forecastle I heard a deep, quiet, trustful sigh of some sleeper inside. And suddenly I rejoiced in the great security of the sea as compared with the unrest of the land, in my choice of that untempted life presenting no disquieting problems, invested with an elementary moral beauty by the absolute straightforwardness of its appeal and by the singleness of its purpose.

The riding-light in the fore-rigging burned with a clear, untroubled, as if symbolic, flame, confident and bright in the mysterious shades of the night. Passing on my way aft along the other side of the ship, I observed that the rope side-ladder, put over, no doubt, for the master of the tug when he came to fetch away our letters, had not been hauled in as it should have been. I became annoyed at this, for exactitude in small matters is the very soul of discipline. Then I reflected that I had myself peremptorily dismissed my officers from duty, and by my own act had prevented the anchor-watch being formally set and things properly attended to. I asked myself whether it was wise ever to interfere with the established routine of duties even from the kindest of motives. My action might have made me appear eccentric. Goodness only knew how that absurdly whiskered mate would "account" for my conduct, and what the whole ship thought of that informality of their new captain. I was vexed with myself.

Not from compunction certainly, but, as it were mechanically, I proceeded to get the ladder in myself. Now a side-ladder of that sort is a light affair and comes in easily, yet my vigorous tug, which should have brought it flying on board, merely recoiled upon my body in a totally unexpected jerk. What the devil! . . . I was so astounded by the immovableness of that ladder that I remained stock-still, trying to account for it to myself like that imbecile mate of mine. In the end, of course, I put my head over the rail.

The side of the ship made an opaque belt of shadow on the darkling glassy shimmer of the sea. But I saw at once something elongated and pale floating very close to the ladder. Before I could form a guess a faint flash of phosphorescent light, which seemed to issue suddenly from the naked body of a man, flickered in the sleeping water with the elusive, silent play of summer lightning in a night sky. With a gasp I saw revealed to my stare a pair of feet, the long legs, a broad livid back immersed right up to the neck in a greenish cadaverous glow. One hand, awash, clutched the bottom rung of the ladder. He was complete but for the head. A headless corpse! The cigar dropped out of my gaping mouth with a tiny plop and a short hiss quite audible in the absolute stillness of all things under heaven. At that I suppose he raised up his face, a dimly pale oval in the shadow of the ship's side. But even then I could only barely make out down there the shape of his black-haired head. However, it was enough for the horrid, frost-bound sensation which had gripped me about the chest to pass off. The moment of vain exclamations was past, too. I only climbed on the spare spar and leaned over the rail as far as I could, to bring my eyes nearer to that mystery floating alongside.

As he hung by the ladder, like a resting swimmer, the sea-lightning played about his limbs at every stir; and he appeared in it ghastly, silvery, fish-like. He remained as mute as a fish, too. He made no motion to get out of the water, either. It was inconceivable that he should not attempt to come on board, and strangely troubling to suspect that perhaps he did not want to. And my first words were prompted by just that troubled incertitude.

"What's the matter?" I asked in my ordinary tone, speaking down to the face upturned exactly under mine.

"Cramp," it answered, no louder. Then slightly anxious, "I say, no need to call anyone."

"I was not going to," I said.

"Are you alone on deck?"

"Yes."

I had somehow the impression that he was on the point of letting go the ladder to swim away beyond my ken—mysterious as he came. But, for the moment, this being appearing as if he had risen from the bottom of the sea (it was certainly the nearest land to the ship) wanted only to know the time. I told him. And he, down there, tentatively:

"I suppose your captain's turned in?"

"I am sure he isn't," I said.

He seemed to struggle with himself, for I heard something like the low, bitter murmur of doubt. "What's the good?" His next words came out with a hesitating effort.

"Look here, my man. Could you call him out quietly?"

I thought the time had come to declare myself.

"I am the captain."

I heard a "By Jove!" whispered at the level of the water. The phosphorescence flashed in the swirl of the water all about his limbs, his other hand seized the ladder.

"My name's Leggatt."

The voice was calm and resolute. A good voice. The self-possession of that man had somehow induced a corresponding state in myself. It was very quietly that I remarked:

"You must be a good swimmer."

"Yes. I've been in the water practically since nine o'clock. The question for me now is whether I am to let go this ladder and go on swimming till I sink from exhaustion, or—to come on board here."

I felt this was no mere formula of desperate speech, but a real alternative in the view of a strong soul. I should have gathered from this that he was young; indeed, it is only the young who are ever confronted by such clear issues. But at the time it was pure intuition on my part. A mysterious communication was established already between us two—in the face of that silent, darkened tropical sea. I was young, too; young enough to make no comment. The man in the water began suddenly to climb up the ladder, and I hastened away from the rail to fetch some clothes.

Before entering the cabin I stood still, listening in the lobby at the foot of the stairs. A faint snore came through the closed door of the chief mate's room. The second mate's door was on the hook, but the darkness in there was absolutely soundless. He, too, was young and could sleep like a stone. Remained the steward, but he was not likely to wake up before he was called. I got a sleeping-suit out of my room and, coming back on deck, saw the naked man from the sea sitting on the main-hatch, glimmering white in the darkness, his elbows on his knees and his head in his hands. In a moment he had concealed his damp body in a sleeping-suit of the same gray-stripe pattern as the one I was wearing and followed me like my double on the poop. Together we moved right aft, barefooted, silent.

"What is it?" I asked in a deadened voice, taking the lighted lamp out of the binnacle, and raising it to his face.

"An ugly business."

He had rather regular features; a good mouth; light eyes under somewhat heavy, dark eyebrows; a smooth, square forehead; no growth on his cheeks; a small, brown mustache, and a well-shaped, round chin. His expression was concentrated, meditative, under the inspecting light of the lamp I held up to his face; such as a man thinking hard in solitude might wear. My sleeping-suit was just right for his size. A well-knit young fellow of twenty-five at most. He caught his lower lip with the edge of white, even teeth.

"Yes," I said, replacing the lamp in the binnacle. The warm, heavy tropical night closed upon his head again.

"There's a ship over there," he murmured.

"Yes, I know. The *Sephora*. Did you know of us?"

"Hadn't the slightest idea. I am the mate of her—" He paused and corrected himself. "I should say I *was*."

"Aha! Something wrong?"

"Yes. Very wrong indeed. I've killed a man."

"What do you mean? Just now?"

"No, on the passage. Weeks ago. Thirty-nine south. When I say a man—"

"Fit of temper," I suggested, confidently.

The shadowy, dark head, like mine, seemed to nod imperceptibly above the ghostly gray of my sleeping-suit. It was, in the night, as though I had been faced by my own reflection in the depths of a somber and immense mirror.

"A pretty thing to have to own up to for a Conway boy," murmured my double, distinctly.

"You're a Conway boy?"

"I am," he said, as if startled. Then, slowly . . . "Perhaps you too—"

It was so; but being a couple of years older I had left before he joined. After a quick interchange of dates a silence fell; and I thought suddenly of my absurd mate with his terrific whiskers and the "Bless my soul—you don't say so" type of intellect. My double gave me an inkling of his thoughts by saying: "My father's a parson in Norfolk. Do you see me before a judge and jury on that charge? For myself I can't see the necessity. There are fellows that an angel from heaven—And I am not that. He was one of those creatures that are just simmering all the time with a silly sort of wickedness. Miserable devils that have no business to live at all. He wouldn't do his duty and wouldn't let anybody else do theirs. But what's the good of talking! You know well enough the sort of ill-conditioned snarling cur—"

He appealed to me as if our experiences had been as identical as our clothes. And I knew well enough the pestiferous danger of such a character where there are no means of legal repression. And I knew well enough also that my double there was no homicidal ruffian. I did not think of asking him for details, and he told me the story roughly in brusque, disconnected sentences. I needed no more. I saw it all going on as though I were myself inside that other sleeping-suit.

"It happened while we were setting a reefed foresail, at dusk. Reefed foresail! You understand the sort of weather. The only sail we had left to keep the ship running; so you may guess what it had been like for days.

Anxious sort of job, that. He gave me some of his cursed insolence at the sheet. I tell you I was overdone with this terrific weather that seemed to have no end to it. Terrific, I tell you—and a deep ship. I believe the fellow himself was half crazed with funk. It was no time for gentlemanly reproof, so I turned round and felled him like an ox. He up and at me. We closed just as an awful sea made for the ship. All hands saw it coming and took to the rigging, but I had him by the throat, and went on shaking him like a rat, the men above us yelling, 'Look out! look out!' Then a crash as if the sky had fallen on my head. They say that for over ten minutes hardly anything was to be seen of the ship—just the three masts and a bit of the forecastle head and of the poop all awash driving along in a smother of foam. It was a miracle that they found us, jammed together behind the forebits. It's clear that I meant business, because I was holding him by the throat still when they picked us up. He was black in the face. It was too much for them. It seems they rushed us aft together, gripped as we were, screaming 'Murder!' like a lot of lunatics, and broke into the cuddy. And the ship running for her life, touch and go all the time, any minute her last in a sea fit to turn your hair gray only a-looking at it. I understand that the skipper, too, started raving like the rest of them. The man had been deprived of sleep for more than a week, and to have this sprung on him at the height of a furious gale nearly drove him out of his mind. I wonder they didn't fling me overboard after getting the carcass of their precious shipmate out of my fingers. They had rather a job to separate us, I've been told. A sufficiently fierce story to make an old judge and a respectable jury sit up a bit. The first thing I heard when I came to myself was the maddening howling of that endless gale, and on that the voice of the old man. He was hanging on to my bunk, staring into my face out of his sou-wester.

" 'Mr. Leggatt, you have killed a man. You can act no longer as chief mate of this ship.' "

His care to subdue his voice made it sound monotonous. He rested a hand on the end of the skylight to steady himself with, and all that time did not stir a limb, so far as I could see. "Nice little tale for a quiet tea-party," he concluded in the same tone.

One of my hands, too, rested on the end of the skylight; neither did I stir a limb, so far as I knew. We stood less than a foot from each other. It occurred to me that if old "Bless my soul—you don't say so" were to put his head up the companion and catch sight of us, he would think he was seeing double, or imagine himself come upon a scene of weird witchcraft; the strange captain having a quiet confabulation by the wheel with his own gray ghost. I became very much concerned to prevent anything of the sort. I heard the other's soothing undertone.

"My father's a parson in Norfolk," it said. Evidently he had forgotten he had told me this important fact before. Truly a nice little tale.

"You had better slip down into my stateroom now," I said, moving off stealthily. My double followed my movements; our bare feet made no sound; I let him in, closed the door with care, and, after giving a call to the second mate, returned on deck for my relief.

"Not much sign of any wind yet," I remarked when he approached.

"No, sir. Not much," he assented, sleepily, in his hoarse voice, with just enough deference, no more, and barely suppressing a yawn.

"Well, that's all you have to look out for. You have got your orders."

"Yes, sir."

I paced a turn or two on the poop and saw him take up his position face forward with his elbows in the ratlines of the mizzen-rigging before I went below. The mate's faint snoring was still going on peacefully. The cuddy lamp was burning over the table on which stood a vase with flowers, a polite attention from the ship's provision merchant—the last flowers we should see for the next three months at the very least. Two bunches of bananas hung from the beam symmetrically, one on each side of the rudder-casing. Everything was as before in the ship—except that two of her captain's sleeping-suits were simultaneously in use, one motionless in the cuddy, the other keeping very still in the captain's stateroom.

It must be explained here that my cabin had the form of the capital letter L, the door being within the angle and opening into the short part of the letter. A couch was to the left, the bed-place to the right; my writing-desk and the chronometers' table faced the door. But anyone opening it, unless he stepped right inside, had no view of what I call the long (or vertical) part of the letter. It contained some lockers surmounted by a book-case; and a few clothes, a thick jacket or two, caps, oilskin coat, and such like, hung on hooks. There was at the bottom of that part a door opening into my bathroom, which could be entered also directly from the saloon. But that way was never used.

The mysterious arrival had discovered the advantage of this particular shape. Entering my room, lighted strongly by a big bulkhead lamp swung on gimbals above my writing-desk, I did not see him anywhere till he stepped out quietly from behind the coats hung in the recessed part.

"I heard somebody moving about, and went in there at once," he whispered.

I, too, spoke under my breath.

"Nobody is likely to come in here without knocking and getting permission."

He nodded. His face was thin and the sunburn faded, as though he had been ill. And no wonder. He had been, I heard presently, kept under arrest in his cabin for nearly seven weeks. But there was nothing sickly in his eyes or in his expression. He was not a bit like me, really; yet, as we stood leaning over my bed-place, whispering side by side, with our dark heads together and our backs to the door, anybody bold enough to open it stealthily would have been treated to the uncanny sight of a double captain busy talking in whispers with his other self.

"But all this doesn't tell me how you came to hang on to our side-ladder," I inquired, in the hardly audible murmurs we used, after he had told me something more of the proceedings on board the *Sephora* once the bad weather was over.

"When we sighted Java Head I had had time to think all those matters out several times over. I had six weeks of doing nothing else, and with only an hour or so every evening for a tramp on the quarter-deck."

He whispered, his arms folded on the side of my bed-place, staring through the open port. And I could imagine perfectly the manner of this thinking out—a stubborn if not a steadfast operation; something of which I should have been perfectly incapable.

"I reckoned it would be dark before we closed with the land," he continued, so low that I had to strain my hearing, near as we were to each other, shoulder touching shoulder almost. "So I asked to speak to the old man. He always seemed very sick when he came to see me—as if he could not look me in the face. You know, that foresail saved the ship. She was too deep to have run long under bare poles. And it was I that managed to set it for him. Anyway, he came. When I had him in my cabin—he stood by the door looking at me as if I had the halter round my neck already— I asked him right away to leave my cabin door unlocked at night while the ship was going through Sunda Straits. There would be the Java coast within two or three miles, off Angier Point. I wanted nothing more. I've had a prize for swimming my second year in the Conway."

"I can believe it," I breathed out.

"God only knows why they locked me in every night. To see some of their faces you'd have thought they were afraid I'd go about at night strangling people. Am I a murdering brute? Do I look it? By Jove! if I had been he wouldn't have trusted himself like that into my room. You'll say I might have chucked him aside and bolted out, there and then—it was dark already. Well, no. And for the same reason I wouldn't think of trying to smash the door. There would have been a rush to stop me at the noise, and I did not mean to get into a confounded scrimmage. Somebody else might have got killed—for I would not have broken out only to get chucked back, and I did not want any more of that work. He refused, looking more sick than ever. He was afraid of the men, and also of that old second mate of his who had been sailing with him for years—a gray-headed old humbug; and his steward, too, had been with him devil knows how long—seventeen years or more—a dogmatic sort of loafer who hated me like poison, just because I was the chief mate. No chief mate ever made more than one voyage in the *Sephora*, you know. Those two old chaps ran the ship. Devil only knows what the skipper wasn't afraid of (all his nerve went to pieces altogether in that hellish spell of bad weather we had)—of what the law would do to him—of his wife, perhaps. Oh, yes! she's on board. Though I don't think she would have meddled. She would have been only too glad to have me out of the ship in any way. The 'brand of Cain' business, don't you see. That's all right. I was ready enough to go off wandering on the face of the earth—and that was price enough to pay for an Abel of that sort. Anyhow, he wouldn't listen to me. 'This thing must take its course. I represent the law here.' He was shaking like a leaf. 'So you won't?' 'No!' 'Then I hope you will be able to sleep on that,' I said, and turned my back on him. 'I wonder that *you* can,' cries he, and locks the door.

"Well, after that, I couldn't. Not very well. That was three weeks ago. We have had a slow passage through the Java Sea; drifted about Carimata for ten days. When we anchored here they thought, I suppose, it was all right. The nearest land (and that's five miles) is the ship's destination; the consul would soon set about catching me; and there would have been no object in bolting to these islets there. I don't suppose there's a drop of water on them. I don't know how it was, but tonight that steward, after bringing me my supper, went out to let me eat it, and left the door unlocked. And I ate it—all there was, too. After I had finished I strolled out on the quarter-deck. I don't know that I meant to do anything. A breath of fresh air was all I wanted, I believe. Then a sudden temptation came over me. I kicked off my slippers and was in the water before I had made up my mind fairly. Somebody heard the splash and they raised an awful hullabaloo. 'He's gone! Lower the boats! He's committed suicide! No, he's swimming.' Certainly I was swimming. It's not so easy for a swimmer like me to commit suicide by drowning. I landed on the nearest islet before the boat left the ship's side. I heard them pulling about in the dark, hailing, and so on, but after a bit they gave up. Everything quieted down and the anchorage became as still as death. I sat down on a stone and began to think. I felt certain they would start searching for me at daylight. There was no place to hide on those stony things—and if there had been, what would have been the good? But now I was clear of that ship, I was not going back. So after a while I took off all my clothes, tied them up in a bundle with a stone inside, and dropped them in the deep water on the outer side of that islet. That was suicide enough for me. Let them think what they like, but I didn't mean to drown myself. I meant to swim till I sank—but that's not the same thing. I struck out for another of these little islands, and it was from that one that I first saw your riding-light. Something to swim for. I went on easily, and on the way I came upon a flat rock a foot or two above water. In the daytime, I dare say, you might make it out with a glass from your poop. I scrambled up on it and rested myself for a bit. Then I made another start. That last spell must have been over a mile."

His whisper was getting fainter and fainter, and all the time he stared straight out through the port-hole, in which there was not even a star to be seen. I had not interrupted him. There was something that made comment impossible in his narrative, or perhaps in himself; a sort of feeling, a quality, which I can't find a name for. And when he ceased, all I found was a futile whisper: "So you swam for our light?"

"Yes—straight for it. It was something to swim for. I couldn't see any stars low down because the coast was in the way, and I couldn't see the land, either. The water was like glass. One might have been swimming in a confounded thousand-feet deep cistern with no place for scrambling out anywhere; but what I didn't like was the notion of swimming round and round like a crazed bullock before I gave out; and as I didn't mean to go back . . . No. Do you see me being hauled back, stark naked, off one of these little islands by the scruff of the neck and fighting like a wild beast? Somebody would have got killed for certain, and I did not want any of that. So I went on. Then your ladder—"

"Why didn't you hail the ship?" I asked, a little louder.

He touched my shoulder lightly. Lazy footsteps came right over our heads and stopped. The second mate had crossed from the other side of the poop and might have been hanging over the rail, for all we knew.

"He couldn't hear us talking—could he?" My double breathed into my very ear, anxiously.

His anxiety was an answer, a sufficient answer, to the question I had put to him. An answer containing all the difficulty of that situation. I closed the port-hole quietly, to make sure. A louder word might have been overheard.

"Who's that?" he whispered then.

"My second mate. But I don't know much more of the fellow than you do."

And I told him a little about myself. I had been appointed to take charge while I least expected anything of the sort, not quite a fortnight ago. I didn't know either the ship or the people. Hadn't had the time in port to look about me or size anybody up. And as to the crew, all they knew was that I was appointed to take the ship home. For the rest, I was almost as much of a stranger on board as himself, I said. And at the moment I felt it most acutely. I felt that it would take very little to make me a suspect person in the eyes of the ship's company.

He had turned about meantime; and we, the two strangers in the ship, faced each other in identical attitudes.

"Your ladder—" he murmured, after a silence. "Who'd have thought of finding a ladder hanging over at night in a ship anchored out here! I felt just then a very unpleasant faintness. After the life I've been leading for nine weeks, anybody would have got out of condition. I wasn't capable of swimming round as far as your rudder-chains. And, lo and behold! there was a ladder to get hold of. After I gripped it I said to myself, 'What's the good?' When I saw a man's head looking over I thought I would swim away presently and leave him shouting—in whatever language it was. I didn't mind being looked at. I—I liked it. And then you speaking to me so quietly—as if you had expected me—made me hold on a little longer. It had been a confounded lonely time—I don't mean while swimming. I was glad to talk a little to somebody that didn't belong to the *Sephora*. As to asking for the captain, that was a mere impulse. It could have been no use, with all the ship knowing about me and the other people pretty certain to be round here in the morning. I don't know—I wanted to be seen, to talk with somebody, before I went on. I don't know what I would have said. . . . 'Fine night, isn't it?' or something of the sort."

"Do you think they will be round here presently?" I asked with some incredulity.

"Quite likely," he said, faintly.

He looked extremely haggard all of a sudden. His head rolled on his shoulders.

"H'm. We shall see then. Meantime get into that bed," I whispered. "Want help? There."

It was a rather high bed-place with a set of drawers underneath. This amazing swimmer really needed the lift I gave him by seizing his leg. He tumbled in, rolled over on his back, and flung one arm across his eyes. And then, with his face nearly hidden, he must have looked exactly as I used to look in that bed. I gazed upon my other self for a while before drawing across carefully the two green serge curtains which ran on a brass rod. I thought for a moment of pinning them together for greater safety, but I sat down on the couch, and once there I felt unwilling to rise and hunt for a pin. I would do it in a moment. I was extremely tired, in a peculiarly intimate way, by the strain of stealthiness, by the effort of whispering and the general secrecy of this excitement. It was three o'clock by now and I had been on my feet since nine, but I was not sleepy; I could not have gone to sleep. I sat there, fagged out, looking at the curtains, trying to clear my mind of the confused sensation of being in two places at once, and greatly bothered by an exasperating knocking in my head. It was a relief to discover suddenly that it was not in my head at all, but on the outside of the door. Before I could collect myself the words "Come in" were out of my mouth, and the steward entered with a tray, bringing in my morning coffee. I had slept, after all, and I was so frightened that I shouted, "This way! I am here, steward," as though he had been miles away. He put down the tray on the table next the couch and only then said, very quietly, "I can see you are here, sir." I felt him give me a keen look, but I dared not meet his eyes just then. He must have wondered why I had drawn the curtains of my bed before going to sleep on the couch. He went out, hooking the door open as usual.

I heard the crew washing decks above me. I knew I would have been told at once if there had been any wind. Calm, I thought, and I was doubly vexed. Indeed, I felt dual more than ever. The steward reappeared suddenly in the doorway. I jumped up from the couch so quickly that he gave a start.

"What do you want here?"

"Close your port, sir—they are washing decks."

"It is closed," I said, reddening.

"Very well, sir." But he did not move from the doorway and returned my stare in an extraordinary, equivocal manner for a time. Then his eyes wavered, all his expression changed, and in a voice unusually gentle, almost coaxingly:

"May I come in to take the empty cup away, sir?"

"Of course!" I turned my back on him while he popped in and out. Then I unhooked and closed the door and even pushed the bolt. This sort of thing could not go on very long. The cabin was as hot as an oven, too. I took a peep at my double, and discovered that he had not moved, his arm was still over his eyes; but his chest heaved; his hair was wet; his chin glistened with perspiration. I reached over him and opened the port.

"I must show myself on deck," I reflected.

Of course, theoretically, I could do what I liked, with no one to say nay to me within the whole circle of the horizon; but to lock my cabin door and take the key away I did not dare. Directly I put my head out of the companion I saw the group of my two officers, the second mate barefooted, the chief mate in long india-rubber boots, near the break of the poop, and the steward half-way down the poop-ladder talking to them eagerly. He happened to catch sight of me and dived, the second ran down on the main-deck shouting some order or other, and the chief mate came to meet me, touching his cap.

There was a sort of curiosity in his eyes that I did not like. I don't know whether the steward had told them that I was "queer" only, or downright drunk, but I know the man meant to have a good look at me. I watched him coming with a smile which, as he got into point-blank range, took effect and froze his very whiskers. I did not give him time to open his lips.

"Square the yards by lifts and braces before the hands go to breakfast."

It was the first particular order I had given on board that ship; and I stayed on deck to see it executed, too. I had felt the need of asserting myself without loss of time. That sneering young cub got taken down a peg or two on that occasion, and I also seized the opportunity of having a good look at the face of every foremast man as they filed past me to go to the after braces. At breakfast time, eating nothing myself, I presided with such frigid dignity that the two mates were only too glad to escape from the cabin as soon as decency permitted; and all the time the dual working of my mind distracted me almost to the point of insanity. I was constantly watching myself, my secret self, as dependent on my actions as my own personality, sleeping in that bed, behind that door which faced me as I sat at the head of the table. It was very much like being mad, only it was worse because one was aware of it.

I had to shake him for a solid minute, but when at last he opened his eyes it was in the full possession of his senses, with an inquiring look.

"All's well so far," I whispered. "Now you must vanish into the bath-room."

He did so, noiseless as a ghost, and then I rang for the steward, and facing him boldly, directed him to tidy up my stateroom while I was having my bath—"and be quick about it." As my tone admitted of no excuses, he said, "Yes, sir," and ran off to fetch his dust-pan and brushes. I took a bath and did most of my dressing, splashing, and whistling softly for the steward's edification, while the secret sharer of my life stood drawn up bold upright in that little space, his face looking very sunken in daylight, his eyelids lowered under the stern, dark line of his eyebrows drawn together by a slight frown.

When I left him there to go back to my room the steward was finishing dusting. I sent for the mate and engaged him in some insignificant conversation. It was, as it were, trifling with the terrific character of his whiskers; but my object was to give him an opportunity for a good look at my cabin. And then I could at last shut, with a clear conscience, the door of my stateroom and get my double back into the recessed part. There was nothing else for it. He had to sit still on a small folding stool, half smothered by the heavy coats hanging there. We listened to the steward going into the bathroom out of the saloon, filling the water-bottles there, scrubbing the bath, setting things to rights, whisk, bang, clatter—out again into the saloon—turn the key—click. Such was my scheme for keeping my second self invisible. Nothing better could be contrived under the circumstances. And there we sat; I at my writing-desk ready to appear busy with some papers, he behind me out of sight of the door. It would not have been prudent to talk in daytime; and I could not have stood the excitement of that queer sense of whispering to myself. Now and then, glancing over my shoulder, I saw him far back there, sitting rigidly on the low stool, his bare feet close together, his arms folded, his head hanging on his breast—and perfectly still. Anybody would have taken him for me.

I was fascinated by it myself. Every moment I had to glance over my shoulder. I was looking at him when a voice outside the door said:

"Beg pardon, sir."

"Well!" . . . I kept my eyes on him, and so when the voice outside the door announced, "There's a ship's boat coming our way, sir," I saw him give a start—the first movement he had made for hours. But he did not raise his bowed head.

"All right. Get the ladder over."

I hesitated. Should I whisper something to him? But what? His immobility seemed to have been never disturbed. What could I tell him he did not know already? . . . Finally I went on deck.

II

The skipper of the *Sephora* had a thin red whisker all round his face, and the sort of complexion that goes with hair of that color; also the particular, rather smeary shade of blue in the eyes. He was not exactly a showy figure; his shoulders were high, his stature but middling—one leg slightly more bandy than the other. He shook hands, looking vaguely around. A spiritless tenacity was his main characteristic, I judged. I behaved with a politeness which seemed to disconcert him. Perhaps he was shy. He mumbled to me as if he were ashamed of what he was saying; gave his name (it was something like Archbold—but at this distance of years I hardly am sure), his ship's name, and a few other particulars of that sort, in the manner of a criminal making a reluctant and doleful confession. He had had terrible weather on the passage out—terrible—terrible—wife aboard, too.

By this time we were seated in the cabin and the steward brought in a tray with a bottle and glasses. "Thanks! No." Never took liquor. Would have some water, though. He drank two tumblerfuls. Terrible thirsty work. Ever since daylight had been exploring the islands round his ship.

"What was that for—fun?" I asked, with an appearance of polite interest.

"No!" He sighed. "Painful duty."

As he persisted in his mumbling and I wanted my double to hear every word, I hit upon the notion of informing him that I regretted to say I was hard of hearing.

"Such a young man, too!" he nodded, keeping his smeary blue, unintelligent eyes fastened upon me. "What was the cause of it—some disease?" he inquired, without the least sympathy and as if he thought that, if so, I'd got no more than I deserved.

"Yes; disease," I admitted in a cheerful tone which seemed to shock him. But my point was gained, because he had to raise his voice to give me his tale. It is not worth while to record that version. It was just over two months since all this had happened, and he had thought so much about it that he seemed completely muddled as to its bearings, but still immensely impressed.

"What would you think of such a thing happening on board your own ship? I've had the *Sephora* for these fifteen years. I am a well-known shipmaster."

He was densely distressed—and perhaps I should have sympathized with him if I had been able to detach my mental vision from the unsuspected sharer of my cabin as though he were my second self. There he was on the other side of the bulkhead, four or five feet from us, no more, as we sat in the saloon. I looked politely at Captain Archbold (if that was his name), but it was the other I saw, in a gray sleeping-suit, seated on a low stool, his bare feet close together, his arms folded, and every word said between us falling into the ears of his dark head bowed on his chest.

"I have been at sea now, man and boy, for seven-and-thirty years, and I've never heard of such a thing happening in an English ship. And that it should be my ship. Wife on board, too."

I was hardly listening to him.

"Don't you think," I said, "that the heavy sea which, you told me, came aboard just then might have killed the man? I have seen the sheer weight of a sea kill a man very neatly, by simply breaking his neck."

"Good God!" he uttered, impressively fixing his smeary blue eyes on me. "The sea! No man killed by the sea ever looked like that." He seemed positively scandalized at my suggestion. And as I gazed at him, certainly not prepared for anything original on his part, he advanced his head close to mine and thrust his tongue out at me so suddenly that I couldn't help starting back.

After scoring over my calmness in this graphic way he nodded wisely. If I had seen the sight, he assured me, I would never forget it as long as I lived. The weather was too bad to give the corpse a proper sea burial. So next day at dawn they took it up on the poop, covering its face with a bit of bunting; he read a short prayer, and then, just as it was, in its oilskins and long boots, they launched it amongst those mountainous seas that seemed ready every moment to swallow up the ship herself and the terrified lives on board of her.

"That reefed foresail saved you," I threw in.

"Under God—it did," he exclaimed fervently. "It was by a special mercy, I firmly believe, that it stood some of those hurricane squalls."

"It was the setting of that sail which—" I began.

"God's own hand in it," he interrupted me. "Nothing less could have done it. I don't mind telling you that I hardly dared give the order. It seemed impossible that we could touch anything without losing it, and then our last hope would have been gone."

The terror of that gale was on him yet. I let him go on for a bit, then said, casually—as if returning to a minor subject:

"You were very anxious to give up your mate to the shore people, I believe?"

He was. To the law. His obscure tenacity on that point had in it something incomprehensible and a little awful; something, as it were, mystical,

quite apart from his anxiety that he should not be suspected of "counte-
nancing any doings of that sort." Seven-and-thirty virtuous years at sea, of
which over twenty of immaculate command, and the last fifteen in the
Sephora, seemed to have laid him under some pitiless obligation.

"And you know," he went on, groping shamefacedly amongst his feelings, "I did not engage that young fellow. His people had some interest
with my owners. I was in a way forced to take him on. He looked very
smart, very gentlemanly, and all that. But do you know—I never liked
him, somehow. I am a plain man. You see, he wasn't exactly the sort for
the chief mate of a ship like the *Sephora*."

I had become so connected in thoughts and impressions with the secret
sharer of my cabin that I felt as if I, personally, were being given to understand that I, too, was not the sort that would have done for the chief mate
of a ship like the *Sephora*. I had no doubt of it in my mind.

"Not at all the style of man. You understand," he insisted, superfluously,
looking hard at me.

I smiled urbanely. He seemed at a loss for a while.

"I suppose I must report a suicide."

"Beg pardon?"

"Sui-cide! That's what I'll have to write to my owners directly I get in."

"Unless you manage to recover him before tomorrow," I assented, dis-
passionately. . . . "I mean, alive."

He mumbled something which I really did not catch, and I turned my
ear to him in a puzzled manner. He fairly bawled:

"The land—I say, the mainland is at least seven miles off my anchorage."

"About that."

My lack of excitement, of curiosity, of surprise, of any sort of pronounced
interest, began to arouse his distrust. But except for the felicitous pretense
of deafness I had not tried to pretend anything. I had felt utterly incapable
of playing the part of ignorance properly, and therefore was afraid to try.
It is also certain that he had brought some ready-made suspicions with him,
and that he viewed my politeness as a strange and unnatural phenomenon.
And yet how else could I have received him? Not heartily! That was impossible for psychological reasons, which I need not state here. My only object
was to keep off his inquiries. Surlily? Yes, but surliness might have provoked a point-blank question. From its novelty to him and from its nature,
punctilious courtesy was the manner best calculated to restrain the man.
But there was the danger of his breaking through my defense bluntly. I
could not, I think, have met him by a direct lie, also for psychological (not
moral) reasons. If he had only known how afraid I was of his putting my
feeling of identity with the other to the test! But, strangely enough—(I
thought of it only afterwards)—I believe that he was not a little disconcerted by the reverse side of that weird situation, by something in me that

reminded him of the man he was seeking—suggested a mysterious similitude to the young fellow he had distrusted and disliked from the first.

However that might have been, the silence was not very prolonged. He took another oblique step.

"I reckon I had no more than a two-mile pull to your ship. Not a bit more."

"And quite enough, too, in this awful heat," I said.

Another pause full of mistrust followed. Necessity, they say, is mother of invention, but fear, too, is not barren of ingenious suggestions. And I was afraid he would ask me point-blank for news of my other self.

"Nice little saloon, isn't it?" I remarked, as if noticing for the first time the way his eyes roamed from one closed door to the other. "And very well fitted out, too. Here, for instance," I continued, reaching over the back of my seat negligently and flinging the door open, "is my bath-room."

He made an eager movement, but hardly gave it a glance. I got up, shut the door of the bath-room, and invited him to have a look round, as if I were very proud of my accommodation. He had to rise and be shown round, but he went through the business without any raptures whatever.

"And now we'll have a look at my stateroom," I declared, in a voice as loud as I dared to make it, crossing the cabin to the starboard side with purposely heavy steps.

He followed me in and gazed around. My intelligent double had vanished. I played my part.

"Very convenient—isn't it?"

"Very nice. Very comf . . ." He didn't finish and went out brusquely as if to escape from some unrighteous wiles of mine. But it was not to be. I had been too frightened not to feel vengeful; I felt I had him on the run, and I meant to keep him on the run. My polite insistence must have had something menacing in it, because he gave in suddenly. And I did not let him off a single item; mate's room, pantry, storerooms, the very sail-locker which was also under the poop—he had to look into them all. When at last I showed him out on the quarter-deck he drew a long, spiritless sigh, and mumbled dismally that he must really be going back to his ship now. I desired my mate, who had joined us, to see to the captain's boat.

The man of whiskers gave a blast on the whistle which he used to wear hanging round his neck, and yelled, "*Sephora's* away!" My double down there in my cabin must have heard, and certainly could not feel more relieved than I. Four fellows came running out from somewhere forward and went over the side, while my own men, appearing on deck too, lined the rail. I escorted my visitor to the gangway ceremoniously, and nearly overdid it. He was a tenacious beast. On the very ladder he lingered, and in that unique, guiltily conscientious manner of sticking to the point:

"I say . . . you . . . you don't think that—"

I covered his voice loudly:

"Certainly not. . . . I am delighted. Good-by."

I had an idea of what he meant to say, and just saved myself by the privilege of defective hearing. He was too shaken generally to insist, but my mate, close witness of that parting, looked mystified and his face took on a thoughtful cast. As I did not want to appear as if I wished to avoid all communication with my officers, he had the opportunity to address me.

"Seems a very nice man. His boat's crew told our chaps a very extraordinary story, if what I am told by the steward is true. I suppose you had it from the captain, sir?"

"Yes. I had a story from the captain."

"A very horrible affair—isn't it, sir?"

"It is."

"Beats all these tales we hear about murders in Yankee ships."

"I don't think it beats them. I don't think it resembles them in the least."

"Bless my soul—you don't say so! But of course I've no acquaintance whatever with American ships, not I, so I couldn't go against your knowledge. It's horrible enough for me. . . . But the queerest part is that those fellows seemed to have some idea the man was hidden aboard here. They had really. Did you ever hear of such a thing?"

"Preposterous—isn't it?"

We were walking to and fro athwart the quarter-deck. No one of the crew forward could be seen (the day was Sunday), and the mate pursued:

"There was some little dispute about it. Our chaps took offense. 'As if we would harbor a thing like that,' they said. 'Wouldn't you like to look for him in our coal-hole?' Quite a tiff. But they made it up in the end. I suppose he did drown himself. Don't you, sir?"

"I don't suppose anything."

"You have no doubt in the matter, sir?"

"None whatever."

I left him suddenly. I felt I was producing a bad impression, but with my double down there it was most trying to be on deck. And it was almost as trying to be below. Altogether a nerve-trying situation. But on the whole I felt less torn in two when I was with him. There was no one in the whole ship whom I dared take into my confidence. Since the hands had got to know his story, it would have been impossible to pass him off for anyone else, and an accidental discovery was to be dreaded now more than ever. . . .

The steward being engaged in laying the table for dinner, we could talk only with our eyes when I first went down. Later in the afternoon we had a cautious try at whispering. The Sunday quietness of the ship was against us; the stillness of air and water around her was against us; the elements, the men were against us—everything was against us in our secret partnership; time itself—for this could not go on forever. The very trust in Providence was, I suppose, denied to his guilt. Shall I confess that this thought cast me down very much? And as to the chapter of accidents which counts for so much in the book of success, I could only hope that it was closed. For what favorable accident could be expected?

"Did you hear everything?" were my first words as soon as we took up our position side by side, leaning over my bed-place.

He had. And the proof of it was his earnest whisper, "The man told you he hardly dared to give the order."

I understood the reference to be to that saving foresail.

"Yes. He was afraid of it being lost in the setting."

"I assure you he never gave the order. He may think he did, but he never gave it. He stood there with me on the break of the poop after the maintopsail blew away, and whimpered about our last hope—positively whimpered about it and nothing else—and the night coming on! To hear one's skipper go on like that in such weather was enough to drive any fellow out of his mind. It worked me up into a sort of desperation. I just took it into my own hands and went away from him, boiling, and— But what's the use telling you? *You* know! . . . Do you think that if I had not been pretty fierce with them I should have got the men to do anything? Not it! The bo's'n perhaps? Perhaps! It wasn't a heavy sea—it was a sea gone mad! I suppose the end of the world will be something like that; and a man may have the heart to see it coming once and be done with it— but to have to face it day after day—I don't blame anybody. I was precious little better than the rest. Only—I was an officer of that old coal-wagon, anyhow—"

"I quite understand," I conveyed that sincere assurance into his ear. He was out of breath with whispering; I could hear him pant slightly. It was all very simple. The same strung-up force which had given twenty-four men a chance, at least, for their lives, had, in a sort of recoil, crushed an unworthy mutinous existence.

But I had no leisure to weigh the merits of the matter—footsteps in the saloon, a heavy knock. "There's enough wind to get under way with, sir." Here was the call of a new claim upon my thoughts and even upon my feelings.

"Turn the hands up," I cried through the door. "I'll be on deck directly."

I was going out to make the acquaintance of my ship. Before I left the cabin our eyes met—the eyes of the only two strangers on board. I pointed to the recessed part where the little campstool awaited him and laid my finger on my lips. He made a gesture—somewhat vague—a little mysterious, accompanied by a faint smile, as if of regret.

This is not the place to enlarge upon the sensations of a man who feels for the first time a ship move under his feet to his own independent word. In my case they were not unalloyed. I was not wholly alone with my command; for there was that stranger in my cabin. Or rather, I was not completely and wholly with her. Part of me was absent. That mental feeling of being in two places at once affected me physically as if the mood of secrecy had penetrated my very soul. Before an hour had elapsed since the ship had begun to move, having occasion to ask the mate (he stood by my side) to take a compass bearing of the Pagoda, I caught myself reaching up to his ear in whispers. I say I caught myself, but enough had escaped to startle the man. I can't describe it otherwise than by saying that he shied. A grave, preoccupied manner, as though he were in possession of some perplexing intelligence, did not leave him henceforth. A little later I moved away from the rail to look at the compass with such a stealthy gait that the helmsman noticed it—and I could not help noticing the unusual roundness of his eyes. These are trifling instances, though it's to no commander's advantage to be suspected of ludicrous eccentricities. But I was also more seriously affected. There are to a seaman certain words, gestures, that should in given conditions come as naturally, as instinctively as the winking of a menaced eye. A certain order should spring on to his lips without thinking; a certain sign should get itself made, so to speak, without reflection. But all unconscious alertness had abandoned me. I had to make an effort of will to recall myself back (from the cabin) to the conditions of the moment. I felt that I was appearing an irresolute commander to those people who were watching me more or less critically.

And, besides, there were the scares. On the second day out, for instance, coming off the deck in the afternoon (I had straw slippers on my bare feet) I stopped at the open pantry and spoke to the steward. He was doing something there with his back to me. At the sound of my voice he nearly jumped out of his skin, as the saying is, and incidentally broke a cup.

"What on earth's the matter with you?" I asked, astonished.

He was extremely confused. "Beg your pardon, sir. I made sure you were in your cabin."

"You see I wasn't."

"No, sir. I could have sworn I heard you moving in there not a moment ago. It's most extraordinary . . . very sorry, sir."

I passed on with an inward shudder. I was so identified with my secret double that I did not even mention the fact in those scanty, fearful whispers we exchanged. I suppose he had made some slight noise of some kind or other. It would have been miraculous if he hadn't at one time or another. And yet, haggard as he appeared, he looked always perfectly self-controlled, more than calm—almost invulnerable. On my suggestion he remained almost entirely in the bath-room, which, upon the whole, was the safest place. There could be really no shadow of an excuse for anyone ever wanting to go in there, once the steward had done with it. It was a very tiny place. Sometimes he reclined on the floor, his legs bent, his head sustained on one elbow. At others I would find him on the camp-stool, sitting in his gray sleeping-suit and with his cropped dark hair like a patient, unmoved convict. At night I would smuggle him into my bed-place, and we would whisper together, with the regular footfalls of the officer of the watch passing and repassing over our heads. It was an infinitely miserable time. It was lucky that some tins of fine preserves were stowed in a locker in my stateroom; hard bread I could always get hold of; and so he lived on stewed chicken, paté de foie gras, asparagus, cooked oysters, sardines—on all sorts of abominable sham delicacies out of tins. My early morning coffee he always drank; and it was all I dared do for him in that respect.

Every day there was the horrible maneuvering to go through so that my room and then the bath-room should be done in the usual way. I came to hate the sight of the steward, to abhor the voice of that harmless man. I felt that it was he who would bring on the disaster of discovery. It hung like a sword over our heads.

The fourth day out, I think (we were then working down the east side of the Gulf of Siam, tack for tack, in light winds and smooth water)—the fourth day, I say, of this miserable juggling with the unavoidable, as we sat at our evening meal, that man, whose slightest movement I dreaded, after putting down the dishes ran up on deck busily. This could not be dangerous. Presently he came down again; and then it appeared that he had remembered a coat of mine which I had thrown over a rail to dry after having been wetted in a shower which had passed over the ship in the afternoon. Sitting stolidly at the head of the table I became terrified at the sight of the garment on his arm. Of course he made for my door. There was no time to lose.

"Steward," I thundered. My nerves were so shaken that I could not govern my voice and conceal my agitation. This was the sort of thing that made my terrifically whiskered mate tap his forehead with his forefinger. I had detected him using that gesture while talking on deck with a confidential air to the carpenter. It was too far to hear a word, but I had no doubt that this pantomime could only refer to the strange new captain.

"Yes, sir," the pale-faced steward turned resignedly to me. It was this maddening course of being shouted at, checked without rhyme or reason, arbitrarily chased out of my cabin, suddenly called into it, sent flying out of his pantry on incomprehensible errands, that accounted for the growing wretchedness of his expression.

"Where are you going with that coat?"

"To your room, sir."

"Is there another shower coming?"

"I'm sure I don't know, sir. Shall I go up again and see, sir?"

"No! never mind."

My object was attained, as of course my other self in there would have heard everything that passed. During this interlude my two officers never raised their eyes off their respective plates; but the lip of that confounded cub, the second mate, quivered visibly.

I expected the steward to hook my coat on and come out at once. He was very slow about it; but I dominated my nervousness sufficiently not to shout after him. Suddenly I became aware (it could be heard plainly enough) that the fellow for some reason or other was opening the door of the bath-room. It was the end. The place was literally not big enough to swing a cat in. My voice died in my throat and I went stony all over. I expected to hear a yell of surprise and terror, and made a movement, but had not the strength to get on my legs. Everything remained still. Had my second self taken the poor wretch by the throat? I don't know what I could have done next moment if I had not seen the steward come out of my room, close the door, and then stand quietly by the sideboard.

"Saved," I thought. "But, no! Lost! Gone! He was gone!"

I laid my knife and fork down and leaned back in my chair. My head swam. After a while, when sufficiently recovered to speak in a steady voice, I instructed my mate to put the ship round at eight o'clock himself.

"I won't come on deck," I went on. "I think I'll turn in, and unless the wind shifts I don't want to be disturbed before midnight. I feel a bit seedy."

"You did look middling bad a little while ago," the chief mate remarked without showing any great concern.

They both went out, and I stared at the steward clearing the table. There was nothing to be read on that wretched man's face. But why did he avoid my eyes, I asked myself. Then I thought I should like to hear the sound of his voice.

"Steward!"

"Sir!" Startled as usual.

"Where did you hang up that coat?"

"In the bath-room, sir." The usual anxious tone. "It's not quite dry yet, sir."

For some time longer I sat in the cuddy. Had my double vanished as he had come? But of his coming there was an explanation, whereas his disappearance would be inexplicable. . . . I went slowly into my dark room, shut the door, lighted the lamp, and for a time dared not turn round. When at last I did, I saw him standing bolt-upright in the narrow recessed part. It would not be true to say I had a shock, but an irresistible doubt of his bodily existence flitted through my mind. Can it be, I asked myself, that he is not visible to other eyes than mine? It was like being haunted. Motionless, with a grave face, he raised his hands slightly at me in a gesture which meant clearly, "Heavens! what a narrow escape!" Narrow indeed. I think I had come creeping quietly as near insanity as any man who has not actually gone over the border. That gesture restrained me, so to speak.

The mate with the terrific whiskers was now putting the ship on the other tack. In the moment of profound silence which follows upon the hands going to their stations I heard on the poop his raised voice: "Hard alee!" and the distance shout of the order repeated on the maindeck. The sails, in that light breeze, made but a faint fluttering noise. It ceased. The ship was coming round slowly; I held my breath in the renewed stillness of expectation; one wouldn't have thought that there was a single living soul on her decks. A sudden brisk shout, "Mainsail haul!" broke the spell, and in the noisy cries and rush overhead of the men running away with the main-brace we two, down in my cabin, came together in our usual position by the bed-place.

He did not wait for my question. "I heard him fumbling here and just managed to squat myself down in the bath," he whispered to me. "The fellow only opened the door and put his arm in to hang the coat up. All the same—"

"I never thought of that," I whispered back, even more appalled than before at the closeness of the shave, and marveling at that something unyielding in his character which was carrying him through so finely. There was no agitation in his whisper. Whoever was being driven distracted, it was not he. He was sane. And the proof of his sanity was continued when he took up the whispering again.

"It would never do for me to come to life again."

It was something that a ghost might have said. But what he was alluding to was his old captain's reluctant admission of the theory of suicide. It would obviously serve his turn—if I had understood at all the view which seemed to govern the unalterable purpose of his action.

"You must maroon me as soon as ever you can get amongst these islands off the Cambodge shore," he went on.

"Maroon you! We are not living in a boy's adventure tale," I protested. His scornful whispering took me up.

"We aren't indeed! There's nothing of a boy's tale in this. But there's nothing else for it. I want no more. You don't suppose I am afraid of what can be done to me? Prison or gallows or whatever they may please. But you don't see me coming back to explain such things to an old fellow in a wig and twelve respectable tradesmen, do you? What can they know whether I am guilty or not—or of *what* I am guilty, either? That's my affair. What does the Bible say? 'Driven off the face of the earth.' Very well. I am off the face of the earth now. As I came at night so I shall go."

"Impossible!" I murmured. "You can't."

"Can't? . . . Not naked like a soul on the Day of Judgment. I shall freeze on to this sleeping-suit. The Last Day is not yet—and . . . you have understood thoroughly. Didn't you?"

I felt suddenly ashamed of myself. I may say truly that I understood—and my hesitation in letting that man swim away from my ship's side had been a mere sham sentiment, a sort of cowardice.

"It can't be done now till next night," I breathed out. "The ship is on the off-shore tack and the wind may fail us."

"As long as I know that you understand," he whispered. "But of course you do. It's a great satisfaction to have got somebody to understand. You seem to have been there on purpose." And in the same whisper, as if we two whenever we talked had to say things to each other which were not fit for the world to hear, he added, "It's very wonderful."

We remained side by side talking in our secret way—but sometimes silent or just exchanging a whispered word or two at long intervals. And as usual he stared through the port. A breath of wind came now and again into our faces. The ship might have been moored in dock, so gently and on an even keel she slipped through the water, that did not murmur even at our passage, shadowy and silent like a phantom sea.

At midnight I went on deck, and to my mate's great surprise put the ship round on the other tack. His terrible whiskers flitted round me in silent criticism. I certainly should not have done it if it had been only a question of getting out of that sleepy gulf as quickly as possible. I believe he told the second mate, who relieved him, that it was a great want of judgment. The other only yawned. That intolerable cub shuffled about so sleepily and lolled against the rails in such a slack, improper fashion that I came came down on him sharply.

"Aren't you properly awake yet?"

"Yes, sir! I am awake."

"Well, then, be good enough to hold yourself as if you were. And keep a look-out. If there's any current we'll be closing with some islands before daylight."

The east side of the gulf is fringed with islands, some solitary, others in groups. On the blue background of the high coast they seem to float on silvery patches of calm water, arid and gray, or dark green and rounded like clumps of evergreen bushes, with the larger ones, a mile or two long, showing the outlines of ridges, ribs of gray rock under the dank mantle of matted leafage. Unknown to trade, to travel, almost to geography, the manner of life they harbor is an unsolved secret. There must be villages—settlements of fishermen at least—on the largest of them, and some communication with the world is probably kept up by native craft. But all that forenoon, as we headed for them, fanned along by the faintest of breezes, I saw no sign of man or canoe in the field of the telescope I kept on pointing at the scattered group.

At noon I gave no orders for a change of course, and the mate's whiskers became much concerned and seemed to be offering themselves unduly to my notice. At last I said:

"I am going to stand right in. Quite in—as far as I can take her."

The stare of extreme surprise imparted an air of ferocity also to his eyes, and he looked truly terrific for a moment.

"We're not doing well in the middle of the gulf," I continued, casually. "I am going to look for the land breezes tonight."

"Bless my soul! Do you mean, sir, in the dark amongst the lot of all them islands and reefs and shoals?"

"Well—if there are any regular land breezes at all on this coast one must get close inshore to find them, mustn't one?"

"Bless my soul!" he exclaimed again under his breath. All that afternoon he wore a dreamy, contemplative appearance which in him was a mark of perplexity. After dinner I went into my stateroom as if I meant to take some rest. There we two bent our dark heads over a half-unrolled chart lying on my bed.

"There," I said. "It's got to be Koh-ring. I've been looking at it ever since sunrise. It has got two hills and a low point. It must be inhabited. And on the coast opposite there is what looks like the mouth of a biggish river—with some town, no doubt, not far up. It's the best chance for you that I can see."

"Anything. Koh-ring let it be."

He looked thoughtfully at the chart as if surveying chances and distances from a lofty height—and following with his eyes his own figure wandering on the blank land of Cochin-China, and then passing off that piece of paper clean out of sight into uncharted regions. And it was as if the ship had two captains to plan her course for her. I had been so worried and restless running up and down that I had not had the patience to dress that day. I had remained in my sleeping-suit, with straw slippers and a soft floppy hat. The closeness of the heat in the gulf had been most oppressive, and the crew were used to see me wandering in that airy attire.

"She will clear the south point as she heads now," I whispered into his ear. "Goodness only knows when, though, but certainly after dark. I'll edge her in to half a mile, as far as I may be able to judge in the dark—"

"Be careful," he murmured, warningly—and I realized suddenly that all my future, the only future for which I was fit, would perhaps go irretrievably to pieces in any mishap to my first command.

I could not stop a moment longer in the room. I motioned him to get out of sight and made my way to the poop. That unplayful cub had the watch. I walked up and down for a while thinking things out, then beckoned him over.

"Send a couple of hands to open the two quarter-deck ports," I said, mildly.

He actually had the impudence, or else so forgot himself in his wonder at such an incomprehensible order, as to repeat:

"Open the quarter-deck ports! What for, sir?"

"The only reason you need concern yourself about is because I tell you to do so. Have them opened wide and fastened properly."

He reddened and went off, but I believe made some jeering remark to the carpenter as to the sensible practice of ventilating a ship's quarter-deck. I know he popped into the mate's cabin to impart the fact to him because the whiskers came on deck, as it were by chance, and stole glances at me from below—for signs of lunacy or drunkenness, I suppose.

A little before supper, feeling more restless than ever, I rejoined, for a moment, my second self. And to find him sitting so quietly was surprising, like something against nature, inhuman.

I developed my plan in a hurried whisper.

"I shall stand in as close as I dare and then put her round. I will presently find means to smuggle you out of here into the sail-locker, which communicates with the lobby. But there is an opening, a sort of square for hauling the sails out, which gives straight on the quarter-deck and which is never closed in fine weather, so as to give air to the sails. When the ship's way is deadened in stays and all the hands are aft at the main-braces you will have a clear road to slip out and get overboard through the open quarter-deck port. I've had them both fastened up. Use a rope's end to lower yourself into the water so as to avoid a splash—you know. It could be heard and cause some beastly complication."

He kept silent for a while, then whispered, "I understand."

"I won't be there to see you go," I began with an effort. "The rest . . . I only hope I have understood, too."

"You have. From first to last"—and for the first time there seemed to be a faltering, something strained in his whisper. He caught hold of my arm, but the ringing of the supper bell made me start. He didn't, though; he only released his grip.

After supper I didn't come below again till well past eight o'clock. The faint, steady breeze was loaded with dew; and the wet, darkened sails held all there was of propelling power in it. The night, clear and starry, sparkled darkly, and the opaque, lightless patches shifting slowly against the low stars were the drifting islets. On the port bow there was a big one more distant and shadowly imposing by the great space of sky it eclipsed.

On opening the door I had a back view of my very own self looking at a chart. He had come out of the recess and was standing near the table.

"Quite dark enough," I whispered.

He stepped back and leaned against my bed with a level, quiet glance. I sat on the couch. We had nothing to say to each other. Over our heads the officer of the watch moved here and there. Then I heard him move quickly. I knew what that meant. He was making for the companion; and presently his voice was outside my door.

"We are drawing in pretty fast, sir. Land looks rather close."

"Very well," I answered. "I am coming on deck directly."

I waited till he was gone out of the cuddy, then rose. My double moved too. The time had come to exchange our last whispers, for neither of us was ever to hear each other's natural voice.

"Look here!" I opened a drawer and took out three sovereigns. "Take this anyhow. I've got six and I'd give you the lot, only I must keep a little money to buy some fruit and vegetables for the crew from native boats as we go through Sundra Straits."

He shook his head.

"Take it," I urged him, whispering desperately. "No one can tell what—"

He smiled and slapped meaningly the only pocket of the sleeping-jacket. It was not safe, certainly. But I produced a large old silk handkerchief of mine, and tying the three pieces of gold in a corner, pressed it on him. He was touched, I suppose, because he took it at last and tied it quickly round his waist under the jacket, on his bare skin.

Our eyes met; several seconds elapsed, till, our glances still mingled, I extended my hand and turned the lamp out. Then I passed through the cuddy, leaving the door of my room wide open. . . . "Steward!"

He was still lingering in the pantry in the greatness of his zeal, giving a rub-up to a plated cruet stand the last thing before going to bed. Being careful not to wake up the mate, whose room was opposite, I spoke in an undertone.

He looked round anxiously. "Sir!"

"Can you get me a little hot water from the galley?"

"I am afraid, sir, the galley fire's been out for some time now."

"Go and see."

He flew up the stairs.

"Now," I whispered, loudly, into the saloon—too loudly, perhaps, but I was afraid I couldn't make a sound. He was by my side in an instant— the double captain slipped past the stairs—through a tiny dark passage . . . a sliding door. We were in the sail-locker, scrambling on our knees over the sails. A sudden thought struck me. I saw myself wandering barefooted, bareheaded, the sun beating on my dark poll. I snatched off my floppy hat and tried hurriedly in the dark to ram it on my other self. He dodged and fended off silently. I wonder what he thought had come to me before he understood and suddenly desisted. Our hands met gropingly, lingered united in a steady, motionless clasp for a second. . . . No word was breathed by either of us when they separated.

I was standing quietly by the pantry door when the steward returned.

"Sorry, sir. Kettle barely warm. Shall I light the spirit-lamp?"

"Never mind."

I came out on deck slowly. It was now a matter of conscience to shave the land as close as possible—for now he must go overboard whenever the ship was put in stays. Must! There could be no going back for him. After a moment I walked over to leeward and my heart flew into my mouth at the nearness of the land on the bow. Under any other circumstances I would not have held on a minute longer. The second mate had followed me anxiously.

I looked on till I felt I could command my voice.

"She will weather," I said then in a quiet tone.

"Are you going to try that, sir?" he stammered out incredulously.

I took no notice of him and raised my tone just enough to be heard by the helmsman.

"Keep her good full."

"Good full, sir."

The wind fanned my cheek, the sails slept, the world was silent. The strain of watching the dark loom of the land grow bigger and denser was too much for me. I had shut my eyes—because the ship must go closer. She must! The stillness was intolerable. Were we standing still?

When I opened my eyes the second view started my heart with a thump. The black southern hill of Koh-ring seemed to hang right over the ship like a towering fragment of the everlasting night. On that enormous mass of blackness there was not a gleam to be seen, not a sound to be heard. It was gliding irresistibly towards us and yet seemed already within reach of the land. I saw the vague figures of the watch grouped in the waist, gazing in awed silence.

"Are you going on, sir?" inquired an unsteady voice at my elbow.

I ignored it. I had to go on.

"Keep her full. Don't check her way. That won't do now," I said, warningly.

"I can't see the sails very well," the helmsman answered me, in strange, quavering tones.

Was she close enough? Already she was, I won't say in the shadow of the land, but in the very blackness of it, already swallowed up as it were, gone too close to be recalled, gone from me altogether.

"Give the mate a call," I said to the young man who stood at my elbow as still as death. "And turn all hands up."

My tone had a borrowed loudness reverberated from the height of the land. Several voices cried out together: "We are all on deck, sir."

Then stillness again, with the great shadow gliding closer, towering higher, without a light, without a sound. Such a hush had fallen on the ship that she might have been a bark of the dead floating in slowly under the very gate of Erebus.

"My God! Where are we?"

It was the mate moaning at my elbow. He was thunderstruck, and as it were deprived of the moral support of his whiskers. He clapped his hands and absolutely cried out, "Lost!"

"Be quiet," I said, sternly.

He lowered his tone, but I saw the shadowy gesture of his despair. "What are we doing here?"

"Looking for the land wind."

He made as if to tear his hair, and addressed me recklessly.

"She will never get out. You have done it, sir. I knew it'd end in something like this. She will never weather, and you are too close now to stay. She'll drift ashore before she's round. O my God!"

I caught his arm as he was raising it to batter his poor devoted head, and shook it violently.

"She's ashore already," he wailed, trying to tear himself away.

"Is she? . . . Keep good full there!"

"Good full, sir," cried the helmsman in a frightened, thin, child-like voice.

I hadn't let go the mate's arm and went on shaking it. "Ready about, do you hear? You go forward"—shake—"and stop there"—shake—"and hold your noise"—shake—"and see these head-sheets properly overhauled"— shake, shake—shake.

And all the time I dared not look towards the land lest my heart should fail me. I released my grip at last and he ran forward as if fleeing for dear life.

I wondered what my double there in the sail-locker thought of this commotion. He was able to hear everything—and perhaps he was able to understand why, on my conscience, it had to be thus close—no less. My first order "Hard alee!" re-echoed ominously under the towering shadow of Koh-ring as if I had shouted in a mountain gorge. And then I watched the land intently. In that smooth water and light wind it was impossible to feel the ship coming-to. No! I could not feel her. And my second self was making now ready to slip out and lower himself overboard. Perhaps he was gone already . . . ?

The great black mass brooding over our very mastheads began to pivot away from the ship's side silently. And now I forgot the secret stranger ready to depart, and remembered only that I was a total stranger to the ship. I did not know her. Would she do it? How was she to be handled?

I swung the mainyard and waited helplessly. She was perhaps stopped, and her very fate hung in balance, with the black mass of Koh-ring like the gate of the everlasting night towering over her taffrail. What would she do now? Had she way on her yet? I stepped to the side swiftly, and on the shadowy water I could see nothing except a faint phosphorescent flash revealing the glassy smoothness of the sleeping surface. It was impossible to tell—and I had not learned yet the feel of my ship. Was she moving? What I needed was something easily seen, a piece of paper, which I could throw overboard and watch. I had nothing on me. To run down for it I didn't dare. There was no time. All at once my strained, yearning stare distinguished a white object floating within a yard of the ship's side. White on the black water. A phosphorescent flash passed under it. What was that thing? . . . I recognized my own floppy hat. It must have fallen off his head . . . and he didn't bother. Now I had what I wanted—the saving mark for my eyes. But I hardly thought of my other self, now gone from the ship, to be hidden forever from all friendly faces, to be a fugitive and a vagabond on the earth, with no brand of the curse on his sane forehead to stay a slaying hand . . . too proud to explain.

And I watched the hat—the expression of my sudden pity for his mere flesh. It had been meant to save his homeless head from the dangers of the sun. And now—behold—it was saving the ship, by serving me for a mark to help out the ignorance of my strangeness. Ha! It was drifting forward, warning me just in time that the ship had gathered sternway.

"Shift the helm," I said in a low voice to the seaman standing still like a statue.

The man's eyes glistened wildly in the binnacle light as he jumped round to the other side and spun round the wheel.

I walked to the break of the poop. On the overshadowed deck all hands stood by the forebraces waiting for my order. The stars ahead seemed to be gliding from right to left. And all was so still in the world that I heard the quiet remark, "She's round," passed in a tone of intense relief between two seamen.

"Let go and haul."

The foreyards ran round with a great noise, amidst cheery cries. And now the frightful whiskers made themselves heard giving orders. Already the ship was drawing ahead. And I was alone with her. Nothing! no one in the world should stand now between us, throwing a shadow on the way of silent knowledge and mute affection, the perfect communion of a seaman with his first command.

Walking to the taffrail, I was in time to make out, on the very edge of a darkness thrown by a towering black mass like the very gateway of Erebus—yes, I was in time to catch an evanescent glimpse of my white hat left behind to mark the spot where the secret sharer of my cabin and of my thoughts, as though he were my second self, had lowered himself into the water to take his punishment: a free man, a proud swimmer striking out for a new destiny.

Anton Chekhov 1860–1904

The Bet

I

I T was a dark autumn night. The old banker was walking up and down his study and remembering how, fifteen years before, he had given a party one autumn evening. There had been many clever men there, and there had been interesting conversations. Among other things they had talked of capital punishment. The majority of the guests, among whom were many journalists and intellectual men, disapproved of the death penalty. They considered that form of punishment out of date, immoral, and unsuitable for Christian states. In the opinion of some of them the death penalty ought to be replaced everywhere by imprisonment for life.

"I don't agree with you," said their host the banker. "I have not tried either the death penalty or imprisonment for life, but if one may judge *a priori*, the death penalty is more moral and more humane than imprisonment for life. Capital punishment kills a man at once, but lifelong imprisonment kills him slowly. Which executioner is the more humane, he who kills you in a few minutes or he who drags the life out of you in the course of many years?"

"Both are equally immoral," observed one of the guests, "for they both have the same object—to take away life. The State is not God. It has not the right to take away what it cannot restore when it wants to."

Among the guests was a young lawyer, a young man of five-and-twenty. When he was asked his opinion, he said:

"The death sentence and the life sentence are equally immoral, but if I had to choose between the death penalty and imprisonment for life, I would certainly choose the second. To live anyhow is better than not at all."

A lively discussion arose. The banker, who was younger and more nervous in those days, was suddenly carried away by excitement; he struck the table with his fist and shouted at the young man:

"It's not true! I'll bet you two millions you wouldn't stay in solitary confinement for five years."

"If you mean that in earnest," said the young man, "I'll take the bet, but I would stay not five but fifteen years."

85

"Fifteen? Done!" cried the banker. "Gentlemen, I stake two millions!"
"Agreed! You stake two millions and I stake my freedom!" said the young man.

And this wild, senseless bet was carried out! The banker, spoilt and frivolous, with millions beyond his reckoning, was delighted at the bet. At supper he made fun of the young man, and said:

"Think better of it, young man, while there is still time. To me two millions are a trifle, but you are losing three or four of the best years of your life. I say three or four, because you won't stay longer. Don't forget either, you unhappy man, that voluntary confinement is a great deal harder to bear than compulsory. The thought that you have the right to step out in liberty at any moment will poison your whole existence in prison. I am sorry for you."

And now the banker, walking to and fro, remembered all this, and asked himself: "What was the object of that bet? What is the good of that man's losing fifteen years of his life and my throwing away two millions? Can it prove that the death penalty is better or worse than imprisonment for life? No, no. It was all nonsensical and meaningless. On my part it was the caprice of a pampered man, and on his part simple greed for money. . . ."

Then he remembered what followed that evening. It was decided that the young man should spend the years of his captivity under the strictest supervision in one of the lodges in the banker's garden. It was agreed that for fifteen years he should not be free to cross the threshold of the lodge, to see human beings, to hear the human voice, or to receive letters and newspapers. He was allowed to have a music instrument and books, and was allowed to write letters, to drink wine, and to smoke. By the terms of the agreement, the only relations he could have with the outer world were by a little window made purposely for that object. He might have anything he wanted—books, music, wine, and so on—in any quantity he desired by writing an order, but could only receive them through the window. The agreement provided for every detail and every trifle that would make his imprisonment strictly solitary, and bound the young man to stay there *exactly* fifteen years, beginning from twelve o'clock of November 14, 1870, and ending at twelve o'clock of November 14, 1885. The slightest attempt on his part to break the conditions, if only two minutes before the end, released the banker from the obligation to pay him two millions.

For the first year of his confinement, as far as one could judge from his brief notes, the prisoner suffered severely from loneliness and depression. The sounds of the piano could be heard continually day and night from his lodge. He refused wine and tobacco. Wine, he wrote, excites the desires, and desires are the worst foes of the prisoner; and besides, nothing could be more dreary than drinking good wine and seeing no one. And tobacco spoilt the air of his room. In the first year the books he sent for were principally of a light character; novels with a complicated love plot, sensational and fantastic stories, and so on.

In the second year the piano was silent in the lodge, and the prisoner asked only for the classics. In the fifth year music was audible again, and the prisoner asked for wine. Those who watched him through the window said that all that year he spent doing nothing but eating and drinking and lying on his bed, frequently yawning and angrily talking to himself. He did not read books. Sometimes at night he would sit down to write; he he would spend hours writing, and in the morning tear up all that he had written. More than once he could be heard crying.

In the second half of the sixth year the prisoner began zealously studying languages, philosophy, and history. He threw himself eagerly into these studies—so much so that the banker had enough to do to get him the books he ordered. In the course of four years some six hundred volumes were procured at his request. It was during this period that the banker received the following letter from his prisoner:

"My dear Jailer, I write you these lines in six languages. Show them to people who know the languages. Let them read them. If they find not one mistake I implore you to fire a shot in the garden. That shot will show me that my efforts have not been thrown away. The geniuses of all ages and of all lands speak different languages, but the same flame burns in them all. Oh, if you only knew what unearthly happiness my soul feels now from being able to understand them!" The prisoner's desire was fulfilled. The banker ordered two shots to be fired in the garden.

Then after the tenth year, the prisoner sat immovably at the table and read nothing but the Gospel. It seemed strange to the banker that a man who in four years had mastered six hundred learned volumes should waste nearly a year over one thin book easy of comprehension. Theology and histories of religion followed the Gospels.

In the last two years of his confinement the prisoner read an immense quantity of books quite indiscriminately. At one time he was busy with the natural sciences, then he would ask for Byron or Shakespeare. There were notes in which he demanded at the same time books on chemistry, and a manual of medicine, and a novel, and some treatise on philosophy or theology. His reading suggested a man swimming in the sea among the wreckage of his ship, and trying to save his life by greedily clutching first at one spar and then at another.

II

The old banker remembered all this, and thought:

"To-morrow at twelve o'clock he will regain his freedom. By our agreement I ought to pay him two millions. If I do pay him, it is all over with me: I shall be utterly ruined."

Fifteen years before, his millions had been beyond his reckoning; now he was afraid to ask himself which were greater, his debts or his assets. Desperate gambling on the Stock Exchange, wild speculation, and the excitability which he could not get over even in advancing years, had by degrees led to the decline of his fortune, and the proud, fearless, self-confident millionaire had become a banker of middling rank, trembling at every rise and fall in his investments. "Cursed bet!" muttered the old man, clutching his head in despair. "Why didn't the man die? He is only forty now. He will take my last penny from me, he will marry, will enjoy life, will gamble on the Exchange; while I shall look at him with envy like a beggar, and hear from him every day the same sentence: 'I am indebted to you for the happiness of my life; let me help you!' No, it is too much! The one means of being saved from bankruptcy and disgrace is the death of that man!"

It struck three o'clock, the banker listened; everyone was asleep in the house, and nothing could be heard outside but the rustling of the chilled trees. Trying to make no noise, he took from a fireproof safe the key of the door which had not been opened for fifteen years, put on his overcoat and went out of the house.

It was dark and cold in the garden. Rain was falling. A damp cutting wind was racing about the garden, howling and giving the trees no rest. The banker strained his eyes, but could see neither the earth nor the white statues, nor the lodge, nor the trees. Going to the spot where the lodge stood, he twice called the watchman. No answer followed. Evidently the watchman had sought shelter from the weather, and was now asleep somewhere either in the kitchen or in the greenhouse.

"If I had the pluck to carry out my intention," thought the old man, "suspicion would fall first upon the watchman."

He felt in the darkness for the steps and the door, and went into the entry of the lodge. Then he groped his way into a little passage and lighted a match. There was not a soul there. There was a bedstead with no bedding on it, and in the corner there was a dark cast-iron stove. The seals on the door leading to the prisoner's rooms were intact.

When the match went out the old man, trembling with emotion, peeped through the little window. A candle was burning dimly in the prisoner's room. He was sitting at the table. Nothing could be seen but his back, the hair on his head, and his hands. Open books were lying on the table, on the two easy-chairs, and on the carpet near the table.

Five minutes passed and the prisoner did not once stir. Fifteen years' imprisonment had taught him to sit still. The banker tapped at the window with his finger, and the prisoner made no movement whatever in response.

Then the banker cautiously broke the seals off the door and put the key in the keyhole. The rusty lock gave a grating sound and the door creaked. The banker expected to hear at once footsteps and a cry of astonishment, but three minutes passed and it was as quiet as ever in the room. He made up his mind to go in.

At the table a man unlike ordinary people was sitting motionless. He was a skeleton with the skin drawn tight over his bones, with long curls like a woman's, and a shaggy beard. His face was yellow with an earthy tint in it, his cheeks were hollow, his back long and narrow, and the hand on which his shaggy head was propped was so thin and delicate that it was dreadful to look at it. His hair was already streaked with silver, and seeing his emaciated, aged-looking face, no one would have believed that he was only forty. He was asleep. . . . In front of his bowed head there lay on the table a sheet of paper on which there was something written in fine handwriting.

"Poor creature!" thought the banker, "he is asleep and most likely dreaming of the millions. And I have only to take this half-dead man, throw him on the bed, stifle him a little with the pillow, and the most conscientious expert would find no sign of a violent death. But let us first read what he has written here. . . ."

The banker took the page from the table and read as follows:

"To-morrow at twelve o'clock I regain my freedom and the right to associate with other men, but before I leave this room and see the sunshine, I think is necessary to say a few words to you. With a clear conscience I tell you, as before God, who beholds me, that I despise freedom and life and health, and all that in your books is called the good things of the world.

"For fifteen years I have been intently studying earthly life. It is true I have not seen the earth nor men, but in your books I have drunk fragrant wine, I have sung songs, I have hunted stags and wild boars in the forests, have loved women. . . . Beauties as ethereal as clouds, created by the magic of your poets and geniuses, have visited me at night, and have whispered in my ears wonderful tales that have set my brain in a whirl. In your books I have climbed to the peaks of Elbruz and Mount Blanc, and from there I have seen the sun rise and have watched it at evening flood the sky, the ocean, and the mountain-tops with gold and crimson. I have watched from there the lightning flashing over my head and cleaving the storm-clouds. I have seen green forest, fields, rivers, lakes, towns. I have heard the singing of the sirens, and the strains of the shepherds' pipes; I have touched the wings of comely devils who flew down to converse with me of God. . . . In your books I have flung myself into the bottomless pit, performed miracles, slain, burned towns, preached new religions, conquered whole kingdoms. . . .

"Your books have given me wisdom. All that the unresting thought of man has created in the ages is compressed into a small compass in my brain. I know that I am wiser than all of you.

"And I despise your books, I despise wisdom and the blessings of this world. It is all worthless, fleeting, illusory, and deceptive, like a mirage. You may be proud, wise, and fine, but death will wipe you off the face of the earth as though you were no more than mice burrowing under the floor, and your posterity, your history, your immortal geniuses will burn or freeze together with the earthly globe.

"You have lost your reason and taken the wrong path. You have taken lies for truth, and hideousness for beauty. You would marvel if, owing to strange events of some sorts, frogs and lizards suddenly grew on apple and orange trees instead of fruit, or if roses began to smell like a sweating horse; so I marvel at you who exchange heaven for earth. I don't want to understand you.

"To prove to you in action how I despise all that you live by, I renounce the two millions of which I once dreamed as of paradise and which now I despise. To deprive myself of the right to the money I shall go out from here five hours before the time fixed, and so break the compact. . . ."

When the banker had read this he laid the page on the table, kissed the strange man on the head, and went out of the lodge, weeping. At no other time, even when he had lost heavily on the Stock Exchange, had he felt so great a contempt for himself. When he got home he lay on his bed, but his tears and emotion kept him for hours from sleeping.

Next morning the watchmen ran in with pale faces, and told him they had seen the man who lived in the lodge climb out of the window into the garden, go to the gate, and disappear. The banker went at once with the servants to the lodge and made sure of the flight of his prisoner. To avoid arousing unnecessary talk, he took from the table the writing in which the millions were renounced, and when he got home locked it up in the fireproof safe.

James Joyce 1882–1941

Eveline

SHE sat at the window watching the evening invade the avenue. Her head was leaned against the window curtains and in her nostrils was the odor of dusty cretonne. She was tired.

Few people passed. The man out of the last house passed on his way home; she heard his footsteps clacking along the concrete pavement and afterwards crunching on the cinder path before the new red houses. One time there used to be a field there in which they used to play every evening with other people's children. Then a man from Belfast bought the field and built houses in it—not like their little brown houses but bright brick houses with shining roofs. The children of the avenue used to play together in that field—the Devines, the Waters, the Dunns, little Keogh the cripple, she and her brothers and sisters. Ernest, however, never played: he was too grown up. Her father used often to hunt them in out of the field with his blackthorn stick; but usually little Keogh used to keep *nix* and call out when he saw her father coming. Still they seemed to have been rather happy then. Her father was not so bad then; and besides, her mother was alive. That was a long time ago; she and her brothers and sisters were all grown up; her mother was dead. Tizzie Dunn was dead, too, and the Waters had gone back to England. Everything changes. Now she was going to go away like the others, to leave her home.

Home! She looked round the room, reviewing all its familiar objects which she had dusted once a week for so many years, wondering where on earth all the dust came from. Perhaps she would never see again those familiar objects from which she had never dreamed of being divided. And yet during all those years she had never found out the name of the priest whose yellowing photograph hung on the wall above the broken harmonium beside the colored print of the promises made to Blessed Margaret Mary Alacoque. He had been a school friend of her father. Whenever he showed the photograph to a visitor her father used to pass it with a casual word:

"He is in Melbourne now."

91

She had consented to go away, to leave her home. Was that wise? She tried to weigh each side of the question. In her home anyway she had shelter and food; she had those whom she had known all her life about her. Of course she had to work hard, both in the house and at business. What would they say of her in the Stores when they found out that she had run away with a fellow? Say she was a fool, perhaps; and her place would be filled up by advertisement. Miss Gavan would be glad. She had always had an edge on her, especially whenever there were people listening.

"Miss Hill, don't you see these ladies are waiting?"

"Look lively, Miss Hill, please."

She would not cry many tears at leaving the Stores.

But in her new home, in a distant unknown country, it would not be like that. That she would be married—she, Eveline. People would treat her with respect then. She would not be treated as her mother had been. Even now, though she was over nineteen, she sometimes felt herself in danger of her father's violence. She knew it was that that had given her the palpitations. When they were growing up he had never gone for her, like he used to go for Harry and Ernest, because she was a girl; but latterly he had begun to threaten her and say what he would do to her only for her dead mother's sake. And now she had nobody to protect her. Ernest was dead and Harry, who was in the church decorating business, was nearly always down somewhere in the country. Besides, the invariable squabble for money on Saturday nights had begun to weary her unspeakably. She always gave her entire wages—seven shillings—and Harry always sent up what he could but the trouble was to get any money from her father. He said she used to squander the money, that she had no head, that he wasn't going to give her his hard-earned money to throw about the streets, and much more, for he was usually fairly bad on Saturday night. In the end he would give her the money and ask her had she any intention of buying Sunday's dinner. Then she had to rush out as quickly as she could and do her marketing, holding her black leather purse tightly in her hand as she elbowed her way through the crowds and returning home late under her load of provisions. She had hard work to keep the house together and to see that the two young children who had been left to her charge went to school regularly and got their meals regularly. It was hard work—a hard life—but now that she was about to leave it she did not find it a wholly undesirable life.

She was about to explore another life with Frank. Frank was very kind, manly, open hearted. She was to go away with him by the night-boat to be his wife and to live with him in Buenos Ayres where he had a home waiting for her. How well she remembered the first time she had seen him; he was lodging in a house on the main road where she used to visit. It seemed a few weeks ago. He was standing at the gate, his peaked cap pushed back on his head and his hair tumbled forward over a face of bronze. Then they had come to know each other. He used to meet her outside the Stores every evening and see her home. He took her to see *The Bohemian Girl* and she felt elated as she sat in an unaccustomed part of the theater with him. He was awfully fond of music and sang a little. People knew that they were courting and, when he sang about the lass that loves a sailor, she always felt pleasantly confused. He used to call her Poppens out of fun. First of all it had been an excitement for her to have a fellow and then she had begun to like him. He had tales of distant countries. He had started as a deck boy at a pound a month on a ship of the Allan Line going out to Canada. He told her the names of the ships he had been on and the names of the different services. He had sailed through the Straits of Magellan and he told her stories of the terrible Patagonians. He had fallen on his feet in Buenos Ayres, he said, and had come over to the old country just for a holiday. Of course, her father had found out the affair and had forbidden her to have anything to say to him.

"I know these sailor chaps," he said.

One day he had quarreled with Frank and after that she had to meet her lover secretly.

The evening deepened in the avenue. The white of two letters in her lap grew indistinct. One was to Harry; the other was to her father. Ernest had been her favorite but she liked Harry too. Her father was becoming old lately, she noticed; he would miss her. Sometimes he could be very nice. Not long before, when she had been laid up for a day, he had read her out a ghost story and made toast for her at the fire. Another day, when their mother was alive, they had all gone for a picnic to the Hill of Howth. She remembered her father putting on her mother's bonnet to make the children laugh.

Her time was running out but she continued to sit by the window, leaning her head against the window curtain, inhaling the odor of dusty cretonne. Down far in the avenue she could hear a street organ playing. She knew the air. Strange that it should come that very night to remind her of the promise to her mother, her promise to keep the home together as long as she could. She remembered the last night of her mother's illness; she was again in the close dark room at the other side of the hall and outside she heard a melancholy air of Italy. The organ player had been ordered to go away and given sixpence. She remembered her father strutting back into the sickroom saying:

"Damned Italians! coming over here!"

As she mused the pitiful vision of her mother's life laid its spell on the very quick of her being—that life of commonplace sacrifices closing in final craziness. She trembled as she heard again her mother's voice saying constantly with foolish insistence:

"Derevaun Seraun! Derevaun Seraun!" [1]

---

[1] One interpretation: "The end of pleasure is pain."

She stood up in a sudden impulse of terror. Escape! She must escape! Frank would save her. He would give her life, perhaps love, too. But she wanted to live. Why should she be unhappy? She had a right to happiness. Frank would take her in his arms, fold her in his arms. He would save her.

She stood among the swaying crowd in the station at the North Wall. He held her hand and she knew that he was speaking to her, saying something about the passage over and over again. The station was full of soldiers with brown baggage. Through the wide doors of the sheds she caught a glimpse of the black mass of the boat, lying in beside the quay wall, with illumined portholes. She answered nothing. She felt her cheek pale and cold and, out of a maze of distress, she prayed to God to direct her, to show her what was her duty. The boat blew a long mournful whistle into the mist. If she went, tomorrow she would be on the sea with Frank, steaming towards Buenos Ayres. Their passage had been booked. Could she still draw back after all he had done for her? Her distress awoke a nausea in her body and she kept moving her lips in silent fervent prayer.

A bell clanged upon her heart. She felt him seize her hand:

"Come!"

All the seas of the world tumbled about her heart. He was drawing her into them: he would drown her. She gripped with both hands at the iron railing.

"Come!"

No! No! No! It was impossible. Her hands clutched the iron in frenzy. Amid the seas she sent a cry of anguish!

"Eveline! Evvy!"

He rushed beyond the barrier and called to her to follow. He was shouted at to go on but he still called to her. She set her white face to him, passive, like a helpless animal. Her eyes gave him no sign of love or farewell or recognition.

Franz Kafka 1893–1924

A Country Doctor

I W A S I N great perplexity; I had to start on an urgent journey; a seriously ill patient was waiting for me in a village ten miles off; a thick blizzard of snow filled all the wide spaces between him and me; I had a gig, a light gig with big wheels, exactly right for our country roads; muffled in furs, my bag of instruments in my hand, I was in the courtyard all ready for the journey; but there was no horse to be had, no horse. My own horse had died in the night, worn out by the fatigues of this icy winter; my servant girl was now running round the village trying to borrow a horse; but it was hopeless, I knew it, and I stood there forlornly, with the snow gathering more and more thickly upon me, more and more unable to move. In the gateway the girl appeared, alone, and waved the lantern; of course, who would lend a horse at this time for such a journey? I strode through the courtyard once more; I could see no way out; in my confused distress I kicked at the dilapidated door of the year-long uninhabited pigsty. It flew open and flapped to and fro on its hinges. A steam and smell as of horses came out from it. A dim stable lantern was swinging inside from a rope. A man, crouching on his hams in that low space, showed an open blue-eyed face. "Shall I yoke up?" he asked, crawling out on all fours. I did not know what to say and merely stooped down to see what else was in the sty. The servant girl was standing beside me. "You never know what you're going to find in your own house," she said, and we both laughed. "Hey there, Brother, hey there, Sister!" called the groom, and two horses, enormous creatures with powerful flanks, one after the other, their legs tucked close to their bodies, each well-shaped head lowered like a camel's, by sheer strength of buttocking squeezed out through the door hole which they filled entirely. But at once they were standing up, their legs long and their bodies steaming thickly. "Give him a hand," I said, and the willing girl hurried to help the groom with the harnessing. Yet hardly was she beside him when the groom clipped hold of her and pushed his face against hers. She screamed and fled back to me; on her cheek stood out in red the marks of two rows of teeth. "You brute," I yelled in fury, "do you want a

95

whipping?" but in the same moment reflected that the man was a stranger; that I did not know where he came from, and that of his own free will he was helping me out when everyone else had failed me. As if he knew my thoughts he took no offense at my threat but, still busied with the horses, only turned round once towards me. "Get in," he said then, and indeed: everything was ready. A magnificent pair of horses, I observed, such as I had never sat behind, and I climbed in happily. "But I'll drive, you don't know the way," I said. "Of course," said he, "I'm not coming with you anyway, I'm staying with Rose." "No," shrieked Rose, fleeing into the house with a justified presentiment that her fate was inescapable; I heard the door chain rattle as she put it up; I heard the key turn in the lock; I could see, moreover, how she put out the lights in the entrance hall and in further flight all through the rooms to keep herself from being discovered. "You're coming with me," I said to the groom, "or I won't go, urgent as my journey is. I'm not thinking of paying for it by handing the girl over to you." Gee up!" he said; clapped his hands; the gig whirled off like a log in a freshet; I could just hear the door of my house splitting and bursting as the groom charged at it and then I was deafened and blinded by a storming rush that steadily buffeted all my senses. But this only for a moment, since, as if my patient's farmyard had opened out just before my courtyard gate, I was already there; the horses had come quietly to a standstill; the blizzard had stopped; moonlight all around; my patient's parents hurried out of the house, his sister behind them; I was almost lifted out of the gig; from their confused ejaculations I gathered not a word; in the sickroom the air was almost unbreathable; the neglected stove was smoking; I wanted to push open a window; but first I had to look at my patient. Gaunt, without any fever, not cold, not warm, with vacant eyes, without a shirt, the youngster heaved himself up from under the feather bedding, threw his arms round my neck, and whispered in my ear: "Doctor, let me die." I glanced round the room; no one had heard it; the parents were leaning forward in silence waiting for my verdict; the sister had set a chair for my handbag; I opened the bag and hunted among my instruments; the boy kept clutching at me from his bed to remind me of his entreaty; I picked up a pair of tweezers, examined them in the candlelight and laid them down again. "Yes," I thought blasphemously, "in cases like this the gods are helpful, send the missing horse, add to it a second because of the urgency, and to crown everything bestow even a groom—" And only now did I remember Rose again; what was I to do, how could I rescue her, how could I pull her away from under that groom at ten miles' distance, with a team of horses I couldn't control. These horses, now, they had somehow slipped the reins loose, pushed the windows open from the outside, I did not know how; each of them had stuck a head in at a window and, quite unmoved by the startled cries of the family, stood eyeing the patient. "Better go back at once," I thought, as if the horses were summoning me to the return journey, yet I permitted the patient's sister, who fancied that I was dazed by the heat, to take my fur coat from me. A glass of rum was poured out for me, the old man clapped me on the shoulder, a familiarity justified by this offer of his treasure. I shook my head; in the narrow confines of the old man's thoughts I felt ill; that was my only reason for refusing the drink. The mother stood by the bedside and cajoled me towards it; I yielded, and, while one of the horses whinnied loudly to the ceiling, laid my head to the boy's breast, which shivered under my wet beard. I confirmed what I already knew; the boy was quite sound, something a little wrong with his circulation, saturated with coffee by his solicitous mother, but sound and best turned out of bed with one shove. I am no world reformer and so I let him lie. I was the district doctor and did my duty to the uttermost, to the point where it became almost too much. I was badly paid and yet generous and helpful to the poor. I had still to see that Rose was all right, and then the boy might have his way and I wanted to die too. What was I doing there in that endless winter! My horse was dead, and not a single person in the village would lend me another. I had to get my team out of the pigsty; if they hadn't chanced to be horses I should have had to travel with swine. That was how it was. And I nodded to the family. They knew nothing about it, and, had they known, would not have believed it. To write prescriptions is easy, but to come to an understanding with people is hard. Well, this should be the end of my visit, I had once more been called out needlessly, I was used to that, the whole district made my life a torment with my night bell, but that I should have to sacrifice Rose this time as well, the pretty girl who had lived in my house for years almost without my noticing her— that sacrifice was too much to ask, and I had somehow to get it reasoned out in my head with the help of what craft I could muster, in order not to let fly at this family, which with the best will in the world could not restore Rose to me. But as I shut my bag and put an arm out for my fur coat, the family meanwhile standing together, the father sniffing at the glass of rum in his hand, the mother, apparently disappointed in me—why, what do people expect?—biting her lips with tears in her eyes, the sister fluttering a blood-soaked towel, I was somehow ready to admit conditionally that the boy might be ill after all. I went towards him, he welcomed me smiling as if I were bringing him the most nourishing invalid broth—ah, now both horses were whinnying together; the noise, I suppose, was ordained by heaven to assist my examination of the patient—and this time I discovered that the boy was indeed ill. In his right side, near the hip, was an open wound as big as the palm of my hand. Rose-red, in many variations of shade, dark in the hollows, lighter at the edges, softly granulated, with irregular clots of blood, open as a surface mine to the daylight. That was how it looked from a distance. But on a closer inspection there was another complication. I could not help a low whistle of surprise. Worms, as thick and as long as my little finger, themselves rose-red and blood-spotted as well, were wriggling from their fastness in the interior of the wound towards the light, with small white heads and many little legs. Poor boy, you were past helping. I had discovered your great wound; this blossom in your side was destroying you. The family was pleased; they saw me busying myself; the sister told the mother, the mother the father, the father told several guests who were coming in, through the moonlight at the open door, walking on tiptoe, keeping their balance with outstretched arms. "Will you save me?" whispered the boy with a sob, quite blinded by the life within his wound. That is what people are like in my district. Always expecting the impossible from the doctor. They have lost their ancient beliefs; the parson sits at home and unravels his vestments, one after another; but the doctor is supposed to be omnipotent with his merciful surgeon's hand. Well, as it pleases them; I have not thrust my services on them; if they misuse me for sacred ends, I let that happen to me too; what better do I want, old country doctor that I am, bereft of my servant girl! And so they came, the family and the village elders, and stripped my clothes off me; a school choir with the teacher at the head of it stood before the house and sang these words to an utterly simple tune:

> Strip his clothes off, then he'll heal us,
> If he doesn't, kill him dead!
> Only a doctor, only a doctor.

Then my clothes were off and I looked at the people quietly, my fingers in my beard and my head cocked to one side. I was altogether composed and equal to the situation and remained so, although it was no help to me, since they now took me by the head and feet and carried me to the bed. They laid me down in it next to the wall, on the side of the wound. Then they all left the room; the door was shut; the singing stopped; clouds covered the moon; the bedding was warm around me; the horses' heads in the open windows wavered like shadows. "Do you know," said a voice in my ear, "I have very little confidence in you. Why, you were only blown in here, you didn't come on your own own feet. Instead of helping me, you're cramping me on my deathbed. What I'd like best is to scratch your eyes out." "Right," I said, "it is a shame. And yet I am a doctor. What am I to do? Believe me, it is not too easy for me either." "Am I supposed to be content with this apology? Oh, I must be, I can't help it. I always have to put up with things. A fine wound is all I brought into the world; that was my sole endowment." "My young friend," said I, "your mistake is: you have not a wide enough view. I have been in all the sickrooms, far and wide, and I tell you: your wound is not so bad. Done in a tight corner with two strokes of the ax. Many a one proffers his side and can hardly hear the ax in the forest, far less that it is coming nearer to him." "Is that really so, or are you deluding me in my fever?" "It is really so, take the word of honor of an official doctor." And he took it and lay still. But now it was time for me to think of escaping. The horses were still standing faithfully in their places. My clothes, my fur coat, my bag were quickly collected; I didn't want to waste time dressing; if the horses raced home as they had come, I should only be springing, as it were, out of this bed into my own. Obediently a horse backed away from the window; I threw my bundle into the gig; the fur coat missed its mark and was caught on a hook only by the sleeve. Good enough. I swung myself onto the horse. With the reins loosely trailing, one horse barely fastened to the other, the gig swaying behind, my fur coat last of all in the snow. "Gee up!" I said, but there was no galloping; slowly, like old men, we crawled through the snowy wastes; a long time echoed behind us the new but faulty song of the children:

> O be joyful, all you patients,
> The doctor's laid in bed beside you!

Never shall I reach home at this rate; my flourishing practice is done for; my successor is robbing me, but in vain, for he cannot take my place; in my house the disgusting groom is raging; Rose is his victim; I do not want to think about it any more. Naked, exposed to the frost of this most unhappy of ages, with an earthly vehicle, unearthly horses, old man that I am, I wander astray. My fur coat is hanging from the back of the gig, but I cannot reach it, and none of my limber pack of patients lifts a finger. Betrayed! Betrayed! A false alarm on the night bell once answered—it cannot be made good, not ever.

D. H. Lawrence 1885–1930

The Horse Dealer's Daughter

W ELL , Mabel, and what are you going to do with yourself?" asked Joe, with foolish flippancy. He felt quite safe himself. Without listening for an answer, he turned aside, worked a grain of tobacco to the tip of his tongue, and spat it out. He did not care about anything, since he felt safe himself.

The three brothers and the sister sat round the desolate breakfast table, attempting some sort of desultory consultation. The morning's post had given the final tap to the family fortune, and all was over. The dreary dining-room itself, with its heavy mahogany furniture, looked as if it were waiting to be done away with.

But the consultation amounted to nothing. There was a strange air of ineffectuality about the three men, as they sprawled at table, smoking and reflecting vaguely on their own condition. The girl was alone, a rather short, sullen-looking young woman of twenty-seven. She did not share the same life as her brothers. She would have been good-looking, save for the impassive fixity of her face, "bull-dog," as her brothers called it.

There was a confused tramping of horses' feet outside. The three men all sprawled round in their chairs to watch. Beyond the dark holly-bushes that separated the strip of lawn from the highroad, they could see a cavalcade of shire horses swinging out of their own yard, being taken for exercise. This was the last time. These were the last horses that would go through their hands. The young men watched with critical, callous look. They were all frightened at the collapse of their lives, and the sense of of disaster in which they were involved left them no inner freedom.

Yet they were three fine, well-set fellows enough. Joe, the eldest, was a man of thirty-three, broad and handsome in a hot, flushed way. His face was red, he twisted his black moustache over a thick finger, his eyes were shallow and restless. He had a sensual way of uncovering his teeth when he laughed, and his bearing was stupid. Now he watched the horses with a glazed look of helplessness in his eyes, a certain stupor of downfall.

The great draught-horses swung past. They were tied head to tail, four of

100

them, and they heaved along to where a lane branched off from the high-road, planting their great hoofs floutingly in the fine black mud, swinging their great rounded haunches sumptuously, and trotting a few sudden steps as they were led into the lane, round the corner. Every movement showed a massive, slumbrous strength, and a stupidity which held them in subjection. The groom at the head looked back, jerking the leading rope. And the cavalcade moved out of sight up the lane, the tail of the last horse, bobbed up tight and stiff, held out taut from the swinging great haunches as they rocked behind the hedges in a motion-like sleep.

Joe watched with glazed hopeless eyes. The horses were almost like his own body to him. He felt he was done for now. Luckily he was engaged to a woman as old as himself, and therefore her father, who was steward of a neighboring estate, would provide him with a job. He would marry and go into harness. His life was over, he would be a subject animal now.

He turned uneasily aside, the retreating steps of the horses echoing in his ears. Then, with foolish restlessness, he reached for the scraps of bacon-rind from the plates, and making a faint whistling sound, flung them to the terrier that lay against the fender. He watched the dog swallow them, and waited till the creature looked into his eyes. Then a faint grin came on his face, and in a high, foolish voice he said:

"You won't get much more bacon, shall you, you little bitch?"

The dog faintly and dismally wagged its tail, then lowered its haunches, circled round, and lay down again.

There was another helpless silence at the table. Joe, sprawled uneasily in his seat, not willing to go till the family conclave was dissolved. Fred Henry, the second brother, was erect, clean-limbed, alert. He had watched the passing of the horses with more sang-froid. If he was an animal, like Joe, he was an animal which controls, not one which is controlled. He was master of any horse, and he carried himself with a well-tempered air of mastery. But he was not master of the situations of life. He pushed his coarse brown moustache upwards, off his lip, and glanced irritably at his sister, who sat impassive and inscrutable.

"You'll go and stop with Lucy for a bit, shan't you?" he asked. The girl did not answer.

"I don't see what else you can do," persisted Fred Henry.

"Go as a skivvy," Joe interpolated laconically.

The girl did not move a muscle.

"If I was her, I should go in for training for a nurse," said Malcolm, the youngest of them all. He was the baby of the family, a young man of twenty-two, with a fresh, jaunty *museau*.

But Mabel did not take any notice of him. They had talked at her and round her for so many years, that she hardly heard them at all.

The marble clock on the mantelpiece, softly chimed the half-hour, the dog rose uneasily from the hearthrug and looked at the party at the break-fast table. But still they sat on in ineffectual conclave.

"Oh, all right," said Joe suddenly, apropos of nothing. "I'll get a move on."

He pushed back his chair, straddled his knees with a downward jerk, to get them free, in horsey fashion, and went to the fire. Still he did not go out of the room; he was curious to know what the others would do or say. He began to charge his pipe, looking down at the dog and saying, in a high, affected voice:

"Going wi' me? Going wi' me are ter? Tha'rt goin' further tha that counts on just now, dost hear?"

The dog faintly wagged its tail, the man stuck out his jaw and covered his pipe with his hands, and puffed intently, losing himself in the tobacco, looking down all the while at the dog with an absent brown eye. The dog looked up at him in mournful distrust. Joe stood with his knees stuck out, in real horsey fashion.

"Have you had a letter from Lucy?" Fred Henry asked of his sister.

"Last week," came the neutral reply.

"And what does she say?"

There was no answer.

"Does she *ask* you to go and stop there?" persisted Fred Henry.

"She says I can if I like."

"Well, then, you'd better. Tell her you'll come on Monday."

This was received in silence.

"That's what you'll do then, is it?" said Fred Henry, in some exaspera-tion.

But she made no answer. There was a silence of futility and irritation in the room. Malcolm grinned fatuously.

"You'll have to make up your mind between now and next Wednesday," said Joe loudly, "or else find yourself lodgings on the curbstone."

The face of the young woman darkened, but she sat on immutable.

"Here's Jack Fergusson!" exclaimed Malcolm, who was looking aimlessly out of the window.

"Where?" exclaimed Joe, loudly. ·

"Just gone past."

"Coming in?"

Malcolm craned his neck to see the gate.

"Yes," he said.

There was a silence. Mabel sat on like one condemned, at the head of the table. Then a whistle was heard from the kitchen. The dog got up and barked sharply. Joe opened the door and shouted:

"Come on."

After a moment a young man entered. He was muffled up in overcoat and a purple woolen scarf, and his tweed cap, which he did not remove, was pulled down on his head. He was of medium height, his face was rather long and pale, his eyes looked tired.

"Hello, Jack! Well, Jack!" exclaimed Malcolm and Joe. Fred Henry merely said, "Jack."

"What's doing?" asked the newcomer, evidently addressing Fred Henry.

"Same. We've got to be out by Wednesday. Got a cold?"

"I have—got it bad, too."

"Why don't you stop in?"

"*Me* stop in? When I can't stand on my legs, perhaps I shall have a chance." The young man spoke huskily. He had a slight Scotch accent.

"It's a knock-out, isn't it," said Joe, boisterously, "if a doctor goes round croaking with a cold. Looks bad for the patients, doesn't it?"

The young doctor looked at him slowly.

"Any thing the matter with *you*, then?" he asked sarcastically.

"Not as I know of. Damn your eyes, I hope not. Why?"

"I thought you were very concerned about the patients, wondered if you might be one yourself."

"Damn it, no, I've never been patient to no flaming doctor, and hope I never shall be," returned Joe.

At this point Mabel rose from the table, and they all seemed to become aware of her existence. She began putting the dishes together. The young doctor looked at her, but did not address her. He had not greeted her. She went out of the room with the tray, her face impassive and unchanged.

"When are you off then, all of you?" asked the doctor.

"I'm catching the eleven-forty," replied Malcolm. "Are you goin' down wi' th' trap, Joe?"

"Yes, I've told you I'm going down wi' th' trap, haven't I?"

"We'd better be getting her in then. So long, Jack, if I don't see you before I go," said Malcolm, shaking hands.

He went out, followed by Joe, who seemed to have his tail between his legs.

"Well, this is the devil's own," exclaimed the doctor, when he was left alone with Fred Henry. "Going before Wednesday, are you?"

"That's the orders," replied the other.

"Where, to Northampton?"

"That's it."

"The devil!" exclaimed Fergusson, with quiet chagrin.

And there was silence between the two.

"All settled up, are you?" asked Fergusson.

"About."

There was another pause.

"Well, I shall miss yer, Freddy, boy," said the young doctor.

"And I shall miss thee, Jack," returned the other.

"Miss you like hell," mused the doctor.

Fred Henry turned aside. There was nothing to say. Mabel came in again, to finish clearing the table.

"What are *you* going to do, then, Miss Pervin?" asked Fergusson. "Going to your sister's, are you?"

Mabel looked at him with her steady, dangerous eyes, that always made him uncomfortable, unsettling his superficial ease.

"No," she said.

"Well, what in the name of fortune *are* you going to do? Say what you mean to do," cried Fred Henry, with futile intensity.

But she only averted her head, and continued her work. She folded the white table-cloth, and put on the chenille cloth.

"The sulkiest bitch that ever trod!" muttered her brother.

But she finished her task with perfectly impassive face, the young doctor watching her interestedly all the while. Then she went out.

Fred Henry stared after her, clenching his lips, his blue eyes fixing in sharp antagonism, as he made a grimace of sour exasperation.

"You could bray her into bits, and that's all you'd get out of her," he said in a small, narrowed tone.

The doctor smiled faintly.

"What's she *going* to do, then?" he asked.

"Strike me if *I* know!" returned the other.

There was a pause. Then the doctor stirred.

"I'll be seeing you to-night, shall I?" he said to his friend.

"Ay—where's it to be? Are we going over to Jessdale?"

"I don't know. I've got such a cold on me. I'll come round to the Moon and Stars, anyway."

"Let Lizzie and May miss their night for once, eh?"

"That's it—if I feel as I do now."

"All's one—"

The two young men went through the passage and down to the back door together. The house was large, but it was servantless now, and desolate. At the back was a small bricked house-yard, and beyond that a big square, graveled fine and red, and having stables on two sides. Sloping, dank, winter-dark fields stretched away on the open sides.

But the stables were empty. Joseph Pervin, the father of the family, had been a man of no education, who had become a fairly large horse dealer. The stables had been full of horses, there was a great turmoil and come-and-go of horses and of dealers and grooms. Then the kitchen was full of servants. But of late things had declined. The old man had married a second time, to retrieve his fortunes. Now he was dead and everything was gone to the dogs, there was nothing but debt and threatening.

For months, Mabel had been servantless in the big house, keeping the home together in penury for her ineffectual brothers. She had kept house for ten years. But previously it was with unstinted means. Then, however brutal and coarse everything was, the sense of money had kept her proud, confident. The men might be foul-mouthed, the women in the kitchen might have bad reputations, her brothers might have illegitimate children. But so long as there was money, the girl felt herself established, and brutally proud, reserved.

No company came to the house, save dealers and coarse men. Mabel had no associates of her own sex, after her sister went away. But she did not mind. She went regularly to church, she attended to her father. And she lived in the memory of her mother, who had died when she was fourteen, and whom she had loved. She had loved her father, too, in a different way, depending upon him, and feeling secure in him, until at the age of fifty-four he married again. And then she had set hard against him. Now he had died and left them all hopelessly in debt.

She had suffered badly during the period of poverty. Nothing, however, could shake the curious sullen, animal pride that dominated each member of the family. Now, for Mabel, the end had come. Still she would not cast about her. She would follow her own way just the same. She would always hold the keys of her own situation. Mindless and persistent, she endured from day to day. Why should she think? Why should she answer anybody? It was enough that this was the end, and there was no way out. She need not pass any more darkly along the main street of the small town, avoiding every eye. She need not demean herself any more, going into the shops and buying the cheapest food. This was at an end. She thought of nobody, not even of herself. Mindless and persistent, she seemed in a sort of ecstasy to be coming nearer to her fulfilment, her own glorification, approaching her dead mother, who was glorified.

In the afternoon she took a little bag, with shears and sponge and a small scrubbing brush, and went out. It was a gray, wintry day, with saddened, dark green fields and an atmosphere blackened by the smoke of foundries not far off. She went quickly, darkly along the causeway, heeding nobody, through the town to the churchyard.

There she always felt secure, as if no one could see her, although as a matter of fact she was exposed to the stare of every one who passed along under the churchyard wall. Nevertheless, once under the shadow of the great looming church, among the graves, she felt immune from the world, reserved within the thick churchyard wall as in another country.

Carefully she clipped the grass from the grave, and arranged the pinky white, small chrysanthemums in the tin cross. When this was done, she took an empty jar from a neighboring grave, brought water, and carefully, most scrupulously sponged the marble headstone and the coping-stone.

It gave her sincere satisfaction to do this. She felt in immediate contact with the world of her mother. She took minute pains, went through the park in a state bordering on pure happiness, as if in performing this task she came into a sublte, intimate connection with her mother. For the life she followed here in the world was far less real than the world of death she inherited from her mother.

The doctor's house was just by the church. Fergusson, being a mere hired assistant, was slave to the countryside. As he hurried now to attend to the outpatients in the surgery, glancing across the graveyard with his quick eyes, he saw the girl at her task at the grave. She seemed so intent and remote, it was like looking into another world. Some mystical element was touched in him. He slowed down as he walked, watching her as if spellbound.

She lifted her eyes, feeling him looking. Their eyes met. And each looked away again at once, each feeling, in some way, found out by the other. He lifted his cap and passed on down the road. There remained distinct in his consciousness, like a vision, the memory of her face, lifted from the tombstone in the churchyard, and looking at him with slow, large, portentous eyes. It *was* portentous, her face. It seemed to mesmerize him. There was a heavy power in her eyes which laid hold of his whole being, as if he had drunk some powerful drug. He had been feeling weak and done before. Now the life came back into him, he felt delivered from his own fretted, daily self.

He finished his duties at the surgery as quickly as might be, hastily filling up the bottles of the waiting people with cheap drugs. Then, in perpetual haste, he set off again to visit several cases in another part of his round, before teatime. At all times he preferred to walk if he could, but particularly when he was not well. He fancied the motion restored him.

The afternoon was falling. It was gray, deadened, and wintry, with a slow, moist, heavy coldness sinking in and deadening all the faculties. But why should he think or notice? He hastily climbed the hill and turned across the dark green fields, following the black cinder-track. In the distance, across a shallow dip in the country, the small town was clustered like smouldering ash, a tower, a spire, a heap of low, raw, extinct houses. And on the nearest fringe of the town, sloping into the dip, was Oldmeadow, the Pervins' house. He could see the stables and the outbuildings distinctly, as they lay towards him on the slope. Well, he would not go there many more times! Another resource would be lost to him, another place gone: the only company he cared for in the alien, ugly little town he was losing. Nothing but work, drudgery, constant hastening from dwelling to dwelling among the colliers and the iron-workers. It wore him out, but at the same time he had a craving for it. It was a stimulant to him to be in the homes of the working people, moving as it were through the innermost body of their life. His nerves were excited and gratified. He could come so near, into the very lives of the rough, inarticulate, powerfully emotional men and women. He grumbled, he said he hated the hellish hole. But as a matter of fact it excited him, the contact with the rough, strongly-feeling people was a stimulant applied direct to his nerves.

Below Oldmeadow, in the green, shallow, soddened hollow of fields, lay a square, deep pond. Roving across the landscape, the doctor's quick eye detected a figure in black passing through the gate of the field, down towards the pond. He looked again. It would be Mabel Pervin. His mind suddenly became alive and attentive.

Why was she going down there? He pulled up on the path on the slope above, and stood staring. He could just make sure of the small black figure moving in the hollow of the failing day. He seemed to see her in the midst of such obscurity, that he was like a clairvoyant, seeing rather with the mind's eye than with ordinary sight. Yet he could see her positively enough, whilst he kept his eye attentive. He felt, if he looked away from her, in the thick, ugly falling dusk, he would lose her altogether.

He followed her minutely as she moved, direct and intent, like something transmitted rather than stirring in voluntary activity, straight down the field towards the pond. There she stood on the bank for a moment. She never raised her head. Then she waded slowly into the water.

He stood motionless as the small black figure walked slowly and deliberately towards the center of the pond, very slowly, gradually moving deeper into the motionless water, and still moving forward as the water got up to her breast. Then he could see her no more in the dusk of the dead afternoon.

"There!" he exclaimed. "Would you believe it?"

And he hastened straight down, running over the wet, soddened fields, pushing through the hedges, down into the depression of callous wintry obscurity. It took him several minutes to come to the pond. He stood on the bank, breathing heavily. He could see nothing. His eyes seemed to penetrate the dead water. Yes, perhaps that was the dark shadow of her black clothing beneath the surface of the water.

He slowly ventured into the pond. The bottom was deep, soft clay, he sank in, and the water clasped dead cold round his legs. As he stirred he could smell the cold, rotten clay that fouled up into the water. It was objectionable in his lungs. Still, repelled and yet not heeding, he moved deeper into the pond. The cold water rose over his thighs, over his loins, upon his abdomen. The lower part of his body was all sunk in the hideous cold element. And the bottom was so deeply soft and uncertain he was afraid of pitching with his mouth underneath. He could not swim, and was afraid.

He crouched a little, spreading his hands under the water and moving them round, trying to feel for her. The dead cold pond swayed upon his chest. He moved again, a little deeper, and again, with his hands underneath, he felt all around under the water. And he touched her clothing. But it evaded his fingers. He made a desperate effort to grasp it.

And so doing he lost his balance and went under, horribly, suffocating in the foul earthy water, struggling madly for a few moments. At last, after what seemed an eternity, he got his footing, rose again into the air and looked around. He gasped, and knew he was in the world. Then he looked at the water. She had risen near him. He grasped her clothing, and drawing her nearer, turned to take his way to land again.

He went very slowly, carefully, absorbed in the slow progress. He rose higher, climbing out of the pond. The water was now only about his legs; he was thankful, full of relief to be out of the clutches of the pond. He lifted her and staggered on to the bank, out of the horror of wet, gray clay.

He laid her down on the bank. She was quite unconscious and running with water. He made the water come from her mouth, he worked to restore her. He did not have to work very long before he could feel the breathing begin again in her; she was breathing naturally. He worked a little longer. He could feel her live beneath his hands; she was coming back. He wiped her face, wrapped her in his overcoat, looked round into the dim, dark gray world, then lifted her and staggered down the bank and across the fields.

It seemed an unthinkably long way, and his burden so heavy he felt he would never get to the house. But at last he was in the stable-yard, and then in the house-yard. He opened the door and went into the house. In the kitchen he laid her down on the hearthrug, and called. The house was empty. But the fire was burning in the grate.

Then again he kneeled to attend to her. She was breathing regularly, her eyes were wide open and as if conscious, but there seemed something missing in her look. She was conscious in herself, but unconscious of her surroundings.

He ran upstairs, took blankets from a bed, and put them before the fire to warm. Then he removed her saturated, earthy-smelling clothing, rubbed her dry with a towel, and wrapped her naked in the blankets. Then he went into the dining-room, to look for spirits. There was a little whisky. He drank a gulp himself, and put some into her mouth.

The effect was instantaneous. She looked full into his face, as if she had been seeing him for some time, and yet had only just become conscious of him.

"Dr. Fergusson?" she said.

"What?" he answered.

He was divesting himself of his coat, intending to find some dry clothing upstairs. He could not bear the smell of the dead, clayey water, and he was mortally afraid for his own health.

"What did I do?" she asked.

"Walked into the pond," he replied. He had begun to shudder like one sick, and could hardly attend to her. Her eyes remained full on him, he seemed to be going dark in his mind, looking back at her helplessly. The shuddering became quieter in him, his life came back in him, dark and unknowing, but strong again.

"Was I out of my mind?" she asked, while her eyes were fixed on him all the time.

"Maybe, for the moment," he replied. He felt quiet, because his strength had come back. The strange fretful strain had left him.

"Am I out of my mind now?" she asked.

"Are you?" he reflected a moment. "No," he answered truthfully, "I don't see that you are." He turned his face aside. He was afraid now, because he felt dazed, and felt dimly that her power was stronger than his, in this issue. And she continued to look at him fixedly all the time. "Can you tell me where I shall find some dry things to put on?" he asked.

"Did you dive into the pond for me?" she asked.

"No," he answered. "I walked in. But I went in overhead as well."

There was silence for a moment. He hesitated. He very much wanted to go upstairs to get into dry clothing. But there was another desire in him. And she seemed to hold him. His will seemed to have gone to sleep, and left him, standing there slack before her. But he felt warm inside himself. He did not shudder at all, though his clothes were sodden on him.

"Why did you?" she asked.

"Because I didn't want you to do such a foolish thing," he said.

"It wasn't foolish," she said, still gazing at him as she lay on the floor, with a sofa cushion under her head. "It was the right thing to do. *I* knew best, then."

"I'll go and shift these wet things," he said. But still he had not the power to move out of her presence, until she sent him. It was as if she had the life of his body in her hands, and he could not extricate himself. Or perhaps he did not want to.

Suddenly she sat up. Then she became aware of her own immediate condition. She felt the blankets about her, she knew her own limbs. For a moment it seemed as if her reason were going. She looked round, with wild eye, as if seeking something. He stood still with fear. She saw her clothing lying scattered.

"Who undressed me?" she asked, her eyes resting full and inevitable on his face.

"I did," he replied, "to bring you round."

For some moments she sat and gazed at him awfully, her lips parted. "Do you love me, then?" she asked.

He only stood and stared at her, fascinated. His soul seemed to melt.

She shuffled forward on her knees, and put her arms round him, round his legs, as he stood there, pressing her breasts against his knees and thighs, clutching him with strange, convulsive certainty, pressing his thighs against her, drawing him to her face, her throat, as she looked up at him with flaring, humble eyes of transfiguration, triumphant in first possession.

"You love me," she murmured, in strange transport, yearning and triumphant and confident. "You love me. I know you love me, I know."

And she was passionately kissing his knees, through the wet clothing, passionately and indiscriminately kissing his knees, his legs, as if unaware of everything.

He looked down at the tangled wet hair, the wild, bare, animal shoulders. He was amazed, bewildered, and afraid. He had never thought of loving her. He had never wanted to love her. When he rescued her and restored her, he was a doctor, and she was a patient. He had had no single personal thought of her. Nay, this introduction of the personal element was very distasteful to him, a violation of his professional honor. It was horrible to have her there embracing his knees. It was horrible. He revolted from it, violently. And yet—and yet—he had not the power to break away.

She looked at him again, with the same supplication of powerful love, and that same transcendent, frightening light of triumph. In view of the delicate flame which seemed to come from her face like a light, he was powerless. And yet he had never intended to love her. He had never intended. And something stubborn in him could not give way.

"You love me," she repeated, in a murmur of deep, rhapsodic assurance. "You love me."

Her hands were drawing him, drawing him down to her. He was afraid, even a little horrified. For he had, really, no intention of loving her. Yet her hands were drawing him towards her. He put out his hand quickly to steady himself, and grasped her bare shoulder. A flame seemed to burn the hand that grasped her soft shoulder. He had no intention of loving her: his whole will was against his yielding. It was horrible. And yet wonderful was the touch of her shoulders, beautiful the shining of her face. Was she perhaps mad? He had a horror of yielding to her. Yet something in him ached also.

He had been staring away at the door, away from her. But his hand remained on her shoulder. She had gone suddenly very still. He looked down at her. Her eyes were now wide with fear, with doubt, the light was dying from her face, a shadow of terrible grayness was returning. He could not bear the touch of her eyes' question upon him, and the look of death behind the question.

With an inward groan he gave way, and let his heart yield towards her. A sudden gentle smile came on his face. And her eyes, which never left his face, slowly, slowly filled with tears. He watched the strange water rise in her eyes, like some slow fountain coming up. And his heart seemed to burn and melt away in his breast.

He could not bear to look at her any more. He dropped on his knees and caught her head with his arms and pressed her face against his throat. She was very still. His heart, which seemed to have broken, was burning with a kind of agony in his breast. And he felt her slow, hot tears wetting his throat. But he could not move.

He felt the hot tears wet his neck and the hollows of his neck, and he remained motionless, suspended through one of man's eternities. Only now it had become indispensable to him to have her face pressed close to him; he could never let her go again. He could never let her head go away from the close clutch of his arm. He wanted to remain like that for ever, with his heart hurting him in a pain that was also life to him. Without knowing, he was looking down on her damp, soft brown hair.

Then, as it were suddenly, he smelt the horrid stagnant smell of that water. And at the same moment she drew away from him and looked at him. Her eyes were wistful and unfathomable. He was afraid of them, and he fell to kissing her, not knowing what he was doing. He wanted her eyes not to have that terrible, wistful, unfathomable look.

When she turned her face to him again, a faint delicate flush was glowing, and there was again dawning that terrible shining of joy in her eyes, which really terrified him, and yet which he now wanted to see, because he feared the look of doubt still more.

"You love me?" she said, rather faltering.

"Yes." The word cost him a painful effort. Not because it wasn't true. But because it was too newly true, the *saying* seemed to tear open again his newly-torn heart. And he hardly wanted it to be true, even now.

She lifted her face to him, and he bent forward and kissed her on the mouth, gently, with the one kiss that is an eternal pledge. And as he kissed her his heart strained again in his breast. He never intended to love her. But now it was over. He had crossed over the gulf to her, and all that he had left behind had shriveled and become void.

After the kiss, her eyes again slowly filled with tears. She sat still, away from him, with her face drooped aside, and her hands folded in her lap. The tears fell very slowly. There was complete silence. He too sat there motionless and silent on the hearthrug. The strange pain of his heart that was broken seemed to consume him. That he should love her? That this was love! That he should be ripped open in this way! Him, a doctor! How they would all jeer if they knew! It was agony to him to think they might know.

In the curious naked pain of the thought he looked again to her. She was sitting there drooped into a muse. He saw a tear fall, and his heart flared hot. He saw for the first time that one of her shoulders was quite uncovered, one arm bare, he could see one of her small breasts; dimly, because it had become almost dark in the room.

"Why are you crying?" he asked, in an altered voice.

She looked up at him, and behind her tears the consciousness of her situation for the first time brought a dark look of shame to her eyes.

"I'm not crying, really," she said, watching him half frightened.

He reached his hand, and softly closed it on her bare arm.

"I love you! I love you!" he said in a soft, low vibrating voice, unlike himself.

She shrank, and dropped her head. The soft, penetrating grip of his hand on her arm distressed her. She looked up at him.

"I want to go," she said. "I want to go and get you some dry things."

"Why?" he said. "I'm all right."

"But I want to go," she said. "And I want you to change your things."

He released her arm, and she wrapped herself in the blanket, looking at him rather frightened. And still she did not rise.

"Kiss me," she said wistfully.

He kissed her, but briefly, half in anger.

Then, after a second, she rose nervously, all mixed up in the blanket. He watched her in her confusion, as she tried to extricate herself and wrap herself up so that she could walk. He watched her relentlessly, as she knew. And as she went, the blanket trailing, and as he saw a glimpse of her feet and her white leg, he tried to remember her as she was when he had wrapped her in the blanket. But then he didn't want to remember, because she had been nothing to him then, and his nature revolted from remembering her as she was when she was nothing to him.

A tumbling, muffled noise from within the dark house startled him. Then he heard her voice:—"There are clothes." He rose and went to the foot of the stairs, and gathered up the garments she had thrown down. Then he came back to the fire, to rub himself down and dress. He grinned at his own appearance when he had finished.

The fire was sinking, so he put on coal. The house was now quite dark, save for the light of a street-lamp that shone in faintly from beyond the holly trees. He lit the gas with matches he found on the mantelpiece. Then he emptied the pockets of his own clothes, and threw all his wet things in a heap into the scullery. After which he gathered up her sodden clothes, gently, and put them in a separate heap on the copper-top in the scullery.

It was six o'clock on the clock. His own watch had stopped. He ought to go back to the surgery. He waited, and still she did not come down. So he went to the foot of the stairs and called:

"I shall have to go."

Almost immediately he heard her coming down. She had on her best dress of black voile, and her hair was tidy, but still damp. She looked at him—and in spite of herself, smiled.

"I don't like you in those clothes," she said.

"Do I look a sight?" he answered.

They were shy of one another.

"I'll make you some tea," she said.

"No, I must go."

"Must you?" And she looked at him again with the wide, strained, doubtful eyes. And again, from the pain of his breast, he knew how he loved her. He went and bent to kiss her, gently, passionately, with his heart's painful kiss.

"And my hair smells so horrible," she murmured in distraction. "And I'm so awful, I'm so awful! Oh, no, I'm too awful." And she broke into bitter, heart-broken sobbing. "You can't want to love me, I'm horrible."

"Don't be silly, don't be silly," he said, trying to comfort her, kissing her, holding her in his arms. "I want you, I want to marry you, we're going to be married, quickly, quickly—tomorrow if I can."

But she only sobbed terribly, and cried:

"I feel awful. I feel awful. I feel I'm horrible to you."

"No, I want you, I want you," was all he answered, blindly, with that terrible intonation which frightened her almost more than her horror lest he should *not* want her.

Katherine Mansfield 1888–1923

The Fly

Y' A R E very snug in here," piped old Mr. Woodifield, and he peered out of the great, green leather armchair by his friend the boss's desk as a baby peers out of its pram. His talk was over; it was time for him to be off. But he did not want to go. Since he had retired, since his . . . stroke, the wife and the girls kept him boxed up in the house every day of the week except Tuesday. On Tuesday he was dressed up and brushed and allowed to cut back to the City for the day. Though what he did there the wife and girls couldn't imagine. Made a nuisance of himself to his friends, they supposed. . . . Well, perhaps so. All the same, we cling to our last pleasures as the tree clings to its last leaves. So there sat old Woodifield, smoking a cigar and staring almost greedily at the boss, who rolled in his office chair, stout, rosy, five years older than he, and still going strong, still at the helm. It did one good to see him.

Wistfully, admiringly, the old voice added, "It's snug in here, upon my word!"

"Yes, it's comfortable enough," agreed the boss, and he flipped the *Financial Times* with a paper-knife. As a matter of fact he was proud of his room; he liked to have it admired, especially by old Woodifield. It gave him a feeling of deep, solid satisfaction to be planted there in the midst of it in full view of that frail old figure in the muffler.

"I've had it done up lately," he explained, as he had explained for the past—how many?—weeks. "New carpet," and he pointed to the bright red carpet with a pattern of large white rings. "New furniture," and he nodded towards the massive bookcase and the table with legs like twisted treacle. "Electric heating!" He waved almost exultantly towards the five transparent, pearly sausages glowing so softly in the tilted copper pan.

But he did not draw old Woodifield's attention to the photograph over the table of a grave-looking boy in uniform standing in one of those spectral photographers' parks with photographers' storm-clouds behind him. It was not new. It had been there for over six years.

"There was something I wanted to tell you," said old Woodifield, and

114

his eyes grew dim remembering. "Now what was it? I had it in my mind when I started out this morning." His hands began to tremble, and patches of red showed above his beard.

Poor old chap, he's on his last pins, thought the boss. And, feeling kindly, he winked at the old man, and said jokingly, "I tell you what. I've got a little drop of something here that'll do you good before you go out into the cold again. It's beautiful stuff. It wouldn't hurt a child." He took a key off his watch-chain, unlocked a cupboard below his desk, and drew forth a dark, squat bottle. "That's the medicine," said he. "And the man from whom I got it told me on the strict Q. T. it came from the cellars at Windsor Cassel."

Old Woodifield's mouth fell open at the sight. He couldn't have looked more surprised if the boss had produced a rabbit.

"It's whisky, ain't it?" he piped, feebly.

The boss turned the bottle and lovingly showed him the label. Whisky it was.

"D'you know," said he, peering up at the boss wonderingly, "they won't let me touch it at home." And he looked as though he was going to cry.

"Ah, that's where we know a bit more than the ladies," cried the boss, swooping across for two tumblers that stood on the table with the water-bottle, and pouring a generous finger into each. "Drink it down. It'll do you good. And don't put any water with it. It's sacrilege to tamper with stuff like this. Ah!" He tossed off his, pulled out his handkerchief, hastily wiped his moustaches, and cocked an eye at old Woodifield, who was rolling his in his chaps.

The old man swallowed, was silent a moment, and then said faintly, "It's nutty!"

But it warmed him; it crept into his chill old brain—he remembered.

"That was it," he said, heaving himself out of his chair. "I thought you'd like to know. The girls were in Belgium last week having a look at poor Reggie's grave, and they happened to come across your boy's. They're quite near each other, it seems."

Old Woodifield paused, but the boss made no reply. Only a quiver in his eyelids showed that he heard.

"The girls were delighted with the way the place is kept," piped the old voice. "Beautifully looked after. Couldn't be better if they were at home. You've not been across, have yer?"

"No, no!" For various reasons the boss had not been across.

"There's miles of it," quavered old Woodifield, "and it's all as neat as a garden. Flowers growing on all the graves. Nice broad paths." It was plain from his voice how much he liked a nice broad path.

The pause came again. Then the old man brightened wonderfully.

"D'you know what the hotel made the girls pay for a pot of jam?" he piped. "Ten francs! Robbery, I call it. It was a little pot, so Gertrude says, no bigger than a half-crown. And she hadn't taken more than a spoonful when they charged her ten francs. Gertrude brought the pot away with her to teach 'em a lesson. Quite right, too; it's trading on our feelings. They think because we're over there having a look around we're ready to pay anything. That's what it is." And he turned towards the door.

"Quite right, quite right!" cried the boss, though what was quite right he hadn't the least idea. He came round by his desk, followed the shuffling footsteps to the door, and saw the old fellow out. Woodifield was gone.

For a long moment the boss stayed, staring at nothing, while the grey-haired office messenger, watching him, dodged in and out of his cubby-hole like a dog that expects to be taken for a run. Then: "I'll see nobody for half an hour, Macey," said the boss. "Understand? Nobody at all."

"Very good, sir."

The door shut, the firm heavy steps recrossed the bright carpet, the fat body plumped down in the spring chair, and leaning forward, the boss covered his face with his hands. He wanted, he intended, he had arranged to weep. . . .

It had been a terrible shock to him when old Woodifield sprang that remark upon him about the boy's grave. It was exactly as though the earth had opened and he had seen the boy lying there with Woodifield's girls staring down at him. For it was strange. Although over six years had passed away, the boss never thought of the boy except as lying unchanged, unblemished in his uniform, asleep for ever. "My son!" groaned the boss. But no tears came yet. In the past, in the first months and even years after the boy's death, he had only to say those words to be overcome by such grief that nothing short of a violent fit of weeping could relieve him. Time, he had declared then, he had told everybody, could make no difference. Other men perhaps might recover, might live their loss down, but not he. How was it possible? His boy was an only son. Ever since his birth the boss had worked at building up this business for him; it had no other meaning if it was not for the boy. Life itself had come to have no other meaning. How on earth could he have slaved, denied himself, kept going all those years without the promise for ever before him of the boy's stepping into his shoes and carrying on where he left off?

And that promise had been so near being fulfilled. The boy had been in the office learning the ropes for a year before the war. Every morning they had started off together; they had come back by the same train. And what congratulations he had received as the boy's father! No wonder; he had taken to it marvellously. As to his popularity with the staff, every man jack of them down to old Macey couldn't make enough of the boy. And he wasn't in the least spoilt. No, he was just his bright, natural self, with the right word for everybody, with that boyish look and his habit of saying, "Simply splendid!"

But all that was over and done with as though it never had been. The day had come when Macey had handed him the telegram that brought the whole place crashing about his head. "Deeply regret to inform you . . ." And he had left the office a broken man with his life in ruins.

Six years ago, six years . . . How quickly time passed! It might have happened yesterday. The boss took his hands from his face; he was puzzled. Something seemed to be wrong with him. He wasn't feeling as he wanted to feel. He decided to get up and have a look at the boy's photograph. But it wasn't a favorite photograph of his; the expression was unnatural. It was cold, even stern-looking. The boy had never looked like that.

At that moment the boss noticed that a fly had fallen into his broad inkpot, and was trying feebly but desperately to clamber out again. Help! help! said those struggling legs. But the sides of the inkpot were wet and slippery; it fell back again and began to swim. The boss took up a pen, picked the fly out of the ink, and shook it onto a piece of blotting-paper. For a fraction of a second it lay still on the dark patch that oozed round it. Then the front legs waved, took hold, and, pulling it small sodden body up, it began the immense task of cleaning the ink from its wings. Over and under, over and under, went a leg along a wing, as the stone goes over and under the scythe. Then there was a pause, while the fly, seeming to stand on the tip of its toes, tried to expand first one wing and then the other. It succeeded at last, and sitting down, it began, like a minute cat, to clean its face. Now one could imagine that the little front legs rubbed against each other lightly, joyfully. The horrible danger was over; it had escaped; it was ready for life again.

But just then the boss had an idea. He plunged his pen back into the ink, leaned his thick wrist on the blotting paper, and as the fly tried its wings down came a great heavy blot. What would it make of that? What indeed! The little beggar seemed absolutely cowed, stunned, and afraid to move because of what would happen next. But then, as if painfully, it dragged itself forward. The front legs waved, caught hold, and, more slowly this time, the task began from the beginning.

He's a plucky little devil, thought the boss, and he felt a real admiration for the fly's courage. That was the way to tackle things; that was the right spirit. Never say die; it was only a question of . . . But the fly had again finished its laborious task, and the boss had just time to refill his pen, to shake fair and square on the new-cleaned body yet another dark drop. What about it this time? A painful moment of suspense followed. But behold, the front legs were again waving; the boss felt a rush of relief. He leaned over the fly and said to it tenderly, "You artful little b . . ." And he actually had the brilliant notion of breathing on it to help the drying process. All the same, there was something timid and weak about its efforts now, and the boss decided that this time should be the last, as he dipped the pen into the inkpot.

It was. The last blot fell on the soaked blotting-paper, and the draggled fly lay in it and did not stir. The black legs were stuck to the body; the front legs were not to be seen.

"Come on," said the boss. "Look sharp!" And he stirred it with his pen— in vain. Nothing happened or was likely to happen. The fly was dead.

The boss lifted the corpse on the end of the paper-knife and flung it into the waste-paper basket. But such a grinding feeling of wretchedness seized him that he felt positively frightened. He started forward and pressed the bell for Macey.

"Bring me some fresh blotting-paper," he said sternly, "and look sharp about it."

And while the old dog padded away he fell to wondering what it was he had been thinking about before. What was it? It was . . . He took out his handkerchief and passed it inside his collar. For the life of him he could not remember.

James Thurber 1894–1961

The Catbird Seat

M R . M A R T I N bought the pack of camels on Monday night in the most crowded cigar store on Broadway. It was theatre time and seven or eight men were buying cigarettes. The clerk didn't even glance at Mr. Martin, who put the pack in his overcoat pocket and went out. If any of the staff at F & S had seen him buy the cigarettes, they would have been astonished, for it was generally known that Mr. Martin did not smoke, and never had. No one saw him.

It was just a week to the day since Mr. Martin had decided to rub out Mrs. Ulgine Barrows. The term "rub out" pleased him because it suggested nothing more than the correction of an error—in this case an error of Mr. Fitweiler. Mr. Martin had spent each night of the past week working out his plan and examining it. As he walked home now he went over it again. For the hundredth time he resented the element of imprecision, the margin of guesswork that entered into the business. The project as he had worked it out was casual and bold, the risks were considerable. Something might go wrong anywhere along the line. And therein lay the cunning of his scheme. No one would ever see in it the cautious, painstaking hand of Erwin Martin, head of the filing department at F & S, of whom Mr. Fitweiler had once said, "Man is fallible but Martin isn't." No one would see his hand, that is, unless it were caught in the act.

Sitting in his apartment, drinking a glass of milk, Mr. Martin reviewed his case against Mrs. Ulgine Barrows, as he had every night for seven nights. He began at the beginning. Her quacking voice and braying laugh had first profaned the halls of F & S on March 7, 1941 (Mr. Martin had a head for dates). Old Roberts, the personnel chief, had introduced her as the newly appointed special adviser to the president of the firm, Mr. Fitweiler. The woman had appalled Mr. Martin instantly, but he hadn't shown it. He had given her his dry hand, a look of studious concentration, and a faint smile. "Well," she had said, looking at the papers on his desk, "are you lifting the oxcart out of the ditch?" As Mr. Martin recalled that moment, over his milk, he squirmed slightly. He must keep his mind on her crimes as a spe-

119

cial adviser, not on her peccadillos as a personality. This he found difficult to do, in spite of entering an objection and sustaining it. The faults of the woman as a woman kept chattering on in his mind like an unruly witness. She had, for almost two years now, baited him. In the halls, in the elevator, even in his own office, into which she romped now and then like a circus horse, she was constantly shouting these silly questions at him. "Are you lifting the oxcart out of the ditch? Are you tearing up the pea patch? Are you hollering down the rain barrel? Are you scraping around the bottom of the pickle barrel? Are you sitting in the catbird seat?"

It was Joey Hart, one of Mr. Martin's two assistants, who had explained what the gibberish meant. "She must be a Dodger fan," he had said. "Red Barber announces the Dodger games over the radio and he uses those expressions—picked 'em up down South." Joey had gone on to explain one or two. "Tearing up the pea patch" meant going on a rampage; "sitting in the catbird seat" meant sitting pretty, like a batter with three balls and no strikes on him. Mr. Martin dismissed all this with an effort. It had been annoying, it had driven him near to distraction, but he was too solid a man to be moved to murder by anything so childish. It was fortunate, he reflected as he passed on to the important charges against Mrs. Barrows, that he had stood up under it so well. He had maintained always an outward appearance of polite tolerance. "Why, I even believe you like the woman," Miss Paird, his other assistant, had once said to him. He had simply smiled.

A gavel rapped in Mr. Martin's mind and the case proper was resumed. Mrs. Ulgine Barrows stood charged with willful, blatant, and persistent attempts to destroy the efficiency and system of F & S. It was competent, material, and relevant to review her advent and rise to power. Mr. Martin had got the story from Miss Paird, who seemed always able to find things out. According to her, Mrs. Barrows had met Mr. Fitweiler at a party, where she had rescued him from the embraces of a powerfully built drunken man who had mistaken the president of F & S for a famous retired Middle Western football coach. She had led him to a sofa and somehow worked upon him a monstrous magic. The aging gentleman had jumped to the conclusion there and then that this was a woman of singular attainments, equipped to bring out the best in him and in the firm. A week later he had introduced her into F & S as his special adviser. On that day confusion got its foot in the door. After Miss Tyson, Mr. Brundage, and Mr. Bartlett had been fired and Mr. Munson had taken his hat and stalked out, mailing in his resignation later, old Roberts had been emboldened to speak to Mr. Fitweiler. He mentioned that Mr. Munson's department had been "a little disrupted" and hadn't they perhaps better resume the old system there? Mr. Fitweiler had said certainly not. He had the greatest faith in Mrs. Barrows' ideas. "They require a little seasoning, a little seasoning, is all," he had added. Mr. Roberts had given it up. Mr. Martin reviewed in detail all the changes wrought by Mrs. Barrows. She had begun chipping at the cornices of the firm's edifice and now she was swinging at the foundation stones with a pickaxe.

Mr. Martin came now, in his summing up, to the afternoon of Monday, November 2, 1942—just one week ago. On that day, at 3 p. m., Mrs. Barrows had bounced into his office. "Boo!" she had yelled. "Are you scraping around the bottom of the pickle barrel?" Mr. Martin had looked at her from under his green eyeshade, saying nothing. She had begun to wander about the office, taking it in with her great, popping eyes. "Do you really need *all* these filing cabinets?" she had demanded suddenly. Mr. Martin's heart had jumped. "Each of these files," he had said, keeping his voice even, "plays an indispensable part in the system of F & S." She had brayed at him, "Well, don't tear up the pea patch!" and gone to the door. From there she had bawled, "But you sure have got a lot of fine scrap in here!" Mr. Martin could no longer doubt that the finger was on his beloved department. Her pickaxe was on the upswing, poised for the first blow. It had not come yet; he had received no blue memo from the enchanted Mr. Fitweiler bearing nonsensical instructions deriving from the obscene woman. But there was no doubt in Mr. Martin's mind that one would be forthcoming. He must act quickly. Already a precious week had gone by. Mr. Martin stood up in his living room, still holding his milk glass. "Gentlemen of the jury," he said to himself, "I demand the death penalty for this horrible person."

The next day Mr. Martin followed his routine, as usual. He polished his glasses more often and once sharpened an already sharp pencil, but not even Miss Paird noticed. Only once did he catch sight of his victim; she swept past him in the hall with a patronizing "Hi!" At five-thirty he walked home, as usual, and had a glass of milk, as usual. He had never drunk anything stronger in his life—unless you could count ginger ale. The late Sam Schlosser, the S of F & S, had praised Mr. Martin at a staff meeting several years before for his temperate habits. "Our most efficient worker neither drinks nor smokes," he had said. "The results speak for themselves." Mr. Fitweiler had sat by, nodding approval.

Mr. Martin was still thinking about that red-letter day as he walked over to the Schrafft's on Fifth Avenue near Forty-Sixth Street. He got there, as he always did, at eight o'clock. He finished his dinner and the financial page of the *Sun* at a quarter to nine, as he always did. It was his custom after dinner to take a walk. This time he walked down Fifth Avenue at a casual pace. His gloved hands felt moist and warm, his forehead cold. He transferred the Camels from his overcoat to a jacket pocket. He wondered, as he did so, if they did not represent an unnecessary note of strain. Mrs. Barrows smoked only Luckies. It was his idea to puff a few puffs on a Camel (after the rubbing-out), stub it out in the ashtray holding her lipstick-stained Luckies, and thus drag a small red herring across the trail. Perhaps it was not a good idea. It would take time. He might even choke, too loudly.

Mr. Martin had never seen the house on West Twelfth Street where Mrs. Barrows lived, but he had a clear enough picture of it. Fortunately, she had bragged to everybody about her ducky first-floor apartment in the perfectly darling three-story red-brick. There would be no doorman or other attendants; just the tenants of the second and third floors. As he walked along, Mr. Martin realized that he would get there before nine-thirty. He had considered walking north on Fifth Avenue from Schrafft's to a point from which it would take him until ten o'clock to reach the house. At that hour people were less likely to be coming in or going out. But the procedure would have made an awkward loop in the straight thread of his casualness, and he had abandoned it. It was impossible to figure when people would be entering or leaving the house, anyway. There was a great risk at any hour. If he ran into anybody, he would simply have to place the rubbing-out of Ulgine Barrows in the inactive file forever. The same thing would hold true if there were someone in her apartment. In that case he would just say that he had been passing by, recognized her charming house, and thought to drop in.

It was eighteen minutes after nine when Mr. Martin turned into Twelfth Street. A man passed him, and a man and a woman, talking. There was no one within fifty paces when he came to the house, halfway down the block. He was up the steps and in the small vestibule in no time, pressing the bell under the card that said "Mrs. Ulgine Barrows." When the clicking in the lock started, he jumped forward against the door. He got inside fast, closing the door behind him. A bulb in a lantern hung from the hall ceiling on a chain seemed to give a monstrously bright light. There was nobody on the stair, which went up ahead of him along the left wall. A door opened down the hall in the wall on the right. He went toward it swiftly, on tiptoe.

"Well, for God's sake, look who's here!" bawled Mrs. Barrows, and her braying laugh rang out like the report of a shotgun. He rushed past her like a football tackle, bumping her. "Hey, quit shoving!" she said, closing the door behind them. They were in her living room, which seemed to Mr. Martin to be lighted by a hundred lamps. "What's after you?" she said. "You're as jumpy as a goat." He found he was unable to speak. His heart was wheezing in his throat. "I—yes," he finally brought out. She was jabbering and laughing as she started to help him off with his coat. "No, no," he said. "I'll put it here." He took it off and put it on a chair near the door. "Your hat and gloves, too," she said. "You're in a lady's house." He put his hat on top of the coat. Mrs. Barrows seemed larger than he had thought. He kept his gloves on. "I was passing by," he said. "I recognized—is there anyone here?" She laughed louder than ever. "No," she said, "we're all alone. You're as white as a sheet, you funny man. Whatever *has* come over you? I'll mix you a toddy." She started toward a door across the room. "Scotch-and-soda be all right? But say, you don't drink, do you?" She turned and gave him her amused look. Mr. Martin pulled himself together. "Scotch-and-soda will be all right," he heard himself say. He could hear her laughing in the kitchen.

Mr. Martin looked quickly around the living room for the weapon. He had counted on finding one there. There were andirons and a poker and something in a corner that looked like an Indian club. None of them would do. It couldn't be that way. He began to pace around. He came to a desk. On it lay a metal paper knife with an ornate handle. Would it be sharp enough? He reached for it and knocked over a small brass jar. Stamps spilled out of it and it fell to the floor with a clatter. "Hey," Mrs. Barrows yelled from the kitchen, "are you tearing up the pea patch?" Mr. Martin gave a strange laugh. Picking up the knife, he tried its point against his left wrist. It was blunt. It wouldn't do.

When Mrs. Barrows reappeared, carrying two highballs, Mr. Martin, standing there with his gloves on, became acutely conscious of the fantasy he had wrought. Cigarettes in his pocket, a drink prepared for him—it was all too grossly improbable. It was more than that; it was impossible. Somewhere in the back of his mind a vague idea stirred, sprouted. "For heaven's sake, take off those gloves," said Mrs. Barrows. "I always wear them in the house," said Mr. Martin. The idea began to bloom, strange and wonderful. She put the glasses on a coffee table in front of a sofa and sat on the sofa. "Come over here, you odd little man," she said. Mr. Martin went over and sat beside her. It was difficult getting a cigarette out of the pack of Camels, but he managed it. She held a match for him, laughing. "Well," she said, handing him his drink, "this is perfectly marvelous. You with a drink and a cigarette."

Mr. Martin puffed, not too awkwardly, and took a gulp of the highball. "I drink and smoke all the time," he said. He clinked his glass against hers. "Here's nuts to that old windbag, Fitweiler," he said, and gulped again. The stuff tasted awful, but he made no grimace. "Really, Mr. Martin," she said, her voice and posture changing, "you are insulting our employer." Mrs. Barrows was now all special adviser to the president. "I am preparing a bomb," said Mr. Martin, "which will blow the old goat higher than hell." He had only a little of the drink, which was not strong. It couldn't be that. "Do you take dope or something?" Mrs. Barrows asked coldly. "Heroin," said Mr. Martin. "I'll be coked to the gills when I bump that old buzzard off." "Mr. Martin!" she shouted, getting to her feet. "That will be all of that. You must go at once." Mr. Martin took another swallow of his drink.

He tapped his cigarette out in the ashtray and put the pack of Camels on the coffee table. Then he got up. She stood glaring at him. He walked over and put on his hat and coat. "Not a word about this," he said, and laid an index finger against his lips. All Mrs. Barrows could bring out was "Really!" Mr. Martin put his hand on the doorknob. "I'm sitting in the catbird seat," he said. He stuck his tongue out at her and left. Nobody saw him go.

Mr. Martin got to his apartment, walking, well before eleven. No one saw him go in. He had two glasses of milk after brushing his teeth, and he felt elated. It wasn't tipsiness, because he hadn't been tipsy. Anyway, the walk had worn off all effects of the whiskey. He got in bed and read a magazine for a while. He was asleep before midnight.

Mr. Martin got to the office at eight-thirty the next morning, as usual. At a quarter to nine, Ulgine Barrows, who had never before arrived at work before ten, swept into his office. "I'm reporting to Mr. Fitweiler now!" she shouted. "If he turns you over to the police, it's no more than you deserve!" Mr. Martin gave her a look of shocked surprise. "I beg your pardon?" he said. Mrs. Barrows snorted and bounced out of the room, leaving Miss Paird and Joey Hart staring after her. "What's the matter with that old devil now?" asked Miss Paird. "I have no idea," said Mr. Martin, resuming his work. The other two looked at him and then at each other. Miss Paird got up and went out. She walked slowly past the closed door of Mr. Fitweiler's office. Mrs. Barrows was yelling inside, but she was not braying. Miss Paird could not hear what the woman was saying. She went back to her desk.

Forty-five minutes later, Mrs. Barrows left the president's office and went into her own, shutting the door. It wasn't until half an hour later that Mr. Fitweiler sent for Mr. Martin. The head of the filing department, neat, quiet, attentive, stood in front of the old man's desk. Mr. Fitweiler was pale and nervous. He took his glasses off and twiddled them. He made a small, bruffing sound in his throat. "Martin," he said, "you have been with us more than twenty years." "Twenty-two, sir," said Mr. Martin. "In that time," pursued the president, "your work and your—uh—manner have been exemplary." "I trust so, sir," said Mr. Martin. "I have understood, Martin," said Mr. Fitweiler, "that you have never taken a drink or smoked." "That is correct, sir," said Mr. Martin. "Ah, yes." Mr. Fitweiler polished his glasses. "You may describe what you did after leaving the office yesterday, Martin," he said. Mr. Martin allowed less than a second for his bewildered pause. "Certainly, sir," he said. "I walked home. Then I went to Schrafft's for dinner. Afterward I walked home again. I went to bed early, sir, and read a magazine for a while. I was asleep before eleven." "Ah, yes," said Mr. Fitweiler again. He was silent for a moment, searching for the proper words to say to the head of the filing department. "Mrs. Barrows," he said finally, "Mrs. Barrows has worked hard, Martin, very hard. It grieves me to report

that she has suffered a severe breakdown. It has taken the form of a persecution complex accompanied by distressing hallucinations." "I am very
sorry, sir," said Mr. Martin. "Mrs. Barrows is under the delusion," continued Mr. Fitweiler, "that you visited her last evening and behaved yourself in an—uh—unseemly manner." He raised his hand to silence Mr.
Martin's little pained outcry. "It is the nature of these psychological diseases," Mr. Fitweiler said, "to fix upon the least likely and most innocent
party as the—uh—source of persecution. These matters are not for the lay
mind to grasp, Martin. I've just had my psychiatrist, Doctor Fitch, on the
phone. He would not, of course, commit himself, but he made enough
generalizations to substantiate my suspicions. I suggested to Mrs. Barrows,
when she had completed her—uh—story to me this morning, that she visit
Doctor Fitch, for I suspected a condition at once. She flew, I regret to say,
into a rage, and demanded—uh—requested that I call you on the carpet.
You may not know, Martin, but Mrs. Barrows had planned a reorganiza-
tion of your department—subject to my approval, of course, subject to my
approval. This brought you, rather than anyone else, to her mind—but
again that is a phenomenon for Doctor Fitch and not for us. So, Martin,
I am afraid Mrs. Barrows' usefulness here is at an end." "I am dreadfully
sorry, sir," said Mr. Martin.

It was at this point that the door to the office blew open with the suddenness of a gas-main explosion and Mrs. Barrows catapulted through it.
"Is the little rat denying it?" she screamed. "He can't get away with that!"
Mr. Martin got up and moved discreetly to a point beside Mr. Fitweiler's
chair. "You drank and smoked at my apartment," she bawled at Mr. Martin, "and you know it! You called Mr. Fitweiler an old windbag and said
you were going to blow him up when you got coked to the gills on your
heroin!" She stopped yelling to catch her breath and a new glint came into
her popping eyes. "If you weren't such a drab, ordinary little man," she
said, "I'd think you'd planned it all. Sticking your tongue out, saying you
were sitting in the catbird seat, because you thought no one would believe
me when I told it! My God, it's really too perfect!" She brayed loudly and
hysterically, and the fury was on her again. She glared at Mr. Fitweiler.
"Can't you see how he has tricked up, you old fool? Can't you see his little
game?" But Mr. Fitweiler had been surreptitiously pressing all the buttons
under the top of his desk and employees of F & S began pouring into the
room. "Stockton," said Mr. Fitweiler, "you and Fishbein will take Mrs.
Barrows to her home. Mrs. Powell, you will go with them." Stockton, who
had played a little football in high school, blocked Mrs. Barrows as she
made for Mr. Martin. It took him and Fishbein together to force her out
of the door into the hall, crowded with stenographers and office boys. She
was still screaming imprecations at Mr. Martin, tangled and contradictory
imprecations. The hubbub finally died down the corridor.

"I regret that this has happened," said Mr. Fitweiler. "I shall ask you to dismiss it from your mind, Martin." "Yes, sir," said Mr. Martin, anticipating his chief's "That will be all" by moving to the door. "I will dismiss it." He went out and shut the door, and his step was light and quick in the hall. When he entered his department he had slowed down to his customary gait, and he walked quietly across the room to the W20 file, wearing a look of studious concentration.

Katherine Anne Porter 1894–

Pale Horse, Pale Rider

I N S L E E P she knew she was in her bed, but not the bed she had lain down in a few hours since, and the room was not the same but it was a room she had known somwhere. Her heart was a stone lying upon her breast outside of her; her pulses lagged and paused, and she knew that something strange was going to happen, even as the early morning winds were cool through the lattice, the streaks of light were dark blue and the whole house was snoring in its sleep.

Now I must get up and go while they are all quiet. Where are my things? Things have a will of their own in this place and hide where they like. Daylight will strike a sudden blow on the roof startling them all up to their feet; faces will beam asking, Where are you going, What are you doing, What are you thinking, How do you feel, Why do you say such things, What do you mean? No more sleep. Where are my boots and what horse shall I ride? Fiddler or Graylie or Miss Lucy with the long nose and the wicked eye? How I have loved this house in the morning before we are all awake and tangled together like badly cast fishing lines. Too many people have been born here, and have wept too much here, and have laughed too much, and have been too angry and outrageous with each other here. Too many have died in this bed already, there are far too many ancestral bones propped up on the mantelpieces, there have been too damned many anti-macassars in this house, she said loudly, and oh, what accumulation of storied dust never allowed to settle in peace for one moment.

And the stranger? Where is that lank greenish stranger I remember hanging about the place, welcomed by my grandfather, my great-aunt, my five times removed cousin, my decrepit hound and my silver kitten? Why did they take to him, I wonder? And where are they now? Yet I saw him pass the window in the evening. What else besides them did I have in the world? Nothing. Nothing is mine, I have only nothing but it is enough, it is beautiful and it is all mine. Do I even walk about in my own skin or is it something I have borrowed to spare my modesty? Now what horse shall I borrow for this journey I do not mean to take, Graylie or Miss Lucy or

Fiddler who can jump ditches in the dark and knows how to get the bit between his teeth? Early morning is best for me because trees are trees in one stroke, stones are stones set in shades known to be grass, there are no false shapes or surmises, the road is still asleep with the crust of dew unbroken. I'll take Graylie because he is not afraid of bridges.

Come now, Graylie, she said, taking his bridle, we must outrun Death and the Devil. You are no good for it, she told the other horses standing saddled before the stable gate, among them the horse of the stranger, gray also, with tarnished nose and ears. The stranger swung into his saddle beside her, leaned far towards her and regarded her without meaning, the blank still stare of mindless malice that makes no threats and can bide its time. She drew Graylie around sharply, urged him to run. He leaped the low rose hedge and the narrow ditch beyond, and the dust of the lane flew heavily under his beating hoofs. The stranger rode beside her, easily, lightly, his reins loose in his half-closed hand, straight and elegant in dark shabby garments that flapped upon his bones; his pale face smiled in an evil trance, he did not glance at her. Ah, I have seen this fellow before, I know this man if I could place him. He is no stranger to me.

She pulled Graylie up, rose in her stirrups and shouted, I'm not going with you this time—ride on! Without pausing or turning his head the stranger rode on. Graylie's ribs heaved under her, her own ribs rose and fell, Oh, why am I so tired, I must wake up. "But let me get a fine yawn first," she said, opening her eyes and stretching, "a slap of cold water in my face, for I've been talking in my sleep again, I heard myself but what was I saying?"

Slowly, unwillingly, Miranda drew herself up inch by inch out of the pit of sleep, waited in a daze for life to begin again. A single word struck in her mind, a gong of warning, reminding her for the daylong what she forgot happily in sleep, and only in sleep. The war, said the gong, and she shook her head. Dangling her feet idly with their slippers hanging, she was reminded of the way all sorts of persons sat upon her desk at the newspaper office. Every day she found someone there, sitting upon her desk instead of the chair provided, dangling his legs, eyes roving, full of his important affairs, waiting to pounce about something or other. "*Why* won't they sit in the chair? Should I put a sign on it, saying, 'For God's sake, sit here'?"

Far from putting up a sign, she did not even frown at her visitors. Usually she did not notice them at all until their determination to be seen was greater than her determination not to see them. Saturday, she thought, lying comfortably in her tub of hot water, will be payday, as always. Or I hope always. Her thoughts roved hazily in a continual effort to bring together and unite firmly the disturbing oppositions in her day-to-day existence, where survival, she could see clearly, had become a series of feats of sleight of hand. I owe—let me see, I wish I had pencil and paper—well, suppose I *did* pay five dollars now on a Liberty Bond, I couldn't possibly keep it up. Or maybe. Eighteen dollars a week. So much for rent, so much for food, and I mean to have a few things besides. About five dollars' worth. Will leave me twenty-seven cents. I suppose I can make it. I suppose I should be worried. I am worried. Very well, now I am worried and what next? Twenty-seven cents. That's not so bad. Pure profit, really. Imagine if they should suddenly raise me to twenty I should then have two dollars and twenty-seven cents left over. But they aren't going to raise me to twenty. They are in fact going to throw me out if I don't buy a Liberty Bond. I hardly believe that. I'll ask Bill. (Bill was the city editor.) I wonder if a threat like that isn't a kind of blackmail. I don't believe even a Lusk Committeeman can get away with that.

Yesterday there had been two pairs of legs dangling, on either side of her typewriter, both pairs stuffed thickly into funnels of dark expensive-looking material. She noticed at a distance that one of them was oldish and one was youngish, and they both of them had a stale air of borrowed importance which apparently they had got from the same source. They were both much too well nourished and the younger one wore a square little mustache. Being what they were, no matter what their business was it would be something unpleasant. Miranda had nodded at them, pulled out her chair and without removing her cap or gloves had reached into a pile of letters and sheets from the copydesk as if she had not a moment to spare. They did not move, or take off their hats. At last she had said "Good morning" to them, and asked if they were, perhaps, waiting for her?

The two men slid off the desk, leaving some of her papers rumpled, and the oldish man had inquired why she had not bought a Liberty Bond. Miranda had looked at him then, and got a poor impression. He was a pursy-faced man, gross-mouthed, with little lightless eyes, and Miranda wondered why nearly all of those selected to do the war work at home were of his sort. He might be anything at all, she thought; advance agent for a road show, promoter of a wildcat oil company, a former saloon keeper announcing the opening of a new cabaret, an automobile salesman—any follower of any one of the crafty, haphazard callings. But he was now all Patriot, working for the government. "Look here," he asked her, "do you know there's a war, or don't you?"

Did he expect an answer to that? Be quiet, Miranda told herself, this was bound to happen. Sooner or later it happens. Keep your head. The man wagged his finger at her. "Do you?" he persisted, as if he were prompting an obstinate child.

"Oh, the war," Miranda had echoed on a rising note and she almost smiled at him. It was habitual, automatic, to give that solemn, mystically uplifted grin when you spoke the words or heard them spoken. *"C'est la guerre,"* whether you could pronounce it or not, was even better, and always, always, you shrugged.

"Yeah," said the younger man in a nasty way, "the war." Miranda, startled by the tone, met his eye; his stare was really stony, really viciously cold, the kind of thing you might expect to meet behind a pistol on a deserted corner. This expression gave temporary meaning to a set of features otherwise nondescript, the face of those men who have no business of their own. "We're having a war, and some people are buying Liberty Bonds and others just don't seem to get around to it," he said. "That's what we mean."

Miranda frowned with nervousness, the sharp beginnings of fear. "Are you selling them?" she asked, taking the cover off her typewriter and putting it back again.

"No, we're not selling them," said the older man. "We're just asking you why you haven't bought one." The voice was persuasive and ominous.

Miranda began to explain that she had no money, and did not know where to find any, when the older man interrupted: "That's no excuse, no excuse at all, and you know it, with the Huns overrunning martyred Belgium."

"With our American boys fighting and dying in Belleau Wood," said the younger man, "anybody can raise fifty dollars to help beat the Boche."

Miranda said hastily, "I have eighteen dollars a week and not another cent in the world. I simply cannot buy anything."

"You can pay for it five dollars a week," said the older man (they had stood there cawing back and forth over her head), "like a lot of other people in this office, and a lot of other offices besides are doing."

Miranda, desperately silent, had thought, "Suppose I were not a coward, but said what I really thought? Suppose I said to hell with this filthy war? Suppose I asked that little thug, What's the matter with you, why aren't you rotting in Belleau Wood? I wish you were. . . ."

She began to arrange her letters and notes, her fingers refusing to pick up things properly. The older man went on making his little set speech. It was hard, of course. Everybody was suffering, naturally. Everybody had to do his share. But as to that, a Liberty Bond was the safest investment you could make. It was just like having the money in the bank. Of course. The government was back of it and where better could you invest?

"I agree with you about that," said Miranda, "but I haven't any money to invest."

And of course, the man had gone on, it wasn't so much her fifty dollars that was going to make any difference. It was just a pledge of good faith on her part. A pledge of good faith that she was a loyal American doing her duty. And the thing was safe as a church. Why, if he had a million dollars he'd be glad to put every last cent of it in these Bonds. . . . "You can't lose by it," he said, almost benevolently, "and you can lose a lot if you don't. Think it over. You're the only one in this whole newspaper office that hasn't come in. And every firm in this city has come in one hundred per cent. Over at the *Daily Clarion* nobody had to be asked twice."

"They pay better over there," said Miranda. "But next week, if I can. Not now, next week."

"See that you do," said the younger man. "This ain't any laughing matter."

They lolled away, past the Society Editor's desk, past Bill the City Editor's desk, past the long copydesk where old man Gibbons sat all night shouting at intervals, "Jarge! Jarge!" and the copyboy would come flying. "Never say *people* when you mean *persons*," old man Gibbons had instructed Miranda, "and never say *practically*, say *virtually*, and don't for God's sake ever so long as I am at this desk use the barbarism *inasmuch* under any circumstances whatsoever. Now you're educated, you may go." At the head of the stairs her inquisitors had stopped in their fussy pride and vainglory, lighting cigars and wedging their hats more firmly over their eyes.

Miranda turned over in the soothing water, and wished she might fall asleep there, to wake up only when it was time to sleep again. She had a burning slow headache, and noticed it now, remembering she had waked up with it and it had in fact begun the evening before. While she dressed she tried to trace the insidious career of her headache, and it seemed reasonable to suppose it had started with the war. "It's been a headache, all right, but not quite like this." After the Committeemen had left, yesterday, she had gone to the cloakroom and had found Mary Townsend, the Society Editor, quietly hysterical about something. She was perched on the edge of the shabby wicker couch with ridges down the center, knitting on something rose-colored. Now and then she would put down her knitting, seize her head with both hands and rock, saying, "My *God*," in a surprised, inquiring voice. Her column was called Ye Towne Gossyp, so of course everybody called her Towney. Miranda and Towney had a great deal in common, and liked each other. They had both been real reporters once, and had been sent together to "cover" a scandalous elopement in which no marriage had taken place, after all, and the recaptured girl, her face swollen, had sat with her mother who was moaning steadily under a mound of blankets. They had both wept painfully and implored the young reporters to suppress the worst of the story. They had suppressed it, and the rival newspaper printed it all the next day. Miranda and Towney had then taken their punishment together, and had been degraded publicly to routine female jobs, one to the theaters, the other to society. They had this in common, that neither of them could see what else they could possibly have done, and they knew they were considered fools by the rest of the staff— nice girls, but fools. At sight of Miranda, Towney had broken out in a rage, "I can't do it, I'll never be able to raise the money, I told them, I can't, I can't, but they wouldn't listen."

Miranda said, "I knew I wasn't the only person in this office who couldn't raise five dollars. I told them I couldn't, too, and I can't."

"My God," said Towney, in the same voice, "they told me I'd lose my job—"

"I'm going to ask Bill," Miranda said; "I don't believe Bill would do that."

"It's not up to Bill," said Towney. "He'd have to if they got after him. Do you suppose they could put us in jail?"

"I don't know," said Miranda. "If they do, we won't be lonesome." She sat down beside Towney and held her own head. "What kind of soldier are you knitting that for? It's a sprightly color, it ought to cheer him up."

"Like hell," said Towney, her needles going again. "I'm making this for myself. That's that."

"Well," said Miranda, "we won't be lonesome and we'll catch up on our sleep." She washed her face and put on fresh makeup. Taking clean gray gloves out of her pocket she went out to join a group of young women fresh from the country club dances, the morning bridge, the charity bazaar, the Red Cross workrooms, who were wallowing in good works. They gave tea dances and raised money, and with the money they bought quantities of sweets, fruit, cigarettes, and magazines for the men in the cantonment hospitals. With this loot they were now setting out, a gay procession of high-powered cars and brightly tinted faces to cheer the brave boys who already, you might very well say, had fallen in defense of their country. It must be frightfully hard on them, the dears, to be floored like this when they're all crazy to get overseas and into the trenches as quickly as possible. Yes, and some of them are the cutest things you ever saw, I didn't know there were so many good-looking men in this country, good heavens, I said, where do they come from? Well, my dear, you may ask yourself that question, who knows where they did come from? You're quite right, the way I feel about it is this, we must do everything we can to make them contented, but I draw the line at talking to them. I told the chaperons at those dances for enlisted men, I'll dance with them, every dumbbell who asks me, but I will NOT talk to them, I said, even if there is a war. So I danced hundreds of miles without opening my mouth except to say, Please keep your knees to yourself. I'm glad we gave those dances up. Yes, and the men stopped coming, anyway. But listen, I've heard that a great many of the enlisted men come from very good families; I'm not good at catching names, and those I did catch I'd never heard before, so I don't know . . . but it seems to me if they were from good families, you'd know it, wouldn't you? I mean, if a man is well bred he doesn't step on your feet, does he? At least not that. I used to have a pair of sandals ruined at every one of those dances. Well, I think any kind of social life is in very poor taste just now, I think we should all put on our Red Cross headdresses and wear them for the duration of the war—

Miranda, carrying her basket and her flowers, moved in among the young women, who scattered out and rushed upon the ward uttering girlish laughter meant to be refreshingly gay, but there was a grim determined clang in it calculated to freeze the blood. Miserably embarrassed at the idiocy of her errand, she walked rapidly between the long rows of high beds, set foot to foot with a narrow aisle between. The men, a selected presentable lot, sheets drawn up to their chins, not seriously ill, were bored and restless, most of them willing to be amused at anything. They were for the most part picturesquely bandaged as to arm or head, and those who were not visibly wounded invariably replied "Rheumatism" if some tactless girl, who had been solemnly warned never to ask this question, still forgot and asked a man what his illness was. The good-natured, eager ones, laughing and calling out from their hard narrow beds, were soon surrounded. Miranda, with her wilting bouquet and her basket of sweets and cigarettes, looking about, caught the unfriendly bitter eye of a young fellow lying on his back, his right leg in a cast and pulley. She stopped at the foot of his bed and continued to look at him, and he looked back with an unchanged, hostile face. Not having any, thank you and be damned to the whole business, his eyes said plainly to her, and will you be so good as to take your trash off my bed? For Miranda had set it down, leaning over to place it where he might be able to reach it if he would. Having set it down, she was incapable of taking it up again, but hurried away, her face burning, down the long aisle and out into the cool October sunshine, where the dreary raw barracks swarmed and worked with an aimless life of scurrying, dun-colored insects; and going around to a window near where he lay, she looked in, spying upon her soldier. He was lying with his eyes closed, his eyebrows in a sad bitter frown. She could not place him at all, she could not imagine where he came from nor what sort of being he might have been "in life," she said to herself. His face was young and the features sharp and plain, the hands were not laborer's hands but not well-cared-for hands either. They were good useful properly shaped hands, lying there on the coverlet. It occurred to her that it would be her luck to find him, instead of a jolly hungry puppy glad of a bite to eat and a little chatter. It is like turning a corner absorbed in your painful thoughts and meeting your state of mind embodied, face to face, she said. "My own feelings about this whole thing, made flesh. Never again will I come here, this is no sort of thing to be doing. This is disgusting," she told herself plainly. "Of course I would pick him out," she thought, getting into the back seat of the car she came in, "serves me right, I know better."

Another girl came out looking very tired and climbed in beside her. After a short silence, the girl said in a puzzled way, "I don't know what good it does, really. Some of them wouldn't take anything at all. I don't like this, do you?"

"I hate it," said Miranda.

"I suppose it's all right, though," said the girl, cautiously.

"Perhaps," said Miranda, turning cautious also.

That was for yesterday. At this point Miranda decided there was no good in thinking of yesterday, except for the hour after midnight she had spent dancing with Adam. He was in her mind so much, she hardly knew when she was thinking about him directly. His image was simply always present in more or less degree, he was sometimes nearer the surface of her thoughts, the pleasantest, the only really pleasant thought she had. She examined her face in the mirror between the windows and decided that her uneasiness was not all imagination. For three days at least she had felt odd and her expression was unfamiliar. She would have to raise that fifty dollars somehow, she supposed, or who knows what can happen? She was hardened to stories of personal disaster, of outrageous accusations and extraordinarily bitter penalties that had grown monstrously out of incidents very little more important than her failure—her refusal—to buy a Bond. No, she did not find herself a pleasing sight, flushed and shiny, and even her hair felt as if it had decided to grow in the other direction. I must do something about this, I can't let Adam see me like this, she told herself, knowing that even now at that moment he was listening for the turn of her doorknob, and he would be in the hallway, or on the porch when she came out, as if by sheerest coincidence. The noon sunlight cast cold slanting shadows in the room where, she said, I suppose I live, and this day is beginning badly, but they all do now, for one reason or another. In a drowse, she sprayed perfume on her hair, put on her moleskin cap and jacket, now in their second winter, but still good, still nice to wear, again being glad she had paid a frightening price for them. She had enjoyed them all this time, and in no case would she have had the money now. Maybe she could manage for that Bond. She could not find the lock without leaning to search for it, then stood undecided a moment possessed by the notion that she had forgotten something she would miss seriously later on.

Adam was in the hallway, a step outside his own door; he swung about as if quite startled to see her, and said, "Hello, I don't have to go back to camp today after all—isn't that luck?"

Miranda smiled at him gaily because she was always delighted at the sight of him. He was wearing his new uniform, and he was all olive and tan and tawny, hay colored and sand colored from hair to boots. She half noticed again that he always began by smiling at her; that his smile faded gradually; that his eyes became fixed and thoughtful as if he were reading in a poor light.

They walked out together into the fine fall day, scuffling bright ragged leaves under their feet, turning their faces up to a generous sky really blue and spotless. At the first corner they waited for a funeral to pass, the mourners seated straight and firm as if proud in their sorrow.

"I imagine I'm late," said Miranda, "as usual. What time is it?"

"Nearly half past one," he said, slipping back his sleeve with an exaggerated thrust of his arm upward. The young soldiers were still self-conscious about their wristwatches. Such of them as Miranda knew were boys from southern and southwestern towns, far off the Atlantic seaboard, and they had always believed that only sissies wore wristwatches. "I'll slap you on the wristwatch," one vaudeville comedian would simper to another, and it was always a good joke, never stale.

"I think it's a most sensible way to carry a watch," said Miranda. "You needn't blush."

"I'm nearly used to it," said Adam, who was from Texas. "We've been told time and again how all the he-manly regular army men wear them. It's the horrors of war," he said; "are we downhearted? I'll say we are."

It was the kind of patter going the rounds. "You look it," said Miranda.

He was tall and heavily muscled in the shoulders, narrow in the waist and flanks, and he was infinitely buttoned, strapped, harnessed into a uniform as tough and unyielding in cut as a straitjacket, though the cloth was fine and supple. He had his uniforms made by the best tailor he could find, he confided to Miranda one day when she told him how squish he was looking in his new soldier suit. "Hard enough to make anything of the outfit, anyhow," he told her. "It's the least I can do for my beloved country, not to go around looking like a tramp." He was twenty-four years old and a Second Lieutenant in an Engineers Corps, on leave because his outfit expected to be sent over shortly. "Came in to make my will," he told Miranda, "and get a supply of toothbrushes and razor blades. By what gorgeous luck do you suppose," he asked her, "I happened to pick on your rooming house? How did I know you were there?"

Strolling, keeping step, his stout polished well-made boots setting themselves down firmly beside her thin-soled black suede, they put off as long as they could the end of their moment together, and kept up as well as they could their small talk that flew back and forth over little grooves worn in the thin upper surface of the brain, things you could say and hear clink reassuringly at once without disturbing the radiance which played and darted about the simple and lovely miracle of being two persons named Adam and Miranda, twenty-four years old each, alive and on the earth at the same moment: "Are you in the mood for dancing, Miranda?" and "I'm always in the mood for dancing, Adam!" but there were things in the way, the day that ended with dancing was a long way to go.

He really did look, Miranda thought, like a fine healthy apple this morning. One time or another in their talking, he had boasted that he had never had a pain in his life that he could remember. Instead of being horrified at this monster, she approved his monstrous uniqueness. As for herself, she had had too many pains to mention, so she did not mention them. After working for three years on a morning newspaper she had an illusion of maturity and experience; but it was fatigue merely, she decided, from keeping what she had been brought up to believe were unnatural hours, eating casually at dirty little restaurants, drinking bad coffee all night, and smoking too much. When she said something of her way of living to Adam, he studied her face a few seconds as if he had never seen it before, and said in a forthright way, "Why, it hasn't hurt you a bit, I think you're beautiful," and left her dangling there, wondering if he had thought she wished to be praised. She did wish to be praised, but not at that moment. Adam kept unwholesome hours too, or had in the ten days they had known each other, staying awake until one o'clock to take her out for supper; he smoked also continually, though if she did not stop him he was apt to explain to her exactly what smoking did to the lungs. "But," he said, "does it matter so much if you're going to war, anyway?"

"No," said Miranda, "and it matters even less if you're staying at home knitting socks. Give me a cigarette, will you?" They paused at another corner, under a half-foliaged maple, and hardly glanced at a funeral procession approaching. His eyes were pale tan with orange flecks in them, and his hair was the color of a haystack when you turn the weathered top back to the clear straw beneath. He fished out his cigarette case and snapped his silver lighter at her, snapped it several times in his own face, and they moved on, smoking.

"I can see you knitting socks," he said. "That would be just your speed. You know perfectly well you can't knit."

"I do worse," she said, soberly; "I write pieces advising other young women to knit and roll bandages and do without sugar and help win the war."

"Oh, well," said Adam, with the easy masculine morals in such questions, "that's merely your job, that doesn't count."

"I wonder," said Miranda. "How did you manage to get an extension of leave?"

"They just gave it," said Adam, "for no reason. The men are dying like flies out there, anyway. This funny new disease. Simply knocks you into a cocked hat."

"It seems to be a plague," said Miranda, "something out of the Middle Ages. Did you ever see so many funerals, ever?"

"Never did. Well, let's be strong-minded and not have any of it. I've got four days more straight from the blue and not a blade of grass must grow under our feet. What about tonight?"

"Same thing," she told him, "but make it about half past one. I've got a special job beside my usual run of the mill."

"What a job you've got," said Adam, "nothing to do but run from one dizzy amusement to another and then write a piece about it."

"Yes, it's too dizzy for words," said Miranda. They stood while a funeral passed, and this time they watched it in silence. Miranda pulled her cap to an angle and winked in the sunlight, her head swimming slowly "like goldfish," she told Adam, "my head swims. I'm only half awake, I must have some coffee."

They lounged on their elbows over the counter of a drugstore. "No more cream for the stay-at-homes," she said, "and only one lump of sugar. I'll have two or none; that's the kind of martyr I'm being. I mean to live on boiled cabbage and wear shoddy from now on and get in good shape for the next round. No war is going to sneak up on me again."

"Oh, there won't be any more wars, don't you read the newspapers?" asked Adam. "We're going to mop 'em up this time, and they're going to stay mopped, and this is going to be all."

"So they told me," said Miranda, tasting her bitter lukewarm brew and making a rueful face. Their smiles approved of each other, they felt they had got the right tone, they were taking the war properly. Above all, thought Miranda, no tooth-gnashing, no hair-tearing, it's noisy and unbecoming and it doesn't get you anywhere.

"Swill," said Adam rudely, pushing back his cup. "Is that all you're having for breakfast?"

"It's more than I want," said Miranda.

"I had buckwheat cakes, with sausage and maple syrup, and two bananas, and two cups of coffee, at eight o'clock, and right now, again, I feel like a famished orphan left in the ashcan. I'm all set," said Adam, "for broiled steak and fried potatoes and—"

"Don't go on with it," said Miranda, "it sounds delirious to me. Do all that after I'm gone." She slipped from the high seat, leaned against it slightly, glanced at her face in her round mirror, rubbed rouge on her lips and decided that she was past praying for.

"There's something terribly wrong," she told Adam. "I feel too rotten. It can't just be the weather, and the war."

"The weather is perfect," said Adam, "and the war is simply too good to be true. But since when? You were all right yesterday."

"I don't know," she said slowly, her voice sounding small and thin. They stopped as always at the open door before the flight of littered steps leading up to the newspaper loft. Miranda listened for a moment to the rattle of typewriters above, the steady rumble of presses below. "I wish we were going to spend the whole afternoon on a park bench," she said, "or drive to the mountains."

"I do too," he said; "let's do that tomorrow."

"Yes, tomorrow, unless something else happens. I'd like to run away," she told him; "let's both."

"Me?" said Adam. "Where I'm going there's no running to speak of. You mostly crawl about on your stomach here and there among the debris. You know, barbed wire and such stuff. It's going to be the kind of thing that happens once in a lifetime." He reflected a moment, and went on, "I don't know a darned thing about it, really, but they make it sound awfully messy. I've heard so much about it I feel as if I had been there and back. It's going to be an anticlimax," he said, "like seeing the pictures of a place so often you can't see it at all when you actually get there. Seems to me I've been in the army all my life."

Six months, he meant. Eternity. He looked so clear and fresh, and he had never had a pain in his life. She had seen them when they had been there and back and they never looked like this again. "Already the returned hero," she said, "and don't I wish you were."

"When I learned the use of the bayonet in my first training camp," said Adam, "I gouged the vitals out of more sandbags and sacks of hay than I could keep track of. They kept bawling at us, 'Get him, get that Boche, stick him before he sticks you'—and we'd go for those sandbags like wildfire, and honestly, sometimes I felt a perfect fool for getting so worked up when I saw the sand trickling out. I used to wake up in the night sometimes feeling silly about it."

"I can imagine," said Miranda. "It's perfect nonsense." They lingered, unwilling to say good-by. After a little pause, Adam, as if keeping up the conversation, asked, "Do you know what the average life expectation of a sapping party is after it hits the job?"

"Something speedy, I suppose."

"Just nine minutes," said Adam; "I read that in your own newspaper not a week ago."

"Make it ten and I'll come along," said Miranda.

"Not another second," said Adam, "exactly nine minutes, take it or leave it."

"Stop bragging," said Miranda. "Who figured that out?"

"A noncombatant," said Adam, "a fellow with rickets."

This seemed very comic, they laughed and leaned towards each other and Miranda heard herself being a little shrill. She wiped the tears from her eyes. "My, it's a funny war," she said; "isn't it? I laugh every time I think about it."

Adam took her hand in both of his and pulled a little at the tips of her gloves and sniffed them. "What nice perfume you have," he said, "and such a lot of it, too. I like a lot of perfume on gloves and hair," he said, sniffing again.

"I've got probably too much," she said. "I can't smell or see or hear today. I must have a fearful cold."

"Don't catch cold," said Adam; "my leave is nearly up and it will be the last, the very last." She moved her fingers in her gloves as he pulled at the fingers and turned her hands as if they were something new and curious and of great value, and she turned shy and quiet. She liked him, she liked him, and there was more than this but it was no good even imagining, because he was not for her nor for any woman, being beyond experience already, committed without any knowledge or act of his own to death. She took back her hands. "Good-by," she said finally, "until tonight."

She ran upstairs and looked back from the top. He was still watching her, and raised his hand without smiling. Miranda hardly ever saw anyone look back after he had said good-by. She could not help turning sometimes for one glimpse more of the person she had been talking with, as if that would save too rude and too sudden a snapping of even the lightest bond. But people hurried away, their faces already changed, fixed, in their straining towards their next stopping place, already absorbed in planning their next act or encounter. Adam was waiting as if he expected her to turn, and under his brows fixed in a strained frown, his eyes were very black.

At her desk she sat without taking off jacket or cap, slitting envelopes and pretending to read the letters. Only Chuck Rouncivale, the sports reporter, and Ye Towne Gossyp were sitting on her desk today, and them she liked having there. She sat on theirs when she pleased. Towney and Chuck were talking and they went on with it.

"They say," said Towney, "that it is really caused by germs brought by a German ship to Boston, a camouflaged ship, naturally, it didn't come in under its own colors. Isn't that ridiculous?"

"Maybe it was a submarine," said Chuck, "sneaking in from the bottom of the sea in the dead of night. Now that sounds better."

"Yes, it does," said Towney; "they always slip up somewhere in these details . . . and they think the germs were sprayed over the city—it started in Boston, you know—and somebody reported seeing a strange, thick, greasy-looking cloud float up out of Boston Harbor and spread slowly all over that end of town. I think it was an old woman who saw it."

"Should have been," said Chuck.

"I read it in a New York newspaper," said Towney; "so it's bound to be true."

Chuck and Miranda laughed so loudly at this that Bill stood up and glared at them. "Towney still reads the newspapers," explained Chuck.

"Well, what's funny about that?" asked Bill, sitting down again and frowning into the clutter before him.

"It was a noncombatant saw that cloud," said Miranda.

"Naturally," said Towney.

"Member of the Lusk Committee, maybe," said Miranda.

"The Angel of Mons," said Chuck, "or a dollar-a-year man."

Miranda wished to stop hearing and talking, she wished to think for just five minutes of her own about Adam, really to think about him, but there was no time. She had seen him first ten days ago, and since then they had been crossing streets together, darting between trucks and limousines and pushcarts and farm wagons; he had waited for her in doorways and in little restaurants that smelled of stale frying fat; they had eaten and danced to the urgent whine and bray of jazz orchestras, they had sat in dull theaters because Miranda was there to write a piece about the play. Once they had gone to the mountains and, leaving the car, had climbed a stony trail, and had come out on a ledge upon a flat stone, where they sat and watched the lights change on a valley landscape that was, no doubt, Miranda said, quite apocryphal—"We need not believe it, but it is fine poetry," she told him; they had leaned their shoulders together there, and had sat quite still, watching. On two Sundays they had gone to the geological museum, and had pored in shared fascination over bits of meteors, rock formations, fossilized tusks and trees, Indian arrows, grottoes from the silver and gold lodes. "Think of those old miners washing out their fortunes in little pans beside the streams," said Adam, "and inside the earth there was this—" and he had told her he liked better those things that took long to make; he loved airplanes too, all sorts of machinery, things carved out of wood or stone. He knew nothing much about them, but he recognized them when he saw them. He had confessed that he simply could not get through a book, any kind of book except textbooks on engineering; reading bored him to crumbs; he regretted now he hadn't brought his roadster, but he hadn't thought he would need a car; he loved driving, he wouldn't expect her to believe how many hundreds of miles he could get over in a day . . . he had showed her snapshots of himself at the wheel of his roadster; of himself sailing a boat, looking very free and windblown, all angles, hauling on the ropes; he would have joined the air force but his mother had hysterics every time he mentioned it. She didn't seem to realize that dogfighting in the air was a good deal safer than sapping parties on the ground at night. But he hadn't argued, because of course she did not realize about sapping parties. And here he was, stuck, on a plateau a mile high with no water for a boat and his car at home, otherwise they could really have had a good time. Miranda knew he was trying to tell her what kind of person he was when he had his machinery with him. She felt she knew pretty well what kind of person he was, and would have liked to tell him that if he thought he had left himself at home in a boat or an automobile, he was much mistaken. The telephones were ringing, Bill was shouting at somebody who kept saying, "Well, but listen, well, but listen—" but nobody was going to listen, of course, nobody. Old man Gibbons bellowed in despair, "Jarge, Jarge—"

"Just the same," Towney was saying in her most complacent patriotic voice, "Hut Service is a fine idea, and we should all volunteer even if they don't want us." Towney does well at this, thought Miranda, look at her; remembering the rose-colored sweater and the tight rebellious face in the cloakroom. Towney was now all open-faced glory and goodness, willing to sacrifice herself for her country. "After all," said Towney, "I *can* sing and dance well enough for the Little Theater, and I could write their letters for them, and at a pinch I might drive an ambulance. I have driven a Ford for years."

Miranda joined in: "Well, I can sing and dance too, but who's going to do the bed-making and the scrubbing up? Those huts are hard to keep, and it would be a dirty job and we'd be perfectly miserable; and as I've got a hard dirty job and am perfectly miserable, I'm going to stay at home."

"I think the women should keep out of it," said Chuck Rouncivale. "They just add skirts to the horrors of war." Chuck had bad lungs and fretted a good deal about missing the show. "I could have been there and back with a leg off by now; it would have served the old man right. Then he'd either have to buy his own hooch or sober up."

Miranda had seen Chuck on payday giving the old man money for hooch. He was a good-humored ingratiating old scoundrel, too, that was the worst of him. He slapped his son on the back and beamed upon him with the bleared eye of paternal affection while he took his last nickel.

"It was Florence Nightingale ruined wars," Chuck went on. "What's the idea of petting soldiers and binding up their wounds and soothing their fevered brows? That's not war. Let 'em perish where they fall. That's what they're there for."

"You can talk," said Towney, with a slantwise glint at him.

"What's the idea?" asked Chuck, flushing and hunching his shoulders. "You know I've got this lung, or maybe half of it anyway by now."

"You're much too sensitive," said Towney. "I didn't mean a thing."

Bill had been raging about, chewing his half-smoked cigar, his hair standing up in a brush, his eyes soft and lambent but wild, like a stag's. He would never, thought Miranda, be more than fourteen years old if he lived for a century, which he would not at the rate he was going. He behaved exactly like city editors in the moving pictures, even to the chewed cigar. Had he formed his style on the films, or had scenario writers seized once for all on the type Bill in its inarguable purity? Bill was shouting to Chuck: "*And* if he comes back here take him up the alley and saw his head off *by hand!*"

Chuck said, "He'll be back, don't worry." Bill said mildly, already off on another track, "Well, saw him off." Towney went to her own desk, but Chuck sat waiting amiably to be taken to the new vaudeville show. Miranda, with two tickets, always invited one of the reporters to go with her on Monday. Chuck was lavishly hardboiled and professional in his sports writing, but he had told Miranda that he didn't give a damn about sports, really; the job kept him out in the open, and paid him enough to buy the old man's hooch. He preferred shows and didn't see why women always had the job.

"Who does Bill want sawed today?" asked Miranda.

"That hoofer you panned in this morning's," said Chuck. "He was up here bright and early asking for the guy that writes up the show business. He said he was going to take the goof who wrote that piece up the alley and bop him in the nose. He said . . ."

"I hope he's gone," said Miranda; "I do hope he had to catch a train."

Chuck stood up and arranged his maroon-colored turtle-necked sweater, glanced down at the peasoup tweed plus fours and the hobnailed tan boots which he hoped would help to disguise the fact that he had a bad lung and didn't care for sports, and said, "He's long gone by now, don't worry. Let's get going; you're late as usual."

Miranda, facing about, almost stepped on the toes of a little drab man in a derby hat. He might have been a pretty fellow once, but now his mouth drooped where he had lost his side teeth, and his sad red-rimmed eyes had given up coquetry. A thin brown wave of hair was combed out with brilliantine and curled against the rim of the derby. He didn't move his feet, but stood planted with a kind of inert resistance, and asked Miranda: "Are you the so-called dramatic critic on this hick newspaper?"

"I'm afraid I am," said Miranda.

"Well," said the little man, "I'm just asking for one minute of your valuable time." His underlip shot out, he began with shaking hands to fish about in his waistcoat pocket. "I just hate to let you get away with it, that's all." He riffled through a collection of shabby newspaper clippings. "Just give these the once-over, will you? And then let me ask you if you think I'm gonna stand for being knocked by a tanktown critic," he said, in a toneless voice; "look here, here's Buffalo, Chicago, Saint Looey, Philadelphia, Frisco, besides New York. Here's the best publications in the business, *Variety*, the *Billboard*, they all broke down and admitted that Danny Dickerson knows his stuff. So you don't think so, hey? That's all I wanta ask you."

"No, I don't," said Miranda, as bluntly as she could, "and I can't stop to talk about it."

The little man leaned nearer, his voice shook as if he had been nervous for a long time. "Look here, what was there you didn't like about me? Tell me that."

Miranda said, "You shouldn't pay any attention at all. What does it matter what I think?"

"I don't care what you think, it ain't that," said the little man, "but these things get round and booking agencies back East don't know how it is out here. We get panned in the sticks and they think it's the same as getting panned in Chicago, see? They don't know the difference. They don't know that the more high class an act is the more the hick critics pan it. But I've been called the best in the business by the best in the business and I wanta know what you think is wrong with me."

Chuck said, "Come on, Miranda, curtain's going up." Miranda handed the little man his clippings, they were mostly ten years old, and tried to edge past him. He stepped before her again and said without much conviction, "If you was a man I'd knock your block off." Chuck got up at that and lounged over, taking his hands out of his pockets, and said, "Now you've done your song and dance you'd better get out. Get the hell out now before I throw you downstairs."

The little man pulled at the top of his tie, a small blue tie with red polka dots, slightly frayed at the knot. He pulled it straight and repeated as if he had rehearsed it, "Come out in the alley." The tears filled his thickened red lids. Chuck said, "Ah, shut up," and followed Miranda, who was running towards the stairs. He overtook her on the sidewalk. "I left him sniveling and shuffling his publicity trying to find the joker," said Chuck, "the poor old heel."

Miranda said, "There's too much of everything in this world just now. I'd like to sit down here on the curb, Chuck, and die, and never again see—I wish I could lose my memory and forget my own name. . . . I wish—"

Chuck said, "Toughen up, Miranda. This is no time to cave in. Forget that fellow. For every hundred people in show business, there are ninety-nine like him. But you don't manage right, anyway. You bring it on yourself. All you have to do is play up the headliners, and you needn't even mention the also-rans. Try to keep in mind that Rypinsky has got show business cornered in this town; please Rypinsky and you'll please the advertising department, please them and you'll get a raise. Hand-in-glove, my poor dumb child, will you never learn?"

"I seem to keep learning all the wrong things," said Miranda hopelessly.

"You do for a fact," Chuck told her cheerfully. "You are as good at it as I ever saw. Now do you feel better?"

"This is a rotten show you've invited me to," said Chuck. "Now what are you going to do about it? If I were writing it up, I'd—"

"Do write it up," said Miranda. "You write it up this time. I'm getting ready to leave, anyway, but don't tell anybody yet."

"You mean it? All my life," said Chuck, "I've yearned to be a so-called dramatic critic on a hick newspaper, and this is positively my first chance."

"Better take it," Miranda told him. "It may be your last." She thought, This is the beginning of the end of something. Something terrible is going to happen to me. I shan't need bread and butter where I'm going. I'll will it to Chuck, he has a venerable father to buy hooch for. I hope they let him have it. Oh, Adam, I hope I see you once more before I go under with whatever is the matter with me. "I wish the war were over," she said to Chuck, as if they had been talking about that. "I wish it were over and I wish it had never begun."

Chuck had got out his pad and pencil and was already writing his review. What she had said seemed safe enough but how would he take it? "I don't care how it started or when it ends," said Chuck, scribbling away. "I'm not going to be there."

All the rejected men talked like that, thought Miranda. War was the only thing they wanted, now they couldn't have it. Maybe they had wanted badly to go, some of them. All of them had a sidelong eye for the women they talked with about it, a guarded resentment which said. "Don't pin a white feather on me, you bloodthirsty female. I've offered my meat to the crows and they won't have it." The worst thing about war for the stay-at-homes is there isn't anyone to talk to any more. The Lusk Committee will get you if you don't watch out. Bread will win the war. Work will win, sugar will win, peach pits will win the war. Nonsense. Not nonsense, I tell you, there's some kind of valuable high explosive to be got out of peach pits. So all the happy housewives hurry during the canning season to lay their baskets of peach pits on the altar of their country. It keeps them busy and makes them feel useful, and all these women running wild with the men away are dangerous, if they aren't given something to keep their little minds out of mischief. So rows of young girls, the intact cradles of the future, with their pure serious faces framed becomingly in Red Cross wimples, roll cockeyed bandages that will never reach a base hospital, and knit sweaters that will never warm a manly chest, their minds dwelling lovingly on all the blood and mud and the next dance at the Acanthus Club for the officers of the flying corps. Keeping still and quiet will win the war.

"I'm simply not going to be there," said Chuck, absorbed in his review. No, Adam will be there, thought Miranda. She slipped down in the chair and leaned her head against the dusty plush, closed her eyes and faced for one instant that was a lifetime the certain, the overwhelming and awful knowledge that there was nothing at all ahead for Adam and for her.

Nothing. She opened her eyes and held her hands together palms up, gazing at them and trying to understand oblivion.

"Now look at this," said Chuck, for the lights had come on and the audience was rustling and talking again. "I've got it all done, even before the headliner comes on. It's old Stella Mayhew, and she's always good, she's been good for forty years, and she's going to sing 'O the blues ain't nothin' but the easy-going heart disease.' That's all you need to know about her. Now just glance over this. Would you be willing to sign it?"

Miranda took the pages and stared at them conscientiously, turning them over, she hoped, at the right moment, and gave them back. "Yes, Chuck, yes, I'd sign that. But I won't. We must tell Bill you wrote it, because it's your start, maybe."

"You don't half appreciate it," said Chuck. "You read it too fast. Here, listen to this—" and he began to mutter excitedly. While he was reading she watched his face. It was a pleasant face with some kind of spark of life in it, and a good severity in the modeling of the brow above the nose. For the first time since she had known him she wondered what Chuck was thinking about. He looked preoccupied and unhappy, he wasn't so frivolous as he sounded. The people were crowding into the aisle, bringing out their cigarette cases ready to strike a match the instant they reached the lobby; women with waved hair clutched at their wraps, men stretched their chins to ease them of their stiff collars, and Chuck said, "We might as well go now." Miranda, buttoning her jacket, stepped into the moving crowd, thinking, What did I ever know about them? There must be a great many of them here who think as I do, and we dare not say a word to each other of our desperation, we are speechless animals letting ourselves be destroyed, and why? Does anybody here believe the things we say to each other?

Stretched in unease on the ridge of the wicker couch in the cloakroom, Miranda waited for time to pass and leave Adam with her. Time seemed to proceed with more thàn usual eccentricity, leaving twilight gaps in her mind for thirty minutes which seemed like a second, and then hard flashes of light that shone clearly on her watch proving that three minutes is an intolerable stretch of waiting, as if she were hanging by her thumbs. At last it was reasonable to imagine Adam stepping out of the house in the early darkness into the blue mist that might soon be rain, he would be on the way, and there was nothing to think about him, after all. There was only the wish to see him and the fear, the present threat, of not seeing him again; for every step they took towards each other seemed perilous, drawing them apart instead of together, as a swimmer in spite of his most determined strokes is yet drawn slowly backward by the tide. "I don't want to love," she would think in spite of herself, "not Adam, there is no time and we are not ready for it and yet this is all we have—"

And there he was on the sidewalk, with his foot on the first step, and Miranda almost ran down to meet him. Adam, holding her hands, asked, "Do you feel well now? Are you hungry? Are you tired? Will you feel like dancing after the show?"

"Yes to everything," said Miranda, "yes, yes. . . ." Her head was like a feather, and she steadied herself on his arm. The mist was still mist that might be rain later, and though the air was sharp and clean in her mouth, it did not, she decided, make breathing any easier. "I hope the show is good, or at least funny," she told him, "but I promise nothing."

It was a long, dreary play, but Adam and Miranda sat very quietly together waiting patiently for it to be over. Adam carefully and seriously pulled off her glove and held her hand as if he were accustomed to holding her hand in theaters. Once they turned and their eyes met, but only once, and the two pairs of eyes were equally steady and noncommittal. A deep tremor set up in Miranda, and she set about resisting herself methodically as if she were closing windows and doors and fastening down curtains against a rising storm. Adam sat watching the monotonous play with a strange shining excitement, his face quite fixed and still.

When the curtain rose for the third act, the third act did not take place at once. There was instead disclosed a backdrop almost covered with an American flag improperly and disrespectfully exposed, nailed at each upper corner, gathered in the middle and nailed again, sagging dustily. Before it posed a local dollar-a-year man, now doing his bit as a Liberty Bond salesman. He was an ordinary man past middle life, with a neat little melon buttoned into his trousers and waistcoat, an opinionated tight mouth, a face and figure in which nothing could be read save the inept sensual record of fifty years. But for once in his life he was an important fellow in an impressive situation, and he reveled, rolling his words in an actorish tone.

"Looks like a penguin," said Adam. They moved, smiled at each other, Miranda reclaimed her hand, Adam folded his together and they prepared to wear their way again through the same old moldy speech with the same old dusty backdrop. Miranda tried not to listen, but she heard. These vile Huns—glorious Belleau Wood—our keyword is Sacrifice—Martyred Belgium—give till it hurts—our noble boys Over There—Big Berthas—the death of civilization—the Boche—

"My head aches," whispered Miranda. "Oh, why won't he hush?"

"He won't," whispered Adam. "I'll get you some aspirin."

"In Flanders Field the poppies grow, Between the crosses row on row"—

"He's getting into the home stretch," whispered Adam—atrocities, innocent babes hoisted on Boche bayonets—your child and my child—if our children are spared these things, then let us say with all reverence that these dead have not died in vain—the war, the *war*, the WAR to end WAR, war for Democracy, for humanity, a safe world forever and ever—and to prove our faith in Democracy to each other, and to the world, let everybody get together and buy Liberty Bonds and do without sugar and wool socks—was that it? Miranda asked herself, Say that over, I didn't catch the last line. Did you mention Adam? If you didn't I'm not interested. What about Adam, you little pig? And what are we going to sing this time, "Tipperary" or "There's a Long, Long Trail"? Oh, please do let the show go on and get over with. I must write a piece about it before I can go dancing with Adam and we have no time. Coal, oil, iron, gold, international finance, why don't you tell us about them, you little liar?

The audience rose and sang, "There's a Long, Long Trail A-winding," their opened mouths black and faces pallid in the reflected footlights; some of the faces grimaced and wept and had shining streaks like snail's tracks on them. Adam and Miranda joined in at the tops of their voices, grinning shamefacedly at each other once or twice.

In the street, they lit their cigarettes and walked slowly as always. "Just another nasty old man who would like to see the young ones killed," said Miranda in a low voice; "the tomcats try to eat the little tomkittens, you know. They don't fool you really, do they, Adam?"

The young people were talking like that about the business by then. They felt they were seeing pretty clearly through that game. She went on, "I hate these potbellied baldheads, too fat, too old, too cowardly, to go to war themselves, they know they're safe; it's you they are sending instead—"

Adam turned eyes of genuine surprise upon her. "Oh, *that* one," he said. "Now what could the poor sap do if they did take him? It's not his fault," he explained, "he can't do anything but talk." His pride in his youth, his forbearance and tolerance and contempt for that unlucky being breathed out of his very pores as he strolled, straight and relaxed in his strength. "What *could* you expect of him, Miranda?"

She spoke his name often, and he spoke hers rarely. The little shock of pleasure the sound of her name in his mouth gave her stopped her answer. For a moment she hesitated, and began at another point of attack. "Adam," she said, "the worst of war is the fear and suspicion and the awful expression in all the eyes you meet . . . as if they had pulled down the shutters over their minds and their hearts and were peering out at you, ready to leap if you make one gesture or say one word they do not understand instantly. It frightens me; I live in fear too, and no one should have to live in fear. It's the skulking about, and the lying. It's what war does to the mind and the heart, Adam, and you can't separate these two— what it does to them is worse than what it can do to the body."

Adam said soberly, after a moment, "Oh, yes, but suppose one comes back whole? The mind and the heart sometimes get another chance, but if anything happens to the poor old human frame, why, it's just out of luck, that's all."

"Oh, yes," mimicked Miranda. "It's just out of luck, that's all."

"If I didn't go," said Adam, in a matter-of-fact voice, "I couldn't look myself in the face."

So that's all settled. With her fingers flattened on his arm, Miranda was silent, thinking about Adam. No, there was no resentment or revolt in him. Pure, she thought, all the way through, flawless, complete, as the sacrificial lamb must be. The sacrificial lamb strode along casually, accommodating his long pace to hers, keeping her on the inside of the walk in the good American style, helping her across street corners as if she were a cripple —"I hope we don't come to a mud puddle, he'll carry me over it"—giving off whiffs of tobacco smoke, a manly smell of scentless soap, freshly cleaned leather and freshly washed skin, breathing through his nose and carrying his chest easily. He threw back his head and smiled into the sky which still misted, promising rain. "Oh, boy," he said, "what a night. Can't you hurry that review of yours so we can get started?"

He waited for her before a cup of coffee in the restaurant next to the pressroom, nicknamed The Greasy Spoon. When she came down at last, freshly washed and combed and powdered, she saw Adam first, sitting near the dingy big window, face turned to the streeet, but looking down. It was an extraordinary face, smooth and fine and golden in the shabby light, but now set in a blind melancholy, a look of pained suspense and disillusion. For just one split second she got a glimpse of Adam when he would have been older, the face of the man he would not live to be. He saw her then, rose, and the bright glow was there.

Adam pulled their chairs together at their table; they drank hot tea and listened to the orchestra jazzing "Pack Up Your Troubles."

"In an old kit bag, and smoil, smoil, smoil," shouted half a dozen boys under the draft age, gathered around a table near the orchestra. They yelled incoherently, laughed in great hysterical bursts of something that appeared to be merriment, and passed around under the tablecloth flat bottles containing a clear liquid—for in this western city founded and built by roaring drunken miners, no one was allowed to take his alcohol openly —splashed it into their tumblers of ginger ale, and went on singing, "It's a Long Way to Tipperary." When the tune changed to "Madelon," Adam said, "Let's dance." It was a tawdry little place, crowded and hot and full of smoke, but there was nothing better. The music was gay; and life is completely crazy anyway, thought Miranda, so what does it matter? This is what we have, Adam and I, this is all we're going to get, this is the way it is with us. She wanted to say, "Adam, come out of your dream and listen to me. I have pains in my chest and my head and my heart and they're real. I am in pain all over, and you are in such danger as I can't bear to think about, and why can we not save each other?" When her hand tightened on his shoulder his arm tightened about her waist instantly, and stayed there, holding firmly. They said nothing but smiled continually at each other, odd changing smiles as though they had found a new language. Miranda, her face near Adam's shoulder, noticed a dark young pair sitting at a corner table, each with an arm around the waist of the other, their heads together, their eyes staring at the same thing, whatever it was, that hovered in space before them. Her right hand lay on the table, his hand over it, and her face was a blur with weeping. Now and then he raised her hand and kissed it, and set it down and held it, and her eyes would fill again. They were not shameless, they had merely forgotten where they were, or they had no other place to go, perhaps. They said not a word, and the small pantomime repeated itself, like a melancholy short film running monotonously over and over again. Miranda envied them. She envied that girl. At least she can weep if that helps, and he does not even have to ask, What is the matter? Tell me. They had cups of coffee before them, and after a long while—Miranda and Adam had danced and sat down again twice—when the coffee was quite cold, they drank it suddenly, then embraced as before, without a word and scarcely a glance at each other. Something was done and settled between them, at least; it was enviable, enviable, that they could sit quietly together and have the same expression on their faces while they looked into the hell they shared, no matter what kind of hell, it was theirs, they were together.

At the table nearest Adam and Miranda a young woman was leaning on her elbow, telling her young man a story. "And I don't like him because he's too fresh. He kept on asking me to take a drink and I kept telling him, I don't drink and he said, Now look here, I want a drink the worst way and I think it's mean of you not to drink with me, I can't sit up here and drink by myself, he said. I told him, You're not by yourself in the first place; I like that, I said, and if you want a drink go ahead and have it, I told him, why drag *me* in? So he called the waiter and ordered ginger ale and two glasses and I drank straight ginger ale like I always do but he poured a shot of hooch in his. He was awfully proud of that hooch, said he made it himself out of potatoes. Nice homemade likker, warm from the pipe, he told me, three drops of this and your ginger ale will taste like Mumm's Extry. But I said, No, and I mean no, can't you get that through your bean? He took another drink and said, Ah, come on, honey, don't be so stubborn, this'll make your shimmy shake. So I just got tired of the argument, and I said, I don't need to drink, to shake my shimmy, I can strut my stuff on tea, I said. Well, why don't you then, he wanted to know, and I just told him—"

She knew she had been asleep for a long time when all at once without even a warning footstep or creak of the door hinge, Adam was in the room turning on the light, and she knew it was he, though at first she was blinded and turned her head away. He came over at once and sat on the side of the bed and began to talk as if he were going on with something they had been talking about before. He crumpled a square of paper and tossed it in the fireplace.

"You didn't get my note," he said. "I left it under the door. I was called back suddenly to camp for a lot of inoculations. They kept me longer than I expected, I was late. I called the office and they told me you were not coming in today. I called Miss Hobbe here and she said you were in bed and couldn't come to the telephone. Did she give you my message?"

"No," said Miranda drowsily, "but I think I have been asleep all day. Oh, I do remember. There was a doctor here. Bill sent him. I was at the telephone once, for Bill told me he would send an ambulance and have me taken to the hospital. The doctor tapped my chest and left a prescription and said he would be back, but he hasn't come."

"Where is it, the prescription?" asked Adam.

"I don't know. He left it, though, I saw him."

Adam moved about searching the tables and the mantelpiece. "Here it is," he said. "I'll be back in a few minutes. I must look for an all-night drugstore. It's after one o'clock. Good-by."

Good-by, good-by. Miranda watched the door where he had disappeared for quite a while, then closed her eyes, and thought, When I am not here I cannot remember anything about this room where I have lived for nearly a year, except that the curtains are too thin and there was never any way of shutting out the morning light. Miss Hobbe had promised heavier curtains, but they had never appeared. When Miranda in her dressing gown had been at the telephone that morning, Miss Hobbe had passed through, carrying a tray. She was a little red-haired nervously friendly creature, and her manner said all too plainly that the place was not paying and she was on the ragged edge.

"My dear *child*," she said sharply, with a glance at Miranda's attire, "what is the matter?"

Miranda, with the receiver to her ear, said, "Influenza, I think."

"*Horrors*," said Miss Hobbe, in a whisper, and the tray wavered in her hands. "Go back to bed at once . . . go at *once!*"

"I must talk to Bill first," Miranda had told her, and Miss Hobbe had hurried on and had not returned. Bill had shouted directions at her, promising everything, doctor, nurse, ambulance, hospital, her check every week as usual, everything, but she was to get back to bed and stay there. She dropped into bed, thinking that Bill was the only person she had ever seen who actually tore his own hair when he was excited enough . . . I suppose I should ask to be sent home, she thought, it's a respectable old custom to inflict your death on the family if you can manage it. No, I'll stay here, this is my business, but not in this room, I hope. . . . I wish I were in the cold mountains in the snow, that's what I should like best; and all about her rose the measured ranges of the Rockies wearing their perpetual snow, their majestic blue laurels of cloud, chilling her to the bone with their sharp breath. Oh, no, I must have warmth—and her memory turned and roved after another place she had known first and loved best, that now she could see only in drifting fragments of palm and cedar, dark shadows and a sky that warmed without dazzling, as this strange sky had dazzled without warming her; there was the long slow wavering of gray moss in the drowsy oak shade, the spacious hovering of buzzards overhead, the smell of crushed water herbs along a bank, and without warning a broad tranquil river into which flowed all the rivers she had known. The walls shelved away in one deliberate silent movement on either side, and a tall sailing ship was moored near by, with a gangplank weathered to blackness touching the foot of her bed. Back of the ship was jungle, and even as it appeared before her, she knew it was all she had ever read or had been told or felt or thought about jungles; a writhing terribly alive and secret place of death, creeping with tangles of spotted serpents, rainbow-colored birds with malign eyes, leopards with humanly wise faces and extravagantly crested lions; screaming long-armed monkeys tumbling among broad fleshy leaves that glowed with sulphur-colored light and exuded the ichor of death, and rotting trunks of unfamiliar trees sprawled in crawling slime. Without surprise, watching from her pillow, she saw herself run swiftly down this gangplank to the slanting deck, and standing there, she leaned on the rail and waved gaily to herself in bed, and the slender ship spread its wings and sailed away into the jungle. The air trembled with the shattering scream and the hoarse bellow of voices all crying together, rolling and colliding above her like ragged stormclouds, and the words became two words only rising and falling and clamoring about her head. Danger, danger, danger, the voices said, and War, war, war. There was her door half open, Adam standing with his hand on the knob, and Miss Hobbe with her face all out of shape with terror was crying shrilly, "I tell you, they must come for her *now*, or I'll put her on the sidewalk. . . . I tell you, this is a plague, a plague, my God, and I've got a houseful of people to think about!"

Adam said, "I know that. They'll come for her tomorrow morning."

"Tomorrow morning, my God, they'd better come now!"

"They can't get an ambulance," said Adam, "and there aren't any beds.

And we can't find a doctor or a nurse. They're all busy. That's all there is to it. You stay out of the room, and I'll look after her."

"Yes, you'll look after her, I can see that," said Miss Hobbe, in a particularly unpleasant tone.

"Yes, that's what I said," answered Adam, drily, "and you keep out."

He closed the door carefully. He was carrying an assortment of misshapen packages, and his face was astonishingly impassive.

"Did you hear that?" he asked, leaning over and speaking very quietly.

"Most of it," said Miranda, "it's a nice prospect, isn't it?"

"I've got your medicine," said Adam, "and you're to begin with it this minute. She can't put you out."

"So it's really as bad as that," said Miranda.

"It's as bad as anything can be," said Adam, "all the theaters and nearly all the shops and restaurants are closed, and the streets have been full of funerals all day and ambulances all night—"

"But not one for me," said Miranda, feeling hilarious and lightheaded. She sat up and beat her pillow into shape and reached for her robe. "I'm glad you're here, I've been having a nightmare. Give me a cigarette, will you, and light one for yourself and open all the windows and sit near one of them. You're running a risk," she told him, "don't you know that? Why do you do it?"

"Never mind," said Adam, "take your medicine," and offered her two large cherry-colored pills. She swallowed them promptly and instantly vomited them up. "Do excuse me," she said, beginning to laugh. "I'm so sorry." Adam without a word and with a very concerned expression washed her face with a wet towel, gave her some cracked ice from one of the packages, and firmly offered her two more pills. "That's what they always did at home," she explained to him, "and it worked." Crushed with humiliation, she put her hands over her face and laughed again, painfully.

"There are two more kinds yet," said Adam, pulling her hands from her face and lifting her chin. "You've hardly begun. And I've got other things, like orange juice and ice cream—they told me to feed you ice cream—and coffee in a thermos bottle, and a thermometer. You have to work through the whole lot so you'd better take it easy."

"This time last night we were dancing," said Miranda, and drank something from a spoon. Her eyes followed him about the room, as he did things for her with an absentminded face, like a man alone; now and again he would come back, and slipping his hand under her head, would hold a cup or a tumbler to her mouth, and she drank, and followed him with her eyes again, without a clear notion of what was happening.

"Adam," she said, "I've just thought of something. Maybe they forgot St. Luke's Hospital. Call the sisters there and ask them not to be so selfish with their silly old rooms. Tell them I only want a very small dark ugly one for three days, or less. Do try them, Adam."

He believed, apparently, that she was still more or less in her right mind, for she heard him at the telephone explaining in his deliberate voice. He was back again almost at once, saying, "This seems to be my day for getting mixed up with peevish old maids. The sister said that even if they had a room you couldn't have it without doctor's orders. But they didn't have one, anyway. She was pretty sour about it."

"Well," said Miranda in a thick voice, "I think that's abominably rude and mean, don't you?" She sat up with a wide gesture of both arms, and began to retch again, violently.

"Hold it, as you were," called Adam, fetching the basin. He held her head, washed her face and hands with ice water, put her head straight on the pillow, and went over and looked out of the window. "Well," he said at last, sitting beside her again, "they haven't got a room. They haven't got a bed. They haven't even got a baby crib, the way she talked. So I think that's straight enough, and we may as well dig in."

"Isn't the ambulance coming?"

"Tomorrow, maybe."

He took off his tunic and hung it on the back of a chair. Kneeling before the fireplace, he began carefully to set kindling sticks in the shape of an Indian tepee, with a little paper in the center for them to lean upon. He lighted this and placed other sticks upon them, and larger bits of wood. When they were going nicely he added still heavier wood, and coal a few lumps at a time, until there was a good blaze, and a fire that would not need rekindling. He rose and dusted his hands together, the fire illuminated him from the back and his hair shone.

"Adam," said Miranda, "I think you're very beautiful." He laughed out at this, and shook his head at her. "What a hell of a word," he said, "for me." "It was the first that occurred to me," she said, drawing up on her elbow to catch the warmth of the blaze. "That's a good job, that fire."

He sat on the bed again, dragging up a chair and putting his feet on the rungs. They smiled at each other for the first time since he had come in that night. "How do you feel now?" he asked.

"Better, much better," she told him. "Let's talk. Let's tell each other what we meant to do."

"You tell me first," said Adam. "I want to know about you."

"You'd get the notion I had a very sad life," she said, "and perhaps it was, but I'd be glad enough to have it now. If I could have it back, it would be easy to be happy about almost anything at all. That's not true, but that's the way I feel now." After a pause, she said, "There's nothing to tell, after all, if it ends now, for all this time I was getting ready for something that was going to happen later, when the time came. So now it's nothing much."

"But it must have been worth having until now, wasn't it?" he asked seriously as if it were something important to know.

"Not if this is all," she repeated obstinately.

"Weren't you ever—happy?" asked Adam, and he was plainly afraid of the word; he was shy of it as he was of the word *love*, he seemed never to have spoken it before, and was uncertain of its sound or meaning.

"I don't know," she said, "I just lived and never thought about it. I remember things I liked, though, and things I hoped for."

"I was going to be an electrical engineer," said Adam. He stopped short. "And I shall finish up when I get back," he added, after a moment.

"Don't you love being alive?" asked Miranda. "Don't you love weather and the colors at different times of the day, and all the sounds and noises like children screaming in the next lot, and automobile horns and little bands playing in the street and the smell of food cooking?"

"I love to swim, too," said Adam.

"So do I," said Miranda; "we never did swim together."

"Do you remember any prayers?" she asked him suddenly. "Did you ever learn anything at Sunday School?"

"Not much," confessed Adam without contrition. "Well, the Lord's Prayer."

"Yes, and there's Hail Mary," she said, "and the really useful one beginning, I confess to Almighty God and to blessed Mary ever virgin and to the holy Apostles Peter and Paul—"

"Catholic," he commented.

"Prayers just the same, you big Methodist. I'll bet you *are* a Methodist."

"No, Presbyterian."

"Well, what others do you remember?"

"Now I lay me down to sleep—" said Adam.

"Yes, that one, and Blessed Jesus meek and mild—you see that my religious education wasn't neglected either. I even know a prayer beginning O Apollo. Want to hear it?"

"No," said Adam, "you're making fun."

"I'm not," said Miranda, "I'm trying to keep from going to sleep. I'm afraid to go to sleep, I may not wake up. Don't let me go to sleep, Adam. Do you know Matthew, Mark, Luke and John? Bless the bed I lie upon?"

"If I should die before I wake, I pray the Lord my soul to take. Is that it?" asked Adam. "It doesn't sound right, somehow."

"Light me a cigarette, please, and move over and sit near the window. We keep forgetting about fresh air. You must have it." He lighted the cigarette and held it to her lips. She took it between her fingers and dropped it under the edge of her pillow. He found it and crushed it out in the saucer under the water tumbler. Her head swam in darkness for an instant, cleared, and she sat up in panic, throwing off the covers and breaking into a sweat. Adam leaped up with an alarmed face, and almost at once was holding a cup of hot coffee to her mouth.

"You must have some too," she told him, quiet again, and they sat huddled together on the edge of the bed, drinking coffee in silence.

Adam said, "You must lie down again. You're awake now."

"Let's sing," said Miranda. "I know an old spiritual, I can remember some of the words." She spoke in a natural voice. "I'm fine now." She began in a hoarse whisper, " 'Pale horse, pale rider, done taken my lover away. . . .' Do you know that song?"

"Yes," said Adam, "I heard Negroes in Texas sing it, in an oil field."

"I heard them sing it in a cotton field," she said; "it's a good song."

They sang that line together. "But I can't remember what comes next," said Adam.

" 'Pale horse, pale rider,' " said Miranda. "(We really need a good banjo) 'done taken my lover away—' " Her voice cleared and she said, "But we ought to get on with it. What's the next line?"

"There's a lot more to it than that," said Adam, "about forty verses, the rider done taken away mammy, pappy, brother, sister, the whole family besides the lover—"

"But not the singer, not yet," said Miranda. "Death always leaves one singer to mourn. 'Death,' " she sang, " 'oh, leave one singer to mourn—' "

" 'Pale horse, pale rider,' " chanted Adam, coming in on the beat, " 'done taken my lover away!' (I think we're good, I think we ought to get up an act—)"

"Go in Hut Service," said Miranda, "entertain the poor defenseless heroes Over There."

"We'll play banjos," said Adam; "I always wanted to play the banjo."

Miranda sighed, and lay back on the pillow and thought, I must give up, I can't hold out any longer. There was only that pain, only that room, and only Adam. There were no longer any multiple planes of living, no tough filaments of memory and hope pulling taut backwards and forwards holding her upright between them. There was only this one moment and it was a dream of time, and Adam's face, very near hers, eyes still and intent, was a shadow, and there was to be nothing more. . . .

"Adam," she said out of the heavy soft darkness that drew her down, down, "I love you, and I was hoping you would say that to me, too."

He lay down beside her with his arm under her shoulder, and pressed his smooth face against hers, his mouth moved towards her mouth and stopped. "Can you hear what I am saying? . . . What do you think I have been trying to tell you all this time?"

She turned towards him, the cloud cleared and she saw his face for an instant. He pulled the covers about her and held her, and said, "Go to sleep, darling, darling, if you will go to sleep now for one hour I will wake you up and bring you hot coffee and tomorrow we will find somebody to help. I love you, go to sleep—"

Almost with no warning at all, she floated into the darkness, holding his hand, in sleep that was not sleep but clear evening light in a small green wood, an angry dangerous wood full of inhuman concealed voices singing sharply like the whine of arrows and she saw Adam transfixed by a flight of these singing arrows that struck him in the heart and passed shrilly cutting their path through the leaves. Adam fell straight back before her eyes, and rose again unwounded and alive; another flight of arrows loosed from the invisible bow struck him again and he fell, and yet he was there before her untouched in a perpetual death and resurrection. She threw herself before him, angrily and selfishly she interposed between him and the track of the arrow, crying, No, no, like a child cheated in a game, It's my turn now, why must you always be the one to die? and the arrows struck her cleanly through the heart and through his body and he lay dead, and she still lived, and the wood whistled and sang and shouted, every branch and leaf and blade of grass had its own terrible accusing voice. She ran then, and Adam caught her in the middle of the room, running, and said, "Darling, I must have been asleep too. What happened, you screamed terribly?"

After he had helped her to settle again, she sat with her knees drawn up under her chin, resting her head on her folded arms and began carefully searching for her words because it was important to explain clearly. "It was a very odd sort of dream, I don't know why it could have frightened me. There was something about an old-fashioned valentine. There were two hearts carved on a tree, pierced by the same arrow—you know, Adam—"

"Yes, I know, honey," he said in the gentlest sort of way, and sat kissing her on the cheek and forehead with a kind of accustomedness, as if he had been kissing her for years, "one of those lace paper things."

"Yes, and yet they were alive, and were us, you understand—this doesn't seem to be quite the way it was, but it was something like that. It was in a wood—"

"Yes," said Adam. He got up and put on his tunic and gathered up the thermos bottle. "I'm going back to that little stand and get us some ice cream and hot coffee," he told her, "and I'll be back in five minutes, and you keep quiet. Good-by for five minutes," he said, holding her chin in the palm of his hand and trying to catch her eye, "and you be very quiet."

"Good-by," she said. "I'm awake again." But she was not, and the two alert young internes from the County hospital who had arrived, after frantic urgings from the noisy city editor of the Blue Mountain *News*, to carry her away in a police ambulance, decided that they had better go down and get the stretcher. Their voices roused her, she sat up, got out of bed at once and stood glancing about brightly. "Why, you're all right," said the darker and stouter of the two young men, both extremely fit and competent-looking in their white clothes, each with a flower in his buttonhole. "I'll just carry you." He unfolded a white blanket and wrapped it around her. She gathered up the folds and asked, "But where is Adam?" taking hold of the doctor's arm. He laid a hand on her drenched forehead, shook his head, and gave her a shrewd look. "Adam?"

"Yes," Miranda told him, lowering her voice confidentially, "he was here and now he is gone."

"Oh, he'll be back," the interne told her easily, "he's just gone round the block to get cigarettes. Don't worry about Adam. He's the least of your troubles."

"Will he know where to find me?" she asked, still holding back.

"We'll leave him a note," said the interne. "Come now, it's time we got out of here."

He lifted and swung her up to his shoulder. "I feel very badly," she told him; "I don't know why."

"I'll bet you do," said he, stepping out carefully, the other doctor going before them, and feeling for the first step of the stairs. "Put your arms around my neck," he instructed her. "It won't do you any harm and it's a great help to me."

"What's your name?" Miranda asked as the other doctor opened the front door and they stepped out into the frosty sweet air.

"Hildesheim," he said, in the tone of one humoring a child.

"Well, Dr. Hidlesheim, aren't we in a pretty mess?"

"We certainly are," said Dr. Hildesheim.

The second young interne, still quite fresh and dapper in his white coat, though his carnation was withering at the edges, was leaning over listening to her breathing through a stethoscope, whistling thinly, "There's a Long, Long Trail—" From time to time he tapped her ribs smartly with two fingers, whistling. Miranda observed him for a few moments until she fixed his bright busy hazel eye not four inches from hers. "I'm not unconscious," she explained, "I know what I want to say." Then to her horror she heard herself babbling nonsense, knowing it was nonsense though she could not hear what she was saying. The flicker of attention in the eye near her vanished, the second interne went on tapping and listening, hissing softly under his breath.

"I wish you'd stop whistling," she said clearly. The sound stopped. "It's a beastly tune," she added. Anything, anything at all to keep her small hold on the life of human beings, a clear line of communication, no matter what, between her and the receding world. "Please let me see Dr. Hildesheim," she said, "I have something important to say to him. I must say it now." The second interne vanished. He did not walk away, he fled into the air without a sound, and Dr. Hildesheim's face appeared in his stead.

"Dr. Hildesheim, I want to ask you about Adam."

"That young man? He's been here, and left you a note, and has gone again," said Dr. Hildesheim, "and he'll be back tomorrow and the day after." His tone was altogether too merry and flippant.

"I don't believe you," said Miranda bitterly, closing her lips and eyes and hoping she might not weep.

"Miss Tanner," called the doctor, "have you got that note?"

Miss Tanner appeared beside her, handed her an unsealed envelope, took it back, unfolded the note and gave it to her.

"I can't see it," said Miranda, after a pained search of the page full of hasty scratches in black ink.

"Here, I'll read it," said Miss Tanner. "It says, 'They came and took you while I was away and now they will not let me see you. Maybe tomorrow they will, with my love, Adam,'" read Miss Tanner in a firm dry voice, pronouncing the words distinctly. "Now, do you see?" she asked soothingly.

Miranda, hearing the words one by one, forgot them one by one. "Oh, read it again, what does it say?" she called out over the silence that pressed upon her, reaching towards the dancing words that just escaped as she almost touched them. "That will do," said Dr. Hildesheim, calmly authoritarian. "Where is that bed?"

"There is no bed yet," said Miss Tanner, as if she said, We are short of oranges. Dr. Hildesheim said, "Well, we'll manage something," and Miss Tanner drew the narrow trestle with bright crossed metal supports and small rubbery wheels into a deep jut of the corridor, out of the way of the swift white figures darting about, whirling and skimming like water flies all in silence. The white walls rose sheer as cliffs, a dozen frosted moons followed each other in perfect self-possession down a white lane and dropped mutely one by one into a snowy abyss.

What is this whiteness and silence but the absence of pain? Miranda lay lifting the nap of her white blanket softly between eased fingers, watching a dance of tall deliberate shadows moving behind a wide screen of sheets spread upon a frame. It was there, near her, on her side of the wall where she could see it clearly and enjoy it, and it was so beautiful she had no curiosity as to its meaning. Two dark figures nodded, bent, curtsied to each other, retreated and bowed again, lifted long arms and spread great hands against the white shadow of the screen; then with a single round movement, the sheets were folded back, disclosing two speechless men in white, standing, and another speechless man in white, lying on the bare springs of a white iron bed. The man on the springs was swathed smoothly from head to foot in white, with folded bands across the face, and a large stiff bow like merry rabbit ears dangled at the crown of his head.

The two living men lifted a mattress standing hunched against the wall, spread it tenderly and exactly over the dead man. Wordless and white they vanished down the corridor, pushing the wheeled bed before them. It had been an entrancing and leisurely spectacle, but now it was over. A pallid white fog rose in their wake insinuatingly and floated before Miranda's eyes, a fog in which was concealed all terror and all weariness, all the wrung faces and twisted backs and broken feet of abused, outraged living things, all the shapes of their confused pain and their estranged hearts; the fog might part at any moment and loose the horde of human torments. She put up her hands and said, Not yet, not yet, but it was too late. The fog parted and two executioners, white clad, moved towards her pushing between them with marvelously deft and practiced hands the misshapen figure of an old man in filthy rags whose scanty beard waggled under his opened mouth as he bowed his back and braced his feet to resist and delay the fate they had prepared for him. In a high weeping voice he was trying to explain to them that the crime of which he was accused did not merit the punishment he was about to receive; and except for this whining cry there was silence as they advanced. The soiled cracked bowls of the old man's hands were held before him beseechingly as a beggar's as he said, "Before God I am not guilty," but they held his arms and drew him onward, passed, and were gone.

The road to death is a long march beset with all evils, and the heart fails little by little at each new terror, the bones rebel at each step, the mind sets up its own bitter resistance and to what end? The barriers sink one by one, and no covering of the eyes shuts out the landscape of disaster, nor the sight of crimes committed there. Across the field came Dr. Hildesheim, his face a skull beneath his German helmet, carrying a naked infant writhing on the point of his bayonet, and a huge stone pot marked Poison in Gothic letters. He stopped before the well that Miranda remembered in a pasture on her father's farm, a well once dry but now bubbling with living water, and into its pure depths he threw the child and the poison, and the violated water sank back soundlessly into the earth. Miranda, screaming, ran with her arms above her head; her voice echoed and came back to her like a wolf's howl, Hildeshem is a Boche, a spy, a Hun, kill him, kill him before he kills you. . . . She woke howling, she heard the foul words accusing Dr. Hildesheim tumbling from her mouth; opened her eyes and knew she was in a bed in a small white room, with Dr. Hildesheim sitting beside her, two firm fingers on her pulse. His hair was brushed sleekly and his buttonhole flower was fresh. Stars gleamed through the window, and Dr. Hildesheim seemed to be gazing at them with no particular expression, his stethoscope dangling around his neck. Miss Tanner stood at the foot of the bed writing something on a chart.

"Hello," said Dr. Hildesheim, "at least you take it out in shouting. You don't try to get out of bed and go running around." Miranda held her eyes open with a terrible effort, saw his rather heavy, patient face clearly even as her mind tottered and slithered again, broke from its foundation and spun like a cast wheel in a ditch. "I didn't mean it, I never believed it, Dr. Hildesheim, you mustn't remember it—" and was gone again, not being able to wait for an answer.

The wrong she had done followed her and haunted her dream: this wrong took vague shapes of horror she could not recognize or name, though her heart cringed at sight of them. Her mind, split in two, acknowledged and denied what she saw in the one instant, for across an abyss of complaining darkness her reasoning coherent self watched the strange frenzy of the other coldly, reluctant to admit the truth of its visions, its tenacious remorses and despairs.

"I know those are your hands," she told Miss Tanner, "I know it, but to me they are white tarantulas, don't touch me."

"Shut your eyes," said Miss Tanner.

"Oh, no," said Miranda, "for then I see worse things," but her eyes closed in spite of her will, and the midnight of her internal torment closed about her.

Oblivion, thought Miranda, her mind feeling among her memories of words she had been taught to describe the unseen, the unknowable, is a whirlpool of gray water turning upon itself for all eternity . . . eternity is perhaps more than the distance to the farthest star. She lay on a narrow ledge over a pit that she knew to be bottomless, though she could not comprehend it; the ledge was her childhood dream of danger, and she strained back against a reassuring wall of granite at her shoulders, staring into the pit, thinking. There it is, there it is at last, it is very simple; and soft carefully shaped words like oblivion and eternity are curtains hung before nothing at all. I shall not know when it happens, I shall not feel or remember, why can't I consent now, I am lost, there is no hope for me. Look, she told herself, there it is, that is death and there is nothing to fear. But she could not consent, still shrinking stiffly against the granite wall that was her childhood dream of safety, breathing slowly for fear of squandering breath, saying desperately, Look, don't be afraid, it is nothing, it is only eternity.

Granite walls, whirlpools, stars, are things. None of them is death, nor the image of it. Death is death, said Miranda, and for the dead it has no attributes. Silenced, she sank easily through deeps under deeps of darkness until she lay like a stone at the farthest bottom of life, knowing herself to be blind, deaf, speechless, no longer aware of the members of her own body, entirely withdrawn from all human concerns, yet alive with a peculiar lucidity and coherence; all notions of the mind, the reasonable inquiries of doubt, all ties of blood and the desires of the heart, dissolved and fell away from her, and there remained of her only a minute fiercely burning particle of being that knew itself alone, that relied upon nothing beyond itself for its strength; not susceptible to any appeal or inducement, being itself composed entirely of one single motive, the stubborn will to live. This fiery motionless particle set itself unaided to resist destruction, to survive and to be in its own madness of being, motiveless and planless beyond that one essential end. Trust me, the hard unwinking angry point of light said. Trust me. I stay.

At once it grew, flattened, thinned to a fine radiance, spread like a great fan and curved out into a rainbow through which Miranda, enchanted, altogether believing, looked upon a deep clear landscape of sea and sand, of soft meadow and sky, freshly washed and glistening with transparencies of blue. Why, of course, of course, said Miranda, without surprise but with serene rapture as if some promise made to her had been kept long after she had ceased to hope for it. She rose from her narrow ledge and ran lightly through the tall portals of the great bow that arched in its splendor over the burning blue of the sea and the cool green of the meadow on either hand.

The small waves rolled in and over unhurriedly, lapped upon the sand in silence and retreated; the grasses flurried before a breeze that made no sound. Moving towards her leisurely as clouds through the shimmering air came a great company of human beings, and Miranda saw in an amazement of joy that they were all the living she had known. Their faces were transfigured, each in its own beauty, beyond what she remembered of them, their eyes were clear and untroubled as good weather, and they cast no shadows. They were pure identities and she knew them every one without calling their names or remembering what relation she bore to them. They surrounded her smoothly on silent feet, then turned their entranced faces again towards the sea, and she moved among them easily as a wave among waves. The drifting circle widened, separated, and each figure was alone but not solitary; Miranda, alone too, questioning nothing, desiring nothing, in the quietude of her ecstasy, stayed where she was, eyes fixed on the overwhelming deep sky where it was always morning.

Lying at ease, arms under her head, in the prodigal warmth which flowed evenly from sea and sky and meadow, within touch but not touching the serenely smiling familiar beings about her, Miranda felt without warning a vague tremor of apprehension, some small flick of distrust in her joy; a thin frost touched the edges of this confident tranquillity; something, somebody, was missing, she had lost something, she had left something valuable in another country, oh, what could it be? There are no trees, no trees here, she said in fright, I have left something unfinished. A thought struggled at the back of her mind, came clearly as a voice in her ear. Where are the dead? We have forgotten the dead, oh, the dead, where are they? At once as if a curtain had fallen, the bright landscape faded, she was alone in a strange stony place of bitter cold, picking her way along a steep path of slippery snow, calling out, Oh, I must go back! But in what direction? Pain returned, a terrible compelling pain running through her veins like heavy fire, the stench of corruption filled her nostrils, the sweetish sickening smell of rotting flesh and pus; she opened her eyes and saw pale light through a coarse white cloth over her face, knew that the smell of death was in her own body, and struggled to lift her hand. The cloth was drawn away; she saw Miss Tanner filling a hypodermic needle in her methodical expert way, and heard Dr. Hildesheim saying, "I think that will do the trick. Try another." Miss Tanner plucked firmly at Miranda's arm near the shoulder, and the unbelievable current of agony ran burning through her veins again. She struggled to cry out, saying, Let me go, let me go; but heard only incoherent sounds of animal suffering. She saw doctor and nurse glance at each other with the glance of initiates at a mystery, nodding in silence, their eyes alive with knowledgeable pride. They looked briefly at their handiwork and hurried away.

Bells screamed all off key, wrangling together as they collided in midair, horns and whistles mingled shrilly with cries of human distress; sulphur-colored light exploded through the black windowpane and flashed away in darkness. Miranda waking from a dreamless sleep asked without expecting an answer, "What is happening?" for there was a bustle of voices and footsteps in the corridor, and a sharpness in the air; the far clamor went on, a furious exasperated shrieking like a mob in revolt.

The light came on, and Miss Tanner said in a furry voice, "Hear that? They're celebrating. It's the Armistice. The war is over, my dear." Her hands trembled. She rattled a spoon in a cup, stopped to listen, held the cup out to Miranda. From the ward for old bedridden women down the hall floated a ragged chorus of cracked voices singing, "My country, 'tis of thee . . ."

Sweet land . . . oh, terrible land of this bitter world where the sound of rejoicing was a clamor of pain, where ragged tuneless old women, sitting up waiting for their evening bowl of cocoa, were singing, "Sweet land of Liberty—"

"Oh, say, can you see?" their hopeless voices were asking next, the hammer strokes of metal tongues drowning them out. "The war is over," said Miss Tanner, her underlip held firmly, her eyes blurred. Miranda said, "Please open the window, please, I smell death in here."

Now if real daylight such as I remember having seen in this world would only come again, but it is always twilight or just before morning, a promise of day that is never kept. What has become of the sun? That was the longest and loneliest night and yet it will not end and let the day come. Shall I ever see light again?

Sitting in a long chair, near a window, it was in itself a melancholy wonder to see the colorless sunlight slanting on the snow, under a sky drained of its blue. "Can this be my face?" Miranda asked her mirror. "Are these my own hands?" she asked Miss Tanner, holding them up to show the yellow tint like melted wax glimmering between the closed fingers. The body is a curious monster, no place to live in, how could anyone feel at home there? Is it possible I can ever accustom myself to this place? she asked herself. The human faces around her semed dulled and tired, with no radiance of skin and eyes as Miranda remembered radiance; the once white walls of her room were now a soiled gray. Breathing slowly, falling asleep and waking again, feeling the splash of water on her flesh, taking food, talking in bare phrases with Dr. Hildesheim and Miss Tanner, Miranda looked about her with the covertly hostile eyes of an alien who does not like the country in which he finds himself, does not understand the language nor wish to learn it, does not mean to live there and yet is helpless, unable to leave it at his will.

"It is morning," Miss Tanner would say, with a sigh, for she had grown old and weary once for all in the past month, "morning again, my dear," showing Miranda the same monotonous landscape of dulled evergreens and leaden snow. She would rustle about in her starched skirts, her face bravely powdered, her spirit unbreakable as good steel, saying, "Look, my dear, what a heavenly morning, like a crystal," for she had an affection for the salvaged creature before her, the silent ungrateful human being whom she, Cornelia Tanner, a nurse who knew her business, had snatched back from death with her own hands. "Nursing is nine-tenths, just the same," Miss Tanner would tell the other nurses; "keep that in mind." Even the sunshine was Miss Tanner's own prescription for the further recovery of Miranda, this patient the doctors had given up for lost, and who yet sat here, visible proof of Miss Tanner's theory. She said, "Look at the sunshine, now," as she might be saying, "I ordered this for you, my dear, do sit up and take it."

"It's beautiful," Miranda would answer, even turning her head to look, thanking Miss Tanner for her goodness, most of all her goodness about the weather, "beautiful, I always loved it." And I might love it again if I saw it, she thought, but truth was, she could not see it. There was no light, there might never be light again, compared as it must always be with the light she had seen beside the blue sea that lay so tranquilly along the shore of her paradise. That was a child's dream of the heavenly meadow, the vision of repose that comes to a tired body in sleep, she thought, but I have seen it when I did not know it was a dream. Closing her eyes she would rest for a moment remembering that bliss which had repaid all the pain of the journey to reach it; opening them again she saw with a new anguish the dull world to which she was condemned, where the light seemed filmed over with cobwebs, all the bright surfaces corroded, the sharp planes melted and formless, all objects and beings meaningless, ah, dead and withered things that believed themselves alive!

At night, after the long effort of lying in her chair, in her extremity of grief for what she had so briefly won, she folded her painful body together and wept silently, shamelessly, in pity for herself and her lost rapture. There was no escape. Dr. Hildesheim, Miss Tanner, the nurses in the diet kitchen, the chemist, the surgeon, the precise machine of the hospital, the whole humane conviction and custom of society, conspired to pull her inseparable rack of bones and wasted flesh to its feet, to put in order her disordered mind, and to set her once more safely in the road that would lead her again to death.

Chuck Rouncivale and Mary Townsend came to see her, bringing her a bundle of letters they had guarded for her. They brought a basket of delicate small hot-house flowers, lilies of the valley with sweet peas and feathery fern, and above these blooms their faces were merry and haggard.

Mary said, "You *have* had a tussle, haven't you?" and Chuck said, "Well, you made it back, didn't you?" Then after an uneasy pause, they told her that everybody was waiting to see her again at her desk. "They've put me back on sports already, Miranda," said Chuck. For ten minutes Miranda smiled and told them how gay and what a pleasant surprise it was to find herself alive. For it will not do to betray the conspiracy and tamper with the courage of the living; there is nothing better than to be alive, everyone has agreed on that; it is past argument, and who attempts to deny it is justly outlawed. "I'll be back in no time at all," she said; "this is almost over."

Her letters lay in a heap in her lap and beside her chair. Now and then she turned one over to read the inscription, recognizing this handwriting or that, examined the blotted stamps and the postmarks, and let them drop again. For two or three days they lay upon the table beside her, and she continued to shrink from them. "They will all be telling me again how good it is to be alive, they will say again they love me, they are glad I am living too, and what can I answer to that?" and her hardened, indifferent heart shuddered in despair at itself, because before it had been tender and capable of love.

Dr. Hildesheim said, "What, all these letters not opened yet?" and Miss Tanner said, "Read your letters, my dear, I'll open them for you." Standing beside the bed, she slit them cleanly with a paper knife. Miranda, cornered, picked and chose until she found a thin one in an unfamiliar handwriting. "Oh, no, now," said Miss Tanner, "take them as they come. Here, I'll hand them to you." She sat down, prepared to be helpful to the end.

What a victory, what triumph, what happiness to be alive, sang the letters in a chorus. The names were signed with flourishes like the circles in air of bugle notes, and they were the names of those she had loved best; some of those she had known well and pleasantly; and a few who meant nothing to her, then or now. The thin letter in the unfamiliar handwriting was from a strange man at the camp where Adam had been, telling her that Adam had died of influenza in the camp hospital. Adam had asked him, in case anything happened, to be sure to let her know.

If anything happened. To be sure to let her know. If anything happened. "Your friend, Adam Barclay," wrote the strange man. It had happened—she looked at the date—more than a month ago.

"I've been here a long time, haven't I?" she asked Miss Tanner, who was folding letters and putting them back in their proper envelopes.

"Oh, quite a while," said Miss Tanner, "but you'll be ready to go soon now. But you must be careful of yourself and not overdo, and you should come back now and then and let us look at you, because sometimes the after-effects are very—"

Miranda, sitting up before the mirror, wrote carefully: "One lipstick, medium, one ounce flask Bois d'Hiver perfume, one pair of gray suede gauntlets without straps, two pair gray sheer stockings without clocks—"

Towney, reading after her, said, "Everything without something so that it will be almost impossible to get?"

"Try it, though," said Miranda, "they're nicer without. One walking stick of silvery wood with a silver knob."

"That's going to be expensive," warned Towney. "Walking is hardly worth it."

"You're right," said Miranda, and wrote in the margin, "a nice one to match my other things. Ask Chuck to look for this, Mary. Good-looking and not too heavy." Lazarus, come forth. Not unless you bring me my top hat and stick. Stay where you are then, you snob. Not at all, I'm coming forth. "A jar of cold cream," wrote Miranda, "a box of apricot powder—and, Mary, I don't need eye shadow, do I?" She glanced at her face in the mirror and away again. "Still, no one need pity this corpse if we look properly to the art of the thing."

Mary Townsend said, "You won't recognize yourself in a week."

"Do you suppose, Mary," asked Miranda, "I could have my old room back again?"

"That should be easy," said Mary. "We stored away all your things there with Miss Hobbe." Miranda wondered again at the time and trouble the living took to be helpful to the dead. But not quite dead now, she reassured herself, one foot in either world now; soon I shall cross back and be at home again. The light will seem real and I shall be glad when I hear that someone I know has escaped from death. I shall visit the escaped ones and help them dress and tell them how lucky they are, and how lucky I am still to have them. Mary will be back soon with my gloves and my walking stick, I must go now, I must begin saying good-by to Miss Tanner and Dr. Hildesheim. Adam, she said, now you need not die again, but still I wish you were here; I wish you had come back, what do you think I came back for, Adam, to be deceived like this?

At once he was there beside her, invisible but urgently present, a ghost but more alive than she was, the last intolerable cheat of her heart; for knowing it was false she still clung to the lie, the unpardonable lie of her bitter desire. She said, "I love you," and stood up trembling, trying by the mere act of her will to bring him to sight before her. If I could call you up from the grave I would, she said, if I could see your ghost I would say, I believe. . . . "I believe," she said aloud. "Oh, let me see you once more." The room was silent, empty, the shade was gone from it, struck away by the sudden violence of her rising and speaking aloud. She came to herself as if out of sleep. Oh, no, that is not the way, I must never do that, she warned herself. Miss Tanner said, "Your taxicab is waiting, my dear," and there was Mary. Ready to go.

No more war, no more plague, only the dazed silence that follows the ceasing of the heavy guns; noiseless houses with the shades drawn, empty streets, the dead cold light of tomorrow. Now there would be time for everything.

William Faulkner 1897–1962

Barn Burning

T H E   S T O R E in which the Justice of the Peace's court was sitting smelled of cheese. The boy, crouched on his nail keg at the back of the crowded room, knew he smelled cheese, and more: from where he sat he could see the ranked shelves close-packed with the solid, squat, dynamic shapes of tin cans whose labels his stomach read, not from the lettering which meant nothing to his mind but from the scarlet devils and the silver curve of fish —this, the cheese which he knew he smelled and the hermetic meat which his intestines believed he smelled coming intermittent gusts momentary and brief between the other constant one, the smell and sense just a little of fear because mostly of despair and grief, the old fierce pull of blood. He could not see the table where the Justice sat and before which his father and his father's enemy (*our enemy* he thought in that despair; *ourn! mine and hisn both! He's my father!*) stood, but he could hear them, the two of them that is, because his father had said no word yet:

"But what proof have you, Mr. Harris?"

"I told you. The hog got into my corn. I caught it up and sent it back to him. He had no fence that would hold it. I told him so, warned him. The next time I put the hog in my pen. When he came to get it I gave him enough wire to patch up his pen. The next time I put the hog up and kept it. I rode down to his house and saw the wire I gave him still rolled on to the spool in his yard. I told him he could have the hog when he paid me a dollar pound fee. That evening a nigger came with the dollar and got the hog. He was a strange nigger. He said, 'He say to tell you wood and hay kin burn.' I said, 'What?' 'That whut he say to tell you,' the nigger said. 'Wood and hay kin burn.' That night my barn burned. I got the stock out but I lost the barn."

"Where is the nigger? Have you got him?"

"He was a strange nigger, I tell you. I don't know what became of him."

"But that's not proof. Don't you see that's not proof?"

"Get that boy up here. He knows." For a moment the boy thought too that the man meant his older brother until Harris said, "Not him. The

167

little one. The boy," and, crouching, small for his age, small and wiry like his father, in patched and faded jeans even too small for him, with straight, uncombed, brown hair and eyes gray and wild as storm scud, he saw the men between himself and the table part and become a lane of grim faces, at the end of which he saw the Justice, a shabby, collarless, graying man in spectacles, beckoning him. He felt no floor under his bare feet; he seemed to walk beneath the palpable weight of the grim turning faces. His father, stiff in his black Sunday coat donned not for the trial but for the moving, did not even look at him. *He aims for me to lie,* he thought, again with that frantic grief and despair. *And I will have to do hit.*

"What's your name, boy?" the Justice said.

"Colonel Sartoris Snopes," the boy whispered.

"Hey?" the Justice said. "Talk louder. Colonel Sartoris? I reckon anybody named for Colonel Sartoris in this country can't help but tell the truth, can they?" The boy said nothing. *Enemy! Enemy!* he thought; for a moment he could not even see, could not see that the Justice's face was kindly nor discern that his voice was troubled when he spoke to the man named Harris: "Do you want me to question this boy?" But he could hear, and during those subsequent long seconds while there was absolutely no sound in the crowded little room save that of quiet and intent breathing it was as if he had swung outward at the end of a grape vine, over a ravine, and at the top of the swing had been caught in a prolonged instant of mesmerized gravity, weightless in time.

"No!" Harris said violently, explosively. "Damnation! Send him out of here!" Now time, the fluid world, rushed beneath him again, the voices coming to him again through the smell of cheese and sealed meat, the fear and despair and the old grief of blood:

"This case is closed. I can't find against you, Snopes, but I can give you advice. Leave this country and don't come back to it."

His father spoke for the first time, his voice cold and harsh, level, without emphasis: "I aim to. I don't figure to stay in a country among people who . . ." he said something unprintable and vile, addressed to no one.

"That'll do," the Justice said. "Take your wagon and get out of this country before dark. Case dismissed."

His father turned, and he followed the stiff black coat, the wiry figure walking a little stiffly from where a Confederate provost's man's musket ball had taken him in the heel on a stolen horse thirty years ago, followed the two backs now, since his older brother had appeared from somewhere in the crowd, no taller than the father but thicker, chewing tobacco steadily, between the two lines of grim-faced men and out of the store and across the worn gallery and down the sagging steps and among the dogs and half-grown boys in the mild May dust, where as he passed a voice hissed:

"Barn burner!"

Again he could not see, whirling; there was a face in a red haze, moon-like, bigger than the full moon, the owner of it half again his size, he leaping in the red haze toward the face, feeling no blow, feeling no shock when his head struck the earth, scrabbling up and leaping again, feeling no blow this time either and tasting no blood, scrabbling up to see the other boy in full flight and himself already leaping into pursuit as his father's hand jerked him back, the harsh, cold voice speaking above him: "Go get in the wagon."

It stood in a grove of locusts and mulberries across the road. His two hulking sisters in their Sunday dresses and his mother and her sister in calico and sunbonnets were already in it, sitting on and among the sorry residue of the dozen and more movings which even the boy could remember—the battered stove, the broken beds and chairs, the clock inlaid with mother-of-pearl, which would not run, stopped at some fourteen minutes past two o'clock of a dead and forgotten day and time, which had been his mother's dowry. She was crying, though when she saw him she drew her sleeve across her face and began to descend from the wagon. "Get back," the father said.

"He's hurt. I got to get some water and wash his . . ."

"Get back in the wagon," his father said. He got in too, over the tail-gate. His father mounted to the seat where the older brother already sat and struck the gaunt mules two savage blows with the peeled willow, but without heat. It was not even sadistic; it was exactly that same quality which in later years would cause his descendants to over-run the engine before putting a motor car into motion, striking and reining back in the same movement. The wagon went on, the store with its quiet crowd of grimly watching men dropped behind; a curve in the road hid it. *Forever* he thought. *Maybe he's done satisfied now, now that he has* . . . stopping himself, not to say it aloud even to himself. His mother's hand touched his shoulder.

"Does hit hurt?" she said.

"Naw," he said. "Hit don't hurt. Lemme be."

"Can't you wipe some of the blood off before hit dries?"

"I'll wash to-night," he said. "Lemme be, I tell you."

The wagon went on. He did not know where they were going. None of them ever did or ever asked, because it was always somewhere, always a house of sorts waiting for them a day or two days or even three days away. Likely his father had already arranged to make a crop on another farm before he . . . Again he had to stop himself. He (the father) always did. There was something about his wolflike independence and even courage when the advantage was at least neutral which impressed strangers, as if they got from his latent ravening ferocity not so much a sense of dependability as a feeling that his ferocious conviction in the rightness of his own actions would be of advantage to all whose interest lay with his.

That night they camped in a grove of oaks and beeches where a spring ran. The nights were still cool and they had a fire against it, of a rail lifted from a nearby fence and cut into lengths—a small fire, neat, niggard almost, a shrewd fire; such fires were his father's habit and custom always, even in freezing weather. Older, the boy might have remarked this and wondered why not a big one; why should not a man who had not only seen the waste and extravagance of war, but who had in his blood an inherent voracious prodigality with material not his own, have burned everything in sight? Then he might have gone a step farther and thought that that was the reason: that niggard blaze was the living fruit of nights passed during those four years in the woods hiding from all men, blue or gray, with his strings of horses (captured horses, he called them). And older still, he might have divined the true reason: that the element of fire spoke to some deep mainspring of his father's being, as the element of steel or of powder spoke to other men, as the one weapon for the preservation of integrity, else breath were not worth the breathing, and hence to be regarded with respect and used with discretion.

But he did not think this now and he had seen those same niggard blazes all his life. He merely ate his supper beside it and was already half asleep over his iron plate when his father called him, and once more he followed the stiff back, the stiff and ruthless limp, up the slope and on to the starlit road where, turning, he could see his father against the stars but without face or depth—a shape black, flat, and bloodless as though cut from tin in the iron folds of the frockcoat which had not been made for him, the voice harsh like tin and without heat like tin:

"You were fixing to tell them. You would have told him." He didn't answer. His father struck him with the flat of his hand on the side of the head, hard but without heat, exactly as he had struck the two mules at the store, exactly as he would strike either of them with any stick in order to kill a horse fly, his voice still without heat or anger: "You're getting to be a man. You got to learn. You got to learn to stick to your own blood or you ain't going to have any blood to stick to you. Do you think either of them, any man there this morning, would? Don't you know all they wanted was a chance to get at me because they knew I had them beat? Eh?" Later, twenty years later, he was to tell himself, "If I had said they wanted only truth, justice, he would have hit me again." But now he said nothing. He was not crying. He just stood there. "Answer me," his father said.

"Yes," he whispered. His father turned.

"Get on to bed. We'll be there tomorrow."

Tomorrow they were there. In the early afternoon the wagon stopped before a paintless two-room house identical almost with the dozen others it had stopped before even in the boy's ten years, and again, as on the other dozen occasions, his mother and aunt got down and began to unload the wagon, although his two sisters and his father and brother had not moved.

"Likely hit ain't fitten for hawgs," one of the sisters said.

"Nevertheless, fit it will and you'll hog it and like it," his father said. "Get out of them chairs and help your Ma unload."

The two sisters got down, big, bovine, in a flutter of cheap ribbons; one of them drew from the jumbled wagon bed a battered lantern, the other a worn broom. His father handed the reins to the older son and began to climb stiffly over the wheel. "When they get unloaded, take the team to the barn and feed them." Then he said, and at first the boy thought he was still speaking to his brother: "Come with me."

"Me?" he said.

"Yes," his father said. "You."

"Abner," his mother said. His father paused and looked back—the harsh level stare beneath the shaggy, graying, irascible brows.

"I reckon I'll have a word with the man that aims to begin tomorrow owning me body and soul for the next eight months."

They went back up the road. A week ago—or before last night, that is —he would have asked where they were going, but not now. His father had struck him before last night but never before had he paused afterward to explain why; it was as if the blow and the following calm, outrageous voice still rang, repercussed, divulging nothing to him save the terrible handicap of being young, the light weight of his few years, just heavy enough to prevent his soaring free of the world as it seemed to be ordered but not heavy enough to keep him footed solid in it, to resist it and try to change the course of its events.

Presently he could see the grove of oaks and cedars and the other flowering trees and shrubs where the house would be, though not the house yet. They walked beside a fence massed with honeysuckle and Cherokee roses and came to a gate swinging open between two brick pillars, and now, beyond a sweep of drive, he saw the house for the first time and at that instant he forgot his father and the terror and despair both, and even when he remembered his father again (who had not stopped) the terror and despair did not return. Because, for all the twelve movings, they had sojourned until now in a poor country, a land of small farms and fields and houses, and he had never seen a house like this before. *Hit's big as a courthouse* he thought quietly, with a surge of peace and joy whose reason he could not have thought into words, being too young for that: *They are safe from him. People whose lives are a part of this peace and dignity are beyond his touch, he no more to them than a buzzing wasp: capable of stinging for a little moment but that's all; the spell of this peace and dignity rendering even the barns and stable and cribs which belong to it impervious to the puny flames he might contrive*

. . . this, the peace and joy, ebbing for an instant as he looked again at the stiff black back, the stiff and implacable limp of the figure which was not dwarfed by the house, for the reason that it had never looked big anywhere and which now, against the serene columned backdrop, had more than ever that impervious quality of something cut ruthlessly from tin, depthless, as though, sidewise to the sun, it would cast no shadow. Watching him, the boy remarked the absolutely undeviating course which his father held and saw the stiff foot come squarely down in a pile of fresh droppings where a horse had stood in the drive and which his father could have avoided by a simple change of stride. But it ebbed only for a moment, though he could not have thought this into words either, walking on in the spell of the house, which he could even want but without envy, without sorrow, certainly never with that ravening and jealous rage which unknown to him walked in the ironlike black coat before him. *Maybe he will feel it too. Maybe it will even change him now from what maybe he couldn't help but be.*

They crossed the portico. Now he could hear his father's stiff foot as it came down on the boards with clocklike finality, a sound out of all proportion to the displacement of the body it bore and which was not dwarfed either by the white door before it, as though it had attained to a sort of vicious and ravening minimum not to be dwarfed by anything— the flat, wide, black hat, the formal coat of broadcloth which had once been black but which had now the friction-glazed greenish cast of the bodies of old house flies, the lifted sleeve which was too large, the lifted hand like a curled claw. The door opened so promptly that the boy knew the Negro must have been watching them all the time, an old man with neat grizzled hair, in a linen jacket, who stood barring the door with his body, saying, "Wipe yo foots, white man, fo you come in here. Major ain't home nohow."

"Get out of my way, nigger," his father said, without heat too, flinging the door back and the Negro also and entering, his hat still on his head. And now the boy saw the prints of the stiff foot on the doorjamb and saw them appear on the pale rug behind the machinelike deliberation of the foot which seemed to bear (or transmit) twice the weight which the body compassed. The Negro was shouting "Miss Lulu! Miss Lulu!" somewhere behind them, then the boy, deluged as though by a warm wave by a suave turn of carpeted stair and a pendant glitter of chandeliers and a mute gleam of gold frames, heard the swift feet and saw her too, a lady— perhaps he had never seen her like before either—in a gray, smooth gown with lace at the throat and an apron tied at the waist and the sleeves turned back, wiping cake or biscuit dough from her hands with a towel as she came up the hall, looking not at his father at all but at the tracks on the blond rug with an expression of incredulous amazement.

"I tried," the Negro cried. "I tole him to . . ."

"Will you please go away?" she said in a shaking voice. "Major de Spain is not at home. Will you please go away?"

His father had not spoken again. He did not speak again. He did not even look at her. He just stood stiff in the center of the rug, in his hat, the shaggy iron-gray brows twitching slightly above the pebble-colored eyes as he appeared to examine the house with brief deliberation. Then with the same deliberation he turned; the boy watched him pivot on the good leg and saw the stiff foot drag round the arc of the turning, leaving a final long and fading smear. His father never looked at it, he never once looked down at the rug. The Negro held the door. It closed behind them, upon the hysteric and indistinguishable woman-wail. His father stopped at the top of the steps and scraped his boot clean on the edge of it. At the gate he stopped again. He stood for a moment, planted stiffly on the stiff foot, looking back at the house. "Pretty and white, ain't it?" he said. "That's sweat. Nigger sweat. Maybe it ain't white enough yet to suit him. Maybe he wants to mix some white sweat with it."

Two hours later the boy was chopping wood behind the house within which his mother and aunt and the two sisters (the mother and aunt, not the two girls, he knew that; even at this distance and muffled by walls the flat loud voices of the two girls emanated an incorrigible idle inertia) were setting up the stove to prepare a meal, when he heard the hooves and saw the linen-clad man on a fine sorrel mare, whom he recognized even before he saw the rolled rug in front of the Negro youth following on a fat bay carriage horse—a suffused, angry face vanishing, still at full gallop, beyond the corner of the house where his father and brother were sitting in the two tilted chairs; and a moment later, almost before he could have put the axe down, he heard the hooves again and watched the sorrel mare go back out of the yard, already galloping again. Then his father began to shout one of the sisters' names, who presently emerged backward from the kitchen door dragging the rolled rug along the ground by one end while the other sister walked behind it.

"If you ain't going to tote, go on and set up the wash pot," the first said.

"You, Sarty!" the second shouted, "Set up the wash pot!" His father appeared at the door, framed against that shabbiness, as he had been against that other bland perfection, impervious to either, the mother's anxious face at his shoulder.

"Go on," the father said. "Pick it up." The two sisters stooped, broad, lethargic; stooping, they presented an incredible expanse of pale cloth and a flutter of tawdry ribbons.

"If I thought enough of a rug to have to git hit all the way from France I wouldn't keep hit where folks coming in would have to tromp on hit," the first said. They raised the rug.

"Abner," the mother said. "Let me do it."

"You go back and git dinner," his father said. "I'll tend to this."

From the woodpile through the rest of the afternoon the boy watched them, the rug spread flat in the dust beside the bubbling wash-pot, the two sisters stooping over it with that profound and lethargic reluctance, while the father stood over them in turn, implacable and grim, driving them though never raising his voice again. He could smell the harsh homemade lye they were using; he saw his mother come to the door once and look toward them with an expression not anxious now but very like despair; he saw his father turn, and he fell to with the axe and saw from the corner of his eye his father raise from the ground a flattish fragment of field stone and examine it and return to the pot, and this time his mother actually spoke: "Abner. Abner. Please don't. Please, Abner."

Then he was done too. It was dusk; the whippoorwills had already begun. He could smell coffee from the room where they would presently eat the cold food remaining from the mid-afternoon meal, though when he entered the house he realized they were having coffee again probably because there was a fire on the hearth, before which the rug now lay spread over the backs of the two chairs. The tracks of his father's foot were gone. Where they had been were now long, water-cloudy scoriations resembling the sporadic course of a lilliputian mowing machine.

It still hung there while they ate the cold food and then went to bed, scattered without order or claim up and down the two rooms, his mother in one bed, where his father would later lie, the older brother in the other, himself, the aunt, and the two sisters on pallets on the floor. But his father was not in bed yet. The last thing the boy remembered was the depthless, harsh silhouette of the hat and coat bending over the rug and it seemed to him that he had not even closed his eyes when the silhouette was standing over him, the fire almost dead behind it, the stiff foot prodding him awake. "Catch up the mule," his father said.

When he returned with the mule his father was standing in the black door, the rolled rug over his shoulder. "Ain't you going to ride?" he said.

"No. Give me your foot."

He bent his knee into his father's hand, the wiry, surprising power flowed smoothly, rising, he rising with it, on to the mule's bare back (they had owned a saddle once; the boy could remember it though not when or where) and with the same effortlessness his father swung the rug up in front of him. Now in the starlight they retraced the afternoon's path, up the dusty road rife with honeysuckle, through the gate and up the black tunnel of the drive to the lightless house, where he sat on the mule and felt the rough warp of the rug drag across his thighs and vanish.

"Don't you want me to help?" he whispered. His father did not answer and now he heard again that stiff foot striking the hollow portico with that wooden and clocklike deliberation, that outrageous overstatement of the weight it carried. The rug, hunched, not flung (the boy could tell that even in the darkness) from his father's shoulder struck the angle of wall and floor with a sound unbelievably loud, thunderous, then the foot again, unhurried and enormous; a light came on in the house and the boy sat, tense, breathing steadily and quietly and just a little fast, though the foot itself did not increase its beat at all, descending the steps now; now the boy could see him.

"Don't you want to ride now?" he whispered. "We kin both ride now," the light within the house altering now, flaring up and sinking. *He's coming down the stairs now,* he thought. He had already ridden the mule up beside the horse block; presently his father was up behind him and he doubled the reins over and slashed the mule across the neck, but before the animal could begin to trot the hard, thin arm came around him, the hard, knotted hand jerking the mule back to a walk.

In the first red rays of the sun they were in the lot, putting plow gear on the mules. This time the sorrel mare was in the lot before he heard it at all, the rider collarless and even bareheaded, trembling, speaking in a shaking voice as the woman in the house had done, his father merely looking up once before stooping again to the hame he was buckling, so that the man on the mare spoke to his stooping back:

"You must realize you have ruined that rug. Wasn't there anybody here, any of your women . . ." he ceased, shaking, the boy watching him, the older brother leaning now in the stable door, chewing, blinking slowly and steadily at nothing apparently. "It cost a hundred dollars. But you never had a hundred dollars. You never will. So I'm going to charge you twenty bushels of corn against your crop. I'll add it in your contract and when you come to the commissary you can sign it. That won't keep Mrs. de Spain quiet but maybe it will teach you to wipe your feet off before you enter her house again."

Then he was gone. The boy looked at his father, who still had not spoken or even looked up again, who was now adjusting the logger-head in the hame.

"Pap," he said. His father looked at him—the inscrutable face, the shaggy brows beneath which the gray eyes glinted coldly. Suddenly the boy went toward him, fast, stopping as suddenly. "You done the best you could!" he cried. "If he wanted hit done different why didn't he wait and tell you how? He won't git no twenty bushels! He won't git none! We'll gether hit and hide hit! I kin watch . . ."

"Did you put the cutter back in the straight stock like I told you?"

"No, sir," he said.

"Then go do it."

That was Wednesday. During the rest of that week he worked steadily, at what was within his scope and some which was beyond it, with an industry that did not need to be driven nor even commanded twice; he had this from his mother, with the difference that some at least of what he did he liked to do, such as splitting wood with the half-size axe which his mother and aunt had earned, or saved money somehow, to present him with at Christmas. In company with the two older women (and on one afternoon, even one of the sisters), he built pens for the shoat and the cow which were a part of his father's contract with the landlord, and one afternoon, his father being absent, gone somewhere on one of the mules, he went to the field.

They were running a middle buster now, his brother holding the plow straight while he handled the reins, and walking beside the straining mule, the rich black soil shearing cool and damp against his bare ankles, he thought *Maybe this is the end of it. Maybe even that twenty bushels that seems hard to have to pay for just a rug will be a cheap price for him to stop forever and always from being what he used to be*; thinking, dreaming now, so that his brother had to speak sharply to him to mind the mule: *Maybe he even won't collect the twenty bushels. Maybe it will all add up and balance and vanish—corn, rug, fire; the terror and grief, the being pulled two ways like between two teams of horses—gone, done with for ever and ever.*

Then it was Saturday; he looked up from beneath the mule he was harnessing and saw his father in the black coat and hat. "Not that," his father said. "The wagon gear." And then, two hours later, sitting in the wagon bed behind his father and brother on the seat, the wagon accomplished a final curve, and he saw the weathered paintless store with its tattered tobacco and patent-medicine posters and the tethered wagons and saddle animals below the gallery. He mounted the gnawed steps behind his father and brother, and there again was the lane of quiet, watching faces for the three of them to walk through. He saw the man in spectacles sitting at the plank table and he did not need to be told this was a Justice of the Peace; he sent one glare of fierce, exultant, partisan defiance at the man in collar and cravat now, whom he had seen but twice before in his life, and that on a galloping horse, who now wore on his face an expression not of rage but of amazed unbelief which the boy could not have known was at the incredible circumstance of being sued by one of his own tenants, and came and stood against his father and cried at the Justice: "He ain't done it! He ain't burnt . . ."

"Go back to the wagon," his father said.

"Burnt?" the Justice said. "Do I understand this rug was burned too?"

"Does anybody here claim it was?" his father said. "Go back to the wagon." But he did not, he merely retreated to the rear of the room, crowded as that other had been, but not to sit down this time, instead, to stand pressing among the motionless bodies, listening to the voices:

"And you claim twenty bushels of corn is too high for the damage you did to the rug?"

"He brought the rug to me and said he wanted the tracks washed out of it. I washed the tracks out and took the rug back to him."

"But you didn't carry the rug back to him in the same condition it was in before you made the tracks on it."

His father did not answer, and now for perhaps half a minute there was no sound at all save that of breathing, the faint, steady suspiration of complete and intent listening.

"You decline to answer that, Mr. Snopes?" Again his father did not answer. "I'm going to find against you, Mr. Snopes. I'm going to find that you were responsible for the injury to Major de Spain's rug and hold you liable for it. But twenty bushels of corn seems a little high for a man in your circumstances to have to pay. Major de Spain claims it cost a hundred dollars. October corn will be worth about fifty cents. I figure that if Major de Spain can stand a ninety-five dollar loss on something he paid cash for, you can stand a five-dollar loss you haven't earned yet. I hold you in damages to Major de Spain to the amount of ten bushels of corn over and above your contract with him, to be paid to him out of your crop at gathering time. Court adjourned."

It had taken no time hardly, the morning was but half begun. He thought they would return home and perhaps back to the field, since they were late, far behind all other farmers. But instead his father passed on behind the wagon, merely indicating with his hand for the older brother to follow with it, and crossed the road toward the blacksmith shop opposite, pressing on after his father, overtaking him, speaking, whispering up at the harsh, calm face beneath the weathered hat: "He won't git no ten bushels neither. He won't git one. We'll . . ." until his father glanced for an instant down at him, the face absolutely calm, the grizzled eyebrows tangled above the cold eyes, the voice almost pleasant, almost gentle:

"You think so? Well, we'll wait till October anyway."

The matter of the wagon—the setting of a spoke or two and the tightening of the tires—did not take long either, the business of the tires accomplished by driving the wagon into the spring branch behind the shop and letting it stand there, the mules nuzzling into the water from time to time, and the boy on the seat with the idle reins, looking up the slope and through the sooty tunnel of the shed where the slow hammer rang and where his father sat on an upended cypress bolt, easily, either talking or listening, still sitting there when the boy brought the dripping wagon up out of the branch and halted it before the door.

"Take them on to the shade and hitch," his father said. He did so and returned. His father and the smith and a third man squatting on his heels inside the door were talking, about crops and animals; the boy, squatting too in the ammoniac dust and hoof-parings and scales of rust, heard his father tell a long and unhurried story out of the time before the birth of the older brother even when he had been a professional horse-trader. And then his father came up beside him where he stood before a tattered last year's circus poster on the other side of the store, gazing rapt and quiet at the scarlet horses, the incredible poisings and convolutions of tulle and tights and the painted leers of comedians, and said, "It's time to eat."

But not at home. Squatting beside his brother against the front wall, he watched his father emerge from the store and produce from a paper sack a segment of cheese and divide it carefully and deliberately into three with his pocket knife and produce crackers from the same sack. They all three squatted on the gallery and ate, slowly, without talking; then in the store again, they drank from a tin dipper tepid water smelling of the cedar bucket and of living beech trees. And still they did not go home. It was a horse lot this time, a tall rail fence upon and along which men stood and sat and out of which one by one horses were led, to be walked and trotted and then cantered back and forth along the road while the slow swapping and buying went on and the sun began to slant westward, they—the three of them—watching and listening, the older brother with his muddy eyes and his steady, inevitable tobacco, the father commenting now and then on certain of the animals, to no one in particular.

It was after sundown when they reached home. They ate supper by lamplight, then, sitting on the doorstep, the boy watched the night fully accomplished, listening to the whippoorwills and the frogs, when he heard his mother's voice: "Abner! No! No! Oh, God. Oh, God. Abner!" and he rose, whirled, and saw the altered light through the door where a candle stub now burned in a bottle neck on the table and his father, still in the hat and coat, at once formal and burlesque as though dressed carefully for some shabby and ceremonial violence, emptying the reservoir of the lamp back into the five-gallon kerosene can from which it had been filled, while the mother tugged at his arm until he shifted the lamp to the other hand and flung her back, not savagely or viciously, just hard, into the wall, her hands flung out against the wall for balance, her mouth open and in her face the same quality of hopeless despair as had been in her voice. Then his father saw him standing in the door.

"Go to the barn and get that can of oil we were oiling the wagon with," he said. The boy did not move. Then he could speak.

"What . . ." he cried. "What are you . . ."

"Go get that oil," his father said. "Go."

Then he was moving, running, outside the house, toward the stable: this the old habit, the old blood which he had not been permitted to choose for himself, which had been bequeathed him willy nilly and which had run for so long (and who knew where, battening on what of outrage and savagery and lust) before it came to him. *I could keep on*, he thought.

*I could run on and on and never look back, never need to see his face
again. Only I can't.* I can't, the rusted can in his hand now, the liquid
sploshing in it as he ran back to the house and into it, into the sound of
his mother's weeping in the next room, and handed the can to his father.

"Ain't you going to even send a nigger?" he cried. "At least you sent
a nigger before!"

This time his father didn't strike him. The hand came even faster than
the blow had, the same hand which had set the can on the table with
almost excruciating care flashing from the can toward him too quick for
him to follow it, gripping him by the back of his shirt and on to tiptoe
before he had seen it quit the can, the face stooping at him in breathless
and frozen ferocity, the cold, dead voice speaking over him to the older
brother who leaned against the table, chewing with that steady, curious,
sidewise motion of cows:

"Empty the can into the big one and go on. I'll ketch up with you."

"Better tie him up to the bedpost," the brother said.

"Do like I told you," the father said. Then the boy was moving, his
bunched shirt and the hard, bony hand between his shoulder-blades, his
toes just touching the floor, across the room and into the other one, past
the sisters sitting with spread heavy thighs in the two chairs over the cold
hearth, and to where his mother and aunt sat side by side on the bed, the
aunt's arms about his mother's shoulders.

"Hold him," the father said. The aunt made a startled movement. "Not
you," the father said. "Lennie. Take hold of him. I want to see you do it."
His mother took him by the wrist. "You'll hold him better than that. If
he gets loose don't you know what he is going to do? He will go up
yonder." He jerked his head toward the road. "Maybe I'd better tie him."

"I'll hold him," his mother whispered.

"See you do then." Then his father was gone, the stiff foot heavy and
measured upon the boards, ceasing at last.

Then he began to struggle. His mother caught him in both arms, he
jerking and wrenching at them. He would be stronger in the end, he knew
that. But he had no time to wait for it. "Lemme go!" he cried. "I don't
want to have to hit you!"

"Let him go!" the aunt said. "If he don't go, before God, I am going
up there myself!"

"Don't you see I can't?" his mother cried. "Sarty! Sarty! No! No! Help
me, Lizzie!"

Then he was free. His aunt grasped at him but it was too late. He
whirled, running, his mother stumbled forward on to her knees behind
him, crying to the nearer sister: "Catch him, Net! Catch him!" But that
was too late too, the sister (the sisters were twins, born at the same time,
yet either of them now gave the impression of being, encompassing as
much living meat and volume and weight as any other two of the family)

not yet having begun to rise from the chair, her head, face, alone merely turned, presenting to him in the flying instant an astonishing expanse of young female features untroubled by any surprise even, wearing only an expression of bovine interest. Then he was out of the room, out of the house, in the mild dust of the starlit road and the heavy rifeness of honeysuckle, the pale ribbon unspooling with terrific slowness under his running feet, reaching the gate at last and turning in, running, his heart and lungs drumming, on up the drive toward the lighted house, the lighted door. He did not knock, he burst in, sobbing for breath, incapable for the moment of speech; he saw the astonished face of the Negro in the linen jacket without knowing when the Negro had appeared.

"De Spain!" he cried, panted. "Where's . . ." then he saw the white man too emerging from a white door down the hall. "Barn!" he cried. "Barn!"

"What?" the white man said. "Barn?"

"Yes!" the boy cried. "Barn!"

"Catch him!" the white man shouted.

But it was too late this time too. The Negro grasped his shirt, but the entire sleeve, rotten with washing, carried away, and he was out that door too and in the drive again, and had actually never ceased to run even while he was screaming into the white man's face.

Behind him the white man was shouting, "My horse! Fetch my horse!" and he thought for an instant of cutting across the park and climbing the fence into the road, but he did not know the park nor how high the vine-massed fence might be and he dared not risk it. So he ran on down the drive, blood and breath roaring; presently he was in the road again though he could not see it. He could not hear either: the galloping mare was almost upon him before he heard her, and even then he held his course, as if the very urgency of his wild grief and need must in a moment more find him wings, waiting until the ultimate instant to hurl himself aside and into the weed-choked roadside ditch as the horse thundered past and on, for an instant in furious silhouette against the stars, the tranquil early summer night sky, which, even before the shape of the horse and rider vanished, stained abruptly and violently upward: a long, swirling roar incredible and soundless, blotting the stars, and he springing up and into the road again, running again, knowing it was too late yet still running even after he heard the shot and, an instant later, two shots, pausing now without knowing he had ceased to run, crying "Pap! Pap!", running again before he knew he had begun to run, stumbling, tripping over something and scrabbling up again without ceasing to run, looking backward over his shoulder at the glare as he got up, running on among the invisible trees, panting, sobbing, "Father! Father!"

At midnight he was sitting on the crest of a hill. He did not know it was midnight and he did not know how far he had come. But there was no glare behind him now and he sat now, his back toward what he had called home for four days anyhow, his face toward the dark woods which he would enter when breath was strong again, small, shaking steadily in the chill darkness, hugging himself into the remainder of his thin, rotten shirt, the grief and despair now no longer terror and fear but just grief and despair. *Father. My father*, he thought. "He was brave!" he cried suddenly, aloud but not loud, no more than a whisper: "He was! He was in the war! He was in Colonel Sartoris' cav'ry!" not knowing that his father had gone to that war a private in the fine old European sense, wearing no uniform, admitting the authority of and giving fidelity to no man or army or flag, going to war as Malbrouck himself did: for booty—it meant nothing and less than nothing to him if it were enemy booty or his own.

The slow constellations wheeled on. It would be dawn and then sun-up after a while and he would be hungry. But that would be tomorrow and now he was only cold, and walking would cure that. His breathing was easier now and he decided to get up and go on, and then he found that he had been asleep because he knew it was almost dawn, the night almost over. He could tell that from the whippoorwills. They were everywhere now among the dark trees below him, constant and inflectioned and ceaseless, so that, as the instant for giving over to the day birds drew nearer and nearer, there was no interval at all between them. He got up. He was a little stiff, but walking would cure that too as it would the cold, and soon there would be the sun. He went on down the hill, toward the dark woods within which the liquid silver voices of the birds called unceasing—the rapid and urgent beating of the urgent and quiring heart of the late spring night. He did not look back.

Ernest Hemingway 1898–1961

In Another Country

IN THE FALL the war was always there, but we did not go to it anymore. It was cold in the fall in Milan and the dark came very early. Then the electric lights came on, and it was pleasant along the streets looking in the windows. There was much game hanging outside the shops, and the snow powdered in the fur of the foxes and the wind blew their tails. The deer hung stiff and heavy and empty, and small birds blew in the wind and the wind turned their feathers. It was a cold fall and the wind came down from the mountains.

We were all at the hospital every afternoon, and there were different ways of walking across the town through the dusk to the hospital. Two of the ways were alongside canals, but they were long. Always, though, you crossed a bridge across a canal to enter the hospital. There was a choice of three bridges. On one of them a woman sold roasted chestnuts. It was warm, standing in front of her charcoal fire, and the chestnuts were warm afterward in your pocket. The hospital was very old and very beautiful, and you entered through a gate and walked across a courtyard and out a gate on the other side. There were usually funerals starting from the courtyard. Beyond the old hospital were the new brick pavilions, and there we met every afternoon and were all very polite and interested in what was the matter, and sat in the machines that were to make so much difference.

The doctor came up to the machine where I was sitting and said: "What did you like best to do before the war? Did you practice a sport?"

I said: "Yes, football."

"Good," he said. "You will be able to play football again better than ever."

My knee did not bend and the leg dropped straight from the knee to the ankle without a calf, and the machine was to bend the knee and make it move as in riding a tricycle. But it did not bend yet, and instead the machine lurched when it came to the bending part. The doctor said: "That will all pass. You are a fortunate young man. You will play football again like a champion."

182

In the next machine was a major who had a little hand like a baby's. He winked at me when the doctor examined his hand, which was between two leather straps that bounced up and down and flapped the stiff fingers, and said: "And will I too play football, captain-doctor?" He had been a very great fencer, and before the war the greatest fencer in Italy.

The doctor went to his office in a back room and brought a photograph which showed a hand that had been withered almost as small as the major's, before it had taken a machine course, and after was a little larger. The major held the photograph with his good hand and looked at it very carefully. "A wound?" he asked.

"An industrial accident," the doctor said.

"Very interesting, very interesting," the major said, and handed it back to the doctor.

"You have confidence?"

"No," said the major.

There were three boys who came each day who were about the same age I was. They were all three from Milan, and one of them was to be a lawyer, and one was to be a painter, and one had intended to be a soldier, and after we were finished with the machines, sometimes we walked back together to the Café Cova, which was next door to the Scala. We walked the short way through the communist quarter because we were four together. The people hated us because we were officers, and from a wine-shop someone called out, "A basso gli ufficiali!" as we passed. Another boy who walked with us sometimes and made us five wore a black silk handkerchief across his face because he had no nose then and his face was to be rebuilt. He had gone out to the front from the military academy and been wounded within an hour after he had gone into the front line for the first time. They rebuilt his face, but he came from a very old family and they could never get the nose exactly right. He went to South America and worked in a bank. But this was a long time ago, and then we did not any of us know how it was going to be afterward. We only knew then that there was always the war, but that we were not going to it any more.

We all had the same medals, except the boy with the black silk bandage across his face, and he had not been at the front long enough to get any medals. The tall boy with a very pale face who was to be a lawyer had been a lieutenant of Arditi and had three medals of the sort we each had only one of. He had lived a very long time with death and was a little detached. We were all a little detached, and there was nothing that held us together except that we met every afternoon at the hospital. Although, as we walked to the Cova through the tough part of town, walking in the dark, with light and singing coming out of the wine-shops, and sometimes having to walk into the street when the men and women would crowd together on the sidewalk so that we would have had to jostle them to get by, we felt held together by there being something that had happened that they, the people who disliked us, did not understand.

We ourselves all understood the Cova, where it was rich and warm and not too brightly lighted, and noisy and smoky at certain hours, and there were always girls at the tables and the illustrated papers on a rack on the wall. The girls at the Cova were very patriotic, and I found that the most patriotic people in Italy were the café girls—and I believe they are still patriotic.

The boys at first were very polite about my medals and asked me what I had done to get them. I showed them the papers, which were written in very beautiful language and full of *fratellanza* and *abnegazione*, but which really said, with the adjectives removed, that I had been given the medals because I was an American. After that their manner changed a little toward me, although I was their friend against outsiders. I was a friend, but I was never really one of them after they had read the citations, because it had been different with them and they had done very different things to get their medals. I had been wounded, it was true; but we all knew that being wounded, after all, was really an accident. I was never ashamed of the ribbons, though, and sometimes, after the cocktail hour, I would imagine myself having done all the things they had done to get their medals; but walking home at night through the empty streets with the cold wind and all the shops closed, trying to keep near the street lights, I knew that I would never have done such things, and I was very much afraid to die, and often lay in bed at night by myself, afraid to die and wondering how I would be when I went back to the front again.

The three with the medals were like hunting-hawks; and I was not a hawk, although I might seem a hawk to those who had never hunted; they, the three, knew better and so we drifted apart. But I stayed good friends with the boy who had been wounded his first day at the front, because he would never know now how he would have turned out; so he could never be accepted either, and I liked him because I thought perhaps he would not have turned out to be a hawk either.

The major, who had been the great fencer, did not believe in bravery, and spent much time while we sat in the machines correcting my grammar. He had complimented me on how I spoke Italian, and we talked together very easily. One day I had said that Italian seemed such an easy language to me that I could not take a great interest in it; everything was so easy to say. "Ah, yes," the major said. "Why, then, do you not take up the use of grammar?" So we took up the use of grammar, and soon Italian was such a difficult language that I was afraid to talk to him until I had the grammar straight in my mind.

The major came very regularly to the hospital. I do not think he ever missed a day, although I am sure he did not believe in the machines. There was a time when none of us believed in the machines, and one day the major said it was all nonsense. The machines were new then and it was we who were to prove them. It was an idiotic idea, he said, "a theory, like another." I had not learned my grammar, and he said I was a stupid impossible disgrace, and he was a fool to have bothered with me. He was a small man and he sat straight up in his chair with his right hand thrust into the machine and looked straight ahead at the wall while the straps thumped up and down with his fingers in them.

"What will you do when the war is over if it is over?" he asked me. "Speak grammatically!"

"I will go to the States."

"Are you married?"

"No, but I hope to be."

"The more of a fool you are," he said. He seemed very angry. "A man must not marry."

"Why, Signor Maggiore?"

"Don't call me 'Signor Maggiore.'"

"Why must not a man marry?"

"He cannot marry. He cannot marry," he said angrily. "If he is to lose everything, he should not place himself in a position to lose that. He should not place himself in a position to lose. He should find things he cannot lose."

He spoke very angrily and bitterly, and looked straight ahead while he talked.

"But why should he necessarily lose it?"

"He'll lose it," the major said. He was looking at the wall. Then he looked down at the machine and jerked his little hand out from between the straps and slapped it hard against his thigh. "He'll lose it," he almost shouted. "Don't argue with me!" Then he called to the attendant who ran the machines. "Come and turn this damned thing off."

He went back into the other room for the light treatment and the massage. Then I heard him ask the doctor if he might use his telephone and he shut the door. When he came back into the room, I was sitting in another machine. He was wearing his cape and had his cap on, and he came directly toward my machine and put his arm on my shoulder.

"I am so sorry," he said, and patted me on the shoulder with his good hand. "I would not be rude. My wife has just died. You must forgive me."

"Oh—" I said, feeling sick for him. "I am *so* sorry."

He stood there biting his lower lip. "It is very difficult," he said. "I cannot resign myself."

He looked straight past me and out through the window. Then he began to cry. "I am utterly unable to resign myself," he said and choked.

And then crying, his head up looking at nothing, carrying himself straight and soldierly, with tears on both his cheeks and biting his lips, he walked past the machines and out the door.

The doctor told me that the major's wife, who was very young and whom he had not married until he was definitely invalided out of the war, had died of pneumonia. She had been sick only a few days. No one expected her to die. The major did not come to the hospital for three days. Then he came at the usual hour, wearing a black band on the sleeve of his uniform. When he came back, there were large framed photographs around the wall, of all sorts of wounds before and after they had been cured by the machines. In front of the machine the major used were three photographs of hands like his that were completely restored. I do not know where the doctor got them. I always understood we were the first to use the machines. The photographs did not make much difference to the major because he only looked out of the window.

Vladimir Nabokov 1899–

"That in Aleppo Once . . ." [1]

D E A R V.—Among other things, this is to tell you that at last I am here, in the country whither so many sunsets have led. One of the first persons I saw was our good old Gleb Alexandrovich Gekko gloomily crossing Columbus Avenue in quest of the *petit café du coin* which none of us three will ever visit again. He seemed to think that somehow or other you were betraying our national literature, and he gave me your address with a deprecatory shake of his gray head, as if you did not deserve the treat of hearing from me.

I have a story for you. Which reminds me—I mean putting it like this reminds me—of the days when we wrote our first udder-warm bubbling verse, and all things, a rose, a puddle, a lighted window, cried out to us: "I'm a rhyme!" Yes, this is a most useful universe. We play, we die: *ig-rhyme, umi-rhyme*. And the sonorous souls of Russian verbs lend a meaning to the wild gesticulation of trees or to some discarded newspaper sliding and pausing, and shuffling again, with abortive flaps and apterous jerks along an endless wind-swept embankment. But just now I am not a poet. I come to you like that gushing lady in Chekhov who was dying to be described.

I married, let me see, about a month after you left France and a few weeks before the gentle Germans roared into Paris. Although I can produce documentary proofs of matrimony, I am positive now that my wife never existed. You may know her name from some other source, but that does not matter: it is the name of an illusion. Therefore, I am able to speak of her with as much detachment as I would of a character in a story (one of your stories, to be precise).

It was love at first touch rather than at first sight, for I had met her several times before without experiencing any special emotions; but one night, as I was seeing her home, something quaint she had said made me stoop with a laugh and lightly kiss her on the hair—and of course we all know of that blinding blast which is caused by merely picking up a small

[1] *Othello* Act V, sc. ii, l. 352.

187

doll from the floor of a carefully abandoned house: the soldier involved hears nothing; for him it is but an ecstatic soundless and boundless expansion of what had been during his life a pin point of light in the dark center of his being. And really, the reason we think of death in celestial terms is that the visible firmament, especially at night (above our blacked-out Paris with the gaunt arches of its Boulevard Exelmans and the ceaseless Alpine gurgle of desolate latrines), is the most adequate and ever-present symbol of that vast silent explosion.

But I cannot discern her. She remains as nebulous as my best poem—the one you made such gruesome fun of in the *Literaturnïe Zapiski*. When I want to imagine her, I have to cling mentally to a tiny brown birthmark on her downy forearm, as one concentrates upon a punctuation mark in an illegible sentence. Perhaps, had she used a greater amount of make-up or used it more constantly, I might have visualized her face today, or at least the delicate transverse furrows of dry, hot rouged lips; but I fail, I fail—although I still feel their elusive touch now and then in the blind-man's buff of my senses, in that sobbing sort of dream when she and I clumsily clutch at each other through a heartbreaking mist and I cannot see the color of her eyes for the blank luster of brimming tears drowning their irises.

She was much younger than I—not as much younger as was Nathalie of the lovely bare shoulders and long earrings in relation to swarthy Push-kin; but still there was a sufficient margin for that kind of retrospective romanticism which finds pleasure in imitating the destiny of a unique genius (down to the jealousy, down to the filth, down to the stab of seeing her almond-shaped eyes turn to her blond Cassio behind her peacock-feathered fan) even if one cannot imitate his verse. She liked mine though, and would scarcely have yawned as the other was wont to do every time her husband's poem happened to exceed the length of a sonnet. If she has remained a phantom to me, I may have been one to her; I suppose she had been solely attracted by the obscurity of my poetry; then tore a hole through its veil and saw a stranger's unlovable face.

As you know, I had been for some time planning to follow the example of your fortunate flight. She described to me an uncle of hers who lived, she said, in New York: he had taught riding at a Southern college and had wound up by marrying a wealthy American woman; they had a little daughter born deaf. She said she had lost their address long ago, but a few days later it miraculously turned up, and we wrote a dramatic letter to which we never received any reply. This did not much matter, as I had already obtained a sound affidavit from Professor Lomchenko of Chicago; but little else had been done in the way of getting the necessary papers, when the invasion began, whereas I foresaw that if we stayed on in Paris some helpful compatriot of mine would sooner or later point out to the interested party sundry passages in one of my books where I argued that, with all her many black sins, Germany was still bound to remain forever and ever the laughing stock of the world.

So we started upon our disastrous honeymoon. Crushed and jolted amid the apocalyptic exodus, waiting for unscheduled trains that were bound for unknown destinations, walking through the stale stage setting of abstract towns, living in a permanent twilight of physical exhaustion, we fled; and the farther we fled, the clearer it became that what was driving us on was something more than a booted and buckled fool with his assortment of variously propelled junk—something of which he was a mere symbol, something monstrous and impalpable, a timeless and faceless mass of immemorial horror that still keeps coming at me from behind even here, in the green vacuum of Central Park.

Oh, she bore it gamely enough—with a kind of dazed cheerfulness. Once, however, quite suddenly she started to sob in a sympathetic railway carriage. "The dog," she said, "the dog we left. I cannot forget the poor dog." The honesty of her grief shocked me, as we had never had any dog. "I know," she said, "but I tried to imagine we had actually bought that setter. And just think, he would be now whining behind a locked door." There had never been any talk of buying a setter.

I should also not like to forget a certain stretch of highroad and the sight of a family of refugees (two women, a child) whose old father, or grandfather, had died on the way. The sky was a chaos of black and flesh-colored clouds with an ugly sunburst beyond a hooded hill, and the dead man was lying on his back under a dusty plane tree. With a stick and their hands the women had tried to dig a roadside grave, but the soil was too hard; they had given it up and were sitting side by side, among the anemic poppies, a little apart from the corpse and its upturned beard. But the little boy was still scratching and scraping and tugging until he tumbled a flat stone and forgot the object of his solemn exertions as he crouched on his haunches, his thin, eloquent neck showing all its vertebrae to the headsman, and watched with surprise and delight thousands of minute brown ants seething, zigzagging, dispersing, heading for places of safety in the Gard, and the Aude, and the Drôme, and the Var, and the Basses-Pyrénées—we two paused only in Pau.

Spain proved too difficult and we decided to move on to Nice. At a place called Faugères (a ten-minute stop) I squeezed out of the train to buy some food. When a couple of minutes later I came back, the train was gone, and the muddled old man responsible for the atrocious void that faced me (coal dust glittering in the heat between naked indifferent rails, and a lone piece of orange peel) brutally told me that, anyway, I had had no right to get out.

In a better world I could have had my wife located and told what to do

(I had both tickets and most of the money); as it was, my nightmare struggle with the telephone proved futile, so I dismissed the whole series of diminutive voices barking at me from afar, sent two or three telegrams which are probably on their way only now, and late in the evening took the next local to Montpellier, farther than which her train would not stumble. Not finding her there, I had to choose between two alternatives: going on because she might have boarded the Marseilles train which I had just missed, or going back because she might have returned to Faugères. I forgot now what tangle of reasoning led me to Marseilles and Nice.

Beyond such routine action as forwarding false data to a few unlikely places, the police did nothing to help: one man bellowed at me for being a nuisance; another sidetracked the question by doubting the authenticity of my marriage certificate because it was stamped on what he contended to be the wrong side; a third, a fat *commissaire* with liquid brown eyes confessed that he wrote poetry in his spare time. I looked up various acquaintances among the numerous Russians domiciled or stranded in Nice. I heard those among them who chanced to have Jewish blood talk of their doomed kinsmen crammed into hell-bound trains; and my own plight, by contrast, acquired a commonplace air of irreality while I sat in some crowded café with the milky blue sea in front of me and a shell-hollow murmur behind telling and retelling the tale of massarcre and misery, and the gray paradise beyond the ocean, and the ways and whims of harsh consuls.

A week after my arrival an indolent plain-clothes man called upon me and took me down a crooked and smelly street to a black-stained house with the word "hotel" almost erased by dirt and time; there, he said, my wife had been found. The girl he produced was an absolute stranger, of course; but my friend Holmes kept on trying for some time to make her and me confess we were married, while her taciturn and muscular bedfellow stood by and listened, his bare arms crossed on his striped chest.

When at length I got rid of those people and had wandered back to my neighborhood, I happened to pass by a compact queue waiting at the entrance of a food store; and there, at the very end, was my wife, straining on tiptoe to catch a glimpse of what exactly was being sold. I think the first thing she said to me was that she hoped it was oranges.

Her tale seemed a trifle hazy, but perfectly banal. She had returned to Faugères and gone straight to the Commissariat instead of making inquiries at the station, where I had left a message for her. A party of refugees suggested that she join them; she spent the night in a bicycle shop with no bicycles, on the floor, together with three elderly women who lay, she said, like three logs in a row. Next day she realized that she had not enough money to reach Nice. Eventually she borrowed some from one of the log-women. She got into the wrong train, however, and traveled to a town the name of which she could not remember. She had arrived at Nice two days ago and had found some friends at the Russian church. They had told her I was somewhere around, looking for her, and would surely turn up soon.

Some time later, as I sat on the edge of the only chair in my garret and held her by her slender young hips (she was combing her soft hair and tossing her head back with every stroke), her dim smile changed all at once into an odd quiver and she placed one hand on my shoulder, staring down at me as if I were a reflection in a pool, which she had noticed for the first time.

"I've been lying to you, dear," she said. "*Ya lgunia.* I stayed for several nights in Montpellier with a brute of a man I met on the train. I did not want it at all. He sold hair lotions."

The time, the place, the torture. Her fan, her gloves, her mask. I spent that night and many others getting it out of her bit by bit, but not getting it all. I was under the strange delusion that first I must find out every detail, reconstruct every minute, and only then decide whether I could bear it. But the limit of desired knowledge was unattainable, nor could I ever foretell the approximate point after which I might imagine myself satiated, because of course the denominator of every fraction of knowledge was potentially as infinite as the number of intervals between the fractions themselves.

Oh, the first time she had been too tired to mind, and the next had not minded because she was sure I had deserted her; and she apparently considered that such explanations ought to be a kind of consolation prize for me instead of the nonsense and agony they really were. It went on like that for eons, she breaking down every now and then, but soon rallying again, answering my unprintable questions in a breathless whisper or trying with a pitiful smile to wriggle into the semisecurity of irrelevant commentaries, and I crushing and crushing the mad molar till my jaw almost burst with pain, a flaming pain which seemed somehow preferable to the dull, humming ache of humble endurance.

And mark, in between the periods of this inquest, we were trying to get from reluctant authorities certain papers which in their turn would make it lawful to apply for a third kind which would serve as a steppingstone towards a permit enabling the holder to apply for yet other papers which might or might not give him the means of discovering how and why it had happened. For even if I could imagine the accursed recurrent scene, I failed to link up its sharp-angled grotesque shadows with the dim limbs of my wife as she shook and rattled and dissolved in my violent grasp.

So nothing remained but to torture each other, to write for hours on end in the Prefecture, filling forms, conferring with friends who had already probed the innermost viscera of all visas, pleading with secretaries, and filling forms again, with the result that her lusty and versatile traveling salesman became blended in a ghastly mix-up with rat-whiskered snarling officials, rotting bundles of obsolete records, the reek of violet ink, bribes slipped under gangrenous blotting paper, fat flies tickling moist necks with their rapid cold padded feet, new-laid clumsy concave photographs of your six subhuman doubles, the tragic eyes and patient politeness of petitioners born in Slutzk, Starodub, or Bobruisk, the funnels and pulleys of the Holy Inquisition, the awful smile of the bald man with the glasses, who had been told that his passport could not be found.

I confess that one evening, after a particularly abominable day, I sank down on a stone bench weeping and cursing a mock world where millions of lives were being juggled by the clammy hands of consuls and *commissaires*. I noticed she was crying too, and then I told her that nothing would really have mattered the way it mattered now, had she not gone and done what she did.

"You will think me crazy," she said with a vehemence that, for a second, almost made a real person of her, "but I didn't—I swear that I didn't. Perhaps I live several lives at once. Perhaps I wanted to test you. Perhaps this bench is a dream and we are in Saratov or on some star."

It would be tedious to niggle the different stages through which I passed before accepting finally the first version of her delay. I did not talk to her and was a good deal alone. She would glimmer and fade, and reappear with some trifle she thought I would appreciate—a handful of cherries, three precious cigarettes or the like—treating me with the unruffled mute sweetness of a nurse that trips from and to a gruff convalescent. I ceased visiting most of our mutual friends because they had lost all interest in my passport affairs and seemed to have turned vaguely inimical. I composed several poems. I drank all the wine I could get. I clasped her one day to my groaning breast, and we went for a week to Caboule and lay on the round pink pebbles of the narrow beach. Strange to say, the happier our new relations seemed, the stronger I felt an undercurrent of poignant sadness, but I kept telling myself that this was an intrinsic feature of all true bliss.

In the meantime, something had shifted in the moving pattern of our fates and at last I emerged from a dark and hot office with a couple of plump *visas de sortie* cupped in my trembling hands. Into these the U.S.A. serum was duly injected, and I dashed to Marseilles and managed to get tickets for the very next boat. I returned and tramped up the stairs. I saw a rose in a glass on the table—the sugar pink of its obvious beauty, the parasitic air bubbles clinging to its stem. Her two spare dresses were gone, her comb was gone, her checkered coat was gone, and so was the mauve hairband with a mauve bow that had been her hat. There was no note pinned to the pillow, nothing at all in the room to enlighten me, for of course the rose was merely what French rhymesters call *une cheville*.

I went to the Veretennikovs, who could tell me nothing; to the Hellmans, who refused to say anything; and to the Elagins, who were not sure whether to tell me or not. Finally the old lady—and you know what Anna Vladimirovna is like at crucial moments—asked for her rubber-tipped cane, heavily but energetically dislodged her bulk from her favorite armchair, and took me into the garden. There she informed me that, being twice my age, she had the right to say I was a bully and a cad.

You must imagine the scene: the tiny graveled garden with its blue Arabian Nights jar and solitary cypress; the cracked terrace where the old lady's father had dozed with a rug on his knees when he retired from his Novgorod governorship to spend a few last evenings in Nice; the pale-green sky; a whiff of vanilla in the deepening dusk; the crickets emitting their metallic trill pitched at two octaves above middle C; and Anna Vladimirovna, the folds of her cheeks jerkily dangling as she flung at me a motherly but quite undeserved insult.

During several preceding weeks, my dear V., every time she had visited by herself the three or four families we both knew, my ghostly wife had filled the eager ears of all those kind people with an extraordinary story. To wit: that she had madly fallen in love with a young Frenchman who could give her a turreted home and a crested name; that she had implored me for a divorce and I had refused; that in fact I had said I would rather shoot her and myself than sail to New York alone; that she had said her father in a similar case had acted like a gentleman; that I had answered I did not give a hoot for her *cocu de père*.

There were loads of other preposterous details of the kind—but they all hung together in such a remarkable fashion that no wonder the old lady made me swear I would not seek to pursue the lovers with a cocked pistol. They had gone, she said, to a château in Lozère. I inquired whether she had ever set eyes upon the man. No, but she had been shown his picture. As I was about to leave, Anna Vladimirovna, who had slightly relaxed and had even given me her five fingers to kiss, suddenly flared up again, struck the gravel with her cane, and said in her deep strong voice: "But one thing I shall never forgive you—her dog, that poor beast which you hanged with your own hands before leaving Paris."

Whether the gentleman of leisure had changed into a traveling salesman, or whether the metamorphosis had been reversed, or whether again he was neither the one nor the other, but the nondescript Russian who had courted her before our marriage—all this was absolutely inessential. She had gone. That was the end. I should have been a fool had I begun the nightmare business of searching and waiting for her all over again.

On the fourth morning of a long and dismal sea voyage, I met on the deck a solemn but pleasant old doctor with whom I had played chess in Paris. He asked me whether my wife was very much incommoded by the rough seas. I answered that I had sailed alone; whereupon he looked taken aback and then said he had seen her a couple of days before going on board, namely in Marseilles, walking, rather aimlessly he thought, along the embankment. She said that I would presently join her with bag and tickets.

This is, I gather, the point of the whole story—although if you write it, you had better not make him a doctor, as that kind of thing has been overdone. It was at that moment that I suddenly knew for certain that she had never existed at all. I shall tell you another thing. When I arrived I hastened to satisfy a certain morbid curiosity: I went to the address she had given me once; it proved to be an anonymous gap between two office buildings; I looked for her uncle's name in the directory; it was not there; I made some inquiries, and Gekko, who knows everything, informed me that the man and his horsey wife existed all right, but had moved to San Francisco after their deaf little girl had died.

Viewing the past graphically, I see our mangled romance engulfed in a deep valley of mist between the crags of two matter-of-fact mountains: life had been real before, life will be real from now on, I hope. Not tomorrow, though. Perhaps after tomorrow. You, happy mortal, with your lovely family (how is Ines? how are the twins?) and your diversified work (how are the lichens?), can hardly be expected to puzzle out my misfortune in terms of human communion, but you may clarify things for me through the prism of your art.

Yet the pity of it. Curse your art, I am hideously unhappy. She keeps on walking to and fro where the brown nets are spread to dry on the hot stone slabs and the dappled light of the water plays on the side of a moored fishing boat. Somewhere, somehow, I have made some fatal mistake. There are tiny pale bits of broken fish scales glistening here and there in the brown meshes. It may all end in *Aleppo* if I am not careful. Spare me, V.: you would load your dice with an unbearable implication if you took that for a title.

John Steinbeck 1902–

The Chrysanthemums

The high gray-flannel fog of winter closed the Salinas Valley from the sky and from all the rest of the world. On every side it sat like a lid on the mountains and made of the great valley a closed pot. On the broad, level land floor the gang plows bit deep and left the black earth shining like metal where the shares had cut. On the foot-hill ranches across the Salinas River the yellow stubble fields seemed to be bathed in pale cold sunshine; but there was no sunshine in the valley now in December. The thick willow scrub along the river flamed with sharp and positive yellow leaves.

It was a time of quiet and of waiting. The air was cold and tender. A light wind blew up from the southwest so that the farmers were mildly hopeful of a good rain before long; but fog and rain do not go together.

Across the river, on Henry Allen's foot-hill ranch there was little work to be done, for the hay was cut and stored and the orchards were plowed up to receive the rain deeply when it should come. The cattle on the higher slopes were becoming shaggy and rough-coated.

Elisa Allen, working in her flower garden, looked down across the yard and saw Henry, her husband, talking to two men in business suits. The three of them stood by the tractor shed, each man with one foot on the side of the Little Fordson. They smoked cigarettes and studied the machine as they talked.

Elisa watched them for a moment and then went back to her work. She was thirty-five. Her face was lean and strong and her eyes were as clear as water. Her figure looked blocked and heavy in her gardening costume, a man's black hat pulled low down over her eyes, clodhopper shoes, a figured print dress almost completely covered by a big corduroy apron with four big pockets to hold the snips, the trowel and scratcher, the seeds and the knife she worked with. She wore heavy leather gloves to protect her hands while she worked.

She was cutting down the old year's chrysanthemum stalks with a pair of short and powerful scissors. She looked down toward the men by the tractor shed now and then. Her face was eager and mature and handsome;

even her work with the scissors was over-eager, over-powerful. The chrysan-themum stems seemed too small and easy for her energy.

She brushed a cloud of hair out of her eyes with the back of her glove, and left a smudge of earth on her cheek in doing it. Behind her stood the neat white farmhouse with red geraniums close-banked round it as high as the windows. It was a hard-swept looking little house, with hard-polished windows, and a clean mat on the front steps.

Elisa cast another glance toward the tractor shed. The stranger men were getting into their Ford coupé. She took off a glove and put her strong fingers down into the forest of new green chysanthemum sprouts that were growing round the old roots. She spread the leaves and looked down among the close-growing stems. No aphids were there, no sow bugs nor snails nor cutworms. Her terrier fingers destroyed such pests before they could get started.

Elisa started at the sound of her husband's voice. He had come near quietly and he leaned over the wire fence that protected her flower garden from cattle and dogs and chickens.

"At it again," he said. "You've got a strong new crop coming."

Elisa straightened her back and pulled on the gardening glove again. "Yes. They'll be strong this coming year." In her tone and on her face there was a little smugness.

"You've got a gift with things," Henry observed. "Some of those yellow chrysanthemums you had last year were ten inches across. I wish you'd work out in the orchard and raise some apples that big."

Her eyes sharpened. "Maybe I could do it too. I've a gift with things all right. My mother had it. She could stick anything in the ground and make it grow. She said it was having planter's hands that knew how to do it."

"Well, it sure works with flowers," he said.

"Henry, who were those men you were talking to?"

"Why, sure, that's what I came to tell you. They were from the Western Meat Company. I sold those thirty head of three-year-old steers. Got nearly my own price too."

"Good," she said. "Good for you."

"And I thought," he continued, "I thought how it's Saturday afternoon, and we might go into Salinas for dinner at a restaurant and then to a pic-ture show—to celebrate, you see."

"Good," she repeated. "Oh, yes. That will be good."

Henry put on his joking tone. "There's fights to-night. How'd you like to go to the fights?"

"Oh, no," she said breathlessly. "No, I wouldn't like fights."

"Just fooling, Elisa. We'll go to a movie. Let's see. It's two now. I'm going to take Scotty and bring down those steers from the hill. It'll take us maybe two hours. We'll go in town about five and have dinner at the Co-minos Hotel. Like that?"

"Of course I'll like it. It's good to eat away from home."

"All right, then. I'll go get up a couple of horses."

She said, "I'll have plenty of time to transplant some of these sets, I guess."

She heard her husband calling Scotty down by the barn. And a little later she saw the two men ride up the pale-yellow hillside in search of the steers.

There was a little square sandy bed kept for rooting the chrysanthemums. With her trowel she turned the soil over and over and smoothed it and patted it firm. Then she dug ten parallel trenches to receive the sets. Back at the chrysanthemum bed she pulled out the little crisp shoots, trimmed off the leaves of each one with her scissors, and laid it on a small orderly pile.

A squeak of wheels and plod of hoofs came from the road. Elisa looked up. The country road ran along the dense bank of willows and cottonwoods that bordered the river, and up this road came a curious vehicle, curiously drawn. It was an old spring-wagon, with a round canvas top on it like the cover of a prairie schooner. It was drawn by an old bay horse and a little gray-and-white burro. A big stubble-bearded man sat between the cover flaps and drove the crawling team. Underneath the wagon, between the hind wheels, a lean and rangy mongrel dog walked sedately. Words were painted on the canvas in clumsy, crooked letters. "Pots, pans, knives, scissors, lawn mowers, Fixed." Two rows of articles, and the triumphantly definitive "Fixed" below. The black paint had run down in little sharp points beneath each letter.

Elisa, squatting on the ground, watched to see the crazy loose-jointed wagon pass by. But it didn't pass. It turned into the farm road in front of her house, crooked old wheels skirling and squeaking. The rangy dog darted from beneath the wheels and ran ahead. Instantly the two ranch shepherds flew out at him. Then all three stopped, and with stiff and quivering tails, with taut straight legs, with ambassadorial dignity, they slowly circled, sniffing daintily. The caravan pulled up to Elisa's wire fence and stopped. Now the newcomer dog, feeling outnumbered, lowered his tail and retired under the wagon with raised hackles and bared teeth.

The man on the wagon seat called out, "That's a bad dog in a fight when he gets started."

Elisa laughed. "I see he is. How soon does he generally get started?"

The man caught up her laughter and echoed it heartily. "Sometimes not for weeks and weeks," he said. He climbed stiffly down over the wheel. The horse and the donkey dropped like unwatered flowers.

Elisa saw that he was a very big man. Although his hair and beard were graying, he did not look old. His worn black suit was wrinkled and spotted with grease. The laughter had disappeared from his face and eyes the moment his laughing voice ceased. His eyes were dark and they were full of the brooding that gets in the eyes of teamsters and of sailors. The calloused hands he rested on the fence were cracked, and every crack was a black line. He took off his battered hat.

"I'm off my general road, ma'am," he said. "Does this dirt road cut over across the river to the Los Angeles highway?"

Elisa stood up and shoved the thick scissors in her apron pocket. "Well, yes, it does, but it winds around and then fords the river. I don't think your team could pull through the sand."

He replied with some asperity, "It might surprise you what them beasts can pull through."

"When they get started?" she asked.

He smiled for a second. "Yes. When they get started."

"Well," said Elisa, "I think you'll save time if you go back to the Salinas road and pick up the highway there."

He drew a big finger down the chicken wire and made it sing. "I ain't in any hurry, ma'am. I go from Seattle to San Diego and back every year. Takes all my time. About six months each way. I aim to follow nice weather."

Elisa took off her gloves and stuffed them in the apron pocket with the scissors. She touched the under edge of her man's hat, searching for fugitive hairs. "That sounds like a nice kind of a way to live," she said.

He leaned confidentially over the fence. "Maybe you noticed the writing on my wagon. I mend pots and sharpen knives and scissors. You got any of them things to do?"

"Oh, no," she said quickly. "Nothing like that." Her eyes hardened with resistance.

"Scissors is the worst thing," he explained. "Most people just ruin scissors trying to sharpen 'em, but I know how. I got a special tool. It's a little bobbit kind of thing and patented. But it sure does the trick."

"No. My scissors are all sharp."

"All right, then. Take a pot," he continued earnestly, "a bent pot or a pot with a hole. I can make it like new so you don't have to buy no new ones. That's a saving for you."

"No," she said shortly. "I tell you I have nothing like that for you to do."

His face fell to an exaggerated sadness. His voice took on a whining undertone. "I ain't had a thing to do to-day. Maybe I won't have no supper to-night. You see I'm off my regular road. I know folks on the highway clear from Seattle to San Diego. They save their things for me to sharpen up because they know I do it so good and save them money."

"I'm sorry," Elisa said irritably. "I haven't anything for you to do."

His eyes left her face and fell to searching the ground. They roamed about until they came to the chrysanthemum bed where she had been working. "What's them plants, ma'am?"

The irritation and resistance melted from Elisa's face. "Oh, those are chrysanthemums, giant whites and yellows. I raise them every year, bigger than anybody around here."

"Kind of a long-stemmed flower? Looks like a quick puff of colored smoke?" he asked.

"That's it. What a nice way to describe them."

"They smell kind of nasty till you get used to them," he said.

"It's a good bitter smell," she retorted, "not nasty at all."

He changed his tone quickly. "I like the smell myself."

"I had ten-inch blooms this year," she said.

The man leaned farther over the fence. "Look. I know a lady down the road a piece has got the nicest garden you ever seen. Got nearly every kind of flower but no chrysanthemums. Last time I was mending a copper-bottom wash tub for her (that's a hard job but I do it good), she said to me, 'If you ever run acrost some nice chrysanthemums I wish you'd try to get me a few seeds.' That's what she told me."

Elisa's eyes grew alert and eager. "She couldn't have known much about chrysanthemums. You *can* raise them from seed, but it's much easier to root the little sprouts you see there."

"Oh," he said. "I s'pose I can't take none to her, then."

"Why, yes, you can," Elisa cried. "I can put some in damp sand, and you can carry them right along with you. They'll take root in the pot if you keep them damp. And then she can transplant them."

"She'd sure like to have some, ma'am. You say they're nice ones?"

"Beautiful," she said. "Oh, beautiful." Her eyes shone. She tore off the battered hat and shook out her dark pretty hair. "I'll put them in a flower pot, and you can take them right with you. Come into the yard."

While the man came through the picket gate Elisa ran excitedly along the geranium-bordered path to the back of the house. And she returned carrying a big red flower pot. The gloves were forgotten now. She kneeled on the ground by the starting bed and dug up the sandy soil with her fingers and scooped it into the bright new flower pot. Then she picked up the little pile of shoots she had prepared. With her strong fingers she pressed them into the sand and tamped round them with her knuckles. The man stood over her. "I'll tell you what to do," she said. "You remember so you can tell the lady."

"Yes, I'll try to remember."

"Well, look. These will take root in about a month. Then she must set them out, about a foot apart in good rich earth like this, see?" She lifted a handful of dark soil for him to look at. "They'll grow fast and tall. Now remember this. In July tell her to cut them down, about eight inches from the ground."

"Before they bloom?" he asked.

"Yes, before they bloom." Her face was tight with eagerness. "They'll grow right up again. About the last of September the buds will start."

She stopped and seemed perplexed. "It's the budding that takes the most care," she said hesitantly. "I don't know how to tell you." She looked deep into his eyes searchingly. Her mouth opened a little, and she seemed to be listening. "I'll try to tell you," she said. "Did you ever hear of planting hands?"

"Can't say I have, ma'am."

"Well, I can only tell you what it feels like. It's when you're picking off the buds you don't want. Everything goes right down into your fingertips. You watch your fingers work. They do it themselves. You can feel how it is. They pick and pick the buds. They never make a mistake. They're with the plant. Do you see? Your fingers and the plant. You can feel that, right up your arm. They know. They never make a mistake. You can feel it. When you're like that, you can't do anything wrong. Do you see that? Can you understand that?"

She was kneeling on the ground looking up at him. Her breast swelled passionately.

The man's eyes narrowed. He looked away self-consciously. "Maybe I know," he said. "Sometimes in the night in the wagon there—"

Elisa's voice grew husky. She broke in on him. "I've never lived as you do, but I know what you mean. When the night is dark—the stars are sharp-pointed, and there's quiet. Why, you rise up and up!"

Kneeling there, her hand went out toward his legs in the greasy black trousers. Her hesitant fingers almost touched the cloth. Then her hand dropped to the ground.

He said, "It's nice, just like you say. Only when you don't have no dinner it ain't."

She stood up, then, very straight, and her face was ashamed. She held the flower pot out to him and placed it gently in his arms. "Here. Put it in your wagon, on the seat, where you can watch it. Maybe I can find something for you to do."

At the back of the house she dug in the can pile and found two old and battered aluminum saucepans. She carried them back and gave them to him. "Here, maybe you can fix these."

His manner changed. He became professional. "Good as new I can fix them." At the back of his wagon he set a little anvil, and out of an oily tool box dug a small machine hammer. Elisa came through the gate to watch him while he pounded out the dents in the kettles. His mouth grew sure and knowing. At a difficult part of the work he sucked his underlip.

"You sleep right in the wagon?" Elisa asked.

"Right in the wagon, ma'am. Rain or shine I'm dry as a cow in there."

"It must be nice," she said. "It must be very nice. I wish women could do such things."

"It ain't the right kind of a life for a woman."

Her upper lip raised a little, showing her teeth. "How do you know? How can you tell?" she said.

"I don't know, ma'am," he protested. "Of course I don't know. Now here's your kettles, done. You don't have to buy no new ones."

"How much?"

"Oh, fifty cents'll do. I keep my prices down and my work good. That's why I have all them satisfied customers up and down the highway."

Elisa brought him a fifty-cent piece from the house and dropped it in his hand. "You might be surprised to have a rival sometime. I can sharpen scissors too. And I can beat the dents out of little pots. I could show you what a woman might do."

He put his hammer back in the oily box and shoved the little anvil out of sight. "It would be a lonely life for a woman, ma'am, and a scary life, too, with animals creeping under the wagon all night." He climbed over the singletree, steadying himself with a hand on the burro's white rump. He settled himself in the seat, picked up the lines. "Thank you kindly, ma'am," he said. "I'll do like you told me; I'll go back and catch the Salinas road."

"Mind," she called, "if you're long in getting there, keep the sand damp."

"Sand, ma'am—sand? Oh, sure. You mean around the chrysanthemums. Sure I will." He clucked his tongue. The beasts leaned luxuriously into their collars. The mongrel dog took his place between the back wheels. The wagon turned and crawled out the entrance road and back the way it had come, along the river.

Elisa stood in front of her wire fence watching the slow progress of the caravan. Her shoulders were straight, her head thrown back, her eyes half-closed, so that the scene came vaguely into them. Her lips moved silently, forming the words "Good-by—good-by." Then she whispered, "That's a bright direction. There's a glowing there." The sound of her whisper startled her. She shook herself free and looked about to see whether anyone had been listening. Only the dogs had heard. They lifted their heads toward her from their sleeping in the dust, and then stretched out their chins and settled asleep again. Elisa turned and ran hurriedly into the house.

In the kitchen she reached behind the stove and felt the water tank. It was full of hot water from the noonday cooking. In the bathroom she tore off her soiled clothes and flung them into the corner. And then she scrubbed herself with a little block of pumice, legs and thighs, loins and chest and arms, until her skin was scratched and red. When she had dried herself she stood in front of a mirror in her bedroom and looked at her body. She tightened her stomach and threw out her chest. She turned and looked over her shoulder at her back.

After a while she began to dress slowly. She put on her newest underclothing and her nicest stockings and the dress which was the symbol of her prettiness. She worked carefully on her hair, pencilled her eyebrows, and rouged her lips.

Before she was finished, she heard the little thunder of hoofs and the shouts of Henry and his helper as they drove the red steers into the corral. She heard the gate bang shut and set herself for Henry's arrival.

His step sounded on the porch. He entered the house, calling, "Elisa, where are you?"

"In my room, dressing. I'm not ready. There's hot water for your bath. Hurry up. It's getting late."

When she heard him splashing in the tub, Elisa laid his dark suit on the bed, and shirt and socks and tie beside it. She stood his polished shoes on the floor beside the bed. Then she went to the porch and sat primly and stiffly down. She looked toward the river road where the willow-line was still yellow with frosted leaves so that under the high gray fog they seemed a thin band of sunshine. This was the only color in the gray afternoon. She sat unmoving for a long time.

Henry came banging out of the door, shoving his tie inside his vest as he came. Elisa stiffened and her face grew tight. Henry stopped short and looked at her. "Why—why, Elisa. You look so nice!"

"Nice? You think I look nice? What do you mean by 'nice'?"

Henry blundered on. "I don't know. I mean you look different, strong and happy."

"I am strong? Yes, strong. What do you mean 'strong'?"

He looked bewildered. "You're playing some kind of a game," he said helplessly. "It's a kind of a play. You look strong enough to break a calf over your knee, happy enough to eat it like a watermelon."

For a second she lost her rigidity. "Henry! Don't talk like that. You didn't know what you said." She grew complete again. "I am strong," she boasted. "I never knew before how strong."

Henry looked down toward the tractor shed, and when he brought his eyes back to her, they were his own again. "I'll get out the car. You can put on your coat while I'm starting."

Elisa went into the house. She heard him drive to the gate and idle down his motor, and then she took a long time to put on her hat. She pulled it here and pressed it there. When Henry turned the motor off she slipped into her coat and went out.

The little roadster bounced along on the dirt road by the river, raising the birds and driving the rabbits into the brush. Two cranes flapped heavily over the willow-line and dropped into the river-bed.

Far ahead on the road Elisa saw a dark speck in the dust. She suddenly felt empty. She did not hear Henry's talk. She tried not to look; she did not want to see the little heap of sand and green shoots, but she could not help herself. The chrysanthemums lay in the road close to the wagon tracks. But not the pot; he had kept that. As the car passed them, she remembered the good bitter smell, and a little shudder went through her. She felt ashamed of her strong planter's hands, that were no use, lying palms up in her lap.

The roadster turned a bend and she saw the caravan ahead. She swung full round toward her husband so that she could not see the little covered wagon and the mismatched team as the car passed.

In a moment they had left behind them the man who had not known or needed to know what she said, the bargainer. She did not look back.

To Henry she said loudly, to be heard above the motor, "It will be good, to-night, a good dinner."

"Now you're changed again," Henry complained. He took one hand from the wheel and patted her knee. "I ought to take you in to dinner oftener. It would be good for both of us. We get so heavy out on the ranch."

"Henry," she asked, "could we have wine at dinner?"

"Sure. Say! That will be fine."

She was silent for a while; then she said, "Henry, at those prize-fights do the men hurt each other very much?"

"Sometimes a little, not often. Why?"

"Well, I've read how they break noses, and blood runs down their chests. I've read how the fighting gloves get heavy and soggy with blood."

He looked round at her. "What's the matter, Elisa? I didn't know you read things like that." He brought the car to a stop, then turned to the right over the Salinas River bridge.

"Do any women ever go to the fights?" she asked.

"Oh, sure, some. What's the matter, Elisa? Do you want to go? I don't think you'd like it, but I'll take you if you really want to go."

She relaxed limply in the seat. "Oh, no. No, I don't want to go. I'm sure I don't." Her face was turned away from him. "It will be enough if we can have wine. It will be plenty." She turned up her coat collar so he could not see that she was crying weakly—like an old woman.

Lionel Trilling 1905–

Of This Time, Of That Place

I T W A S A fine September day. By noon it would be summer again but
now it was true autumn with a touch of chill in the air. As Joseph Howe
stood on the porch of the house in which he lodged, ready to leave for his
first class of the year, he thought with pleasure of the long indoor days that
were coming. It was a moment when he could feel glad of his profession.

On the lawn the peach tree was still in fruit and young Hilda Aiken was
taking a picture of it. She held the camera tight against her chest. She
wanted the sun behind her but she did not want her own long morning
shadow in the foreground. She raised the camera but that did not help,
and she lowered it but that made things worse. She twisted her body to the
left, then to the right. In the end she had to step out of the direct line of
the sun. At last she snapped the shutter and wound the film with intense
care.

Howe, watching her from the porch, waited for her to finish and called
good morning. She turned, startled, and almost sullenly lowered her glance.
In the year Howe had lived at the Aikens', Hilda had accepted him as one
of her family, but since his absence of the summer she had grown shy.
Then suddenly she lifted her head and smiled at him, and the humorous
smile confirmed his pleasure in the day. She picked up her bookbag and set
off for school.

The handsome houses on the streets to the college were not yet fully
awake but they looked very friendly. Howe went by the Bradby house
where he would be a guest this evening at the first dinner-party of the year.
When he had gone the length of the picket fence, the whitest in town, he
turned back. Along the path there was a fine row of asters and he went
through the gate and picked one for his buttonhole. The Bradbys would
be pleased if they happened to see him invading their lawn and the knowledge of this made him even more comfortable.

He reached the campus as the hour was striking. The students were hurrying to their classes. He himself was in no hurry. He stopped at his dim
cubicle of an office and lit a cigarette. The prospect of facing his class had

204

suddenly presented itself to him and his hands were cold, the lawful seizure of power he was about to make seemed momentous. Waiting did not help. He put out his cigarette, picked up a pad of theme paper and went to his classroom.

As he entered, the rattle of voices ceased and the twenty-odd freshmen settled themselves and looked at him appraisingly. Their faces seemed gross, his heart sank at their massed impassivity, but he spoke briskly.

"My name is Howe," he said and turned and wrote it on the blackboard. The carelessness of the scrawl confirmed.his authority. He went on: "My office is 412 Slemp Hall and my office hours are Monday, Wednesday, and Friday from eleven-thirty to twelve-thirty."

He wrote: "M., W., F., 11.30–12.30." He said: "I'll be very glad to see any of you at that time. Or if you can't come then, you can arrange with me for some other time."

He turned again to the blackboard and spoke over his shoulder. "The text for the course is Jarman's _Modern Plays_, revised edition. The Co-op has it in stock." He wrote the name, underlined "revised edition" and waited for it to be taken down in the new note-books.

When the bent heads were raised again he began his speech of prospectus. "It is hard to explain——" he said, and paused as they composed themselves. "It is hard to explain what a course like this is intended to do. We are going to try to learn something about modern literature and something about prose composition."

As he spoke, his hands warmed and he was able to look directly at the class. Last year on the first day the faces had seemed just as cloddish, but as the term wore on they became gradually alive and quite likeable. It did not seem possible that the same thing could happen again.

"I shall not lecture in this course," he continued. "Our work will be carried on by discussion and we will try to learn by an exchange of opinion. But you will soon recognize that my opinion is worth more than anyone else's here."

He remained grave as he said it, but two boys understood and laughed. The rest took permission from them and laughed too. All Howe's private ironies protested the vulgarity of the joke but the laughter made him feel benign and powerful.

When the little speech was finished, Howe picked up the pad of paper he had brought. He announced that they would write an extemporaneous theme. Its subject was traditional: "Who I am and why I came to Dwight College." By now the class was more at ease and it gave a ritualistic groan of protest. Then there was a stir as fountain-pens were brought out and the writing arms of the chairs were cleared and the paper was passed about. At last all the heads bent to work and the room became still.

Howe sat idly at his desk. The sun shone through the tall clumsy windows. The cool of the morning was already passing. There was a scent of autumn and of varnish, and the stillness of the room was deep and oddly touching. Now and then a student's head was raised and scratched in the old elaborate students' pantomime that calls the teacher to witness honest intellectual effort.

Suddenly a tall boy stood within the frame of the open door. "Is this," he said, and thrust a large nose into a college catalogue, "is this the meeting place of English 1A? The section instructed by Dr. Joseph Howe?"

He stood on the very sill of the door, as if refusing to enter until he was perfectly sure of all his rights. The class looked up from work, found him absurd and gave a low mocking cheer.

The teacher and the new student, with equal pointedness, ignored the disturbance. Howe nodded to the boy, who pushed his head forward and then jerked it back in a wide elaborate arc to clear his brow of a heavy lock of hair. He advanced into the room and halted before Howe, almost at attention. In a loud clear voice he announced: "I am Tertan, Ferdinand R., reporting at the direction of Head of Department Vincent."

The heraldic formality of this statement brought forth another cheer. Howe looked at the class with a sternness he could not really feel, for there was indeed something ridiculous about this boy. Under his displeased regard the rows of heads dropped to work again. Then he touched Tertan's elbow, led him up to the desk and stood so as to shield their conversation from the class.

"We are writing an extemporaneous theme," he said. "The subject is: 'Who I am and why I came to Dwight College.' "

He stripped a few sheets from the pad and offered them to the boy. Tertan hesitated and then took the paper, but he held it only tentatively. As if with the effort of making something clear, he gulped, and a slow smile fixed itself on his face. It was at once knowing and shy.

"Professor," he said, "to be perfectly fair to my classmates"—he made a large gesture over the room—"and to you"—he inclined his head to Howe —"this would not be for me an extemporaneous subject."

Howe tried to understand. "You mean you've already thought about it —you've heard we always give the same subject? That doesn't matter."

Again the boy ducked his head and gulped. It was the gesture of one who wishes to make a difficult explanation with perfect candor. "Sir," he said, and made the distinction with great care, "the topic I did not expect but I have given much ratiocination to the subject."

Howe smiled and said: "I don't think that's an unfair advantage. Just go ahead and write."

Tertan narrowed his eyes and glanced sidewise at Howe. His strange mouth smiled. Then in quizzical acceptance, he ducked his head, threw back the heavy dank lock, dropped into a seat with a great loose noise and began to write rapidly.

The room fell silent again and Howe resumed his idleness. When the bell rang, the students who had groaned when the task had been set now groaned again because they had not finished. Howe took up the papers and held the class while he made the first assignment. When he dismissed it, Tertan bore down on him, his slack mouth held ready for speech.

"Some professors," he said, "are pedants. They are Dryasdusts. However, some professors are free souls and creative spirits. Kant, Hegel, and Nietzsche were all professors." With this pronouncement he paused. "It is my opinion," he continued, "that you occupy the second category."

Howe looked at the boy in surprise and said with good-natured irony: "With Kant, Hegel, and Nietzsche?"

Not only Tertan's hand and head but his whole awkward body waved away the stupidity. "It is the kind and not the quantity of the kind," he said sternly.

Rebuked, Howe said as simply and seriously as he could: "It would be nice to think so." He added: "Of course, I am not a professor."

This was clearly a disappointment but Tertan met it. "In the French sense," he said with composure. "Generically, a teacher."

Suddenly he bowed. It was such a bow, Howe fancied, as a stage-director might teach an actor playing a medieval student who takes leave of Abelard —stiff, solemn, with elbows close to the body and feet together. Then, quite as suddenly, he turned and left.

A queer fish, and as soon as Howe reached his office he sifted through the batch of themes and drew out Tertan's. The boy had filled many sheets with his unformed headlong scrawl. "Who am I?" he had begun. "Here, in a mundane, not to say commercialized academe, is asked the question which from time long immemorably out of mind has accreted doubts and thoughts in the psyche of man to pester him as a nuisance. Whether in St. Augustine (or Austin as sometimes called) or Miss Bashkirtsieff or Frederic Amiel or Empedocles, or in less lights of the intellect than these, this posed question has been ineluctable."

Howe took out his pencil. He circled "academe" and wrote "vocab." in the margin. He underlined "time long immemorably out of mind" and wrote "Diction!" But this seemed inadequate for what was wrong. He put down his pencil and read ahead to discover the principle of error in the theme. "To-day as ever, in spite of gloomy prophets of the dismal science (economics) the question is uninvalidated. Out of the starry depths of heaven hurtles this spear of query demanding to be caught on the shield of the mind ere it pierces the skull and the limbs be unstrung."

Baffled but quite caught, Howe read on. "Materialism, by which is meant the philosophic concept and not the moral idea, provides no aegis against the question which lies beyond the tangible (metaphysics). Existence without alloy is the question presented. Environment and heredity relegated aside, the rags and old clothes of practical life discarded, the name and the instrumentality of livelihood do not, as the prophets of the dismal science insist on in this connection, give solution to the interrogation which not from the professor merely but veritably from the cosmos is given. I think, therefore I am (cogito etc.) but who am I? Tertan I am, but what is Tertan? Of this time, of that place, of some parentage, what does it matter?"

Existence without alloy: the phrase established itself. Howe put aside Tertan's paper and at random picked up another. "I am Arthur J. Casebeer, Jr.," he read. "My father is Arthur J. Casebeer and my grandfather was Arthur J. Casebeer before him. My mother is Nina Wimble Casebeer. Both of them are college graduates and my father is in insurance. I was born in St. Louis eighteen years ago and we still make our residence there."

Arthur J. Casebeer, who knew who he was, was less interesting than Tertan, but more coherent. Howe picked up Tertan's paper again. It was clear that none of the routine marginal comments, no "sent. str." or "punct." or "vocab." could cope with this torrential rhetoric. He read ahead, contenting himself with underscoring the errors against the time when he should have the necessary "conference" with Tertan.

It was a busy and official day of cards and sheets, arrangements and small decisions, and it gave Howe pleasure. Even when it was time to attend the first of the weekly Convocations he felt the charm of the beginning of things when intention is still innocent and uncorrupted by effort. He sat among the young instructors on the platform and joined in their humorous complaints at having to assist at the ceremony, but actually he got a clear satisfaction from the ritual of prayer and prosy speech and even from wearing his academic gown. And when the Convocation was over the pleasure continued as he crossed the campus, exchanging greetings with men he had not seen since the spring. They were people who did not yet, and perhaps never would, mean much to him, but in a year they had grown amiably to be part of his life. They were his fellow-townsmen.

The day had cooled again at sunset and there was a bright chill in the September twilight. Howe carried his voluminous gown over his arm, he swung his doctoral hood by its purple neckpiece and on his head he wore his mortarboard with its heavy gold tassel bobbing just over his eye. These were the weighty and absurd symbols of his new profession and they pleased him. At twenty-six Joseph Howe had discovered that he was neither so well off nor so bohemian as he had once thought. A small income, adequate when supplemented by a sizable cash legacy, was genteel poverty when the cash was all spent. And the literary life—the room at the Lafayette or the small apartment without a lease, the long summers on the Cape, the long afternoons and the social evenings—began to weary him. His writing filled his mornings and should perhaps have filled his life, yet it did not. To the amusement of his friends and with a certain sense that he was betraying his own freedom, he had used the last of his legacy for a year at Harvard.

The small but respectable reputation of his two volumes of verse had proved useful—he continued at Harvard on a fellowship and when he emerged as Dr. Howe he received an excellent appointment, with prospects, at Dwight.

He had his moments of fear when all that had ever been said of the dangers of the academic life had occurred to him. But after a year in which he had tested every possibility of corruption and seduction he was ready to rest easy. His third volume of verse, most of it written in his first year of teaching, was not only ampler but, he thought, better than its predecessors.

There was a clear hour before the Bradby dinner-party and Howe looked forward to it. But he was not to enjoy it, for lying with his mail on the hall table was a copy of this quarter's issue of *Life and Letters*, to which his landlord subscribed. Its severe cover announced that its editor, Frederic Woolley, had this month contributed an essay called "Two Poets," and Howe, picking it up, curious to see who the two poets might be, felt his own name start out at him with cabalistic power—Joseph Howe. As he continued to turn the pages his hand trembled.

Standing in the dark hall, holding the neat little magazine, Howe knew that his literary contempt for Frederic Woolley meant nothing, for he suddenly understood how he respected Woolley in the way of the world. He knew this by the trembling of his hand. And of the little world as well as the great, for although the literary groups of New York might dismiss Woolley, his name carried high authority in the academic world. At Dwight it was even a revered name, for it had been here at the college that Frederic Woolley had made the distinguished scholarly career from which he had gone on to literary journalism. In middle life he had been induced to take the editorship of *Life and Letters*, a literary monthly not widely read but heavily endowed and in its pages he had carried on the defence of what he sometimes called the older values. He was not without wit, he had great knowledge and considerable taste and even in the full movement of the "new" literature he had won a certain respect for his refusal to accept it. In France, even in England, he would have been connected with a more robust tradition of conservatism, but America gave him an audience not much better than genteel. It was known in the college that to the subsidy of *Life and Letters* the Bradbys contributed a great part.

As Howe read, he saw that he was involved in nothing less than an event. When the Fifth Series of *Studies in Order and Value* came to be collected, this latest of Frederic Woolley's essays would not be merely another step in the old direction. Clearly and unmistakably, it was a turning-point. All his literary life Woolley had been concerned with the relation of literature to morality, religion, and the private and delicate pieties, and he had been unalterably opposed to all that he had called "inhuman humanitarianism." But here, suddenly, dramatically late, he had made an about-face, turning to the public life and to the humanitarian politics he had so long despised. This was the kind of incident the histories of literature make much of. Frederic Woolley was opening for himself a new career and winning a kind of new youth. He contrasted the two poets, Thomas Wormser who was admirable, Joseph Howe who was almost dangerous. He spoke of the "precious subjectivism" of Howe's verse. "In times like ours," he wrote, "with millions facing penury and want, one feels that the qualities of the *tour d'ivoire* are well nigh inhuman, nearly insulting. The *tour d'ivoire* becomes the *tour d'ivresse* and it is not self-intoxicated poets that our people need." The essay said more: "The problem is one of meaning. I am not ignorant that the creed of the esoteric poets declares that a poem does not and should not *mean* anything, that it *is* something. But poetry is what the poet makes it, and if he is a true poet he makes what his society needs. And what is needed now is the tradition in which Mr. Wormser writes, the true tradition of poetry. The Howes do no harm, but they do no good when positive good is demanded of all responsible men. Or do the Howes indeed do no harm? Perhaps Plato would have said they do, that in some ways theirs is the Phrygian music that turns men's minds from the struggle. Certainly it is true that Thomas Wormser writes in the lucid Dorian mode which sends men into battle with evil."

It was easy to understand why Woolley had chosen to praise Thomas Wormser. The long, lilting lines of *Corn Under Willows* hymned, as Woolley put it, the struggle for wheat in the Iowa fields and expressed the real lives of real people. But why out of the dozen more notable examples he had chosen Howe's little volume as the example of "precious subjectivism" was hard to guess. In a way it was funny, this multiplication of himself into "the Howes." And yet this becoming the multiform political symbol by whose creation Frederic Woolley gave the sign of a sudden new life, this use of him as a sacrifice whose blood was necessary for the rites of rejuvenation, made him feel oddly unclean.

Nor could Howe get rid of a certain practical resentment. As a poet he had a special and respectable place in the college life. But it might be another thing to be marked as the poet of a wilful and selfish obscurity.

As he walked to the Bradbys Howe ·was a little tense and defensive. It seemed to him that all the world knew of the "attack" and agreed with it. And indeed the Bradbys had read the essay, but Professor Bradby, a kind and pretentious man, said, "I see my old friend knocked you about a bit, my boy," and his wife Eugenia looked at Howe with her child-like blue eyes and said: "I shall *scold* Frederic for the untrue things he wrote about you. You aren't the least obscure." They beamed at him. In their genial snobbery they seemed to feel that he had distinguished himself. He was the leader of Howeism. He enjoyed the dinner-party as much as he had thought he would.

And in the following days, as he was more preoccupied with his duties, the incident was forgotten. His classes had ceased to be mere groups. Student after student detached himself from the mass and required or claimed a place in Howe's awareness. Of them all it was Tertan who first and most violently signalled his separate existence. A week after classes had begun Howe saw his silhouette on the frosted glass of his office door. It was motionless for a long time, perhaps stopped by the problem of whether or not to knock before entering. Howe called, "Come in!" and Tertan entered with his shambling stride.

He stood beside the desk, silent and at attention. When Howe asked him to sit down, he responded with a gesture of head and hand as if to say that such amenities were beside the point. Nevertheless he did take the chair. He put his ragged crammed brief-case between his legs. His face, which Howe now observed fully for the first time, was confusing, for it was made up of florid curves, the nose arched in the bone and voluted in the nostril, the mouth loose and soft and rather moist. Yet the face was so thin and narrow as to seem the very type of asceticism. Lashes of unusual length veiled the eyes and, indeed, it seemed as if there were a veil over the whole countenance. Before the words actually came, the face screwed itself into an attitude of preparation for them.

"You can confer with me now?" Tertan said.

"Yes, I'd be glad to. There are several things in your two themes I want to talk to you about." Howe reached for the packet of themes on his desk and sought for Tertan's. But the boy was waving them away.

"These are done perforce," he said. "Under the pressure of your requirement. They are not significant, mere duties." Again his great hand flapped vaguely to dismiss his themes. He leaned forward and gazed at his teacher.

"You are," he said, "a man of letters? You are a poet?" It was more declaration than question.

"I should like to think so," Howe said.

At first Tertan accepted the answer with a show of appreciation, as though the understatement made a secret between himself and Howe. Then he chose to misunderstand. With his shrewd and disconcerting control of expression, he presented to Howe a puzzled grimace. "What does that mean?" he said.

Howe retracted the irony. "Yes. I am a poet." It sounded strange to say.

"That," Tertan said, "is a wonder." He corrected himself with his ducking head. "I mean that is wonderful."

Suddenly he dived at the miserable brief-case between his legs, put it on his knees and began to fumble with the catch, all intent on the difficulty it presented. Howe noted that his suit was worn thin, his shirt almost unclean. He became aware, even, of a vague and musty odor of garments worn too long in unaired rooms. Tertan conquered the lock and began to concentrate upon a search into the interior. At last he held in his hand what he was after, a torn and crumpled copy of *Life and Letters*.

"I learned it from here," he said, holding it out.

Howe looked at him sharply, his hackles a little up. But the boy's face was not only perfectly innocent, it even shone with a conscious admiration. Apparently nothing of the import of the essay had touched him except the wonderful fact that his teacher was a "man of letters." Yet this seemed too stupid and Howe, to test it, said: "The man who wrote that doesn't think it's wonderful."

Tertan made a moist hissing sound as he cleared his mouth of saliva. His head, oddly loose on his neck, wove a pattern of contempt in the air. "A critic," he said, "who admits *prima facie* that he does not understand." Then he said grandly: "It is the inevitable fate."

It was absurd, yet Howe was not only aware of the absurdity but of a tension suddenly and wonderfully relaxed. Now that the "attack" was on the table between himself and this strange boy and subject to the boy's funny and absolutely certain contempt, the hidden force of his feeling was revealed to him in the very moment that it vanished. All unsuspected, there had been a film over the world, a transparent but discoloring haze of danger. But he had no time to stop over the brightened aspect of things. Tertan was going on. "I also am a man of letters. Putative."

"You have written a good deal?" Howe meant to be no more than polite and he was surprised at the tenderness he heard in his words.

Solemnly the boy nodded, threw back the dank lock and sucked in a deep anticipatory breath. "First, a work of homiletics, which is a defence of the principles of religious optimism against the pessimism of Schopenhauer and the humanism of Nietzsche."

"Humanism? Why do you call it humanism?"

"It is my nomenclature for making a deity of man," Tertan replied negligently. "Then three fictional works, novels. And numerous essays in science, combating materialism. Is it your duty to read these if I bring them to you?"

Howe answered simply: "No, it isn't exactly my duty, but I shall be happy to read them."

Tertan stood up and remained silent. He rested his bag on the chair. With a certain compunction—for it did not seem entirely proper that, of two men of letters, one should have the right to blue-pencil the other, to grade him or to question the quality of his "sentence structure"— Howe reached for Tertan's papers. But before he could take them up, the boy suddenly made his bow-to-Abelard, the stiff inclination of the body with the hands seeming to emerge from the scholar's gown. Then he was gone.

But after his departure something was still left of him. The timbre of his curious sentences, the downright finality of so quaint a phrase as "It is the inevitable fate" still rang in the air. Howe gave the warmth of his feeling to the new visitor who stood at the door announcing himself with a genteel clearing of the throat.

"Dr. Howe, I believe?" the student said. A large hand advanced into the room and grasped Howe's hand. "Blackburn, sir, Theodore Blackburn, vice-president of the Student Council. A great pleasure, sir."

Out of a pair of ruddy cheeks a pair of small eyes twinkled good-naturedly. The large face, the large body were not so much fat as beefy and suggested something "typical," monk, politician, or innkeeper.

Blackburn took the seat beside Howe's desk. "I may have seemed to introduce myself in my public capacity, sir," he said. "But it is really as an individual that I came to see you. That is to say, as one of your students to be."

He spoke with an "English" intonation and he went on: "I was once an English major, sir."

For a moment Howe was startled, for the roast-beef look of the boy and the manner of his speech gave a second's credibility to one sense of his statement. Then the collegiate meaning of the phrase asserted itself, but some perversity made Howe say what was not really in good taste even with so forward a student: "Indeed? What regiment?"

Blackburn stared and then gave a little pouf-pouf of laughter. He waved the misapprehension away. "*Very* good, sir. It certainly is an ambiguous term." He chuckled in appreciation of Howe's joke, then cleared his throat to put it aside. "I look forward to taking your course in the romantic poets, sir," he said earnestly. "To me the romantic poets are the very crown of English literature."

Howe made a dry sound, and the boy, catching some meaning in it, said: "Little as I know them, of course. But even Shakespeare who is so dear to us of the Anglo-Saxon tradition is in a sense but the preparation for Shelley, Keats and Byron. And Wadsworth."

Almost sorry for him, Howe dropped his eyes. With some embarrassment, for the boy was not actually his student, he said softly: "Wordsworth."

"Sir?"

"Wordsworth, not Wadsworth. You said Wadsworth."

"Did I, sir?" Gravely he shook his head to rebuke himself for the error. "Wordsworth, of course—slip of the tongue." Then, quite in command again, he went on. "I have a favor to ask of you, Dr. Howe. You see. I began my college course as an English major"—he smiled—"as I said."

"Yes?"

"But after my first year I shifted. I shifted to the social sciences. Sociology and government—I find them stimulating and very *real*." He paused, out of respect for reality. "But now I find that perhaps I have neglected the other side."

"The other side?" Howe said.

"Imagination, fancy, culture. A well-rounded man." He trailed off as if there were perfect understanding between them. "And so, sir, I have decided to end my senior year with your course in the romantic poets."

His voice was filled with an indulgence which Howe ignored as he said flatly and gravely: "But that course isn't given until the spring term."

"Yes, sir, and that is where the favor comes in. Would you let me take your romantic prose course? I can't take it for credit, sir, my program is full, but just for background it seems to me that I ought to take it. I do hope," he concluded in a manly way, "that you will consent."

"Well, it's no great favor, Mr. Blackburn. You can come if you wish, though there's not much point in it if you don't do the reading."

The bell rang for the hour and Howe got up.

"May I begin with this class, sir?" Blackburn's smile was candid and boyish.

Howe nodded carelessly and together, silently, they walked to the classroom down the hall. When they reached the door Howe stood back to let his student enter, but Blackburn moved adroitly behind him and grasped him by the arm to urge him over the threshold. They entered together with Blackburn's hand firmly on Howe's biceps, the student inducting the teacher into his own room. Howe felt a surge of temper rise in him and almost violently he disengaged his arm and walked to the desk, while Blackburn found a seat in the front row and smiled at him.

II

The question was: At whose door must the tragedy be laid?

All night the snow had fallen heavily and only now was abating in sparse little flurries. The windows were valanced high with white. It was very quiet, something of the quiet of the world had reached the class and Howe found that everyone was glad to talk or listen. In the room there was a comfortable sense of pleasure in being human.

Casebeer believed that the blame for the tragedy rested with heredity. Picking up the book he read: "The sins of the fathers are visited on their children." This opinion was received with general favor. Nevertheless Johnson ventured to say that the fault was all Pastor Manders' because the Pastor had made Mrs. Alving go back to her husband and was always hiding the truth. To this Hibbard objected with logic enough: "Well, then, it was really all her husband's fault. He *did* all the bad things." De Witt, his face bright with an impatient idea, said that the fault was all society's. "By society I don't mean upper-crust society," he said. He looked around a little defiantly, taking in any members of the class who might be members of upper-crust society. "'Not in that sense. I mean the social unit."

Howe nodded and said: "Yes, of course."

"If the society of the time had progressed far enough in science," De Witt went on, "then there would be no problem for Mr. Ibsen to write about. Captain Alving plays around a little, gives way to perfectly natural biological urges, and he gets a social disease, a venereal disease. If the disease is cured, no problem. Invent salvarsan and the disease is cured. The problem of heredity disappears and li'l Oswald just doesn't get paresis. No paresis, no problem—no problem, no play."

This was carrying the ark into battle and the class looked at De Witt with respectful curiosity. It was his usual way and on the whole they were sympathetic with his struggle to prove to Howe that science was better than literature. Still, there was something in his reckless manner that alienated them a little.

"Or take birth-control, for instance," De Witt went on. "If Mrs. Alving had had some knowledge of contraception, she wouldn't have had to have li'l Oswald at all. No li'l Oswald, no play."

The class was suddenly quieter. In the back row Stettenhover swung his great football shoulders in a righteous sulking gesture, first to the right, then to the left. He puckered his mouth ostentatiously. Intellect was always ending up by talking dirty.

Tertan's hand went up and Howe said: "Mr. Tertan." The boy shambled to his feet and began his long characteristic gulp. Howe made a motion with his fingers, as small as possible, and Tertan ducked his head and smiled in apology. He sat down. The class laughed. With more than half the term gone, Tertan had not been able to remember that one did not rise to speak. He seemed unable to carry on the life of the intellect without this mark of respect for it. To Howe the boy's habit of rising seemed to accord with the formal shabbiness of his dress. He never wore the casual sweaters and jackets of his classmates. Into the free and comfortable air of the college classroom he brought the stuffy sordid strictness of some crowded metropolitan high school.

"Speaking from one sense," Tertan began slowly, "there is no blame ascribable. From the sense of determinism, who can say where the blame lies? The preordained is the preordained and it cannot be said without rebellion against the universe, a palpable absurdity."

In the back row Stettenhover slumped suddenly in his seat, his heels held out before him, making a loud dry disgusted sound. His body sank until his neck rested on the back of his chair. He folded his hands across his belly and looked significantly out of the window, exasperated not only with Tertan but with Howe, with the class, with the whole system designed to encourage this kind of thing. There was a certain insolence in the movement and Howe flushed. As Tertan continued to speak, Howe walked casually towards the window and placed himself in the line of Stettenhover's vision. He stared at the great fellow, who pretended not to see him.

There was so much power in the big body, so much contempt in the Greek-athlete face under the crisp Greek-athlete curls, that Howe felt almost physical fear. But at last Stettenhover admitted him to focus and under his disapproving gaze sat up with slow indifference. His eyebrows raised high in resignation, he began to examine his hands. Howe relaxed and turned his attention back to Tertan.

"Flux of existence," Tertan was saying, "produces all things, so that judgment wavers. Beyond the phenomena, what? But phenomena are adumbrated and to them we are limited."

Howe saw it for a moment as perhaps it existed in the boy's mind— the world of shadows which are cast by a great light upon a hidden reality as in the old myth of the Cave. But the little brush with Stettenhover had tired him and he said irritably: "But come to the point, Mr. Tertan."

He said it so sharply that some of the class looked at him curiously. For three months he had gently carried Tertan through his verbosities, to the vaguely respectful surprise of the other students, who seemed to conceive that there existed between this strange classmate and their teacher some special understanding from which they were content to be excluded. Tertan looked at him mildly and at once came brilliantly to the point. "This is the summation of the play," he said and took up his book and read: " 'Your poor father never found any outlet for the overmastering joy of life that was in him. And I brought no holiday into his home, either. Everything seemed to turn upon duty and I am afraid I made your poor father's home unbearable to him, Oswald.' Spoken by Mrs. Alving."

Yes, that was surely the "summation" of the play and Tertan had hit it, as he hit, deviously and eventually, the literary point of almost everything. But now, as always, he was wrapping it away from sight. "For most mortals," he said, "there are only joys of biological urgings, gross and crass, such as the sensuous Captain Alving. For certain few there are the transmutations beyond these to a contemplation of the utter whole."

Oh, the boy was mad. And suddenly the word, used in hyperbole, intended almost for the expression of exasperated admiration, became literal. Now that the word was used, it became simply apparent to Howe that Tertan was mad.

It was a monstrous word and stood like a bestial thing in the room. Yet it so completely comprehended everything that had puzzled Howe, it so arranged and explained what for three months had been perplexing him that almost at once its horror became domesticated. With this word Howe was able to understand why he had never been able to communicate to Tertan the value of a single criticism or correction of his wild, verbose themes. Their conferences had been frequent and long but had done nothing to reduce to order the splendid confusion of the boy's ideas. Yet, impossible though its expression was, Tertan's incandescent mind could always strike for a moment into some dark corner of thought.

And now it was suddenly apparent that it was not a faulty rhetoric that Howe had to contend with. With his new knowledge he looked at Tertan's face and wondered how he could have so long deceived himself. Tertan was still talking and the class had lapsed into a kind of patient unconsciousness, a coma of respect for words which, for all that most of them knew, might be profound. Almost with a suffusion of shame, Howe believed that in some dim way the class had long ago had some intimation of Tertan's madness. He reached out as decisively as he could to seize the thread of Tertan's discourse before it should be entangled further.

"Mr. Tertan says that the blame must be put upon whoever kills the joy of living in another. We have been assuming that Captain Alving was a wholly bad man, but what if we assume that he became bad only because Mrs. Alving, when they were first married, acted towards him in the prudish way she says she did?"

It was a ticklish idea to advance to freshmen and perhaps not profitable. Not all of them were following.

"That would put the blame on Mrs. Alving herself, whom most of you admire. And she herself seems to think so." He glanced at his watch. The hour was nearly over. "What do you think, Mr. De Witt?"

De Witt rose to the idea, wanted to know if society couldn't be blamed for educating Mrs. Alving's temperament in the wrong way. Casebeer was puzzled, Stettenhover continued to look at his hands until the bell rang.

Tertan, his brows louring in thought, was making as always for a private word. Howe gathered his books and papers to leave quickly. At this moment of his discovery and with the knowledge still raw, he could not engage himself with Tertan. Tertan sucked in his breath to prepare for speech and Howe made ready for the pain and confusion. But at that moment Casebeer detached himself from the group with which he had been conferring and which he seemed to represent. His constituency remained at a tactful distance. The mission involved the time of an assigned essay. Casebeer's presentation of the plea—it was based on the freshmen's heavy duties at the fraternities during Carnival Week—cut across Tertan's preparations for speech. "And so some of us fellows thought," Casebeer concluded with heavy solemnity, "that we could do a better job, give our minds to it more, if we had more time."

Tertan regarded Casebeer with mingled curiosity and revulsion. Howe not only said that he would postpone the assignment but went on to talk about the Carnival and even drew the waiting constituency into the conversation. He was conscious of Tertan's stern and astonished stare, then of his sudden departure.

Now that the fact was clear, Howe knew that he must act on it. His course was simple enough. He must lay the case before the Dean. Yet he hesitated. His feeling for Tertan must now, certainly, be in some way invalidated. Yet could he, because of a word, hurry to assign to official and reasonable solicitude what had been, until this moment, so various and warm? He could at least delay and, by moving slowly, lend a poor grace to the necessary, ugly act of making his report.

It was with some notion of keeping the matter in his own hands that he went to the Dean's office to look up Tertan's records. In the outer office the Dean's secretary greeted him brightly and at his request brought him the manila folder with the small identifying photograph pasted in the corner. She laughed. "He was looking for the birdie in the wrong place," she said.

Howe leaned over her shoulder to look at the picture. It was as bad as all the Dean's office photographs were, but it differed from all that Howe had ever seen. Tertan, instead of looking into the camera, as no doubt he had been bidden, had, at the moment of exposure, turned his eyes upward. His mouth, as though conscious of the trick played on the photographer, had the sly superior look that Howe knew.

The secretary was fascinated by the picture. "What a funny boy," she said. "He looks like Tartuffe!"

And so he did, with the absurd piety of the eyes and the conscious slyness of the mouth and the whole face bloated by the bad lens.

"Is he *like* that?" the secretary said.

"Like Tartuffe? No."

From the photograph there was little enough comfort to be had. The records themselves gave no clue to madness, though they suggested sadness enough. Howe read of a father, Stanislaus Tertan, born in Budapest and trained in engineering in Berlin, once employed by the Hercules Chemical Corporation—this was one of the factories that dominated the south end of the town—but now without employment. He read of a mother Erminie (Youngfellow) Tertan, born in Manchester, educated at a Normal School at Leeds, now housewife by profession. The family lived on Greenbriar Street, which Howe knew as a row of once elegant homes near what was now the factory district. The old mansions had long ago been divided into small and primitive apartments. Of Ferdinand himself there was little to learn. He lived with his parents, had attended a Detroit high school and had transferred to the local school in his last year. His rating for intelligence, as expressed in numbers, was high, his scholastic record was remarkable, he held a college scholarship for his tuition.

Howe laid the folder on the secretary's desk. "Did you find what you wanted to know?" she asked.

The phrases from Tertan's momentous first theme came back to him. "Tertan I am, but what is Tertan? Of this time, of that place, of some parentage, what does it matter?"

"No, I didn't find it," he said.

Now that he had consulted the sad half-meaningless record he knew all the more firmly that he must not give the matter out of his own hands. He must not release Tertan to authority. Not that he anticipated from the Dean anything but the greatest kindness for Tertan. The Dean would have the experience and skill which he himself could not have. One way or another the Dean could answer the question: "What is Tertan?" Yet this was precisely what he feared. He alone could keep alive—not for ever but for a somehow important time—the question: "What is Tertan?" He alone could keep it still a question. Some sure instinct told him that he must not surrender the question to a clean official desk in a clear official light to be dealt with, settled and closed.

He heard himself saying: "Is the Dean busy at the moment? I'd like to see him."

His request came thus unbidden, even forbidden, and it was one of the surprising and startling incidents of his life. Later, when he reviewed the events, so disconnected in themselves or so merely odd, of the story that unfolded for him that year, it was over this moment, on its face the least notable, that he paused longest. It was frequently to be with fear and never without a certainty of its meaning in his own knowledge of himself that he would recall this simple, routine request and the feeling of shame and freedom it gave him as he sent everything down the official chute. In the end, of course, no matter what he did to "protect" Tertan, he would have had to make the same request and lay the matter on the Dean's clean desk. But it would always be a landmark of his life that, at the very moment when he was rejecting the official way, he had been, without will or intention, so gladly drawn to it.

After the storm's last delicate flurry, the sun had come out. Reflected by the new snow, it filled the office with a golden light which was almost musical in the way it made all the commonplace objects of efficiency shine with a sudden sad and noble significance. And the light, now that he noticed it, made the utterance of his perverse and unwanted request even more momentous.

The secretary consulted the engagement pad. "He'll be free any minute. Don't you want to wait in the parlor?"

She threw open the door of the large and pleasant room in which the Dean held his Committee meetings and in which his visitors waited. It was designed with a homely elegance on the masculine side of the eighteenth-century manner. There was a small coal fire in the grate and the handsome mahogany table was strewn with books and magazines. The large windows gave on the snowy lawn and there was such a fine width of window that the white casements and walls seemed at this moment but a continuation of the snow, the snow but an extension of casement and walls. The outdoors seemed taken in and made safe, the indoors seemed luxuriously freshened and expanded.

Howe sat down by the fire and lighted a cigarette. The room had its intended effect upon him. He felt comfortable and relaxed, yet nicely organized, some young diplomatic agent of the eighteenth century, the newly fledged Swift carrying out Sir William Temple's business. The rawness of Tertan's case quite vanished. He crossed his legs and reached for a magazine.

It was that famous issue of *Life and Letters* that his idle hand had found and his blood raced as he sifted through it and the shape of his own name, Joseph Howe, sprang out at him, still cabalistic in its power. He tossed the magazine back on the table as the door of the Dean's office opened and the Dean ushered out Theodore Blackburn.

"Ah, Joseph!" the Dean said.

Blackburn said: "Good morning, Doctor." Howe winced at the title and caught the flicker of amusement over the Dean's face. The Dean stood with his hand high on the door-jamb and Blackburn, still in the doorway, remained standing almost under his long arm.

Howe nodded briefly to Blackburn, snubbing his eager deference. "Can you give me a few minutes?" he said to the Dean.

"All the time you want. Come in." Before the two men could enter the office, Blackburn claimed their attention with a long full "Er." As they turned to him, Blackburn said: "Can *you* give *me* a few minutes, Dr. Howe?" His eyes sparkled at the little audacity he had committed, the slightly impudent play with hierarchy. Of the three of them Blackburn kept himself the lowest, but he reminded Howe of his subaltern relation to the Dean.

"I mean, of course," Blackburn went on easily, "when you've finished with the Dean."

"I'll be in my office shortly," Howe said, turned his back on the ready "Thank you, sir," and followed the Dean into the inner room.

"Energetic boy," said the Dean. "A bit beyond himself but very energetic. Sit down."

The Dean lighted a cigarette, leaned back in his chair, sat easy and silent for a moment, giving Howe no signal to go ahead with business. He was a young Dean, not much beyond forty, a tall handsome man with sad, ambitious eyes. He had been a Rhodes scholar. His friends looked for great things from him and it was generally said that he had notions of education which he was not yet ready to try to put into practice.

His relaxed silence was meant as a compliment to Howe. He smiled and said: "What's the business, Joseph?"

"Do you know Tertan—Ferdinand Tertan, a freshman?"

The Dean's cigarette was in his mouth and his hands were clasped behind his head. He did not seem to search his memory for the name. He said: "What about him?"

Clearly the Dean knew something and he was waiting for Howe to tell him more. Howe moved only tentatively. Now that he was doing what he had resolved not to do, he felt more guilty at having been so long deceived by Tertan and more need to be loyal to his error.

"He's a strange fellow," he ventured. He said stubbornly: "In a strange way he's very brilliant." He concluded: "But very strange."

The springs of the Dean's swivel chair creaked as he came out of his sprawl and leaned forward to Howe. "Do you mean he's so strange that it's something you could give a name to?"

Howe looked at him stupidly. "What do you mean?" he said.

"What's his trouble?" the Dean said more neutrally.

"He's very brilliant, in a way. I looked him up and he has a top intelligence rating. But somehow, and it's hard to explain just how, what he says is always on the edge of sense and doesn't quite make it."

The Dean looked at him and Howe flushed up. The Dean had surely read Woolley on the subject of "the Howe's" and the *tour d'ivresse*. Was that quick glance ironical?

The Dean picked up some papers from his desk and Howe could see that they were in Tertan's impatient scrawl. Perhaps the little gleam in the Dean's glance had come only from putting facts together.

"He sent me this yesterday," the Dean said. "After an interview I had with him. I haven't been able to do more than glance at it. When you said what you did, I realized there was something wrong."

Twisting his mouth, the Dean looked over the letter. "You seem to be involved," he said without looking up. "By the way, what did you give him at mid-term?"

Flushing, setting his shoulders, Howe said firmly: "I gave him A-minus."

The Dean chuckled. "Might be a good idea if some of our nicer boys went crazy—just a little." He said, "Well," to conclude the matter and handed the papers to Howe. "See if this is the same thing you've been finding. Then we can go into the matter again."

Before the fire in the parlor, in the chair that Howe had been occupying, sat Blackburn. He sprang to his feet as Howe entered.

"I said my office, Mr. Blackburn." Howe's voice was sharp. Then he was almost sorry for the rebuke, so clearly and naïvely did Blackburn seem to relish his stay in the parlor, close to authority.

"I'm in a bit of a hurry, sir," he said, "and I did want to be sure to speak to you, sir."

He was really absurd, yet fifteen years from now he would have grown up to himself, to the assurance and mature beefiness. In banks, in consular offices, in brokerage firms, on the bench, more seriously affable, a little sterner, he would make use of his ability to be administered by his job. It was almost reassuring. Now he was exercising his too-great skill on Howe. "I owe you an apology, sir," he said.

Howe knew that he did but he showed surprise.

"I mean, Doctor, after your having been so kind about letting me attend your class, I stopped coming." He smiled in deprecation. "Extra-curricular activities take up so much of my time. I'm afraid I undertook more than I could perform."

Howe had noticed the absence and had been a little irritated by it after Blackburn's elaborate plea. It was an absence that might be interpreted as a comment on the teacher. But there was only one way for him to answer. "You've no need to apologize," he said. "It's wholly your affair."

Blackburn beamed. "I'm so glad you feel that way about it, sir. I was worried you might think I had stayed away because I was influenced by—" He stopped and lowered his eyes.

Astonished, Howe said: "Influenced by what?"

"Well, by—" Blackburn hesitated and for answer pointed to the table on which lay the copy of *Life and Letters*. Without looking at it, he knew where to direct his hand. "By the unfavorable publicity, sir." He hurried on. "And that brings me to another point, sir. I am secretary of Quill and Scroll, sir, the student literary society, and I wonder if you would address us. You could read your own poetry, sir, and defend your own point of view. It would be very interesting."

It was truly amazing. Howe looked long and cruelly into Blackburn's face, trying to catch the secret of the mind that could have conceived this way of manipulating him, this way so daring and inept—but not entirely inept—with its malice so without malignity. The face did not yield its secret. Howe smiled broadly and said: "Of course I don't think you were influenced by the unfavorable publicity."

"I'm still going to take—regularly, for credit—your romantic poets course next term," Blackburn said.

"Don't worry, my dear fellow, don't worry about it."

Howe started to leave and Blackburn stopped him with: "But about Quill, sir?"

"Suppose we wait until next term? I'll be less busy then."

And Blackburn said: "Very good, sir, and thank you."

In his office the little encounter seemed less funny to Howe, was even in some indeterminate way disturbing. He made an effort to put it from his mind by turning to what was sure to disturb him more, the Tertan letter read in the new interpretation. He found what he had always found, the same florid leaps beyond fact and meaning, the same headlong certainty. But as his eye passed over the familiar scrawl it caught his own name and for the second time that hour he felt the race of his blood.

"The Paraclete," Tertan had written to the Dean, "from a Greek word meaning to stand in place of, but going beyond the primitive idea to mean traditionally the helper, the one who comforts and assists, cannot without fundamental loss be jettisoned. Even if taken no longer in the supernatural sense, the concept remains deeply in the human consciousness inevitably. Humanitarianism is no reply, for not every man stands in the place of every other man for this other's comrade comfort. But certain are chosen out of the human race to be the consoler of some other. Of these, for example, is Joseph Barker Howe, Ph.D. of intellects not the first yet of true intellect and lambent instructions, given to that which is intuitive and irrational, not to what is logical in the strict word, what is judged by him is of the heart and not the head. Here is one chosen, in that he chooses himself to stand in the place of another for comfort and consolation. To him more than another I give my gratitude, with all respect to our Dean who reads this, a noble man, but merely dedicated, not consecrated. But not in the aspect of the Paraclete only is Dr. Joseph Barker Howe established, for he must be the Paraclete to another aspect of himself, that which is driven and persecuted by the lack of understanding in the world at large, so that he in himself embodies the full history of man's tribulations and, overflowing upon others, notably the present writer, is the ultimate end."

This was love. There was no escape from it. Try as Howe might to remember that Tertan was mad and all his emotions invalidated, he could not destroy the effect upon him of his student's stern, affectionate regard. He had betrayed not only a power of mind but a power of love. And however firmly he held before his attention the fact of Tertan's madness, he could do nothing to banish the physical sensation of gratitude he felt. He had never thought of himself as "driven and persecuted" and he did not now. But still he could not make meaningless his sensation of gratitude. The pitiable Tertan sternly pitied him, and comfort came from Tertan's never-to-be-comforted mind.

III

In an academic community, even an efficient one, official matters move slowly. The term drew to a close with no action in the case of Tertan, and Joseph Howe had to confront a curious problem. How should he grade his strange student, Tertan?

Tertan's final examination had been no different from all his other writing, and what did one "give" such a student? De Witt must have his A, that was clear. Johnson would get a B. With Casebeer it was a question of a B-minus or a C-plus, and Stettenhover, who had been crammed by the team tutor to fill half a blue-book with his thin feminine scrawl, would have his C-minus which he would accept with mingled indifference and resentment. But with Tertan it was not so easy.

The boy was still in the college process and his name could not be omitted from the grade sheet. Yet what should a mind under suspicion of madness be graded? Until the medical verdict was given, it was for Howe to continue as Tertan's teacher and to keep his judgment peda-gogical. Impossible to give him an F: he had not failed. B was for Johnson's stolid mediocrity. He could not be put on the edge of passing with Stetten-hover, for he exactly did not pass. In energy and richness of intellect he was perhaps even De Witt's superior, and Howe toyed grimly with the notion of giving him an A, but that would lower the value of the A De Witt had won with his beautiful and clear, if still arrogant, mind. There was a notation which the Registrar recognized—Inc. for Incomplete and in the horrible comedy of the situation, Howe considered that. But really only a mark of M for Mad would serve.

In his perplexity, Howe sought the Dean, but the Dean was out of town. In the end, he decided to maintain the A-minus he had given Tertan at mid-term. After all, there had been no falling away from that quality. He entered it on the grade sheet with something like bravado.

Academic time moves quickly. A college year is not really a year, lacking as it does three months. And it is endlessly divided into units which, at their beginning, appear larger than they are—terms, half-terms, months, weeks. And the ultimate unit, the hour, is not really an hour, lacking as it does ten minutes. And so the new term advanced rapidly and one day the fields about the town were all brown, cleared of even the few thin patches of snow which had lingered so long.

Howe, as he lectured on the romantic poets, became conscious of Blackburn emanating wrath. Blackburn did it well, did it with enormous dignity. He did not stir in his seat, he kept his eyes fixed on Howe in perfect attention, but he abstained from using his notebook, there was no mistaking what he proposed to himself as an attitude. His elbow on the writing-wing of the chair, his chin on the curled fingers of his hand, he was the embodiment of intellectual indignation. He was thinking his own thoughts, would give no public offence, yet would claim his due, was not to be intimidated. Howe knew that he would present himself at the end of the hour.

Blackburn entered the office without invitation. He did not smile, there was no cajolery about him. Without invitation he sat down beside Howe's desk. He did not speak until he had taken the blue-book from his pocket. He said: "What does this mean, sir?"

It was a sound and conservative student tactic. Said in the usual way it meant: "How could you have so misunderstood me?" or "What does this mean for my future in the course?" But there were none of the humbler tones in Blackburn's way of saying it.

Howe made the established reply: "I think that's for you to tell me."

Blackburn continued icy. "I'm sure I can't, sir."

There was a silence between them. Both dropped their eyes to the blue-book on the desk. On its cover Howe had penciled: "F. This is very poor work."

Howe picked up the blue-book. There was always the possibility of injustice. The teacher may be bored by the mass of papers and not wholly attentive. A phrase, even the student's handwriting, may irritate him unreasonably. "Well," said Howe, "let's go through it."

He opened the first page. "Now here: you write: 'In *The Ancient Mariner*, Coleridge lives in and transports us to a honey-sweet world where all is rich and strange, a world of charm to which we can escape from the humdrum existence of our daily lives, the world of romance. Here, in this warm and honey-sweet land of charming dreams we can relax and enjoy ourselves.' "

Howe lowered the paper and waited with a neutral look for Blackburn to speak. Blackburn returned the look boldly, did not speak, sat stolid and lofty. At last Howe said, speaking gently: "Did you mean that, or were you just at a loss for something to say?"

"You imply that I was just 'bluffing'?" The quotation marks hung palpable in the air about the word.

"I'd like to know. I'd prefer believing that you were bluffing to believing that you really thought this."

Blackburn's eyebrows went up. From the height of a great and firmbased idea he looked at his teacher. He clasped the crags for a moment and then pounced, craftily, suavely. "Do you mean, Dr. Howe, that there aren't two opinions possible?"

It was superbly done in its air of putting all of Howe's intellectual life into the balance. Howe remained patient and simple. "Yes, many opinions are possible, but not this one. Whatever anyone believes of *The Ancient Mariner*, no one can in reason believe that it represents a—a honey-sweet world in which we can relax."

"But that is what I *feel*, sir."

This was well done too. Howe said: "Look, Mr. Blackburn. Do you really relax with hunger and thirst, the heat and the sea-serpents, the dead men with staring eyes, Life in Death and the skeletons? Come now, Mr. Blackburn."

Blackburn made no answer and Howe pressed forward. "Now you say of Wordsworth: 'Of peasant stock himself, he turned from the effete life of the salons and found in the peasant the hope of a flaming revolution which would sweep away all the old ideas. This is the subject of his best poems.' "

Beaming at his teacher with youthful eagerness, Blackburn said: "Yes, sir, a rebel, a bringer of light to suffering mankind. I see him as a kind of Prothemeus."

"A kind of what?"

"Prothemeus, sir."

"Think, Mr. Blackburn. We were talking about him only today and I mentioned his name a dozen times. You don't mean Prothemeus. You mean—" Howe waited but there was no response.

"You mean Prometheus."

Blackburn gave no assent and Howe took the reins. "You've done a bad job here, Mr. Blackburn, about as bad as could be done." He saw Blackburn stiffen and his genial face harden again. "It shows either a lack of preparation or a complete lack of understanding." He saw Blackburn's face begin to go to pieces and he stopped.

"Oh, sir," Blackburn burst out, "I've never had a mark like this before, never anything below a B, never. A thing like this has never happened to me before."

It must be true, it was a statement too easily verified. Could it be that other instructors accepted such flaunting nonsense? Howe wanted to end the interview. "I'll set it down to lack of preparation," he said. "I know you're busy. That's not an excuse but it's an explanation. Now suppose you really prepare and then take another quiz in two weeks. We'll forget this one and count the other."

Blackburn squirmed with pleasure and gratitude. "Thank you, sir. You're really very kind, very kind."

Howe rose to conclude the visit. "All right then—in two weeks."

It was that day that the Dean imparted to Howe the conclusion of the case of Tertan. It was simple and a little anticlimactic. A physician had been called in, and had said the word, given the name.

"A classic case, he called it," the Dean said. "Not a doubt in the world," he said. His eyes were full of miserable pity and he clutched at a word. "A classic case, a classic case." To his aid and to Howe's there came the Parthenon and the form of the Greek drama, the Aristotelian logic, Racine and the Well-Tempered Clavichord, the blueness of the Aegean and its clear sky. Classic—that is to say, without a doubt, perfect in its way, a veritable model, and, as the Dean had been told, sure to take a perfectly predictable and inevitable course to a foreknown conclusion.

It was not only pity that stood in the Dean's eyes. For a moment there was fear too. "Terrible," he said, "it is simply terrible."

Then he went on briskly. "Naturally we've told the boy nothing. And naturally we won't. His tuition's paid by his scholarship and we'll continue him on the rolls until the end of the year. That will be kindest. After that the matter will be out of our control. We'll see, of course, that he gets into the proper hands. I'm told there will be no change, he'll go on like this, be as good as this, for four to six months. And so we'll just go along as usual."

So Tertan continued to sit in Section 5 of English 1A, to his classmates still a figure of curiously dignified fun, symbol to most of them of the respectable but absurd intellectual life. But to his teacher he was now very different. He had not changed—he was still the greyhound casting for the scent of ideas and Howe could see that he was still the same Tertan, but he could not feel it. What he felt as he looked at the boy sitting in his accustomed place was the hard blank of a fact. The fact itself was formidable and depressing. But what Howe was chiefly aware of was that he had permitted the metamorphosis of Tertan from person to fact.

As much as possible he avoided seeing Tertan's upraised hand and eager eye. But the fact did not know of its mere factuality, it continued its existence as if it were Tertan, hand up and eye questioning, and one day it appeared in Howe's office with a document.

"Even the spirit who lives egregiously, above the herd, must have its relations with the fellow-man," Tertan declared. He laid the document on Howe's desk. It was headed "Quill and Scroll Society of Dwight College. Application for Membership."

"In most ways these are crass minds," Tertan said, touching the paper. "Yet as a whole, bound together in their common love of letters, they transcend their intellectual lacks, since it is not a paradox that the whole is greater than the sum of its parts."

"When are the elections?" Howe asked.

"They take place to-morrow."

"I certainly hope you will be successful."

"Thank you. Would you wish to implement that hope?" A rather dirty finger pointed to the bottom of the sheet. "A faculty recommender is necessary," Tertan said stiffly, and waited.

"And you wish me to recommend you?"

"It would be an honor."

"You may use my name."

Tertan's finger pointed again. "It must be a written sponsorship, signed by the sponsor." There was a large blank space on the form under the heading: "Opinion of Faculty Sponsor."

This was almost another thing and Howe hesitated. Yet there was nothing else to do and he took out his fountain-pen. He wrote: "Mr. Ferdinand Tertan is marked by his intense devotion to letters and by his exceptional love of all things of the mind." To this he signed his name which looked bold and assertive on the white page. It disturbed him, the strange affirming power of a name. With a business-like air, Tertan whipped up the paper, folded it with decision and put it into his pocket. He bowed and took his departure, leaving Howe with the sense of having done something oddly momentous.

And so much now seemed odd and momentous to Howe that should not have seemed so. It was odd and momentous, he felt, when he sat with

Blackburn's second quiz before him and wrote in an excessively firm hand the grade of C-minus. The paper was a clear, an indisputable failure. He was carefully and consciously committing a cowardice. Blackburn had told the truth when he had pleaded his past record. Howe had consulted it in the Dean's office. It showed no grade lower than a B-minus. A canvass of some of Blackburn's previous instructors had brought vague attestations to the adequate powers of a student imperfectly remembered and sometimes surprise that his abilities could be questioned at all.

As he wrote the grade, Howe told himself that this cowardice sprang from an unwillingness to have more dealings with a student he disliked. He knew it was simpler than that. He knew he feared Blackburn: that was the absurd truth. And cowardice did not solve the matter after all. Blackburn, flushed with a first success, attacked at once. The minimal passing grade had not assuaged his feelings, and he sat at Howe's desk and again the blue-book lay between them. Blackburn said nothing. With an enormous impudence, he was waiting for Howe to speak and explain himself.

At last Howe said sharply and rudely: "Well?" His throat was tense and the blood was hammering in his head. His mouth was tight with anger at himself for his disturbance.

Blackburn's glance was almost baleful. "This is impossible, sir."

"But there it is," Howe answered.

"Sir?" Blackburn had not caught the meaning but his tone was still haughty.

Impatiently Howe said: "There it is, plain as day. Are you here to complain again?"

"Indeed I am, sir." There was surprise in Blackburn's voice that Howe should ask the question.

"I shouldn't complain if I were you. You did a thoroughly bad job on your first quiz. This one is a little, only a very little, better." This was not true. If anything, it was worse.

"That might be a matter of opinion, sir."

"It is a matter of opinion. Of my opinion."

"Another opinion might be different, sir."

"You really believe that?" Howe said.

"Yes." The omission of the "sir" was monumental.

"Whose, for example?"

"The Dean's, for example." Then the fleshy jaw came forward a little. "Or a certain literary critic's, for example."

It was colossal and almost too much for Blackburn himself to handle. The solidity of his face almost crumpled under it. But he withstood his own audacity and went on. "And the Dean's opinion might be guided by the knowledge that the person who gave me this mark is the man whom a famous critic, the most eminent judge of literature in this country, called a drunken man. The Dean might think twice about whether such a man is fit to teach Dwight students."

Howe said in quiet admonition, "Blackburn, you're mad," meaning no more than to check the boy's extravagance.

But Blackburn paid no heed. He had another shot in the locker. "And the Dean might be guided by the information, of which I have evidence, documentary evidence"—he slapped his breast-pocket twice—"that this same person personally recommended to the college literary society, the oldest in the country, that he personally recommended a student who is crazy, who threw the meeting into an uproar, a psychiatric case. The Dean might take that into account."

Howe was never to learn the details of that "uproar." He had always to content himself with the dim but passionate picture which at that moment sprang into his mind, of Tertan standing on some abstract height and madly denouncing the multitude of Quill and Scroll who howled him down.

He sat quiet a moment and looked at Blackburn. The ferocity had entirely gone from the student's face. He sat regarding his teacher almost benevolently. He had played a good card and now, scarcely at all unfriendly, he was waiting to see the effect. Howe took up the blue-book and negligently sifted through it. He read a page, closed the book, struck out the C-minus and wrote an F.

"Now you may take the paper to the Dean," he said. "You may tell him that after reconsidering it, I lowered the grade."

The gasp was audible. "Oh, sir!" Blackburn cried. "Please!" His face was agonized. "It means my graduation, my livelihood, my future. Don't do this to me."

"It's done already."

Blackburn stood up. "I spoke rashly, sir, hastily. I had no intention, no real intention, of seeing the Dean. It rests with you—entirely, entirely. I *hope* you will restore the first mark."

"Take the matter to the Dean or not, just as you choose. The grade is what you deserve and it stands."

Blackburn's head dropped. "And will I be failed at mid-term, sir?"

"Of course."

From deep out of Blackburn's great chest rose a cry of anguish. "Oh, sir, if you want me to go down on my knees to you, I will, I will."

Howe looked at him in amazement.

"I will, I will. On my knees, sir. This mustn't, mustn't happen."

He spoke so literally, meaning so very truly that his knees and exactly his knees were involved and seeming to think that he was offering something of tangible value to his teacher, that Howe, whose head had become icy clear in the nonsensical drama, thought, "The boy is mad," and began to speculate fantastically whether something in himself attracted or developed aberration. He could see himself standing absurdly before the Dean and saying: "I've found another. This time it's the vice-president of the Council, the manager of the debating team, and secretary of Quill and Scroll."

One more such discovery, he thought, and he himself would be discovered! And there, suddenly, Blackburn was on his knees with a thump, his huge thighs straining his trousers, his hands outstretched in a great gesture of supplication.

With a cry, Howe shoved back his swivel chair and it rolled away on its casters half across the little room. Blackburn knelt for a moment to nothing at all, then got to his feet.

Howe rose abruptly. He said: "Blackburn, you will stop acting like an idiot. Dust your knees off, take your paper and get out. You've behaved like a fool and a malicious person. You have half a term to do a decent job. Keep your silly mouth shut and try to do it. Now get out."

Blackburn's head was low. He raised it and there was a pious light in his eyes. "Will you shake hands, sir?" he said. He thrust out his hand.

"I will not," Howe said.

Head and hand sank together. Blackburn picked up his blue-book and walked to the door. He turned and said: "Thank you, sir." His back, as he departed, was heavy with tragedy and stateliness.

IV

After years of bad luck with the weather, the College had a perfect day for Commencement. It was wonderfully bright, the air so transparent, the wind so brisk that no one could resist talking about it.

As Howe set out for the campus he heard Hilda calling from the back yard. She called, "Professor, professor," and came running to him.

Howe said: "What's this 'professor' business?"

"Mother told me," Hilda said. "You've been promoted. And I want to take your picture."

"Next year," said Howe. "I won't be a professor until next year. And you know better than to call anybody 'professor.' "

"It was just in fun," Hilda said. She seemed disappointed.

"But you can take my picture if you want. I won't look much different next year." Still, it was frightening. It might mean that he was to stay in this town all his life.

Hilda brightened. "Can I take it in this?" she said, and touched the gown he carried over his arm.

Howe laughed. "Yes, you can take it in this."

"I'll get my things and meet you in front of Otis," Hilda said. "I have the background all picked out."

On the campus the Commencement crowd was already large. It stood about in eager, nervous little family groups. As he crossed, Howe was greeted by a student, capped and gowned, glad of the chance to make an event for his parents by introducing one of his teachers. It was while Howe stood there chatting that he saw Tertan.

He had never seen anyone quite so alone, as though a circle had been woven about him to separate him from the gay crowd on the campus. Not that Tertan was not gay—he was the gayest of all. Three weeks had passed since Howe had last seen him, the weeks of examination, the lazy week before Commencement, and this was now a different Tertan. On his head he wore a panama hat, broad-brimmed and fine, of the shape associated with South American planters. He wore a suit of raw silk, luxurious but yellowed with age and much too tight, and he sported a whangee cane. He walked sedately, the hat tilted at a devastating angle, the stick coming up and down in time to his measured tread. He had, Howe guessed, outfitted himself to greet the day in the clothes of that ruined father whose existence was on record in the Dean's office. Gravely and arrogantly he surveyed the scene—in it, his whole bearing seemed to say, but not of it. With his haughty step, with his flashing eye, Tertan was coming nearer. Howe did not wish to be seen. He shifted his position slightly. When he looked again, Tertan was not in sight.

The chapel clock struck the quarter hour. Howe detached himself from his chat and hurried to Otis Hall at the far end of the campus. Hilda had not yet come. He went up into the high portico and, using the glass of the door for a mirror, put on his gown, adjusted the hood on his shoulders and set the mortar-board on his head. When he came down the steps Hilda had arrived.

Nothing could have told him more forcibly that a year had passed than the development of Hilda's photographic possessions from the box camera of the previous fall. By a strap about her neck was hung a leather case, so thick and strong, so carefully stitched and so moulded to its contents that it could only hold a costly camera. The appearance was deceptive, Howe knew, for he had been present at the Aikens' pre-Christmas conference about its purchase. It was only a fairly good domestic camera. Still, it looked very impressive. Hilda carried another leather case from which she drew a collapsible tripod. Decisively she extended each of its gleaming legs and set it up on the path. She removed the camera from its case and fixed it to the tripod. In its compact efficiency the camera almost had a life of its own, but Hilda treated it with easy familiarity, looked into its eye, glanced casually at its gauges. Then from a pocket she took still another leather case and drew from it a small instrument through which she looked first at Howe, who began to feel inanimate and lost, and then at the sky. She made some adjustment on the instrument, then some adjustment on the camera. She swept the scene with her eye, found a spot and pointed the camera in its direction. She walked to the spot, stood on it and beckoned to Howe. With each new leather case, with each new instrument and with each new adjustment she had grown in ease and now she said: "Joe, will you stand here?"

Obediently Howe stood where he was bidden. She had yet another instrument. She took out a tape-measure on a mechanical spool. Kneeling down before Howe, she put the little metal ring of the tape under the tip of his shoe. At her request, Howe pressed it with his toe. When she had measured her distance, she nodded to Howe who released the tape. At a touch, it sprang back into the spool. "You have to be careful if you're going to get what you want," Hilda said. "I don't believe in all this snap-snap-snapping," she remarked loftily. Howe nodded in agreement, although he was beginning to think Hilda's care excessive.

Now at last the moment had come. Hilda squinted into the camera, moved the tripod slightly. She stood to the side, holding the plunger of the shutter-cable. "Ready," she said. "Will you relax, Joseph, please?" Howe realized that he was standing frozen. Hilda stood poised and precise as a setter, one hand holding the little cable, the other extended with curled dainty fingers like a dancer's, as if expressing to her subject the precarious delicacy of the moment. She pressed the plunger and there was the click. At once she stirred to action, got behind the camera, turned a new exposure. "Thank you," she said. "Would you stand under that tree and let me do a character study with light and shade?"

The childish absurdity of the remark restored Howe's ease. He went to the little tree. The pattern the leaves made on his gown was what Hilda was after. He had just taken a satisfactory position when he heard in the unmistakable voice: "Ah, Doctor! Having your picture taken?"

Howe gave up the pose and turned to Blackburn who stood on the walk, his hands behind his back, a little too large for his bachelor's gown. Annoyed that Blackburn should see him posing for a character study in light and shade, Howe said irritably: "Yes, having my picture taken."

Blackburn beamed at Hilda. "And the little photographer," he said. Hilda fixed her eyes on the ground and stood closer to her brilliant and aggressive camera. Blackburn, teetering on his heels, his hands behind his back, wholly prelatical and benignly patient, was not abashed at the silence. At last Howe said: "If you'll excuse us, Mr. Blackburn, we'll go on with the picture."

"Go right ahead, sir. I'm running along," But he only came closer. "Dr. Howe," he said fervently, "I want to tell you how glad I am that I was able to satisfy your standards at last."

Howe was surprised at the hard insulting brightness of his own voice and even Hilda looked up curiously as he said: "Nothing you have ever done has satisfied me and nothing you could ever do would satisfy me, Blackburn."

With a glance at Hilda, Blackburn made a gesture as if to hush Howe— as though all his former bold malice had taken for granted a kind of understanding between himself and his teacher, a secret which must not be betrayed to a third person. "I only meant, sir," he said, "that I was able to pass your course after all."

Howe said: "You didn't pass my course. I passed you out of my course. I passed you without even reading your paper, I wanted to be sure the college would be rid of you. And when all the grades were in and I did read your paper, I saw I was right not to have read it first."

Blackburn presented a stricken face. "It was very bad, sir?"

But Howe had turned away. The paper had been fantastic. The paper had been, if he wished to see it so, mad. It was at this moment that the Dean came up behind Howe and caught his arm. "Hello, Joseph," he said. "We'd better be getting along, it's almost late."

He was not a familiar man, but when he saw Blackburn, who approached to greet him, he took Blackburn's arm too. "Hello, Theodore," he said. Leaning forward on the Howe's arm and on Blackburn's, he said: "Hello, Hilda dear." Hilda replied quietly: "Hello, Uncle George."

Still clinging to their arms, still linking Howe and Blackburn, the Dean said: "Another year gone, Joe, and we've turned out another crop. After you've been here a few years, you'll find it reasonably upsetting—you wonder how there can be so many graduating classes while you stay the same. But, of course, you don't stay the same." Then he said, "Well," sharply, to dismiss the thought. He pulled Blackburn's arm and swung him around to Howe. "Have you heard about Teddy Blackburn?" he asked. "He has a job already, before graduation, the first man of his class to be placed." Expectant of congratulations, Blackburn beamed at Howe, Howe remained silent.

"Isn't that good?" the Dean said. Still Howe did not answer and the Dean, puzzled and put out, turned to Hilda. "That's a very fine-looking camera, Hilda." She touched it with affectionate pride.

"Instruments of precision," said a voice. "Instruments of precision." Of the three with joined arms, Howe was the nearest to Tertan, whose gaze took in all the scene except the smile and the nod which Howe gave him. The boy leaned on his cane. The broad-brimmed hat, canting jauntily over his eye, confused the image of his face that Howe had established, suppressed the rigid lines of the ascetic and brought out the baroque curves. It made an effect of perverse majesty.

"Instruments of precision," said Tertan for the last time, addressing no one, making a casual comment to the universe. And it occurred to Howe that Tertan might not be referring to Hilda's equipment. The sense of the thrice-woven circle of the boy's loneliness smote him fiercely. Tertan stood in majestic jauntiness, superior to all the scene, but his isolation made Howe ache with a pity of which Tertan was more the cause than the object, so general and indiscriminate was it.

Whether in his sorrow he made some unintended movement towards Tertan which the Dean checked or whether the suddenly tightened grip on his arm was the Dean's own sorrow and fear, he did not know. Tertan watched them in the incurious way people watch a photograph being taken and suddenly the thought that, to the boy, it must seem that the three were posing for a picture together made Howe detach himself almost rudely from the Dean's grasp.

"I promised Hilda another picture," he announced—needlessly, for Tertan was no longer there, he had vanished in the last sudden flux of visitors who, now that the band had struck up, were rushing nervously to find seats.

"You'd better hurry," the Dean said. "I'll go along, it's getting late for me." He departed and Blackburn walked stately by his side.

Howe again took his position under the little tree which cast its shadow over his face and gown. "Just hurry, Hilda, won't you?" he said. Hilda held the cable at arm's-length, her other arm crooked and her fingers crisped. She rose on her toes and said "Ready," and pressed the release. "Thank you," she said gravely and began to dismantle her camera as he hurried off to join the procession.

Eudora Welty 1909–

Livvie

SOLOMON carried Livvie twenty-one miles away from her home when he married her. He carried her away up on the Old Natchez Trace into the deep country to live in his house. She was sixteen—an only girl, then. Once people said he thought nobody would ever come along there. He told her himself that it had been a long time, and a day she did not know about, since that road was a travelled road with *people* coming and going. He was good to her, but he kept her in the house. She had not thought that she could not get back. Where she came from, people said an old man did not want anybody in the world to ever find his wife, for fear they would steal her back from him. Solomon asked her before he took her, "Would she be happy?"—very dignified, for he was a colored man that owned his land and had it written down in the courthouse; and she said, "Yes, sir," since he was an old man and she was young and just listened and answered. He asked her, if she was choosing winter, would she pine for spring, and she said, "No indeed." Whatever she said, always, was because he was an old man . . . while nine years went by. All the time, he got old, and he got so old he gave out. At last he slept the whole day in bed, and she was young still.

It was a nice house, inside and outside both. In the first place, it had three rooms. The front room was papered in holly paper, with green palmettos from the swamp spaced at careful intervals over the walls. There was fresh newspaper cut with fancy borders on the mantel-shelf, on which were propped photographs of old or very young men printed in faint yellow—Solomon's people. Solomon had a houseful of furniture. There was a double settee, a tall scrolled rocker and an organ in the front room, all around a three-legged table with a pink marble top, on which was set a lamp with three gold feet, besides a jelly glass with pretty hen feathers in it. Behind the front room, the other room had the bright iron bed with the polished knobs like a throne, in which Solomon slept all day. There were snow-white curtains of wiry lace at the window, and a lace bedspread belonged on the bed. But what old Solomon slept so sound under was a big feather-stitched piece-quilt in the pattern "Trip Around the World," which had twenty-one different colors, four hundred and forty pieces, and a thousand yards of thread, and that was what Solomon's mother made in her life and old age. There was a table holding the Bible, and a trunk with a key. On the wall were two calendars, and a diploma from somewhere in Solomon's family, and under that Livvie's one possession was nailed, a picture of the little white baby of the family she worked for, back in Natchez before she was married. Going through that room and on to the kitchen, there was a big wood stove and a big round table always with a wet top and with the knives and forks in one jelly glass and the spoons in another, and a cut-glass vinegar bottle between, and going out from those, many shallow dishes of pickled peaches, fig preserves, watermelon pickles and blackberry jam always sitting there. The churn sat in the sun, the doors of the safe were always both shut, and there were four baited mouse-traps in the kitchen, one in every corner.

The outside of Solomon's house looked nice. It was not painted, but across the porch was an even balance. On each side there was one easy chair with high springs, looking out, and a fern basket hanging over it from the ceiling, and a dishpan of zinnia seedlings growing at its foot on the floor. By the door was a plow-wheel, just a pretty iron circle, nailed up on one wall and a square mirror on the other, a turquoise-blue comb stuck up in the frame, with the wash stand beneath it. On the door was a wooden knob with a pearl in the end, and Solomon's black hat hung on that, if he was in the house.

Out front was a clean dirt yard with every vestige of grass patiently uprooted and the ground scarred in deep whorls from the strike of Livvie's broom. Rose bushes with tiny blood-red roses blooming every month grew in threes on either side of the steps. On one side was a peach tree, on the other a pomegranate. Then coming around up the path from the deep cut of the Natchez Trace below was a line of bare crape-myrtle trees with every branch of them ending in a colored bottle, green or blue. There was no word that fell from Solomon's lips to say what they were for, but Livvie knew that there could be a spell put in trees, and she was familiar from the time she was born with the way bottle trees kept evil spirits from coming into the house—by luring them inside the colored bottles, where they cannot get out again. Solomon had made the bottle trees with his own hands over the nine years, in labor amounting to about a tree a year, and without a sign that he had any uneasiness in his heart, for he took as much pride in his precautions against spirits coming in the house as he took in the house, and sometimes in the sun the bottle trees looked prettier than the house did.

It was a nice house. It was in a place where the days would go by and surprise anyone that they were over. The lamplight and the firelight would shine out the door after dark, over the still and breathing country, lighting the roses and the bottle trees, and all was quiet there.

But there was nobody, nobody at all, not even a white person. And if there had been anybody, Solomon would not have let Livvie look at them, just as he would not let her look at a field hand, or a field hand look at her. There was no house near, except for the cabins of the tenants that were forbidden to her, and there was no house as far as she had been, stealing away down the still, deep Trace. She felt as if she waded a river when she went, for the dead leaves on the ground reached as high as her knees, and when she was all scratched and bleeding she said it was not like a road that went anywhere. One day, climbing up the high bank, she had found a graveyard without a church, with ribbon-grass growing about the foot of an angel (she had climbed up because she thought she saw angel wings), and in the sun, trees shining like burning flames through the great caterpillar nets which enclosed them. Scarey thistles stood looking like the prophets in the Bible in Solomon's house. Indian paint brushes grew over her head, and the mourning dove made the only sound in the world. Oh for a stirring of the leaves, and a breaking of the nets! But not by a ghost, prayed Livvie, jumping down the bank. After Solomon took to his bed, she never went out, except one more time.

Livvie knew she made a nice girl to wait on anybody. She fixed things to eat on a tray like a surprise. She could keep from singing when she ironed, and to sit by a bed and fan away the flies, she could be so still she could not hear herself breathe. She could clean up the house and never drop a thing, and wash the dishes without a sound, and she would step outside to churn, for churning sounded too sad to her, like sobbing, and if it made her home-sick and not Solomon, she did not think of that.

But Solomon scarcely opened his eyes to see her, and scarcely tasted his food. He was not sick or paralyzed or in any pain that he mentioned, but he was surely wearing out in the body, and no matter what nice hot thing Livvie would bring him to taste, he would only look at it now, as if he were past seeing how he could add anything more to himself. Before she could beg him, he would go fast asleep. She could not surprise him any more, if he would not taste, and she was afraid that he was never in the world going to taste another thing she brought him—and so how could he last?

But one morning it was breakfast time and she cooked his eggs and grits, carried them in on a tray, and called his name. He was sound asleep. He lay in a dignified way with his watch beside him, on his back in the middle of the bed. One hand drew the quilt up high, though it was the first day of spring. Through the white lace curtains a little puffy wind was blowing as if it came from round checks. All night the frogs had sung out in the swamp, like a commotion in the room, and he had not stirred, though she lay wide awake and saying "Shh, frogs!" for fear he would mind them.

He looked as if he would like to sleep a little longer, and so she put back the tray and waited a little. When she tiptoed and stayed so quiet, she surrounded herself with a little reverie, and sometimes it seemed to her when she was so stealthy that the quiet she kept was for a sleeping baby, and that she had a baby and was its mother. When she stood at Solomon's bed and looked down at him, she would be thinking, "He sleeps so well," and she would hate to wake him up. And in some other way, too, she was afraid to wake him up because even in his sleep he seemed to be such a strict man.

Of course, nailed to the wall over the bed—only she would forget who it was—there was a picture of him when he was young. Then he had a fan of hair over his forehead like a king's crown. Now his hair lay down on his head, the spring had gone out of it. Solomon had a lightish face, with eyebrows scattered but rugged, the way privet grows, strong eyes, with second sight, a strict mouth, and a little gold smile. This was the way he looked in his clothes, but in bed in the daytime he looked like a different and smaller man, even when he was wide awake, and holding the Bible. He looked like somebody kin to himself. And then sometimes when he lay in sleep and she stood fanning the flies away, and the light came in, his face was like new, so smooth and clear that it was like a glass of jelly held to the window, and she could almost look through his forehead and see what he thought.

She fanned him and at length he opened his eyes and spoke her name, but he would not taste the nice eggs she had kept warm under a pan.

Back in the kitchen she ate heartily, his breakfast and hers, and looked out the open door at what went on. The whole day, and the whole night before, she had felt the stir of spring close to her. It was as present in the house as a young man would be. The moon was in the last quarter and outside they were turning the sod and planting peas and beans. Up and down the red fields, over which smoke from the brush-burning hung showing like a little skirt of sky, a white horse and a white mule pulled the plow. At intervals hoarse shouts came through the air and roused her as if she dozed neglectfully in the shade, and they were telling her, "Jump up!" She could see how over each ribbon of field were moving men and girls, on foot and mounted on mules, with hats set on their heads and bright with tall hoes and forks as if they carried streamers on them and were going to some place on a journey—and how as if at a signal now and then they would all start at once shouting, hollering, cajoling, calling and answering back, running, being leaped on and breaking away, flinging to earth with a shout and lying motionless in the trance of twelve o'clock. The old women came out of the cabins and brought them food they had ready for them, and then all worked together, spread evenly out. The little children came too, like a bouncing stream overflowing the fields, and set upon the men, the women, the dogs, the rushing birds, and the wave-like rows of earth, their little voices almost too high to be heard. In the middle distance like some white-and-gold towers were the haystacks, with black cows coming around to eat their edges. High above everything, the wheel of fields, house, and cabins, and the deep road surrounding like a moat to keep them in, was the turning sky, blue with long, far-flung white mare's-tail clouds, serene and still as high flames. And sound asleep while all this went around him that was his, Solomon was like a little still spot in the middle.

Even in the house the earth was sweet to breathe. Solomon had never let Livvie go any farther than the chicken house and the well. But what if she would walk now into the heart of the fields and take a hoe and work until she fell stretched out and drenched with her efforts, like other girls, and laid her cheek against the laid-open earth, and shamed the old man with her humbleness and delight? To shame him! A cruel wish could come in uninvited and so fast while she looked out the back door. She washed the dishes and scrubbed the table. She could hear the cries of the little lambs. Her mother, that she had not seen since her wedding day, had said one time, "I rather a man be anything, than a woman be mean."

So all morning she kept tasting the chicken broth on the stove, and when it was right she poured off a nice cupful. She carried it in to Solomon, and there he lay having a dream. Now what did he dream about? For she saw him sigh gently as if not to disturb some whole thing he held round in his mind, like a fresh egg. So even an old man dreamed about something pretty. Did he dream of her, while his eyes were shut and sunken, and his small hand with the wedding ring curled close in sleep around the quilt? He might be dreaming of what time it was, for even through his sleep he kept track of it like a clock, and knew how much of it went by, and waked up knowing where the hands were even before he consulted the silver watch that he never let go. He would sleep with the watch in his palm, and even holding it to his cheek like a child that loves a plaything. Or he might dream of journeys and travels on a steamboat to Natchez. Yet she thought he dreamed of her; but even while she scrutinized him, the rods of the foot of the bed seemed to rise up like a rail fence between them, and she could see that people never could be sure of anything as long as one of them was asleep and the other awake. To look at him dreaming of her when he might be going to die frightened her a little, as if he might carry her with him that way, and she wanted to run out of the room. She took hold of the bed and held on, and Solomon opened his eyes and called her name, but he did not want anything. He would not taste the good broth.

Just a little after that, as she was taking up the ashes in the front room for the last time in the year, she heard a sound. It was somebody coming. She pulled the curtains together and looked through the slit.

Coming up the path under the bottle trees was a white lady. At first she looked young, but then she looked old. Marvelous to see, a little car stood steaming like a kettle out in the field-track—it had come without a road.

Livvie stood listening to the long, repeated knockings at the door, and after a while she opened it just a little. The lady came in through the crack, though she was more than middle-sized and wore a big hat.

"My name is Miss Baby Marie," she said.

Livvie gazed respectfully at the lady and at the little suitcase she was holding close to her by the handle until the proper moment. The lady's eyes were running over the room, from palmetto to palmetto, but she was saying, "I live at home . . . out from Natchez . . . and get out and show these pretty cosmetic things to the white people and the colored people both . . . all around . . . years and years. . . . Both shades of powder and rouge. . . . It's the kind of work a girl can do and not go clear 'way from home . . ." And the harder she looked, the more she talked. Suddenly she turned up her nose and said, "It is not Christian or sanitary to put feathers in a vase," and then she took a gold key out of the front of her dress and began unlocking the locks on her suitcase. Her face drew the light, the way it was covered with intense white and red, with a little patty-cake of white between the wrinkles by her upper lip. Little red tassels of hair bobbed under the rusty wires of her picture-hat, as with an air of triumph and secrecy she now drew open her little suitcase and brought out bottle after bottle and jar after jar, which she put down on the table, the mantel-piece, the settee, and the organ.

"Did you ever see so many cosmetics in your life?" cried Miss Baby Marie.

"No'm," Livvie tried to say, but the cat had her tongue.

"Have you ever applied cosmetics?" asked Miss Baby Marie next.

"No'm," Livvie tried to say.

"Then look!" she said, and pulling out the last thing of all, "Try this!" she said. And in her hand was unclenched a golden lipstick which popped open like magic. A fragrance came out of it like incense, and Livvie cried out suddenly, "Chinaberry flowers!"

Her hand took the lipstick, and in an instant she was carried away in the air through the spring, and looking down with a half-drowsy smile from a purple cloud she saw from above a chinaberry tree, dark and smooth and neatly leaved, neat as a guinea hen in the dooryard, and there was her home that she had left. On one side of the tree was her mama holding up her heavy apron, and she could see it was loaded with ripe figs, and on the other side was her papa holding a fish-pole over the pond, and she could see it transparently, the little clear fishes swimming up to the brim.

"Oh, no, not chinaberry flowers—secret ingredients," said Miss Baby Marie. "My cosmetics have secret ingredients—not chinaberry flowers."

"It's purple," Livvie breathed, and Miss Baby Marie said, "Use it freely. Rub it on."

Livvie tiptoed out to the wash stand on the front porch and before the mirror put the paint on her mouth. In the wavery surface her face danced before her like a flame. Miss Baby Marie followed her out, took a look at what she had done, and said, "That's it."

Livvie tried to say "Thank you" without moving her parted lips where the paint lay so new.

By now Miss Baby Marie stood behind Livvie and looked in the mirror over her shoulder, twisting up the tassels of her hair. "The lipstick I can let you have for only two dollars," she said, close to her neck.

"Lady, but I don't have no money, never did have," said Livvie.

"Oh, but you don't pay the first time. I make another trip, that's the way I do. I come back again—later."

"Oh," said Livvie, pretending she understood everything so as to please the lady.

"But if you don't take it now, this may be the last time I'll call at your house," said Miss Baby Marie sharply. "It's far away from anywhere, I'll tell you that. You don't live close to anywhere."

"Yes'm. My husband, he keep the *money*," said Livvie, trembling. "He is strict as he can be. He don't know *you* walk in here—Miss Baby Marie!"

"Where is he?"

"Right now, he in yonder sound asleep, an old man. I wouldn't ever ask him for anything."

Miss Baby Marie took back the lipstick and packed it up. She gathered up the jars for both black and white and got them all inside the suitcase, with the same little fuss of triumph with which she had brought them out. She started away.

"Goodbye," she said, making herself look grand from the back, but at the last minute she turned around in the door. Her old hat wobbled as she whispered, "Let me see your husband."

Livvie obediently went on tiptoe and opened the door to the other room. Miss Baby Marie came behind her and rose on her toes and looked in.

"My, what a little tiny old, old man!" she whispered, clasping her hands and shaking her head over them. "What a beautiful quilt! What a tiny old, old man!"

"He can sleep like that all day," whispered Livvie proudly.

They looked at him awhile so fast asleep, and then all at once they looked at each other. Somehow that was as if they had a secret, for he had never stirred. Livvie then politely, but all at once, closed the door.

"Well! I'd certainly like to leave you with a lipstick!" said Miss Baby Marie vivaciously. She smiled in the door.

"Lady, but I told you I don't have no money, and never did have."

"And never will?" In the air and all around, like a bright halo around the white lady's nodding head, it was a true spring day.

"Would you take eggs, lady?" asked Livvie softly.

"No, I have plenty of eggs—plenty," said Miss Baby Marie.

"I still don't have no money," said Livvie, and Miss Baby Marie took her suitcase and went on somewhere else.

Livvie stood watching her go, and all the time she felt her heart beating in her left side. She touched the place with her hand. It seemed as if her heart beat and her whole face flamed from the pulsing color of her lips. She went to sit by Solomon and when he opened his eyes he could not see a change in her. "He's fixin' to die," she said inside. That was the secret. That was when she went out of the house for a little breath of air.

She went down the path and down the Natchez Trace a way, and she did not know how far she had gone, but it was not far, when she saw a sight. It was a man, looking like a vision—she standing on one side of the Old Natchez Trace and he standing on the other.

As soon as this man caught sight of her, he began to look himself over. Starting at the bottom with his pointed shoes, he began to look up, lifting his peg-top pants the higher to see fully his bright socks. His coat long and wide and leaf-green he opened like doors to see his high-up tawny pants and his pants he smoothed downward from the points of his collar, and he wore a luminous baby-pink satin shirt. At the end, he reached gently above his wide platter-shaped round hat, the color of a plum, and one finger touched at the feather, emerald green, blowing in the spring winds.

No matter how she looked, she could never look so fine as he did, and she was not sorry for that, she was pleased.

He took three jumps, one down and two up, and was by her side.

"My name is Cash," he said.

He had a guinea pig in his pocket. They began to walk along. She stared on and on at him, as if he were doing some daring spectacular thing, instead of just walking beside her. It was not simply the city way he was dressed that made her look at him and see hope in its insolence looking back. It was not only the way he moved along kicking the flowers as if he could break through everything in the way and destroy anything in the world, that made her eyes grow bright. It might be, if he had not appeared the way he did appear that day she would never have looked so closely at him, but the time people come makes a difference.

They walked through the still leaves of the Natchez Trace, the light and the shade falling through trees about them, the white irises shining like candles on the banks and the new ferns shining like green stars up in the oak branches. They came out at Solomon's house, bottle trees and all. Livvie stopped and hung her head.

Cash began whistling a little tune. She did not know what it was, but she had heard it before from a distance, and she had a revelation. Cash was a field hand. He was a transformed field hand. Cash belonged to Solomon. But he had stepped out of his overalls into this. There in front of Solomon's house he laughed. He had a round head, a round face, all of him was young, and he flung his head up, rolled it against the mare's-tail sky in his round hat, and he could laugh just to see Solomon's house sitting there. Livvie looked at it, and there was Solomon's black hat hanging on the peg on the front door, the blackest thing in the world.

"I been to Natchez," Cash said, wagging his head around against the sky. "*I* taken a trip, *I* ready for Easter!"

How was it possible to look so fine before the harvest? Cash must have stolen the money, stolen it from Solomon. He stood in the path and lifted his spread hand high and brought it down again and again in his laughter. He kicked up his heels. A little chill went through her. It was as if Cash was bringing that strong hand down to beat a drum or to rain blows upon a man, such an abandon and menace were in his laugh. Frowning, she went closer to him and his swinging arm drew her in at once and the fright was crushed from her body, as a little match-flame might be smothered out by what it lighted. She gathered the folds of his coat behind him and fastened her red lips to his mouth, and she was dazzled by herself then, the way he had been dazzled at himself to begin with.

In that instant she felt something that could not be told—that Solomon's death was at hand, that he was the same to her as if he were dead now. She cried out, and uttering little cries turned and ran for the house.

At once Cash was coming, following after, he was running behind her. He came close, and half-way up the path he laughed and passed her. He even picked up a stone and sailed it into the bottle trees. She put her hands over her head, and sounds clattered through the bottle trees like cries of outrage. Cash stamped and plunged zigzag up the front steps and in at the door.

When she got there, he had stuck his hands in his pockets and was turning slowly about in the front room. The little guinea pig peeped out. Around Cash, the pinned-up palmettos looked as if a lazy green monkey had walked up and down and around the walls leaving green prints of his hands and feet.

She got through the room and his hands were still in his pockets, and she fell upon the closed door to the other room and pushed it open. She ran to Solomon's bed, calling "Solomon! Solomon!" The little shape of the old man never moved at all, wrapped under the quilt as if it were winter still.

"Solomon!" She pulled the quilt away, but there was another one under that, and she fell on her knees beside him. He made no sound except a sigh, and then she could hear in the silence the light springy steps of Cash walking and walking in the front room, and the ticking of Solomon's silver watch, which came from the bed. Old Solomon was far away in his sleep, his face looked small, relentless, and devout, as if he were walking somewhere where she could imagine the snow falling.

Then there was a noise like a hoof pawing the floor, and the door gave a creak, and Cash appeared beside her. When she looked up, Cash's face was so black it was bright, and so bright and bare of pity that it looked sweet to her. She stood up and held up her head. Cash was so powerful that his presence gave her strength even when she did not need any.

Under their eyes Solomon slept. People's faces tell of things and places not known to the one who looks at them while they sleep, and while Solomon slept under the eyes of Livvie and Cash his face told them like a mythical story that all his life he had built, little scrap by little scrap, respect. A beetle could not have been more laborious or more ingenious in the task of its destiny. When Solomon was young, as he was in his picture overhead, it was the infinite thing wth him, and he could see no end to the respect he would contrive and keep in a house. He had built a lonely house, the way he would make a cage, but it grew to be the same with him as a great monumental pyramid and sometimes in his absorption of getting it erected he was like the builder-slaves of Egypt who forgot or never knew the origin and meaning of the thing to which they gave all the strength of their bodies and used up all their days. Livvie and Cash could see that as a man might rest from a life-labor he lay in his bed, and they could hear how, wrapped in his quilt, he sighed to himself comfortably in sleep, while in his dreams he might have been an ant, a beetle, a bird, an Egyptian, assembling and carrying on his back and building with his hands, or he might have been an old man of India or a swaddled baby, about to smile and brush all away.

Then without warning old Solomon's eyes flew wide open under the hedgelike brows. He was wide awake.

And instantly Cash raised his quick arm. A radiant sweat stood on his temples. But he did not bring his arm down—it stayed in the air, as if something might have taken hold.

It was not Livvie—she did not move. As if something said "Wait," she stood waiting. Even while her eyes burned under motionless lids, her lips parted in a stiff grimace, and with her arms stiff at her sides she stood above the prone old man and the panting young one, erect and apart.

Movement when it came came in Solomon's face. It was an old and strict face, a frail face, but behind it, like a covered light, came an animation that could play hide and seek, that would dart and escape, had always escaped. The mystery flickered in him, and invited from his eyes. It was that very mystery that Cash with his quick arm would have to strike, and that Livvie could not weep for. But Cash only stood holding his arm in the air, when the gentlest flick of his great strength, almost a puff of his breath, would have been enough, if he had known how to give it, to send the old man over the obstruction that kept him away from death.

If it could not be that the tiny illumination in the fragile and ancient face caused a crisis, a mystery in the room that would not permit a blow to fall, at least it was certain that Cash, throbbing in his Easter clothes, felt a pang of shame that the vigor of a man would come to such an end that he could not be struck without warning. He took down his hand and stepped back behind Livvie, like a round-eyed schoolboy on whose unsuspecting head the dunce cap has been set.

"Young ones can't wait," said Solomon.

Livvie shuddered violently, and then in a gush of tears she stooped for a glass of water and handed it to him, but he did not see her.

"So here come the young man Livvie wait for. Was no prevention. No prevention. Now I lay eyes on young man and it come to be somebody I know all the time, and been knowing since he were born in a cotton patch, and watched grow up year to year, Cash McCord, growed to size, growed up to come in my house in the end—ragged and barefoot."

Solomon gave a cough of distaste. Then he shut his eyes vigorously, and his lips began to move like a chanter's.

"When Livvie married, her husband were already somebody. He had paid great cost for his land. He spread sycamore leaves over the ground from wagon to door, day he brought her home, so her foot would not have to touch ground. He carried her through his door. Then he growed old and could not lift her, and she were still young."

Livvie's sobs followed his words like a soft melody repeating each thing as he stated it. His lips moved for a little without sound, or she cried too fervently, and unheard he might have been telling his whole life, and then he said, "God forgive Solomon for sins great and small. God forgive Solomon for carrying away too young girl for wife and keeping her away from her people and from all the young people would clamor for her back."

Then he lifted up his right hand toward Livvie where she stood by the bed and offered her his silver watch. He dangled it before her eyes, and she hushed crying; her tears stopped. For a moment the watch could be heard ticking as it always did, precisely in his proud hand. She lifted it away. Then he took hold of the quilt; then he was dead.

Livvie left Solomon dead and went out of the room. Stealthily, nearly without noise, Cash went beside her. He was like a shadow, but his shiny shoes moved over the floor in spangles, and the green downy feather shone like a light in his hat. As they reached the front room, he seized her deftly as a long black cat and dragged her hanging by the waist round and round him, while he turned in a circle, his face bent down to hers. The first moment, she kept one arm and its hand stiff and still, the one that held Solomon's watch. Then the fingers softly let go, all of her was limp, and the watch fell somewhere on the floor. It ticked away in the still room, and all at once there began outside the full song of a bird.

They moved around and around the room and into the brightness of the open door, then he stopped and shook her once. She rested in silence in his trembling arms, unprotesting as a bird on a nest. Outside the redbirds were flying and criss-crossing, the sun was in all the bottles on the prisoned trees, and the young peach was shining in the middle of them with the bursting light of spring.

Albert Camus 1913–1960

The Guest

T H E schoolmaster was watching the two men climb toward him. One was on horseback, the other on foot. They had not yet tackled the abrupt rise leading to the schoolhouse built on the hillside. They were toiling onward, making slow progress in the snow, among the stones, on the vast expanse of the high, deserted plateau. From time to time the horse stumbled. Without hearing anything yet, he could see the breath issuing from the horse's nostrils. One of the men, at least, knew the region. They were following the trail although it had disappeared days ago under a layer of dirty white snow. The schoolmaster calculated that it would take them half an hour to get onto the hill. It was cold; he went back into the school to get a sweater.

He crossed the empty frigid classroom. On the blackboard the four rivers of France, drawn with four different colored chalks, had been flowing toward their estuaries for the past three days. Snow had suddenly fallen in mid-October after eight months of drought without the transition of rain, and the twenty pupils, more or less, who lived in the villages scattered over the plateau had stopped coming. With fair weather they would return. Daru now heated only the single room that was his lodging, adjoining the classroom and giving also onto the plateau to the east. Like the class windows, his window looked to the south too. On that side the school was a few kilometers from the point where the plateau began to slope toward the south. In clear weather could be seen the purple mass of the mountain range where the gap opened onto the desert.

Somewhat warmed, Daru returned to the window from which he had first seen the two men. They were no longer visible. Hence they must have tackled the rise. The sky was not so dark, for the snow had stopped falling during the night. The morning had opened with a dirty light which had scarcely become brighter as the ceiling of clouds lifted. At two in the afternoon it seemed as if the day were merely beginning. But still this was better than those three days when the thick snow was falling amidst unbroken darkness with little gusts of wind that rattled the double door of the classroom. Then Daru had spent long hours in his room, leaving it only to go to the shed and feed the chickens or get some coal. Fortunately the delivery truck from Tadjid, the nearest village to the north, had brought his supplies two days before the blizzard. It would return in forty-eight hours.

Besides, he had enough to resist a siege, for the little room was cluttered with bags of wheat that the administration left as a stock to distribute to those of his pupils whose families had suffered from the drought. Actually they had all been victims because they were all poor. Every day Daru would distribute a ration to the children. They had missed it, he knew, during these bad days. Possibly one of the fathers or big brothers would come this afternoon and he could supply them with grain. It was just a matter of carrying them over to the next harvest. Now shiploads of wheat were arriving from France and the worst was over. But it would be hard to forget that poverty, that army of ragged ghosts wandering in the sunlight, the plateaus burned to a cinder month after month, the earth shriveled up little by little, literally scorched, every stone bursting into dust under one's foot. The sheep had died then by thousands and even a few men, here and there, sometimes without anyone's knowing.

In contrast with such poverty, he who lived almost like a monk in his remote schoolhouse, nonetheless satisfied with the little he had and with the rough life, had felt like a lord with his whitewashed walls, his narrow couch, his unpainted shelves, his well, and his weekly provision of water and food. And suddenly this snow, without warning, without the foretaste of rain. This is the way the region was, cruel to live in, even without men —who didn't help matters either. But Daru had been born here. Everywhere else, he felt exiled.

He stepped out onto the terrace in front of the schoolhouse. The two men were now halfway up the slope. He recognized the horseman as Balducci, the old gendarme he had known for a long time. Balducci was holding on the end of a rope an Arab who was walking behind him with hands bound and head lowered. The gendarme waved a greeting to which Daru did not reply, lost as he was in contemplation of the Arab dressed in a faded blue jellaba, his feet in sandals but covered with socks of heavy raw wool, his head surmounted by a narrow, short *chèche*. They were approaching. Balducci was holding back his horse in order not to hurt the Arab, and the group was advancing slowly.

Within earshot, Balducci shouted: "One hour to do the three kilometers from El Ameur!" Daru did not answer. Short and square in his thick sweater, he watched them climb. Not once had the Arab raised his head. "Hello," said Daru when they got up onto the terrace. "Come in and warm up." Balducci painfully got down from his horse without letting go of the rope. From under his bristling moustache he smiled at the schoolmaster. His little dark eyes, deepset under a tanned forehead, and his mouth surrounded with wrinkles made him look attentive and studious. Daru took the bridle, led the horse to the shed, and came back to the two men, who were now waiting for him in the school. He led them into his room. "I am going to heat up the classroom," he said. "We'll be more comfortable there." When he entered the room again, Balducci was on the couch. He had undone the rope tying him to the Arab, who had squatted near the stove. His hands still bound, the *chèche* pushed back on his head, he was looking toward the window. At first Daru noticed only his huge lips, fat, smooth, almost Negroid; yet his nose was straight, his eyes were dark and full of fever. The *chèche* revealed an obstinate forehead and, under the weathered skin now rather discolored by the cold, the whole face had a restless and rebellious look that struck Daru when the Arab, turning his face toward him, looked him straight in the eyes. "Go into the other room," said the schoolmaster, "and I'll make you some mint tea." "Thanks," Balducci said. "What a chore! How I long for retirement." And addressing his prisoner in Arabic: "Come on, you." The Arab got up and, slowly, holding his bound wrists in front of him, went into the classroom.

With the tea, Daru brought a chair. But Balducci was already enthroned on the nearest pupil's desk and the Arab had squatted against the teacher's platform facing the stove, which stood between the desk and the window. When he held out the glass of tea to the prisoner, Daru hesitated at the sight of his bound hands. "He might perhaps be untied." "Sure," said Balducci. "That was for the trip." He started to get to his feet. But Daru, setting the glass on the floor, had knelt beside the Arab. Without saying anything, the Arab watched him with his feverish eyes. Once his hands were free, he rubbed his swollen wrists against each other, took the glass of tea, and sucked up the burning liquid in swift little sips.

"Good," said Daru. "And where are you headed?"

Balducci withdrew his moustache from the tea. "Here, son."

"Odd pupils! And you're spending the night?"

"No. I'm going back to El Ameur. And you will deliver this fellow to Tinguit. He is expected at police headquarters."

Balducci was looking at Daru with a friendly little smile.

"What's this story?" asked the schoolmaster. "Are you pulling my leg?"

"No, son. Those are the orders."

"The orders? I'm not . . ." Daru hesitated, not wanting to hurt the old Corsican. "I mean, that's not my job."

"What! What's the meaning of that? In wartime people do all kinds of jobs."

"Then I'll wait for the declaration of war!"

Balducci nodded.

"O.K. But the orders exist and they concern you too. Things are brewing, it appears. There is talk of a forthcoming revolt. We are mobilized, in a way."

Daru still had his obstinate look.

"Listen, son," Balducci said. "I like you and you must understand. There's only a dozen of us at El Ameur to patrol throughout the whole territory of a small department and I must get back in a hurry. I was told to hand this guy over to you and return without delay. He couldn't be kept there. His village was beginning to stir; they wanted to take him back. You must take him to Tinguit tomorrow before the day is over. Twenty kilometers shouldn't faze a husky fellow like you. After that, all will be over. You'll come back to your pupils and your comfortable life."

Behind the wall the horse could be heard snorting and pawing the earth. Daru was looking out the window. Decidedly, the weather was clearing and the light was increasing over the snowy plateau. When all the snow was melted, the sun would take over again and once more would burn the fields of stone. For days, still, the unchanging sky would shed its dry light on the solitary expanse where nothing had any connection with man.

"After all," he said, turning around toward Balducci, "what did he do?" And, before the gendarme had opened his mouth, he asked: "Does he speak French?"

"No, not a word. We had been looking for him for a month, but they were hiding him. He killed his cousin."

"Is he against us?"

"I don't think so. But you can never be sure."

"Why did he kill?"

"A family squabble, I think. One owed the other grain, it seems. It's not at all clear. In short, he killed his cousin with a billhook. You know, like a sheep, *kreezk!*"

Balducci made the gesture of drawing a blade across his throat and the Arab, his attention attracted, watched him with a sort of anxiety. Daru felt a sudden wrath against the man, against all men with their rotten spite, their tireless hates, their blood lust.

But the kettle was singing on the stove. He served Balducci more tea, hesitated, then served the Arab again, who, a second time, drank avidly. His raised arms made the jellaba fall open and the schoolmaster saw his thin, muscular chest.

"Thanks, kid," Balducci said. "And now, I'm off."

He got up and went toward the Arab, taking a small rope from his pocket.

"What are you doing?" Daru asked dryly.

Balducci, disconcerted, showed him the rope.

"Don't bother."

The old gendarme hesitated. "It's up to you. Of course, you are armed?"

"I have my shotgun."

"Where?"

"In the trunk."

"You ought to have it near your bed."

"Why? I have nothing to fear."

"You're crazy, son. If there's an uprising, no one is safe, we're all in the same boat."

"I'll defend myself. I'll have time to see them coming."

Balducci began to laugh, then suddenly the moustache covered the white teeth. "You'll have time? O.K. That's just what I was saying. You have always been a little cracked. That's why I like you, my son was like that."

At the same time he took out his revolver and put it on the desk.

"Keep it; I don't need two weapons from here to El Ameur."

The revolver shone against the black paint of the table. When the gendarme turned toward him, the schoolmaster caught the smell of leather and horseflesh.

"Listen, Balducci," Daru said suddenly, "every bit of this disgusts me, and first of all your fellow here. But I won't hand him over. Fight, yes, if I have to. But not that."

The old gendarme stood in front of him and looked at him severely.

"You're being a fool," he said slowly. "I don't like it either. You don't get used to putting a rope on a man even after years of it, and you're even ashamed—yes, ashamed. But you can't let them have their way."

"I won't hand him over," Daru said again.

"It's an order, son, and I repeat it."

"That's right. Repeat to them what I've said to you: I won't hand him over."

Balducci made a visible effort to reflect. He looked at the Arab and at Daru. At last he decided.

"No, I won't tell them anything. If you want to drop us, go ahead; I'll not denounce you. I have an order to deliver the prisoner and I'm doing so. And now you'll just sign this paper for me."

"There's no need. I'll not deny that you left him with me."

"Don't be mean with me. I know you'll tell the truth. You're from hereabouts and you are a man. But you must sign, that's the rule."

Daru opened his drawer, took out a little square bottle of purple ink, the red wooden penholder with the "sergeant-major" pen he used for making models of penmanship, and signed. The gendarme carefully folded the paper and put it into his wallet. Then he moved toward the door.

"I'll see you off," Daru said.

"No," said Balducci. "There's no use being polite. You insulted me."

He looked at the Arab, motionless in the same spot, sniffed peevishly, and turned away toward the door. "Good-by, son," he said. The door shut behind him. Balducci appeared suddenly outside the window and then disappeared. His footsteps were muffled by the snow. The horse stirred on the other side of the wall and several chickens fluttered in fright. A moment later Balducci reappeared outside the window leading the horse by the bridle. He walked toward the little rise without turning around and disappeared from sight with the horse following him. A big stone could be heard bouncing down. Daru walked back toward the prisoner, who, without stirring, never took his eyes off him. "Wait," the school-master said in Arabic and went toward the bedroom. As he was going through the door, he had a second thought, went to the desk, took the revolver, and stuck it in his pocket. Then, without looking back, he went into his room.

For some time he lay on his couch watching the sky gradually close over, listening to the silence. It was this silence that had seemed painful to him during the first days here, after the war. He had requested a post in the little town at the base of the foothills separating the upper plateaus from the desert. There, rocky walls, green and black to the north, pink and lavender to the south, marked the frontier of eternal summer. He had been named to a post farther north, on the plateau itself. In the beginning, the solitude and the silence had been hard for him on these wastelands peopled only by stones. Occasionally, furrows suggested cultivation, but they had been dug to uncover a certain kind of stone good for building. The only plowing here was to harvest rocks. Elsewhere a thin layer of soil accumulated in the hollows would be scraped out to enrich paltry village gardens. This is the way it was: bare rock covered three quarters of the region. Towns sprang up, flourished, then disappeared; men came by, loved one another or fought bitterly, then died. No one in this desert, neither he nor his guest, mattered. And yet, outside this desert neither of them, Daru knew, could have really lived.

When he got up, no noise came from the classroom. He was amazed at the unmixed joy he derived from the mere thought that the Arab might have fled and that he would be alone with no decision to make. But the prisoner was there. He had merely stretched out between the stove and the desk. With eyes open, he was staring at the ceiling. In that position, his thick lips were particularly noticeable, giving him a pouting look. "Come," said Daru. The Arab got up and followed him. In the bedroom, the schoolmaster pointed to a chair near the table under the window. The Arab sat down without taking his eyes off Daru.

"Are you hungry?"

"Yes," the prisoner said.

Daru set the table for two. He took flour and oil, shaped a cake in a frying-pan, and lighted the little stove that functioned on bottled gas. While the cake was cooking, he went out to the shed to get cheese, eggs, dates, and condensed milk. When the cake was done he set it on the window sill to cool, heated some condensed milk diluted with water, and beat up the eggs into an omelette. In one of his motions he knocked against the revolver stuck in his right pocket. He set the bowl down, went into the classroom, and put the revolver in his desk drawer. When he came back to the room, night was falling. He put on the light and served the Arab. "Eat," he said. The Arab took a piece of the cake, lifted it eagerly to his mouth, and stopped short.

"And you?" he asked.

"After you. I'll eat too."

The thick lips opened slightly. The Arab hesitated, then bit into the cake determinedly.

The meal over, the Arab looked at the schoolmaster. "Are you the judge?"

"No, I'm simply keeping you until tomorrow."

"Why do you eat with me?"

"I'm hungry."

The Arab fell silent. Daru got up and went out. He brought back a folding bed from the shed, set it up between the table and the stove, perpendicular to his own bed. From a large suitcase which, upright in a corner, served as a shelf for papers, he took two blankets and arranged them on the camp bed. Then he stopped, felt useless, and sat down on his bed. There was nothing more to do or to get ready. He had to look at this man. He looked at him, therefore, trying to imagine his face bursting with rage. He couldn't do so. He could see nothing but the dark yet shining eyes and the animal mouth.

"Why did you kill him?" he asked in a voice whose hostile tone surprised him.

The Arab looked away. "He ran away. I ran after him."

He raised his eyes to Daru again and they were full of a sort of woeful interrogation. "Now what will they do to me?"

"Are you afraid?"

He stiffened, turning his eyes away.

"Are you sorry?"

The Arab stared at him openmouthed. Obviously he did not understand. Daru's annoyance was growing. At the same time he felt awkward and self-conscious with his big body wedged between the two beds.

"Lie down there," he said impatiently. "That's your bed."

The Arab didn't move. He called to Daru:

"Tell me!"

The schoolmaster looked at him.

"Is the gendarme coming back tomorrow?"

"I don't know."

"Are you coming with us?"

"I don't know. Why?"

The prisoner got up and stretched out on top of the blankets, his feet toward the window. The light from the electric bulb shone straight into his eyes and he closed them at once.

"Why?" Daru repeated, standing beside the bed.

The Arab opened his eyes under the blinding light and looked at him, trying not to blink.

"Come with us," he said.

In the middle of the night, Daru was still not asleep. He had gone to bed after undressing completely; he generally slept naked. But when he suddenly realized that he had nothing on, he hesitated. He felt vulnerable and the temptation came to him to put his clothes back on. Then he shrugged his shoulders; after all, he wasn't a child and, if need be, he could break his adversary in two. From his bed he could observe him, lying on his back, still motionless with his eyes closed under the harsh light. When Daru turned out the light, the darkness seemed to coagulate all of a sudden. Little by little, the night came back to life in the window where the starless sky was stirring gently. The schoolmaster soon made out the body lying at his feet. The Arab still did not move, but his eyes seemed open. A faint wind was prowling around the schoolhouse. Perhaps it would drive away the clouds and the sun would reappear.

During the night the wind increased. The hens fluttered a little and then were silent. The Arab turned over on his side with his back to Daru, who thought he heard him moan. Then he listened for his guest's breathing, become heavier and more regular. He listened to that breath so close to him and mused without being able to go to sleep. In this room where he had been sleeping alone for a year, this presence bothered him. But it bothered him also by imposing on him a sort of brotherhood he knew well but refused to accept in the present circumstances. Men who share the same rooms, soldiers or prisoners, develop a strange alliance as if, having cast off their armor with their clothing, they fraternized every evening, over and above their differences, in the ancient community of dream and fatigue. But Daru shook himself; he didn't like such musings, and it was essential to sleep.

A little later, however, when the Arab stirred slightly, the schoolmaster was still not asleep. When the prisoner made a second move, he stiffened, on the alert. The Arab was lifting himself slowly on his arms with almost the motion of a sleepwalker. Seated upright in bed, he waited motionless without turning his head toward Daru, as if he were listening attentively. Daru did not stir; it had just occurred to him that the revolver was still in the drawer of his desk. It was better to act at once. Yet he continued to observe the prisoner, who, with the same slithery motion, put his feet on the ground, waited again, then began to stand up slowly. Daru was about to call out to him when the Arab began to walk, in a quite natural but extraordinary silent way. He was heading toward the door at the end of the room that opened into the shed. He lifted the latch with precaution and went out, pushing the door behind him but without shutting it. Daru had not stirred. "He is running away," he merely thought. "Good riddance!" Yet he listened attentively. The hens were not fluttering; the guest must be on the plateau. A faint sound of water reached him, and he didn't know what it was until the Arab again stood framed in the doorway, closed the door carefully, and came back to bed without a sound. Then Daru turned his back on him and fell asleep. Still later he seemed, from the depths of his sleep, to hear furtive steps around the schoolhouse. "I'm dreaming! I'm dreaming!" he repeated to himself. And he went on sleeping.

When he awoke, the sky was clear; the loose window let in a cold, pure air. The Arab was asleep, hunched up under the blankets now, his mouth open, utterly relaxed. But when Daru shook him, he started dreadfully, staring at Daru with wild eyes as if he had never seen him and such a frightened expression that the schoolmaster stepped back. "Don't be afraid. It's me. You must eat." The Arab nodded his head and said yes. Calm had returned to his face, but his expression was vacant and listless.

The coffee was ready. They drank it seated together on the folding bed as they munched their pieces of the cake. Then Daru led the Arab under the shed and showed him the faucet where he washed. He went back into the room, folded the blankets and the bed, made his own bed and put the room in order. Then he went through the classroom and out onto the terrace. The sun was already rising in the blue sky; a soft, bright light was bathing the deserted plateau. On the ridge the snow was melting in spots. The stones were about to reappear. Crouched on the edge of the plateau, the schoolmaster looked at the deserted expanse. He thought of Balducci. He had hurt him, for he had sent him off in a way as if he didn't want to be associated with him. He could still hear the gendarme's farewell and, without knowing why, he felt strangely empty and vulnerable. At that moment, from the other side of the schoolhouse, the prisoner coughed. Daru listened to him almost despite himself and then, furious, threw a pebble that whistled through the air before sinking into the snow. That man's stupid crime revolted him, but to hand him over was contrary to honor. Merely thinking of it made him smart with humiliation. And he cursed at one and the same time his own people who had sent him this Arab and the Arab too who had dared to kill and not managed to get away. Daru got up, walked in a circle on the terrace, waited motionless, and then went back into the schoolhouse.

The Arab, leaning over the cement floor of the shed, was washing his teeth with two fingers. Daru looked at him and said: "Come." He went back into the room ahead of the prisoner. He slipped a hunting-jacket on over his sweater and put on walking-shoes. Standing, he waited until the Arab had put on his *chèche* and sandals. They went into the classroom and the schoolmaster pointed to the exit, saying: "Go ahead." The fellow didn't budge. "I'm coming." said Daru. The Arab went out. Daru went back into the room and made a package of pieces of rusk, dates, and sugar. In the classroom, before going out, he hesitated a second in front of his desk, then crossed the threshold and locked the door. "That's the way," he said. He started toward the east, followed by the prisoner. But, a short distance from the schoolhouse, he thought he heard a slight sound behind them. He retraced his steps and examined the surroundings of the house; there was no one there. The Arab watched him without seeming to understand. "Come on," said Daru.

They walked for an hour and rested beside a sharp peak of limestone. The snow was melting faster and faster and the sun was drinking up the puddles at once, rapidly cleaning the plateau, which gradually dried and vibrated like the air itself. When they resumed walking, the ground rang under their feet. From time to time a bird rent the space in front of them with a joyful cry. Daru breathed in deeply the fresh morning light. He felt a sort of rapture before the vast familiar expanse, now almost entirely yellow under its dome of blue sky. They walked an hour more, descending toward the south. They reached a level height made up of crumbly rocks. From there on, the plateau sloped down, eastward toward a low plain where there were a few spindly trees and, to the south, toward outcroppings of rock that gave the landscape a chaotic look.

Daru surveyed the two directions. There was nothing but the sky on the horizon. Not a man could be seen. He turned toward the Arab, who was looking at him blankly. Daru held out the package to him. "Take it," he said. "There are dates, bread, and sugar. You can hold out for two days. Here are a thousand francs too." The Arab took the package and the money but kept his full hands at chest level as if he didn't know what to do with what was being given him. "Now look," the schoolmaster said as he pointed in the direction of the east, "there's the way to Tinguit. You have a two-hour walk. At Tinguit you'll find the administration and the police. They are expecting you." The Arab looked toward the east, still holding the package and the money against his chest. Daru took his elbow and turned him rather roughly toward the south. At the foot of the height on which they stood could be seen a faint path. "That's the trail across the plateau. In a day's walk from here you'll find pasturelands and the first nomads. They'll take you in and shelter you according to their law." The Arab had now turned toward Daru and a sort of panic was visible in his expression. "Listen," he said. Daru shook his head: "No, be quiet. Now I'm leaving you." He turned his back on him, took two long steps in the direction of the school, looked hesitantly at the motionless Arab, and started off again. For a few minutes he heard nothing but his own step resounding on the cold ground and did not turn his head. A moment later, however, he turned around. The Arab was still there on the edge of the hill, his arms hanging now, and he was looking at the school-master. Daru felt something rise in his throat. But he swore with impatience, waved vaguely, and started off again. He had already gone some distance when he again stopped and looked. There was no longer anyone on the hill.

Daru hesitated. The sun was now rather high in the sky and was beginning to beat down on his head. The schoolmaster retraced his steps, at first somewhat uncertaintly, then with decision. When he reached the little hill, he was bathed in sweat. He climbed it as fast as he could and stopped, out of breath, at the top. The rock-fields to the south stood out sharply against the blue sky, but on the plain to the east a steamy heat was already rising. And in that slight haze, Daru, with heavy heart, made out the Arab walking slowly on the road to prison.

A little later, standing before the window of the classroom, the school-master was watching the clear light bathing the whole surface of the plateau, but he hardly saw it. Behind him on the blackboard, among the winding French rivers, sprawled the clumsily chalked-up words he had just read: "You handed over our brother. You will pay for this." Daru looked at the sky, the plateau, and, beyond, the invisible lands stretching all the way to the sea. In this vast landscape he had loved so much he was alone.

Delmore Schwartz 1913–1966

In Dreams Begin Responsibilities

I THINK it is the year 1909. I feel as if I were in a moving-picture theater, the long arm of light crossing the darkness and spinning, my eyes
fixed upon the screen. It is a silent picture, as if an old Biograph one, in
which the actors are dressed in ridiculously old-fashioned clothes, and
one flash succeeds another with sudden jumps, and the actors, too, seem
to jump about, walking too fast. The shots are full of rays and dots, as
if it had been raining when the picture was photographed. The light
is bad.

It is Sunday afternoon, June 12th, 1909, and my father is walking down
the quiet streets of Brooklyn on his way to visit my mother. His clothes are
newly pressed, and his tie is too tight in his high collar. He jingles the
coins in his pocket, thinking of the witty things he will say. I feel as if
I had by now relaxed entirely in the soft darkness of the theater; the
organist peals out the obvious approximate emotions on which the audience rocks unknowingly. I am anonymous. I have forgotten myself: it is
always so when one goes to a movie, it is, as they say, a drug.

My father walks from street to street of trees, lawns and houses, once
in a while coming to an avenue on which a streetcar skates and yaws,
progressing slowly. The motorman, who has a handlebar mustache, helps
a young lady wearing a hat like a feathered bowl onto the car. He leisurely
makes change and rings his bell as the passengers mount the car. It is
obviously Sunday, for everyone is wearing Sunday clothes and the streetcar's noises emphasize the quiet of the holiday (Brooklyn is said to be
the city of churches). The shops are closed and their shades drawn but
for an occasional stationery store or drugstore with great green balls in
the window.

My father has chosen to take this long walk because he likes to walk
and think. He thinks about himself in the future and so arrives at the
place he is to visit in a mild state of exaltation. He pays no attention
to the houses he is passing, in which the Sunday dinner is being eaten,
nor to the many trees which line each street, now coming to their full

258

green and the time when they will enclose the whole street in leafy shadow. An occasional carriage passes, the horses' hooves falling like stones in the quiet afternoon, and once in a while an automobile, looking like an enormous upholstered sofa, puffs and passes.

My father thinks of my mother, of how lady-like she is, and of the pride which will be his when he introduces her to his family. They are not yet engaged and he is not yet sure that he loves my mother, so that, once in a while, he becomes panicky about the bond already established. But then he reassures himself by thinking of the big men he admires who are married: William Randolph Hearst and William Howard Taft, who has just become the President of the United States.

My father arrives at my mother's house. He has come too early and so is suddenly embarrassed. My aunt, my mother's younger sister, answers the loud bell with her napkin in her hand, for the family is still at dinner. As my father enters, my grandfather rises from the table and shakes hands with him. My mother has run upstairs to tidy herself. My grandmother asks my father if he has had dinner and tells him that my mother will be down soon. My grandfather opens the conversation by remarking about the mild June weather. My father sits uncomfortably near the table, holding his hat in his hand. My grandmother tells my aunt to take my father's hat. My uncle, twelve years old, runs into the house, his hair tousled. He shouts a greeting to my father, who has often given him nickels, and then runs upstairs, as my grandmother shouts after him. It is evident that the respect in which my father is held in this house is tempered by a good deal of mirth. He is impressive, but also very awkward.

II

Finally my mother comes downstairs and my father, being at the moment engaged in conversation with my grandfather, is made uneasy by her entrance, for he does not know whether to greet my mother or to continue the conversation. He gets up from his chair clumsily and says "Hello" gruffly. My grandfather watches this, examining their congruence, such as it is, with a critical eye, and meanwhile rubbing his bearded cheek roughly, as he always does when he reasons. He is worried; he is afraid that my father will not make a good husband for his oldest daughter. At this point something happens to the film, just as my father says something funny to my mother: I am awakened to myself and my unhappiness just as my interest has become most intense. The audience begins to clap impatiently. Then the trouble is attended to, but the film has been returned to a portion just shown, and once more I see my grandfather rubbing his bearded cheek, pondering my father's character. It is difficult to get back into the picture once more and forget myself, but as my mother giggles at my father's words, the darkness drowns me.

My father and mother depart from the house, my father shaking hands with my grandfather once more, out of some unknown uneasiness. I stir uneasily also, slouched in the hard chair of the theater. Where is the older uncle, my mother's older brother? He is studying in his bedroom upstairs, studying for his final examinations at the College of the City of New York, having been dead of double pneumonia for the last twenty-one years. My mother and father walk down the same quiet streets once more. My mother is holding my father's arm and telling him of the novel she has been reading and my father utters judgments of the characters as the plot is made clear to him. This is a habit which he very much enjoys, for he feels the utmost superiority and confidence when he is approving or condemning the behavior of other people. At times he feels moved to utter a brief "Ugh," whenever the story becomes what he would call sugary. This tribute is the assertion of his manliness. My mother feels satisfied by the interest she has awakened; and she is showing my father how intelligent she is and how interesting.

They reach the avenue, and the streetcar leisurely arrives. They are going to Coney Island this afternoon, although my mother really considers such pleasures inferior. She has made up her mind to indulge only in a walk on the boardwalk and a pleasant dinner, avoiding the riotous amusements as being beneath the dignity of so dignified a couple.

My father tells my mother how much money he has made in the week just past, exaggerating an amount which need not have been exaggerated. But my father has always felt that actualities somehow fall short, no matter how fine they are. Suddenly I begin to weep. The determined old lady who sits next to me in the theater is annoyed and looks at me with an angry face, and being intimidated, I stop. I drag out my handkerchief and dry my face, licking the drop which has fallen near my lips. Meanwhile I have missed something, for here are my father and mother alighting from the streetcar at the last stop, Coney Island.

III

They walk toward the boardwalk and my mother commands my father to inhale the pungent air from the sea. They both breathe in deeply, both of them laughing as they do so. They have in common a great interest in health, although my father is strong and husky, and my mother is frail. They are both full of theories about what is good to eat and not good to eat, and sometimes have heated discussions about it, the whole matter ending in my father's announcement, made with a scornful bluster, that you have to die sooner or later anyway. On the boardwalk's flagpole, the American flag is pulsing in an intermittent wind from the sea.

My father and mother go to the rail of the boardwalk and look down on the beach where a good many bathers are casually walking about. A few are in the surf. A peanut whistle pierces the air with its pleasant and active whine, and my father goes to buy peanuts. My mother remains at the rail and stares at the ocean. The ocean seems merry to her; it pointedly sparkles and again and again the pony waves are released. She notices the children digging in the wet sand, and the bathing costumes of the girls who are her own age. My father returns with the peanuts. Overhead the sun's lightning strikes and strikes, but neither of them are at all aware of it. The boardwalk is full of people dressed in their Sunday clothes and casually strolling. The tide does not reach as far as the boardwalk, and the strollers would feel no danger if it did. My father and mother lean on the rail of the boardwalk and absently stare at the ocean. The ocean is becoming rough; the waves come in slowly, tugging strength from far back. The moment before they somersault, the moment when they arch their backs so beautifully, showing white veins in the green and black, that moment is intolerable. They finally crack, dashing fiercely upon the sand, actually driving, full force downward, against it, bouncing upward and forward, and at last petering out into a small stream of bubbles which slides up the beach and then is recalled. The sun overhead does not disturb my father and my mother. They gaze idly at the ocean, scarcely interested in its harshness. But I stare at the terrible sun which breaks up sight, and the fatal merciless passionate ocean. I forget my parents. I stare fascinated, and finally, shocked by their indifference, I burst out weeping once more. The old lady next to me pats my shoulder and says: "There, there, young man, all of this is only a movie, only a movie," but I look up once more at the terrifying sun and the terrifying ocean, and being unable to control my tears I get up and go to the men's room, stumbling over the feet of the other people seated in my row.

IV

When I return, feeling as if I had just awakened in the morning sick for lack of sleep, several hours have apparently passed and my parents are riding on the merry-go-round. My father is on a black horse, my mother on a white one, and they seem to be making an eternal circuit for the single purpose of snatching the nickel rings which are attached to an arm of one of the posts. A hand-organ is playing; it is inseparable from the ceaseless circling of the merry-go-round.

For a moment it seems that they will never get off the carousel, for it will never stop, and I feel as if I were looking down from the fiftieth story of a building. But at length they do get off; even the hand-organ has ceased for a moment. There is a sudden and sweet stillness, as if the achievement of so much motion. My mother has acquired only two rings, my father, however, ten of them, although it was my mother who really wanted them.

They walk on along the boardwalk as the afternoon descends by imperceptible degrees into the incredible violet of dusk. Everything fades into a relaxed glow, even the ceaseless murmuring from the beach. They look for a place to have dinner. My father suggests the best restaurant on the boardwalk and my mother demurs, according to her principles of economy and housewifeliness.

However they do go to the best place, asking for a table near the window so that they can look out upon the boardwalk and the mobile ocean. My father feels omnipotent as he places a quarter in the waiter's hand in asking for a table. The place is crowded and here too there is music, this time from a kind of string trio. My father orders with a fine confidence.

As their dinner goes on, my father tells of his plans for the future and my mother shows with expressive face how interested she is, and how impressed. My father becomes exultant, lifted up by the waltz that is being played and his own future begins to intoxicate him. My father tells my mother that he is going to expand his business, for there is a great deal of money to be made. He wants to settle down. After all, he is twenty-nine, he has lived by himself since his thirteenth year, he is making more and more money, and he is envious of his friends when he visits them in the security of their homes, surrounded, it seems, by the calm domestic pleasures, and by delightful children, and then as the waltz reaches the moment when the dancers all swing madly, then, then with awful daring, then he asks my mother to marry him, although awkwardly enough and puzzled as to how he had arrived at the question, and she, to make the whole business worse, begins to cry, and my father looks nervously about, not knowing at all what to do now, and my mother says: "It's all I've wanted from the first moment I saw you," sobbing, and he finds all of this very difficult, scarcely to his taste, scarcely as he thought it would be, on his long walks over Brooklyn Bridge in the revery of a fine cigar, and it was then, at that point, that I stood up in the theater and shouted: "Don't do it! It's not too late to change your minds, both of you. Nothing good will come of it, only remorse, hatred, scandal, and two children whose characters are monstrous." The whole audience turned to look at me, annoyed, the usher came hurrying down the aisle flashing his searchlight, and the old lady next to me tugged me down into my seat, saying: "Be quiet. You'll be put out, and you paid thirty-five cents to come in." And so I shut my eyes because I could not bear to see what was happening. I sat there quietly.

V

But after a while I begin to take brief glimpses and at length I watch again with thirsty interest, like a child who tries to maintain his sulk when he is offered a bribe of candy. My parents are now having their picture taken in a photographer's booth along the boardwalk. The place is shadowed in the mauve light which is apparently necessary. The camera is set to the side on its tripod and looks like a Martian man. The photographer is instructing my parents in how to pose. My father has his arm over my mother's shoulder, and both of them smile emphatically. The photographer brings my mother a bouquet of flowers to hold in her hand, but she holds it at the wrong angle. Then the photographer covers himself with the black cloth which drapes the camera and all that one sees of him is one protruding arm and his hand with which he holds tightly to the rubber ball which he squeezes when the picture is taken. But he is not satisfied with their appearance. He feels that somehow there is something wrong in their pose. Again and again he comes out from his hiding place with new directions. Each suggestion merely makes matters worse. My father is becoming impatient. They try a seated pose. The photographer explains that he has his pride, he wants to make beautiful pictures, he is not merely interested in all of this for the money. My father says: "Hurry up, will you? We haven't got all night." But the photographer only scurries about apologetically, issuing new directions. The photographer charms me, and I approve of him with all my heart, for I know exactly how he feels, and as he criticizes each revised pose according to some obscure idea of rightness, I become quite hopeful. But then my father says angrily: "Come on, you've had enough time, we're not going to wait any longer." And the photographer, sighing unhappily, goes back into the black covering, and holds out his hand, saying: "One, two, three, Now!" and the picture is taken, with my father's smile turned to a grimace and my mother's bright and false. It takes a few minutes for the picture to be developed and as my parents sit in the curious light they become depressed.

VI

They have passed a fortune-teller's booth and my mother wishes to go in, but my father does not. They begin to argue about it. My mother becomes stubborn, my father once more impatient. What my father would like to do now is walk off and leave my mother there, but he knows that that would never do. My mother refuses to budge. She is near tears, but she feels an uncontrollable desire to hear what the palm-reader will say. My father consents angrily and they both go into the booth which is, in a way, like the photographer's, since it is draped in black cloth and its light is colored and shadowed. The place is too warm, and my father keeps saying that this is all nonsense, pointing to the crystal ball on the table. The fortune-teller, a short, fat woman garbed in robes supposedly exotic, comes into the room and greets them, speaking with an accent, but suddenly my father feels that the whole thing is intolerable; he tugs at my mother's arm but my mother refuses to budge. And then, in terrible anger, my father lets go of my mother's arm and strides out, leaving my mother stunned. She makes a movement as if to go after him, but the fortune-teller holds her and begs her not to do so, and I in my seat in the darkness am shocked and horrified. I feel as if I were walking a tight-rope one hundred feet over a circus audience and suddenly the rope is showing signs of breaking, and I get up from my seat and begin to shout once more the first words I can think of to communicate my terrible fear, and once more the usher comes hurrying down the aisle flashing his searchlight, and the old lady pleads with me, and the shocked audience has turned to stare at me, and I keep shouting: "What are they doing? Don't they know what they are doing? Why doesn't my mother go after my father and beg him not to be angry? If she does not do that, what will she do? Doesn't my father know what he is doing?" But the usher has seized my arm, and is dragging me away, and as he does so, he says: "What are *you* doing? Don't you know you can't do things like this, you can't do whatever you want to do, even if other people aren't about? You will be sorry if you do not do what you should do. You can't carry on like this, it is not right, you will find that out soon enough, everything you do matters too much," and as he said that, dragging me through the lobby of the theater, into the cold light, I woke up into the bleak winter morning of my twenty-first birthday, the window-sill shining with its lip of snow, and the morning already begun.

Flannery O'Connor 1925–1965

Everything That Rises Must Converge

H ER DOCTOR had told Julian's mother that she must lose twenty pounds on account of her blood pressure, so on Wednesday nights Julian had to take her downtown on the bus for a reducing class at the Y. The reducing class was designed for working girls over fifty, who weighed from 165 to 200 pounds. His mother was one of the slimmer ones, but she said ladies did not tell their age or weight. She would not ride the buses by herself at night since they had been integrated, and because the reducing class was one of her few pleasures, necessary for her health, and *free*, she said Julian could at least put himself out to take her, considering all she did for him. Julian did not like to consider all she did for him, but every Wednesday night he braced himself and took her.

She was almost ready to go, standing before the hall mirror, putting on her hat, while he, his hands behind him, appeared pinned to the door frame, waiting like Saint Sebastian for the arrows to begin piercing him. The hat was new and had cost her seven dollars and a half. She kept saying, "Maybe I shouldn't have paid that for it. No, I shouldn't have. I'll take it off and return it tomorrow. I shouldn't have bought it."

Julian raised his eyes to heaven. "Yes, you should have bought it," he said. "Put it on and let's go." It was a hideous hat. A purple velvet flap came down on one side of it and stood up on the other; the rest of it was green and looked like a cushion with the stuffing out. He decided it was less comical than jaunty and pathetic. Everything that gave her pleasure was small and depressed him.

She lifted the hat one more time and set it down slowly on top of her head. Two wings of gray hair protruded on either side of her florid face, but her eyes, sky-blue, were as innocent and untouched by experience as they must have been when she was ten. Were it not that she was a widow who had struggled fiercely to feed and clothe and put him through school and who was supporting him still, "until he got on his feet," she might have been a little girl that he had to take to town.

"It's all right, it's all right," he said. "Let's go." He opened the door

265

himself and started down the walk to get her going. The sky was a dying violet and the houses stood out darkly against it, bulbous liver-colored monstrosities of a uniform ugliness though no two were alike. Since this had been a fashionable neighborhood forty years ago, his mother persisted in thinking they did well to have an apartment in it. Each house had a narrow collar of dirt around it in which sat, usually a grubby child. Julian walked with his hands in his pockets, his head down and thrust forward and his eyes glazed with the determination to make himself completely numb during the time he would be sacrificed to her pleasure.

The door closed and he turned to find the dumpy figure, surmounted by the atrocious hat, coming toward him. "Well," she said, "you only live once and paying a little more for it, I at least won't meet myself coming and going."

"Some day I'll start making money," Julian said gloomily—he knew he never would—"and you can have one of those jokes whenever you take the fit." But first they would move. He visualized a place where the nearest neighbors would be three miles away on either side.

"I think you're doing fine," she said, drawing on her gloves. "You've only been out of school a year. Rome wasn't built in a day."

She was one of the few members of the Y reducing class who arrived in hat and gloves and who had a son who had been to college. "It takes time," she said, "and the world is in such a mess. This hat looked better on me than any of the others, though when she brought it out I said, 'Take that thing back. I wouldn't have it on my head,' and she said, 'Now wait till you see it on,' and when she put it on me, I said, 'We-ull,' and she said, 'If you ask me, that hat does something for you and you do something for the hat, and besides,' she said 'with that hat, you won't meet yourself coming and going.'"

Julian thought he could have stood his lot better if she had been selfish, if she had been an old hag who drank and screamed at him. He walked along, saturated in depression, as if in the midst of his martyrdom he had lost his faith. Catching sight of his long, hopeless, irritated face, she stopped suddenly with a grief-stricken look, and pulled back on his arm. "Wait on me," she said. "I'm going back to the house and take this thing off and tomorrow I'm going to return it. I was out of my head. I can pay the gas bill with that seven-fifty."

He caught her arm in a vicious grip. "You are not going to take it back," he said. "I like it."

"Well," she said, "I don't think I ought . . ."

"Shut up and enjoy it," he muttered, more depressed than ever.

"With the world in the mess it's in," she said, "it's a wonder we can enjoy anything. I tell you, the bottom rail is on the top."

Julian sighed.

"Of course," she said, "if you know who you are, you can go anywhere." She said this every time he took her to the reducing class. "Most of them in it are not our kind of people," she said, "but I can be gracious to anybody. I know who I am."

"They don't give a damn for your graciousness," Julian said savagely. "Knowing who you are is good for one generation only. You haven't the foggiest idea where you stand now or who you are."

She stopped and allowed her eyes to flash at him. "I most certainly do know who I am," she said, "and if you don't know who you are, I'm ashamed of you."

"Oh hell," Julian said.

"Your great-grandfather was a former governor of this state," she said. "Your grandfather was a prosperous landowner. Your grandmother was a Godhigh."

"Will you look around you," he said tensely, "and see where you are now?" and he swept his arm jerkily out to indicate the neighborhood, which the growing darkness at least made less dingy.

"You remain what you are," she said. "Your great-grandfather had a plantation and two hundred slaves."

"There are no more slaves," he said irritably.

"They were better off when they were," she said. He groaned to see that she was off on that topic. She rolled onto it every few days like a train on an open track. He knew every stop, every junction, every swamp along the way, and knew the exact point at which her conclusion woud roll majestically into the station: "It's ridiculous. It's simply not realistic. They should rise, yes, but on their own side of the fence."

"Let's skip it," Julian said.

"The ones I feel sorry for," she said, "are the ones that are half white. They're tragic."

"Will you skip it?"

"Suppose we were half white. We would certainly have mixed feelings."

"I have mixed feelings now," he groaned.

"Well let's talk about something pleasant," she said. "I remember going to Grandpa's when I was a little girl. Then the house had double stairways that went up to what was really the second floor—all the cooking was done on the first. I used to like to stay down in the kitchen on account of the way the walls smelled. I would sit with my nose pressed against the plaster and take deep breaths. Actually the place belonged to the Godhighs but your grandfather Chestny paid the mortgage and saved it for them. They were in reduced circumstances," she said, "but reduced or not, they never forgot who they were."

"Doubtless that decayed mansion reminded them," Julian muttered. He never spoke of it without contempt or thought of it without longing.

He had seen it once when he was a child before it had been sold. The double stairways had rotted and been torn down. Negroes were living in it. But it remained in his mind as his mother had known it. It appeared in his dreams regularly. He would stand on the wide porch, listening to the rustle of oak leaves, then wander through the high-ceilinged hall into the parlor that opened onto it and gaze at the worn rugs and faded draperies. It occurred to him that it was he, not she, who could have appreciated it. He preferred its threadbare elegance to anything he could name and it was because of it that all the neighborhoods they had lived in had been a torment to him—whereas she had hardly known the difference. She called her insensitivity "being adjustable."

"And I remember the old darky who was my nurse, Caroline. There was no better person in the world. I've always had a great respect for my colored friends," she said. "I'd do anything in the world for them and they'd . . ."

"Will you for God's sake get off that subject?" Julian said. When he got on a bus by himself, he made it a point to sit down beside a Negro, in reparation as it were for his mother's sins.

"You're mighty touchy tonight," she said. "Do you feel all right?"

"Yes I feel all right," he said. "Now lay off."

She pursed her lips. "Well, you certainly are in a vile humor," she observed. "I just won't speak to you at all."

They had reached the bus stop. There was no bus in sight and Julian, his hands still jammed in his pockets and his head thrust forward, scowled down the empty street. The frustration of having to wait on the bus as well as ride on it began to creep up his neck like a hot hand. The presence of his mother was borne in upon him as she gave a pained sigh. He looked at her bleakly. She was holding herself very erect under the preposterous hat, wearing it like a banner of her imaginary dignity. There was in him an evil urge to break her spirit. He suddenly unloosened his tie and pulled it off and put it in his pocket.

She stiffened. "Why must you look like *that* when you take me to town?" she said. "Why must you deliberately embarrass me?"

"If you'll never learn where you are," he said, "you can at least learn where I am."

"You look like a—thug," she said.

"Then I must be one," he murmured.

"I'll just go home," she said. "I will not bother you. If you can't do a little thing like that for me . . ."

Rolling his eyes upward, he put his tie back on. "Restored to my class," he muttered. He thrust his face toward her and hissed, "True culture is in the mind, the *mind*," he said, and tapped his head, "the mind."

"It's in the heart," she said, "and in how you do things and how you do things is because of who you *are*."

"Nobody in the damn bus cares who you are."

"I care who I am," she said icily.

The lighted bus appeared on top of the next hill and as it approached, they moved out into the street to meet it. He put his hand under her elbow and hoisted her up on the creaking step. She entered with a little smile, as if she were going into a drawing room where everyone had been waiting for her. While he put in the tokens, she sat down on one of the broad front seats for three which faced the aisle. A thin woman with protruding teeth and long yellow hair was sitting on the end of it. His mother moved up beside her and left room for Julian beside herself. He sat down and looked at the floor across the aisle where a pair of thin feet in red and white canvas sandals were planted.

His mother immediately began a general conversation meant to attract anyone who felt like talking. "Can it get any hotter?" she said and removed from her purse a folding fan, black with a Japanese scene on it, which she began to flutter before her.

"I reckon it might could," the woman with the protruding teeth said, "but I know for a fact my apartment couldn't get no hotter."

"It must get the afternoon sun," his mother said. She sat forward and looked up and down the bus. It was half filled. Everybody was white. "I see we have the bus to ourselves," she said. Julian cringed.

"For a change," said the woman across the aisle, the owner of the red and white canvas sandals. "I come on one the other day and they were thick as fleas—up front and all through."

"The world is in a mess everywhere," his mother said. "I don't know how we've let it get in this fix."

"What gets my goat is all those boys from good families stealing automobile tires," the woman with the protruding teeth said. "I told my boy, I said you may not be rich but you been raised right and if I ever catch you in any such mess, they can send you on to the reformatory. Be exactly where you belong."

"Training tells," his mother said. "Is your boy in high school?"

"Ninth grade," the woman said.

"My son just finished college last year. He wants to write but he's selling typewriters until he gets started," his mother said.

The woman leaned forward and peered at Julian. He threw her such a malevolent look that she subsided against the seat. On the floor across the aisle there was an abandoned newspaper. He got up and got it and opened it out in front of him. His mother discreetly continued the conversation in a lower tone but the woman across the aisle said in a loud voice, "Well that's nice. Selling typewriters is close to writing. He can go right from one to the other."

"I tell him," his mother said, "that Rome wasn't built in a day."

Behind the newspaper Julian was withdrawing into the inner compartment of his mind where he spent most of his time. This was a kind of mental bubble in which he established himself when he could not bear to be a part of what was going on around him. From it he could see out and judge but in it he was safe from any kind of penetration from without. It was the only place where he felt free of the general idiocy of his fellows. His mother had never entered it but from it he could see her with absolute clarity.

The old lady was clever enough and he thought that if she had started from any of the right premises, more might have been expected of her. She lived according to the laws of her own fantasy world, outside of which he had never seen her set foot. The law of it was to sacrifice herself for him after she had first created the necessity to do so by making a mess of things. If he had permitted her sacrifices, it was only because her lack of foresight had made them necessary. All of her life had been a struggle to act like a Chestny without the Chestny goods, and to give him everything she thought a Chestny ought to have; but since, said she, it was fun to struggle, why complain? And when you had won, as she had won, what fun to look back on the hard times! He could not forgive her that she had enjoyed the struggle and that she thought *she* had won.

What she meant when she said she had won was that she had brought him up successfully and had sent him to college and that he had turned out so well—good looking (her teeth had gone unfilled so that his could be straightened), intelligent (he realized he was too intelligent to be a success), and with a future ahead of him (there was of course no future ahead of him). She excused his gloominess on the grounds that he was still growing up and his radical ideas on his lack of practical experience. She said he didn't yet know a thing about "life," that he hadn't even entered the real world—when already he was as disenchanted with it as a man of fifty.

The further irony of all this was that in spite of her, he had turned out so well. In spite of going to only a third-rate college, he had, on his own initiative, come out with a first-rate education; in spite of growing up dominated by a small mind, he had ended up with a large one; in spite of all her foolish views, he was free of prejudice and unafraid to face facts. Most miraculous of all, instead of being blinded by love for her as she was for him, he had cut himself emotionally free of her and could see her with complete objectivity. He was not dominated by his mother.

The bus stopped with a sudden jerk and shook him from his meditation. A woman from the back lurched forward with little steps and barely escaped falling in his newspaper as she righted herself. She got off and a large Negro got on. Julian kept his paper lowered to watch. It gave him a certain satisfaction to see injustice in daily operation. It confirmed his view that with a few exceptions there was no one worth knowing within a radius of three hundred miles. The Negro was well dressed and carried a briefcase. He looked around and then sat down on the other end of the seat where the woman with the red and white canvas sandals was sitting. He immediately unfolded a newspaper and obscured himself behind it. Julian's mother's elbow at once prodded insistently into his ribs. "Now you see why I won't ride on these buses by myself," she whispered.

The woman with the red and white canvas sandals had risen at the same time the Negro sat down and had gone further back in the bus and taken the seat of the woman who had got off. His mother leaned forward and cast her an approving look.

Julian rose, crossed the aisle, and sat down in the place of the woman with the canvas sandals. From this position, he looked serenely across at his mother. Her face had turned an angry red. He stared at her, making his eyes the eyes of a stranger. He felt his tension suddenly lift as if he had openly declared war on her.

He would have liked to get in conversation with the Negro and to talk with him about art or politics or any subject that would be above the comprehension of those around them, but the man remained entrenched behind his paper. He was either ignoring the change of seating or had never noticed it. There was no way for Julian to convey his sympathy.

His mother kept her eyes fixed reproachfully on his face. The woman with the protruding teeth was looking at him avidly as if he were a type of monster new to her.

"Do you have a light?" he asked the Negro.

Without looking away from his paper, the man reached in his pocket and handed him a packet of matches.

"Thanks," Julian said. For a moment he held the matches foolishly. A NO SMOKING sign looked down upon him from over the door. This alone would not have deterred him; he had no cigarettes. He had quit smoking some months before because he could not afford it. "Sorry," he muttered and handed back the matches. The Negro lowered the paper and gave him an annoyed look. He took the matches and raised the paper again.

His mother continued to gaze at him but she did not take advantage of his momentary discomfort. Her eyes retained their battered look. Her face seemed to be unnaturally red, as if her blood pressure had risen. Julian allowed no glimmer of sympathy to show on his face. Having got the advantage, he wanted desperately to keep it and carry it through. He would have liked to teach her a lesson that would last her a while, but there seemed no way to continue the point. The Negro refused to come out from behind his paper.

Julian folded his arms and looked stolidly before him, facing her but as if he did not see her, as if he had ceased to recognize her existence. He visualized a scene in which, the bus having reached their stop, he would remain in his seat and when she said, "Aren't you going to get off?" he would look at her as at a stranger who had rashly addressed him. The corner they got off on was usually deserted, but it was well lighted and it would not hurt her to walk by herself the four blocks to the Y. He decided to wait until the time came and then decide whether or not he would let her get off by herself. He would have to be at the Y at ten to bring her back, but he could leave her wondering if he was going to show up. There was no reason for her to think she could always depend on him.

He retired again into the high-ceilinged room sparsely settled with large pieces of antique furniture. His soul expanded momentarily but then he became aware of his mother across from him and the vision shriveled. He studied her coldly. Her feet in little pumps dangled like a child's and did not quite reach the floor. She was training on him an exaggerated look of reproach. He felt completely detached from her. At that moment he could with pleasure have slapped her as he would have slapped a particularly obnoxious child in his charge.

He began to imagine various unlikely ways by which he could teach her a lesson. He might make friends with some distinguished Negro professor or lawyer and bring him home to spend the evening. He would be entirely justified but her blood pressure would rise to 300. He could not push her to the extent of making her have a stroke, and moreover, he had never been successful at making any Negro friends. He had tried to strike up an acquaintance on the bus with some of the better types, with ones that looked like professors or ministers or lawyers. One morning he had sat down next to a distinguished-looking dark brown man who had answered his questions with a sonorous solemnity but who had turned out to be an undertaker. Another day he had sat down beside a cigar-smoking Negro with a diamond ring on his finger, but after a few stilted pleasantries, the Negro had rung the buzzer and risen, slipping two lottery tickets into Julian's hand as he climbed over him to leave.

He imagined his mother lying desperately ill and his being able to secure only a Negro doctor for her. He toyed with that idea for a few minutes and then dropped it for a momentary vision of himself participating as a sympathizer in a sit-in demonstration. This was possible but he did not linger with it. Instead, he approached the ultimate horror. He brought home a beautiful suspiciously Negroid woman. Prepare yourself, he said. There is nothing you can do about it. This is the woman I've chosen. She's intelligent, dignified, even good, and she's suffered and she hasn't thought it *fun*. Now persecute us, go ahead and persecute us. Drive her out of here, but remember, you're driving me too. His eyes were narrowed and through the indignation he had generated, he saw his mother across the aisle, purple-faced, shrunken to the dwarf-like proportions of her moral nature, sitting like a mummy beneath the ridiculous banner of her hat.

He was tilted out of his fantasy again as the bus stopped. The door opened with a sucking hiss and out of the dark a large, gaily dressed, sullen-looking colored woman got on with a little boy. The child, who might have been four, had on a short plaid suit and a Tyrolean hat with a blue feather in it. Julian hoped that he would sit down beside him and that the woman would push in beside his mother. He could think of no better arrangement.

As she waited for her tokens, the woman was surveying the seating possibilities—he hoped with the idea of sitting where she was least wanted. There was something familiar-looking about her but Julian could not place what it was. She was a giant of a woman. Her face was set not only to meet opposition but to seek it out. The downward tilt of her large lower lip was like a warning sign: DON'T TAMPER WITH ME. Her bulging figure was encased in a green crepe dress and her feet overflowed in red shoes. She had on a hideous hat. A purple velvet flap came down on one side of it and stood up on the other; the rest of it was green and looked like a cushion with the stuffing out. She carried a mammoth red pocketbook that bulged throughout as if it were stuffed with rocks.

To Julian's disappointment, the little boy climbed up on the empty seat beside his mother. His mother lumped all children, black and white, into the common category, "cute," and she thought little Negroes were on the whole cuter than little white children. She smiled at the little boy as he climbed on the seat.

Meanwhile the woman was bearing down upon the empty seat beside Julian. To his annoyance, she squeezed herself into it. He saw his mother's face change as the woman settled herself next to him and he realized with satisfaction that this was more objectionable to her than it was to him. Her face seemed almost gray and there was a look of dull recognition in her eyes, as if suddenly she had sickened at some awful confrontation. Julian saw that it was because she and the woman had, in a sense, swapped sons. Though his mother would not realize the symbolic significance of this, she would feel it. His amusement showed plainly on his face.

The woman next to him muttered something unintelligible to herself. He was conscious of a kind of bristling next to him, a muted growling like that of an angry cat. He could not see anything but the red pocketbook upright on the bulging green thighs. He visualized the woman as she had stood waiting for her tokens—the ponderous figure, rising from the red shoes upward over the solid hips, the mammoth bosom, the haughty face, to the green and purple hat.

His eyes widened.

The vision of the two hats, identical, broke upon him with the radiance of a brilliant sunrise. His face was suddenly lit with joy. He could not believe that Fate had thrust upon his mother such a lesson. He gave a loud chuckle so that she would look at him and see that he saw. She turned her eyes on him slowly. The blue in them seemed to have turned a bruised purple. For a moment he had an uncomfortable sense of her innocence, but it lasted only a second before principle rescued him. Justice entitled him to laugh. His grin hardened until it said to her as plainly as if he were saying aloud: Your punishment exactly fits your pettiness. This should teach you a permanent lesson.

Her eyes shifted to the woman. She seemed unable to bear looking at him and to find the woman preferable. He became conscious again of the bristling presence at his side. The woman was rumbling like a volcano about to become active. His mother's mouth began to twitch slightly at one corner. With a sinking heart, he saw incipient signs of recovery on her face and realized that this was going to strike her suddenly as funny and was going to be no lesson at all. She kept her eyes on the woman and an amused smile came over her face as if the woman were a monkey that had stolen her hat. The little Negro was looking up at her with large fascinated eyes. He had been trying to attract her attention for some time.

"Carver!" the woman said suddenly. "Come heah!"

When he saw that the spotlight was on him at last, Carver drew his feet up and turned himself toward Julian's mother and giggled.

"Carver!" the woman said. "You heah me? Come heah!"

Carver slid down from the seat but remained squatting with his back against the base of it, his head turned slyly around toward Julian's mother, who was smiling at him. The woman reached a hand across the aisle and snatched him to her. He righted himself and hung backwards on her knees, grinning at Julian's mother. "Isn't he cute?" Julian's mother said to the woman with the protruding teeth.

"I reckon he is," the woman said without conviction.

The Negress yanked him upright but he eased out of her grip and shot across the aisle and scrambled, giggling wildly, onto the seat beside his love.

"I think he likes me," Julian's mother said, and smiled at the woman. It was the smile she used when she was being particularly gracious to an inferior. Julian saw everything lost. The lesson had rolled off her like rain on a roof.

The woman stood up and yanked the little boy off the seat as if she were snatching him from contagion. Julian could feel the rage in her at having no weapon like his mother's smile. She gave the child a sharp slap across his leg. He howled once and then thrust his head into her stomach and kicked his feet against her shins. "Be-have," she said vehemently.

The bus stopped and the Negro who had been reading the newspaper got off. The woman moved over and set the little boy down with a thump between herself and Julian. She held him firmly by the knee. In a moment he put his hands in front of his face and peeped at Julian's mother through his fingers.

"I see yoooooooo!" she said and put her hand in front of her face and peeped at him.

The woman slapped his hand down. "Quit yo' foolishness," she said, "before I knock the living Jesus out of you!"

Julian was thankful that the next stop was theirs. He reached up and pulled the cord. The woman reached up and pulled it at the same time. Oh my God, he thought. He had the terrible intuition that when they got off the bus together, his mother would open her purse and give the little boy a nickel. The gesture would be as natural to her as breathing. The bus stopped and the woman got up and lunged to the front, dragging the child, who wished to stay on, after her. Julian and his mother got up and followed. As they neared the door, Julian tried to relieve her of her pocketbook.

"No," she murmured, "I want to give the little boy a nickel."

"No!" Julian hissed. "No!"

She smiled down at the child and opened her bag. The bus door opened and the woman picked him up by the arm and descended with him, hanging at her hip. Once in the street she set him down and shook him.

Julian's mother had to close her purse while she got down the bus step but as soon as her feet were on the ground, she opened it again and began to rummage inside. "I can't find but a penny," she whispered, "but it looks like a new one."

"Don't do it!" Julian said fiercely between his teeth. There was a streetlight on the corner and she hurried to get under it so that she could better see into her pocketbook. The woman was heading off rapidly down the street with the child still hanging backward on her hand.

"Oh little boy!" Julian's mother called and took a few quick steps and caught up with them just beyond the lamppost. "Here's a bright new penny for you," and she held out the coin, which shone bronze in the dim light.

The huge woman turned and for a moment stood, her shoulders lifted and her face frozen with frustrated rage, and stared at Julian's mother. Then all at once she seemed to explode like a piece of machinery that had been given one ounce of pressure too much. Julian saw the black fist swing out with the red pocketbook. He shut his eyes and cringed as he heard the woman shout, "He don't take nobody's pennies!" When he opened his eyes, the woman was disappearing down the street with the little boy staring wide-eyed over her shoulder. Julian's mother was sitting on the sidewalk.

"I told you not to do that," Julian said angrily. "I told you not to do that!"

He stood over her for a minute, gritting his teeth. Her legs were stretched out in front of her and her hat was on her lap. He squatted down and looked her in the face. It was totally expressionless. "You got exactly what you deserved," he said. "Now get up."

He picked up her pocketbook and put what had fallen out back in it. He picked the hat up off her lap. The penny caught his eye on the sidewalk and he picked that up and let it drop before her eyes into the purse. Then he stood up and leaned over and held his hands out to pull her up. She remained immobile. He sighed. Rising above them on either side were black apartment buildings, marked with irregular rectangles of light. At the end of the block a man came out of a door and walked off in the opposite direction. "All right," he said, "suppose somebody happens by and wants to know why you're sitting on the sidewalk?"

She took the hand and, breathing hard, pulled heavily up on it and then stood for a moment, swaying slightly as if the spots of light in the darkness were circling around her. Her eyes, shadowed and confused, finally settled on his face. He did not try to conceal his irritation. "I hope this teaches you a lesson," he said. She leaned forward and her eyes raked his face. She seemed trying to determine his identity. Then, as if she found nothing familiar about him, she started off with a headlong movement in the wrong direction.

"Aren't you going on to the Y?" he asked.

"Home," she muttered.

"Well, are we walking?"

For answer she kept going. Julian followed along, his hands behind him. He saw no reason to let the lesson she had had go without backing it up with an explanation of its meaning. She might as well be made to understand what had happened to her. "Don't think that was just an uppity Negro woman," he said. "That was the whole colored race which will no longer take your condescending pennies. That was your black double. She can wear the same hat as you, and to be sure," he added gratuitously (because he thought it was funny), "it looked better on her than it did on you. What all this means," he said, "is that the old world is gone. The old manners are obsolete and your graciousness is not worth a damn." He thought bitterly of the house that had been lost for him. "You aren't who you think you are," he said.

She continued to plow ahead, paying no attention to him. Her hair had come undone on one side. She dropped her pocketbook and took no notice. He stooped and picked it up and handed it to her but she did not take it.

"You needn't act as if the world had come to an end," he said, "because it hasn't. From now on you've got to live in a new world and face a few realities for a change. Buck up," he said, "it won't kill you."

She was breathing fast.

"Let's wait on the bus," he said.

"Home," she said thickly.

"I hate to see you behave like this," he said. "Just like a child. I should be able to expect more of you." He decided to stop where he was and make her stop and wait for a bus. "I'm not going any farther," he said, stopping. "We're going on the bus."

She continued to go on as if she had not heard him. He took a few steps and caught her arm and stopped her. He looked into her face and caught his breath. He was looking into a face he had never seen before. "Tell Grandpa to come get me," she said.

He stared, stricken.

"Tell Caroline to come get me," she said.

Stunned, he let her go and she lurched forward again, walking as if one leg were shorter than the other. A tide of darkness seemed to be sweeping her from him. "Mother!" he cried. "Darling, sweetheart, wait!" Crumpling, she fell to the pavement. He dashed forward and fell at her side, crying, "Mamma, Mamma!" He turned her over. Her face was fiercely distorted. One eye, large and staring, moved slightly to the left as if it had become unmoored. The other remained fixed on him, raked his face again, found nothing and closed.

"Wait here, wait here!" he cried and jumped up and began to run for help toward a cluster of lights he saw in the distance ahead of him. "Help, help!" he shouted, but his voice was thin, scarcely a thread of sound. The lights drifted farther away the faster he ran and his feet moved numbly as if they carried him nowhere. The tide of darkness seemed to sweep him back to her, postponing from moment to moment his entry into the world of guilt and sorrow.

Drama

Sophocles   495–406 B.C.

King Oedipus

A Version for the Modern Stage by
William Butler Yeats

PERSONS IN THE PLAY

OEDIPUS, King of Thebes
JOCASTA, wife of Oedipus
ANTIGONE, daughter of Oedipus
ISMENE, daughter of Oedipus
CREON, brother-in-law of Oedipus

TIRESIAS, a seer
A PRIEST
MESSENGERS
A HERDSMAN
CHORUS

SCENE

The Palace of KING OEDIPUS *at Thebes*

OEDIPUS. Children, descendants of old Cadmus, why do you come before me, why do you carry the branches of suppliants, while the city smokes with incense and murmurs with prayer and lamentation? I would not learn from any mouth but yours, old man, therefore I question you myself. Do you know of anything that I can do and have not done? How can I, being the man I am, being King Oedipus, do other than all I know? I were indeed hard of heart did I not pity such suppliants.

PRIEST. Oedipus, King of my country, we who stand before your door are of all ages, some too young to have walked so many miles, some—priests of Zeus such as I—too old. Among us stand the pick of the young men,   10 and behind in the market-places the people throng, carrying suppliant branches. We all stand here because the city stumbles towards death, hardly able to raise up its head. A blight has fallen upon the fruitful

---

1. *Cadmus,* founder of Thebes, great-great grandfather of Oedipus.

281

blossoms of the land, a blight upon flock and field and upon the bed of marriage—plague ravages the city. Oedipus, King, not God but foremost of living men, seeing that when you first came to this town of Thebes you freed us from that harsh singer, the riddling Sphinx, we beseech you, all we suppliants, to find some help; whether you find it by your power as a man, or because, being near the Gods, a God has whispered you.

20   Uplift our State; think upon your fame; your coming brought us luck, be lucky to us still; remember that it is better to rule over men than over a waste place, since neither walled town nor ship is anything if it be empty and no man within it.

OEDIPUS. My unhappy children! I know well what need has brought you, what suffering you endure; yet, sufferers though you be, there is not a single one whose suffering is as mine—each mourns himself, but my soul mourns the city, myself, and you. It is not therefore as if you came to arouse a sleeping man. No! Be certain that I have wept many tears and searched hither and thither for some remedy. I have already done the

30   only thing that came into my head for all my search. I have sent the son of Menoeceus, Creon, my own wife's brother, to the Pythian House of Phoebus, to hear if deed or word of mine may yet deliver this town. I am troubled, for he is a long time away—a longer time than should be— but when he comes I shall not be an honest man unless I do whatever the God commands.

PRIEST. You have spoken at the right time. They have just signalled to us that Creon has arrived.

OEDIPUS. O King Apollo, may he bring brighter fortune, for his face is shining!

40   PRIEST. He brings good news, for he is crowned with bay.

OEDIPUS. We shall know soon. Brother-in-law, Menoeceus' son, what news from the God?

CREON. Good news; for pain turns to pleasure when we have set the crooked straight.

OEDIPUS. But what is the oracle?—so far the news is neither good nor bad.

CREON. If you would hear it with all these about you, I am ready to speak. Or do we go within?

OEDIPUS. Speak before all. The sorrow I endure is less for my own life than these.

50   CREON. Then, with your leave, I speak. Our lord Phoebus bids us drive out a defiling thing that has been cherished in this land.

OEDIPUS. By what purification?

CREON. King Laius was our King before you came to pilot us.

OEDIPUS. I know—but not of my own knowledge, for I never saw him.

31. *Pythian House of Phoebus,* oracle of Phoebus Apollo at Delphi.

CREON. He was killed; and the God now bids us revenge it on his murderers, whoever they be.

OEDIPUS. Where shall we come upon their track after all these years? Did he meet his death in house or field, at home or in some foreign land?

CREON. In a foreign land: he was journeying to Delphi.

OEDIPUS. Did no fellow-traveller see the deed? Was there none there who 60 could be questioned?

CREON. All perished but one man who fled in terror and could tell for certain but one thing of all he had seen.

OEDIPUS. One thing might be a clue to many things.

CREON. He said that they were fallen upon by a great troop of robbers.

OEDIPUS What robbers would be so daring unless bribed from here?

CREON. Such things were indeed guessed at, but Laius once dead no avenger arose. We were amid our troubles.

OEDIPUS. But when royalty had fallen what troubles could have hindered search? 70

CREON. The riddling Sphinx put those dark things out of our thoughts—we thought of what had come to our own doors.

OEDIPUS. But I will start afresh and make the dark things plain. In doing right by Laius I protect myself, for whoever slew Laius might turn a hand against me. Come, my children, rise up from the altar steps; lift up these suppliant boughs and let all the children of Cadmus be called hither that I may search out everything and find for all happiness or misery as God wills.

PRIEST. May Phoebus, sender of the oracle, come with it and be our saviour and deliverer! 80

[*The* CHORUS *enter.*]

CHORUS.

What message comes to famous Thebes from the Golden House?
What message of disaster from that sweet-throated Zeus?
What monstrous thing our fathers saw do the seasons bring?
Or what that no man ever saw, what new monstrous thing?
Trembling in every limb I raise my loud importunate cry.
And in a sacred terror wait the Delian God's reply.

Apollo chase the God of Death that leads no shouting men,
Bears no rattling shield and yet consumes this form with pain.
Famine takes what the plague spares, and all the crops are lost;
No new life fills the empty place—ghost flits after ghost 90

71. *riddling Sphinx*, mythical monster whose riddle Oedipus solved, thus saving the citizens of Thebes, whom she was slaying. 86. *Delian God*, Phoebus, reputedly born as a son of Zeus on the island of Delos.

To that God-trodden western shore, as flit benighted birds.
Sorrow speaks to sorrow, but no comfort finds in words.

Hurry him from the land of Thebes with a fair wind behind
Out on to that formless deep where not a man can find
Hold for an anchor-fluke, for all is world-enfolding sea;
Master of the thunder-cloud, set the lightning free,
And add the thunder-stone to that and fling them on his head,
For death is all the fashion now, till even Death be dead.

We call against the pallid face of this God-hated God
100   The springing heel of Artemis in the hunting sandal shod,
The tousle-headed Maenads, blown torch and drunken sound,
The stately Lysian king himself with golden fillet crowned,
And in his hands the golden bow and the stretched golden string,
And Bacchus' wine-ensanguined face that all the Maenads sing.

OEDIPUS. You are praying, and it may be that your prayer will be answered;
that if you hear my words and do my bidding you may find help out of
all your trouble. This is my proclamation, children of Cadmus. Whoever
among you knows by what man Laius, son of Labdacus, was killed, must
tell all he knows. If he fear for himself and being guilty denounce him-
110   self, he shall be in the less danger, suffering no worse thing than banishment. If on the other hand there be one that knows that a foreigner did
the deed, let him speak, and I shall give him a reward and my thanks:
but if any man keep silent from fear or to screen a friend, hear all what
I will do to that man. No one in this land shall speak to him, nor offer
sacrifice beside him; but he shall be driven from their homes as if he
himself had done the deed. And in this I am the ally of the Pythian
God and of the murdered man, and I pray that the murderer's life may,
should he be so hidden and screened, drop from him and perish away,
whoever he may be, whether he did the deed with others or by himself
120   alone: and on you I lay it to make—so far as man may—these words
good, for my sake, and for the God's sake, and for the sake of this land.
And even if the God had not spurred us to it, it were a wrong to leave
the guilt unpurged, when one so noble, and he your King, had perished;
and all have sinned that could have searched it out and did not: and
now since it is I who hold the power which he held once, and have his
wife for wife—she who would have borne him heirs had he but lived—
I take up this cause even as I would were it that of my own father. And
if there be any who do not obey me in it, I pray that the Gods send

---

100. *Artemis*, chaste goddess of the hunt, sister of Phoebus.   101. *Maenads*, or Bacchantes, frenzied, female worshrippers of Bacchus (Dionysius).   102. *Lysian king*,
Phoebus.

them neither harvest of the earth nor fruit of the womb; but let them be wasted by this plague, or by one more dreadful still. But may all be 130 blessed for ever who hear my words and do my will!

CHORUS. We do not know the murderer, and it were indeed more fitting that Phoebus, who laid the task upon us, should name the man.

OEDIPUS. No man can make the Gods speak against their will.

CHORUS. Then I will say what seems the next best thing.

OEDIPUS. If there is a third course, show it.

CHORUS. I know that our lord Tiresias is the seer most like to our lord Phoebus, and through him we may unravel all.

OEDIPUS. So I was advised by Creon, and twice already have I sent to bring him. 140

CHORUS. If we lack his help we have nothing but vague and ancient rumours.

OEDIPUS. What rumours are they? I would examine every story.

CHORUS. Certain wayfarers were said to have killed the King.

OEDIPUS. I know, I know. But who was there that saw it?

CHORUS. If there is such a man, and terror can move him, he will not keep silence when they have told him of your curses.

OEDIPUS. He that such a deed did not terrify will not be terrified because of a word.

CHORUS. But there is one who shall convict him. For the blind prophet 150 comes at last—in whom alone of all men the truth lives.

[*Enter* TIRESIAS, *led by a boy.*]

OEDIPUS. Tiresias, master of all knowledge, whatever may be spoken, whatever is unspeakable, whatever omens of earth and sky reveal, the plague is among us, and from that plague, Great Prophet, protect us and save us. Phoebus in answer to our question says that it will not leave us till we have found the murderers of Laius, and driven them into exile or put them to death. Do you therefore neglect neither the voice of birds, nor any other sort of wisdom, but rescue yourself, rescue the State, rescue me, rescue all that are defiled by the deed. For we are in your hands, and what greater task falls to a man than to help other men with all he 160 knows and has?

TIRESIAS. Aye, and what worse task than to be wise and suffer for it? I know this well; it slipped out of mind, or I would never have come.

OEDIPUS. What now?

TIRESIAS. Let me go home. You will bear your burden to the end more easily, and I bear mine—if you but give me leave for that.

OEDIPUS. Your words are strange and unkind to the State that bred you.

TIRESIAS. I see that you, on your part, keep your lips tight shut, and therefore I have shut mine that I may come to no misfortune.

170 Oedipus. For God's love do not turn away—if you have knowledge. We suppliants implore you on our knees.

Tiresias. You are fools—I will bring misfortune neither upon you nor upon myself.

Oedipus. What is this? You know all and will say nothing? You are minded to betray me and Thebes?

Tiresias. Why do you ask these things? You will not learn them from me.

Oedipus. What! Basest of the base! You would enrage the very stones. Will you never speak out? Cannot anything touch you?

Tiersias. The future will come of itself though I keep silent.

180 Oedipus. Then seeing that come it must, you had best speak out.

Tiresias. I will speak no further. Rage if you have a mind to; bring out all the fierceness that is in your heart.

Oedipus. That will I. I will not spare to speak my thoughts. Listen to what I have to say. It seems to me that you have helped to plot the deed; and, short of doing it with your own hands, have done the deed yourself. Had you eyesight I would declare that you alone had done it.

Tiresias. So that is what you say? I charge you to obey the decree that you yourself have made, and from this day out to speak neither to these nor
190 to me. You are the defiler of this land.

Oedipus. So brazen in your impudence? How do you hope to escape punishment?

Tiresias. I have escaped; my strength is in my truth.

Oedipus. Who taught you this? You never got it by your art.

Tiresias. You, because you have spurred me to speech against my will.

Oedipus. What speech? Speak it again that I may learn it better.

Tiresias. You are but tempting me—you understood me well enough.

Oedipus. No; not so that I can say I know it; speak it again.

Tiresias. I say that you are yourself the murderer that you seek.

200 Oedipus. You shall rue it for having spoken twice such outrageous words.

Tiresias. Would you that I say more that you may be still angrier?

Oedipus. Say what you will. I will not let it move me.

Tiresias. I say that you are living with your next of kin in unimagined shame.

Oedipus. Do you think you can say such things and never smart for it?

Tiresias. Yes, if there be strength in truth.

Oedipus. There is; yes—for everyone but you. But not for you that are maimed in ear and in eye and in wit.

Tiresias. You are but a poor wretch flinging taunts that in a little while
210 everyone shall fling at you.

Oedipus. Night, endless night has covered you up so that you can neither hurt me nor any man that looks upon the sun.

TIRESIAS. Your doom is not to fall by me. Apollo is enough: it is his business to work out your doom.

OEDIPUS. Was it Creon that planned this or you yourself?

TIRESIAS. Creon is not your enemy; you are your own enemy.

OEDIPUS. Power, ability, position, you bear all burdens, and yet what envy you create! Great must that envy be if envy of my power in this town— a power put into my hands unsought—has made trusty Creon, my old friend Creon, secretly long to take that power from me; if he has ₂₂₀ suborned this scheming juggler, this quack and trickster, this man with eyes for his gains and blindness in his art. Come, come, where did you prove yourself a seer? Why did you say nothing to set the townsmen free when the riddling Sphinx was here? Yet that riddle was not for the first-comer to read; it needed the skill of a seer. And none such had you! Neither found by help of birds, nor straight from any God. No, I came; I silenced her, I the ignorant Oedipus, it was I that found the answer in my mother-wit, untaught by any birds. And it is I that you would pluck out of my place, thinking to stand close to Creon's throne. But you and the plotter of all this shall mourn despite your zeal to purge the land. ₂₃₀ Were you not an old man, you had already learnt how bold you are and learnt it to your cost.

CHORUS. Both this man's words and yours, Oedipus, have been said in anger. Such words cannot help us here, nor any but those that teach us to obey the oracle.

TIRESIAS. King though you are, the right to answer when attacked belongs to both alike. I am not subject to you, but to Loxias; and therefore I shall never be Creon's subject. And I tell you, since you have taunted me with blindness, that though you have your sight, you cannot see in what misery you stand, nor where you are living, nor with whom, un- ₂₄₀ knowing what you do—for you do not know the stock you come of—you have been your own kin's enemy be they living or be they dead. And one day a mother's curse and father's curse alike shall drive you from this land in dreadful haste with darkness upon those eyes. Therefore, heap your scorn on Creon and on my message if you have a mind to; for no one of living men shall be crushed as you shall be crushed.

OEDIPUS. Begone this instant! Away, away! Get you from these doors!

TIRESIAS. I had never come but that you sent for me.

OEDIPUS. I did not know you were mad.

TIRESIAS. I may seem mad to you, but your parents thought me sane. ₂₅₀

OEDIPUS. My parents! Stop! Who was my father?

TIRESIAS. This day shall you know your birth; and it will ruin you.

OEDIPUS. What dark words you always speak!

TIRESIAS. But are you not most skilful in the unravelling of dark words?

OEDIPUS. You mock me for that which made me great?

TIRESIAS. It was that fortune that undid you.

OEDIPUS. What do I care? For I delivered all this town.

TIRESIAS. Then I will go: boy, lead me out of this.

OEDIPUS. Yes, let him lead you. You take vexation with you.

260 TIRESIAS. I will go: but first I will do my errand. For frown though you may you cannot destroy me. The man for whom you look, the man you have been threatening in all the proclamations about the death of Laius, that man is here. He seems, so far as looks go, an alien; yet he shall be found a native Theban and shall nowise be glad of that fortune. A blind man, though now he has his sight; a beggar, though now he is most rich; he shall go forth feeling the ground before him with his stick; so you go in and think on that, and if you find I am in fault say that I have no skill in prophecy.

[TIRESIAS *is led out by the boy.* OEDIPUS *enters the palace.*]

CHORUS

The Delphian rock has spoken out, now must a wicked mind,
270   Planner of things I dare not speak and of this bloody wrack,
Pray for feet that are as fast as the four hoofs of the wind:
Cloudy Parnassus and the Fates thunder at his back.

That sacred crossing-place of lines upon Parnassus' head,
Lines that have run through North and South, and run through
     West and East,
That navel of the world bids all men search the mountain wood,
The solitary cavern, till they have found that infamous beast.

[CREON *enters from the house.*]

CREON. Fellow-citizens, having heard that King Oedipus accuses me of dreadful things, I come in my indignation. Does he think that he has
280   suffered wrong from me in these present troubles, or anything that could lead to wrong, whether in word or deed? How can I live under blame like that? What life would be worth having if by you here, and by my nearest friends, called a traitor through the town?

CHORUS. He said it in anger, and not from his heart out.

CREON. He said it was I put up the seer to speak those falsehoods.

CHORUS. Such things were said.

CREON. And had he his right mind saying it?

CHORUS. I do not know—I do not know what my masters do.

[OEDIPUS *enters.*]

272. *Parnassus,* mountain on which the Delphic oracle was situated, thought to be the center of the world.

OEDIPUS. What brought you here? Have you a face so brazen that you come to my house—you, the proved assassin of its master—the certain 290 robber of my crown? Come, tell me in the face of the Gods what cowardice, or folly, did you discover in me that you plotted this? Did you think that I would not see what you were at till you had crept upon me, or seeing it would not ward it off? What madness to seek a throne, having neither friends nor followers!

CREON. Now, listen, hear my answer, and then you may with knowledge judge between us.

OEDIPUS. You are plausible, but waste words now that I know you.

CREON. Hear what I have to say. I can explain it all.

OEDIPUS. One thing you will not explain away—that you are my enemy. 300

CREON. You are a fool to imagine that senseless stubbornness sits well upon you.

OEDIPUS. And you to imagine that you can wrong a kinsman and escape the penalty.

CREON. That is justly said, I grant you; but what is this wrong that you complain of?

OEDIPUS. Did you advise, or not, that I should send for that notorious prophet?

CREON. And I am of the same mind still.

OEDIPUS. How long is it, then, since Laius—   310

CREON. What, what about him?

OEDIPUS. Since Laius was killed by an unknown hand?

CREON. That was many years ago.

OEDIPUS. Was this prophet at his trade in those days?

CREON. Yes; skilled as now and in equal honour.

OEDIPUS. Did he ever speak of me?

CREON. Never certainly when I was within earshot.

OEDIPUS. And did you enquire into the murder?

CREON. We did enquire but learnt nothing.

OEDIPUS. And why did he not tell out his story then?   320

CREON. I do not know. When I know nothing I say nothing.

OEDIPUS. This much at least you know and can say out.

CREON. What is that? If I know it I will say it.

OEDIPUS. That if he had not consulted you he would never have said that it was I who killed Laius.

CREON. You know best what he said; but now, question for question.

OEDIPUS. Question your fill—I cannot be proved guilty of that blood.

CREON. Answer me then. Are you not married to my sister?

OEDIPUS. That cannot be denied.

CREON. And do you not rule as she does? And with a like power?   330

OEDIPUS. I give her all she asks for.

CREON. And am not I the equal of you both?

OEDIPUS. Yes: and that is why you are so false a friend.

CREON. Not so; reason this out as I reason it, and first weigh this: who would prefer to lie awake amid terrors rather than to sleep in peace, granting that his power is equal in both cases? Neither I nor any sober-minded man. You give me what I ask and let me do what I want, but were I King I would have to do things I did not want to do. Is not influence and no trouble with it better than any throne, am I such a fool as to hunger after unprofitable honours? Now all are glad to see me, every one wishes me well, all that want a favour from you ask speech of me—finding in that their hope. Why should I give up these things and take those? No wise mind is treacherous. I am no contriver of plots, and if another took to them he would not come to me for help. And in proof of this go to the Pythian Oracle, and ask if I have truly told what the Gods said: and after that, if you have found that I have plotted with the Soothsayer, take me and kill me; not by the sentence of one mouth only—but of two mouths, yours and my own. But do not condemn me in a corner, upon some fancy and without proof. What right have you to declare a good man bad or a bad good? It is as bad a thing to cast off a true friend as it is for a man to cast away his own life—but you will learn these things with certainty when the time comes; for time alone shows a just man; though a day can show a knave.

CHORUS. King! He has spoken well, he gives himself time to think; a headlong talker does not know what he is saying.

OEDIPUS. The plotter is at his work, and I must counterplot headlong, or he will get his ends and I miss mine.

CREON. What will you do then? Drive me from the land?

OEDIPUS. Not so; I do not desire your banishment—but your death.

CREON. You are not sane.

OEDIPUS. I am sane at least in my own interest.

CREON. You should be in mine also.

OEDIPUS. No, for you are false.

CREON. But if you understand nothing?

OEDIPUS. Yet I must rule.

CREON. Not if you rule badly.

OEDIPUS. Hear him, O Thebes!

CREON. Thebes is for me also, not for you alone.

CHORUS. Cease, princes: I see Jocasta coming out of the house; she comes just in time to quench the quarrel.

[JOCASTA *enters.*]

JOCASTA. Unhappy men! Why have you made this crazy uproar? Are you not ashamed to quarrel about your own affairs when the whole country is in trouble? Go back into the palace, Oedipus, and you, Creon, to your own house. Stop making all this noise about some petty thing.

CREON. Your husband is about to kill me—or to drive me from the land of my fathers.

OEDIPUS. Yes: for I have convicted him of treachery against me.

CREON. Now may I perish accursed if I have done such a thing!

JOCASTA. For God's love believe it, Oedipus. First, for the sake of his oath, and then for my sake, and for the sake of these people here.   380

CHORUS. [*all*]. King, do what she asks.

OEDIPUS. What would you have me do?

CHORUS. Not to make a dishonourable charge, with no more evidence than rumour, against a friend who has bound himself with an oath.

OEDIPUS. Do you desire my exile or my death?

CHORUS. No, by Helios, by the first of all the Gods, may I die abandoned by Heaven and earth if I have that thought! What breaks my heart is that our public griefs should be increased by your quarrels.

OEDIPUS. Then let him go, though I am doomed thereby to death or to be thrust dishonoured from the land; it is your lips, not his, that move 390 me to compassion; wherever he goes my hatred follows him.

CREON. You are as sullen in yielding as you were vehement in anger, but such natures are their own heaviest burden.

OEDIPUS. Why will you not leave me in peace and begone?

CREON. I will go away; what is your hatred to me? In the eyes of all here I am a just man.

[*He goes.*]

CHORUS. Lady, why do you not take your man in to the house?

JOCASTA. I will do so when I have learned what has happened.

CHORUS. The half of it was blind suspicion bred of talk; the rest the wounds left by injustice.   400

JOCASTA. It was on both sides?

CHORUS. Yes.

JOCASTA. What was it?

CHORUS. Our land is vexed enough. Let the thing alone now that it is over.

[*Exit leader of* CHORUS.]

JOCASTA. In the name of the Gods, King, what put you in this anger?

OEDIPUS. I will tell you; for I honour you more than these men do. The cause is Creon and his plots against me.

JOCASTA. Speak on, if you can tell clearly how this quarrel arose.

OEDIPUS. He says that I am guilty of the blood of Laius.

---

386. *Helios,* another name for Phoebus Apollo, the sun god.

410 JOCASTA. On his own knowledge, or on hearsay?

OEDIPUS. He has made a rascal of a seer his mouthpiece.

JOCASTA. Do not fear that there is truth in what he says. Listen to me, and learn to your comfort that nothing born of woman can know what is to come. I will give you proof of that. An oracle came to Laius once, I will not say from Phoebus, but from his ministers, that he was doomed to die by the hand of his own child sprung from him and me. When his child was but three days old, Laius bound its feet together and had it thrown by sure hands upon a trackless mountain; and when Laius was murdered at the place where three highways meet, it was, or so at

420 least the rumour says, by foreign robbers. So Apollo did not bring it about that the child should kill its father, nor did Laius die in the dreadful way he feared by his child's hand. Yet that was how the message of the seers mapped out the future. Pay no attention to such things. What the God would show he will need no help to show it, but bring it to light himself.

OEDIPUS. What restlessness of soul, lady, has come upon me since I heard you speak, what a tumult of the mind!

JOCASTA. What is this new anxiety? What has startled you?

OEDIPUS. You said that Laius was killed where three highways meet.

430 JOCASTA. Yes: that was the story.

OEDIPUS. And where is the place?

JOCASTA. In Phocis where the road divides branching off to Delphi and to Daulia.

OEDIPUS. And when did it happen? How many years ago?

JOCASTA. News was published in this town just before you came into power.

OEDIPUS. O Zeus! What have you planned to do unto me?

JOCASTA. He was tall; the silver had just come into his hair; and in shape not greatly unlike to you.

OEDIPUS. Unhappy that I am! It seems that I have laid a dreadful curse

440 upon myself, and did not know it.

JOCASTA. What do you say? I tremble when I look on you, my King.

OEDIPUS. And I have a misgiving that the seer can see indeed. But I will know it all more clearly, if you tell me one thing more.

JOCASTA. Indeed, though I tremble I will answer whatever you ask.

OEDIPUS. Had he but a small troop with him; or did he travel like a great man with many followers?

JOCASTA. There were but five in all—one of them a herald; and there was one carriage with Laius in it.

OEDIPUS. Alas! It is now clear indeed. Who was it brought the news, lady?

450 JOCASTA. A servant—the one survivor.

OEDIPUS. Is he by chance in the house now?

JOCASTA. No; for when he found you reigning instead of Laius he besought

me, his hand clasped in mine, to send him to the fields among the
cattle that he might be far from the sight of this town; and I sent him.
He was a worthy man for a slave and might have asked a bigger thing.

OEDIPUS. I would have him return to us without delay.

JOCASTA. Oedipus, it is easy. But why do you ask this?

OEDIPUS. I fear that I have said too much, and therefore I would question
him.

JOCASTA. He shall come, but I too have a right to know what lies so heavy 460
upon your heart, my King.

OEDIPUS. Yes: and it shall not be kept from you now that my fear has
grown so heavy. Nobody is more to me than you, nobody has the same
right to learn my good or evil luck. My father was Polybus of Corinth,
my mother the Dorian Merope, and I was held the foremost man in all
that town until a thing happened—a thing to startle a man, though not
to make him angry as it made me. We were sitting at the table, and a
man who had drunk too much cried out that I was not my father's son
—and I, though angry, restrained my anger for that day; but the next
day went to my father and my mother and questioned them. They 470
were indignant at the taunt and that comforted me—and yet the man's
words rankled, for they had spread a rumour through the town. Without
consulting my father or my mother I went to Delphi, but Phoebus told
me nothing of the thing for which I came, but much of other things
—things of sorrow and of terror: that I should live in incest with my
mother, and beget a brood that men would shudder to look upon; that
I should be my father's murderer. Hearing those words I fled out of
Corinth, and from that day have but known where it lies when I have
found its direction by the stars. I sought where I might escape those
infamous things—the doom that was laid upon me. I came in my flight 480
to that very spot where you tell me this king perished. Now, lady, I will
tell you the truth. When I had come close up to those three roads, I
came upon a herald, and a man like him you have described seated in
a carriage. The man who held the reins and the old man himself would
not give me room, but thought to force me from the path, and I struck
the driver in my anger. The old man, seeing what I had done, waited
till I was passing him and then struck me upon the head. I paid him
back in full, for I knocked him out of the carriage with a blow of my
stick. He rolled on his back, and after that I killed them all. If this
stranger were indeed Laius, is there a more miserable man in the world 490
than the man before you? Is there a man more hated of Heaven? No
stranger, no citizen, may receive him into his house, not a soul may speak

---

464. *Polybus,* king of Corinth, with his wife, Merope, had reared Oedipus as their son.
Oedipus had assumed that the oracle's prophecy that he will kill his father and marry
his mother refers to them.

to him, and no mouth but my own mouth has laid this curse upon me. Am I not wretched? May I be swept from this world before I have endured this doom!

CHORUS. These things, O King, fill us with terror; yet hope till you speak with him that saw the deed, and have learnt all.

OEDIPUS. Till I have learnt all, I may hope. I await the man that is coming from the pastures.

500 JOCASTA. What is it that you hope to learn?

OEDIPUS. I will tell you. If his tale agrees with yours, then I am clear.

JOCASTA. What tale of mine?

OEDIPUS. He told you that Laius met his death from robbers; if he keeps to that tale now and speaks of several slayers, I am not the slayer. But if he says one lonely wayfarer, then beyond a doubt the scale dips to me.

JOCASTA. Be certain of this much at least, his first tale was of robbers. He cannot revoke that tale—the city heard it and not I alone. Yet, if he should somewhat change his story, King, at least he cannot make the murder of Laius square with prophecy; for Loxias plainly said of Laius

510 that he would die by the hand of my child. That poor innocent did not kill him, for it died before him. Therefore from this out I would not, for all divination can do, so much as look to my right hand or to my left hand, or fear at all.

OEDIPUS. You have judged well; and yet for all that, send and bring this peasant to me.

JOCASTA. I will send without delay. I will do all that you would have of me —but let us come in to the house.

[*They go in to the house.*]

CHORUS

    For this one thing above all I would be praised as a man,
    That in my words and my deeds I have kept those laws in mind,
520   Olympian Zeus, and that high clear Empyrean,
    Fashioned, and not some man or people of mankind,
    Even those sacred laws nor age nor sleep can blind.

    A man becomes a tyrant out of insolence
    He climbs and climbs, until all people call him great,
    He seems upon the summit, and God flings him thence;
    Yet an ambitious man may lift up a whole State,
    And in his death be blessed, in his life fortunate.

    And all men honour such; but should a man forget
    The holy images, the Delphian Sibyl's trance,

529. *Delphian Sibyl*, the oracle.

And the world's navel-stone, and not be punished for it 530
And seem most fortunate, or even blessed perchance,
Why should we honour the Gods, or join the sacred dance?

[JOCASTA *enters from the palace.*]

JOCASTA. It has come into my head, citizens of Thebes, to visit every altar
of the Gods, a wreath in my hand and a dish of incense. For all manner
of alarms trouble the soul of Oedipus, who instead of weighing new
oracles by old, like a man of sense, is at the mercy of every mouth that
speaks terror. Seeing that my words are nothing to him, I cry to you,
Lysian Apollo, whose altar is the first I meet: I come, a suppliant, bearing symbols of prayer; O, make us clean, for now we are all afraid, seeing
him afraid, even as they who see the helmsman afraid. 540

[*Enter* MESSENGER.]

MESSENGER. May I learn from you, strangers, where is the home of King
Oedipus? Or better still, tell me where he himself is, if you know.
CHORUS. This is his house, and he himself, stranger, is within it, and this
lady is the mother of his children.
MESSENGER. Then I call a blessing upon her, seeing what man she has
married.
JOCASTA. May God reward those words with a like blessing, stranger! But
what have you come to seek or to tell?
MESSENGER. Good news for your house, lady, and for your husband.
JOCASTA. What news? From whence have you come? 550
MESSENGER. From Corinth, and you will rejoice at the message I am about
to give you; yet, maybe, it will grieve you.
JOCASTA. What is it? How can it have this double power?
MESSENGER. The people of Corinth, they say, will take him for king.
JOCASTA. How then? Is old Polybus no longer on the throne?
MESSENGER. No. He is in his tomb.
JOCASTA. What do you say? Is Polybus dead, old man?
MESSENGER. May I drop dead if it is not the truth.
JOCASTA. Away! Hurry to your master with this news. O oracle of the
Gods, where are you now? This is the man whom Oedipus feared and 560
shunned lest he should murder him, and now this man has died a
natural death, and not by the hand of Oedipus.

[*Enter* OEDIPUS.]

OEDIPUS. Jocasta, dearest wife, why have you called me from the house?
JOCASTA. Listen to this man, and judge to what the oracles of the Gods
have come.
OEDIPUS. And he—who may he be? And what news has he?

JOCASTA. He has come from Corinth to tell you that your father, Polybus, is dead.

OEDIPUS. How, stranger? Let me have it from your own mouth.

570 MESSENGER. If I am to tell the story, the first thing is that he is dead and gone.

OEDIPUS. By some sickness or by treachery?

MESSENGER. A little thing can bring the aged to their rest.

OEDIPUS. Ah! He died, it seems, from sickness?

MESSENGER. Yes; and of old age.

OEDIPUS. Alas! Alas! Why, indeed, my wife, should one look to that Pythian seer, or to the birds that scream above our heads? For they would have it that I was doomed to kill my father. And now he is dead —hid already beneath the earth. And here am I—who had no part in it,
580 unless indeed he died from longing for me. If that were so, I may have caused his death; but Polybus has carried the oracles with him into Hades—the oracles as men have understood them—and they are worth nothing.

JOCASTA. Did I not tell you so, long since?

OEDIPUS. You did, but fear misled me.

JOCASTA. Put this trouble from you.

OEDIPUS. Those bold words would sound better, were not my mother living. But as it is—I have some grounds for fear; yet you have said well.

JOCASTA. Yet your father's death is a sign that all is well.

590 OEDIPUS. I know that: but I fear because of her who lives.

MESSENGER. Who is this woman who makes you afraid?

OEDIPUS. Merope, old man, the wife of Polybus.

MESSENGER. What is there in her to make you afraid?

OEDIPUS. A dreadful oracle sent from Heaven, stranger.

MESSENGER. Is it a secret, or can you speak it out?

OEDIPUS. Loxias said that I was doomed to marry my own mother, and to shed my father's blood. For that reason I fled from my house in Corinth; and I did right, though there is great comfort in familiar faces.

MESSENGER. Was it indeed for that reason that you went into exile?

600 OEDIPUS. I did not wish, old man, to shed my father's blood.

MESSENGER. King, have I not freed you from that fear?

OEDIPUS. You shall be fittingly rewarded.

MESSENGER. Indeed, to tell the truth, it was for that I came; to bring you home and be the better for it—

OEDIPUS. No! I will never go to my parents' home.

MESSENGER. Ah, my son, it is plain enough, you do not know what you do.

OEDIPUS. How, old man? For God's love, tell me.

MESSENGER. If for these reasons you shrink from going home.

OEDIPUS. I am afraid lest Phoebus has spoken true.

MESSENGER. You are afraid of being made guilty through Merope? 610
OEDIPUS. That is my constant fear.
MESSENGER. A vain fear.
OEDIPUS. How so, if I was born of that father and mother?
MESSENGER. Because they were nothing to you in blood.
OEDIPUS. What do you say? Was Polybus not my father?
MESSENGER. No more nor less than myself.
OEDIPUS. How can my father be no more to me than you who are nothing to me?
MESSENGER. He did not beget you any more than I.
OEDIPUS. No? Then why did he call me his son? 620
MESSENGER. He took you as a gift from these hands of mine.
OEDIPUS. How could he love so dearly what came from another's hands?
MESSENGER. He had been childless.
OEDIPUS. If I am not your son, where did you get me?
MESSENGER. In a wooded valley of Cithaeron.
OEDIPUS. What brought you wandering there?
MESSENGER. I was in charge of mountain sheep.
OEDIPUS. A shepherd—a wandering, hired man.
MESSENGER. A hired man who came just in time.
OEDIPUS. Just in time—had it come to that? 630
MESSENGER. Have not the cords left their marks upon your ankles?
OEDIPUS. Yes, that is an old trouble.
MESSENGER. I took your feet out of the spancel.
OEDIPUS. I have had those marks from the cradle.
MESSENGER. They have given you the name your bear.
OEDIPUS. Tell me, for God's sake, was that deed my mother's or my father's?
MESSENGER. I do not know—he who gave you to me knows more of that than I.
OEDIPUS. What? You had me from another? You did not chance on me 640 yourself?
MESSENGER. No. Another shepherd gave you to me.
OEDIPUS. Who was he? Can you tell me who he was?
MESSENGER. I think that he was said to be of Laius' household.
OEDIPUS. The king who ruled this country long ago?
MESSENGER. The same—the man was herdsman in his service.
OEDIPUS. Is he alive, that I might speak with him?
MESSENGER. You people of this country should know that.
OEDIPUS. Is there any one here present who knows the herd he speaks of?

625. *Cithaeron,* the mountain where Oedipus as a baby had been left to die. 635. *the name you bear.* Oedipus means swollen foot.

650   Any one who has seen him in the town pastures? The hour has come when all must be made clear.

CHORUS. I think he is the very herd you sent for but now; Jocasta can tell you better than I.

JOCASTA. Why ask about that man? Why think about him? Why waste a thought on what this man has said? What he has said is of no account.

OEDIPUS. What, with a clue like that in my hands and fail to find out my birth?

JOCASTA. For God's sake, if you set any value upon your life, give up this search—my misery is enough.

660 OEDIPUS. Though I be proved the son of a slave, yes, even of three generations of slaves, you cannot be made base-born.

JOCASTA. Yet, hear me, I implore you. Give up this search.

OEDIPUS. I will not hear of anything but searching the whole thing out.

JOCASTA. I am only thinking of your good—I have advised you for the best.

OEDIPUS. Your advice makes me impatient.

JOCASTA. May you never come to know who you are, unhappy man!

OEDIPUS. Go, some one, bring the herdsman here—and let that woman glory in her noble blood.

JOCASTA. Alas, alas, miserable man! Miserable! That is all that I can call
670   you now or for ever.

[*She goes out.*]

CHORUS. Why has the lady gone, Oedipus, in such a transport of despair? Out of this silence will burst a storm of sorrows.

OEDIPUS. Let come what will. However lowly my origin I will discover it. That woman, with all a woman's pride, grows red with shame at my base birth. I think myself the child of Good Luck, and that the years are my foster-brothers. Sometimes they have set me up, and sometimes thrown me down, but he that has Good Luck for mother can suffer no dishonour. That is my origin, nothing can change it, so why should I renounce this search into my birth?

CHORUS

680   Oedipus' nurse, mountain of many a hidden glen,
    Be honoured among men;
    A famous man, deep-thoughted, and his body strong;
    Be honoured in dance and song.
    Who met in the hidden glen? Who let his fancy run
    Upon nymph of Helicon?
    Lord Pan or Lord Apollo or the mountain Lord
    By the Bacchantes adored?

OEDIPUS. If I, who have never met the man, may venture to say so, I think that the herdsman we await approaches; his venerable age matches
690   with this stranger's, and I recognise as servants of mine those who bring

him. But you, if you have seen the man before, will know the man better than I.

CHORUS. Yes, I know the man who is coming; he was indeed in Laius' service, and is still the most trusted of the herdsmen.

OEDIPUS. I ask you first, Corinthian stranger, is this the man you mean?

MESSENGER. He is the very man.

OEDIPUS. Look at me, old man! Answer my questions. Were you once in Laius' service?

HERDSMAN. I was: not a bought slave, but reared up in the house.

OEDIPUS. What was your work—your manner of life? 700

HERDSMAN. For the best part of my life I have tended flocks.

OEDIPUS. Where, mainly?

HERDSMAN. Cithaeron or its neighbourhood.

OEDIPUS. Do you remember meeting with this man there?

HERDSMAN. What man do you mean?

OEDIPUS. This man. Did you ever meet him?

HERDSMAN. I cannot recall him to mind.

MESSENGER. No wonder in that, master; but I will bring back his memory. He and I lived side by side upon Cithaeron. I had but one flock and he had two. Three full half-years we lived there, from spring to autumn, and 710 every winter I drove my flock to my own fold, while he drove his to the fold of Laius. Is that right? Was it not so?

HERDSMAN. True enough; though it was long ago.

MESSENGER. Come, tell me now—do you remember giving me a boy to rear as my own foster-son?

HERDSMAN. What are you saying? Why do you ask me that?

MESSENGER. Look at that man, my friend, he is the child you gave me.

HERDSMAN. A plague upon you! Cannot you hold your tongue?

OEDIPUS. Do not blame him, old man; your own words are more blameable.

HERDSMAN. And how have I offended, master? 720

OEDIPUS. In not telling of that boy he asks of.

HERDSMAN. He speaks from ignorance, and does not know what he is saying.

OEDIPUS. If you will not speak with a good grace you shall be made to speak.

HERDSMAN. Do not hurt me for the love of God, I am an old man.

OEDIPUS. Some one there, tie his hands behind his back.

HERDSMAN. Alas! Wherefore! What more would you learn?

OEDIPUS. Did you give this man the child he speaks of?

HERDSMAN. I did: would I had died that day! 730

OEDIPUS. Well, you may come to that unless you speak the truth.

HERDSMAN. Much more am I lost if I speak it.

OEDIPUS. What! Would the fellow make more delay?

HERDSMAN. No, no. I said before that I gave it to him.

OEDIPUS. Where did you come by it? Your own child, or another?

HERDSMAN. It was not my own child—I had it from another.

OEDIPUS. From any of those here? From what house?

HERDSMAN. Do not ask any more, master; for the love of God do not ask.

OEDIPUS. You are lost if I have to question you again.

740 HERDSMAN. It was a child from the house of Laius.

OEDIPUS. A slave? Or one of his own race?

HERDSMAN. Alas! I am on the edge of dreadful words.

OEDIPUS. And I of hearing: yet hear I must.

HERDSMAN. It was said to have been his own child. But your lady within can tell you of these things best.

OEDIPUS. How? It was she who gave it to you?

HERDSMAN. Yes, King.

OEDIPUS. To what end?

HERDSMAN. That I should make away with it.

750 OEDIPUS. Her own child?

HERDSMAN. Yes: from fear of evil prophecies.

OEDIPUS. What prophecies?

HERDSMAN. That he should kill his father.

OEDIPUS. Why, then, did you give him up to this old man?

HERDSMAN. Through pity, master, believing that he would carry him to whatever land he had himself come from—but he saved him for dreadful misery; for if you are what this man says, you are the most miserable of all men.

OEDIPUS. O! O! All brought to pass! All truth! Now, O light, may I look
760   my last upon you, having been found accursed in bloodshed, accursed in marriage, and in my coming into the world accursed!

[*He rushes into the palace.*]

CHORUS

What can the shadow-like generations of man attain
But build up a dazzling mockery of delight that under their touch dissolves again?
Oedipus seemed blessed, but there is no man blessed amongst men.

Oedipus overcame the woman-breasted Fate;
He seemed like a strong tower against Death and first among the fortunate;
He sat upon the ancient throne of Thebes, and all men called him
770   great.

But, looking for a marriage-bed, he found the bed of his birth,
Tilled the field his father had tilled, cast seed into the same abounding earth;
Entered through the door that had sent him wailing forth.

Begetter and begot as one! How could that be hid?
What darkness cover up that marriage-bed? Time watches, he is
eagle-eyed,
And all the works of man are known and every soul is tried.

Would you had never come to Thebes, nor to this house,
Nor riddled with the woman-breasted Fate, beaten off Death and 780
succoured us,
That I had never raised this song, heartbroken Oedipus!

SECOND MESSENGER [*coming from the house*]. Friends and kinsmen of this
house! What deeds must you look upon, what burden of sorrow bear,
if true to race you still love the House of Labdacus. For not Ister nor
Phasis could wash this house clean, so many misfortunes have been
brought upon it, so many has it brought upon itself, and those misfortunes are always the worst that a man brings upon himself.

CHORUS. Great already are the misfortunes of this house, and you bring
us a new tale.   790

SECOND MESSENGER. A short tale in the telling: Jocasta, our Queen, is dead.

CHORUS. Alas, miserable woman, how did she die?

SECOND MESSENGER. By her own hand. It cannot be as terrible to you
as to one that saw it with his eyes, yet so far as words can serve, you
shall see it. When she had come into the vestibule, she ran half
crazed towards her marriage-bed, clutching at her hair with the fingers
of both hands, and once within the chamber dashed the doors together behind her. Then called upon the name of Laius, long since
dead, remembering that son who killed the father and upon the mother
begot an accursed race. And wailed because of that marriage wherein 800
she had borne a two-fold race—husband by husband, children by her
child. Then Oedipus with a shriek burst in and running here and there
asked for a sword, asked where he would find the wife that was no
wife but a mother who had borne his children and himself. Nobody
answered him, we all stood dumb; but supernatural power helped him,
for, with a dreadful shriek, as though beckoned, he sprang at the double
doors, drove them in, burst the bolts out of their sockets, and ran into
the room. There we saw the woman hanging in a swinging halter, and
with a terrible cry he loosened the halter from her neck. When that
unhappiest woman lay stretched upon the ground, we saw another 810
dreadful sight. He dragged the golden brooches from her dress and lifting
them struck them upon his eyeballs, crying out, 'You have looked
enough upon those you ought never to have looked upon, failed long
enough to know those that you should have known; henceforth you shall
be dark'. He struck his eyes, not once, but many times, lifting his hands

---

785–6. *not Ister nor Phasis*, Greek rivers.

and speaking such or like words. The blood poured down and not with a few slow drops, but all at once over his beard in a dark shower as it were hail.

[*The* CHORUS *wails and he steps further on to the stage.*]

Such evils have come forth from the deeds of those two and fallen not
820   on one alone but upon husband and wife. They inherited much happiness, much good fortune; but to-day, ruin, shame, death, and loud crying, all evils that can be counted up, all, all are theirs.

CHORUS. Is he any quieter?

SECOND MESSENGER. He cries for some one to unbar the gates and to show to all the men of Thebes his father's murderer, his mother's—the unholy word must not be spoken. It is his purpose to cast himself out of the land that he may not bring all this house under his curse. But he has not the strength to do it. He must be supported and led away. The curtain is parting; you are going to look upon a sight which even those
830   who shudder must pity.

[*Enter* OEDIPUS.]

OEDIPUS. Woe, woe is me! Miserable, miserable that I am! Where am I? Where am I going? Where am I cast away? Who hears my words?

CHORUS. Cast away indeed, dreadful to the sight of the eye, dreadful to the ear.

OEDIPUS. Ah, friend, the only friend left to me, friend still faithful to the blind man! I know that you are there; blind though I am, I recognise your voice.

CHORUS. Where did you get the courage to put out your eyes? What unearthly power drove you to that?

840   OEDIPUS. Apollo, friends, Apollo, but it was my own hand alone, wretched that I am, that quenched these eyes.

CHORUS. You were better dead than blind.

OEDIPUS. No, it is better to be blind. What sight is there that could give me joy? How could I have looked into the face of my father when I came among the dead, aye, or on my miserable mother, since against them both I sinned such things that no halter can punish? And what to me this spectacle, town, statue, wall, and what to me this people, since I, thrice wretched, I, noblest of Theban men, have doomed myself to banishment, doomed myself when I commanded all to thrust out
850   the unclean thing?

CHORUS. It had indeed been better if that herdsman had never taken your feet out of the spancel or brought you back to life.

OEDIPUS. O three roads, O secret glen; O coppice and narrow way where three roads met; you that drank up the blood I spilt, the blood that was my own, my father's blood: remember what deeds I wrought for you to look upon, and then, when I had come hither, the new deeds that I wrought. O marriage-bed that gave me birth and after that gave children to your child, creating an incestuous kindred of fathers, brothers, sons, wives, and mothers. Yes, all the shame and the uncleanness that I have wrought among men. 860

CHORUS. For all my pity I shudder and turn away.

OEDIPUS. Come near, condescend to lay your hands upon a wretched man; listen, do not fear. My plague can touch no man but me. Hide me somewhere out of this land for God's sake, or kill me, or throw me into the sea where you shall never look upon me more.

[*Enter* CREON *and attendants.*]

CHORUS. Here Creon comes at a fit moment; you can ask of him what you will, help or counsel, for he is now in your place. He is King.

OEDIPUS. What can I say to him? What can I claim, having been altogether unjust to him?

CREON. I have not come in mockery, Oedipus, nor to reproach you. Lead 870 him in to the house as quickly as you can. Do not let him display his misery before strangers.

OEDIPUS. I must obey, but first, since you have come in so noble a spirit, you will hear me.

CREON. Say what you will.

OEDIPUS. I know that you will give her that lies within such a tomb as befits your own blood, but there is something more, Creon. My sons are men and can take care of themselves, but my daughters, my two unhappy daughters, that have ever eaten at my own table and shared my food, watch over my daughters, Creon. If it is lawful, let me touch them 880 with my hands. Grant it, Prince, grant it, noble heart. I would believe, could I touch them, that I still saw them.

[ISMENE *and* ANTIGONE *are led in by attendants.*]

But do I hear them sobbing? Has Creon pitied me and sent my children, my darlings? Has he done this?

CREON. Yes, I ordered it, for I know how greatly you have always loved them.

OEDIPUS. Then may you be blessed, and may Heaven be kinder to you than it has been to me! My children, where are you? Come hither—hither—come to the hands of him whose mother was your mother; the hands that put out your father's eyes, eyes once as bright as your own; 890 his who, understanding nothing, seeing nothing, became your father by her that bore him. I weep when I think of the bitter life that men will make you live, and the days that are to come. Into what company dare you go, to what festival, but that you shall return home from it not sharing in the joys, but bathed in tears? When you are old enough to be married, what man dare face the reproach that must cling to you and to your children? What misery is there lacking? Your father killed his father, he begat you at the spring of his own being, offspring of her that bore him. That is the taunt that would be cast upon you and on the

900 man that you should marry. That man is not alive; my children, you must wither away in barrenness. Ah, son of Menoeceus, listen. Seeing that you are the only father now left to them, for we their parents are lost, both of us lost, do not let them wander in beggary—are they not your own kindred?—do not let them sink down into my misery. No, pity them, seeing them utterly wretched in helpless childhood if you do not protect them. Show me that you promise, generous man, by touching me with your hand. [CREON *touches him.*] My children, there is much advice that I would give you were you but old enough to understand, but all I can do now is bid you pray that you may live wherever you

910 are let live, and that your life be happier than your father's.

CREON. Enough of tears. Pass into the house.

OEDIPUS. I will obey, though upon conditions.

CREON. Conditions?

OEDIPUS. Banish me from this country. I know that nothing can destroy me, for I wait some incredible fate; yet cast me upon Cithaeron, chosen by my father and my mother for my tomb.

CREON. Only the Gods can say yes or no to that.

OEDIPUS No, for I am hateful to the Gods.

CREON. If that be so you will get your wish the quicker. They will banish

920 that which they hate.

OEDIPUS. Are you certain of that?

CREON. I would not say it if I did not mean it.

OEDIPUS. Then it is time to lead me within.

CREON. Come, but let your children go.

OEDIPUS. No, do not take them from me.

CREON. Do not seek to be master; you won the mastery but could not keep it to the end.

[*He leads* OEDIPUS *into the palace, followed by* ISMENE, ANTIGONE, *and attendants.*]

CHORUS

Make way for Oedipus. All people said,
'That is a fortunate man;'
930 And now what storms are beating on his head!
Call no man fortunate that is not dead.
The dead are free from pain.

William Shakespeare 1564–1616

Antony and Cleopatra

DRAMATIS PERSONÆ

MARK ANTONY,
OCTAVIUS CÆSAR, } triumvirs.
M. ÆMILIUS LEPIDUS,
SEXTUS POMPEIUS.
DOMITIUS ENOBARBUS,
VENTIDIUS,
EROS,
SCARUS, } friends to Antony.
DERCETAS,
DEMETRIUS,
PHILO,
MECÆNAS,
AGRIPPA,
DOLABELLA,
PROCULEIUS, } friends to Cæsar.
THYREUS,
GALLUS,
MENAS,
MENECRATES, } friends to Pompey.
VARRIUS,

TAURUS, lieutenant-general to Cæsar.
CANIDIUS, lieutenant-general to Antony.
SILIUS, an officer in Ventidius's army.
EUPHRONIUS, an ambassador from Antony to Cæsar.
ALEXAS,
MARDIAN, a Eunuch, } attendants on Cleopatra.
SELEUCUS,
DIOMEDES,
A SOOTHSAYER.
A CLOWN.
CLEOPATRA, queen of Egypt
OCTAVIA, sister to Cæsar and wife to Antony.
CHARMIAN, } attendants on Cleopatra
IRAS,
OFFICERS, SOLDIERS, MESSENGERS, and other ATTENDANTS.
SCENE: In several parts of the Roman empire.

ACT I

SCENE I. Alexandria. A room in CLEOPATRA's palace.

[Enter DEMETRIUS and PHILO.]

PHI. Nay, but this dotage of our general's
O'erflows the measure: those his goodly eyes,
That o'er the files and musters of the war
Have glow'd like plated Mars, now bend, now turn,

Act I, Scene i: 3. files and musters, troops in battle array.   4. plated, clad in armor.

305

5 The office and devotion of their view
Upon a tawny front: his captain's heart,
Which in the scuffles of great fights hath burst
The buckles on his breast, reneges all temper,
And is become the bellows and the fan
To cool a gipsy's lust.

[*Flourish. Enter* ANTONY, CLEOPATRA, *her* LADIES, *the Train, with Eunuchs fanning her.*]

10   Look, where they come:
Take but good note, and you shall see in him
The triple pillar of the world transform'd
Into a strumpet's fool: behold and see.
CLEO. If it be love indeed, tell me how much.
15 ANT. There's beggary in the love that can be reckon'd.
CLEO. I'll set a bourn how far to be beloved.
ANT. Then must thou needs find out new heaven, new earth.

[*Enter an* ATTENDANT.]

ATT. News, my good lord, from Rome.
ANT.   Grates me: the sum.
CLEO. Nay, hear them, Antony:
20 Fulvia perchance is angry; or, who knows
If the scarce-bearded Cæsar have not sent
His powerful mandate to you, "Do this, or this;
Take in that kingdom, and enfranchise that;
Perform 't, or else we damn thee."
ANT.   How, my love!
25 CLEO. Perchance! nay, and most like:
You must not stay here longer, your dismission
Is come from Cæsar; therefore hear it, Antony.
Where's Fulvia's process? Cæsar's I would say? both?
Call in the messengers. As I am Egypt's queen,
30 Thou blushest, Antony; and that blood of thine
Is Cæsar's homager: else so thy cheek pays shame
When shrill-tongued Fulvia scolds. The messengers!

---

5. *office,* special duty. 6. *tawny front,* brown-skinned face. 8. *reneges all temper,* renounces all his self-control. 10. *gipsy's,* the gypsies were supposed to come from Egypt. 12. *triple pillar,* one of the triumvirs, the other two being Octavius Cæsar and Lepidus. 16. *bourn,* limit. 18. *Grates me: the sum,* It annoys me: What is its purport? 20. *Fulvia,* Antony's wife, a notorious shrew. 21. *Cæsar,* Octavius, grand-nephew and adopted son of Julius Cæsar, later Emperor Augustus. 23. *Take in,* occupy. 24. *damn,* condemn to death. 28. *process,* summons. 31. *homager,* vassal.

ANT. Let Rome in Tiber melt, and the wide arch
   Of the ranged empire fall! Here is my space.
   Kingdoms are clay: our dungy earth alike
   Feeds beast as man: the nobleness of life   36
   Is to do thus; when such a mutual pair

[*Embracing.*]

   And such a twain can do 't, in which I bind,
   On pain of punishment, the world to weet
   We stand up peerless.
CLEO.   Excellent falsehood!   40
   Why did he marry Fulvia, and not love her?
   I'll seem the fool I am not; Antony
   Will be himself.
ANT.   But stirr'd by Cleopatra.
   Now, for the love of Love and her soft hours,
   Let's not confound the time with conference harsh: 45
   There's not a minute of our lives should stretch
   Without some pleasure now. What sport to-night?
CLEO. Hear the ambassadors.
ANT.   Fie, wrangling queen!
   Whom every thing becomes, to chide, to laugh,
   To weep; whose every passion fully strives   50
   To make itself, in thee, fair and admired!
   No messenger, but thine; and all alone
   To-night we'll wander through the streets and note
   The qualities of people. Come, my queen;
   Last night you did desire it: speak not to us.   55

[*Exeunt* ANT. *and* CLEO. *with their train.*]

DEM. Is Cæsar with Antonius prized so slight?
PHI. Sir, sometimes, when he is not Antony,
   He comes too short of that great property
   Which still should go with Antony.
DEM.   I am full sorry
   That he approves the common liar, who   60
   Thus speaks of him at Rome: but I will hope
   Of better deeds to-morrow. Rest you happy!

[*Exeunt.*]

34. *ranged*, well-ordered; *space*, empire. 38. *bind*, force. 39. *weet*, know. 40. *peer-less*, without equals. 43. *himself*, i.e., a deceiver ever; *stir'd*, excited. 45. *confound*, waste. 46. *stretch*, pass. 52. *No messenger*, i.e., I will heed no messenger. 58. *prop-erty*, personality. 59. *still*, always. 60. *approves*, corroborates

SCENE II. *The same. Another room.*

[*Enter* CHARMIAN, IRAS, ALEXAS, *and a* SOOTHSAYER.]

CHAR. Lord Alexas, sweet Alexas, most anything Alexas, almost most
absolute Alexas, where's the soothsayer that you praised so to the queen?

3   O, that I knew this husband, which, you say, must charge his horns
with garlands!

ALEX. Soothsayer!

SOOTH. Your will?

CHAR. Is this the man? Is 't you, sir, that know things?

SOOTH. In nature's infinite book of secrecy
A little I can read.

10 ALEX.   Show him your hand.

[*Enter* ENOBARBUS.]

ENO. Bring in the banquet quickly; wine enough
Cleopatra's health to drink.

CHAR. Good sir, give me good fortune.

SOOTH. I make not, but foresee.

15 CHAR. Pray, then, foresee me one.

SOOTH. You shall be yet far fairer than you are.

CHAR. He means in flesh.

IRAS. No, you shall paint when you are old.

CHAR. Wrinkles forbid!

20 ALEX. Vex not his prescience; be attentive.

CHAR. Hush!

SOOTH. You shall be more beloving than beloved.

CHAR. I had rather heat my liver with drinking.

ALEX. Nay, hear him.

CHAR. Good now, some excellent fortune! Let me be married to three
kings in a forenoon, and widow them all: let me have a child at fifty, to

28   whom Herod of Jewry may do homage: find me to marry me with Octavius Cæsar, and companion me with my mistress.

SOOTH. You shall outlive the lady whom you serve.

CHAR. O excellent! I love long life better than figs.

33 SOOTH. You have seen and proved a fairer former fortune
Than that which is to approach.

CHAR. Then belike my children shall have no names; prithee, how many
boys and wenches must I have?

Scene ii: 2. *absolute*, perfect. 3. *charge*, load, like a bull decorated for sacrifice.
11. *banquet*, dessert (of wine and sweets). 20. *prescience*, foreknowledge of events.
23. *liver*, the supposed seat of love. 28. *Herod of Jewry*, i.e., the most ferocious of
tyrants. 33. *proved*, experienced.

SOOTH. If every of your wishes had a womb,
  And fertile every wish, a million.
CHAR. Out, fool! I forgive thee for a witch.   40
ALEX. You think none but your sheets are privy to your wishes.
CHAR. Nay, come, tell Iras hers.
ALEX. We'll know all our fortunes.   45
ENO. Mine, and most of our fortunes, to-night, shall be—drunk to bed.
IRAS. There's a palm presages chastity, if nothing else.
CHAR. E'en as the o'erflowing Nilus presageth famine.   50
IRAS. Go, you wild bedfellow, you cannot soothsay.
CHAR. Nay, if an oily palm be not a fruitful prognostication, I cannot
  scratch mine ear. Prithee, tell her but a worky-day fortune.
SOOTH. Your fortunes are alike.
IRAS. But how, but how? give me particulars.
SOOTH. I have said.
IRAS. Am I not an inch of fortune better than she?   60
CHAR. Well, if you were but an inch of fortune better than I, where would
  you choose it?
IRAS. Not in my husband's nose.
CHAR. Our worser thoughts heavens mend! Alexas,—come, his fortune,
  his fortune! O, let him marry a woman that cannot go, sweet Isis, I be-   64
  seech thee! and let her die too, and give him a worse! and let worse follow worse, till the worst of all follow him laughing to his grave, fifty-fold
  a cuckold! Good Isis, hear me this prayer, though thou deny me a matter
  of more weight; good Isis, I beseech thee!
IRAS. Amen. Dear goddess, hear that prayer of the people! for, as it is a
  heart-breaking to see a handsome man loose-wived, so it is a deadly sor-   75
  row to behold a foul knave uncuckolded: therefore, dear Isis, keep decorum, and fortune him accordingly!
CHAR. Amen.
ALEX. Lo, now, if it lay in their hands to make me a cuckold, they would
  make themselves whores, but they 'ld do 't!
ENO. Hush! here comes Antony.
CHAR.   Not he; the queen.

[*Enter* CLEOPATRA.]

CLEO. Saw you my lord?
ENO.   No, lady.

---

40. *forgive . . . witch*, exonerate you of being a wizard (your prophecies are so trivial).
41. *are privy to*, have secret knowledge of. 52. *oily palm*, a moist palm was thought
to be a sign of an amorous disposition; *fruitful prognostication*, a sign of fecundity.
53. *worky-day*, ordinary. 64. *go*, (1) walk, (2) copulate successfully; *Isis*, Egyptian
goddess of maternity and fertility. 75. *loose-wived*, married to an unfaithful wife.
76. *foul*, ugly. 76. *keep decorum*, observe a sense of what is fitting.

CLEO. Was he not here?

85 CHAR. No, madam.

CLEO. He was disposed to mirth; but on the sudden
A Roman thought hath struck him. Enobarbus!

ENO. Madam?

CLEO. Seek him, and bring him hither. Where's Alexas?

90 ALEX. Here, at your service. My lord approaches.

CLEO. We will not look upon him: go with us.

[*Exeunt.*]

[*Enter* ANTONY *with a* MESSENGER *and* ATTENDANTS.]

MESS. Fulvia thy wife first came into the field.

ANT. Against my brother Lucius?

MESS. Ay:

95 But soon that war had end, and the time's state
Made friends of them, jointing their force 'gainst Cæsar;
Whose better issue in the war, from Italy,
Upon the first encounter, drave them.

ANT. Well, what worst?

MESS. The nature of bad news infects the teller.

100 ANT. When it concerns the fool or coward. On:
Things that are past are done with me. 'Tis thus;
Who tells me true, though in his tale lie death,
I hear him as he flatter'd.

MESS. Labienus—
This is stiff news—hath, with his Parthian force,

105 Extended Asia from Euphrates;
His conquering banner shook from Syria
To Lydia and to Ionia;
Whilst—

ANT. Antony, thou wouldst say,—

MESS. O, my lord!

ANT. Speak to me home, mince not the general tongue:

110 Name Cleopatra as she is call'd in Rome;
Rail thou in Fulvia's phrase; and taunt my faults
With such full license as both truth and malice
Have power to utter. O, then we bring forth weeds,
When our quick minds lie still; and our ills told us

95. *time's state*, the situation at the moment. 97. *issue*, success. 103. *as*, as though; *flattered*, i.e., told good news; *Labienus*, ambassador of Brutus and Cassius to the Parthians, then the commander-in-chief of their army. 105. *Extended*, seized. 109. *home*, bluntly; *general tongue*, common report. 114. *quick*, living, i.e., fertile; *still*, idle, uncultivated.

Is as our earing. Fare thee well awhile.   115
MESS. At your noble pleasure.

[*Exit.*]

ANT. From Sicyon, ho, the news! Speak there!
FIRST ATT. The man from Sicyon,—is there such an one?
SEC. ATT. He stays upon your will.
ANT.   Let him appear.
    These strong Egyptian fetters I must break,   120
    Or lose myself in dotage.

[*Enter another* MESSENGER.]

                                    What are you?
SEC. MESS. Fulvia thy wife is dead.
ANT.   Where died she?
SEC. MESS. In Sicyon:
    Her length of sickness, with what else more serious
    Importeth thee to know, this bears.   125

[*Gives a letter.*]

                                    ANT. Forbear me.

[*Exit* SEC. MESSENGER.]

    There's a great spirit gone! Thus did I desire it:
    What our contempt doth often hurl from us,
    We wish it ours again; the present pleasure,
    By revolution lowering, does become
    The opposite of itself: she's good, being gone;   130
    The hand could pluck her back that shoved her on.
    I must from this enchanting queen break off:
    Ten thousand harms, more than the ills I know,
    My idleness doth hatch. How now! Enobarbus!

[*Re-enter* ENOBARBUS.]

ENO. What's your pleasure, sir?   135
ANT. I must with haste from hence.
ENO. Why, then, we kill all our women: we see how mortal an unkindness
    is to them; if they suffer our departure, death's the word.
ANT. I must be gone.   140

---

115. *earing*, plowing. The phrase means "to have our faults told us is like ploughing
which frees the fields of weeds."   117. *Sicyon*, a town in Greece where Antony had left
his wife.   125. *Importeth*, it concerns; *Forbear*, leave.   129. *revolution*, i.e., the turning of Fortune's wheel.   134. *idleness*, folly.

Eno. Under a compelling occasion, let women die: it were pity to cast them away for nothing; though, between them and a great cause, they
144   should be esteemed nothing. Cleopatra, catching but the least noise of this, dies instantly; I have seen her die twenty times upon far poorer moment: I do think there is mettle in death, which commits some loving act upon her, she hath such a celerity in dying.

Ant. She is cunning past man's thought.

151 Eno. Alack, sir, no; her passions are made of nothing but the finest part of pure love: we cannot call her winds and waters sighs and tears; they are greater storms and tempests than almanacs can report: this cannot be cunning in her; if it be, she makes a shower of rain as well as Jove.

Ant. Would I had never seen her!

Eno. O, sir, you had then left unseen a wonderful piece of work; which
161   not to have been blest withal would have discredited your travel.

Ant. Fulvia is dead.

Eno. Sir?

Ant. Fulvia is dead.

Eno. Fulvia!

166 Ant. Dead.

Eno. Why, sir, give the gods a thankful sacrifice. When it pleaseth their deities to take the wife of a man from him, it shows to man the tailors of the earth; comforting therein, that when old robes are worn out, there
172   are members to make new. If there were no more women but Fulvia, then had you indeed a cut, and the case to be lamented: this grief is crowned with consolation; your old smock brings forth a new petticoat: and indeed the tears live in an onion that should water this sor-
177   row.

Ant. The business she hath broached in the state
Cannot endure my absence.

Eno. And the business you have broached here cannot be without you;
182   especially that of Cleopatra's, which wholly depends on your abode.

Ant. No more light answers. Let our officers
Have notice what we purpose. I shall break
185   The cause of our expedience to the queen,
And get her leave to part. For not alone
The death of Fulvia, with more urgent touches,
Do strongly speak to us; but the letters too
Of many our contriving friends in Rome

144. *noise,* rumor. 145–6. *upon . . . moment,* for a far less important cause. 146. *mettle,* ardor. 151. *passions,* emotion. 161. *discredited your travel,* been a disgrace to you as a sightseer. 172. *members,* persons. 173. *cut,* blow. 184. *break,* tell. 185. *expedience,* haste. 186. *part,* depart. 187. *more . . . touches,* matters of more urgent concern. 189. *our contriving,* scheming in my interest.

Petition us at home: Sextus Pompeius   190
Hath given the dare to Cæsar, and commands
The empire of the sea: our slippery people,
Whose love is never link'd to the deserver
Till his deserts are past, begin to throw
Pompey the Great and all his dignities   195
Upon his son; who, high in name and power,
Higher than both in blood and life, stands up
For the main soldier: whose quality, going on,
The sides o' the world may danger: much is breeding,   199
Which, like the courser's hair, hath yet but life,
And not a serpent's poison. Say our pleasure,
To such whose place is under us, requires
Our quick remove from hence.
ENO. I shall do 't.

[*Exeunt.*]

SCENE III. *The same. Another room.*

[*Enter* CLEOPATRA, CHARMIAN, IRAS, *and* ALEXAS.]

CLEO. Where is he?
CHAR.   I did not see him since.
CLEO. See where he is, who's with him, what he does:
  I did not send you: if you find him sad,
  Say I am dancing; if in mirth, report
  That I am sudden sick: quick, and return.   5

[*Exit* ALEXAS.]

CHAR. Madam, methinks, if you did love him dearly,
  You did not hold the method to enforce
  The like from him.
CLEO.   What should I do, I do not?
CHAR. In each thing give him way, cross him in nothing.
CLEO. Thou teachest like a fool; the way to lose him.   10
CHAR. Tempt him not so too far; I wish, forbear:

190. *Petition . . . home*, urge me to come home; *Sextus Pompeius*, the son of Pompey the Great. 194–6. *throw . . . Upon*, to transfer the title of Pompey the Great and all his high offices to. 197. *blood and life*, spirit and vitality. 197–8. *stands . . . soldier*, takes the position of the foremost soldier. 198. *quality, going on*, soldiership, if it continues to develop. 199. *sides*, i.e., the frame; *danger*, endanger. 200. *courser's hair*, a horse's hair when put into water was thought to turn into a snake. Scene iii: 3. *sad*, serious. 11. *Tempt*, test; *forbear*, i.e., give up (testing him).

In time we hate that which we often fear.
But here comes Antony.

[*Enter* ANTONY.]

CLEO.   I am sick and sullen.
ANT. I am sorry to give breathing to my purpose,—
15 CLEO. Help me away, dear Charmian; I shall fall:
It cannot be thus long, the sides of nature
Will not sustain it.
ANT.   Now, my dearest queen,—
CLEO. Pray you, stand farther from me.
ANT.   What's the matter?
CLEO. I know, by that same eye, there's some good news.
20   What says the married woman? You may go:
Would she had never given you leave to come!
Let her not say 'tis I that keep you here:
I have no power upon you; hers you are.
ANT. The gods best know,—
CLEO.   O, never was there queen
25   So mightily betray'd! yet at the first
I saw the treasons planted.
ANT.   Cleopatra,—
CLEO. Why should I think you can be mine and true,
Though you in swearing shake the thronèd gods,
Who have been false to Fulvia? Riotous madness,
30   To be entangled with those mouth-made vows,
Which break themselves in swearing!
ANT.   Most sweet queen,—
CLEO. Nay, pray you, seek no colour for your going,
But bid farewell, and go: when you sued staying,
Then was the time for words: no going then;
35   Eternity was in our lips and eyes,
Bliss in our brows' bent; none our parts so poor,
But was a race of heaven: they are so still,
Or thou, the greatest soldier of the world,
Art turn'd the greatest liar.
ANT.   How now, lady!
40 CLEO. I would I had thy inches; thou shouldst know
There were a heart in Egypt.

---

13. *sullen*, gloomy.   16. *sides of nature*, my bodily strength.   29. *riotous madness*, I was
completely mad.   32. *colour*, excuse.   33. *sued staying*, begged to stay (with me).   36.
brows' bent, the arch of eyebrows.   37. *race*, flavor, taste.   41. *Egypt*, the Queen
of Egypt.

ANT.   Hear me, queen:
  The strong necessity of time commands
  Our services awhile; but my full heart
  Remains in use with you. Our Italy
  Shines o'er with civil swords: Sextus Pompeius   45
  Makes his approaches to the port of Rome:
  Equality of two domestic powers
  Breed scrupulous faction: the hated, grown to strength,
  Are newly grown to love: the cóndemn'd Pompey,
  Rich in his father's honour, creeps apace   50
  Into the hearts of such as have not thrived
  Upon the present state, whose numbers threaten;
  And quietness, grown sick of rest, would purge
  By any desperate change: my more particular,
  And that which most with you should safe my going,   55
  Is Fulvia's death.
CLEO. Though age from folly could not give me freedom,
  It does from childishness: can Fulvia die?
ANT. She's dead, my queen:
  Look here, and at thy sovereign leisure read   60
  The garboils she awaked; at the last, best:
  See when and where she died.
CLEO.   O most false love!
  Where be the sacred vials thou shouldst fill
  With sorrowful water? Now I see, I see,
  In Fulvia's death, how mine received shall be.   65
ANT. Quarrel no more, but be prepared to know
  The purposes I bear; which are, or cease,
  As you shall give the advice. By the fire
  That quickens Nilus' slime, I go from hence
  Thy soldier, servant; making peace or war   70
  As thou affect'st.
CLEO.   Cut my lace, Charmian, come;
  But let it be: I am quickly ill, and well,
  So Antony loves.

---

44. *use*, usufruct, i.e., on deposit to your account.   46. *port of Rome*, i.e., Ostia, at the
mouth of the Tiber.   47. *Equality*, the equal resources; *two*, i.e., (1) those of Pompey,
(2) those of the Triumvirs.   48. *scrupulous faction*, captious strife, i.e., quarreling over
trivial matters.   52. *state*, administration.   54. *particular*, personal reason (for going).
55. *safe*, make safe (from your point of view).   61. *garboils*, disturbances.   63. *sacred
vials*, i.e., the bottles of tears which supposedly the Romans put into the burial urns of
their dead.   67. *bear*, bring to your notice; *are*, shall be realized.   68. *fire*, i.e., the sun.
69. *quickens*, endows with life, i.e., makes fertile.   71. *affect'st*, please; *lace*, lacing of
my stays.

ANT.   My precious queen, forbear;
 And give true evidence to his love, which stands
 An honourable trial.
75 CLEO.   So Fulvia told me.
 I prithee, turn aside and weep for her;
 Then bid adieu to me, and say the tears
 Belong to Egypt: good now, play one scene
 Of excellent dissembling; and let it look
 Like perfect honour.
80 ANT. You'll heat my blood: no more.
 CLEO. You can do better yet; but this is meetly.
 ANT. Now, by my sword,—
 CLEO.   And target. Still he mends;
 But this is not the best. Look, prithee, Charmian,
 How this Herculean Roman does become
85 The carriage of his chafe.
 ANT. I'll leave you, lady.
 CLEO.   Courteous lord, one word
 Sir, you and I must part, but that's not it:
 Sir, you and I have loved, but there's not it;
 That you know well: something it is I would,—
90 O, my oblivion is a very Antony,
 And I am all forgotten.
 ANT.   But that your royalty
 Holds idleness your subject, I should take you
 For idleness itself.
 CLEO.   'Tis sweating labour
 To bear such idleness so near the heart
95 As Cleopatra this. But, sir, forgive me;
 Since my becomings kill me, when they do not
 Eye well to you: your honour calls you hence;
 Therefore be deaf to my unpitied folly,
 And all the gods go with you! upon your sword
100 Sit laurel victory! and smooth success
 Be strew'd before your feet!
 ANT.   Let us go. Come;
 Our separation so abides, and flies,

---

81. *meetly*, appropriately done. 82. *target*, shield; *Still he mends*, i.e., he plays his part better and better every minute. 84–5. *How . . . chafe*, how well suited to the part of this Roman claiming descent from Hercules is his acting of anger. 89. *would*, wished to say. 90. *oblivion*, forgetfulness. 91. *am all forgotten*, I have completely forgotten (what I was about to say). 92. *Holds . . . subject*, is complete master of foolishness. 96. *becomings*, the qualities that become me. 97. *Eye well*, appear attractive.

That thou, residing here, go'st yet with me,
And I, hence fleeting, here remain with thee.
Away!

[*Exeunt.*]

SCENE IV. *Rome.* CÆSAR'S *house.*

[*Enter* OCTAVIUS CÆSAR, *reading a letter,* LEPIDUS, *and their train.*]

CÆS. You may see, Lepidus, and henceforth know,
   It is not Cæsar's natural vice to hate
   Our great competitor: from Alexandria
   This is the news: he fishes, drinks, and wastes
   The lamps of night in revel; is not more manlike   5
   Than Cleopatra; nor the queen of Ptolemy
   More womanly than he; hardly gave audience, or
   Vouchsafed to think he had partners: you shall find there
   A man who is the abstract of all faults
   That all men follow.
LEP.   I must not think there are   10
   Evils enow to darken all his goodness:
   His faults in him seem as the spots of heaven,
   More fiery by night's blackness; hereditary,
   Rather than purchased; what he cannot change,
   Than what he chooses.   15
CÆS. You are too indulgent. Let us grant, it is not
   Amiss to tumble on the bed of Ptolemy;
   To give a kingdom for a mirth; to sit
   And keep the turn of tippling with a slave;
   To reel the streets at noon, and stand the buffet   20
   With knaves that smell of sweat: say this becomes him,—
   As his composure must be rare indeed
   Whom these things cannot blemish,—yet must Antony
   No way excuse his soils, when we do bear
   So great weight in his lightness. If he fill'd   25
   His vacancy with his voluptuousness,

Scene iv: 3. *competitor*, partner. 6. *Ptolemy*, Cleopatra's husband, whom she is thought to have poisoned, was Ptolemy XII, King of Egypt. 7. *gave audience*, i.e., to their ambassadors. 9. *abstract*, epitome. 11. *enow*, enough. 13. *by*, beside, in contrast to. 14. *purchased*, acquired. 18. *mirth*, joyous entertainment. 19. *keep . . . tippling*, observe the custom of drinking healths in turn. 20. *stand the buffet*, exchange blows (in a pugilistic contest). 22. *composure*, composition, make-up. 24. *soils*, disgraceful acts. 24–5. *bear . . . lightness*, are so greatly involved in the consequences of his levity. 26. *vacancy*, spare time.

Full surfeits, and the dryness of his bones,
Call on him for 't: but to confound such time,
That drums him from his sport, and speaks as loud
30   As his own state and ours,—'tis to be chid
As we rate boys, who, being mature in knowledge,
Pawn their experience to their present pleasure,
And so rebel to judgement.

[*Enter a* Messenger.]

Lep.   Here's more news.
Mess. Thy biddings have been done; and every hour,
35   Most noble Cæsar, shalt thou have report
How 'tis abroad. Pompey is strong at sea;
And it appears he is beloved of those
That only have fear'd Cæsar: to the ports
39   The discontents repair, and men's reports
Give him much wrong'd.
Cæs.   I should have known no less.
It hath been taught us from the primal state,
That he which is was wish'd until he were;
And the ebb'd man, ne'er loved till ne'er worth love,
Comes dear'd by being lack'd. This common body,
45   Like to a vagabond flag upon the stream,
Goes to and back, lackeying the varying tide,
To rot itself with motion.
Mess.   Cæsar, I bring thee word,
Menecrates and Menas, famous pirates,
Make the sea serve them, which they ear and wound
50   With keels of every kind: many hot inroads
They make in Italy; the borders maritime
Lack blood to think on 't, and flush youth revolt:
No vessel can peep forth, but 'tis as soon
Taken as seen; for Pompey's name strikes more
Than could his war resisted.
55   Cæs.   Antony,

27. *Full surfeits,* attacks of indigestion, caused by overeating. 28. *Call on him,* demand payment of him; *confound,* waste. 29. *drums,* gives him a warlike summons. 30. *state,* political importance. 31. *rate, scold;* mature in knowledge, arrived at years of discretion. 32. *Pawn . . . experience,* risk what experience has taught them. 40. *Give him,* make him out. 41. *primal state,* primeval organization of society. 42. *That . . . were,* that the man in power was wanted until he obtained it. 44. *Comes dear'd,* becomes endeared; *body,* i.e., of the people. 45. *flag,* iris. 46. *lackeying,* following like a lackey. 49. *ear,* plough. 52. *Lack blood,* turn pale; *flush,* vigorous; *revolt,* i.e., to join the pirates.

Leave thy lascivious wassails. When thou once
Wast beaten from Modena, where thou slew'st
Hirtius and Pansa, consuls, at thy heel
Did famine follow; whom thou fought'st against,
Though daintily brought up, with patience more   60
Than savages could suffer: thou didst drink
The stale of horses, and the gilded puddle
Which beasts would cough at: thy palate then did deign
The roughest berry on the rudest hedge;
Yea, like the stag, when snow the pasture sheets,   65
The barks of trees thou browsed'st; on the Alps
It is reported thou didst eat strange flesh,
Which some did die to look on: and all this—
It wounds thine honour that I speak it now—
Was borne so like a soldier, that thy cheek   70
So much as lank'd not.
LEP.   'Tis pity of him.
CÆS. Let his shames quickly
Drive him to Rome: 'tis time we twain
Did show ourselves i' the field; and to that end
Assemble we immediate council: Pompey   75
Thrives in our idleness.
LEP.   To-morrow, Cæsar,
I shall be furnish'd to inform you rightly
Both what by sea and land I can be able
To front this present time.
CÆS.   Till which encounter,
It is my business too. Farewell.   80
LEP. Farewell, my lord: what you shall know meantime.
Of stirs abroad, I shall beseech you, sir,
To let me be partaker.
CÆS.   Doubt not, sir;
I knew it for my bond.

[*Exeunt.*]

SCENE V. *Alexandria.* CLEOPATRA's *palace.*

[*Enter* CLEOPATRA, CHARMIAN, IRAS, *and* MARDIAN.]

CLEO. Charmian!

56. *wassails,* carousing. 60. *patience,* fortitude. 61. *suffer,* endure. 62. *stale,* urine;
gilded, covered with yellow slime. 71. *lank'd not,* did not grow thin. 78. *be able,* i.e.,
muster. 79. *front,* meet; *time,* situation; *encounter,* conference. 84. *for my bond,* to
be my bounden duty.

CHAR. Madam?

CLEO. Ha, ha!

    Give me to drink mandragora.

CHAR.   Why, madam?

5 CLEO. That I might sleep out this great gap of time

    My Antony is away.

CHAR.   You think of him too much.

CLEO. O, 'tis treason!

CHAR.   Madam, I trust, not so.

CLEO. Thou, eunuch Mardian!

MAR.   What's your highness' pleasure?

CLEO. Not now to hear thee sing; I take no pleasure

10   In aught an eunuch has: 'tis well for thee,

    That, being unseminar'd, thy freer thoughts

    May not fly forth of Egypt. Hast thou affections?

MAR. Yes, gracious madam.

CLEO. Indeed!

15 MAR. Not in deed, madam; for I can do nothing

    But what indeed is honest to be done:

    Yet have I fierce affections, and think

    What Venus did with Mars.

CLEO.   O Charmian,

    Where think'st thou he is now? Stands he, or sits he?

20   Or does he walk? or is he on his horse?

    O happy horse, to bear the weight of Antony!

    Do bravely, horse! for wot'st thou whom thou movest?

    The demi-Atlas of this earth, the arm

    And burgonet of men. He's speaking now,

25   Or murmuring "Where's my serpent of old Nile?

    For so he calls me: now I feed myself

    With most delicious poison. Think on me,

    That am with Phœbus' amorous pinches black,

    And wrinkled deep in time? Broad-fronted Cæsar,

30   When thou wast here above the ground, I was

    A morsel for a monarch; and great Pompey

    Would stand and make his eyes grow in my brow;

    There would he anchor his aspéct and die

    With looking on his life.

Scene v: 3. *Ha, ha!* i.e., a yawn of boredom.   4. *mandragora*, the juice of mandrake, a narcotic. 11. *unseminar'd*, emasculated. 22. *Do bravely*, act splendidly. 23. *demi-Atlas*, Atlas bore the world on his shoulders. Antony bears half of it, Octavius the other. She ignores Lepidus. 24. *burgonet*, helmet. 28. *black*, tanned. 29. *wrinkled*, Cleopatra was really only thirty years old; *Cæsar*, Julius Cæsar, who was her paramour. 33. *aspéct*, gaze.

[*Enter* ALEXAS.]

ALEX.   Sovereign of Egypt, hail!
CLEO. How much unlike art thou Mark Antony!   35
  Yet, coming from him, that great medicine hath
  With his tinct gilded thee.
  How goes it with my brave Mark Antony?
ALEX. Last thing he did, dear queen,
  He kiss'd,—the last of many doubled kisses,—
  This orient pearl. His speech sticks in my heart.   41
CLEO. Mine ear must pluck it thence.
ALEX.   "Good friend," quoth he,
  "Say, the firm Roman to great Egypt sends
  This treasure of an oyster; at whose foot,
  To mend the petty present, I will piece   45
  Her opulent throne with kingdoms, all the east,
  Say thou, shall call her mistress." So he nodded,
  And soberly did mount an arm-gaunt steed,
  Who neigh'd so high, that what I would have spoke
  Was beastly dumb'd by him.
CLEO   What, was he sad or merry?   50
ALEX. Like to the time o' the year between the extremes
  Of hot and cold, he was nor sad nor merry.
CLEO. O well-divided disposition! Note him,
  Note him, good Charmian, 'tis the man; but note him:
  He was not sad, for he would shine on those   55
  That make their looks by his; he was not merry,
  Which seem'd to tell them his remembrance lay
  In Egypt with his joy; but between both:
  O heavenly mingle! Be'st thou sad or merry,
  The violence of either thee becomes,   60
  So does it no man else. Met'st thou my posts?
ALEX. Ay, madam, twenty several messengers:
  Why do you send so thick?
CLEO.   Who's born that day
  When I forget to send to Antony,
  Shall die a beggar. Ink and paper, Charmian.   65
  Welcome, my good Alexas. Did I, Charmian,
  Ever love Cæsar so?

36. *great medicine*, the elixir of the alchemists which was supposed to turn baser metals
into gold. 37. *his tinct*, its active principle, i.e., its occult power. 41. *orient*, bright.
43. *Egypt*, the Queen of Egypt. 45. *piece*, piece out, extend. 48. *arm-gaunt*, gaunt
from service in war. 50. *beastly dumb'd*, drowned out by the beast's neighing. 54. *'tis
the man*, the man (Antony) to the life! 61. *posts*, messengers.

Char.   O that brave Cæsar!
Cleo. Be choked with such another emphasis!
 Say, the brave Antony.
Char.   The valiant Cæsar!
70 Cleo. By Isis, I will give thee bloody teeth,
 If thou with Cæsar paragon again
 My man of men.
Char.   By your most gracious pardon,
 I sing but after you.
Cleo.   My salad days,
 When I was green in judgement: cold in blood,
75 To say as I said then! But, come, away;
 Get me ink and paper:
 He shall have every day a several greeting,
 Or I'll unpeople Egypt.

[*Exeunt.*]

ACT II

Scene I. *Messina.* Pompey's *house.*

[*Enter* Pompey, Menecrates, *and* Menas, *in warlike manner.*]

Pom. If the great gods be just, they shall assist
 The deeds of justest men.
Mene.   Know, worthy Pompey,
 That what they do delay, they not deny.
Pom. Whiles we are suitors to their throne, decays
 The thing we sue for.
5 Mene.   We, ignorant of ourselves,
 Beg often our own harms, which the wise powers
 Deny us for our good; so find we profit
 By losing of our prayers.
Pom.   I shall do well:
 The people love me, and the sea is mine;
10 My powers are crescent, and my auguring hope
 Says it will come to the full. Mark Antony
 In Egypt sits at dinner, and will make
 No wars without doors: Cæsar gets money where
 He loses hearts: Lepidus flatters both,

Of both is flatter'd; but he neither loves, 15
Nor either cares for him.
MEN.   Cæsar and Lepidus
 Are in the field: a mighty strength they carry.
POM. Where have you this? 'tis false.
MEN.   From Silvius, sir.
POM. He dreams: I know they are in Rome together,
 Looking for Antony. But all the charms of love, 20
 Salt Cleopatra, soften thy wanèd lip!
 Let witchcraft join with beauty, lust with both!
 Tie up the libertine in a field of feasts,
 Keep his brain fuming; Epicurean cooks
 Sharpen with cloyless sauce his appetite; 25
 That sleep and feeding may prorogue his honour
 Even till a Lethe'd dulness!

[*Enter* VARRIUS.]

                              How now, Varrius!
VAR. This is most certain that I shall deliver:
 Mark Antony is every hour in Rome
 Expected: since he went from Egypt 'tis 30
 A space for further travel.
POM.   I could have given less matter
 A better ear. Menas, I did not think
 This amorous surfeiter would have donn'd his helm
 For such a petty war: his soldiership
 Is twice the other twain: but let us rear 35
 The higher our opinion, that our stirring
 Can from the lap of Egypt's widow pluck
 The ne'er-lust-wearied Antony.
MEN.   I cannot hope
 Cæsar and Antony shall well greet together:
 His wife that's dead did trespasses to Cæsar; 40
 His brother warr'd upon him; although, I think,
 Not moved by Antony.
POM.   I know not, Menas,
 How lesser enmities may give way to greater.
 Were 't not that we stand up against them all,

---

21. *Salt*, wanton; *wanèd*, shrunken. 26. *prorogue his honour*, defer considerations of honor. 27. *Lethe'd dulness*, oblivious apathy (overtake him). 28. *deliver*, report. 31. *space*, sufficient time. 36. *opinion*, i.e., of ourselves. 39. *well* . . . *together*, come to a friendly agreement. 40. *Cæsar*, Octavius Cæsar. 41. *brother*, i.e., Lucius Antonius, who joined with Fulvia to make war on Octavius.

45   'Twere pregnant they should square between themselves;
　　　For they have entertainèd cause enough
　　　To draw their swords: but how the fear of us
　　　May cément their divisions and bind up
　　　The petty difference, we yet not know.
50   Be 't as our gods will have 't! It only stands
　　　Our lives upon to use our strongest hands.
　　　Come, Menas.

[*Exeunt.*]

Scene II. *Rome. The house of* Lepidus.

[*Enter* Enobarbus *and* Lepidus.]

Lep.　Good Enobarbus, 'tis a worthy deed,
　　　And shall become you well, to entreat your captain
　　　To soft and gentle speech.
Eno.　　　　　　　　　　I shall entreat him
　　　To answer like himself: if Cæsar move him,
5　　Let Antony look over Cæsar's head
　　　And speak as loud as Mars. By Jupiter,
　　　Were I the wearer of Antonius' beard,
　　　I would not shave 't to-day.
Lep.　　　　　　　　　　'Tis not a time
　　　For private stomaching.
Eno.　　　　　　　　Every time
10　Serves for the matter that is then born in 't.
Lep.　But small to greater matters must give way.
Eno.　Not if the small come first.
Lep.　　　　　　　　　Your speech is passion:
　　　But, pray you, stir no embers up. Here comes
　　　The noble Antony.

[*Enter* Antony *and* Ventidius.]

Eno.　　　　　　　And yonder, Cæsar.

[*Enter* Cæsar, Mecænas, *and* Agrippa.]

15　Ant.　If we compose well here, to Parthia:
　　　Hark, Ventidius.

45. *pregnant,* very probable; *square,* square off, fight.　46. *entertainèd,* received.　50–1. *It . . . upon,* our lives wholly depend upon. Scene ii:　4. *like himself,* in accordance with his best nature; *move,* exasperate.　8. *not shave 't,* i.e., would show disrespect by not trimming my beard.　9. *stomaching,* resentment.　15. *compose,* agree.

CÆS.   I do not know,
Mecænas; ask Agrippa.
LEP.   Noble friends,
That which combined us was most great, and let not
A leaner action rend us. What's amiss,
May it be gently heard: when we debate   20
Our trivial difference loud, we do commit
Murder in healing wounds: then, noble partners,
The rather, for I earnestly beseech,
Touch you the sourest points with sweetest terms,
Nor curstness grow to the matter.
ANT.   'Tis spoken well.   25
Were we before our armies, and to fight,
I should do thus.

[*Flourish.*]

CÆS. Welcome to Rome.
ANT.   Thank you.
CÆS,   Sit.
ANT.   Sit, sir.
CÆS.   Nay, then.
ANT. I learn, you take things ill which are not so,
Or being, concern you not.
CÆS.   I must be laugh'd at,   30
If, or for nothing or a little, I
Should say myself offended, and with you
Chiefly i' the world; more laugh'd at, that I should
Once name you derogately, when to sound your name
It not concern'd me.
ANT.   My being in Egypt, Cæsar,   35
What was 't to you?
CÆS. No more than my residing here at Rome
Might be to you in Egypt: yet, if you there
Did practise on my state, your being in Egypt
Might be my question.
ANT.   How intend you, practisèd?   40
CÆS. You may be pleased to catch at mine intent
By what did here befall me. Your wife and brother
Made wars upon me; and their contestation

19. *What's*, whatever is. 25. *Nor . . . matter*, nor let angry speech play a part in our discussion. 27. *do thus*, i.e., he makes some conciliatory gesture. 34. *derogately*, disparagingly. 39. *practise . . . state*, plot against my administration. 40. *question*, business.

Was theme for you, you were the word of war.
45 ANT. You do mistake your business; my brother never
Did urge me in his act: I did inquire it;
And have my learning from some true reports,
That drew their swords with you. Did he not rather
Discredit my authority with yours;
50 And make the wars alike against my stomach,
Having alike your cause? Of this my letters
Before did satisfy you. If you'll patch a quarrel,
As matter whole you have not to make it with,
It must not be with this.
CÆS.   You praise yourself
55 By laying defects of judgement to me; but
You patch'd up your excuses.
ANT.   Not so, not so;
I know you could not lack, I am certain on 't,
Very necessity of this thought, that I,
Your partner in the cause 'gainst which he fought,
60 Could not with graceful eyes attend those wars
Which fronted mine own peace. As for my wife,
I would you had her spirit in such another:
The third o' the world is yours; which with a snaffle
You may pace easy, but not such a wife.
ENO. Would we had all such wives, that the men might go to wars with
66 the women!
ANT. So much uncurbable, her garboils, Cæsar,
Made out of her impatience, which not wanted
Shrewdness of policy too, I grieving grant
Did you too much disquiet: for that you must
70 But say, I could not help it.
CÆS.   I wrote to you
When rioting in Alexandria; you
Did pocket up my letters, and with taunts
Did gibe my missive out of audience.
ANT.   Sir,
75 He fell upon me ere admitted: then

---

44. *theme for you*, for your benefit; *word,* watchword.   45. *do . . . business*, you are mistaken in the matter you advert to.   46. *urge me*, use my name.   47. *learning*, information; *true reports*, reliable reporters.   50. *stomach*, desire.   51. *alike your cause*, the same cause (of irritation).   52. *patch a quarrel*, trump up a quarrel out of shreds and patches.   54. *this*, i.e., my brother's doings.   58. *Very necessity*, inevitability.   60. *graceful*, favoring; *attend*, regard.   61. *fronted*, opposed.   63. *snaffle*, bridle bit.   64. *pace*, control.   67. *her garboils*, the disturbances she caused.   74. *missive*, messenger.

Three kings I had newly feasted, and did want
Of what I was i' the morning: but next day
I told him of myself; which was as much
As to have ask'd him pardon. Let this fellow
Be nothing of our strife; if we contend, 80
Out of our question wipe him.

CÆS. You have broken
The article of your oath; which you shall never
Have tongue to charge me with.

LEP. Soft, Cæsar!

ANT. No,
Lepidus, let him speak:
The honour is sacred which he talks on now, 85
Supposing that I lack'd it. But, on, Cæsar;
The article of my oath.

CÆS. To lend me arms and aid when I required them;
The which you both denied.

ANT. Neglected, rather;
And then when poison'd hours had bound me up 90
From mine own knowledge. As nearly as I may,
I'll play the penitent to you: but mine honesty
Shall not make poor my greatness, nor my power
Work without it. Truth is, that Fulvia,
To have me out of Egypt, made wars here; 95
For which myself, the ignorant motive, do
So far ask pardon as befits mine honour
To stoop in such a case.

LEP. 'Tis noble spoken.

MEC. If it might please you, to enforce no further
The griefs between ye: to forget them quite 100
Were to remember that the present need
Speaks to atone you.

LEP. Worthily spoken, Mecænas.

ENO. Or, if you borrow one another's love for the instant, you may, when
you hear no more words of Pompey, return it again: you shall have time
to wrangle in when you have nothing else to do. 107

ANT. Thou art a soldier only: speak no more.

ENO. That truth should be silent I had almost forgot.

---

78. *myself,* my (slightly drunken) condition at the time. 82. *article,* essential point.
83. *Soft,* be careful. 91. *From . . . knowledge,* from knowing what I was doing.
92. *honesty,* sense of honor. 93. *make . . . greatness,* subtract from the dignity of
my position. 93–4. *nor . . . without it,* nor shall I exercise my power dishonorably.
99. *enforce,* insist upon. 100. *griefs,* grievances. 102. *atone,* reconcile.

111 Ant. You wrong this presence; therefore speak no more.
Eno. Go to, then; your considerate stone.
Cæs. I do not much dislike the matter, but
The manner of his speech: for 't cannot be
115 We shall remain in friendship, our conditions
So differing in their acts. Yet, if I knew
What hoop should hold us stanch, from edge to edge
O' the world I would pursue it.
Agr.   Give me leave, Cæsar,—
Cæs. Speak, Agrippa.
120 Agr. Thou hast a sister by the mother's side,
Admired Octavia: great Mark Antony
Is now a widower.
Cæs.   Say not so, Agrippa:
If Cleopatra heard you, your reproof
124 Were well deserved of rashness.
Ant. I am not married, Cæsar: let me hear Agrippa further speak.
Agr. To hold you in perpetual amity,
To make you brothers, and to knit your hearts
With an unslipping knot, take Antony
130 Octavia to his wife; whose beauty claims
No worse a husband than the best of men;
Whose virtue and whose general graces speak
That which none else can utter. By this marriage,
All little jealousies, which now seem great,
135 And all great fears, which now import their dangers,
Would then be nothing: truths would be tales,
Where now half tales be truths: her love to both
Would, each to other and all loves to both,
Draw after her. Pardon what I have spoke;
140 For 'tis a studied, not a present thought,
By duty ruminated.
Ant.   Will Cæsar speak?
Cæs. Not till he hears how Antony is touch'd
With what is spoke already.
Ant.   What power is in Agrippa,
If I would say, "Agrippa, be it so,"
To make this good?

---

111. *this presence,* those present at this conference. 112. *your . . . stone,* i.e., I shall
be as silent as a thinking stone. 115. *conditions,* dispositions. 124. *of,* because of your.
134. *jealousies,* suspicions. 135. *import,* carry with them. 137. *half tales be truths,*
rumors be accepted as true. 140. *studied . . . thought,* carefully considered ideas, not
one that has just occurred to me.

CÆS.   The power of Cæsar, and
  His power unto Octavia.
ANT.   May I never   146
  To this good purpose, that so fairly shows,
  Dream of impediment! Let me have thy hand:
  Further this act of grace; and from this hour
  The heart of brothers govern in our loves   150
  And sway our great designs!
CÆS.   There is my hand.
  A sister I bequeath you, whom no brother
  Did ever love so dearly: let her live
  To join our kingdoms and our hearts; and never
  Fly off our loves again!
LEP.   Happily, amen!   155
ANT. I did not think to draw my sword 'gainst Pompey;
  For he hath laid strange courtesies and great
  Of late upon me: I must thank him only,
  Lest my remembrance suffer ill report;
  At heel of that, defy him.
LEP.   Time calls upon 's:
  Of us must Pompey presently be sought,   161
  Or else he seeks out us.
ANT.   Where lies he?
CÆS. About the mount Misenum.
ANT. What is his strength by land?
CÆS. Great and increasing: but by sea   165
  He is an absolute master.
ANT.   So is the fame.
  Would we had spoke together! Haste we for it:
  Yet, ere we put ourselves in arms, dispatch we
  The business we have talk'd of.
CÆS.   With most gladness;
  And do invite you to my sister's view,   170
  Whither straight I'll lead you.
ANT.   Let us, Lepidus,
  Not lack your company.
LEP.   Noble Antony,
  Not sickness should detain me.

[*Flourish. Exeunt* CÆSAR, ANTONY, *and* LEPIDUS.]

147. *so fairly shows,* seems so promising.   149. *grace,* reconciliation.   155. *fly . . . our
loves,* may we never be estranged.   157. *strange,* unusual.   160. *At heel of,* immediately
after.   166. *fame,* report.   170. *to . . . view,* to see my sister.

174 MEC. Welcome from Egypt, sir.

ENO. Half the heart of Cæsar, worthy

MEC. My honourable friend, Agrippa!

AGR. Good Enobarbus!

MEC. We have cause to be glad that matters are so well digested. You
180   stayed well by 't in Egypt.

ENO. Ay, sir; we did sleep day out of countenance, and made the night
light with drinking.

MEC. Eight wild-boars roasted whole at a breakfast, and but twelve persons
185   there; is this true?

ENO. This was but as a fly by an eagle: we had much more monstrous
matter of feast, which worthily deserved noting.

190 MEC. She's a most triumphant lady if report be square to her.

ENO. When she first met Mark Antony, she pursed up his heart, upon the
river of Cydnus.

194 AGR. There she appeared indeed; or my reporter devised well for her.

ENO. I will tell you.

The barge she sat in, like a burnish'd throne,
Burn'd on the water: the poop was beaten gold;
Purple the sails, and so perfumèd that
The winds were love-sick with them; the oars were silver,
200   Which to the tune of flutes kept stroke, and made
The water which they beat to follow faster,
As amorous of their strokes. For her own person,
It beggar'd all description: she did lie
In her pavilion—cloth-of-gold of tissue—
205   O'er-picturing that Venus where we see
The fancy outwork nature: on each side her
Stood pretty dimpled boys, like smiling Cupids,
With divers-colour'd fans, whose wind did seem
To glow the delicate cheeks which they did cool,
And what they undid did.
210 AGR.   O, rare for Antony!

ENO. Her gentlewomen, like the Nereides,
So many mermaids, tended her i' the eyes,

179–80. You . . . by 't, you kept your revels going well.   182. light, giddy (with the
obvious pun).   186. by, compared with.   190. triumphant, splendid; square, just.
191. pursed up, put in the purse, i.e., pocketed.   193. appeared indeed, put on a magnificent show.   194. devised . . . her, exaggerated his description of her.   202. For, as
for.   204. cloth . . . tissue, cloth made of interwoven threads of silk and gold.   205.
that Venus, probably a picture of Venus rising from the sea painted by the Greek artist
Apelles (ca. 330 B.C.).   206. fancy, imagination (of the painter).   209. glow, cause
to glow.   212. i' the eyes, attentive to her slightest glance.

And made their bends adornings: at the helm
A seeming mermaid steers: the silken tackle
Swell with the touches of those flower-soft hands,   215
That yarely frame the office. From the barge
A strange invisible perfume hits the sense
Of the adjacent wharfs. The city cast
Her people out upon her; and Antony,
Enthroned i' the market-place, did sit alone,   220
Whistling to the air; which, but for vacancy,
Had gone to gaze on Cleopatra too
And made a gap in nature.
AGR.   Rare Egyptian!
ENO. Upon her landing, Antony sent to her,
Invited her to supper: she replied,   225
It should be better he became her guest;
Which she entreated: our courteous Antony,
Whom ne'er the word of "No" woman heard speak,
Being barber'd ten times o'er, goes to the feast,
And for his ordinary pays his heart   230
For what his eyes eat only.
AGR.   Royal wench!
She made great Cæsar lay his sword to bed:
He plough'd her, and she cropp'd.
ENO.   I saw her once
Hop forty paces through the public street;
And having lost her breath, she spoke, and panted,   235
That she did make defect perfection,
And, breathless, power breathe forth.
MEC. Now Antony must leave her utterly.
ENO. Never; he will not:
Age cannot wither her, nor custom stale   240
Her infinite variety: other women cloy
The appetites they feed; but she makes hungry
Where most she satisfies: for vilest things
Become themselves in her; that the holy priests
Bless her when she is riggish.   245
MEC. If beauty, wisdom, modesty, can settle
The heart of Antony, Octavia is

213. *made . . . adornings,* their obeisances (were so graceful) that they adorned Cleopatra.   216. *yarely . . . office,* perform their duty dexterously.   218. *wharfs,* banks. 221. *for vacancy,* for fear of forming a vacuum.   230. *ordinary,* meal.   237. *power breathe forth,* i.e., she did breathe forth the power of her charm.   244. *Become themselves,* are becoming.   245. *riggish,* wanton.

A blessed lottery to him.

AGR.   Let us go.
Good Enobarbus, make yourself my guest
250 Whilst you abide here.

ENO. Humbly, sir, I thank you.

[*Exeunt.*]

SCENE III. *The same.* CÆSAR'S *house.*

[*Enter* ANTONY, CÆSAR, OCTAVIA *between them, and* ATTENDANTS.]

ANT. The world and my great office will sometimes
Divide me from your bosom.

OCTA.   All which time
Before the gods my knee shall bow my prayers
To them for you.

4 ANT.   Good night, sir. My Octavia,
Read not my blemishes in the world's report:
I have not kept my square; but that to come
Shall be all done by the rule. Good night, dear lady.
Good night, sir.

CÆSAR. Good night.

[*Exeunt* CÆSAR *and* OCTAVIA.]

[*Enter* SOOTHSAYER.]

10 ANT. Now, sirrah; you do wish yourself in Egypt?

SOOTH. Would I had never come from thence, nor you
Thither!

ANT. If you can, your reason?

SOOTH.   I see it in
My motion, have it not in my tongue: but yet
Hie you to Egypt again.

15 ANT.   Say to me,
Whose fortunes shall rise higher. Cæsar's or mine?

SOOTH. Cæsar's.
Therefore, O Antony, stay not by his side:
Thy demon, that's thy spirit which keeps thee, is
20 Noble, courageous, high, unmatchable,
Where Cæsar's is not; but, near him, thy angel

---

248. *lottery,* prize in a lottery.   Scene iii: 5. *in,* in accordance with.   6. *square,* proper position, i.e., moral control.   13–14. *in My motion,* intuitively.   19. *demon,* guardian spirit; *keeps,* protects.

Becomes a fear, as being o'erpower'd: therefore
Make space enough between you.
ANT.   Speak this no more.
SOOTH. To none but thee; no more, but when to thee.
   If thou dost play with him at any game,   25
   Thou art sure to lose; and, of that natural luck,
   He beats thee 'gainst the odds: thy lustre thickens,
   When he shines by: I say again, thy spirit
   Is all afraid to govern thee near him;
   But, he away, 'tis noble.
ANT.   Get thee gone: 30
   Say to Ventidius I would speak with him:

[*Exit* SOOTHSAYER.]

   He shall to Parthia. Be it art or hap,
   He hath spoken true: the very dice obey him;
   And in our sports my better cunning faints
   Under his chance: if we draw lots, he speeds;   35
   His cocks do win the battle still of mine,
   When it is all to nought; and his quails ever
   Beat mine, inhoop'd, at odds. I will to Egypt:
   And though I make this marriage for my peace,
   I' the east my pleasure lies.

[*Enter* VENTIDIUS.]

                     O, come, Ventidius,   40
   You must to Parthia: your commission's ready;
   Follow me, and receive 't.

[*Exeunt.*]

SCENE IV. *The same. A street.*

[*Enter* LEPIDUS, MECÆNAS, *and* AGRIPPA.]

LEP. Trouble yourselves no further: pray you, hasten
   Your generals after.
AGR.   Sir, Mark Antony
   Will e'en but kiss Octavia, and we'll follow.
LEP. Till I shall see you in your soldier's dress,

---

22. *fear,* frightening thing.   27. *thickens,* grows dim.   34. *cunning,* skill.   35. *chance,*
luck; *speeds,* win.   36. *still,* always.   37. *all to nought,* i.e., when the odds are all to
nothing in my favor.   38. *inhoop'd,* enclosed (for fighting).   Scene iv: 1. *Trouble*
yourselves, i.e., in escorting me.

Which will become you both, farewell.

MEC.   We shall,

6   As I conceive the journey, be at the Mount

Before you, Lepidus.

LEP.   Your way is shorter;

My purposes do draw me much about:

You'll win two days upon me.

MEC. ⎤

AGR. ⎦ Sir, good success!

10 LEP. Farewell.

[*Exeunt.*]

SCENE V. *Alexandria.* CLEOPATRA'S *palace.*

[*Enter* CLEOPATRA, CHARMIAN, IRAS, *and* ALEXAS.]

CLEO. Give me some music; music, moody food

Of us that trade in love.

ATTEND.   The music, ho!

[*Enter* MARDIAN *the Eunuch.*]

CLEO. Let it alone; let's to billiards: come, Charmian.

CHAR. My arm is sore; best play with Mardian.

5 CLEO. As well a woman with an eunuch play'd

As with a woman. Come, you'll play with me, sir?

MAR. As well as I can, madam.

CLEO. And when good will is show'd, though 't come too short,

The actor may plead pardon. I'll none now:

10 Give me mine angle; we'll to the river: there,

My music playing far off, I will betray

Tawny-finn'd fishes; my bended hook shall pierce

Their slimy jaws; and, as I draw them up,

I'll think them every one an Antony,

And say "Ah, ha! you're caught."

CHAR.   'Twas merry when

16 You wager'd on your angling; when your diver

Did hang a salt-fish on his hook, which he

With fervency drew up.

CLEO.   That time,—O times!—

I laugh'd him out of patience; and that night

20 I laugh'd him into patience: and next morn,

6. *Mount,* i.e., Mount Misenum. 8. *much about,* by a very roundabout way. Scene
v: 9. *I'll none,* I don't wish to play (billiards). 10. *angle,* rod and line.

Ere the ninth hour, I drunk him to his bed;
Then put my tires and mantles on him, whilst
I wore his sword Philippan.

[*Enter a* Messenger.]

                    O, from Italy!
Ram thou thy fruitful tidings in mine ears,
That long time have been barren.
Mess.   Madam, madam,—
Cleo. Antonius dead!—If thou say so, villain,   26
   Thou kill'st thy mistress: but well and free,
   If thou so yield him, there is gold, and here
   My bluest veins to kiss; a hand that kings
   Have lipp'd, and trembled kissing.   30
Mess. First, madam, he is well.
Cleo.   Why, there's more gold.
   But, sirrah, mark, we use
   To say the dead are well: bring it to that,
   The gold I give thee will I melt and pour
   Down thy ill-uttering throat.   35
Mess. Good madam, hear me.
Cleo.   Well, go to, I will;
   But there's no goodness in thy face: if Antony
   Be free and healthful,—so tart a favour
   To trumpet such good tidings! If not well,
   Thou shouldst come like a Fury crown'd with snakes,   40
   Not like a formal man.
Mess.   Will 't please you hear me?
Cleo. I have a mind to strike thee ere thou speak'st:
   Yet, if thou say Antony lives, is well,
   Or friends with Cæsar, or not captive to him,
   I'll set thee in a shower of gold, and hail   45
   Rich pearls upon thee.
Mess.   Madam, he's well.
Cleo.   Well said.
Mess. And friends with Cæsar.
Cleo.   Thou 'rt an honest man.
Mess. Cæsar and he are greater friends than ever.
Cleo. Make thee a fortune from me.

22. *tires*, head-dresses.   23. *Philippan*, named for its service in the battle of Philippi,
where he defeated Brutus and Cassius..   28. *yield*, report.   33. *bring it to that*, if that
is what you mean.   38. *tart a favour*, sour an expression.   41. *formal*, normally formed.
47. *honest*, honorable.

MESS.   But yet, madam,—

50 CLEO. I do not like "But yet," it does allay
    The good precedence, fie upon "But yet"!
    "But yet" is as a gaoler to bring forth
    Some monstrous malefactor. Prithee, friend,
    Pour out the pack of matter to mine ear,
55   The good and bad together: he's friends with Cæsar;
    In state of health thou say'st; and thou say'st free.
MESS. Free, madam! no; I made no such report:
    He's bound unto Octavia.
CLEO.   For what good turn?
MESS. For the best turn i' the bed.
CLEO.   I am pale, Charmian.
60 MESS. Madam, he's married to Octavia.
CLEO. The most infectious pestilence upon thee!

[*Strikes him down.*]

MESS. Good madam, patience.
CLEO.   What say you? Hence,

[*Strikes him again.*]

    Horrible villain! or I'll spurn thine eyes
    Like balls before me; I'll unhair thy head:

[*She hales him up and down.*]

65   Thou shalt be whipp'd with wire, and stew'd in brine,
    Smarting in lingering pickle.
MESS.   Gracious madam,
    I that do bring the news made not the match.
CLEO. Say 'tis not so, a province I will give thee,
    And make thy fortunes proud: the blow thou hadst
70   Shall make thy peace for moving me to rage;
    And I will boot thee with what gift beside
    Thy modesty can beg.
MESS.   He's married, madam.
CLEO. Rogue, thou hast lived too long.

[*Draws a knife.*]

MESS.   Nay, then I'll run.

50–1. *it . . . precedence*, dilutes the good news which preceded it; *pack of matter*, all
the contents of the bag.   58. *good turn*, favor.   63. *spurn*, kick. *s.d. hales*, drags.   71.
boot thee, give you to boot.   72. *modesty*, moderation.

What mean you, madam? I have made no fault.

[*Exit.*]

CHAR. Good madam, keep yourself within yourself: 75
  The man is innocent.
CLEO. Some innocents 'scape not the thunderbolt.
  Melt Egypt into Nile! and kindly creatures
  Turn all to serpents! Call the slave again:
  Though I am mad, I will not bite him: call.   80
CHAR. He is afeard to come.
CLEO.   I will not hurt him.

[*Exit* CHARMIAN.]

  These hands do lack nobility, that they strike
  A meaner than myself; since I myself
  Have given myself the cause.

[*Re-enter* CHARMIAN *and* MESSENGER.]

                   Come, hither, sir.
  Though it be honest, it is never good   85
  To bring bad news: give to a gracious message
  An host of tongues: but let ill tidings tell
  Themselves when they be felt.
MESS.   I have done my duty.
CLEO. Is he married?
  I cannot hate thee worser than I do,   90
  If thou again say "Yes."
MESS.   He's married, madam.
CLEO. The gods confound thee! dost thou hold there still?
MESS. Should I lie, madam?
CLEO.   O, I would thou didst,
  So half my Egypt were submerged and made
  A cistern for scaled snakes! Go, get thee hence: 95
  Hadst thou Narcissus in thy face, to me
  Thou wouldst appear most ugly. He is married?
MESS. I crave your highness' pardon.
CLEO.   He is married?
MESS. Take no offence that I would not offend you:
  To punish me for what you make me do   100

78. *kindly*, natural.   84. *the cause*, i.e., my immoderate love.   86. *gracious*, favorable.
92. *hold there still*, persists in this report.   94. *So*, even if.   96. *Narcissus*, a Greek
youth who fell in love with his own beautiful face.   98. *pardon*, i.e., for being afraid
to answer.   99. *would . . . you*, i.e., by answering in the affirmative.

Seems much unequal: he's married to Octavia.
CLEO. O, that his fault should make a knave of thee,
That art not what thou'rt sure of! Get thee hence:
The merchandise which thou hast brought from Rome
105   Are all too dear for me: lie they upon thy hand,
And be undone by 'em!

[*Exit* MESSENGER.]

CHAR.   Good your highness, patience.
CLEO. In praising Antony, I have dispraised Cæsar.
CHAR. Many times, madam.
CLEO.   I am paid for 't now.
Lead me from hence;
110   I faint: O Iras, Charmian! 'tis no matter.
Go to the fellow, good Alexas; bid him
Report the feature of Octavia, her years,
Her inclination, let him not leave out
The colour of her hair: bring me word quickly.

[*Exit* ALEXAS.]

115   Let him for ever go:—let him not—Charmian,
Though he be painted one way like a Gorgon,
The other way 's a Mars. Bid you Alexas

[*To* MARDIAN.]

Bring me word how tall she is. Pity me, Charmian,
But do not speak to me. Lead me to my chamber.

[*Exeunt.*]

SCENE VI. *Near Misenum.*

[*Flourish. Enter* POMPEY *and* MENAS *at one side, with drum and trumpet:
at another,* CÆSAR, ANTONY, LEPIDUS, ENOBARBUS, MECÆNAS, *with* SOLDIERS
marching.]

POM. Your hostages I have, so have you mine;
And we shall talk before we fight.
CÆS.   Most meet

---

101. *unequal,* undeserved.   103. *what . . . sure of,* i.e., his base act.   105. *lie . . .
hand,* i.e., be unsold.   106. *undone,* ruined.   112. *feature,* general appearance.   113.
inclination, disposition.   115. *him,* i.e., Antony.   116–7. *one . . . Mars,* a reference to
a "perspective" picture that showed different objects when looked at from different
angles; *way's,* way he's.

That first we come to words; and therefore have we
Our written purposes before us sent;
Which, if thou hast consider'd, let us know   5
If 'twill tie up thy discontented sword,
And carry back to Sicily much tall youth
That else must perish here.
POM.   To you all three,
The senators alone of this great world,
Chief factors for the gods, I do not know   10
Wherefore my father should revengers want,
Having a son and friends; since Julius Cæsar,
Who at Philippi the good Brutus ghosted,
There saw you labouring for him. What was 't
That moved pale Cassius to conspire; and what   15
Made the all-honour'd, honest Roman, Brutus,
With the arm'd rest, courtiers of beauteous freedom,
To drench the Capitol; but that they would
Have one man but a man? And that is it
Hath made me rig my navy; at whose burthen   20
The anger'd ocean foams; with which I meant
To scourge the ingratitude that despiteful Rome
Cast on my noble father.
CÆS.   Take your time.
ANT. Thou canst not fear us, Pompey, with thy sails;
We'll speak with thee at sea: at land, thou know'st   25
How much we do o'er-count thee.
POM.   At land, indeed,
Thou dost o'er-count me of my father's house:
But, since the cuckoo builds not for himself,
Remain in 't as thou mayst.
LEP.   Be pleased to tell us—
For this is from the present—how you take   30
The offers we have sent you.
CÆS.   There's the point.
ANT. Which do not be entreated to, but weigh
What it is worth embraced.
CÆS.   And what may follow,
To try a larger fortune.
POM.   You have made me offer

Scene vi: 7. *tall,* brave.   10. *factors,* agents.   13. *ghosted,* haunted.   16. *honest,* honorable.   19. *but a man,* i.e., no superman.   24. *fear,* frighten.   25. *speak,* fight.   26.
o'er-count, outnumber.   27. *o'er-count,* overreach, cheat.   30. *from the present,* irrelevant.   33. *embraced,* if accepted.

35 Of Sicily, Sardinia; and I must
Rid all the sea of pirates; then, to send
Measures of wheat to Rome; this 'greed upon,
To part with unhack'd edges, and bear back
Our targes undinted.

Cæs. Ant. Lep.   That's our offer.

40 Pom.   Know, then,
I came before you here a man prepared
To take this offer: but Mark Antony
Put me to some impatience: though I lose
The praise of it by telling, you must know,

45 When Cæsar and your brother were at blows,
Your mother came to Sicily and did find
Her welcome friendly.

Ant.   I have heard it, Pompey;
And am well studied for a liberal thanks
Which I do owe you.

Pom.   Let me have your hand:

50 I did not think, sir, to have met you here.

Ant. The beds i' the east are soft; and thanks to you,
That call'd me timelier than my purpose hither;
For I have gain'd by 't.

Cæs.   Since I saw you last,
There is a change upon you.

Pom.   Well, I know not

55 What counts harsh fortune casts upon my face;
But in my bosom shall she never come,
To make my heart her vassal.

Lep.   Well met here.

Pom. I hope so, Lepidus. Thus we are agreed:
I crave our composition may be written,
And seal'd between us.

60 Cæs.   That's the next to do.

Pom. We'll feast each other ere we part; and let's
Draw lots who shall begin.

Ant.   That will I, Pompey.

Pom. No, Antony, take the lot· but, first
Or last, your fine Egyptian cookery

65 Shall have the fame. I have heard that Julius Cæsar

38. *edges*, swords. 39. *targes*, shields. 45. *your brother*, i.e., Lucius Antonius. 48. *studied*, prepared. 52. *timelier*, earlier; *than my purpose*, than I intended. 55. *What . . . casts*, the figure is from casting accounts; the counts are the lines drawn in the ledger. 59. *composition*, agreement. 65. *have the fame*, have a chance to live up to its reputation.

Grew fat with feasting there.
ANT.   You have heard much.
POM. I have fair meanings, sir.
ANT.   And fair words to them.
POM. Then so much have I heard:
 And I have heard, Apollodorus carried—
ENO. No more of that: he did so.
POM.   What, I pray you?   70
ENO. A certain queen to Cæsar in a mattress.
POM. I know thee now: how farest thou, soldier?
ENO. Well;
 And well am like to do; for, I perceive,   74
 Four feasts are toward.
POM.   Let me shake thy hand;
 I never hated thee: I have seen thee fight,
 When I have envied thy behaviour.
ENO.   Sir,
 I never loved you much; but I ha' praised ye,
 When you have well deserved ten times as much
 As I have said you did.
POM.   Enjoy thy plainness,   80
 It nothing ill becomes thee.
 Aboard my galley I invite you all:
 Will you lead, lords?
CÆS. ANT. LEP. Show us the way, sir.
POM.   Come.

[*Exeunt all but* MENAS *and* ENOBARBUS.]

MEN. [*Aside*] Thy father, Pompey, would ne'er have made this treaty.—
 You and I have known, sir.   86
ENO. At sea, I think.
MEN. We have, sir.
ENO. You have done well by water.
MEN. And you by land.   90
ENO. I will praise any man that will praise me; though it cannot be denied
 what I have done by land.
MEN. Nor what I have done by water.
ENO. Yes, something you can deny for your own safety: you have been a
 great thief by sea.   96

69. *Apollodorus carried,* Plutarch reports that after Julius Cæsar had captured Alexandria, Apollodorus tied Cleopatra in a bundle and so carried her secretly to Cæsar's quarters. 75. *toward,* in preparation. 80. *plainness,* plain-speaking. 86. *known,* met before. 96. *thief by sea,* i.e., pirate.

MEN. And you by land.

ENO. There I deny my land service. But give me your hand, Menas: if our
101   eyes had authority, here they might take two thieves kissing.

MEN. All men's faces are true, whatsome'er their hands are.

105 ENO. But there is never a fair woman has a true face.

MEN. No slander; they steal hearts.

ENO. We came hither to fight with you.

MEN. For my part, I am sorry it is turned to a drinking. Pompey doth this
110   day laugh away his fortune.

ENO. If he do, sure, he cannot weep 't back again.

MEN. You've said, sir. We looked not for Mark Antony here: pray you, is
115   he married to Cleopatra?

ENO. Cæsar's sister is called Octavia.

MEN. True, sir; she was the wife of Caius Marcellus.

ENO. But she is now the wife of Marcus Antonius.

120 MEN. Pray ye, sir?

ENO. 'Tis true.

MEN. Then is Cæsar and he for ever knit together.

124 ENO. If I were bound to divine of this unity, I would not prophesy so.

MEN. I think the policy of that purpose made more in the marriage than
the love of the parties.

ENO. I think so too. But you shall find, the band that seems to tie their
friendship together will be the very strangler of their amity: Octavia is
131   of a holy, cold, and still conversation.

MEN. Who would not have his wife so?

ENO. Not he that himself is not so; which is Mark Antony. He will to his
Egyptian dish again: then shall the sighs of Octavia blow the fire up in
Cæsar; and, as I said before, that which is the strength of their amity
shall prove the immediate author of their variance. Antony will use his
140   affection where it is: he married but his occasion here.

MEN. And thus it may be. Come, sir, will you aboard? I have a health for
you.

ENO. I shall take it, sir: we have used our throats in Egypt.

MEN. Come, let's away.

[*Exeunt.*]

101. *take,* arrest; *thieves,* i.e., our hands.   120. *Pray ye, sir?* Do you really mean it?
124. *divine of,* prophecy about.   125. *made more in,* had more to do with.   131. *con-*
versation, behavior.   139-40. *use his affection,* will continue to bestow his love.   140.
occasion, necessary business.

SCENE VII. *On board* POMPEY's *galley, off Misenum.*

[*Music plays. Enter two or three* SERVANTS *with a banquet.*]

FIRST SERV. Here they'll be, man. Some o' their plants are ill-rooted already; the least wind i' the world will blow them down.

SEC. SERV. Lepidus is high-coloured.

FIRST SERV. They have made him drink alms-drink. 6

SEC. SERV. As they pinch one another by the disposition, he cries out "No more;" reconciles them to his entreaty, and himself to the drink.

FIRST SERV. But it raises the greater war between him and his discretion. 11

SEC. SERV. Why, this it is to have a name in great men's fellowship: I had as lief have a reed that will do me no service as a partisan I could not heave. 15

FIRST SERV. To be called into a huge sphere, and not to be seen to move in 't, are the holes where eyes should be, which pitifully disaster the cheeks.

[*A sennet sounded. Enter* CÆSAR, ANTONY, LEPIDUS, POMPEY, AGRIPPA, MECÆNAS, ENOBARBUS, MENAS, *with other* CAPTAINS.]

ANT. [*To* CÆSAR] Thus do they, sir: they take the flow o' the Nile 20
By certain scales i' the pyramid; they know
By the height, the lowness, or the mean, if dearth
Or foison follow: the higher Nilus swells,
The more it promises: as it ebbs, the seedsman
Upon the slime and ooze scatters his grain, 25
And shortly comes to harvest.

LEP. You've strange serpents there.

ANT. Ay, Lepidus.

LEP. Your serpent of Egypt is bred now of your mud by the operation of your sun: so is your crocodile. 31

ANT. They are so.

POM. Sit,—and some wine! A health to Lepidus!

LEP. I am not so well as I should be, but I'll ne'er out. 36

ENO. Not till you have slept; I fear me you'll be in till then.

LEP. Nay, certainly, I have heard the Ptolemies' pyramises are very goodly things; without contradiction, I have heard that. 41

Scene vii: 1. *their plants,* a pun on the soles of their feet. 6. *alms-drink,* "To relieve a man of his duty by drinking in his place (in a drinking bout) was to drink alms drink." (Kittredge.) 7. *pinch . . . disposition,* fall to quarreling. 14. *partisan,* pike. 15. *heave,* lift. 16. *huge sphere,* i.e., of action. 16-17. *not in 't,* to show no ability to perform the duties it demands. 17. *are . . . should be,* is like having sockets bare of eyes; *disaster,* disfigure. *s.d.,* sennet, a signal call on a trumpet announcing the entrance of an important person. 20. *take the flow,* measure the rise and fall. 23. *foison,* plenty. 36. *out,* quit. 37. *in,* i.e., drunk. 40. *goodly,* handsome.

MEN. [*Aside to* POM.] Pompey, a word.

POM.   [*Aside to* MEN.] Say in mine ear:
what is 't?

MEN. [*Aside to* POM.] Forsake thy seat, I do beseech thee, captain.
And hear me speak a word.

44   POM. [*Aside to* MEN.] Forbear me till anon.
This wine for Lepidus!

LEP. What manner o' thing is your crocodile?

ANT. It is shaped, sir, like itself; and it is as broad as it hath breadth: it is
just so high as it is, and moves with its own organs: it lives by that which
51   nourisheth it; and the elements once out of it, it transmigrates.

LEP. What colour is it of?

ANT. Of it own colour too.

LEP. 'Tis a strange serpent.

ANT. 'Tis so. And the tears of it are wet.

CÆS. Will this description satisfy him?

ANT. With the health that Pompey gives him, else he is a very epicure.

59   POM. [*Aside to* MEN.] Go hang, sir, hang! Tell me of that? away!
Do as I bid you. Where's this cup I call'd for?

MEN. [*Aside to* POM.] If for the sake of merit thou wilt hear me,
Rise from thy stool.

POM. [*Aside to* MEN.] I think thou'rt mad. The matter?

[*Rises, and walks aside.*]

64   MEN. I have ever held my cap off to thy fortunes.

POM. Thou hast served me with much faith. What's else to say?
Be jolly, lords.

ANT.   These quick-sands, Lepidus,
Keep off them, for you sink.

MEN. Wilt thou be lord of all the world?

POM.   What say'st thou?

MEN. Wilt thou be lord of the whole world? That's twice.

POM. How should that be?

69   MEN.   But entertain it,
And, though thou think me poor, I am the man
Will give thee all the world.

POM.   Hast thou drunk well?

MEN. No, Pompey, I have kept me from the cup.
Thou art, if thou darest be, the earthly Jove:

---

44. *Forbear . . . anon*, let me alone for a moment.   51. *elements*, vital constituents,
i.e., life.   59. *that*, i.e., your wish to talk to me secretly.   61. *merit*, i.e., my past achievements.   64. *held . . . off*, assiduously served.   69. *entertain it*, accept my suggestion.

Whate'er the ocean pales, or sky inclips,   74
Is thine, if thou wilt ha 't.
Pom.   Show me which way.
Men. These three world-sharers, these competitors,
   Are in thy vessel: let me cut the cable;
   And, when we are put off, fall to their throats:
   All there is thine.
Pom.   Ah, this thou shouldst have done,
   And not have spoke on 't! In me 'tis villany;
   In thee 't had been good service. Thou must know,   81
   'Tis not my profit that does lead mine honour;
   Mine honour, it. Repent that e'er thy tongue
   Hath so betray'd thine act: being done unknown,
   I should have found it afterwards well done;
   But must condemn it now. Desist, and drink.
Men. [*Aside*] For this,
   I'll never follow thy pall'd fortunes more.   88
   Who seeks, and will not take when once 'tis offer'd,
   Shall never find it more.
Pom.   This health to Lepidus!
Ant. Bear him ashore. I'll pledge it for him, Pompey.
Eno. Here's to thee, Menas!
Men.   Enobarbus, welcome!
Pom. Fill till the cup be hid.
Eno. There's a strong fellow, Menas.

[*Pointing to the* Attendant *who carries off* Lepidus.]

Men. Why?
Eno. A' bears the third part of the world, man; see'st not?
Men. The third part, then, is drunk: would it were all,
   That it might go on wheels!
Eno. Drink thou; increase the reels.   100
Men. Come.
Pom. This is not yet an Alexandrian feast.
Ant. It ripens towards it. Strike the vessels, ho!
   Here is to Cæsar!
Cæs.   I could well forbear 't.
   It's monstrous labour, when I wash my brain,
   And it grows fouler.   106

---

74. *pales*, encloses; *inclips*, embraces. 76. *competitors*, partners. 88. *pall'd*, enfeebled. 99. *go on wheels*, proverbial for "go well," cf. the proverb, "the world runs on wheels." 100. *reels*, reeling. 103. *Strike the vessels*, tap the casks. 105. *monstrous*, unnatural. 106. *fouler*, dirtier.

ANT.   Be a child o' the time.

107 CÆS. Possess it, I'll make answer:
    But I had rather fast from all four days
    Than drink so much in one.

ENO. Ha, my brave emperor!

[*To* ANTONY.]

    Shall we dance now the Egyptian Bacchanals,
    And celebrate our drink?

POM.   Let's ha 't, good soldier.

ANT. Come, let's all take hands,
    Till that the conquering wine hath steep'd our sense
114   In soft and delicate Lethe.

ENO.   All take hands.
    Make battery to our ears with the loud music:
    That while I'll place you: then the boy shall sing;
    The holding every man shall bear as loud
    As his strong sides can volley.

[*Music plays.* ENOBARBUS *places them hand in hand.*]

                    THE SONG

120   Come, thou monarch of the vine,
               Plumpy Bacchus with pink eyne!
               In thy fats our cares be drown'd,
               With thy grapes our hairs be crown'd:
               Cup us, till the world go round,
125   Cup us, till the world go round!

    CÆS. What would you more? Pompey, good night. Good brother,
    Let me request you off: our graver business
    Frowns at this levity. Gentle lords, let's part;
    You see we have burnt our cheeks: strong Enobarb
130   Is weaker than the wine; and mine own tongue
    Splits what it speaks: the wild disguise hath almost
    Antick'd us all. What needs more words? Good night.
    Good Antony, your hand.

POM.   I'll try you on the shore.

ANT. And shall, sir: give 's your hand.

POM.   O Antony,

---

107. *Possess it*, drink it up; *make answer*, drinks a toast in response.   110. *brave*, fine.
114. *Lethe*, i.e., oblivion.   118. *holding*, refrain.   121. *pink*, half-closed.   122. *fats*,
vats.   131. *disguise*, *behavior* (i.e., their dancing and singing).   132. *Antick'd*, made
fools of.   133. *try you*, see how much you can drink.

You have my father's house,—But, what? we are friends.   135
Come, down into the boat.
ENO.   Take heed you fall not.

[*Exeunt all but* ENOBARBUS *and* MENAS.]

Menas, I'll not on shore.
MEN.   No, to my cabin.
These drums; these trumpets, flutes! what!
Let Neptune hear we bid a loud farewell
To these great fellows: sound and be hang'd, sound out!

[*Sound a flourish, with drums.*]

ENO. Ho! says a'. There's my cap.   141
MEN. Ho! Noble captain, come.

[*Exeunt.*]

ACT III

SCENE I. *A plain in Syria.*

[*Enter* VENTIDIUS *as it were in triumph, with* SILIUS, *and other* ROMANS,
OFFICERS, *and* SOLDIERS; *the dead body of* PACORUS *borne before him.*]

VEN. Now, darting Parthia, art thou struck; and now
Pleased fortune does of Marcus Crassus' death
Make me revenger. Bear the king's son's body
Before our army. Thy Pacorus, Orodes,
Pays this for Marcus Crassus.
SIL.   Noble Ventidius,   5
Whilst yet with Parthian blood thy sword is warm,
The fugitive Parthians follow; spur through Media,
Mesopotamia, and the shelters whither
The routed fly: so thy grand captain Antony
Shall set thee on triumphant chariots and   10
Put garlands on thy head.
VEN.   O Silius, Silius,
I have done enough; a lower place, note well,

135. *my father's house*, Antony had confiscated the house of the elder Pompey.   141.
There's . . . cap, i.e., he throws his cap into the air.   Act II, Scene i: 1. *darting*,
skillful in hurling darts.   2. *Marcus Crassus*, member of the first triumvirate with Pompey and Julius Cæsar, defeated and killed in 53 B.C. by the forces of Orodes, King of
Parthia.   5. *this*, i.e., this death.   12. *lower place*, subordinate officer.

May make too great an act: for learn this, Silius;
Better to leave undone, than by our deed
15 Acquire too high a fame when him we serve 's away.
Cæsar and Antony have ever won
More in their officer than person: Sossius,
One of my place in Syria, his lieutenant,
For quick accumulation of renown,
20 Which he achieved by the minute, lost his favour.
Who does i' the wars more than his captain can
Becomes his captain's captain: and ambition,
The soldier's virtue, rather makes choice of loss,
Than gain which darkens him.
25 I could do more to do Antonius good,
But 'twould offend him; and in his offence
Should my performance perish.
Sil.   Thou hast, Ventidius, that
Without the which a soldier, and his sword,
Grants scarce distinction. Thou wilt write to Antony?
30 Ven. I'll humbly signify what in his name,
That magical word of war, we have effected;
How, with his banners and his well-paid ranks,
The ne'er-yet-beaten horse of Parthia
We have jaded out o' the field.
Sil.   Where is he now?
35 Ven. He purposeth to Athens: whither, with what haste
The weight we must convey with 's will permit,
We shall appear before him. On, there; pass along!

[*Exeunt.*]

Scene II. *Rome. An ante-chamber in* Cæsar's *house.*

[*Enter* Agrippa *at one door,* Enobarbus *at another.*]

Agr. What, are the brothers parted?
Eno. They have dispatch'd with Pompey, he is gone;
The other three are sealing. Octavia weeps
To part from Rome; Cæsar is sad; and Lepidus,
5   Since Pompey's feast, as Menas says, is troubled

13. *make,* perform.   24. *darkens him,* puts him into the shade.   26. *offence,* taking
offence.   27. *that,* i.e., discretion.   33. *horse,* cavalry.   34. *jaded,* been driven exhausted
(i.e., like jades).   36. *with 's,* with us. Scene ii: 1. *brothers,* brothers-in-law, Octavius
and Antony.   2. *dispatch'd,* concluded their business.   3. *sealing,* signing the agreement.
4. *sad,* serious.

With the green sickness.

AGR.   'Tis a noble Lepidus.

ENO. A very fine one: O, how he loves Cæsar!

AGR. Nay, but how dearly he adores Mark Antony!

ENO. Cæsar? Why, he's the Jupiter of men.

AGR. What's Antony? The god of Jupiter.

ENO. Spake you of Cæsar? How! the non-pareil!

AGR. O Antony! O thou Arabian bird!

ENO. Would you praise Cæsar, say "Cæsar:" go no further.

AGR. Indeed, he plied them both with excellent praises.

ENO. But he loves Cæsar best; yet he loves Antony:
Ho! hearts, tongues, figures, scribes, bards, poets, cannot
Think, speak, cast, write, sing, number, ho!
His love to Antony. But as for Cæsar,
Kneel down, kneel down, and wonder.

AGR.   Both he loves.

ENO. They are his shards, and he their beetle [*Trumpets within.*] So;
This is to horse. Adieu, noble Agrippa.

AGR. Good fortune, worthy soldier; and farewell.

[*Enter* CÆSAR, ANTONY, LEPIDUS, *and* OCTAVIA.]

ANT. No further, sir.

CÆS. You take from me a great part of myself;
Use me well in 't. Sister, prove such a wife
As my thoughts make thee, and as my farthest band
Shall pass on thy approof. Most noble Antony,
Let not the piece of virtue, which is set
Betwixt us as the cement of our love,
To keep it builded, be the ram to batter
The fortress of it; for better might we
Have loved without this mean, if on both parts
This be not cherish'd.

ANT.   Make me not offended
In your distrust.

CÆS.   I have said.

ANT.   You shall not find,

---

6. *green sickness,* a kind of anæmia to which adolescent girls were supposed to be particularly susceptible. 11. *nonpareil,* man without an equal. 12. *Arabian bird,* the phoenix, of which there was supposed to be but one in the world at any one time. 17. *cast,* compute; *number,* versify. 20. *shards,* wings of a beetle. 23. *No further,* i.e., you need escort me no further. 26. *farthest band,* my bond to any amount. 27. *Shall . . . approof,* shall be given that you will prove to be what I think you. 28. *piece,* masterpiece. 34. *In your distrust,* by your distrust of me.

Though you be therein curious, the least cause
36 For what you seem to fear: so, the gods keep you,
And make the hearts of Romans serve your ends!
We will here part.

Cæs. Farewell, my dearest sister, fare thee well:
40 The elements be kind to thee, and make
Thy spirits all of comfort! fare thee well.

Oct. My noble brother!

Ant. The April's in her eyes: it is love's spring,
And these the showers to bring it on. Be cheerful.

Oct. Sir, look well to my husband's house; and—

45 Cæs. What,
Octavia?

Oct. I'll tell you in your ear.

Ant. Her tongue will not obey her heart, nor can
Her heart inform her tongue,—the swan's down-feather,
That stands upon the swell at full of tide,
50 And neither way inclines.

Eno. [Aside to Agr.] Will Cæsar weep?

Agr.   [Aside to Eno.] He has a cloud in 's face.

Eno. [Aside to Agr.] He were the worse for that, were he a horse.
So is he, being a man.

Agr. [Aside to Eno.] Why, Enobarbus,
When Antony found Julius Cæsar dead,
55 He cried almost to roaring; and he wept
When at Philippi he found Brutus slain.

Eno. [Aside to Agr.] That year, indeed, he was troubled with a rheum;
What willingly he did confound he wail'd,
Believe 't, till I wept too.

Cæs.   No, sweet Octavia,
60 You shall hear from me still; the time shall not
Out-go my thinking on you.

Ant.   Come, sir, come;
I'll wrestle with you in my strength of love:
Look, here I have you; thus I let you go,
And give you to the gods.

Cæs.   Adieu; be happy!

65 Lep. Let all the number of the stars give light

35. *curious*, meticulous (in searching for causes of offence). 36. *keep*, protect. 48–50. *the swan's . . . inclines,* her grief at leaving her brother, and joy at following her husband, are as evenly balanced as a floating swan's feather at turn of the tide. 51. *cloud in 's face,* a dark spot in the forehead of a horse indicating ill temper. 57. *rheum,* cold in the head. 58. *confound,* destroy. 60. *still,* continually. 61. *Out-go,* outstrip. 62. *wrestle,* i.e., he gives him a parting hug.

To thy fair way!
Cæs. Farewell, farewell!

[*Kisses* Octavia.]

Ant.   Farewell!

[*Trumpets sound. Exeunt.*]

Scene III. *Alexandria.* Cleopatra's *palace.*

[*Enter* Cleopatra, Charmian, Iras, *and* Alexas.]

Cleo. Where is the fellow?
Alex.   Half afeard to come.
Cleo. Go to, go to.

[*Enter the* Messenger *as before.*]

                         Come hither, sir.
Alex.   Good majesty,
  Herod of Jewry dare not look upon you
  But when you are well pleased.
Cleo.   That Herod's head
  I'll have: but how, when Antony is gone   5
  Through whom I might command it? Come thou near.
Mess. Most gracious majesty,—
Cleo. Didst thou behold Octavia?
Mess. Ay, dread queen.
Cleo. Where?   10
Mess. Madam, in Rome;
  I look'd her in the face, and saw her led
  Between her brother and Mark Antony.
Cleo. Is she as tall as me?
Mess.   She is not, madam.
Cleo. Didst hear her speak? is she shrill-tongued or low?   15
Mess. Madam, I heard her speak; she is low-voiced.
Cleo. That's not so good: he cannot like her long.
Char. Like her! O Isis! 'tis impossible.
Cleo. I think so, Charmian: dull of tongue, and dwarfish!
  What majesty is in her gait? Remember,   20
  If e'er thou look'dst on majesty.
Mess.   She creeps:
  Her motion and her station are as one;

Scene iii: 2. Go to, about = how absurd!   22. *station,* standing still.

> She shows a body rather than a life,
> A statue than a breather.

24　CLEO.　　　　　　　　　Is this certain?

MESS. Or I have no observance.

CHAR.　　　　　　　　　Three in Egypt
> Cannot make better note.

CLEO.　　　　　　　　　He's very knowing;
> I do perceive 't: there's nothing in her yet:
> The fellow has good judgement.

CHAR.　　　　　　　　　Excellent.

CLEO. Guess at her years, I prithee.

MESS.　　　　　　　　　Madam,
> She was a widow,—

30　CLEO.　　　　　　Widow! Charmian, hark.

MESS. And I do think she's thirty.

CLEO. Bear'st thou her face in mind? Is 't long or round?

MESS. Round even to faultiness.

CLEO. For the most part, too, they are foolish that are so.

35　　Her hair, what colour?

MESS. Brown, madam: and her forehead
> As low as she would wish it.

CLEO.　　　　　　　　　There's gold for thee.
> Thou must not take my former sharpness ill:
> I will employ thee back again; I find thee

40　　Most fit for business: go make thee ready;
> Our letters are prepared.

[*Exit* MESSENGER.]

CHAR.　　　　　　　　　A proper man.

CLEO. Indeed, he is so: I repent me much
> That so I harried him. Why, methinks, by him,
> This creature 's no such thing.

CHAR.　　　　　　　　　Nothing, madam.

45　CLEO. The man hath seen some majesty, and should know.

CHAR. Hath he seen majesty? Isis else defend,
> And serving you so long!

CLEO. I have one thing more to ask him yet, good Charmian:
> But 'tis no matter; thou shalt bring him to me

50　　Where I will write. All may be well enough.

CHAR. I warrant you, madam.

[*Exeunt.*]

23. *shows*, seems to be. 37. *as low*, i.e., fully as low. 41. *proper*, handsome. 44. *no such thing*, about = the colloquial "is not so much." 46. *defend*, forbid.

SCENE IV. *Athens. A room in* ANTONY'S *house.*

[*Enter* ANTONY *and* OCTAVIA.]

ANT. Nay, nay, Octavia, not only that,—
    That were excusable, that, and thousands more
    Of semblable import,—but he hath waged
    New wars 'gainst Pompey; made his will, and read it
    To public ear: 5
    Spoke scantly of me: when perforce he could not
    But pay me terms of honour, cold and sickly
    He vented them; most narrow measure lent me:
    When the best hint was given him, he not took 't,
    Or did it from his teeth.
OCT.   O my good lord,   10
    Believe not all; or, if you must believe,
    Stomach not all. A more unhappy lady,
    If this division chance, ne'er stood between,
    Praying for both parts:
    The good gods will mock me presently,   15
    When I shall pray, "O, bless my lord and husband!"
    Undo that prayer, by crying out as loud,
    "O, bless my brother!" Husband win, win brother,
    Prays, and destroys the prayer; no midway
    'Twixt these extremes at all.
ANT.   Gentle Octavia,   20
    Let your best love draw to that point, which seeks
    Best to preserve it: if I lose mine honour,
    I lose myself: better I were not yours
    Than yours so branchless. But, as you requested,
    Yourself shall go between 's: the mean time, lady,   25
    I'll raise the preparation of a war
    Shall stain your brother: make your soonest haste;
    So your desires are yours.
OCT.   Thanks to my lord.
    The Jove of power make me most weak, most weak,
    Your reconciler—Wars 'twixt you twain would be   30
    As if the world should cleave, and that slain men
    Should solder up the rift.
ANT. When it appears to you where this begins,

Scene iv: 3. *semblable,* similar. 6. *scantly,* grudgingly. 8. *vented,* uttered. 10. *from his teeth,* i.e., not from the heart. 12. *Stomach,* resent. 15. *presently,* immediately. 24. *branchless,* maimed. 27. *Shall stain,* which shall eclipse. 31. *that,* as if. 33. *this,* i.e., alienation.

Turn your displeasure that way; for our faults
35   Can never be so equal, that your love
Can equally move with them. Provide your going;
Choose your own company, and command what cost
Your heart has mind to.

[*Exeunt.*]

SCENE V. *The same. Another room.*

[*Enter* ENOBARBUS *and* EROS, *meeting.*]

ENO. How now, friend Eros!

EROS. There's strange news come, sir.

ENO. What, man?

EROS. Cæsar and Lepidus have made wars upon Pompey.

6 ENO. This is old: what is the success?

EROS. Cæsar, having made use of him in the wars 'gainst Pompey, presently denied him rivality; would not let him partake in the glory of the
action: and not resting here, accuses him of letters he had formerly
wrote to Pompey; upon his own appeal, seizes him: so the poor third is
13 up, till death enlarge his confine.

ENO. Then, world, thou hast a pair of chaps, no more;
And throw between them all the food thou hast,
They'll grind the one the other. Where's Antony?

EROS. He's walking in the garden—thus; and spurns
The rush that lies before him; cried, "Fool Lepidus!"
19 And threats the throat of that his officer
That murder'd Pompey.

ENO.   Our great navy's rigg'd.

EROS. For Italy and Cæsar. More, Domitius;
My lord desires you presently: my news
I might have told hereafter.

ENO.   'Twill be naught:
24 But let it be. Bring me to Antony.

EROS. Come, sir.

[*Exeunt.*]

Scene v: 6. *success,* outcome. 12. *his,* i.e., Cæsar's. 13. *up,* done for; *enlarge his confine,* release him (from prison). 14. *chaps,* jaws. 17. *spurns,* kicks. 20. *murder'd Pompey,* Pompey was supposed to have been murdered at Antony's command.

SCENE VI. *Rome.* CÆSAR'S *house.*

[*Enter* CÆSAR, AGRIPPA, *and* MECÆNAS.]

CÆS. Contemning Rome, he has done all this, and more,
   In Alexandria: here's the manner of 't:
   I' the market-place, on a tribunal silver'd,
   Cleopatra and himself in chairs of gold
   Were publicly enthroned: at the feet sat   5
   Cæsarion, whom they call my father's son,
   And all the unlawful issue that their lust
   Since then hath made between them. Unto her
   He gave the stablishment of Egypt; made her
   Of lower Syria, Cyprus, Lydia,   10
   Absolute queen.
MEC.   This in the public eye?
CÆS. I' the common show-place, where they exercise.
   His sons he there proclaim'd the kings of kings:
   Great Media, Parthia, and Armenia,
   He gave to Alexander; to Ptolemy he assign'd
   Syria, Cilicia, and Phœnecia: she
   In the habiliments of the goddess Isis   17
   That day appear'd; and oft before gave audience,
   As 'tis reported, so.
MEC.   Let Rome be thus
   Inform'd.
AGR.   Who, queasy with his insolence   20
   Already, will their good thoughts call from him.
CÆS. The people know it; and have now received
   His accusations.
AGR.   Who does he accuse?
CÆS. Cæsar: and that, having in Sicily
   Sextus Pompeius spoil'd, we had not rated him   25
   His part o' the isle: then does he say, he lent me
   Some shipping unrestored: lastly, he frets
   That Lepidus of the triumvirate
   Should be deposed; and, being, that we detain
   All his revenue.
AGR.   Sir, this should be answer'd.   30

Scene vi: 1. *Contemning*, despising. 3. *tribunal*, platform. 6. *Cæsarion*, son of Cleopatra and Julius Cæsar; *my father's*, Octavius was the adopted son of Julius Cæsar.
9. *He . . . Egypt*, he settled Egypt as an inheritance. 17. *habiliments*, robes; *Isis*, the
Egyptian moon goddess. 20. *queasy*, nauseated. 25. *spoil'd*, despoiled (of the terri-
tories he ruled); *rated*, assigned, prorated. 29. *being*, being deposed.

Cæs. 'Tis done already, and the messenger gone.
I have told him, Lepidus was grown too cruel;
That he his high authority abused,
And did deserve his change: for what I have conquer'd,
35   I grant him part; but then, in his Armenia,
And other of his conquer'd kingdoms, I
Demand the like.
Mec.   He'll never yield to that.
Cæs. Nor must not then be yielded to in this.

[*Enter* Octavia *with her train.*]

Oct. Hail, Cæsar, and my lord! hail, most dear Cæsar!
40   Cæs. That ever I should call thee castaway!
Oct. You have not call'd me so, nor have you cause.
Cæs. Why have you stol'n upon us thus?
You come not
Like Cæsar's sister: the wife of Antony
Should have an army for an usher, and
45   The neighs of horse to tell of her approach
Long ere she did appear; the trees by the way
Should have borne men; and expectation fainted,
Longing for what it had not; nay, the dust
Should have ascended to the roof of heaven,
50   Raised by your populous troops: but you are come
A market-maid to Rome; and have prevented
The ostentation of our love, which, left unshown,
Is often left unloved: we should have met you
By sea and land; supplying every stage
With an augmented greeting.
55   Oct.   Good my lord,
To come thus was I not constrain'd, but did it
On my free will. My lord, Mark Antony,
Hearing that you prepared for war, acquainted
My grieved ear withal; whereon, I begg'd
His pardon for return.
60   Cæs.   Which soon he granted,
Being an obstruct 'tween his lust and him.
Oct. Do not say so, my lord.
Cæs.   I have eyes upon him,

34. *change,* change of fortune; *for,* as for.   43. *Like,* i.e., with the ceremony befitting.
44. *usher,* attendant.   50. *populous,* numerous.   52. *ostentation,* display.   53. *Is often left unloved,* often becomes no love at all.   59. *withal,* with it (the news).   60. *pardon for,* permission to.   61. *obstruct,* obstruction.

And his affairs come to me on the wind.
Where is he now?
Oct.   My lord, in Athens.
Cæs. No, my most wronged sister; Cleopatra   65
Hath nodded him to her. He hath given his empire
Up to a whore; who now are levying
The kings o' the earth for war: he hath assembled
Bocchus, the king of Libya; Archelaus,
Of Cappadocia; Philadelphos, king   70
Of Paphlagonia; the Thracian king, Adallas;
King Malchus of Arabia; King of Pont;
Herod of Jewry; Mithridates, king
Of Comagene; Polemon and Amyntas,
The kings of Mede and Lycaonia,   75
With a more larger list of sceptres.
Oct.   Ay me, most wretched,
That have my heart parted betwixt two friends
That do afflict each other!
Cæs.   Welcome hither:
Your letters did withhold our breaking forth;
Till we perceived, both how you were wrong led   80
And we in negligent danger. Cheer your heart:
Be you not troubled with the time, which drives
O'er your content these strong necessities;
But let determined things to destiny
Hold unbewail'd their way. Welcome to Rome;   85
Nothing more dear to me. You are abused
Beyond the mark of thought: and the high gods,
To do you justice, make them ministers
Of us and those that love you. Best of comfort;
And ever welcome to us.
Agr.   Welcome lady.   90
Mec. Welcome, dear madam.
Each heart in Rome does love and pity you:
Only the adulterous Antony, most large
In his abominations, turns you off;
And gives his potent regiment to a trull,   95
That noises it against us.

67. *who*, i.e., they. 72. *Pont*, Pontus. 74. *Comagene*, a country in ancient Syria.
75. *Mede*, Media; *Lycaonia*, a province of ancient Asia Minor. 78. *afflict*, attack. 79.
withhold, prevent. 81. *negligent danger*, danger from inaction. 82. *time*, state of
affairs. 83. *content*, happiness. 84. *determined*, foreordained. 87. *mark*, boundary.
93. *large*, unrestrained. 95. *potent regiment*, great authority; *trull*, whore. 96. *noises
it*, raises a disturbance.

Oct.   Is it so, sir?
Cæs. Most certain. Sister, welcome: pray you,
98   Be ever known to patience: my dear'st sister!

[*Exeunt.*]

Scene VII. *Near Actium.* Antony's *camp.*

[*Enter* Cleopatra *and* Enobarbus.]

Cleo. I will be even with thee, doubt it not.
Eno. But why, why, why?
Cleo. Thou hast forspoke my being in these wars,
     And say'st it is not fit.
Eno.   Well, is it, is it?
5 Cleo. If not denounced against us, why should not we
     Be there in person?
Eno. [*Aside*] Well, I could reply:
     If we should serve with horse and mares together,
     The horse were merely lost; the mares would bear
     A soldier and his horse.
10 Cleo.   What is 't you say?
Eno. Your presence needs must puzzle Antony;
     Take from his heart, take from his brain, from 's time,
     What should not then be spared. He is already
     Traduced for levity; and 'tis said in Rome
15   That Photinus an eunuch and your maids
     Manage this war.
Cleo.   Sink Rome, and their tongues rot
     That speak against us! A charge we bear i' the war,
     And, as the president of my kingdom, will
     Appear there for a man. Speak not against it;
     I will not stay behind.
20 Eno.   Nay, I have done.
     Here comes the emperor.

[*Enter* Antony *and* Canidius.]

Ant.   Is it not strange, Canidius,
     That from Tarentum and Brundusium
     He could so quickly cut the Ionian sea,

---

98. *Be . . . patience,* always keep calm. Scene vii: 3. *forspoke,* spoken against.
5. *denounced against,* forbidden. 8. *merely,* completely. 11. *puzzle,* embarrass. 12.
from's time, from his life. 17. *charge,* obligation. 22. *Tarentum and Brundusium,* the
ancient names of Taranto and Brindisi, towns in southern Italy.

And take in Toryne? You have heard on 't, sweet?
CLEO. Celerity is never more admired   25
  Than by the negligent.
ANT.   A good rebuke,
  Which might have well becomed the best of men,
  To taunt at slackness. Canidius, we
  Will fight with him by sea.
CLEO.   By sea! what else?
CAN. Why will my lord do so?
ANT.   For that he dares us to 't.   30
ENO. So hath my lord dared him to single fight.
CAN. Ay, and to wage this battle at Pharsalia.
  Where Cæsar fought with Pompey: but these offers,
  Which serve not for his vantage, he shakes off;
  And so should you.
ENO.   Your ships are not well mann'd;   35
  Your mariners are muleters, reapers, people
  Ingross'd by swift impress; in Cæsar's fleet
  Are those that often have 'gainst Pompey fought:
  Their ships are yare; yours, heavy: no disgrace
  Shall fall you for refusing him at sea,   40
  Being prepared for land.
ANT.   By sea, by sea.
ENO. Most worthy sir, you therein throw away
  The absolute soldiership you have by land;
  Distract your army, which doth most consist
  Of war-mark'd footmen; leave unexecuted   45
  Your own renownèd knowledge; quite forego
  The way which promises assurance; and
  Give up yourself merely to chance and hazard,
  From firm security.
ANT.   I'll fight at sea.
CLEO. I have sixty sails, Cæsar none better.   50
ANT. Our overplus of shipping will we burn;
  And, with the rest full-mann'd, from the head of Actium
  Beat the approaching Cæsar. But if we fail,
  We then can do 't at land.

[*Enter a* MESSENGER.]

---

24. *take in,* capture; *Toryne,* a town on the coast of Epirus.   29. *what else?* i.e., why not?   30. *For that,* because.   37. *Ingross'd,* collected; *impress,* conscription.   39. *yare,* easy to handle.   43. *absolute,* perfect.   44. *Distract,* divide.   48. *merely,* utterly.   52. *head,* headland.

Thy business?

55 MESS. The news is true, my lord; he is descried;
Cæsar has taken Toryne.

ANT. Can he be there in person? 'tis impossible;
Strange that his power should be. Canidius,
Our nineteen legions thou shalt hold by land,
60 And our twelve thousand horse. We'll to our ship:
Away, my Thetis!

[*Enter a* SOLDIER.]

How now, worthy soldier!

SOLD. O noble emperor, do not fight by sea;
Trust not to rotten planks: do you misdoubt
This sword and these my wounds? Let the Egyptians
65 And the Phœnicians go a-ducking: we
Have used to conquer, standing on the earth,
And fighting foot to foot.

ANT.   Well, well; away!

[*Exeunt* ANTONY, CLEOPATRA, *and* ENOBARBUS.]

SOLD. By Hercules, I think I am i' the right.

CAN. Soldier, thou art: but his whole action grows
70 Not in the power on 't: so our leader 's led,
And we are women's men.

SOLD.   You keep by land
The legions and the horse whole, do you not?

CAN. Marcus Octavius, Marcus Justeius,
Publicola, and Cælius, are for sea:
75 But we keep whole by land. This speed of Cæsar's
Carries beyond belief.

SOLD.   While he was yet in Rome,
His power went out in such distractions as
Beguiled all spies.

CAN.   Who's his lieutenant, hear you?

SOLD. They say, one Taurus.

CAN.   Well I know the man.

[*Enter a* MESSENGER.]

80 MESS. The emperor calls Canidius.

---

58. *power*, forces. 61. *Thetis*, a sea-goddess. 65. *a-ducking*, a-diving. 69–70. *action . . . power on 't*, course of action is not developing in a way to prove most effective. 71. *men*, servants. 76. *Carries beyond*, surpasses. 77. *distraction*, small detachments.

CAN. With news the time's with labour, and throes forth,
   Each minute, some.

[*Exeunt.*]

SCENE VIII. *A plain near Actium.*

[*Enter* CÆSAR, *and* TAURUS, *with his army, marching.*]

CÆS. Taurus!
TAUR. My lord?
CÆS. Strike not by land; keep whole: provoke not battle,
   Till we have done at sea. Do not exceed
   The prescript of this scroll: our fortune lies   5
   Upon this jump.

[*Exeunt.*]

SCENE IX. *Another part of the plain.*

[*Enter* ANTONY *and* ENOBARBUS.]

ANT. Set we our squadrons on yond side o' the hill,
   In eye of Cæsar's battle; from which place   2
   We may the number of the ships behold,
   And so proceed accordingly.

[*Exeunt.*]

SCENE X. *Another part of the plain.*

[CANDIDIUS *marcheth with his land army one way over the stage; and*
TAURUS, *the lieutenant of* CÆSAR, *the other way. After their going in, is
heard the noise of a sea-fight.*]

[*Alarum. Enter* ENOBARBUS.]

ENO. Naught, naught, all naught! I can behold no longer:
   The Antoniad, the Egyptian admiral,   2
   With all their sixty, fly and turn the rudder:
   To see 't mine eyes are blasted.

[*Enter* SCARUS.]

SCAR.   Gods and goddesses,

---

81. *throes forth*, gives birth in pain. Scene viii: 5. *prescript*, instruction. 6. *jump*,
risk. Scene ix: 2. *battle*, army in battle array. Scene x: 2. *admiral*, flagship.

All the whole synod of them!

5 ENO.   What's thy passion?

SCAR. The greater cantle of the world is lost
With very ignorance; we have kiss'd away
Kingdoms and provinces.

ENO.   How appears the fight?

SCAR. On our side like the token'd pestilence,
10   Where death is sure. You ribaudrèd nag of Egypt,—
Whom leprosy o'ertake!—i' the midst o' the fight,
When vantage like a pair of twins appear'd,
Both as the same, or rather ours the elder,
The breese upon her, like a cow in June,
15   Hoists sails and flies.

ENO. That I beheld:
Mine eyes did sicken at the sight, and could not
Endure a further view.

SCAR.   She once being loof'd,
The noble ruin of her magic, Antony,
20   Claps on his sea-wing, and, like a doting mallard,
Leaving the fight in height, flies after her:
I never saw an action of such shame;
Experience, manhood, honour, ne'er before
Did violate so itself.

ENO.   Alack, alack!

[*Enter* CANIDIUS.]

25 CAN. Our fortune on the sea is out of breath,
And sinks most lamentably. Had our general
Been what he knew himself, it had gone well:
O, he has given example for our flight,
Most grossly, by his own!

ENO.   Ay, are you thereabouts?
30   Why, then, good night indeed.

CAN. Toward Peloponnesus are they fled.

SCAR. 'Tis easy to 't; and there I will attend
What further comes.

CAN.   To Cæsar will I render
My legions and my horse: six kings already

5. *passion,* excitement about.   6. *cantle,* slice.   7. *With very,* out of sheer.   9. *token'd,*
spotted; the spots were thought to be sent by God as signs (tokens) of approaching
death.   10. *ribaudred,* lewd.   14. *breese,* gadfly.   18. *loof'd,* luffed, brought up into
the wind.   27. *what . . . himself,* true to his better self.   29. *Are you thereabout?*
Are you too thinking of flight?   32. *to 't,* to reach it; *attend,* await.   33. *render,* surrender.

Show me the way of yielding.

ENO.   I'll yet follow   35
  The wounded chance of Antony, though my reason
  Sits in the wind against me.

[*Exeunt.*]

SCENE XI. *Alexandria.* CLEOPATRA'S *palace.*

[*Enter* ANTONY *with* ATTENDANTS.]

ANT. Hark! the land bids me tread no more upon 't;
  It is ashamed to bear me! Friends, come hither.
  I am so lated in the world, that I
  Have lost my way forever: I have a ship
  Laden with gold; take that, divide it; fly,   5
  And make your peace with Cæsar.
ALL.   Fly! not we.
ANT. I have fled myself; and have instructed cowards
  To run and show their shoulders. Friends, be gone;
  I have myself resolved upon a course
  Which has no need of you; be gone: 10
  My treasure's in the harbour, take it. O,
  I follow'd that I blush to look upon:
  My very hairs do mutiny; for the white
  Reprove the brown for rashness, and they them
  For fear and doting. Friends, be gone: you shall   15
  Have letters from me to some friends that will
  Sweep your way for you. Pray you, look not sad,
  Nor make replies of loathness: take the hint
  Which my despair proclaims: let that be left
  Which leaves itself: to the sea-side straightway: 20
  I will possess you of that ship and treasure.
  Leave me, I pray, a little: pray you now:
  Nay, do so; for, indeed, I have lost command,
  Therefore I pray you: I'll see you by and by.

[*Sits down.*]

[*Enter* CLEOPATRA *led by* CHARMIAN *and* IRAS; EROS *following.*]

EROS. Nay, gentle madam, to him, comfort him.   25

---

36. *chance*, fortunes. 37. *sits . . . against*, strongly opposes. Scene xi: 3. *lated*, belated, benighted. 8. *show shoulders*, turn their backs in flight. 12. *that*, what. 18. *loathness*, reluctance.

IRAS. Do, most dear queen.

CHAR. Do! why: what else?

CLEO. Let me sit down. O Juno!

ANT. No, no, no, no, no.

30 EROS. See you here, sir?

ANT. O fie, fie, fie!

CHAR. Madam!

IRAS. Madam, O good empress!

EROS. Sir, sir,—

35 ANT. Yes, my lord, yes; he at Philippi kept
  His sword e'en like a dancer; while I struck
  The lean and wrinkled Cassius; and 'twas I
  That the mad Brutus ended: he alone
  Dealt on lieutenantry, and no practice had
40   In the brave squares of war: yet now—No matter.

CLEO. Ah, stand by.

EROS. The queen, my lord, the queen.

IRAS. Go to him, madam, speak to him:
  He is unqualitied with very shame.

45 CLEO. Well then, sustain me: O!

ENOS. Most noble sir, arise; the queen approaches;
  Her head's declined, and death will seize her, but
  Your comfort makes the rescue.

ANT. I have offended reputation,
  A most unnoble swerving.

50 EROS.   Sir, the queen.

ANT. O, whither hast thou led me, Egypt? See,
  How I convèy my shame out of thine eyes
  By looking back what I have left behind
  'Stroy'd in dishonour.

CLEO.   O my lord, my lord,

55 Forgive my fearful sails! I little thought
  You would have follow'd.

ANT.   Egypt, thou knew'st too well
  My heart was to thy rudder tied by the strings,
  And thou shouldst tow me after: o'er my spirit
  Thy full supremacy thou knew'st, and that

60 Thy beck might from the bidding of the gods

---

35. *he*, i.e., Octavius. 36. *like a dancer*, i.e., sheathed. 39. *Dealt on lieutenantry*, depended on (the fighting of) his lieutenants. 40. *brave squares*, splendid squadrons. 44. *unqualitied*, shorn of his quality (essential nature). 47. *but*, unless. 52. *convey . . . eyes*, hide my shame from your glance. 53. *back*, back at. 57. *strings*, heart strings.

Command me.

CLEO.   O, my pardon!

ANT.   Now I must
To the young man send humble treaties, dodge
And palter in the shifts of lowness; who
With half the bulk o' the world play'd as I pleased,
Making and marring fortunes. You did know   65
How much you were my conquerer; and that
My sword, made weak by my affection, would
Obey it on all cause.

CLEO.   Pardon, pardon!

ANT. Fall not a tear, I say; one of them rates
All that is won and lost: give me a kiss;   70
Even this repays me. We sent our schoolmaster;
Is he come back? Love, I am full of lead.
Some wine, within there, and our viands! Fortune knows
We scorn her most when most she offers blows.

[*Exeunt.*]

SCENE XII. *Egypt.* CÆSAR's *camp.*

[*Enter* CÆSAR, DOLABELLA, THYREUS, *with others.*]

CÆS. Let him appear that's come from Antony.
Know you him?

DOL.   Cæsar, 'tis his schoolmaster:
An argument that he is pluck'd, when hither
He sends so poor a pinion of his wing,
Which had superfluous kings for messengers   5
Not many moons gone by.

[*Enter* EUPHRONIUS, *ambassador from* ANTONY.]

CÆS.   Approach, and speak.

EUPH. Such as I am, I come from Antony:
I was of late as petty to his ends
As is the morn-dew on the myrtle-leaf
To his grand sea.

CÆS.   Be 't so: declare thine office.   10

EUPH. Lord of his fortunes he salutes thee, and

---

62. *young man*, i.e., Octavius; *treaties*, "peace-feelers." 63. *palter*, equivocate; *shifts of lowness*, mean evasions. 69. *rates*, is worth. 71. *schoolmaster*, Euphronius, tutor of his and Cleopatra's children. 72. *full of lead*, leaden, dull. Scene xii: 3. *argument*, proof. 8. *petty*, unimportant; *to his ends*, for his plans. 10. *his*, its.

Requires to live in Egypt: which not granted,
He lessens his requests; and to thee sues
To let him breathe between the heavens and earth,
15   A private man in Athens: this for him.
Next, Cleopatra does confess thy greatness;
Submits her to thy might; and of thee craves
The circle of the Ptolemies for her heirs,
Now hazarded to thy grace.

Cæs.   For Antony,
20   I have no ears to his request. The queen
Of audience nor desire shall fail, so she
From Egypt drive her all-disgracèd friend,
Or take his life there: this if she perform,
She shall not sue unheard. So to them both.

Euph. Fortune pursue thee!

Cæs.   Bring him through the bands.

[*Exit* Euphronius.]

26   [*To* Thyreus] To try thy eloquence, now 'tis time: dispatch;
From Antony win Cleopatra: promise,
And in our name, what she requires; add more,
From thine invention, offers: women are not
30   In their best fortunes strong; but want will perjure
The ne'er-touch'd vestal: try thy cunning, Thyreus;
Make thine own edict for thy pains, which we
Will answer as a law.

Thyr.   Cæsar, I go.

Cæs. Observe how Antony becomes his flaw,
35   And what thou think'st his very action speaks
In every power that moves.

Thyr.   Cæsar, I shall.

[*Exeunt.*]

Scene XIII. *Alexandria.* Cleopatra's *palace.*

[*Enter* Cleopatra, Enobarbus, Charmian, *and* Iras.]

Cleo. What shall we do, Enobarbus?

---

12. *Requires*, requests. 16. *confess*, acknowledge. 18. *circle*, crown. 19. *hazarded*, in hazard; *grace*, kindness, mercy; *For*, as for. 24. *So . . . both*, thus I reply to both. 30. *perjure*, break the vows of. 31. *ne'er touch'd*, pure; *cunning*, skill. 32. *Make . . . edict*, name your own reward. 34. *becomes his flaw*, acts in the face of his disaster. 35–6. *his very action . . . moves*, his essential character is revealed in his every movement.

ENO.   Think, and die.
CLEO. Is Antony or we in fault for this?
ENO. Antony only, that would make his will
  Lord of his reason. What though you fled
  From that great face of war, whose several ranges   5
  Frighted each other? why should he follow?
  The itch of his affection should not then
  Have nick'd his captainship; at such a point,
  When half to half the world opposed, he being
  The meerèd question: 'twas a shame no less   10
  Than was his loss, to course your flying flags,
  And leave his navy gazing.
CLEO.   Prithee, peace.

[*Enter* ANTONY *with* EUPHRONIUS, *the Ambassador.*]

ANT. Is that his answer?
EUPH. Ay, my lord.
ANT. The queen shall then have courtesy, so she   15
  Will yield us up.
EUPH.   He says so.
ANT.   Let her know 't.
  To the boy Cæsar send this grizzled head,
  And he will fill thy wishes to the brim
  With principalities.
CLEO.   That head, my lord?
ANT. To him again: tell him he wears the rose   20
  Of youth upon him; from which the world should note
  Something particular: his coin, ships, legions,
  May be a coward's; whose ministers would prevail
  Under the service of a child as soon
  As i' the command of Cæsar: I dare him therefore   25
  To lay his gay comparisons apart,
  And answer me declinèd, sword against sword,
  Ourselves alone. I'll write it: follow me.

[*Exeunt* ANTONY *and* EUPHRONIUS.]

ENO. [*Aside*] Yes, like enough, high-battled Cæsar will

Scene xiii: 3. *will*, desire.   5. *ranges*, squadrons.   7. *affection*, passion.   8. *nick'd*,
clipped grotesquely, like the head of a clown.   10. *meerèd question*, sole ground for the
dispute.   11. *course*, pursue.   22. *Something particular*, some personal achievement.
23. *ministers*, agents.   26. *gay comparisons apart*, his splendid trappings aside.   27.
answer me declinèd, meet me in a duel on the level of my fallen fortunes.

30   Unstate his happiness, and be staged to the show,
Against a sworder! I see men's judgements are
A parcel of their fortunes; and things outward
Do draw the inward quality after them,
To suffer all alike. That he should dream,
35   Knowing all measures, the full Cæsar will
Answer his emptiness! Cæsar, thou hast subdued
His judgement too.

[*Enter an* ATTENDANT.]

ATT.   A messenger from Cæsar.
CLEO. What, no more ceremony? See, my women!
Against the blown rose may they stop their nose
40   That kneel'd unto the buds. Admit him, sir.

[*Exit* ATTENDANT.]

ENO. [*Aside*] Mine honesty and I begin to square.
The loyalty well held to fools does make
Our faith mere folly: yet he that can endure
To follow with allegiance a fall'n lord
45   Does conquer him that did his master conquer,
And earns a place i' the story.

[*Enter* THYREUS.]

CLEO.   Cæsar's will?
THYR. Hear it apart.
CLEO.   None but friends: say boldly.
THYR. So, haply, are they friends to Antony.
ENO. He needs as many, sir, as Cæsar has;
50   Or needs not us. If Cæsar please, our master
Will leap to be his friend: for us, you know
Whose he is we are, and that is, Cæsar's.
THYR.   So.
Thus then, thou most renown'd: Cæsar entreats,
Not to consider in what case thou stand'st,
55   Further than he is Cæsar.

30. *Unstate his happiness,* divest himself of the advantages of his fortunate position; *staged to the show,* publicly exhibited as a spectacle. 31. *sworder,* gladiator. 32. *A parcel of,* of a piece with. 33. *quality,* nature. 34. *To . . . alike,* so that they (the outward circumstances and the inward nature) exactly correspond. 35. *Knowing . . . measures,* having experienced every kind of fortune; *full,* fully provided with resources. 36. *Answer,* accept the challenge of; *emptiness,* destitution. 39. *blown,* overblown. 41. *square,* quarrel. 43. *mere,* utter. 47. *apart,* in private. 55. *he is Cæsar,* i.e., a ruler with generous impulses.

CLEO.   Go on: right royal.
THYR. He knows that you embrace not Antony
  As you did love, but as you fear'd him.
CLEO.   O!
THYR. The scars upon your honour, therefore, he
  Does pity, as constrainèd blemishes,
  Not as deserved.
CLEO.   He is a god, and knows   60
  What is most right: mine honour was not yielded,
  But conquer'd merely.
ENO.   [*Aside*] To be sure of that,
  I will ask Antony. Sir, sir, thou art so leaky,
  That we must leave thee to thy sinking, for
  Thy dearest quit thee.

[*Exit.*]

THYR.   Shall I say to Cæsar   65
  What you require of him? for he partly begs
  To be desired to give. It much would please him,
  That of his fortunes you should make a staff
  To lean upon: but it would warm his spirits,
  To hear from me you had left Antony,   70
  And put yourself under his shrowd,
  The universal landlord.
CLEO.   What's your name?
THYR. My name is Thyreus.
CLEO.   Most kind messenger,
  Say to great Cæsar this: in deputation
  I kiss his conquering hand: tell him, I am prompt   75
  To lay my crown at 's feet, and there to kneel:
  Tell him, from his all-obeying breath I hear
  The doom of Egypt.
THYR.   'Tis your noblest course.
  Wisdom and fortune combating together,
  If that the former dare but what it can,   80
  No chance may shake it. Give me grace to lay
  My duty on your hand.
CLEO.   Your Cæsar's father oft,
  When he hath mused of taking kingdoms in,

62. *merely,* completely. 71. *shrowd,* shelter, protection. 72. *universal landlord,* ruler
of the whole world. 74. *in deputation,* by proxy. 77. *all-obeying,* obeyed by all. 78.
doom of Egypt, fate of the Queen of Egypt. 81. *Give me grace,* grant me the favor.
83. *taking . . . in,* conquering.

84   Bestow'd his lips on that unworthy place,
      As it rain'd kisses.

[*Re-enter* ANTONY *and* ENOBARBUS.]

ANT.   Favours, by Jove that thunders!
      What art thou, fellow?
THYR.   One that but performs
      The bidding of the fullest man, and worthiest
      To have command obey'd.
ENO.   [*Aside*] You will be whipp'd.
ANT. Approach, there! Ah, you kite! Now, gods and devils!
90   Authority melts from me: of late, when I cried "Ho!"
      Like boys unto a muss, kings would start forth,
      And cry "Your will?" Have you no ears? I am
      Antony yet.

[*Enter* ATTENDANTS.]

            Take hence this Jack, and whip him.
ENO. [*Aside*] 'Tis better playing with a lion's whelp
      Than with an old one dying.
ANT.   Moon and stars!
96   Whip him. Were't twenty of the greatest tributaries
      That do acknowledge Cæsar, should I find them
      So saucy with the hand of—she here,—what's her name,
      Since she was Cleopatra? Whip him, fellows,
100   Till, like a boy, you see him cringe his face,
      And whine aloud for mercy: take him hence.
THYR. Mark Antony!
ANT.   Tug him away: being whipp'd,
      Bring him again: this Jack of Cæsar's shall
      Bear us an errand to him.

[*Exeunt* ATTENDANTS *with* THYREUS.]

105   You were half blasted ere I knew you: ha!
      Have I my pillow left unpress'd in Rome,
      Forborne the getting of a lawful race,
      And by a gem of women, to be abused
      By one that looks on feeders?
CLEO.   Good my lord,—
110 ANT. You have been a boggler ever:

85. *As*, as if. 87. *fullest*, having the most advantages. 89. *kite*, a wanton, i.e.,
Cleopatra. 91. *muss*, scramble. 93. *Jack*, impertinent fellow. 100. *cringe*, distort.
108. *abused*, deceived. 109. *feeders*, menials. 110. *boggler*, a shifty creature.

But when we in our viciousness grow hard—
O misery on 't!—the wise gods seel our eyes;
In our own filth drop our clear judgements; make us
Adore our errors; laugh at 's, while we strut
To our confusion.

CLEO.   O, is 't come to this?   115

ANT. I found you as a morsel cold upon
Dead Cæsar's trencher; nay, you were a fragment
Of Cneius Pompey's; besides what hotter hours,
Unregister'd in vulgar fame, you have
Luxuriously pick'd out: for, I am sure,   120
Though you can guess what temperance should be,
You know not what it is.

CLEO.   Wherefore is this?

ANT. To let a fellow that will take rewards
And say "God quit you!" be familiar with
My playfellow, your hand; this kingly seal   125
And plighter of high hearts! O, that I were
Upon the hill of Basan, to outroar
The hornèd herd! for I have savage cause;
And to proclaim it civilly, were like
A halter'd neck which does the hangman thank   130
For being yare about him.

[*Re-enter* ATTENDANTS *with* THYREUS.]

                        Is he whipp'd?

FIRST ATT. Soundly, my lord.

ANT.   Cried he? and begg'd a pardon?

FIRST ATT. He did ask favour.

ANT. If that thy father live, let him repent
Thou wast not made his daughter; and be thou sorry   135
To follow Cæsar in his triumph, since
Thou hast been whipped for following him: henceforth
The white hand of a lady fever thee,
Shake thou to look on 't. Get thee back to Cæsar,   139
Tell him thy entertainment: look, thou say
He makes me angry with him; for he seems

112. *seel*, sew up (like those of a falcon). 117. *trencher*, wooden plate. 119. *vulgar fame*, common report. 120. *luxuriously*, licentiously. 121. *temperance*, continence. 124. *quit*, repay, the conventional thanks of a beggar. 126. *plighter*, pledger. 127. *Basan*, the bulls of Bashan were strong in body and voice. Cf. Psalms, XXII, 12, 13. 128. *hornèd herd*, i.e., the cuckolds; *savage*, i.e., to be wild. 129. *civilly*, calmly. 131. *yare*, quick, dexterous. 133. *ask favour*, beg me to go easy. 140. *thy entertainment*, the reception you got.

Proud and disdainful, harping on what I am,
Not what he knew I was: he makes me angry;
And at this time most easy 'tis to do 't,

145　When my good stars, that were my former guides,
Have empty left their orbs, and shot their fires
Into the abysm of hell. If he mislike
My speech and what is done, tell him he has
Hipparchus, my enfranchèd bondman, whom

150　He may at pleasure whip, or hang, or torture,
As he shall like, to quit me: urge it thou:
Hence with thy stripes, begone!

[*Exit* THYREUS.]

CLEO. Have you done yet?
ANT.　　　　　　　　　　Alack, our terrene moon
Is now eclipsed; and it portends alone
The fall of Antony!

155 CLEO.　　　　　　　I must stay his time.
ANT. To flatter Cæsar, would you mingle eyes
With one that ties his points?
CLEO.　　　　　　　　　　　　Not know me yet?
ANT. Cold-hearted toward me?
CLEO.　　　　　　　　　　　Ah, dear, if I be so,
From my cold heart let heaven engender hail,

160　And poison it in the source; and the first stone
Drop in my neck: as it determines, so
Dissolve my life! The next Cæsarion smite!
Till by degrees the memory of my womb,
Together with my brave Egyptians all,

165　By the discandying of this pelleted storm,
Lie graveless, till the flies and gnats of Nile
Have buried them for prey!
ANT.　　　　　　　　　　I am satisfied.
Cæsar sits down in Alexandria; where
I will oppose his fate. Our force by land

170　Hath nobly held; our sever'd navy too
Have knit again, and fleet, threatening most sea-like.
Where hast thou been, my heart? Dost thou hear, lady?
If from the field I shall return once more

146. *orbs*, spheres in which the stars were supposed to move.　149. *enfranchèd*, freed;
Hipparchus, says Plutarch, was a deserter.　153. *terrene*, earthly.　157. *points*, laces
which attached the doublet to the breeches.　161. *determines*, ends (by melting).
163. *memory*, memorials (her children).　164. *brave*, splendid.　165. *discandying*,
melting.　171. *fleet*, is afloat.

To kiss these lips, I will appear in blood;
I and my sword will earn our chronicle: 175
There's hope in 't yet.

CLEO. That's my brave lord!

ANT. I will be treble-sinew'd, hearted, breathed,
And fight maliciously: for when mine hours
Were nice and lucky, men did ransom lives 180
Of me for jests; but now I'll set my teeth,
And send to darkness all that stop me. Come,
Let's have one other gaudy night: call to me
All my sad captains; fill our bowls once more;
Let's mock the midnight bell.

CLEO.   It is my birth-day: 185
I had thought to have held it poor; but, since my lord
Is Antony again, I will be Cleopatra.

ANT. We will yet do well.

CLEO. Call all his noble captains to my lord.

ANT. Do so, we'll speak to them; and to-night I'll force 190
The wine peep through their scars. Come on, my queen;
There's sap in 't yet. The next time I do fight,
I'll make death love me; for I will contend
Even with his pestilent scythe.

[*Exeunt all but* ENOBARBUS.]

ENO. Now he'll outstare the lightning. To be furious, 195
Is to be frighted out of fear; and in that mood
The dove will peck the estridge; and I see still,
A diminution in our captain's brain
Restores his heart: when valour preys on reason,
It eats the sword it fights with. I will seek 200
Some way to leave him.

[*Exit.*]

ACT IV

SCENE I. *Before Alexandria.* CÆSAR'S *camp.*

[*Enter* CÆSAR, AGRIPPA, *and* MECÆNAS, *with his army;* CÆSAR *reading a letter.*]

CÆS. He calls me boy; and chides, as he had power

175. *chronicle*, place in history.   179. *maliciously*, with the strength of hatred.   180. *nice*, i.e., spent effeminately.   183. *gaudy*, of wild revel.   193. *contend*, compete.   194. *pestilent*, used in time of the plague.   195. *furious*, frantic.   197. *estridge*, falcon.

To beat me out of Egypt; my messenger
He hath whipp'd with rods; dares me to personal combat,
Cæsar to Antony: let the old ruffian know
5 I have many other ways to die; meantime
Laugh at his challenge.
Mec.   Cæsar must think,
When one so great begins to rage, he's hunted
Even to falling. Give him no breath, but now
Make boot of his distraction: never anger
Made good guard for itself.
10 Cæs.   Let our best heads
Know that to-morrow the last of many battles
We mean to fight: within our files there are,
Of those that served Mark Antony but late,
Enough to fetch him in. See it done:
15 And feast the army; we have store to do 't,
And they have earn'd the waste. Poor Antony!

[*Exeunt.*]

Scene II. *Alexandria.* Cleopatra's *palace.*

[*Enter* Antony, Cleopatra, Enobarbus, Charmian, Iras, Alexas, *with others.*]

Ant. He will not fight with me, Domitius.
Eno.   No.
Ant. Why should he not?
Eno. He thinks, being twenty times of better fortune,
 He is twenty men to one.
Ant.   To-morrow, soldier,
5 By sea and land I'll fight: or I will live,
Or bathe my dying honour in the blood
Shall make it live again. Woo 't thou fight well?
Eno. I'll strike, and cry "Take all."
Ant.   Well said; come on.
Call forth my household servants: let's to-night
Be bounteous at our meal.

[*Enter three or four* Servitors.]

10   Give me thy hand,

Act IV, Scene 1: 7. *rage*, rave. 9. *Make boot*, take advantage. 10. *heads*, leaders.
15. *store*, plenty. 16. *waste* expenditure. Scene ii: 5. *or*, either. 7. *Woo't*, wilt.
8. *Take all*, a gambler's cry, "All or nothing," i.e., I will give and expect no quarter.

Thou hast been rightly honest;—so hast thou;—
Thou,—and thou,—and thou:—you have served me well,
And kings have been your fellows.

CLEO.   [*Aside to* ENO.] What means this?

ENO. [*Aside to* CLEO.] 'Tis one of those odd tricks which sorrow shoots
Out of the mind.

ANT.   And thou art honest too.   15
I wish I could be made so many men,
And all of you clapp'd up together in
An Antony, that I might do you service
So good as you have done.

ALL.   The gods forbid!

ANT. Well, my good fellows, wait on me to-night: 20
Scant not my cups; and make as much of me
As when mine empire was your fellow too,
And suffer'd my command.

CLEO. [*Aside to* ENO.] What does he mean?

ENO. [*Aside to* CLEO.] To make his followers weep.

ANT.   Tend me to-night;
Maybe it is the period of your duty: 25
Haply you shall not see me more; or if,
A mangled shadow: perchance to-morrow
You'll serve another master. I look on you
As one that takes his leave. Mine honest friends,
I turn you not away; but, like a master   30
Married to your good service, stay till death:
Tend me to-night two hours, I ask no more,
And the gods yield you for 't!

ENO.   What mean you, sir,
To give them this discomfort? Look, they weep;
And I, an ass, am onion-eyed: for shame,   35
Transform us not to women.

ANT.   Ho, ho, ho!
Now the witch take me, if I meant it thus!
Grace grow where those drops fall! My hearty friends,
You take me in too dolorous a sense;
For I spake to you for your comfort; did desire you   40
To burn this night with torches: know, my hearts,
I hope well of to-morrow; and will lead you
Where rather I'll expect victorious life

11. *honest*, honorable, faithful.   16. *made*, made into.   17. *clapp'd up*, shut up.   23.
suffer'd, endured.   25. *period*, end.   33. *yield*, reward.   37. *witch take me*, may I be
bewitched.   38. *Grace*, goodness.

45   Than death and honour. Let's to supper, come,
    And drown consideration.

[*Exeunt.*]

SCENE III. *The same. Before the palace.*

[*Enter two* SOLDIERS *to their guard.*]

FIRST SOLD. Brother, good night: to-morrow is the day.
SEC. SOLD. It will determine one way: fare you well.
    Heard you of nothing strange about the streets?
FIRST SOLD. Nothing. What news?
5 SEC. SOLD. Belike 'tis but a rumour. Good night to you.
FIRST SOLD. Well, sir, good night.

[*Enter two other* SOLDIERS.]

SEC. SOLD. Soldiers, have careful watch.
THIRD SOLD. And you. Good night, good night.

[*They place themselves in every corner of the stage.*]

FOURTH SOLD. Here we: and if to-morrow
10   Our navy thrive, I have an absolute hope
    Our landmen will stand up.
THIRD SOLD.   'Tis a brave army,
    And full of purpose.

[*Music of the hautboys as under the stage.*]

FOURTH SOLD. Peace! what noise?
FIRST SOLD.   List, list!
SEC. SOLD. Hark!
FIRST SOLD.   Music i' the air.
THIRD SOLD.   Under the earth.
FOURTH SOLD. It signs well, does it not?
THIRD SOLD.   No.
FIRST SOLD.   Peace, I say!
15   What should this mean?
SEC. SOLD. 'Tis the god Hercules, whom Antony loved,
    Now leaves him.
FIRST SOLD. Walk; let's see if other watchmen

---

46. *consideration*, reflection.   Scene iii: 2. *one way*, i.e., the issue one way or the other.
14. *signs well*, is a good sign.   16. *Hercules*, in Plutarch it is Bacchus, "the God unto
whom Antonius bore singular devotion," who thus signalizes his forsaking of his devotee.

Do hear what we do.

[*They advance to another post.*]

SEC. SOLD. How now, masters.
ALL. [*Speaking together.*] How now!
How now! do you hear this?
FIRST SOLD. Ay; is 't not strange? 20
THIRD SOLD. Do you hear, masters? do you hear?
FIRST SOLD. Follow the noise so far as we have quarter;
Let's see how it will give off.
ALL. Content. 'Tis strange.

[*Exeunt.*]

SCENE IV. *The same. A room in the palace.*

[*Enter* ANTONY *and* CLEOPATRA, CHARMIAN, *and others attending.*]

ANT. Eros! mine armour, Eros!
CLEO. Sleep a little.
ANT. No, my chuck, Eros, come; mine armour, Eros!

[*Enter* EROS *with armour.*]

Come, good fellow, put mine iron on:
If fortune be not ours to-day, it is
Because we brave her: come.
CLEO. Nay, I'll help too. 5
What's this for?
ANT. Ah, let be, let be! thou art
The armourer of my heart: false, false; this, this.
CLEO. Sooth, la, I'll help: thus it must be.
ANT. Well, well;
We shall thrive now. Seest thou, my good fellow?
Go put on thy defences.
EROS. Briefly, sir. 10
CLEO. Is not this buckled well?
ANT. Rarely, rarely:
He that unbuckles this, till we do please
To daff 't for our repose, shall hear a storm.
Thou fumblest, Eros; and my queen's a squire
More tight at this than thou: dispatch. O love, 15

22. *as we have quarter*, as the limits of our post extend. 23. *give off*, stop; *Content*, agreed. Scene iv: 5. *brave*, defy. 8. *Sooth*, in truth. 10. *Briefly*, quickly. 13. *daff 't*, take it off. 15. *tight*, skillful.

That thou couldst see my wars to-day, and knew'st
The royal occupation! thou shouldst see
A workman in 't.

[*Enter an armed* SOLDIER.]

                Good morrow to thee; welcome:
Thou look'st like him that knows a warlike charge:
20   To business that we love we rise betime,
And go to 't with delight.
SOLD.   A thousand, sir,
Early though 't be, have on their riveted trim,
And at the port expect you.

[*Shout. Trumpets flourish.*]

[*Enter* CAPTAINS *and* SOLDIERS.]

CAPT. The morn is fair. Good morrow, general.
ALL. Good morrow, general.
25 ANT.   'Tis well blown, lads:
This morning, like the spirit of a youth
That means to be of note, begins betimes.
So, so; come, give me that: this way; well said.
Fare thee well, dame, whate'er becomes of me:
30   This is a soldier's kiss: rebukeable [*Kisses her.*]
And worthy shameful check it were, to stand
On more mechanic compliment; I'll leave thee
Now, like a man of steel. You that will fight,
Follow me close; I'll bring you to 't. Adieu.

[*Exeunt* ANTONY, EROS, CAPTAINS, *and* SOLDIERS.]

CHAR. Please you, retire to your chamber.
35 CLEO   Lead me.
He goes forth gallantly. That he and Cæsar might
Determine this great war in single fight!
Then, Antony,—but now—Well, on.

[*Exeunt.*]

---

20. *betime*, early.   22. *trim*, gear, i.e., armor.   23. *port . . . you*, wait at the gate.
25. *well blown*, i.e., the morning is dawning (burgeoning) fair. Perhaps he is referring to
a flourish blown by his trumpeters.   28. *said*, done.   31. *check*, reproof.   31–2. *stand
On*, insist on.   32. *mechanic compliment*, vulgar ceremony.

Scene V. *Alexandria.* Antony's *camp.*

[*Trumpets sound. Enter* Antony *and* Eros; *a* Soldier *meeting them.*]

Sold. The gods make this a happy day to Antony!

Ant. Would thou and those thy scars had once prevail'd
  To make me fight at land!

Sold.   Hadst thou done so,
  The kings that have revolted, and the soldier
  That has this morning left thee, would have still   5
  Follow'd thy heels.

Ant.   Who's gone this morning?

Sold.   Who!
  One ever near thee: call for Enobarbus,
  He shall not hear thee; or from Cæsar's camp
  Say "I am none of thine."

Ant.   What say'st thou?

Sold.   Sir,
  He is with Cæsar.

Eros.   Sir, his chests and treasure   10
  He has not with him.

Ant.   Is he gone?

Sold.   Most certain.

Ant. Go, Eros, send his treasure after; do it;
  Detain no jot, I charge thee: write to him—
  I will subscribe—gentle adieus and greetings;
  Say that I wish he never find more cause   15
  To change a master. O, my fortunes have
  Corrupted honest men! Dispatch.—Enobarbus!

[*Exeunt.*]

Scene VI. *Alexandria.* Cæsar's *camp.*

[*Flourish. Enter* Cæsar, Agrippa, *with* Enobarbus, *and others.*]

Cæs. Go forth, Agrippa, and begin the fight:
  Our will is Antony be took alive;
  Make it so known.

Agr. Cæsar, I shall.

[*Exit.*]

Cæs. The time of universal peace is near: 5

Scene v: 2. *once*, on one occasion.   14. *subscribe*, sign.

Prove this a prosperous day, the three-nook'd world
Shall bear the olive freely.

[*Enter a* Messenger.]

Mess.   Antony
Is come into the field.
Cæs.   Go charge Agrippa
Plant those that have revolted in the van,
10   That Antony may seem to spend his fury
Upon himself.

[*Exeunt all but* Enobarbus.]

Eno. Alexas did revolt; and went to Jewry on
Affairs of Antony; there did persuade
Great Herod to incline himself to Cæsar,
15   And leave his master Antony: for this pains
Cæsar hath hang'd him. Canidius and the rest
That fell away have entertainment, but
No honourable trust. I have done ill;
Of which I do accuse myself so sorely,
That I will joy no more.

[*Enter a* Soldier *of* Cæsar's.]

20   Sold.   Enobarbus, Antony
Hath after thee sent all thy treasure, with
His bounty overplus: the messenger
Came on my guard; and at thy tent is now
Unloading of his mules.
Eno.   I give it you.
25   Sold. Mock not, Enobarbus.
I tell you true: best you safed the bringer
Out of the host; I must attend mine office,
Or would have done 't myself. Your emperor
Continues still a Jove.

[*Exit.*]

30   Eno. I am alone the villain of the earth,
And feel I am so most. O Antony,
Thou mine of bounty, how wouldst thou have paid
My better service, when my turpitude

Scene vi: 6. *three-nook'd,* three-cornered, i.e., Europe, Asia and Africa.   17. *entertain-ment,* employment (in Cæsar's army).   22. *bounty overplus,* a liberal gift to boot.   23. *on my guard,* while I was on guard.   26. *safed,* safely convoyed.   27. *office,* duty.

Thou dost so crown with gold! This blows my heart:
If swift thought break it not, a swifter mean   35
Shall outstrike thought: but thought will do 't, I feel.
I fight against thee! No: I will go seek
Some ditch wherein to die; the foul'st best fits
My latter part of life.

[*Exit.*]

SCENE VII. *Field of battle between the camps.*

[*Alarum. Drums and trumpets. Enter* AGRIPPA *and others.*]

AGR. Retire, we have engaged ourselves too far;
    Cæsar himself has work, and our oppression
    Exceeds what we expected.

[*Exeunt.*]

[*Alarums. Enter* ANTONY, *and* SCARUS *wounded.*]

SCAR. O my brave emperor, this is fought indeed!
    Had we done so at first, we had droven them home   5
    With clouts about their heads.
ANT.   Thou bleed'st apace.
SCAR. I had a wound here that was like a T,
    But now 'tis made an H.
ANT.   They do retire.
SCAR. We'll beat 'em into bench-holes: I have yet
    Room for six scotches more.   10

[*Enter* EROS.]

EROS. They are beaten, sir; and our advantage serves
    For a fair victory.
SCAR.   Let us score their backs,
    And snatch 'em up, as we take hares, behind:
    'Tis sport to maul a runner.
ANT.   I will reward thee
    Once for thy spritely comfort, and ten-fold   15
    For thy good valour. Come thee on.

---

34. *blows,* swells to bursting.   35. *thought,* i.e., remorse; *mean,* means, i.e., my sword.
36. *Shall outstrike,* will surely strike sooner, than do it, i.e., break his heart.   Scene vii:
2. *has work,* has plenty to do; *our oppression,* the forces opposing us.   6. *clouts,* bandages.   8. *H,* was pronounced "ache."   9. *bench-holes,* holes in the seat of a privy.
10. *scotches,* cuts.   12. *score,* make notches on as if making a record.

16 SCAR.   I'll halt after.

[*Exeunt.*]

SCENE VIII. *Under the walls of Alexandria.*

[*Alarum. Enter* ANTONY, *in a march;* SCARUS, *with others.*]

ANT. We have beat him to his camp: run one before,
   And let the queen know of our gests. To-morrow,
   Before the sun shall see 's, we'll spill the blood
   That has to-day escaped. I thank you all;
5 For doughty-handed are you, and have fought
   Not as you served the cause, but as 't had been
   Each man's like mine; you have shown all Hectors.
   Enter the city, clip your wives, your friends,
   Tell them your feats; whilst they with joyful tears
10 Wash the congealment from your wounds, and kiss
   The honour'd gashes whole. [*To* SCARUS.] Give me thy hand;

[*Enter* CLEOPATRA, *attended.*]

   To this great fairy I'll commend thy acts,
   Make her thanks bless thee. [*To* CLEO.] O thou day o' the world,
   Chain mine arm'd neck; leap thou, attire and all,
15 Through proof of harness to my heart, and there
   Ride on the pants triumphing!
CLEO.   Lord of lords!
   O infinite virtue, comest thou smiling from
   The world's great snare uncaught?
ANT.   My nightingale,
   We have beat them to their beds. What, girl! though grey
20 Do something mingle with our younger brown, yet ha' we
   A brain that nourishes our nerves, and can
   Get goal for goal of youth. Behold this man;
   Commend unto his lips thy favouring hand:
   Kiss it, my warrior: he hath fought to-day
25 As if a god, in hate of mankind, had
   Destroy'd in such a shape.
CLEO.   I'll give thee, friend,

---

16. *halt,* limp. Scene viii: 2. *gests,* exploits. 7. *you . . . Hectors,* you have all
shown yourselves to be Hectors. 8. *clip,* embrace. 10. *congealment,* clotted blood. 12.
fairy, enchantress. 15. *proof of harness,* sword-proof armor. 16. *pants,* heartbeats.
17. *virtue,* bravery. 21. *nerves,* sinews. 22. *Get . . . youth,* make just as many goals
(in the game of barriers) as young men. 23. *Commend,* commit.

An armour all of gold; it was a king's.
ANT. He has deserved it, were it carbuncled
Like holy Phœbus' car. Give me thy hand:
Through Alexandria make a jolly march;   30
Bear our hack'd targets like the men that owe them:
Had our great palace the capacity
To camp this host, we all would sup together,
And drink carouses to the next day's fate,
Which promises royal peril. Trumpeters,   35
With brazen din blast you the city's ear;
Make mingle with our rattling tambourines;
That heaven and earth may strike their sounds together,
Applauding our approach.

[*Exeunt.*]

SCENE IX. CÆSAR'S *camp.*

[SENTINELS *at their post.*]

FIRST SOLD. If we be not relieved within this hour,
We must return to the court of guard: the night
Is shiny; and they say we shall embattle
By the second hour i' the morn.
SEC. SOLD.   This last day was
A shrewd one to 's.

[*Enter* ENOBARBUS.]

ENO.   O, bear me witness, night,—   5
THIRD SOLD. What man is this?
SEC. SOLD.   Stand close, and list him.
ENO. Be witness to me, O thou blessèd moon,
When men revolted shall upon recórd
Bear hateful memory, poor Enobarbus did
Before thy face repent!
FIRST SOLD.   Enobarbus!
THIRD SOLD.   Peace!   10
Hark further.
ENO. O sovereign mistress of true melancholy,

---

28. *carbuncled,* set with jewels. 31. *targets,* shields; *like . . . them,* with the same triumphant air as those who own them. 34. *carouses,* i.e., "bottoms up." 37. *tambourines,* drums. Scene ix: 2. *court of guard,* guardhouse. 3. *embattle,* form in battle array. 5. *shrewd,* curst, grievous. 6. *close,* hidden.

The poisonous damp of night disponge upon me,
That life, a very rebel to my will,
15   May hang no longer on me: throw my heart
Against the flint and hardness of my fault;
Which, being dried with grief, will break to powder,
And finish all foul thoughts. O Antony,
Nobler than my revolt is infamous,
20   Forgive me in thine own particular;
But let the world rank me in register
A master-leaver and a fugitive:
O Antony! O Antony!

[*Dies.*]

SEC. SOLD.   Let's speak
To him.
25   FIRST SOLD. Let's hear him, for the things he speaks
May concern Cæsar.
THIRD SOLD.   Let's do so. But he sleeps.
FIRST SOLD. Swoons rather, for so bad a prayer as his
Was never yet for sleep.
SEC. SOLD.   Go we to him.
THIRD SOLD. Awake, sir, awake, speak to us.
SEC. SOLD.   Hear you, sir?
FIRST SOLD. The hand of death hath raught him. [*Drums afar off.*] Hark!
30   the drums
Demurely wake the sleepers. Let us bear him
To the court of guard; he is of note: our hour
Is fully out.
THIRD SOLD. Come on, then;
He may recover yet.

[*Exeunt with the body.*]

SCENE X. *Between the two camps.*

[*Enter* ANTONY *and* SCARUS, *with their Army.*]

ANT. Their preparation is to-day by sea;
We please them not by land.
SCAR.   For both, my lord.
ANT. I would they 'ld fight i' the fire or i' the air;
We 'ld fight there too. But this it is; our foot

13. *disponge,* squeeze out (your poisonous dew). 20. *in . . . particular,* as an individual. 21. *in register,* in its records. 30. *raught,* reached. 31. *Demurely,* quietly.

Upon the hills adjoining to the city 5
Shall stay with us: order for sea is given;
They have put forth the haven,
Where their appointment we may best discover,
And look on their endeavour. 9

[*Exeunt.*]

Scene XI. *Another part of the same.*

[*Enter* Cæsar, *and his Army.*]

Cæs. But being charged, we will be still by land,
Which, as I take 't, we shall; for his best force
Is forth to man his galleys. To the vales,
And hold our best advantage.

[*Exeunt.*]

Scene XII. *Another part of the same.*

[*Enter* Antony *and* Scarus.]

Ant. Yet they are not join'd: where yond pine does stand,
I shall discover all: I'll bring thee word
Straight, how 'tis like to go.

[*Exit.*]

Scar.   Swallows have built
In Cleopatra's sails their nests: the augurers
Say they know not, they cannot tell; look grimly, 5
And dare not speak their knowledge. Antony
Is valiant, and dejected; and, by starts,
His fretted fortunes give him hope, and fear,
Of what he has, and has not.

[*Alarum afar off, as at a sea-fight.*]

[*Re-enter* Antony.]

Ant.   All is lost;
This foul Egyptian hath betrayed me: 10
My fleet hath yielded to the foe; and yonder

Scene x: 8. *their appointment*, the equipment (of their ships). Scene xi: 1. *But
. . . charged*, unless we are attacked; *still*, inactive. 2. *we shall*, i.e., remain inactive.
Scene xii: 4. *sails*, ships. 8. *fretted*, eaten away, corroded.

They cast their caps up and carouse together
Like friends long lost. Triple-turn'd whore! 'tis thou
Hath sold me to this novice; and my heart
15 Makes only wars on thee. Bid them all fly;
For when I am revenged upon my charm,
I have done all. Bid them all fly; begone.

[*Exit* SCARUS.]

O sun, thy uprise shall I see no more:
Fortune and Antony part here; even here
20 Do we shake hands. All come to this? The hearts
That spaniel'd me at heels, to whom I gave
Their wishes, do discandy, melt their sweets
On blossoming Cæsar; and this pine is bark'd,
That overtopp'd them all. Betray'd I am:
25 O this false soul of Egypt! this grave charm,—
Whose eye beck'd forth my wars, and call'd them home;
Whose bosom was my crownet, my chief end,—
Like a right gipsy, hath, at fast and loose,
Beguiled me to the very heart of loss.
What, Eros, Eros!

[*Enter* CLEOPATRA.]

30   Ah, thou spell! Avaunt!
CLEO. Why is my lord enraged against his love?
ANT. Vanish, or I shall give thee thy deserving.
And blemish Cæsar's triumph. Let him take thee,
And hoist thee up to the shouting plebeians:
35 Follow his chariot, like the greatest spot
Of all thy sex; most monster-like, be shown
For poor'st diminutives, for doits; and let
Patient Octavia plough thy visage up
With her preparèd nails.

[*Exit* CLEOPATRA.]

                  'Tis well thou'rt gone,
40 If it be well to live: but better 'twere
Thou fell'st into my fury, for one death

13. *Triple-turn'd,* thrice faithless, (1) to Pompey, (2) to Julius Cæsar, (3) to Antony.
16. *charm,* charmer.   22. *discandy,* dissolve.   25. *grave charm,* deadly sorceress.   26.
beck'd, nodded.   27. *crownet,* coronet.   28. *right,* regular; *fast and loose,* a cheating
trick practiced by the gypsies.   35. *spot,* blemish.   36. *monster-like,* i.e., like a freak of
nature in a sideshow.   37. *diminutives,* small coin; *doit,* Dutch coin = half a farthing.
41. *Thou . . . fury,* you had fallen before my fury.

Might have prevented many. Eros, ho!
The shirt of Nessus is upon me: teach me,
Alcides, thou mine ancestor, thy rage:
Let me lodge Lichas on the horns o' the moon;   45
And with those hands, that grasp'd the heaviest club,
Subdue my worthiest self. The witch shall die:
To the young Roman boy she hath sold me, and I fall
Under this plot; she dies for 't. Eros, ho!   49

[*Exit.*]

SCENE XIII. *Alexandria.* CLEOPATRA'S *palace.*

[*Enter* CLEOPATRA, CHARMIAN, IRAS, *and* MARDIAN.]

CLEO. Help me, my women! O, he is more mad
  Than Telamon for his shield; the boar of Thessaly
  Was never so emboss'd.
CHAR.   To the monument!
  There lock yourself, and send him word you are dead.
  The soul and body rive not more in parting   5
  Than greatness going off.
CLEO.   To the monument!
  Mardian, go tell him I have slain myself;
  Say, that the last I spoke was "Antony,"
  And word it, prithee, piteously: hence, Mardian,
  And bring me how he takes my death. To the monument!   10

[*Exeunt.*]

SCENE XIV. *The same. Another room.*

[*Enter* ANTONY *and* EROS.]

ANT. Eros, thou yet behold'st me?
EROS.   Ay, noble lord.
ANT. Sometime we see a cloud that's dragonish;
  A vapour sometime like a bear or lion,
  A tower'd citadel, a pendant rock,

---

43. *shirt of Nessus,* a shirt, soaked in the poisoned blood of the Centaur Nessus, was given to Hercules by his wife, mistakenly thinking it a love-charm. Maddened by the agony of the poison, Hercules seized Lichas, who had brought it to him, and hurled him into the sea. 44. *Alcides,* Hercules. Scene xiii: 2. *Telamon,* Ajax, son of Telamon; *for his shield,* because Achilles' shield was awarded to his rival, Odysseus; *boar of Thessaly,* the boar sent by Diana to ravage Caledon, slain by Meleager. 3. *emboss'd,* foaming with rage. 6. *monument,* tomb. Scene xiv: 2. *dragonish,* shaped like a snake.

5   A forkèd mountain, or blue promontory
      With trees upon 't, that nod unto the world,
      And mock our eyes with air: thou hast seen these signs;
      They are black vesper's pageants.
EROS.   Ay, my lord.
ANT. That which is now a horse, even with a thought
10   The rack dislimns, and makes it indistinct,
      As water is in water.
EROS.   It does, my lord.
ANT. My good knave Eros, now thy captain is
      Even such a body: here I am Antony;
      Yet cannot hold this visible shape, my knave.
15   I made these wars for Egypt; and the queen,—
      Whose heart I thought I had, for she had mine;
      Which whilst it was mine had annex'd unto 't
      A million more, now lost,—she, Eros, has
      Pack'd cards with Cæsar, and false-play'd my glory
20   Unto an enemy's triumph.
      Nay, weep not, gentle Eros; there is left us
      Ourselves to end ourselves.

    [*Enter* MARDIAN.]

                        O, thy vile lady!
      She has robb'd me of my sword.
MAR.   No, Antony;
24   My mistress loved thee, and her fortunes mingled
      With thine entirely.
ANT.   Hence, saucy eunuch; peace!
      She hath betray'd me and shall die the death.
MAR. Death of one person can be paid but once,
      And that she has discharged: what thou wouldst do
      Is done unto thy hand: the last she spake
30   Was "Antony! most noble Antony!"
      Then in the midst a tearing groan did break
      The name of Antony; it was divided
      Between her heart and lips: she render'd life,
      Thy name so buried in her.
ANT.   Dead, then?
MAR.   Dead.

---

8. *Black . . . pageants*, the shows or pageants that greet the coming of evening.   10. *rack dislimns*, light drifting cloud paints it out.   19. *Pack'd*, stacked.   23. *sword*, i.e., the symbol of his soldiership.   28. *discharged*, paid in full.   33. *render'd*, gave up.

ANT. Unarm, Eros; the long day's task is done,   35
And we must sleep. [*To* MAR.] That thou depart'st hence safe,
Does pay thy labour richly; go.

[*Exit* MARDIAN.]

                    Off, pluck off:
The seven-fold shield of Ajax cannot keep
The battery from my heart. O, cleave, my sides!
Heart, once be stronger than thy continent,   40
Crack thy frail case! Apace, Eros, apace.
No more a soldier: bruisèd pieces, go;
You have been nobly borne. From me awhile.

[*Exit* EROS.]

I will o'ertake thee, Cleopatra, and
Weep for my pardon. So it must be, for now   45
All length is torture: since the torch is out,
Lie down, and stray no farther: now all labour
Mars what it does; yea, very force entangles
Itself with strength: seal then, and all is done.
Eros!—I come, my queen:—Eros!—Stay for me: 50
Where souls do couch on flowers, we'll hand in hand,
And with our sprightly port make the ghosts gaze:
Dido and her Æneas shall want troops,
And all the haunt be ours. Come, Eros, Eros!

[*Re-enter* EROS.]

EROS. What would my lord?
ANT.   Since Cleopatra died,   55
I have lived in such dishonour, that the gods
Detest my baseness. I, that with my sword
Quarter'd the world, and o'er green Neptune's back
With ships made cities, condemn myself to lack
The courage of a woman; less noble mind   60
Than she which by her death our Cæsar tells
"I am conqueror of myself." Thou art sworn, Eros,
That, when the exigent should come, which now

37. *thy labour,* i.e., your service as messenger.   39. *battery . . . heart,* assault launched by my heart.   40. *thy continent,* that which contains you.   41. *Apace,* hurry.   42. *bruisèd pieces,* i.e., of armor.   46. *length,* i.e., of life.   47–8. *all . . . it does,* i.e., everything I could do would be futile.   48. *force,* violence of my action.   49. *seal,* put the final seal (of death).   52. *port,* bearing.   53. *want troops,* be without their (usual) crowd of admirers.   54. *haunt,* companionship (with ghosts).   60. *less,* i.e., possessing a less.   63. *exigent,* time of need.

Is come indeed, when I should see behind me
65   The inevitable prosecution of
Disgrace and horror, that, on my command,
Thou then wouldst kill me: do 't; the time is come:
Thou strikest not me, 'tis Cæsar thou defeat'st,
Put colour in thy cheek.
EROS.   The gods withhold me!
Shall I do that which all the Parthian darts,
Though enemy, lost aim, and could not?
71   ANT.   Eros,
Wouldst thou be window'd in great Rome and see
Thy master thus with pleach'd arms, bending down
His corrigible neck, his face subdued
75   To penetrative shame, whilst the wheel'd seat
Of fortunate Cæsar, drawn before him, branded
His baseness that ensued?
EROS.   I would not see 't.
ANT. Come, then; for with a wound I must be cured.
Draw that thy honest sword, which thou hast worn
Most useful for thy country.
80   EROS.   O, sir, pardon me!
ANT. When I did make thee free, sworest thou not then
To do this when I bade thee? Do it at once;
Or thy precédent services are all
But accidents unpurposed. Draw, and come.
85   EROS. Turn from me, then, that noble countenance,
Wherein the worship of the whole world lies.
ANT. Lo thee!

[*Turning from him.*]

EROS. My sword is drawn.
ANT.   Then let it do at once
The thing why thou hast drawn it.
EROS.   My dear master,
90   My captain, and my emperor, let me say,
Before I strike this bloody stroke, farewell.
ANT. 'Tis said, man; and farewell.
EROS. Farewell, great chief. Shall I strike now?
ANT. Now Eros.

65. *prosecution*, pursuit.   73. *pleach'd*, folded.   74. *corrigible*, submissive.   75. *pene-trative*, acute.   76. *branded*, i.e., with shame.   77. *His . . . ensued*, the baseness of him who followed (his chariot).   79. *honest*, honorable.   86. *worship*, all that is worthy of honor.

EROS. Why, there then: thus I do escape the sorrow
Of Antony's death.

[*Kills himself.*]

ANT.   Thrice-nobler than myself!   95
Thou teachest me, O valiant Eros, what
I should, and thou couldst not. My queen and Eros
Have by their brave instruction got upon me
A nobleness in record: but I will be
A bridegroom in my death, and run into 't   100
As to a lover's bed. Come, then; and, Eros,
Thy master dies thy scholar: to do thus

[*Falling on his sword.*]

I learn'd of thee. How! not dead? not dead?
The guard, ho! O, dispatch me!

[*Enter* DERCETAS *and* GUARD.]

FIRST GUARD.   What's the noise?
ANT. I have done my work ill, friends: O make an end   105
Of what I have begun.
SEC. GUARD.   The star is fall'n.
FIRST GUARD. And time is at his period.
ALL.   Alas, and woe!
ANT. Let him that loves me strike me dead.
FIRST GUARD.   Not I.
SEC. GUARD. Nor I.
THIRD GUARD. Nor any one.   110

[*Exeunt* GUARD.]

DER. Thy death and fortunes bid thy followers fly.
This sword but shown to Cæsar, with this tidings,
Shall enter me with him.

[*Enter* DIOMEDES.]

DIO. Where's Antony?
DER.   There, Diomed, there.
DIO.   Lives he?
Wilt thou not answer, man?   115

[*Exit* DERCETAS.]

98–9. *got . . . record,* won an advantage over me by winning a noble reputation in
history.   107. *period,* end.   113. *enter . . . him,* gain me a place in his service.

ANT. Art thou there, Diomed? Draw thy sword, and give me
Sufficing strokes for death.
DIO.   Most absolute lord,
My mistress Cleopatra sent me to thee.
ANT. When did she send thee?
DIO.   Now, my lord.
ANT.   Where is she?
120 DIO. Lock'd in her monument. She had a prophesying fear
Of what hath come to pass: for when she saw—
Which never shall be found—you did suspect
She had disposed with Cæsar, and that your rage
Would not be purged, she sent you word she was dead;
125   But, fearing since how it might work, hath sent
Me to proclaim the truth; and I am come,
I dread, too late.
ANT. Too late, good Diomed: call my guard, I prithee.
DIO. What, ho, the emperor's guard! The guard, what, ho!
130   Come, your lord calls!

[*Enter four or five of the* GUARD *of* ANTONY.]

ANT. Bear me, good friends, where Cleopatra bides;
'Tis the last service that I shall command you.
FIRST GUARD. Woe, woe are we, sir, you may not live to wear
All your true followers out.
ALL.   Most heavy day!
135 ANT. Nay, good my fellows, do not please sharp fate
To grace it with your sorrows: bid that welcome
Which comes to punish us, and we punish it
Seeming to bear it lightly. Take me up:
I have led you oft: carry me now, good friends,
140   And have my thanks for all.

[*Exeunt, bearing* ANTONY.]

SCENE XV. *The same. A monument.*

[*Enter* CLEOPATRA, *and her maids aloft, with* CHARMIAN *and* IRAS.]

CLEO. O Charmian, I will never go from hence.
CHAR. Be comforted, dear madam.
CLEO.   No, I will not:
All strange and terrible events are welcome,

122. *found*, i.e., to be true.   123. *disposed*, come to terms.   134. *heavy*, woeful.
136. *To grace it*, by honoring it.

But comforts we despise; our size of sorrow,
Proportion'd to our cause, must be as great   5
As that which makes it.

[*Enter, below,* DIOMEDES.]

                    How now! is he dead?
DIO. His death's upon him, but not dead.
Look out o' the other side your monument;
His guard have brought him thither.

[*Enter, below,* ANTONY, *borne by the* GUARD.]

CLEO.   O sun,
Burn the great sphere thou movest in! darkling stand   10
The varying shore o' the world. O Antony,
Antony, Antony! Help, Charmian, help, Iras, help;
Help, friends below; let's draw him hither.
ANT.   Peace!
Not Cæsar's valour hath o'erthrown Antony,
But Antony's hath triumph'd on itself.   15
CLEO. So it should be, that none but Antony
Should conquer Antony; but woe 'tis so!
ANT. I am dying, Egypt, dying; only
I here impórtune death awhile, until
Of many thousand kisses the poor last   20
I lay upon thy lips.
CLEO.   I dare not, dear,—
Dear my lord, pardon,—I dare not,
Lest I be taken: not the imperious show
Of the full-fortuned Cæsar ever shall
Be brooch'd with me; if knife, drugs, serpents, have   25
Edge, sting, or operation, I am safe:
Your wife Octavia, with her modest eyes
And still conclusion, shall acquire no honour
Demuring upon me. But come, come, Antony,—
Help me, my women,—we must draw thee up: 30
Assist, good friends.
ANT.   O, quick, or I am gone.
CLEO. Here's sport indeed! How heavy weighs my lord!

Scene xv: 6. *that*, i.e., Antony. 10. *great sphere*, the sun was supposed to be fixed in a hollow sphere which revolved about the earth; *darkling*, in darkness. 11. *varying*, i.e., like the tides between darkness and light. 23. *imperious show*, imperial triumph. 25. *brooch'd*, ornamented. 28. *still conclusion*, quiet inferences. 29. *Demuring*, gazing demurely.

Our strength is all gone into heaviness,
That makes the weight: had I great Juno's power,
35 The strong-wing'd Mercury should fetch thee up,
And set thee by Jove's side. Yet come a little,—
Wishers were ever fools,—O, come, come, come;

[*They heave* ANTONY *aloft to* CLEOPATRA.]

And welcome, welcome! die where thou hast lived:
Quicken with kissing: had my lips that power,
Thus would I wear them out.
40 ALL.   A heavy sight!
ANT. I am dying, Egypt, dying:
Give me some wine, and let me speak a little.
CLEO. No, let me speak; and let me rail so high,
That the false housewife Fortune break her wheel,
Provoked by my offence.
45 ANT.   One word, sweet queen:
Of Cæsar seek your honour, with your safety. O!
CLEO. They do not go together.
ANT.   Gentle, hear me:
None about Cæsar trust but Proculeius.
50 CLEO. My resolution and my hands I'll trust; None about Cæsar.
ANT. The miserable change now at my end
Lament nor sorrow at; but please your thoughts
In feeding them with those my former fortunes
Wherein I lived, the greatest prince o' the world,
55 The noblest; and do now not basely die,
Not cowardly put off my helmet to
My countryman,—a Roman by a Roman
Valiantly vanquish'd. Now my spirit is going;
I can no more.
CLEO.   Noblest of men, woo't die?
60 Hast thou no care of me? shall I abide
In this dull world, which in thy absence is
No better than a sty? O, see, my women,

[ANTONY *dies.*]

The crown o' the earth doth melt. My lord!
O, wither'd is the garland of the war,
65 The soldier's pole is fall'n: young boys and girls

---

39. *Quicken*, revive.   40. *heavy*, grievous.   44. *housewife*, hussy, wench.   45. *offence*, offensive speech.   59. *woo't*, will you.   65. *pole*, standard.

Are level now with men; the odds is gone,
And there is nothing left remarkable
Beneath the visiting moon.

[*Faints.*]

CHAR.   O, quietness, lady!
IRAS. She is dead too, our sovereign.
CHAR.   Lady!
IRAS.   Madam!
CHAR. O madam, madam, madam!
IRAS.   Royal Egypt,   70
 Empress!
CHAR. Peace, peace, Iras!
CLEO. No more, but e'en a woman, and commanded
 By such poor passion as the maid that milks
 And does the meanest chares. It were for me   75
 To throw my sceptre at the injurious gods;
 To tell them that this world did equal theirs
 Till they had stol'n our jewel. All's but naught;
 Patience is sottish, and impatience does
 Become a dog that's mad: then is it sin   80
 To rush into the secret house of death,
 Ere death dare come to us? How do you, women?
 What, what! good cheer! Why, how now, Charmian!
 My noble girls! Ah, women, women, look,
 Our lamp is spent, it's out! Good sirs, take heart: 85
 We'll bury him; and then, what's brave, what's noble,
 Let's do it after the high Roman fashion,
 And make death proud to take us. Come, away:
 This case of that huge spirit now is cold:
 Ah, women, women! come; we have no friend   90
 But resolution, and the briefest end.

[*Exeunt; those above bearing off* ANTONY'S *body.*]

66. *odds*, all characteristics of inequality. 75. *chares*, chores. 79. *sottish*, the part of a fool. 83. *good cheer!* cheer up! 85. *sirs*, addressed to her women. 86. *brave*, fine. 91. *briefest*, quickest.

ACT V

SCENE I. *Alexandria.* CÆSAR'S *camp.*

[*Enter* CÆSAR, AGRIPPA, DOLABELLA, MECÆNAS, GALLUS, PROCULEIUS, *and others, his council of war.*]

CÆS. Go to him, Dolabella, bid him yield;
    Being so frustrate, tell him he mocks
    The pauses that he makes.
DOL.   Cæsar, I shall.

[*Exit.*]

[*Enter* DERCETAS, *with the sword of* ANTONY.]

CÆS. Wherefore is that? and what art thou that darest
    Appear thus to us?
5 DER.   I am call'd Dercetas;
    Mark Antony I served, who best was worthy
    Best to be served: whilst he stood up and spoke,
    He was my master; and I wore my life
    To spend upon his haters. If thou please
10   To take me to thee, as I was to him
    I'll be to Cæsar; if thou pleasest not,
    I yield thee up my life.
CÆS.   What is 't thou say'st?
DER. I say, O Cæsar, Antony is dead.
CÆS. The breaking of so great a thing should make
15   A greater crack: the round world
    Should have shook lions into civil streets,
    And citizens to their dens: the death of Antony
    Is not a single doom; in the name lay
    A moiety of the world.
DER.   He is dead, Cæsar;
20   Not by a public minister of justice,
    Nor by a hired knife; but that self hand,
    Which writ his honour in the acts it did,
    Hath, with the courage which the heart did lend it,
    Splitted the heart. This is his sword;
25   I robb'd his wound of it; behold it stain'd

Act V. Scene i: 2. *frustrate*, baffled. 2–3. *mocks* . . . *makes*, he makes himself ridiculous by his delay. 15. *crack*, loud report. 16. *shook*, i.e., wth an earthquake; *civil*, of a civilized community. 19. *moiety*, one-half.

With his most noble blood.
CÆS.   Look you sad, friends?
The gods rebuke me, but it is tidings
To wash the eyes of kings.
AGR.   And strange it is,
That nature must compel us to lament
Our most persisted deeds.
MEC.   His taints and honours   30
Waged equal with him.
AGR.   A rarer spirit never
Did steer humanity: but you, gods, will give us
Some faults to make us men. Cæsar is touch'd.
MEC. When such a spacious mirror's set before him,
He needs must see himself.
CÆS.   O Antony!   35
I have follow'd thee to this; but we do lance
Diseases in our bodies: I must perforce
Have shown to thee such a declining day,
Or look on thine; we could not stall together
In the whole world: but yet let me lament,   40
With tears as sovereign as the blood of hearts,
That thou, my brother, my competitor
In top of all design, my mate in empire,
Friend and companion in the front of war,
The arm of mine own body, and the heart   45
Where mine his thoughts did kindle,—that our stars,
Unreconcilable, should divide
Our equalness to this. Hear me, good friends,—
But I will tell you at some meeter season:

[*Enter an* EGYPTIAN.]

The business of this man looks out of him;   50
We'll hear him what he says. Whence are you?
EGYP. A poor Egyptian yet. The queen my mistress,
Confined in all she has, her monument,
Of thy intents desires instruction,
That she preparedly may frame herself   55
To the way she's forced to.

27. *but it is*, if it is not.   30. *persisted*, persistently sought.   31. *Waged equal*, contended equally.   32. *will give*, insist on giving.   41. *sovereign*, supremely important.
42. *competitor*, partner.   43. *In . . . design*, in the most important of enterprises.
46. *his*, its.   47–8. *divide Our equalness*, reduce (break up) the likeness of our status.
49. *meeter*, more suitable.   50. *looks . . . him*, appears in his eyes.   55. *frame*, adjust.

CÆS.   Bid her have good heart:
She soon shall know of us, by some of ours,
How honourable and how kindly we
Determine for her, for Cæsar cannot live
To be ungentle.
60 EGYP. So the gods preserve thee!

[*Exit.*]

CÆS. Come hither, Proculeius. Go and say,
We purpose her no shame: give her what comforts
The quality of her passion shall require,
Lest, in her greatness, by some mortal stroke
65 She do defeat us; for her life in Rome
Would be eternal in our triumph: go,
And with your speediest bring us what she says,
And how you find of her.
PRO.   Cæsar, I shall.

[*Exit.*]

CÆS. Gallus, go you along.

[*Exit* GALLUS.]

Where's Dolabella,
To second Proculeius?
70 ALL.   Dolabella!
CÆS. Let him alone, for I remember now
How he's employ'd: he shall in time be ready.
Go with me to my tent; where you shall see
How hardly I was drawn into this war;
75 How calm and gentle I proceeded still
In all my writings: go with me, and see
What I can show in this.

[*Exeunt.*]

SCENE II. *Alexandria. A room in the monument.*

[*Enter* CLEOPATRA, CHARMIAN, *and* IRAS.]

CLEO. My desolation does begin to make
A better life. 'Tis paltry to be Cæsar;

63. *quality of her passion,* nature of her emotion (of grief). 65. *life,* alive. 66. *Would
. . . triumph,* would make my triumphal procession eternally glorious. 68. *how . . .
of her,* what you find out about her. 76. *writings,* written messages.

Not being Fortune, he's but Fortune's knave,
A minister of her will: and it is great
To do that thing that ends all other deeds;   5
Which shackles accidents and bolts up change;
Which sleeps, and never palates more the dung,
The beggar's nurse and Cæsar's.

[*Enter, to the gates of the monument,* PROCULEIUS, GALLUS, *and* SOLDIERS.]

PRO. Cæsar sends greeting to the Queen of Egypt;
And bids thee study on what fair demands   10
Thou mean'st to have him grant thee.
CLEO.   What's thy name?
PRO. My name is Proculeius.
CLEO.   Antony
Did tell me of you, bade me trust you; but
I do not greatly care to be deceived,
That have no use for trusting. If your master   15
Would have a queen his beggar, you must tell him,
That majesty, to keep decorum, must
No less beg than a kingdom: if he please
To give me conquer'd Egypt for my son,
He gives me so much of mine own, as I   20
Will kneel to him with thanks.
PRO.   Be of good cheer;
You're fall'n into a princely hand, fear nothing:
Make your full reference freely to my lord,
Who is so full of grace, that it flows over
On all that need: let me report to him   25
Your sweet dependency; and you shall find
A conqueror that will pray in aid for kindness,
Where he for grace is kneel'd to.
CLEO.   Pray you, tell him
I am his fortune's vassal, and I send him
The greatness he has got. I hourly learn   30
A doctrine of obedience; and would gladly
Look him i' the face.

Scene ii: 3. *knave*, servant. 6. *accidents*, things that happen by chance. 7. *sleeps*, gives me (eternal) sleep; *dung*, the vile food. 8. *nurse*, nourishment. 10. *fair*, for favorable terms. 14. *greatly . . . deceived*, am not much worried about being deceived. 17. *keep decorum*, i.e., act as a king should. 23. *Make . . . freely*, put yourself without reservation into my lord's power. 26. *dependency*, submission. 27. *pray . . . for kindness*, i.e., calls in your aid to help him in thinking of kind deeds. "Pray in aid" is a legal term = "to call in the aid of a person not a party to the suit." 28. *grace*, favors. 30. *got*, i.e., by subduing me. 31. *doctrine*, lesson.

PRO.   This I'll report, dear lady.
Have comfort, for I know your plight is pitied
Of him that caused it.

35   GAL. You see how easily she may be surprised:

[*Here* PROCULEIUS *and two of the Guard ascend the monument by a ladder placed against a window, and, having descended, come behind* CLEOPATRA. *Some of the Guard unbar and open the gates.*]

[*To* PROCULEIUS *and the Guard*] Guard her till Cæsar come.

[*Exit.*]

IRAS. Royal queen!
CHAR. O Cleopatra! thou art taken, queen.
CLEO. Quick, quick, good hands.

[*Drawing a dagger.*]

PRO.   Hold, worthy lady, hold:

[*Seizes and disarms her.*]

40   Do not yourself such wrong, who are in this
Relieved, but not betray'd.
CLEO.   What, of death too,
That rids our dogs of languish?
PRO.   Cleopatra,
Do not abuse my master's bounty by
The undoing of yourself: let the world see
45   His nobleness well acted, which your death
Will never let come forth.
CLEO.   Where art thou, death?
Come hither, come! come, come, and take a queen
Worth many babes and beggars!
PRO.   O, temperance, lady!
CLEO. Sir, I will eat no meat, I'll not drink, sir;
50   If idle talk will once be necessary,
I'll not sleep neither: this mortal house I'll ruin,
Do Cæsar what he can. Know, sir, that I
Will not wait pinion'd at your master's court;
Nor once be chástised with the sober eye
55   Of dull Octavia. Shall they hoist me up

35. *surprised,* taken in.   41. *of,* i.e., cheated out of.   42. *languish,* lingering disease.   43. *abuse,* cheat.   44. *undoing,* destruction.   46. *come forth,* display itself.   48. *temperance,* use self-control.   50. *If . . . necessary,* if it is necessary for once to use meaningless words (the clause is parenthetical).   53. *wait pinion'd,* attend as a slave.

And show me to the shouting varletry
Of censuring Rome? Rather a ditch in Egypt
Be gentle grave unto me! rather on Nilus' mud
Lay me stark naked, and let the water-flies
Blow me into abhorring! rather make   60
My country's high pyramides my gibbet,
And hang me up in chains!

Pro.   You do extend
These thoughts of horror further than you shall
Find cause in Cæsar.

[*Enter* Dolabella.]

Dol.   Proculeius,
What thou hast done thy master Cæsar knows,   65
And he hath sent for thee: for the queen,
I'll take her to my guard.

Pro.   So, Dolabella,
It shall content me best: be gentle to her.
[*To* Cleo.] To Cæsar I will speak what you shall please,
If you'll employ me to him.

Cleo.   Say, I would die.   70

[*Exeunt* Proculeius *and* Soldiers.]

Dol. Most noble empress, you have heard of me?
Cleo. I cannot tell.
Dol.   Assuredly you know me.
Cleo. No matter, sir, what I have heard or known.
You laugh when boys or women tell their dreams;
Is 't not your trick?
Dol.   I understand not, madam.   75
Cleo. I dream'd there was an Emperor Antony:
O, such another sleep, that I might see
But such another man!
Dol.   If it might please ye,—
Cleo. His face was as the heavens; and therein stuck
A sun and moon, which kept their course, and lighted   80
The little O, the earth.
Dol.   Most sovereign creature,—
Cleo. His legs bestrid the ocean: his rear'd arm
Crested the world: his voice was propertied

56. *varletry*, rabble.   57. *censuring*, passing judgment on me.   60. *blow . . . abhorring*, flyblow me until I am a disgusting object.   75. *trick*, custom.   83. *Crested*, served as a crest for, crowned; *propertied*, had the quality of.

As all the tunèd spheres, and that to friends;
85   But when he meant to quail and shake the orb,
He was as rattling thunder. For his bounty,
There was no winter in 't; an autumn 'twas
That grew the more by reaping: his delights
Were dolphin-like; they show'd his back above
90   The element they lived in: in his livery
Walk'd crowns and crownets; realms and islands were
As plates dropp'd from his pocket.
DOL.   Cleopatra!
CLEO. Think you there was, or might be, such a man
As this I dream'd of?
DOL.   Gentle madam, no.
95 CLEO. You lie, up to the hearing of the gods.
But, if there be, or ever were, one such,
It's past the size of dreaming: nature wants stuff
To vie strange forms with fancy; yet, to imagine
An Antony, were nature's piece 'gainst fancy,
Condemning shadows quite.
100 DOL.   Hear me, good madam.
Your loss is as yourself, great; and you bear it
As answering to the weight: would I might never
O'ertake pursued success, but I do feel,
By the rebound of yours, a grief that smites
My very heart at root.
105 CLEO.   I thank you, sir.
Know you what Cæsar means to do with me?
DOL. I am loath to tell you what I would you knew.
CLEO. Nay, pray you, sir,—
DOL.   Though he be honourable,—
CLEO. He'll lead me, then, in triumph?
110 DOL. Madam, he will; I know 't.

[*Flourish, and shout within,* "Make way there: *Cæsar!*"]

[*Enter* CÆSAR, GALLUS, PROCULEIUS, MECÆNAS, SELEUCUS, *and others of his train.*]

CÆS. Which is the Queen of Egypt?

---

84. *all . . . spheres,* i.e., the music of the spheres. 85. *orb,* i.e., the earth. 91. *crownets,* coronets. 92. *plates,* silver coins. 98. *To . . . fancy,* to equal the strange forms produced by the imagination. 99. *piece 'gainst fancy,* masterpiece competing with creatures of the imagination. 102. *As . . . weight,* in accordance with its weight, i.e., heavily. 103. *but I do,* if I do not.

Dol. It is the emperor, madam.

[Cleopatra *kneels*.]

Cæs. Arise, you shall not kneel:
I pray you, rise; rise, Egypt.

Cleo.   Sir, the gods   115
Will have it thus; my master and my lord
I must obey.

Cæs.   Take to you no hard thoughts:
The record of what injuries you did us,
Though written in our flesh, we shall remember
As things but done by chance.

Cleo.   Sole sir o' the world,   120
I cannot project mine own cause so well
To make it clear; but do confess I have
Been laden with like frailties which before
Have often shamed our sex.

Cæs.   Cleopatra, know,
We will extenuate rather than enforce: 125
If you apply yourself to our intents,
Which towards you are most gentle, you shall find
A benefit in this change; but if you seek
To lay on me a cruelty, by taking
Antony's course, you shall bereave yourself   130
Of my good purposes, and put your children
To that destruction which I'll guard them from,
If thereon you rely. I'll take my leave.

Cleo. And may, through all the world: 'tis yours; and we,
Your scutcheons and your signs of conquest, shall   135
Hang in what place you please. Here, my good lord.

Cæs. You shall advise me in all for Cleopatra.

Cleo. This is the brief of money, plate, and jewels,
I am possess'd of: 'tis exactly valued;
Not petty things admitted. Where's Seleucus?   140

Sel. Here, madam.

Cleo. This is my treasurer: let him speak, my lord,
Upon his peril, that I have reserved
To myself nothing. Speak the truth, Seleucus.

Sel. Madam,   145

---

121. *project*, set forth.   125. *enforce*, stress (your offences).   126. *apply yourself*, submit.   129. *lay* . . . *cruelty*, force me to act cruelly.   135. *scutcheons*, shields, hung up as trophies.   138. *brief*, list.   140. *Not* . . . *admitted*, trifles omitted.

I had rather seal my lips, than, to my peril,
Speak that which is not.
CLEO.   What have I kept back?
SEL. Enough to purchase what you have made known.
CÆS. Nay, blush not Cleopatra; I approve
Your wisdom in the deed.
150 CLEO.   See, Cæsar! O, behold,
How pomp is follow'd! mine will now be yours;
And, should we shift estates, yours would be mine.
The ingratitude of this Seleucus does
Even make me wild: O slave, of no more trust
155 Than love that's hired! What, goest thou back? thou shalt
Go back, I warrant thee; but I'll catch thine eyes,
Though they had wings: slave, soulless villain, dog!
O rarely base!
CÆS.   Good queen, let us entreat you.
CLEO. O Cæsar, what a wounding shame is this,
160 That thou, vouchsafing here to visit me,
Doing the honour of thy lordliness
To one so meek, that mine own servant should
Parcel the sum of my disgraces by
Addition of his envy! Say, good Cæsar,
165 That I some lady trifles have reserved,
Immoment toys, things of such dignity
As we greet modern friends withal; and say,
Some nobler token I have kept apart
For Livia and Octavia, to induce
170 Their mediation; must I be unfolded
With one that I have bred? The gods! it smites me
Beneath the fall I have. [To SELEUCUS] Prithee, go hence;
Or I shall show the cinders of my spirits
Through the ashes of my chance; wert thou a man,
Thou wouldst have mercy on me.
175 CÆS.   Forbear, Seleucus.

[Exit SELEUCUS.]

CLEO. Be it known, that we, the greatest, are misthought
For things that others do; and, when we fall,
We answer others' merits in our name,

151. mine, my followers. 152. shift estates, change places. 163. Parcel, add a piece to.
164. envy, malice. 166. Immoment toys, insignificant trinkets. 167. modern, ordinary.
170-1. unfolded With, exposed by. 174. chance, ill fortune. 176. misthought, mis-
judged. 178. others' . . . in our name, the misdeeds of our agents.

Are therefore to be pitied.
CÆS.   Cleopatra,
Not what you have reserved, nor what acknowledged,   180
Put we i' the roll of conquest: still be 't yours,
Bestow it at your pleasure; and believe,
Cæsar's no merchant, to make prize with you
Of things that merchants sold. Therefore be cheer'd;
Make not your thoughts your prisons: no, dear queen;   185
For we intend so to dispose you as
Yourself shall give us counsel. Feed, and sleep:
Our care and pity is so much upon you,
That we remain your friend; and so, adieu.
CLEO. My master, and my lord!
CÆS.   Not so. Adieu.   190

[*Flourish. Exeunt* CÆSAR *and his train.*]

CLEO. He words me, girls, he words me, that I should not
Be noble to myself: but, hark thee, Charmian.

[*Whispers* CHARMIAN.]

IRAS. Finish, good lady; the bright day is done,
And we are for the dark.
CLEO.   Hie thee again:
I have spoke already, and it is provided;   195
Go put it to the haste.
CHAR.   Madam, I will.

[*Re-enter* DOLABELLA.]

DOL. Where is the queen?
CHAR.   Behold, sir. [*Exit.*]
CLEO.   Dolabella!
DOL. Madam, as thereto sworn by your command,
Which my love makes religion to obey,
I tell you this: Cæsar through Syria   200
Intends his journey; and within three days
You with your children will he send before:
Make your best use of this: I have perform'd
Your pleasure and my promise.
CLEO.   Dolabella,
I shall remain your debtor.

181. *roll of conquest*, list of the spoils of our victory.   183. *make prize*, haggle.   185.
Make . . . prisons, do not imagine you are a prisoner.   194. *Hie thee*, make haste.
195. *it*, i.e., the asp.

205 DOL.   I your servant.
    Adieu, good queen; I must attend on Cæsar.
    CLEO. Farewell, and thanks.

[*Exit* DOLABELLA.]

                              Now, Iras, what think'st thou?
    Thou, an Egyptian puppet, shalt be shown
    In Rome, as well as I: mechanic slaves
210 With greasy aprons, rules, and hammers, shall
    Uplift us to the view; in their thick breaths,
    Rank of gross diet, shall we be enclouded,
    And forced to drink their vapour.
    IRAS.   The gods forbid!
    CLEO. Nay, 'tis most certain, Iras: saucy lictors
215 Will catch at us, like strumpets; and scald rhymers
    Ballad us out o' tune: the quick comedians,
    Extemporally will stage us, and present
    Our Alexandrian revels; Antony
    Shall be brought drunken forth, and I shall see
220 Some squeaking Cleopatra boy my greatness
    I' the posture of a whore.
    IRAS.   O the good gods!
    CLEO. Nay, that's certain.
    IRAS. I'll never see 't; for, I am sure, my nails
    Are stronger than mine eyes.
    CLEO.   Why, that's the way
225 To fool their preparation, and to conquer
    Their most absurd intents.

[*Re-enter* CHARMIAN.]

                              Now, Charmian!
    Show me, my women, like a queen: go fetch
    My best attires: I am again for Cydnus,
    To meet Mark Antony: sirrah Iras, go.
230 Now, noble Charmian, we'll dispatch indeed;
    And, when thou hast done this chare, I'll give thee leave
    To play till doomsday. Bring our crown and all.
    Wherefore's this noise?

[*Exit* IRAS. A *noise within.*]

208. *an . . . puppet,* an Egyptian figure in a puppet show. 209. *mechanic slaves,* wretched laborers. 215. *scald,* scabby, contemptible. 216. *Ballad us,* sing ballads about us; *quick,* quick-witted. 220. *squeaking . . . greatness,* boy actor with shrill voice impersonate my majesty. 221. *posture,* demeanor. 231. *chare,* chore, simple task.

[*Enter a* GUARDSMAN.]

GUARD.   Here is a rural fellow
That will not be denied your highness' presence:
He brings you figs.   235
CLEO. Let him come in. [*Exit* GUARDSMAN.]
                    What poor an instrument
May do a noble deed! he brings me liberty.
My resolution's placed, and I have nothing
Of woman in me: now from head to foot
I am marble-constant; now the fleeting moon   240
No planet is of mine.

[*Re-enter* GUARDSMAN, *with* CLOWN *bringing in a basket.*]

GUARD.   This is the man.
CLEO. Avoid, and leave him.

[*Exit* GUARDSMAN.]

Hast thou the pretty worm of Nilus there,
That kills and pains not?
CLOWN. Truly, I have him: but I would not be the party that should
desire you to touch him, for his biting is immortal; those that do die 247
of it do seldom or never recover.
CLEO. Rememberest thou any that have died on 't?
CLOWN. Very many, men and women too. I heard of one of them no
longer than yesterday: a very honest woman, but something given to lie; 252
as a woman should not do, but in the way of honesty: how she died of
the biting of it, what pain she felt: truly, she makes a very good report
o' the worm; but he that will believe all that they say, shall never be
saved by half that they do: but this is most fallible, the worm's an odd 259
worm.
CLEO. Get thee hence; farewell.
CLOWN. I wish you all joy of the worm.

[*Setting down his basket.*]

CLEO. Farewell.
CLOWN. You must think this, look you, that the worm will do his kind.
CLEO. Ay, ay; farewell.   265

---

236. *What*, how.   238. *placed*, fixed.   240. *marble-constant*, as firm in my resolution
as marble; *fleeting*, inconstant.   s.d. *Clown*, country fellow.   242. *Avoid*, depart.
243. *worm*, serpent.   247. *immortal*, clown's mistake for "mortal."   252. *honest*, respectable.   259. *fallible*, mistake for "infallible."   264. *do his kind*, act in accordance
with his nature.

CLOWN. Look you, the worm is not to be trusted but in the keeping of
wise people; for, indeed, there is no goodness in the worm.

269 CLEO. Take thou no care; it shall be heeded.

CLOWN. Very good. Give it nothing, I pray you, for it is not worth the
feeding.

CLEO. Will it eat me?

CLOWN. You must not think I am so simple but I know the devil himself
will not eat a woman: I know that a woman is a dish for the gods, if

276 the devil dress her not. But, truly, these same whoreson devils do the
gods great harm in their women; for in every ten that they make, the
devils mar five.

CLEO. Well, get thee gone; farewell.

CLOWN. Yes, forsooth: I wish you joy o' the worm.

[*Exit.*]

[*Re-enter* IRAS *with a robe, crown, &c.*]

CLEO. Give me my robe, put on my crown; I have
Immortal longings in me: now no more

285 The juice of Egypt's grape shall moist this lip:
Yare, yare, good Iras; quick. Methinks I hear
Antony call; I see him rouse himself
To praise my noble act; I hear him mock
The luck of Cæsar, which the gods give men

290 To excuse their after wrath: husband, I come:
Now to that name my courage prove my title!
I am fire and air; my other elements
I give to baser life. So; have you done?
Come then, and take the last warmth of my lips.

295 Farewell, kind Charmian; Iras, long farewell.

[*Kisses them.* IRAS *falls and dies.*]

Have I the aspic in my lips? Dost fall?
If thou and nature can so gently part,
The stroke of death is as a lover's pinch,
Which hurts, and is desired. Dost thou lie still?

300 If thus thou vanishest, thou tell'st the world
It is not worth leave-taking.

CHAR. Dissolve, thick cloud, and rain; that I may say,

269. *heeded,* looked after.   276. *dress her not,* does not prepare her for cooking.   284.
immortal longings, longings for immortality.   286. *yare,* hurry.   290. *their after,* i.e.,
the gods' subsequent.   292. *other elements,* i.e., earth and water.   293. *baser,* mortal.
296. *aspic,* asp, a small poisonous snake.

The gods themselves do weep!
CLEO.   This proves me base:
　If she first meet the curlèd Antony,
　He'll make demand of her, and spend that kiss   305
　Which is my heaven to have. Come, thou mortal wretch,

[*To an asp, which she applies to her breast.*]

　With thy sharp teeth this knot intrinsicate
　Of life at once untie: poor venomous fool,
　Be angry, and dispatch. O, couldst thou speak,
　That I might hear thee call great Cæsar ass   310
　Unpolicied!
CHAR.   O eastern star!
CLEO.   Peace, peace!
　Dost thou not see my baby at my breast,
　That sucks the nurse asleep?
CHAR.   O, break! O, break!
CLEO. As sweet as balm, as soft as air, as gentle,—
　O Antony!—Nay, I will take thee too: 315

[*Applying another asp to her arm.*]

　What should I stay—

[*Dies.*]

CHAR. In this vile world? So, fare thee well.
　Now boast thee, death, in thy possession lies
　A lass unparallel'd. Downy windows, close;
　And golden Phœbus never be beheld   320
　Of eyes again so royal! Your crown's awry;
　I'll mend it, and then play.

[*Enter the* GUARD, *rushing in.*]

FIRST GUARD. Where is the queen?
CHAR.   Speak softly, wake her not.
FIRST GUARD. Cæsar hath sent—
CHAR.   Too slow a messenger.

[*Applies an asp.*]

　O, come apace, dispatch! I partly feel thee.   325
FIRST GUARD. Approach, ho! All's not well: Cæsar's beguiled.

305. *He'll . . . her*, He'll ask her about me.   306. *mortal*, deadly.   307. *intrinsicate*, intricate.   311. *Unpolicied*, without political cunning.   316. *What*, why.   322. *mend*, fix, straighten.   325. *apace*, quickly.

SEC. GUARD. There's Dolabella sent from Cæsar; call him.
FIRST GUARD. What work is here! Charmian, is this well done?
CHAR. It is well done, and fitting for a princess
330   Descended of so many royal kings.
Ah, soldier!

[*Dies.*]

[*Re-enter* DOLABELLA.]

DOL. How goes it here?
SEC. GUARD.   All dead.
DOL.   Cæsar, thy thoughts
Touch their effects in this: thyself art coming
To see perform'd the dreaded act which thou
335   So sought'st to hinder.

[*Within* "A way there, a way for Cæsar!"]

[*Re-enter* CÆSAR *and all his train, marching.*]

DOL. O sir, you are too sure an augurer;
That you did fear is done.
338 CÆS.   Bravest at the last,
She levell'd at our purposes, and, being royal,
Took her own way. The manner of their deaths?
I do not see them bleed.
DOL.   Who was last with them?
FIRST GUARD. A simple countryman, that brought her figs:
This was his basket.
CÆS.   Poison'd, then.
FIRST GUARD.   O Cæsar,
This Charmian lived but now; she stood and spake:
345   I found her trimming up the diadem
On her dead mistress; tremblingly she stood
And on the sudden dropp'd.
CÆS.   O noble weakness!
If they had swallow'd poison, 'twould appear
By external swelling: but she looks like sleep,
350   As she would catch another Antony
In her strong toil of grace.
DOL.   Here, on her breast,
There is a vent of blood and something blown:

---

333. *Touch their effects*, i.e., your fears are realized.   338. *Bravest*, finest.   339. *levell'd at*, aimed at (and hit).   345. *trimming up*, straightening.   351. *toil of grace*, snare of charm.   352. *vent*, discharge; *something blown*, a somewhat swollen (spot).

The like is on her arm.

FIRST GUARD. This is an aspic's trail: and these fig-leaves
 Have slime upon them, such as the aspic leaves   355
 Upon the caves of Nile.

CÆS.   Most probable
 That so she died; for her physician tells me
 She hath pursued conclusions infinite
 Of easy ways to die. Take up her bed;
 And bear her women from the monument: 360
 She shall be buried by her Antony:
 No grave upon the earth shall clip in it
 A pair so famous. High events as these
 Strike those that make them: and their story is
 No less in pity than his glory which   365
 Brought them to be lamented. Our army shall
 In solemn show attend this funeral;
 And then to Rome. Come, Dolabella, see
 High order in this great solemnity.

[*Exeunt.*]

358. *pursued conclusions*, tried experiments. 362. *clip*, clasp. 365. *his glory which*, the glory of him who. 366. *Brought . . . lamented*, brought such lamentable events to pass. 368–9. *see . . . solemnity*, see that this solemn rite is observed in a stately manner.

Henrik Ibsen 1828–1906

Ghosts

A FAMILY DRAMA IN THREE ACTS*

CHARACTERS

MRS. HELEN ALVING, *widow of Cap-*
tain Alving, late Chamberlain to
the King.
OSWALD ALVING, *her son, a painter.*
PASTOR MANDERS.
JACOB ENGSTRAND, *a carpenter.*

REGINA ENGSTRAND, *Mrs. Alving's*
maid.
The action takes place at MRS. AL-
VING'S *country house, beside one of the*
large fjords in Western Norway.

ACT I

[*A spacious garden-room, with one door to the left, and two doors to the*
right. In the middle of the room a round table, with chairs about it. On
the table lie books, periodicals, and newspapers. In the foreground to the
left a window, and by it a small sofa, with a work table in front of it. In
the background, the room is continued into a somewhat narrower con-
servatory, the walls of which are formed by large panes of glass. In the
right-hand wall of the conservatory is a door leading down into the garden.
Through the glass wall a gloomy fjord-landscape is faintly visible, veiled
by steady rain.]

[ENGSTRAND, *the carpenter, stands by the garden door. His left leg is some-*
what bent; he has a clump of wood under the sole of his boot. REGINA,
with an empty garden syringe in her hand, hinders him from advancing.]

REGINA [*in a low voice*]. What do you want? Stop where you are. You're
positively dripping.
ENGSTRAND. It's the Lord's own rain, my girl.
REGINA. It's the devil's rain, *I* say.

* Translated by William Archer.

412

ENGSTRAND. Lord, how you talk, Regina. [*Limps a step or two forward into the room.*] It's just this as I wanted to say—

REGINA. Don't clatter so with that foot of yours, I tell you! the young master's asleep upstairs.

ENGSTRAND. Asleep? In the middle of the day?

REGINA. It's no business of yours.

ENGSTRAND. I was out on the loose last night—

REGINA. I can quite believe that.

ENGSTRAND. Yes, we're weak vessels, we poor mortals, my girl—

REGINA. So it seems.

ENGSTRAND. —and temptations are manifold in this world, you see. But all the same, I was hard at work, God knows, at half-past five this morning.

REGINA. Very well; only be off now. I won't stop here and have *rendez-vous's* with you.

ENGSTRAND. What do you say you won't have?

REGINA. I won't have any one find you here; so just you go about your business.

ENGSTRAND [*advances a step or two*]. Blest if I go before I've had a talk with you. This afternoon I shall have finished my work at the school-house, and then I shall take to-night's boat and be off home to the town.

REGINA [*mutters*]. Pleasant journey to you!

ENGSTRAND. Thank you, my child. To-morrow the Orphanage is to be opened, and then there'll be fine doings, no doubt, and plenty of intoxi-cating drink going, you know. And nobody shall say of Jacob Engstrand that he can't keep out of temptation's way.

REGINA. Oh!

ENGSTRAND. You see, there's to be heaps of grand folks here to-morrow. Pastor Manders is expected from town, too.

REGINA. He's coming to-day.

ENGSTRAND. There, you see! And I should be cursedly sorry if he found out anything against me, don't you understand?

REGINA. Oho! is that your game?

ENGSTRAND. Is what my game?

REGINA [*looking hard at him*]. What are you going to fool Pastor Man-ders into doing, this time?

ENGSTRAND. Sh! sh! Are you crazy? Do *I* want to fool Pastor Manders? Oh no! Pastor Manders has been far too good a friend to me for that. But I just wanted to say, you know—that I mean to be off home again to-night.

REGINA. The sooner the better, say I.

ENGSTRAND. Yes, but I want you with me, Regina.

REGINA [*open-mouthed*]. You want me—? What are you talking about?

ENGSTRAND. I want you to come home with me, I say.

REGINA [*scornfully*]. Never in this world shall you get me home with you.

ENGSTRAND. Oh, we'll see about that.

REGINA. Yes, you may be sure we'll see about it! Me, that have been brought up by a lady like Mrs. Alving! Me, that am treated almost as a daughter here! Is it me you want to go home with you?—to a house like yours? For shame!

ENGSTRAND. What the devil do you mean? Do you set yourself up against your father, you hussy?

REGINA [mutters without looking at him]. You've said often eough I was no concern of yours.

ENGSTRAND. Pooh! Why should you bother about that—

REGINA. Haven't you many a time sworn at me and called me a—? Fi donc!

ENGSTRAND. Curse me, now, if ever I used such an ugly word.

REGINA. Oh, I remember very well what word you used.

ENGSTRAND. Well, but that was only when I was a bit on, don't you know? Temptations are manifold in this world, Regina.

REGINA. Ugh!

ENGSTRAND. And besides, it was when your mother was that aggravating— I had to find something to twit her with, my child. She was always setting up for a fine lady. [Mimics.] "Let me go, Engstrand; let me be. Remember I was three years in Chamberlain Alving's family at Rosenvold." [Laughs.] Mercy on us! She could never forget that the Captain was made a Chamberlain while she was in service here.

REGINA. Poor mother! you very soon tormented her into her grave.

ENGSTRAND [with a twist of his shoulders]. Oh, of course! I'm to have the blame for everything.

REGINA [turns away; half aloud]. Ugh—! And that leg too!

ENGSTRAND. What do you say, my child?

REGINA. Pied de mouton.

ENGSTRAND. Is that English, eh?

REGINA. Yes.

ENGSTRAND. Ay, ay; you've picked up some learning out here; and that may come in useful now, Regina.

REGINA [after a short silence]. What do you want with me in town?

ENGSTRAND. Can you ask what a father wants with his only child? A'n't I a lonely, forlorn widower?

REGINA. Oh, don't try on any nonsense like that with me! Why do you want me?

ENGSTRAND. Well, let me tell you, I've been thinking of setting up in a new line of business.

REGINA [contemptuously]. You've tried that often enough, and much good you've done with it.

ENGSTRAND. Yes, but this time you shall see, Regina! Devil take me—

REGINA [*stamps*]. Stop your swearing!

ENGSTRAND. Hush, hush; you're right enough there, my girl. What I wanted to say was just this—I've laid by a very tidy pile from this Orphanage job.

REGINA. Have you? That's a good thing for you.

ENGSTRAND. What can a man spend his ha'pence on here in this country hole?

REGINA. Well, what then?

ENGSTRAND. Why, you see, I thought of putting the money into some paying speculation. I thought of a sort of a sailor's tavern—

REGINA. Pah!

ENGSTRAND. A regular high-class affair, of course; not any sort of pig-sty for common sailors. No! damn it! it would be for captains and mates, and—and—regular swells, you know.

REGINA. And I was to—?

ENGSTRAND. You were to help, to be sure. Only for the look of the thing, you understand. Devil a bit of hard work shall you have, my girl. You shall do exactly what you like.

REGINA. Oh, indeed!

ENGSTRAND. But there must be a petticoat in the house; that's as clear as daylight. For I want to have it a bit lively-like in the evenings, with singing and dancing, and so on. You must remember they're weary wanderers on the ocean of life. [*Nearer.*] Now don't be a fool and stand in your own light, Regina. What's to become of you out here? Your mistress has given you a lot of learning; but what good is that to you? You're to look after the children at the new Orphanage, I hear. Is that the sort of thing for you, eh? Are you so dead set on wearing your life out for a pack of dirty brats?

REGINA. No; if things go as I want them to— Well there's no saying—there's no saying.

ENGSTRAND. What do you mean by "there's no saying"?

REGINA. Never you mind.—How much money have you saved?

ENGSTRAND. What with one thing and another, a matter of seven or eight hundred crowns.

REGINA. That's not so bad.

ENGSTRAND. It's enough to make a start with, my girl.

REGINA. Aren't you thinking of giving me any?

ENGSTRAND. No, I'm blest if I am!

REGINA. Not even of sending me a scrap of stuff for a new dress?

ENGSTRAND. Come to town with me, my lass, and you'll soon get dresses enough.

REGINA. Pooh! I can do that on my own account, if I want to.

ENGSTRAND. No, a father's guiding hand is what you want, Regina. Now,

I've got my eye on a capital house in Little Harbour Street. They don't want much ready-money; and it could be a sort of a Sailors' Home, you know.

REGINA. But I will not live with you! I have nothing whatever to do with you. Be off!

ENGSTRAND. You wouldn't stop long with me, my girl. No such luck! If you knew how to play your cards, such a fine figure of a girl as you've grown in the last year or two—

REGINA. Well?

ENGSTRAND. You'd soon get hold of some mate—or maybe even a captain—

REGINA. I won't marry any one of that sort. Sailors have no *savoir vivre*.

ENGSTRAND. What's that they haven't got?

REGINA. I know what sailors are, I tell you. They're not the sort of people to marry.

ENGSTRAND. Then never mind about marrying them. You can make it pay all the same. [*More confidentially.*] He—the Englishman—the man with the yacht—he came down with three hundred dollars, he did; and she wasn't a bit handsomer than you.

REGINA [*making for him*]. Out you go!

ENGSTRAND [*falling back*]. Come, come! You're not going to hit me, I hope.

REGINA. Yes, if you begin talking about mother I shall hit you. Get away with you, I say! [*Drives him back towards the garden door.*] And don't slam the doors. Young Mr. Alving—

ENGSTRAND. He's asleep; I know. You're mighty taken up about young Mr. Alving— [*More softly.*] Oho! you don't mean to say it's him as—?

REGINA. Be off this minute! You're crazy, I tell you! No, not that way. There comes Pastor Manders. Down the kitchen stairs with you.

ENGSTRAND [*towards the right*]. Yes, yes, I'm going. But just you talk to him as is coming there. He's the man to tell you what a child owes its father. For I am your father all the same, you know. I can prove it from the church register.

[*He goes out through the second door to the right, which* REGINA *has opened, and closes again after him.* REGINA *glances hastily at herself in the mirror, dusts herself with her pocket handkerchief, and settles her necktie; then she busies herself with the flowers.*]

[PASTOR MANDERS, *wearing an overcoat, carrying an umbrella, and with a small travelling-bag on a strap over his shoulder, comes through the garden door into the conservatory.*]

MANDERS. Good-morning, Miss Engstrand.

REGINA [*turning round, surprised and pleased*]. No, really! Good-morning, Pastor Manders. Is the steamer in already?

MANDERS. It is just in. [*Enters the sitting-room.*] Terrible weather we have been having lately.

REGINA [*follows him*]. It's such blessed weather for the country, sir.

MANDERS. No doubt; you are quite right. We townspeople give too little thought to that. [*He begins to take off his overcoat.*]

REGINA. Oh, mayn't I help you?—There! Why, how wet it is! I'll just hang it up in the hall. And your umbrella, too—I'll open it and let it dry.

[*She goes out with the things through the second door on the right.* PASTOR MANDERS *takes off his travelling-bag and lays it and his hat on a chair. Meanwhile* REGINA *comes in again.*]

MANDERS. Ah, it's a comfort to get safe under cover. I hope everything is going on well here?

REGINA. Yes, thank you, sir.

MANDERS. You have your hands full, I suppose, in preparation for to-morrow?

REGINA. Yes, there's plenty to do, of course.

MANDERS. And Mrs. Alving is at home, I trust?

REGINA. Oh dear, yes. She's just upstairs, looking after the young master's chocolate.

MANDERS. Yes, by-the-bye—I heard down at the pier that Oswald had arrived.

REGINA. Yes, he came the day before yesterday. We didn't expect him before to-day.

MANDERS. Quite strong and well, I hope?

REGINA. Yes, thank you, quite; but dreadfully tired with the journey. He has made one rush right through from Paris—the whole way in one train, I believe. He's sleeping a little now, I think; so perhaps we'd better talk a little quietly.

MANDERS. Sh!—as quietly as you please.

REGINA [*arranging an arm-chair beside the table*]. Now, do sit down, Pastor Manders, and make yourself comfortable. [*He sits down; she places a footstool under his feet.*] There! Are you comfortable now, sir?

MANDERS. Thanks, thanks, extremely so. [*Looks at her.*] Do you know, Miss Engstrand, I positively believe you have grown since I last saw you.

REGINA. Do you think so, sir? Mrs. Alving says I've filled out too.

MANDERS. Filled out? Well, perhaps a little; just enough.

[*Short pause.*]

REGINA. Shall I tell Mrs. Alving you are here?

MANDERS. Thanks, thanks, there is no hurry, my dear child.—By-the-bye, Regina, my good girl, tell me: how is your father getting on out here?

REGINA. Oh, thank you, sir, he's getting on well enough.

MANDERS. He called upon me last time he was in town.

REGINA. Did he, indeed? He's always so glad of a chance of talking to you, sir.

MANDERS. And you often look in upon him at his work, I daresay?

REGINA. I? Oh, of course, when I have time, I—

MANDERS. Your father is not a man of strong character, Miss Engstrand. He stands terribly in need of a guiding hand.

REGINA. Oh, yes; I daresay he does.

MANDERS. He requires some one near him whom he cares for, and whose judgment he respects. He frankly admitted as much when he last came to see me.

REGINA. Yes, he mentioned something of the sort to me. But I don't know whether Mrs. Alving can spare me; especially now that we've got the new Orphanage to attend to. And then I should be so sorry to leave Mrs. Alving; she has always been so kind to me.

MANDERS. But a daughter's duty, my good girl— Of course, we should first have to get your mistress's consent.

REGINA. But I don't know whether it would be quite proper for me, at my age, to keep house for a single man.

MANDERS. What! My dear Miss Engstrand! When the man is your own father!

REGINA. Yes, that may be; but all the same— Now, if it were in a thoroughly nice house, and with a real gentleman—

MANDERS. Why, my dear Regina—

REGINA. —one I could love and respect, and be a daughter to—

MANDERS. Yes, but my dear, good child—

REGINA. Then I should be glad to go to town. It's very lonely out here; you know yourself, sir, what it is to be alone in the world. And I can assure you I'm both quick and willing. Don't you know of any such place for me, sir?

MANDERS. I? No, certainly not.

REGINA. But, dear, dear sir, do remember me if—

MANDERS [rising]. Yes, yes, certainly, Miss Engstrand.

REGINA. For if I—

MANDERS. Will you be so good as to tell your mistress I am here?

REGINA. I will, at once, sir. [She goes out to the left.]

MANDERS [paces the room two or three times, stands a moment in the background with his hands behind his back, and looks out over the garden. Then he returns to the table, takes up a book, and looks at the title-page; starts, and looks at several books]. Ha—indeed!

[MRS. ALVING enters by the door on the left; she is followed by REGINA, who immediately goes out by the first door on the right.]

MRS. ALVING [*holds out her hand*]. Welcome, my dear Pastor.

MANDERS. How do you do, Mrs. Alving? Here I am as I promised.

MRS. ALVING. Always punctual to the minute.

MANDERS. You may believe it was not easy for me to get away. With all the Boards and Committees I belong to—

MRS. ALVING. That makes it all the kinder of you to come so early. Now we can get through our business before dinner. But where is your portmanteau?

MANDERS [*quickly*]. I left it down at the inn. I shall sleep there to-night.

MRS. ALVING [*suppressing a smile*]. Are you really not to be persuaded, even now, to pass the night under my roof?

MANDERS. No, no, Mrs. Alving; many thanks. I shall stay at the inn, as usual. It is so conveniently near the landing-stage.

MRS. ALVING. Well, you must have your own way. But I really should have thought we two old people—

MANDERS. Now you are making fun of me. Ah, you're naturally in great spirits to-day—what with to-morrow's festival and Oswald's return.

MRS. ALVING. Yes; you can think what a delight it is to me! It's more than two years since he was home last. And now he has promised to stay with me all the winter.

MANDERS. Has he really? That is very nice and dutiful of him. For I can well believe that life in Rome and Paris has very different attractions from any we can offer here.

MRS. ALVING. Ah, but here he has his mother, you see. My own darling boy—he hasn't forgotten his old mother!

MANDERS. It would be grievous indeed, if absence and absorption in art and that sort of thing were to blunt his natural feelings.

MRS. ALVING. Yes, you may well say so. But there's nothing of that sort to fear with him. I'm quite curious to see whether you know him again. He'll be down presently; he's upstairs just now, resting a little on the sofa. But do sit down, my dear Pastor.

MANDERS. Thank you. Are you quite at liberty—?

MRS. ALVING. Certainly. [*She sits by the table.*]

MANDERS. Very well. Then let me show you— [*He goes to the chair where his travelling-bag lies, takes out a packet of papers, sits down on the opposite side of the table, and tries to find a clear space for the papers.*] Now, to begin with, here is— [*Breaking off.*] Tell me, Mrs. Alving, how do these books come to be here?

MRS. ALVING. These books? They are books I am reading.

MANDERS. Do you read this sort of literature?

MRS. ALVING. Certainly I do.

MANDERS. Do you feel better or happier for such reading?

MRS. ALVING. I feel, so to speak, more secure.

MANDERS. That is strange. How do you mean?

MRS. ALVING. Well, I seem to find explanation and confirmation of all sorts of things I myself have been thinking. For that is the wonderful part of it, Pastor Manders—there is really nothing new in these books, nothing but what most people think and believe. Only most people either don't formulate it to themselves, or else keep quiet about it.

MANDERS. Great heavens! Do you really believe that most people—?

MRS. ALVING. I do, indeed.

MANDERS. But surely not in this country? Not here among us?

MRS. ALVING. Yes, certainly; here as elsewhere.

MANDERS. Well, I really must say—!

MRS. ALVING. For the rest, what do you object to in these books?

MANDERS. Object to in them? You surely do not suppose that I have nothing better to do than to study such publications as these?

MRS. ALVING. That is to say, you know nothing of what you are condemning?

MANDERS. I have read enough about these writings to disapprove of them.

MRS. ALVING. Yes; but your own judgment—

MANDERS. My dear Mrs. Alving, there are many occasions in life when one must rely upon others. Things are so ordered in this world; and it is well that they are. Otherwise, what would become of society?

MRS. ALVING. Well, well, I daresay you're right there.

MANDERS. Besides, I of course do not deny that there may be much that is attractive in such books. Nor can I blame you for wishing to keep up with the intellectual movements that are said to be going on in the great world—where you have let your son pass so much of his life. But—

MRS. ALVING. But?

MANDERS [lowering his voice]. But one should not talk about it, Mrs. Alving. One is certainly not bound to account to everybody for what one reads and thinks within one's own four walls.

MRS. ALVING. Of course not; I quite agree with you.

MANDERS. Only think, now, how you are bound to consider the interests of this Orphanage, which you decided on founding at a time when—if I understand you rightly—you thought very differently on spiritual matters.

MRS. ALVING. Oh, yes; I quite admit that. But it was about the Orphanage—

MANDERS. It was about the Orphanage we were to speak; yes. All I say is: prudence, my dear lady! And now let us get to business. [Opens the packet, and takes out a number of papers.] Do you see these?

MRS. ALVING. The documents?

MANDERS. All—and in perfect order. I can tell you it was hard work to get them in time. I had to put on strong pressure. The authorities are almost morbidly scrupulous when there is any decisive step to be taken. But here they are at last. [*Looks through the bundle.*] See! here is the formal deed of gift of the parcel of ground known as Solvik in the Manor of Rosenvold, with all the newly constructed buildings, schoolrooms, master's house, and chapel. And here is the legal fiat for the endowment and for the Bye-laws of the Institution. Will you look at them? [*Reads.*] "Bye-laws for the Children's Home to be known as 'Captain Alving's Foundation.'"

MRS. ALVING [*looks long at the paper*]. So there it is.

MANDERS. I have chosen the designation "Captain" rather than "Chamberlain." "Captain" looks less pretentious.

MRS. ALVING. Oh, yes; just as you think best.

MANDERS. And here you have the Bank Account of the capital lying at interest to cover the current expenses of the Orphanage.

MRS. ALVING. Thank you; but please keep it—it will be more convenient.

MANDERS. With pleasure. I think we will leave the money in the Bank for the present. The interest is certainly not what we could wish—four per cent and six months' notice of withdrawal. If a good mortgage could be found later on—of course it must be a first mortgage and an unimpeachable security—then we could consider the matter.

MRS. ALVING. Certainly, my dear Pastor Manders. You are the best judge in these things.

MANDERS. I will keep my eyes open at any rate.—But now there is one thing more which I have several times been intending to ask you.

MRS. ALVING. And what is that?

MANDERS. Shall the Orphange buildings be insured or not?

MRS. ALVING. Of course they must be insured.

MANDERS. Well, wait a moment, Mrs. Alving. Let us look into the matter a little more closely.

MRS. ALVING. I have everything insured; buildings and movables and stock and crops.

MANDERS. Of course you have—on your own estate. And so have I—of course. But here, you see, it is quite another matter. The Orphanage is to be consecrated, as it were, to a higher purpose.

MRS. ALVING. Yes, but that's no reason—

MANDERS. For my own part, I should certainly not see the smallest impropriety in guarding against all contingencies—

MRS. ALVING. No, I should think not.

MANDERS. But what is the general feeling in the neighbourhood? You, of course, know better than I.

MRS. ALVING. Well—the general feeling—

MANDERS. Is there any considerable number of people—really responsible people—who might be scandalised?

Mrs. Alving. What do you mean by "really responsible people"?

Manders. Well, I mean people in such independent and influential positions that one cannot help attaching some weight to their opinions.

Mrs. Alving. There are several people of that sort here, who would very likely be shocked if—

Manders. There, you see! In town we have many such people. Think of all my colleague's adherents! People would be only too ready to interpret our action as a sign that neither you nor I had the right faith in a Higher Providence.

Mrs. Alving. But for your own part, my dear Pastor, you can at least tell yourself that—

Manders. Yes, I know—I know; my conscience would be quite easy, that is true enough. But nevertheless we should not escape grave misinterpretation; and that might very likely react unfavourably upon the Orphanage.

Mrs. Alving. Well, in that case—

Manders. Nor can I entirely lose sight of the difficult—may even say painful—position in which I might perhaps be placed. In the leading circles of the town, people take a lively interest in this Orphanage. It is, of course, founded partly for the benefit of the town, as well; and it is to be hoped it will, to a considerable extent, result in lightening our Poor Rates. Now, as I have been your adviser, and have had the business arrangements in my hands, I cannot but fear that I may have to bear the brunt of fanaticism—

Mrs. Alving. Oh, you mustn't run the risk of that.

Manders. To say nothing of the attacks that would assuredly be made upon me in certain papers and periodicals, which—

Mrs. Alving. Enough, my dear Pastor Manders. That consideration is quite decisive.

Manders. Then you do not wish the Orphanage to be insured?

Mrs. Alving. No. We will let it alone.

Manders [leaning back in his chair]. But if, now, a disaster were to happen? One can never tell— Should you be able to make good the damage?

Mrs. Alving. No; I tell you plainly I should do nothing of the kind.

Manders. Then I must tell you, Mrs. Alving—we are taking no small responsibility upon ourselves.

Mrs. Alving. Do you think we can otherwise?

Manders. No, that is just the point; we really cannot do otherwise. We ought not to expose ourselves to misinterpretation; and we have no right whatever to give offence to the weaker brethren.

Mrs. Alving. You, as a clergyman, certainly should not.

Manders. I really think, too, we may trust that such an institution has fortune on its side; in fact, that it stands under a special providence.

MRS. ALVING. Let us hope so, Pastor Manders.

MANDERS. Then we will let it take its chance?

MRS. ALVING. Yes, certainly.

MANDERS. Very well. So be it. [*Makes a note.*] Then—no insurance.

MRS. ALVING. It's odd that you should just happen to mention the matter to-day—

MANDERS. I have often thought of asking you about it—

MRS. ALVING. —for we very nearly had a fire down there yesterday.

MANDERS. You don't say so!

MRS. ALVING. Oh, it was a trifling matter. A heap of shavings had caught fire in the carpenter's workshop.

MANDERS. Where Engstrand works?

MRS. ALVING. Yes. They say he's often very careless with matches.

MANDERS. He has so much on his mind, that man—so many things to fight against. Thank God, he is now striving to lead a decent life, I hear.

MRS. ALVING. Indeed! Who says so?

MANDERS. He himself assures me of it. And he is certainly a capital workman.

MRS. ALVING. Oh, yes; so long as he's sober—

MANDERS. Ah, that melancholy weakness? But he is often driven to it by his injured leg, he says. Last time he was in town I was really touched by him. He came and thanked me so warmly for having got him work here, so that he might be near Regina.

MRS. ALVING. He doesn't see much of her.

MANDERS. Oh, yes; he has a talk with her every day. He told me so himself.

MRS. ALVING. Well, it may be so.

MANDERS. He feels so acutely that he needs some one to keep a firm hold on him when temptation comes. That is what I cannot help liking about Jacob Engstrand: he comes to you so helplessly, accusing himself and confessing his own weakness. The last time he was talking to me— Believe me, Mrs. Alving, supposing it were a real necessity for him to have Regina home again—

MRS. ALVING [*rising hastily*]. Regina!

MANDERS. —you must not set yourself against it.

MRS. ALVING. Indeed I shall set my self against it. And besides—Regina is to have a position in the Orphanage.

MANDERS. But, after all, remember he is her father—

MRS. ALVING. Oh, I know very well what sort of a father he has been to her. No! She shall never go to him with my goodwill.

MANDERS [*rising*]. My dear lady, don't take the matter so warmly. You sadly misjudge poor Engstrand. You seem to be quite terrified—

MRS. ALVING [*more quietly*]. It makes no difference. I have taken Regina into my houses, and there she shall stay. [*Listen.*] Hush, my dear Mr. Manders; say no more about it. [*Her face lights up with gladness.*] Listen! there is Oswald coming downstairs. Now we'll think of no one but him.

[Oswald Alving, *in a light overcoat, hat in hand, and smoking a large meerschaum, enters by the door on the left; he stops in the doorway.*]

Oswald. Oh, I beg your pardon; I thought you were in the study. [*Comes forward.*] Good-morning, Pastor Manders.

Manders [*staring*]. Ah— How strange—!

Mrs. Alving. Well now, what do you think of him, Mr. Manders?

Manders. I—I—can it really be—?

Oswald. Yes, it's really the Prodigal Son, sir.

Manders [*protesting*]. My dear young friend—

Oswald. Well, then, the Lost Sheep Found.

Mrs. Alving. Oswald is thinking of the time when you were so much opposed to his becoming a painter.

Manders. To our human eyes many a step seems dubious, which afterwards proves— [*Wrings his hand.*] But first of all, welcome, welcome home! Do not think, my dear Oswald—I suppose I may call you by your Christian name?

Oswald. What else should you call me?

Manders. Very good. What I wanted to say was this, my dear Oswald— you must not think that I utterly condemn the artist's calling. I have no doubt there are many who can keep their inner self unharmed in that profession, as in any other.

Oswald. Let us hope so.

Mrs. Alving [*beaming with delight*]. I know one who has kept both his inner and his outer self unharmed. Just look at him, Mr. Manders.

Oswald [*moves restlessly about the room*]. Yes, yes, my dear mother; let's say no more about it.

Manders. Why, certainly—that is undeniable. And you have begun to make a name for yourself already. The newspapers have often spoken of you, most favourably. Just lately, by-the-bye, I fancy I haven't seen your name quite so often.

Oswald [*up in the conservatory*]. I haven't been able to paint so much lately.

Mrs. Alving. Even a painter needs a little rest now and then.

Manders. No doubt, no doubt. And meanwhile he can be preparing himself and mustering his forces for some great work.

Oswald. Yes.—Mother, will dinner soon be ready?

Mrs. Alving. In less than half an hour. He has a capital appetite, thank God.

MANDERS. And a taste for tobacco, too.

OSWALD. I found my father's pipe in my room—

MANDERS. Aha—then that accounts for it!

MRS. ALVING. For what?

MANDERS. When Oswald appeared there, in the doorway, with the pipe in his mouth, I could have sworn I saw his father, large as life.

OSWALD. No, really?

MRS. ALVING. Oh, how can you say so? Oswald takes after me.

MANDERS. Yes, but there is an expression about the corners of the mouth —something about the lips—that reminds one exactly of Alving: at any rate, now that he is smoking.

MRS. ALVING. Not in the least. Oswald has rather a clerical curve about his mouth, I think.

MANDERS. Yes, yes; some of my colleagues have much the same expression.

MRS. ALVING. But put your pipe away, my dear boy; I won't have smoking in here.

OSWALD [*does so*]. By all means. I only wanted to try it; for I once smoked it when I was a child.

MRS. ALVING. You?

OSWALD. Yes. I was quite small at the time. I recollect I came up to father's room one evening when he was in great spirits.

MRS. ALVING. Oh, you can't recollect anything of those times.

OSWALD. Yes, I recollect it distinctly. He took me on his knee, and gave me the pipe. "Smoke, boy," he said; "smoke away, boy!" And I smoked as hard as I could, until I felt I was growing quite pale, and the perspiration stood in great drops on my forehead. Then he burst out laughing heartily—

MANDERS. That was most extraordinary.

MRS. ALVING. My dear friend, it's only something Oswald has dreamt.

OSWALD. No, mother, I assure you I didn't dream it. For—don't you remember this?—you came and carried me out into the nursery. Then I was sick, and I saw that you were crying.—Did father often play such practical jokes?

MANDERS. In his youth he overflowed with the joy of life—

OSWALD. And yet he managed to do so much in the world; so much that was good and useful; although he died so early.

MANDERS. Yes, you have inherited the name of an energetic and admirable man, my dear Oswald Alving. No doubt it will be an incentive to you—

OSWALD. It ought to, indeed.

MANDERS. It was good of you to come home for the ceremony in his honour.

OSWALD. I could do no less for my father.

MRS. ALVING. And I am to keep him so long! That is the best of all.

Manders. You are going to pass the winter at home, I hear.

Oswald. My stay is indefinite, sir.—But, ah! it is good to be at home!

Mrs. Alving [*beaming*]. Yes, isn't it, dear?

Manders [*looking sympathetically at him*]. You went out into the world early, my dear Oswald.

Oswald. I did. I sometimes wonder whether it wasn't too early.

Mrs. Alving. Oh, not at all. A healthy lad is all the better for it; especially when he's an only child. He oughtn't to hang on at home with his mother and father, and get spoilt.

Manders. That is a very disputable point, Mrs. Alving. A child's proper place is, and must be, the home of his fathers.

Oswald. There I quite agree with you, Pastor Manders.

Manders. Only look at your own son—there is no reason why we should not say it in his presence—what has the consequence been for him? He is six or seven and twenty, and has never had the opportunity of learning what a well-ordered home really is.

Oswald. I beg your pardon, Pastor; there you're quite mistaken.

Manders. Indeed? I thought you had lived almost exclusively in artistic circles.

Oswald. So I have.

Manders. And chiefly among the younger artists?

Oswald. Yes, certainly.

Manders. But I thought few of those young fellows could afford to set up house and support a family.

Oswald. There are many who cannot afford to marry, sir.

Manders. Yes, that is just what I say.

Oswald. But they may have a home for all that. And several of them have, as a matter of fact; and very pleasant, well-ordered homes they are, too.

[Mrs. Alving *follows with breathless interest; nods, but says nothing.*]

Manders. But I'm not talking of bachelors' quarters. By a "home" I understand the home of a family, where a man lives with his wife and children.

Oswald. Yes; or with his children and his children's mother.

Manders [*starts; clasps his hands.*]. But, good heavens—

Oswald. Well?

Manders. Lives with—his children's mother!

Oswald. Yes. Would you have him turn his children's mother out of doors?

Manders. Then it is illicit relations you are talking of! Irregular marriages, as people call them!

Oswald. I have never noticed anything particularly irregular about the life these people lead.

MANDERS. But how is it possible that a—a young man or young woman with any decency of feeling can endure to live in that way?—in the eyes of all the world!

OSWALD. What are they to do? A poor young artist—a poor girl—marriage costs a great deal. What are they to do?

MANDERS. What are they to do? Let me tell you, Mr. Alving, what they ought to do. They ought to exercise self-restraint from the first; that is what they ought to do.

OSWALD. That doctrine will scarcely go down with warm-blooded young people who love each other.

MRS. ALVING. No, scarcely!

MANDERS [continuing]. How can the authorities tolerate such things! Allow them to go on in the light of day! [Confronting MRS. ALVING.] Had I not cause to be deeply concerned about your son? In circles where open immorality prevails, and has even a sort of recognised position—!

OSWALD. Let me tell you, sir, that I have been in the habit of spending nearly all my Sundays in one or two such irregular homes—

MANDERS. Sunday of all days!

OSWALD. Isn't that the day to enjoy one's self? Well, never have I heard an offensive word, and still less have I witnessed anything that could be called immoral. No; do you know when and where I have come across immorality in artistic circles?

MANDERS. No, thank heaven, I don't!

OSWALD. Well, then, allow me to inform you. I have met with it when one or other of our pattern husbands and fathers has come to Paris to have a look round on his own account, and has done the artists the honour of visiting their humble haunts. They knew what was what. These gentlemen could tell us all about places and things we had never dreamt of.

MANDERS. What! Do you mean to say that respectable men from home here would—?

OSWALD. Have you never heard these respectable men, when they got home again, talking about the way in which immorality runs rampant abroad?

MANDERS. Yes, no doubt—

MRS. ALVING. I have too.

OSWALD. Well, you may take their word for it. They know what they are talking about! [Presses his hands to his head.] Oh! that that great, free, glorious life out there should be defiled in such a way!

MRS. ALVING. You mustn't get excited, Oswald. It's not good for you.

OSWALD. Yes; you're quite right, mother. It's bad for me, I know. You see, I'm wretchedly worn out. I shall go for a little turn before dinner. Excuse me, Pastor: I know you can't take my point of view; but I couldn't help speaking out. [*He goes out by the second door to the right.*]

Mrs. Alving. My poor boy!

Manders. You may well say so. Then this is what he has come to!

[Mrs. Alving *looks at him silently.*]

Manders [*walking up and down*]. He called himself the Prodigal Son. Alas! alas!

[Mrs. Alving *continues looking at him.*]

Manders. And what do you say to all this?

Mrs. Alving. I say that Oswald was right in every word.

Manders [*stands still*]. Right? Right! In such principles?

Mrs. Alving. Here, in my loneliness, I have come to the same way of thinking, Pastor Manders. But I have never dared to say anything. Well! now my boy shall speak for me.

Manders. You are greatly to be pitied, Mrs. Alving. But now I must speak seriously to you. And now it is no longer your business manager and adviser, your own and your husband's early friend, who stands before you. It is the priest—the priest who stood before you in the moment of your life when you had gone farthest astray.

Mrs. Alving. And what has the priest to say to me?

Manders. I will first stir up your memory a little. The moment is well chosen. To-morrow will be the tenth anniversary of your husband's death. Tomorrow the memorial in his honour will be unveiled. To-morrow I shall have to speak to the whole assembled multitude. But to-day I will speak to you alone.

Mrs. Alving. Very well, Pastor Manders. Speak.

Manders. Do you remember that after less than a year of married life you stood on the verge of an abyss? That you forsook your house and home? That you fled from your husband? Yes, Mrs. Alving—fled, fled, and refused to return to him, however much he begged and prayed you?

Mrs. Alving. Have you forgotten how infinitely miserable I was in that first year?

Manders. It is the very mark of the spirit of rebellion to crave for happiness in this life. What right have we human beings to happiness? We have simply to do our duty, Mrs. Alving! And your duty was to hold firmly to the man you had once chosen, and to whom you were bound by the holiest ties.

Mrs. Alving. You know very well what sort of life Alving was leading—what excesses he was guilty of.

Manders. I know very well what rumours there were about him; and I am the last to approve the life he led in his young days, if report did not wrong him. But a wife is not appointed to be her husband's judge. It was your duty to bear with humility the cross which a Higher Power had, in its wisdom, laid upon you. But instead of that you rebelliously throw away the cross, desert the backslider whom you should have supported, go and risk your good name and reputation, and—nearly succeed in ruining other people's reputation into the bargain.

Mrs. Alving. Other people's? One other person's, you mean.

Manders. It was incredibly reckless of you to seek refuge with me.

Mrs. Alving. With our clergyman? With our intimate friend?

Manders. Just on that account. Yes, you may thank God that I possessed the necessary firmness; that I succeeded in dissuading you from your wild designs; and that it was vouchsafed me to lead you back to the path of duty, and home to your lawful husband.

Mrs. Alving. Yes, Pastor Manders, that was certainly your work.

Manders. I was but a poor instrument in a Higher Hand. And what a blessing has it not proved to you, all the days of your life, that I induced you to resume the yoke of duty and obedience! Did not everything happen as I foretold? Did not Alving turn his back on his errors, as a man should? Did he not live with you from that time, lovingly and blamelessly, all his days? Did he not become a benefactor to the whole district? And did he not help you to rise to his own level, so that you, little by little, became his assistant in all his undertakings? And a capital assistant, too—oh, I know, Mrs. Alving, that praise is due to you.— But now I come to the next great error in your life.

Mrs. Alving. What do you mean?

Manders. Just as you once disowned a wife's duty, so you have since disowned a mother's.

Mrs. Alving. Ah—!

Manders. You have been all your life under the dominion of a pestilent spirit of self-will. The whole bias of your mind has been towards insubordination and lawlessness. You have never known how to endure any bond. Everything that has weighed upon you in life you have cast away without care or conscience, like a burden you were free to throw off at will. It did not please you to be a wife any longer, and you left your husband. You found it troublesome to be a mother, and you sent your child forth among strangers.

Mrs. Alving. Yes, that is true I did so.

Manders. And thus you have become a stranger to him.

Mrs. Alving. No! no! I am not.

Manders. Yes, you are; you must be. And in what state of mind has he returned to you? Bethink yourself well, Mrs. Alving. You sinned greatly against your husband;—that you recognise by raising yonder memorial to him. Recognise now, also, how you have sinned against your son—

there may yet be time to lead him back from the paths of error. Turn back yourself, and save what may yet be saved in him. For [*with uplifted forefinger*] verily, Mrs. Alving, you are a guilt-laden mother!—This I have thought it my duty to say to you.

[*Silence.*]

Mrs. Alving [*slowly and with self-control*]. You have now spoken out, Pastor Manders; and to-morrow you are to speak publicly in memory of my husband. I shall not speak to-morrow. But now I will speak frankly to you, as you have spoken to me.

Manders. To be sure; you will plead excuses for your conduct—

Mrs. Alving. No. I will only tell you a story.

Manders. Well—?

Mrs. Alving. All that you have just said about my husband and me, and our life after you had brought me back to the path of duty—as you called it—about all that you know nothing from personal observation. From that moment you, who had been our intimate friend, never set foot in our house again.

Manders. You and your husband left the town immediately after.

Mrs. Alving. Yes; and in my husband's lifetime you never came to see us. It was business that forced you to visit me when you undertook the affairs of the Orphanage.

Manders [*softly and hesitatingly*]. Helen—if that is meant as a reproach, I would beg you to bear in mind—

Mrs. Alving. —the regard you owed to your position, yes; and that I was a runaway wife. One can never be too cautious with such unprincipled creatures.

Manders. My dear—Mrs. Alving, you know that is an absurd exaggeration—

Mrs. Alving. Well, well, suppose it is. My point is that your judgment as to my married life is founded upon nothing but common knowledge and report.

Manders. I admit that. What then?

Mrs. Alving. Well, then, Pastor Manders—I will tell you the truth. I have sworn to myself that one day you should know it—you alone!

Manders. What is the truth, then?

Mrs. Alving. The truth is that my husband died just as dissolute as he had lived all his days.

Manders [*feeling after a chair*]. What do you say?

Mrs. Alving. After nineteen years of marriage, as dissolute—in his desires at any rate—as he was before you married us.

Manders. And those—those wild oats—those irregularities—those excesses, if you like—you call "a dissolute life"?

Mrs. Alving. Our doctor used the expression.

MANDERS. I do not understand you.

MRS. ALVING. You need not.

MANDERS. It almost makes me dizzy. Your whole married life, the seeming union of all these years, was nothing more than a hidden abyss!

MRS. ALVING. Neither more nor less. Now you know it.

MANDERS. This is—this is inconceivable to me. I cannot grasp it! I cannot realise it! But how was it possible to—? How could such a state of things be kept secret?

MRS. ALVING. That has been my ceaseless struggle, day after day. After Oswald's birth, I thought Alving seemed to be a little better. But it did not last long. And then I had to struggle twice as hard, fighting as though for life or death, so that nobody should know what sort of man my child's father was. And you know what power Alving had of winning people's hearts. Nobody seemed able to believe anything but good of him. He was one of those people whose life does not bite upon their reputation. But at last, Mr. Manders—for you must know the whole story—the most repulsive thing of all happened.

MANDERS. More repulsive than what you have told me!

MRS. ALVING. I had gone on bearing with him, although I knew very well the secrets of his life out of doors. But when he brought the scandal within our own walls—

MANDERS. Impossible! Here!

MRS. ALVING. Yes; here in our own home. It was there [*pointing towards the first door on the right*], in the dining-room, that I first came to know of it. I was busy with something in there, and the door was standing ajar. I heard our housemaid come up from the garden, with water for those flowers.

MANDERS. Well—?

MRS. ALVING. Soon after, I heard Alving come in too. I heard him say something softly to her. And then I heard—[*with a short laugh*]—oh! it still sounds in my ears, so hateful and yet so ludicrous—I heard my own servant-maid whisper, "Let me go, Mr. Alving! Let me be!"

MANDERS. What unseemly levity on his part! But it cannot have been more than levity, Mrs. Alving; believe me, it cannot.

MRS. ALVING. I soon knew what to believe. Mr. Alving had his way with the girl; and that connection had consequences, Mr. Manders.

MANDERS [*as though petrified*]. Such things in this house! in this house!

MRS. ALVING. I had borne a great deal in this house. To keep him at home in the evenings, and at night, I had to make myself his boon companion in his secret orgies up in his room. There I have had to sit alone with him, to clink glasses and drink with him, and to listen to his ribald, silly talk. I have had to fight with him to get him dragged to bed—

MANDERS [*moved*]. And you were able to bear all this!

Mrs. Alving. I had to bear it for my little boy's sake. But when the last insult was added; when my own servant maid—; then I swore to myself: This shall come to an end! And so I took the reins into my own hand— the whole control—over him and everything else. For now I had a weapon against him, you see; he dared not oppose me. It was then I sent Oswald away from home. He was nearly seven years old, and was beginning to observe and ask questions, as children do. That I could not bear. It seemed to me the child must be poisoned by merely breathing the air of this polluted home. That was why I sent him away. And now you can see, too, why he was never allowed to set foot inside his home so long as his father lived. No one knows what that cost me.

Manders. You have indeed had a life of trial.

Mrs. Alving. I could never have borne it if I had not had my work. For I may truly say that I have worked! All the additions to the estate— all the improvements—all the labour-saving appliances, that Alving was so much praised for having introduced—do you suppose he had energy for anything of the sort?—he, who lay all day on the sofa, reading an old Court Guide! No; but I may tell you this too: when he had his better intervals, it was I who urged him on; it was I who had to drag the whole load when he relapsed into his evil ways, or sank into querulous wretchedness.

Manders. And it is to this man that you raise a memorial?

Mrs. Alving. There you see the power of an evil conscience.

Manders. Evil—? What do you mean?

Mrs. Alving. It always seemed to me impossible but that the truth must come out and be believed. So the Orphanage was to deaden all rumours and set every doubt at rest.

Manders. In that you have certainly not missed your aim, Mrs. Alving.

Mrs. Alving. And besides, I had one other reason. I was determined that Oswald, my own boy, should inherit nothing whatever from his father.

Manders. Then it is Alving's fortune that—?

Mrs. Alving. Yes. The sums I have spent upon the Orphanage, year by year, make up the amount—I have reckoned it up precisely—the amount which made Lieutenant Alving "a good match" in his day.

Manders. I don't understand—

Mrs. Alving. It was my purchase-money. I do not choose that that money should pass into Oswald's hands. My son shall have everything from me —everything.

[Oswald Alving *enters through the second door to the right; he has taken off his hat and overcoat in the hall.*]

Mrs. Alving [*going towards him*]. Are you back again already? My dear, dear boy!

OSWALD. Yes. What can a fellow do out of doors in this eternal rain? But I hear dinner is ready. That's capital!

REGINA [*with a parcel, from the dining-room*]. A parcel has come for you, Mrs. Alving. [*Hands it to her.*]

MRS. ALVING [*with a glance at* MR. MANDERS]. No doubt copies of the ode for to-morrow's ceremony.

MANDERS. H'm—

REGINA. And dinner is ready.

MRS. ALVING. Very well. We will come directly. I will just— [*Begins to open the parcel.*]

REGINA [*to* OSWALD]. Would Mr. Alving like red or white wine?

OSWALD. Both, if you please.

REGINA. *Bien.* Very well, sir. [*She goes into the dining-room.*]

OSWALD. I may as well help to uncork it. [*He also goes into the dining-room, the door of which swings half open behind him.*]

MRS. ALVING [*who has opened the parcel*]. Yes, I thought so. Here is the Ceremonial Ode, Pastor Manders.

MANDERS [*with folded hands*]. With what countenance I am to deliver my discourse to-morrow—!

MRS. ALVING. Oh, you will get through it somehow.

MANDERS [*softly, so as not to be heard in the dining-room*]. Yes; it would not do to provoke scandal.

MRS. ALVING [*under her breath, but firmly*]. No. But then this long, hateful comedy will be ended. From the day after to-morrow, I shall act in every way as though he who is dead had never lived in this house. There shall be no one here but my boy and his mother.

[*From the dining-room comes the noise of a chair overturned, and at the same moment is heard:*]

REGINA [*sharply, but in a whisper*]. Oswald! take care! are you mad? Let me go!

MRS. ALVING [*starts in terror*]. Ah—!

[*She stares wildly towards the half-open door.* OSWALD *is heard laughing and humming. A bottle is uncorked.*]

MANDERS [*agitated*]. What can be the matter? What is it, Mrs. Alving?

MRS. ALVING [*hoarsely*]. Ghosts! The couple from the conservatory—risen again!

MANDERS. Is it possible! Regina—? Is she—?

MRS. ALVING. Yes. Come. Not a word—!

[*She seizes* PASTOR MANDERS *by the arm, and walks unsteadily towards the dining-room.*]

ACT II

[*The same room. The mist still lies heavy over the landscape.*]

[MANDERS *and* MRS. ALVING *enter from the dining-room.*]

MRS. ALVING [*still in the doorway*]. Velbekomme, Mr. Manders. [*Turns back towards the dining-room.*] Aren't you coming too, Oswald?

OSWALD [*from within*]. No, thank you. I think I shall go out a little.

MRS. ALVING. Yes, do. The weather seems a little brighter now. [*She shuts the dining-room door, goes to the hall door, and calls:*] Regina!

REGINA [*outside*]. Yes, Mrs. Alving?

MRS. ALVING. Go down to the laundry, and help with the garlands.

REGINA. Yes, Mrs. Alving.

[MRS. ALVING *assures herself that* REGINA *goes; then shuts the door.*]

MANDERS. I suppose he cannot overhear us in there?

MRS. ALVING. Not when the door is shut. Besides, he's just going out.

MANDERS. I am still quite upset. I don't know how I could swallow a morsel of dinner.

MRS. ALVING [*controlling her nervousness, walks up and down*]. Nor I. But what is to be done now?

MANDERS. Yes; what is to be done? I am really quite at a loss. I am so utterly without experience in matters of this sort.

MRS. ALVING. I feel sure that, so far, no mischief has been done.

MANDERS. No; heaven forbid! But it is an unseemly state of things, nevertheless.

MRS. ALVING. It is only an idle fancy on Oswald's part; you may be sure of that.

MANDERS. Well, as I say, I am not accustomed to affairs of the kind. But I should certainly think—

MRS. ALVING. Out of the house she must go, and that immediately. That is as clear as daylight—

MANDERS. Yes, of course she must.

MRS. ALVING. But where to? It would not be right to—

MANDERS. Where to? Home to her father, of course.

MRS. ALVING. To whom did you say?

MANDERS. To her— But then, Engstrand is not—? Good God, Mrs. Alving, it's impossible! You must be mistaken after all.

MRS. ALVING. Unfortunately there is no possibility of mistake. Johanna confessed everything to me; and Alving could not deny it. So there was nothing to be done but to get the matter hushed up.

MANDERS. No, you could do nothing else.

MRS. ALVING. The girl left our service at once, and got a good sum of money to hold her tongue for the time. The rest she managed for herself when she got to town. She renewed her old acquaintance with Engstrand, no doubt let him see that she had money in her purse, and told him some tale about a foreigner who put in here with a yacht that summer. So she and Engstrand got married in hot haste. Why, you married them yourself.

MANDERS. But then how to account for—? I recollect distinctly Engstrand coming to give notice of the marriage. He was quite overwhelmed with contrition, and bitterly reproached himself for the misbehaviour he and his sweetheart had been guilty of.

MRS. ALVING. Yes; of course he had to take the blame upon himself.

MANDERS. But such a piece of duplicity on his part! And towards me too! I never could have believed it of Jacob Engrstand. I shall not fail to take him seriously to task; he may be sure of that.—And then the immorality of such a connection! For money—! How much did the girl receive?

MRS. ALVING. Three hundred dollars.

MANDERS. Just think of it—for a miserable three hundred dollars, to go and marry a fallen woman!

MRS. ALVING. Then what have you to say of me? I went and married a fallen man.

MANDERS. Why—good heavens!—what are you talking about! A fallen man!

MRS. ALVING. Do you think Alving was any purer when I went with him to the altar than Johanna was when Engstrand married her?

MANDERS. Well, but there is a world of difference between the two cases—

MRS. ALVING. Not so much difference after all—except in the price:—a miserable three hundred dollars and a whole fortune.

MANDERS. How can you compare such absolutely dissimilar cases? You had taken counsel with your own heart and with your natural advisers.

MRS. ALVING [*without looking at him*]. I thought you understood where what you call my heart had strayed to at the time.

MANDERS [*distantly*]. Had I understood anything of the kind, I should not have been a daily guest in your husband's house.

MRS. ALVING. At any rate, the fact remains that with myself I took no counsel whatever.

MANDERS. Well then, with your nearest relatives—as your duty bade you— with your mother and your two aunts.

MRS. ALVING. Yes, that is true. Those three cast up the account for me. Oh, it's marvellous how clearly they made out that it would be downright madness to refuse such an offer. If mother could only see me now, and know what all that grandeur has come to!

MANDERS. Nobody can be held responsible for the result. This, at least, remains clear: your marriage was in full accordance with law and order.

MRS. ALVING [*at the window*]. Oh, that perpetual law and order! I often think that is what does all the mischief in this world of ours.

MANDERS. Mrs. Alving, that is a sinful way of talking.

MRS. ALVING. Well, I can't help it; I must have done with all this constraint and insincerity. I can endure it no longer. I must work my way out to freedom.

MANDERS. What do you mean by that?

MRS. ALVING [*drumming on the window-frame*]. I ought never to have concealed the facts of Alving's life. But at that time I dared not do anything else—I was afraid, partly on my own account. I was such a coward.

MANDERS. A coward?

MRS. ALVING. If people, had come to know anything, they would have said—"Poor man! with a runaway wife, no wonder he kicks over the traces."

MANDERS. Such remarks might have been made with a certain show of right.

MRS ALVING [*looking steadily at him*]. If I were what I ought to be, I should go to Oswald and say, "Listen, my boy: your father led a vicious life—"

MANDERS. Merciful heavens—!

MRS. ALVING. —and then I should tell him all I have told you—every word of it.

MANDERS. You shock me unspeakably, Mrs. Alving.

MRS. ALVING. Yes; I know that. I know that very well. I myself am shocked at the idea. [*Goes away from the window.*] I am such a coward.

MANDERS. You call it "cowardice" to do your plain duty? Have you forgotten that a son ought to love and honour his father and mother?

MRS. ALVING. Do not let us talk in such general terms. Let us ask: Ought Oswald to love and honour Chamberlain Alving?

MANDERS. Is there no voice in your mother's heart that forbids you to destroy your son's ideals?

MRS. ALVING. But what about the truth?

MANDERS. But what about the ideals?

MRS. ALVING. Oh—ideals, ideals! If only I were not such a coward!

MANDERS. Do not despise ideals, Mrs. Alving; they will avenge themselves cruelly. Take Oswald's case: he, unfortunately, seems to have few enough ideals as it is; but I can see that his father stands before him as an ideal.

MRS. ALVING. Yes, that is true.

MANDERS. And this habit of mind you have yourself implanted and fostered by your letters.

MRS. ALVING. Yes; in my superstitious awe for duty and the proprieties, I lied to my boy, year after year. Oh, what a coward—what a coward I have been!

MANDERS. You have established a happy illusion in your son's heart, Mrs. Alving; and assuredly you ought not to undervalue it.

MRS. ALVING. H'm; who knows whether it is so happy after all—? But, at any rate, I will not have any tampering with Regina. He shall not go and wreck the poor girl's life.

MANDERS. No; good God—that would be terrible!

MRS. ALVING. If I knew he was in earnest, and that it would be for his happiness—

MANDERS. What? What then?

MRS. ALVING. But it couldn't be; for unfortunately Regina is not the right sort of woman.

MANDERS. Well, what then? What do you mean?

MRS. ALVING. If I weren't such a pitiful coward, I should say to him, "Marry her, or make what arrangement you please, only let us have nothing underhand about it."

MANDERS. Merciful heavens, would you let them marry! Anything so dreadful—! so unheard of—

MRS. ALVING. Do you really mean "unheard of"? Frankly, Pastor Manders, do you suppose that throughout the country there are not plenty of married couples as closely akin as they?

MANDERS. I don't in the least understand you.

MRS. ALVING. Oh yes, indeed you do.

MANDERS. Ah, you are thinking of the possibility that—Alas! yes, family life is certainly not always so pure as it ought to be. But in such a case as you point to, one can never know—at least with any certainty. Here, on the other hand—that you, a mother, can think of letting your son—!

MRS. ALVING. But I cannot—I wouldn't for anything in the world; that is precisely what I am saying.

MANDERS. No, because you are a "coward," as you put it. But if you were not a "coward," then—? Good God! a connection so shocking!

MRS. ALVING. So far as that goes, they say we are all sprung from connections of that sort. And who is it that arranged the world so, Pastor Manders?

MANDERS. Questions of that kind I must decline to discuss with you, Mrs. Alving; you are far from being in the right frame of mind for them. But that you dare to call your scruples "cowardly"—!

MRS. ALVING. Let me tell you what I mean. I am timid and faint-hearted because of the ghosts that hang about me, and that I can never quite shake off.

MANDERS. What do you say hangs about you?

MRS. ALVING. Ghosts! When I heard Regina and Oswald in there, it was as though ghosts rose up before me. But I almost think we are all of us ghosts, Pastor Manders. It is not only what we have inherited from our father and mother that "walks" in us. It is all sorts of dead ideas, and lifeless old beliefs, and so forth. They have no vitality, but they cling to us all the same, and we cannot shake them off. Whenever I take up a newspaper, I seem to see ghosts gliding between the lines. There must be ghosts all the country over, as thick as the sands of the sea. And then we are, one and all, so pitifully afraid of the light.

MANDERS. Aha—here we have the fruits of your reading. And pretty fruits they are, upon my word! Oh, those horrible, revolutionary, freethinking books!

MRS. ALVING. You are mistaken, my dear Pastor. It was you yourself who set me thinking; and I thank you for it with all my heart.

MANDERS. I!

MRS. ALVING. Yes—when you forced me under the yoke of what you called duty and obligation; when you lauded as right and proper what my whole soul rebelled against as something loathsome. It was then that I began to look into the seams of your doctrines. I wanted only to pick at a single knot; but when I had got that undone, the whole thing ravelled out. And then I understood that it was all machine-sewn.

MANDERS [softly, with emotion]. And was that the upshot of my life's hardest battle?

MRS. ALVING. Call it rather your most pitiful defeat.

MANDERS. It was my greatest victory, Helen—the victory over myself.

MRS. ALVING. It was a crime against us both.

MANDERS. When you went astray, and came to me crying, "Here I am; take me!" I commanded you, saying, "Woman, go home to your lawful husband." Was that a crime?

MRS. ALVING. Yes, I think so.

MANDERS. We two do not understand each other.

MRS. ALVING. Not now, at any rate.

MANDERS. Never—never in my most secret thoughts have I regarded you otherwise than as another's wife.

MRS. ALVING. Oh—indeed?

MANDERS. Helen—!

MRS. ALVING. People so easily forget their past selves.

MANDERS. I do not. I am what I always was.

MRS. ALVING [changing the subject]. Well, well, well; don't let us talk of old times any longer. You are now over head and ears in Boards and Committees, and I am fighting my battle with ghosts, both within me and without.

MANDERS. Those without I shall help you to lay. After all the terrible things I have heard from you to-day, I cannot in conscience permit an unprotected girl to remain in your house.

MRS. ALVING. Don't you think the best plan would be to get her provided for?—I mean, by a good marriage.

MANDERS. No doubt. I think it would be desirable for her in every respect. Regina is now at the age when— Of course I don't know much about these things, but—

MRS. ALVING. Regina matured very early.

MANDERS. Yes, I thought so. I have an impression that she was remarkably well developed, physically, when I prepared her for confirmation. But in the meantime, she ought to be at home, under her father's eye— Ah! but Engstrand is not— That he—that he—could so hide the truth from me!

[*A knock at the door into the hall.*]

MRS. ALVING. Who can this be? Come in!

ENGSTRAND [*in his Sunday clothes, in the doorway*]. I humbly beg your pardon, but—

MANDERS. Aha! H'm—

MRS. ALVING. Is that you, Engstrand?

ENGSTRAND. —there was none of the servants about, so I took the great liberty of just knocking.

MRS. ALVING. Oh, very well. Come in. Do you want to speak to me?

ENGSTRAND [*comes in*]. No, I'm obliged to you, ma'am; it was with his Reverence I wanted to have a word or two.

MANDERS [*walking up and down the room*]. Ah—indeed! You want to speak to me, do you?

ENGSTRAND. Yes, I'd like so terrible much to—

MANDERS [*stops in front of him*]. Well; may I ask what you want?

ENGSTRAND. Well, it was just this, your Reverence: we've been paid off down yonder—my grateful thanks to you, ma'am,—and now everything's finished, I've been thinking it would be but right and proper if we, that have been working so honestly together all this time—well, I was thinking we ought to end up with a little prayer-meeting tonight.

MANDERS. A prayer-meeting? Down at the Orphanage?

ENGSTRAND. Oh, if your Reverence doesn't think it proper—

MANDERS. Oh yes, I do; but—h'm—

ENGSTRAND. I've been in the habit of offering up a little prayer in the evenings, myself—

MRS. ALVING. Have you?

ENGSTRAND. Yes, every now and then—just a little edification, in a manner of speaking. But I'm a poor, common man, and have little enough gift, God help me!—and so I thought as the Reverend Mr. Manders happened to be here, I'd—

MANDERS. Well, you see, Engstrand, I have a question to put to you first. Are you in the right frame of mind for such a meeting? Do you feel your conscience clear and at ease?

ENGSTRAND. Oh, God help us, your Reverence! we'd better not talk about conscience.

MANDERS. Yes, that is just what we must talk about. What have you to answer?

ENGSTRAND. Why—a man's conscience—it can be bad enough now and then.

MANDERS. Ah, you admit that. Then perhaps you will make a clean breast of it, and tell me—the real truth about Regina.

MRS. ALVING [quickly]. Mr. Manders!

MANDERS [reassuringly]. Please allow me—

ENGSTRAND. About Regina! Lord, what a turn you gave me! [Looks at Mrs. Alving.] There's nothing wrong about Regina, is there?

MANDERS. We will hope not. But I mean, what is the truth about you and Regina? You pass for her father, eh!

ENGSTRAND [uncertain]. Well—h'm—your Reverence knows all about me and poor Johanna.

MANDERS. Come now, no more prevarication! Your wife told Mrs. Alving the whole story before quitting her service.

ENGSTRAND. Well, then, may—! Now, did she really?

MANDERS. You see we know you now, Engstrand.

ENGSTRAND. And she swore and took her Bible oath—

MANDERS. Did she take her Bible oath?

ENGSTRAND. No; she only swore; but she did it that solemn-like.

MANDERS. And you have hidden the truth from me all these years? Hidden it from me, who have trusted you without reserve, in everything.

ENGSTRAND. Well, I can't deny it.

MANDERS. Have I deserved this of you, Engstrand? Have I not always been ready to help you in word and deed, so far as it lay in my power? Answer me. Have I not?

ENGSTRAND. It would have been a poor look-out for me many a time but for the Reverend Mr. Manders.

MANDERS. And this is how you reward me! You cause me to enter falsehoods in the Church Register, and you withhold from me, year after year, the explanation you owed alike to me and to the truth. Your conduct has been wholly inexcusable, Engstrand; and from this time forward I have done with you!

ENGSTRAND [with a sigh]. Yes! I suppose there's no help for it.

MANDERS. How can you possibly justify yourself?

ENGSTRAND. Who could ever have thought she'd have gone and made bad worse by talking about it? Will your Reverence just fancy yourself in the same trouble as poor Johanna—

MANDERS. I!

ENGSTRAND. Lord bless you, I don't mean just exactly the same. But I mean, if your Reverence had anything to be ashamed of in the eyes of the world, as the saying goes. We menfolk oughtn't to judge a poor woman too hardly, your Reverence.

MANDERS. I am not doing so. It is you I am reproaching.

ENGSTRAND. Might I make so bold as to ask your Reverence a bit of a question?

MANDERS. Yes, if you want to.

ENGSTRAND. Isn't it right and proper for a man to raise up the fallen?

MANDERS. Most certainly it is.

ENGSTRAND. And isn't a man bound to keep his sacred word?

MANDERS. Why, of course he is; but—

ENGSTRAND. When Johanna had got into trouble through that Englishman—or it might have been an American or a Russian, as they call them —well, you see, she came down into the town. Poor thing, she'd sent me about my business once or twice before: for she couldn't bear the sight of anything as wasn't handsome; and I'd got this damaged leg of mine. Your Reverence recollects how I ventured up into a dancing saloon, where seafaring men was carrying on with drink and devilry, as the saying goes. And then, when I was for giving them a bit of an admonition to lead a new life—

MRS. ALVING [*at the window*]. H'm—

MANDERS. I know all about that, Engstrand; the ruffians threw you downstairs. You have told me of the affair already. Your infirmity is an honour to you.

ENGSTRAND. I'm not puffed up about it, your Reverence. But what I wanted to say was, that when she came and confessed all to me, with weeping and gnashing of teeth, I can tell your Reverence I was sore at heart to hear it.

MANDERS. Were you indeed, Engstrand? Well, go on.

ENGSTRAND. So I says to her, "The American, he's sailing about on the boundless sea. And as for you, Johanna," says I, "you've committed a grievous sin, and you're a fallen creature. But Jacob Engstrand," says I, "he's got two good legs to stand upon, he has—" You see, your Reverence, I was speaking figurative-like.

MANDERS. I understand quite well. Go on.

ENGSTRAND. Well, that was how I raised her up and made an honest woman of her, so as folks shouldn't get to know how as she'd gone astray with foreigners.

MANDERS. In all that you acted very well. Only I cannot approve of your stooping to take money—

ENGSTRAND. Money? I? Not a farthing!

MANDERS [*inquiringly to Mrs. Alving*]. But—

ENGSTRAND. Oh, wait a minute!—now I recollect. Johanna did have a trifle of money. But I would have nothing to do with that. "No," says I, "that's mammon; that's the wages of sin. This dirty gold—or notes, or whatever it was—we'll just fling that back in the American's face," says I. But he was off and away, over the stormy sea, your Reverence.

MANDERS. Was he really, my good fellow?

ENGSTRAND. He was indeed, sir. So Johanna and I, we agreed that the money should go to the child's education; and so it did, and I can account for every blessed farthing of it.

MANDERS. Why, this alters the case considerably.

ENGSTRAND. That's just how it stands, your Reverence. And I make so bold as to say as I've been an honest father to Regina, so far as my poor strength went; for I'm but a weak vessel, worse luck!

MANDERS. Well, well, my good fellow—

ENGSTRAND. All the same, I bear myself witness as I've brought up the child, and lived kindly with poor Johanna, and ruled over my own house, as the Scripture has it. But it couldn't never enter my head to go to your Reverence and puff myself up and boast because even the likes of me had done some good in the world. No, sir; when anything of that sort happens to Jacob Engstrand, he holds his tongue about it. It don't happen so terrible often, I daresay. And when I do come to see your Reverence, I find a mortal deal that's wicked and weak to talk about. For I said it before, and I says it again—a man's conscience isn't always as clean as it might be.

MANDERS. Give me your hand, Jacob Engstrand.

ENGSTRAND. Oh, Lord! your Reverence—

MANDERS. Come, no nonsense. [Wrings his hand.] There we are!

ENGSTRAND. And if I might humbly beg your Reverence's pardon—

MANDERS. You? On the contrary, it is I who ought to beg your pardon—

ENGSTRAND. Lord, no, sir!

MANDERS. Yes, assuredly. And I do it with all my heart. Forgive me for misunderstanding you. I only wish I could give you some proof of my hearty regret, and of my good-will towards you—

ENGSTRAND. Would your Reverence do it?

MANDERS. With the greatest pleasure.

ENGSTRAND. Well then, here's the very chance. With the bit of money I've saved here, I was thinking I might set up a Sailors' Home down in the town.

MRS. ALVING. You?

ENGSTRAND. Yes; it might be a sort of Orphanage, too, in a manner of speaking. There's such a many temptations for seafaring folk ashore. But in this Home of mine, a man might feel like as he was under a father's eye, I was thinking.

MANDERS. What do you say to this, Mrs. Alving?

ENGSTRAND. It isn't much as I've got to start with, Lord help me! But if I could only find a helping hand, why—

MANDERS. Yes, yes; we will look into the matter more closely. I entirely approve of your plan. But now, go before me and make everything ready, and get the candles lighted, so as to give the place an air of festivity. And then we will pass an edifying hour together, my good fellow; for now I quite believe you are in the right frame of mind.

ENGSTRAND. Yes, I trust I am. And so I'll say good-bye, ma'am, and thank you kindly; and take good care of Regina for me—[*wipes a tear from his eye*]—poor Johanna's child. Well, it's a queer thing, now; but it's just like as if she'd growd into the very apple of my eye. It is, indeed. [*He bows and goes out through the hall.*]

MANDERS. Well, what do you say of that man now, Mrs. Alving? That was a very different account of matters, was it not?

MRS. ALVING. Yes, it certainly was.

MANDERS. It only shows how excessively careful one ought to be in judging one's fellow creatures. But what a heartfelt joy it is to ascertain that one has been mistaken! Don't you think so?

MRS. ALVING. I think you are, and will always be, a great baby, Manders.

MANDERS. I?

MRS. ALVING [*laying her two hands upon his shoulders*]. And I say that I have half a mind to put my arms round your neck, and kiss you.

MANDERS [*stepping hastily back*]. No, no! God bless me! What an idea!

MRS. ALVING [*with a smile*]. Oh, you needn't be afraid of me.

MANDERS [*by the table*]. You have sometimes such an exaggerated way of expressing yourself. Now, let me just collect all the documents, and put them in my bag. [*He does so.*] There, that's all right. And now, good-bye for the present. Keep your eyes open when Oswald comes back. I shall look in again later. [*He takes his hat and goes out through the hall door.*]

MRS. ALVING [*sighs, looks for a moment out of the window, sets the room in order a little, and is about to go into the dining-room, but stops at the door with a half-suppressed cry*]. Oswald, are you still at table?

OSWALD [*in the dining-room*]. I'm only finishing my cigar.

MRS. ALVING. I thought you had gone for a little walk.

OSWALD. In such weather as this?

[*A glass clinks.* MRS. ALVING *leaves the door open, and sits down with her knitting on the sofa by the window.*]

OSWALD. Wasn't that Pastor Manders that went out just now?

MRS. ALVING. Yes; he went down to the Orphanage.

OSWALD. H'm. [*The glass and decanter clink again.*]

MRS. ALVING [*with a troubled glance*]. Dear Oswald, you should take care of that liqueur. It is strong.

OSWALD. It keeps out the damp.

MRS. ALVING. Wouldn't you rather come in here, to me?

OSWALD. I mayn't smoke in there.

MRS. ALVING. You know quite well you may smoke cigars.

OSWALD. Oh, all right then; I'll come in. Just a tiny drop more first.—
There! [*He comes into the room with his cigar, and shuts the door after
him. A short silence.*] Where has the pastor gone to?

MRS. ALVING. I have just told you; he went down to the Orphanage.

OSWALD. Oh, yes; so you did.

MRS. ALVING. You shouldn't sit so long at table, Oswald.

OSWALD [*holding his cigar behind him*]. But I find it so pleasant, mother.
[*Strokes and caresses her.*] Just think what it is for me to come home and
sit at mother's own table, in mother's room, and eat mother's delicious
dishes.

MRS. ALVING. My dear, dear boy!

OSWALD [*somewhat impatiently, walks about and smokes*]. And what else
can I do with myself here? I can't set to work at anything.

MRS. ALVING. Why can't you?

OSWALD. In such weather as this? Without a single ray of sunshine the
whole day? [*Walks up the room.*] Oh, not to be able to work—!

MRS. ALVING. Perhaps it was not quite wise of you to come home?

OSWALD. Oh, yes, mother; I had to.

MRS. ALVING. You know I would ten times rather forgo the joy of having
you here, than let you—

OSWALD [*stops beside the table*]. Now just tell me, mother: does it really
make you so very happy to have me home again?

MRS. ALVING. Does it make me happy!

OSWALD [*crumpling up a newspaper*]. I should have thought it must be
pretty much the same to you whether I was in existence or not.

MRS. ALVING. Have you the heart to say that to your mother, Oswald?

OSWALD. But you've got on very well without me all this time.

MRS. ALVING. Yes, I have got on without you. That is true.

[*A silence. Twilight slowly begins to fall.* OSWALD *paces to and fro across
the room. He has laid his cigar down.*]

OSWALD [*stops beside* MRS. ALVING]. Mother, may I sit on the sofa beside
you?

MRS. ALVING [*makes room for him*]. Yes, do, my dear boy.

OSWALD [*sits down*]. There is something I must tell you, mother.

MRS. ALVING [*anxiously*]. Well?

OSWALD [*looks fixedly before him*]. For I can't go on hiding it any longer.

MRS. ALVING. Hiding what? What is it?

OSWALD [*as before*]. I could never bring myself to write to you about it;
and since I've come home—

Mrs. Alving [*seizes him by the arm*]. Oswald, what is the matter?

Oswald. Both yesterday and to-day I have tried to put the thoughts away from me—to cast them off; but it's no use.

Mrs. Alving [*rising*]. Now you must tell me everything, Oswald!

Oswald [*draws her down to the sofa again*]. Sit still; and then I will try to tell you.—I complained of fatigue after my journey—

Mrs. Alving. Well? What then?

Oswald. But it isn't that that is the matter with me; not any ordinary fatigue—

Mrs. Alving [*tries to jump up*]. You are not ill, Oswald?

Oswald [*draws her down again*]. Sit still, mother. Do take it quietly. I'm not downright ill, either; not what is commonly called "ill." [*Clasps his hands above his head.*] Mother, my mind is broken down—ruined—I shall never be able to work again! [*With his hands before his face, he buries his head in her lap, and breaks into bitter sobbing.*]

Mrs. Alving [*white and trembling*]. Oswald! Look at me! No, no; it's not true.

Oswald [*looks up with despair in his eyes*]. Never to be able to work again! Never!—never! A living death! Mother, can you imagine anything so horrible?

Mrs. Alving. My poor boy! How has this horrible thing come upon you?

Oswald [*sitting upright again*]. That's just what I cannot possibly grasp or understand. I have never led a dissipated life—never, in any respect. You mustn't believe that of me, mother! I've never done that.

Mrs. Alving. I am sure you haven't, Oswald.

Oswald. And yet this has come upon me just the same—this awful misfortune!

Mrs. Alving. Oh, but it will pass over, my dear, blessed boy. It's nothing but over-work. Trust me, I am right.

Oswald [*sadly*]. I thought so too, at first; but it isn't so.

Mrs. Alving. Tell me everything, from beginning to end.

Oswald. Yes, I will.

Mrs. Alving. When did you first notice it?

Oswald. It was directly after I had been home last time, and had got back to Paris again. I began to feel the most violent pains in my head—chiefly in the back of my head, they seemed to come. It was as though a tight iron ring was being screwed round my neck and upwards.

Mrs. Alving. Well, and then?

Oswald. At first I thought it was nothing but the ordinary headache I had been so plagued with while I was growing up—

Mrs. Alving. Yes, yes—

Oswald. But it wasn't that. I soon found that out. I couldn't work any more. I wanted to begin upon a big new picture, but my powers seemed to fail me; all my strength was crippled; I could form no definite images;

everything swam before me—whirling round and round. Oh, it was an awful state! At last I sent for a doctor—and from him I learned the truth.

MRS. ALVING. How do you mean?

OSWALD. He was one of the first doctors in Paris. I told him my symptoms; and then he set to work asking me a string of questions which I thought had nothing to do with the matter. I couldn't imagine what the man was after—

MRS. ALVING. Well?

OSWALD. At last he said: "There has been something worm-eaten in you from your birth." He used that very word—*vermoulu*.

MRS. ALVING [*breathlessly*]. What did he mean by that?

OSWALD. I didn't understand either, and begged him to explain himself more clearly. And then the old cynic said—[*Clenching his fist.*] Oh—!

MRS. ALVING. What did he say?

OSWALD. He said, "The sins of the fathers are visited upon the children."

MRS. ALVING [*rising slowly*]. The sins of the fathers—!

OSWALD. I very nearly struck him in the face—

MRS. ALVING [*walks away across the room*]. The sins of the fathers—

OSWALD [*smiles sadly*]. Yes; what do you think of that? Of course I assured him that such a thing was out of the question. But do you think he gave in? No, he stuck to it; and it was only when I produced your letters and translated the passages relating to father—

MRS. ALVING. But then—?

OSWALD. Then of course he had to admit that he was on the wrong track; and so I learned the truth—the incomprehensible truth! I ought not to have taken part with my comrades in that lighthearted, glorious life of theirs. It had been too much for my strength. So I had brought it upon myself!

MRS. ALVING. Oswald! No, no; do not believe it!

OSWALD. No other explanation was possible, he said. That's the awful part of it. Incurably ruined for life—by my own heedlessness! All that I meant to have done in the world—I never dare think of it again—I'm not able to think of it. Oh! if I could only live over again, and undo all I have done! [*He buries his face in the sofa.*]

[MRS. ALVING *wrings her hands and walks, in silent struggle, backwards and forwards.*]

OSWALD [*after a while, looks up and remains resting upon his elbow*]. If it had only been something inherited—something one wasn't responsible for! But this! To have thrown away so shamefully, thoughtlessly, recklessly, one's own happiness, one's own health, everything in the world—one's future, one's very life—!

MRS. ALVING. No, no, my dear, darling boy; this is impossible! [*Bends over him.*] Things are not so desperate as you think.

OSWALD. Oh, you don't know—[*Springs up.*] And then, mother, to cause you all this sorrow! Many a time I have almost wished and hoped that at bottom you didn't care so very much about me.

MRS. ALVING. I, Oswald? My only boy! You are all I have in the world! The only thing I care about!

OSWALD [*seizes both her hands and kisses them*]. Yes, yes, I see it. When I'm at home, I see it, of course; and that's almost the hardest part for me.—But now you know the whole story; and now we won't talk any more about it to-day. I daren't think of it for long together. [*Goes up the room.*] Get me something to drink, mother.

MRS. ALVING. To drink? What do you want to drink now?

OSWALD. Oh, anything you like. You have some cold punch in the house.

MRS. ALVING. Yes, but my dear Oswald—

OSWALD. Don't refuse me, mother. Do be kind, now! I must have something to wash down all these gnawing thoughts. [*Goes into the conservatory.*] And then—it's so dark here! [MRS. ALVING *pulls a bell-rope on the right.*] And this ceaseless rain! It may go on week after week, for months together. Never to get a glimpse of the sun! I can't recollect ever having seen the sun shine all the times I've been at home.

MRS. ALVING. Oswald—you are thinking of going away from me.

OSWALD. H'm—[*Drawing a heavy breath.*]—I'm not thinking of anything. I cannot think of anything. [*In a low voice.*] I let thinking alone.

REGINA [*from the dining-room*]. Did you ring, ma'am?

MRS. ALVING. Yes; let us have the lamp in.

REGINA. Yes, ma'am. It's ready lighted. [*Goes out.*]

MRS. ALVING [*goes across to* OSWALD]. Oswald, be frank with me.

OSWALD. Well, so I am, mother. [*Goes to the table.*] I think I have told you enough.

[REGINA *brings the lamp and sets it upon the table.*]

MRS. ALVING. Regina, you may bring us a small bottle of champagne.

REGINA. Very well, ma'am. [*Goes out.*]

OSWALD [*puts his arm round* MRS. ALVING's *neck*]. That's just what I wanted. I knew mother wouldn't let her boy go thirsty.

MRS. ALVING. My own, poor, darling Oswald; how could I deny you anything now?

OSWALD [*eagerly*]. Is that true, mother? Do you mean it?

MRS. ALVING. How? what?

OSWALD. That you couldn't deny me anything.

MRS. ALVING. My dear Oswald—

OSWALD. Hush!

Regina [*brings a tray with a half-bottle of champagne and two glasses, which she sets on the table*]. Shall I open it?

Oswald. No, thanks. I will do it myself.

[Regina *goes out again.*]

Mrs. Alving [*sits down by the table.*] What was it you meant—that I mustn't deny you?

Oswald [*busy opening the bottle*]. First let us have a glass—or two. [*The cork pops; he pours wine into one glass, and is about to pour it into the other.*]

Mrs. Alving [*holding her hand over it*]. Thanks; not for me.

Oswald. Oh! won't you? Then I will! [*He empties the glass, fills, and empties it again; then he sits down by the table.*]

Mrs. Alving [*in expectancy*]. Well?

Oswald [*without looking at her*]. Tell me—I thought you and Pastor Manders seemed so odd—so quiet—at dinner to-day.

Mrs. Alving. Did you notice it?

Oswald. Yes. H'm— [*After a short silence.*] Tell me: what do you think of Regina?

Mrs. Alving. What do I think?

Oswald. Yes; isn't she splendid?

Mrs. Alving. My dear Oswald, you don't know her as I do—

Oswald. Well?

Mrs. Alving. Regina, unfortunately, was allowed to stay at home too long. I ought to have taken her earlier into my house.

Oswald. Yes, but isn't she splendid to look at, mother? [*He fills his glass.*]

Mrs. Alving. Regina has many serious faults—

Oswald. Oh, what does that matter? [*He drinks again.*]

Mrs. Alving. But I am fond of her, nevertheless, and I am responsible for her. I wouldn't for all the world have any harm happen to her.

Oswald [*springs up*]. Mother, Regina is my only salvation!

Mrs. Alving [*rising*]. What do you mean by that?

Oswald. I cannot go on bearing all this anguish of soul alone.

Mrs. Alving. Have you not your mother to share it with you?

Oswald. Yes; that's what I thought; and so I came home to you. But that will not do. I see it won't do. I cannot endure my life here.

Mrs. Alving. Oswald!

Oswald. I must live differently, mother. That is why I must leave you. I will not have you looking on at it.

Mrs. Alving. My unhappy boy! But, Oswald, while you are so ill as this—

Oswald. If it were only the illness, I should stay with you, mother, you may be sure; for you are the best friend I have in the world.

Mrs. Alving. Yes, indeed I am, Oswald; am I not?

Oswald [*wanders restlessly about*]. But it's all the torment, the gnawing remorse—and then, the great, killing dread. Oh—that awful dread!

Mrs. Alving [*walking after him*]. Dread? What dread? What do you mean?

Oswald. Oh, you mustn't ask me any more. I don't know. I can't describe it.

[Mrs. Alving *goes over to the right and pulls the bell.*]

Oswald. What is it you want?

Mrs. Alving. I want my boy to be happy—that is what I want. He sha'n't go on brooding over things. [*To* Regina, *who appears at the door:*] More champagne—a large bottle.

[Regina *goes.*]

Oswald. Mother!

Mrs. Alving. Do you think we don't know how to live here at home?

Oswald. Isn't she splendid to look at? How beautifully she's built! And so thoroughly healthy!

Mrs. Alving [*sits by the table*]. Sit down, Oswald; let us talk quietly together.

Oswald [*sits*]. I daresay you don't know, mother, that I owe Regina some reparation.

Mrs. Alving. You!

Oswald. For a bit of thoughtlessness, or whatever you like to call it—very innocent, at any rate. When I was home last time—

Mrs. Alving. Well?

Oswald. She used often to ask me about Paris, and I used to tell her one thing and another. Then I recollect I happened to say to her one day, "Shouldn't you like to go there yourself?"

Mrs. Alving. Well?

Oswald. I saw her face flush, and then she said, "Yes, I should like it of all things." "Ah, well," I replied, "it might perhaps be m_naged"—or something like that.

Mrs. Alving. And then?

Oswald. Of course I had forgotten all about it; but the day before yesterday I happened to ask her whether she was glad I was to stay at home so long—

Mrs. Alving. Yes?

Oswald. And then she gave me such a strange look, and asked, "But what's to become of my trip to Paris?"

Mrs. Alving. Her trip!

Oswald. And so it came out that she had taken the thing seriously; that she had been thinking of me the whole time, and had set to work to learn French—

MRS. ALVING. So that was why—!

OSWALD. Mother—when I saw that fresh, lovely, splendid girl standing there, before me—till then I had hardly noticed her—but when she stood there, as though with open arms ready to receive me—

MRS. ALVING. Oswald!

OSWALD. —then it flashed upon me that in her lay my salvation; for I saw that she was full of the joy of life.

MRS. ALVING [starts]. The joy of life—? Can there be salvation in that?

REGINA [from the dining-room, with a bottle of champagne]. I'm sorry to have been so long, but I had to go to the cellar. [Places the bottle on the table.]

OSWALD. And now bring another glass.

REGINA [looks at him in surprise]. There is Mrs. Alving's glass, Mr. Alving.

OSWALD. Yes, but bring one for yourself, Regina. [REGINA starts and gives a lightning-like side glance at MRS. ALVING.] Why do you wait?

REGINA [softly and hesitaingly]. Is it Mrs. Alving's wish?

MRS. ALVING. Bring the glass, Regina. [REGINA goes out into the dining-room.]

OSWALD [follows her with his eyes]. Have you noticed how she walks?—so firmly and lightly!

MRS. ALVING. This can never be, Oswald!

OSWALD. It's a settled thing. Can't you see that? It's no use saying anything against it.

[REGINA enters with an empty glass, which she keeps in her hand.]

OSWALD. Sit down, Regina.

[REGINA looks inquiringly at MRS. ALVING.]

MRS. ALVING. Sit down. [REGINA sits on a chair by the dining-room door, still holding the empty glass in her hand.] Oswald—what were you saying about the joy of life?

OSWALD. Ah, the joy of life, mother—that's a thing you don't know much about in these parts. I have never felt it here.

MRS. ALVING. Not when you are with me?

OSWALD. Not when I'm at home. But you don't understand that.

MRS. ALVING. Yes, yes; I think I almost understand it—now.

OSWALD. And then, too, the joy of work! At bottom, it's the same thing. But that, too, you know nothing about.

MRS. ALVING. Perhaps you are right. Tell me more about it, Oswald.

OSWALD. I only mean that here people are brought up to believe that work is a curse and a punishment for sin, and that life is something miserable, something it would be best to have done with, the sooner the better.

MRS. ALVING. "A vale of tears," yes; and we certainly do our best to make it one.

OSWALD. But in the great world people won't hear of such things. There, nobody really believes such doctrines any longer. There, you feel it a positive bliss and ecstasy merely to draw the breath of life. Mother, have you noticed that everything I have painted has turned upon the joy of life?—always, always upon the joy of life?—light and sunshine and glori-our air—and faces radiant with happiness. That is why I'm afraid of remaining at home with you.

MRS. ALVING. Afraid? What are you afraid of here, with me?

OSWALD. I'm afraid lest all my instincts should be warped into ugliness.

MRS. ALVING [*looks steadily at him.*] Do you think that is what would happen?

OSWALD. I know it. You may live the same life here as there, and yet it won't be the same life.

MRS. ALVING [*who has been listening eagerly, rises, her eyes big with thought, and says:*] Now I see the sequence of things.

OSWALD. What is it you see?

MRS. ALVING. I see it now for the first time. And now I can speak.

OSWALD [*rising*]. Mother, I don't understand you.

REGINA [*who has also risen*]. Perhaps I ought to go?

MRS. ALVING. No. Stay here. Now I can speak. Now, my boy, you shall know the whole truth. And then you can choose. Oswald! Regina!

OSWALD. Hush! The Pastor——

MANDERS [*enters by the hall door*]. There! We have had a most edifying time down there.

OSWALD. So have we.

MANDERS. We must stand by Engstrand and his Sailors' Home. Regina must go to him and help him—

REGINA. No thank you, sir.

MANDERS [*noticing her for the first time*]. What—? You here? And with a glass in your hand!

REGINA [*hastily putting the glass down*]. *Pardon!*

OSWALD. Regina is going with me, Mr. Manders.

MANDERS. Going! With you!

OSWALD. Yes! as my wife—if she wishes it.

MANDERS. But, merciful God—!

REGINA. I can't help it, sir.

OSWALD. Or she'll stay here, if I stay.

REGINA [*involuntarily*]. Here!

MANDERS. I am thunderstruck at your conduct, Mrs. Alving.

MRS. ALVING. They will do neither one thing nor the other; for now I can speak out plainly.

MANDERS. You surely will not do that! No, no, no!

Mrs. Alving. Yes, I can speak and I will. And no ideals shall suffer after all.
Oswald. Mother—what is it you are hiding from me?
Regina [listening]. Oh, ma'am, listen! Don't you hear shouts outside. [She goes into the conservatory and looks out.]
Oswald [at the window on the left]. What's going on? Where does that light come from?
Regina [cries out]. The Orphanage is on fire!
Mrs. Alving [rushing to the window]. On fire!
Manders. On fire! Impossible! I've just come from there.
Oswald. Where's my hat? Oh, never mind it—Father's Orphanage—! [He rushes out through the garden door.]
Mrs. Alving. My shawl, Regina! The whole place is in a blaze!
Manders. Terrible! Mrs. Alving, it is a judgment upon this abode of lawlessness.
Mrs. Alving. Yes, of course. Come, Regina.

[She and Regina hasten out through the hall.]

Manders [clasps his hands together]. And we left it uninsured! [He goes out the same way.]

ACT III

[The room as before. All the doors stand open. The lamp is still burning on the table. It is dark out of doors; there is only a faint glow from the conflagration in the background to the left.]

[Mrs. Alving, with a shawl over her head, stands in the conservatory, looking out. Regina, also with a shawl on, stands a little behind her.]

Mrs. Alving. The whole thing burnt!—burnt to the ground!
Regina The basement is still burning.
Mrs. Alving. How is it Oswald doesn't come home? There's nothing to be saved.
Regina. Should you like me to take down his hat to him?
Mrs. Alving. Has he not even got his hat on?
Regina [pointing to the hall]. No; there it hangs.
Mrs. Alving. Let it be. He must come up now. I shall go and look for him myself. [She goes out through the garden door.]
Manders [comes in from the hall]. Is not Mrs. Alving here?
Regina. She has just gone down the garden.
Manders This is the most terrible night I ever went through.
Regina. Yes; isn't it a dreadful misfortune, sir?

MANDERS. Oh, don't talk about it! I can hardly bear to think of it.

REGINA. How can it have happened—?

MANDERS. Don't ask me, Miss Engstrand! How should *I* know? Do you, too—? Is it not enough that your father—?

REGINA. What about him?

MANDERS. Oh, he has driven me distracted—

ENGSTRAND [*enters through the hall*]. Your Reverence—

MANDERS [*turns round in terror*]. Are you after me here, too?

ENGSTRAND. Yes, strike me dead, but I must—! Oh, Lord! what am I saying? But this is a terrible ugly business, your Reverence.

MANDERS [*walks to and fro*]. Alas! alas!

REGINA. What's the matter?

ENGSTRAND. Why, it all came of this here prayer-meeting, you see. [*Softly.*] The bird's limed, my girl. [*Aloud.*] And to think it should be my doing that such a thing should be his Reverence's doing!

MANDERS. But I assure you, Engstrand—

ENGSTRAND. There wasn't another soul except your Reverence as ever laid a finger on the candles down there.

MANDERS [*stops*]. So you declare. But I certainly cannot recollect that I ever had a candle in my hand.

ENGSTRAND. And I saw as clear as daylight how your Reverence took the candle and snuffed it with your fingers, and threw away the snuff among the shavings.

MANDERS. And you stood and looked on?

ENGSTRAND. Yes; I saw it as plain as a pike-staff, I did.

MANDERS It's quite beyond my comprehension. Besides, it has never been my habit to snuff candles with my fingers.

ENGSTRAND. And terrible risky it looked, too, that it did! But is there such a deal of harm done after all, your Reverence?

MANDERS [*walks restlessly to and fro*]. Oh, don't ask me!

ENGSTRAND [*walks with him*]. And your Reverence hadn't insured it, neither?

MANDERS [*continuing to walk up and down*]. No, no, no; I have told you so.

ENGSTRAND [*following him*]. Not insured! And then to go straight away down and set light to the whole thing! Lord, Lord, what a misfortune!

MANDERS [*wipes the sweat from his forehead*]. Ay, you may well say that, Engstrand.

ENGSTRAND. And to think that such a thing should happen to a benevolent Institution, that was to have been a blessing both to town and country, as the saying goes! The newspapers won't be for handling your Reverence very gently, I expect.

MANDERS. No; that is just what I am thinking of. That is almost the worst of the whole matter. All the malignant attacks and imputations—! Oh, it makes me shudder to think of it!

MRS. ALVING [*comes in from the garden*]. He is not to be persuaded to leave the fire.

MANDERS Ah, there you are, Mrs. Alving.

MRS. ALVING. So you have escaped your Inaugural Address, Pastor Manders.

MANDERS. Oh, I should so gladly—

MRS. ALVING [*in an undertone*]. It is all for the best. That Orphanage would have done no one any good.

MANDERS. Do you think not?

MRS. ALVING. Do you think it would?

MANDERS. It is a terrible misfortune, all the same.

MRS. ALVING. Let us speak of it plainly, as a matter of business—Are you waiting for Mr. Manders, Engstrand?

ENGSTRAND [*at the hall door*]. That's just what I'm a-doing of, ma'am.

MRS. ALVING. Then sit down meanwhile.

ENGSTRAND. Thank you, ma'am; I'd as soon stand.

MRS. ALVING [*to* MANDERS]. I suppose you are going by the steamer?

MANDERS. Yes; it starts in an hour.

MRS. ALVING. Then be so good as to take all the papers with you. I won't hear another word about this affair. I have other things to think of—

MANDERS. Mrs. Alving—

MRS. ALVING. Later on I shall send you a Power of Attorney to settle everything as you please.

MANDERS. That I will very readily undertake. The original destination of the endowment must now be completely changed, alas!

MRS. ALVING. Of course it must.

MANDERS. I think, first of all, I shall arrange that the Solvik property shall pass to the parish. The land is by no means without value. It can always be turned to account for some purpose or other. And the interest of the money in the Bank I could, perhaps, best apply for the benefit of some undertaking of acknowledged value to the town.

MRS. ALVING. Do just as you please. The whole matter is now completely indifferent to me.

ENGSTRAND. Give a thought to my Sailors' Home, your Reverence.

MANDERS. Upon my word, that is not a bad suggestion. That must be considered.

ENGSTRAND. Oh, devil take considering—Lord forgive me!

MANDERS [*with a sigh*]. And unfortunately I cannot tell how long I shall be able to retain control of these things—whether public opinion may not compel me to retire. It entirely depends upon the result of the official inquiry into the fire—

MRS. ALVING. What are you talking about?

MANDERS. And the result can by no means be foretold.

ENGSTRAND [*comes close to him*]. Ay, but it can though. For here stands old Jacob Engstrand.

MANDERS. Well, well, but—?

ENGSTRAND [*more softly*]. And Jacob Engstrand isn't the man to desert a noble benefactor in the hour of need, as the saying goes.

MANDERS. Yes, but my good fellow—how—?

ENGSTRAND. Jacob Engstrand may be likened to a sort of a guardian angel, he may, your Reverence.

MANDERS. No, no; I really cannot accept that.

ENGSTRAND. Oh, that'll be the way of it, all the same. I know a man as has taken others' sins upon himself before now, I do.

MANDERS. Jacob! [*Wrings his hand.*] Yours is a rare nature. Well, you shall be helped with your Sailors' Home. That you may rely upon.

[ENGSTRAND *tries to thank him, but cannot for emotion.*]

MANDERS [*hangs his travelling-bag over his shoulders*]. And now let us set out. We two will go together.

ENGSTRAND [*at the dining-room door, softly to* REGINA]. You come along too, my lass. You shall live as snug as the yolk in an egg.

REGINA [*tosses her head*]. Merci!

[*She goes out into the hall and fetches* MANDERS' *overcoat.*]

MANDERS. Good-bye, Mrs. Alving! and may the spirit of Law and Order descend upon this house, and that quickly.

MRS. ALVING. Good-bye, Pastor Manders. [*She goes up towards the conservatory, as she sees* OSWALD *coming in through the garden door.*]

ENGSTRAND [*while he and* REGINA *help* MANDERS *to get his coat on*]. Good-bye, my child. And if any trouble should come to you, you know where Jacob Engstrand is to be found. [*Softly.*] Little Harbour Street, h'm—! [*To* MRS. ALVING *and* OSWALD.] And the refuge for wandering mariners shall be called "Chamberlain Alving's Home," that it shall! And if so be as I'm spared to carry on that house in my own way, I make so bold as to promise that it shall be worthy of the Chamberlain's memory.

MANDERS [*in the doorway*]. H'm—h'm!—Come along, my dear Engstrand. Good-bye! Good-bye! [*He and* ENGSTRAND *go out through the hall.*]

OSWALD [*goes towards the table*]. What house was he talking about?

MRS. ALVING Oh, a kind of Home that he and Pastor Manders want to set up.

OSWALD. It will burn down like the other.

MRS. ALVING. What makes you think so?

Oswald. Everything will burn. All that recalls father's memory is doomed. Here am I, too, burning down.

[Regina *starts and looks at him.*]

Mrs. Alving. Oswald! You oughtn't to have remained so long down there, my poor boy.

Oswald [*sits down by the table*]. I almost think you are right.

Mrs. Alving. Let me dry your face, Oswald; you are quite wet. [*She dries his face with her pocket-handkerchief.*]

Oswald [*stares indifferently in front of him*]. Thanks, mother.

Mrs. Alving. Are you not tired, Oswald? Should you like to sleep?

Oswald [*nervously*]. No, no—not to sleep! I never sleep. I only pretend to. [*Sadly.*] That will come soon enough.

Mrs. Alving [*looking sorrowfully at him*]. Yes, you really are ill, my blessed boy.

Regina [*eagerly*]. Is Mr. Alving ill?

Oswald [*impatiently*]. Oh, do shut all the doors! This killing dread—

Mrs. Alving Close the doors, Regina.

[Regina *shuts them and remains standing by the hall door.* Mrs. Alving *takes her shawl off.* Regina *does the same.* Mrs. Alving *draws a chair across to* Oswald's *and sits by him.*]

Mrs. Alving. There now! I am going to sit beside you—

Oswald. Yes, do. And Regina shall stay here too. Regina shall be with me always. You will come to the rescue, Regina, won't you?

Regina. I don't understand—

Mrs. Alving. To the rescue?

Oswald. Yes—when the need comes.

Mrs. Alving. Oswald, have you not your mother to come to the rescue?

Oswald. You? [*Smiles.*] No, mother; that rescue you will never bring me. [*Laughs sadly.*] You! ha ha! [*Looks earnestly at her.*] Though, after all, who ought to do it if not you? [*Impetuously.*] Why can't you say "thou" to me, Regina? Why don't you call me "Oswald"?

Regina [*softly*]. I don't think Mrs. Alving would like it.

Mrs. Alving. You shall have leave to, presently. And meanwhile sit over here beside us.

[Regina *seats herself demurely and hesitatingly at the other side of the table.*]

Mrs. Alving. And now, my poor suffering boy, I am going to take the burden off your mind—

Oswald. You, mother?

Mrs. Alving. —all the gnawing remorse and self-reproach you speak of.

OSWALD. And you think you can do that?

MRS. ALVING Yes, now I can, Oswald. A little while ago you spoke of the joy of life; and at that word a new light burst for me over my life and everything connected with it.

OSWALD [*shakes his head*]. I don't understand you.

MRS. ALVING. You ought to have known your father when he was a young lieutenant. He was brimming over with the joy of life!

OSWALD. Yes, I know he was.

MRS. ALVING. It was like a breezy day only to look at him. And what exuberant strength and vitality there was in him!

OSWALD. Well—?

MRS. ALVING. Well then, child of joy as he was—for he was like a child in those days—he had to live at home here in a half-grown town, which had no joys to offer him—only dissipations. He had no object in life— only an official position. He had no work into which he could throw himself heart and soul; he had only business. He had not a single comrade that could realise what the joy of life meant—only loungers and boon-companions—

OSWALD. Mother—!

MRS. ALVING. So the inevitable happened.

OSWALD. The inevitable?

MRS. ALVING. You told me yourself, this evening, what would become of you if you stayed at home.

OSWALD. Do you mean to say that father—?

MRS. ALVING. Your poor father found no outlet for the overpowering joy of life that was in him. And I brought no brightness into his home.

OSWALD. Not even you?

MRS. ALVING. They had taught me a great deal about duties and so forth, which I went on obstinately believing in. Everything was marked out into duties—into my duties, and his duties, and—I am afraid I made his home intolerable for your poor father, Oswald.

OSWALD. Why have you never spoke of this in writing to me?

MRS. ALVING. I have never before seen it in such a light that I could speak of it to you, his son.

OSWALD. In what light did you see it, then?

MRS. ALVING [*slowly*]. I saw only this one thing: that your father was a broken-down man before you were born.

OSWALD [*softly*]. Ah—! [*He rises and walks away to the window.*]

MRS. ALVING. And then, day after day, I dwelt on the one thought that by rights Regina should be at home in this house—just like my own boy.

OSWALD [*turning round quickly*]. Regina—!

REGINA [*springs up and asks, with bated breath*]. I—?

MRS. ALVING. Yes, now you know it, both of you.

OSWALD. Regina!

REGINA [*to herself*]. So mother was that kind of woman.

MRS. ALVING. Your mother had many good qualities, Regina.

REGINA. Yes, but she was one of that sort, all the same. Oh, I've often suspected it; but— And now, if you please, ma'am, may I be allowed to go away at once?

MRS. ALVING. Do you really wish it, Regina?

REGINA. Yes, indeed I do.

MRS. ALVING. Of course you can do as you like; but—

OSWALD [*goes towards* REGINA]. Go away now? Your place is here.

REGINA. *Merci*, Mr. Alving!—or now, I suppose, I may say Oswald. But I can tell you this wasn't at all what I expected.

MRS. ALVING. Regina, I have not been frank with you—

REGINA. No, that you haven't indeed. If I'd known that Oswald was an invalid, why— And now, too, that it can never come to anything serious between us— I really can't stop out here in the country and wear myself out nursing sick people.

OSWALD. Not even one who is so near to you?

REGINA. No, that I can't. A poor girl must make the best of her young days, or she'll be left out in the cold before she knows where she is. And I, too, have the joy of life in me, Mrs. Alving!

MRS. ALVING. Unfortunately, you have. But don't throw yourself away, Regina.

REGINA. Oh, what must be, must be. If Oswald takes after his father, I take after my mother, I dare say.—May I ask, ma'am, if Pastor Manders knows all this about me?

MRS. ALVING. Pastor Manders knows all about it.

REGINA [*busied in putting on her shawl*]. Well then, I'd better make haste and get away by this steamer. The Pastor is such a nice man to deal with; and I certainly think I've as much right to a little of that money as he has—that brute of a carpenter.

MRS. ALVING. You are heartily welcome to it, Regina.

REGINA [*looks hard at her*]. I think you might have brought me up as a gentleman's daughter, ma'am; it would have suited me better. [*Tosses her head.*] But pooh—what does it matter! [*With a bitter side glance at the corked bottle.*] I may come to drink champagne with gentlefolks yet.

MRS. ALVING. And if you ever need a home, Regina, come to me.

REGINA. No, thank you, ma'am. Pastor Manders will look after me, I know. And if the worst comes to the worst, I know of one house where I've every right to a place.

MRS. ALVING. Where is that?

REGINA. "Chamberlain Alving's Home."

MRS. ALVING. Regina—now I see it—you are going to your ruin.

REGINA. Oh, stuff! Good-bye. [*She nods and goes out through the hall.*]

OSWALD [*stands at the window and looks out*]. Is she gone?

MRS. ALVING. Yes.

OSWALD [*murmuring aside to himself*]. I think it was a mistake, this.

MRS. ALVING [*goes up behind him and lays her hands on his shoulders*]. Oswald, my dear boy—has it shaken you very much?

OSWALD [*turns his face towards her*]. All that about father, do you mean?

MRS. ALVING. Yes, about your unhappy father. I am so afraid it may have been too much for you.

OSWALD. Why should you fancy that? Of course it came upon me as a great surprise; but it can make no real difference to me.

MRS. ALVING [*draws her hands away*]. No difference! That your father was so infinitely unhappy!

OSWALD. Of course I can pity him, as I would anybody else; but—

MRS. ALVING Nothing more! Your own father!

OSWALD [*impatiently*]. Oh, "father,"—"father"! I never knew anything of father. I remember nothing about him, except that he once made me sick.

MRS. ALVING. This is terrible to think of! Ought not a son to love his father, whatever happens?

OSWALD. When a son has nothing to thank his father for? has never known him? Do you really cling to that old superstition?—you who are so enlightened in other ways?

MRS. ALVING. Can it be only a superstition—?

OSWALD. Yes; surely you can see that, mother. It's one of those notions that are current in the world, and so—

MRS. ALVING [*deeply moved*]. Ghosts!

OSWALD [*crossing the room*]. Yes; you may call them ghosts.

MRS. ALVING [*wildly*]. Oswald—then you don't love me, either!

OSWALD. You I know, at any rate—

MRS. ALVING. Yes, you know me; but is that all?

OSWALD. And, of course, I know how fond you are of me, and I can't but be grateful to you. And then you can be so useful to me, now that I am ill.

MRS. ALVING. Yes, cannot I, Oswald? Oh, I could almost bless the illness that has driven you home to me. For I see very plainly that you are not mine: I have to win you.

OSWALD [*impatiently*]. Yes, yes, yes; all these are just so many phrases. You must remember that I am a sick man, mother. I can't be much taken up with other people; I have enough to do thinking about myself.

MRS. ALVING [*in a low voice*]. I shall be patient and easily satisfied.

OSWALD. And cheerful too, mother!

MRS. ALVING. Yes, my dear boy, you are quite right. [*Goes towards him.*] Have I relieved you of all remorse and self-reproach now?

OSWALD. Yes, you have. But now who will relieve me of the dread?

MRS. ALVING. The dread?

OSWALD [*walks across the room*]. Regina could have been got to do it.

MRS. ALVING. I don't understand you. What is this about dread—and Regina?

OSWALD. Is it very late, mother?

MRS. ALVING. It is early morning. [*She looks out through the conservatory.*] The day is dawning over the mountains. And the weather is clearing, Oswald. In a little while you shall see the sun.

OSWALD. I'm glad of that. Oh, I may still have much to rejoice in and live for—

MRS. ALVING. I should think so, indeed!

OSWALD. Even if I can't work—

MRS. ALVING. Oh, you'll soon be able to work again, my dear boy—now that you haven't got all those gnawing and depressing thoughts to brood over any longer.

OSWALD. Yes, I'm glad you were able to rid me of all those fancies. And when I've got over this one thing more—[*Sits on the sofa.*] Now we will have a little talk, mother—

MRS. ALVING. Yes, let us. [*She pushes an arm-chair towards the sofa, and sits down close to him.*]

OSWALD. And meantime the sun will be rising. And then you will know all. And then I shall not feel this dread any longer.

MRS. ALVING. What is it that I am to know?

OSWALD [*not listening to her*]. Mother, did you not say a little while ago, that there was nothing in the world you would not do for me, if I asked you?

MRS. ALVING. Yes, indeed I said so!

OSWALD. And you'll stick to it, mother?

MRS. ALVING. You may rely on that, my dear and only boy! I have nothing in the world to live for but you alone.

OSWALD. Very well, then; now you shall hear—Mother, you have a strong, steadfast mind, I know. Now you're to sit quite still when you hear it.

MRS. ALVING. What dreadful thing can it be—?

OSWALD. You're not to scream out. Do you hear? Do you promise me that? We will sit and talk about it quietly. Do you promise me, mother?

MRS. ALVING. Yes, yes; I promise. Only speak!

OSWALD. Well, you must know that all this fatigue—and my inability to think of work—all that is not the illness itself—

MRS. ALVING. Then what is the illness itself?

OSWALD. The disease I have as my birthright—[*he points to his forehead and adds very softly*]—is seated here.

MRS. ALVING [*almost voiceless*]. Oswald! No—no!

OSWALD. Don't scream. I can't bear it. Yes, mother, it is seated here—waiting. And it may break out any day—at any moment.

Mrs. Alving. Oh, what horror—!

Oswald. Now, quiet, quiet. That is how it stands with me—

Mrs. Alving [*springs up*]. It's not true, Oswald! It's impossible! It cannot be so!

Oswald. I have had one attack down there already. It was soon over. But when I came to know the state I had been in, then the dread descended upon me, raging and ravening; and so I set off home to you as fast as I could.

Mrs. Alving. Then this is the dread—!

Oswald. Yes—it's so indescribably loathsome, you know. Oh, if it had only been an ordinary mortal disease—! For I'm not so afraid of death—though I should like to live as long as I can.

Mrs. Alving. Yes, yes, Oswald, you must!

Oswald. But this is so unutterably loathsome. To become a little baby again! To have to be fed! To have to—Oh, it's not to be spoken of!

Mrs. Alving. The child has his mother to nurse him.

Oswald [*springs up*]. No, never that! That is just what I will not have. I can't endure to think that perhaps I should lie in that state for many years—and get old and grey. And in the meantime you might die and leave me. [*Sits in* Mrs. Alving's *chair.*] For the doctor said it wouldn't necessarily prove fatal at once. He called it a sort of softening of the brain—or something like that. [*Smiles sadly.*] I think that expression sounds so nice. It always sets me thinking of cherry-coloured velvet—something soft and delicate to stroke.

Mrs. Alving [*shrieks*]. Oswald!

Oswald [*springs up and paces the room*]. And now you have taken Regina from me. If I could only have had her! She would have come to the rescue, I know.

Mrs. Alving [*goes to him*]. What do you mean by that, my darling boy? Is there any help in the world that I would not give you?

Oswald. When I got over my attack in Paris, the doctor told me that when it comes again—and it will come—there will be no more hope.

Mrs. Alving. He was heartless enough to—

Oswald. I demanded it of him. I told him I had preparations to make— [*He smiles cunningly.*] And so I had. [*He takes a little box from his inner breast pocket and opens it.*] Mother, do you see this?

Mrs. Alving What is it?

Oswald. Morphia.

Mrs. Alving [*looks at him horror-struck*]. Oswald—my boy.

Oswald. I've scraped together twelve pilules—

Mrs. Alving [*snatches at it*]. Give me the box, Oswald.

Oswald. Not yet, mother. [*He hides the box again in his pocket.*]

Mrs. Alving. I shall never survive this!

Oswald. It must be survived. Now if I'd had Regina here, I should have told her how things stood with me—and begged her to come to the rescue at the last. She would have done it. I know she would.

MRS. ALVING. Never!

OSWALD. When the horror had come upon me, and she saw me lying there helpless, like a little new-born baby, impotent, lost, hopeless—past all saving—

MRS. ALVING. Never in all the world would Regina have done this!

OSWALD. Regina would have done it. Regina was so splendidly light-hearted. And she would soon have wearied of nursing an invalid like me.

MRS. ALVING. Then heaven be praised that Regina is not here.

OSWALD. Well then, it is you that must come to the rescue, mother.

MRS. ALVING [shrieks aloud]. I!

OSWALD. Who should do it if not you?

MRS. ALVING. I! your mother!

OSWALD. For that very reason.

MRS. ALVING. I who gave you life!

OSWALD. I never asked you for life. And what sort of a life have you given me? I will not have it! You shall take it back again!

MRS. ALVING. Help! Help! [She runs out into the hall.]

OSWALD [going after her]. Do not leave me! Where are you going?

MRS. ALVING [in the hall]. To fetch the doctor, Oswald! Let me pass!

OSWALD [also outside]. You shall not go out. And no one shall come in.

[The locking of a door is heard.]

MRS. ALVING [comes in again]. Oswald! Oswald—my child!

OSWALD [follows her]. Have you a mother's heart for me—and yet can see me suffer from this unutterable dread?

MRS. ALVING [after a moment's silence, commands herself, and says:] Here is my hand upon it.

OSWALD. Will you—?

MRS. ALVING. If it should ever be necessary. But it will never be necessary. No, no; it is impossible.

OSWALD. Well, let us hope so. And let us live together as long as we can. Thank you, mother. [He seats himself in the arm-chair which MRS. ALVING has moved to the sofa. Day is breaking. The lamp is still burning on the table.]

MRS. ALVING [drawing near cautiously]. Do you feel calm now?

OSWALD. Yes.

MRS. ALVING [bending over him]. It has been a dreadful fancy of yours, Oswald—nothing but a fancy. All this excitement has been too much for you. But now you shall have a long rest; at home with your mother, my own blessed boy. Everything you point to you shall have, just as when you were a little child.—There now. The crisis is over. You see how easily it passed! Oh, I was sure it would.—And do you see, Oswald, what a lovely day we are going to have? Brilliant sunshine! Now you can really see your home. [*She goes to the table and puts out the lamp. Sunrise. The glacier and the snow-peaks in the background glow in the morning light.*]

OSWALD [*sits in the arm-chair with his back towards the landscape, without moving. Suddenly he says:*] Mother, give me the sun.

MRS. ALVING [*by the table, starts and looks at him*]. What do you say?

OSWALD [*repeats, in a dull, toneless voice*]. The sun. The sun.

MRS. ALVING [*goes to him*]. Oswald, what is the matter with you?

[OSWALD *seems to shrink together in the chair; all his muscles relax; his face is expressionless, his eyes have a glassy stare.*]

MRS. ALVING [*quivering with terror*]. What is this? [*Shrieks.*] Oswald! what is the matter with you? [*Falls on her knees beside him and shakes him.*] Oswald! Oswald! look at me! Don't you know me?

OSWALD [*tonelessly as before*]. The sun.—The sun.

MRS. ALVING [*springs up in despair, entwines her hands in her hair and shrieks*]. I cannot bear it! [*Whispers, as though petrified.*] I cannot bear it! Never! [*Suddenly.*] Where has he got them? [*Fumbles hastily in his breast.*] Here! [*Shrinks back a few steps and screams:*] No; no; no!—Yes! —No; no! [*She stands a few steps away from him with her hands twisted in her hair, and stares at him in speechless horror.*]

OSWALD [*sits motionless as before and says:*] The sun.—The sun.

Anton Chekhov 1860–1904

The Sea Gull

DRAMATIS PERSONÆ

IRINA NIKOLAYEVNA ARKADIN (MA-
DAME TREPLEV), *an actress*
KONSTANTIN GAVRILOVITCH TREPLEV,
her son, a young man
PYOTR NIKOLAYEVITCH SORIN, *her
brother*
NINA MIHAILOVNA ZARETCHNY, *a
young girl, the daughter of a wealthy
landowner*
ILYA AFANASYEVITCH SHAMRAEV, *a re-
tired lieutenant,* SORIN's *steward*
POLINA ANDREYEVNA, *his wife*
MASHA, *his daughter*

BORIS ALEXEYEVITCH TRIGORIN, *a
literary man*
YEVGENY SERGEYEVITCH DORN, *a doc-
tor*
SEMYON SEMYONOVITCH MEDVE-
DENKO, *a schoolmaster*
YAKOV, *a labourer*
A MAN COOK
A HOUSEMAID
The action takes place in SORIN's
*house and garden. Between the Third
and Fourth Acts there is an interval
of two years.*

ACT I

[*Part of the park on* SORIN's *estate. Wide avenue leading away from the
spectators into the depths of the park toward the lake is blocked up by a
platform roughly put together for private theatricals, so that the lake is
not visible. To right and left of the platform, bushes. A few chairs, a little
table.*]

[*The sun has just set.* YAKOV *and other labourers are at work on the platform behind the curtain; there is the sound of coughing and hammering.*
MASHA *and* MEDVEDENKO *enter on the left, returning from a walk.*]

MEDVEDENKO. Why do you always wear black?
MASHA. I am in mourning for my life. I am unhappy.
MEDVEDENKO. Why? [*Pondering.*] I don't understand . . . You are in good

464

health; though your father is not very well off, he has got enough. My
life is much harder than yours. I only get twenty-three roubles a month,
and from that they deduct something for the pension fund, and yet I
don't wear mourning. [*They sit down.*]

MASHA. It isn't money that matters. A poor man may be happy.

MEDVEDENKO. Theoretically, yes; but in practice it's like this: there are my
two sisters and my mother and my little brother and I, and my salary is
only twenty-three roubles. We must eat and drink, mustn't we? One
must have tea and sugar. One must have tobacco. It's a tight fit.

MASHA. [*Looking round at the platform.*] The play will soon begin.

MEDVEDENKO. Yes. Miss Zaretchny will act: it is Konstantin Gavrilitch's
play. They are in love with each other and today their souls will be
united in the effort to realize the same artistic effect. But your soul and
mine have not a common point of contact. I love you, I am so wretched
I can't stay at home. Every day I walk four miles here and four miles
back and I meet with nothing but indifference from you. I can quite
understand it. I am without means and have a big family to keep. . . .
Who would care to marry a man who hasn't a penny to bless himself
with?

MASHA. Oh, nonsense! [*Takes a pinch of snuff.*] Your love touches me,
but I can't reciprocate it—that's all. [*Holding out the snuffbox to him.*]
Help yourself.

MEDVEDENKO. I don't feel like it. [*A pause.*]

MASHA. How stifling it is! There must be a storm coming. . . . You're
always discussing theories or talking about money. You think there is
no greater misfortune than poverty, but to my mind it is a thousand
times better to go in rags and be a beggar than . . . But you wouldn't
understand that, though. . . .

[SORIN *and* TREPLEV *enter on the right.*]

SORIN. [*Leaning on his walking stick.*] I am never quite myself in the
country, my boy, and, naturally enough, I shall never get used to it.
Last night I went to bed at ten and woke up this morning at nine feeling
as though my brain were glued to my skull, through sleeping so long.
[*Laughs.*] And after dinner I accidentally dropped off again, and now I
am utterly shattered and feel as though I were in a nightmare, in
fact. . . .

TREPLEV. Yes, you really ought to live in town. [*Catches sight of* MASHA
and MEDVEDENKO.] When the show begins, my friends, you will be
summoned, but you mustn't be here now. You must please go away.

SORIN. [*To* MASHA.] Marya Ilyinishna, will you be so good as to ask your
papa to tell them to take the dog off the chain?—it howls. My sister
could not sleep again last night.

MASHA. Speak to my father yourself; I am not going to. Please don't ask me. [*To* MEDVEDENKO.] Come along!

MEDVEDENKO. [*To* TREPLEV.] So you will send and let us know before it begins. [*Both go out.*]

SORIN. So I suppose the dog will be howling all night again. What a business it is! I have never done as I liked in the country. In old days I used to get leave for twenty-eight days and come here for a rest and so on, but they worried me so with all sorts of trifles that before I had been here two days I was longing to be off again. [*Laughs.*] I've always been glad to get away from here. . . . But now I am on the retired list, and I have nowhere else to go, as a matter of fact. I've got to live here whether I like it or not. . . .

YAKOV. [*To* TREPLEV.] We are going to have a bath, Konstantin Gavrilitch.

TREPLEV. Very well; but don't be more than ten minutes. [*Looks at his watch.*] It will soon begin.

YAKOV. Yes, sir. [*Goes out.*]

TREPLEV. [*Looking round the stage.*] Here is our theater. The curtain, then the first wing, then the second, and beyond that—open space. No scenery of any sort. There is an open view of the lake and the horizon. We shall raise the curtain at exactly half past eight, when the moon rises.

SORIN. Magnificent.

TREPLEV. If Nina is late it will spoil the whole effect. It is time she was here. Her father and her stepmother keep a sharp eye on her, and it is as hard for her to get out of the house as to escape from prison. [*Puts his uncle's cravat straight.*] Your hair and your beard are very untidy. They want clipping or something. . . .

SORIN. [*Combing out his beard.*] It's the tragedy of my life. Even as a young man I looked as though I had been drinking for days or something of the sort. I was never a favourite with the ladies. [*Sitting down.*] Why is your mother out of humor?

TREPLEV. Why? Because she is bored. [*Sitting down beside him.*] She is jealous. She is set against me, and against the performance, and against my play because Nina is acting in it, and she is not. She does not know my play, but she hates it.

SORIN. [*Laughs.*] What an idea!

TREPLEV. She is annoyed to think that even on this little stage Nina will have a triumph and not she. [*Looks at his watch.*] My mother is a psychological freak. Unmistakably talented, intelligent, capable of sobbing over a book, she will reel off all Nekrassov by heart; as a sick nurse she is an angel; but just try praising Duse in her presence! O-ho! You must praise no one but herself, you must write about her, make a fuss over her, be in raptures over her extraordinary acting in *La Dame aux*

Camélias or the *Ferment of Life;* but she has none of this narcotic in the country, she is bored and cross, and we are all her enemies—we are all in fault. Then she is superstitious—she is afraid of three candles, of the number thirteen. She is stingy. She has got seventy thousand roubles in a bank at Odessa—I know that for a fact—but ask her to lend you some money, and she will burst into tears.

SORIN. You imagine your mother does not like your play, and you are already upset and all that. Don't worry; your mother adores you.

TREPLEV. [*Pulling the petals off a flower.*] Loves me, loves me not; loves me, loves me not; loves me, loves me not. [*Laughs.*] You see, my mother does not love me. I should think not! She wants to live, to love, to wear light blouses; and I am twenty-five, and I am a continual reminder that she is no longer young. When I am not there she is only thirty-two, but when I am there she is forty-three, and for that she hates me. She knows, too, that I have no belief in the theater. She loves the stage, she fancies she is working for humanity, for the holy cause of art, while to my mind the modern theater is nothing but tradition and conventionality. When the curtain goes up, and by artificial light, in a room with three walls, these great geniuses, the devotees of holy art, represent how people eat, drink, love, move about, and wear their jackets; when from these commonplace sentences and pictures they try to draw a moral—a petty moral, easy of comprehension and convenient for domestic use; when in a thousand variations I am offered the same thing over and over again—I run away as Maupassant ran away from the Eiffel Tower, which weighed upon his brain with its vulgarity.

SORIN. You can't do without the stage.

TREPLEV. We need new forms of expression. We need new forms, and if we can't have them we had better have nothing. [*Looks at his watch.*] I love my mother—I love her very much—but she leads a senseless sort of life, always taken up with this literary gentleman, her name is always trotted out in the papers—and that wearies me. And sometimes the simple egoism of an ordinary mortal makes me feel sorry that my mother is a celebrated actress, and I fancy that if she were an ordinary woman I should be happier. Uncle, what could be more hopeless and stupid than my position? She used to have visitors, all celebrities—artists and authors—and among them all I was the only one who was nothing, and they only put up with me because I was her son. Who am I? What am I? I left the University in my third year—owing to circumstances "for which we accept no responsibility," as the editors say; I have no talents, I haven't a penny of my own, and on my passport I am described as an artisan of Kiev. You know my father was an artisan of Kiev, though he too was a well-known actor. So, when in her drawing room all these artists and authors graciously noticed me, I always fancied from their faces that they were taking the measure of my insignificance—I guessed their thoughts and suffered from the humiliation. . . .

SORIN. And, by the way, can you tell me, please, what sort of man this literary gentleman is? There's no making him out. He never says anything.

TREPLEV. He is an intelligent man, good-natured and rather melancholy, you know. A very decent fellow. He is still a good distance off forty, but he is already celebrated and has enough and to spare of everything. As for his writings . . . what shall I say? They are charming, full of talent, but . . . after Tolstoy or Zola you do not care to read Trigorin.

SORIN. Well, I am fond of authors, my boy. At one time I had a passionate desire for two things: I wanted to get married, and I wanted to become an author; but I did not succeed in doing either. Yes, it is pleasant to be even a small author, as a matter of fact.

TREPLEV. [Listens.] I hear steps . . . [Embraces his uncle.] I cannot live without her. . . . The very sound of her footsteps is lovely. . . . I am wildly happy. [Goes quickly to meet NINA ZARETCHNY as she enters.] My enchantress—my dream. . . .

NINA. [In agitation.] I am not late. . . . Of course I am not late. . . .

TREPLEV. [Kissing her hands.] No, no, no!

NINA. I have been uneasy all day. I was so frightened. I was afraid father would not let me come. . . . But he has just gone out with my stepmother. The sky is red, the moon is just rising, and I kept urging on the horse. [Laughs.] But I am glad. [Shakes SORIN's hand warmly.]

SORIN. [Laughs.] Your eyes look at though you have been crying. . . . Fie, fie! That's not right!

NINA. Oh, it was nothing. . . . You see how out of breath I am. I have to go in half an hour. We must make haste. I can't stay, I can't! For God's sake don't keep me! My father doesn't know I am here.

TREPLEV. It really is time to begin. We must go and call the others.

SORIN. I'll go this minute. [Goes to the right, singing "To France two grenadiers." Looks round.] Once I sang like that, and a deputy prosecutor said to me, "You have a powerful voice, your Excellency"; then he thought a little and added, "but not a pleasant one." [Laughs and goes off.]

NINA. My father and his wife won't let me come here. They say it is so Bohemian here . . . they are afraid I shall go on the stage. . . . But I feel drawn to the lake here like a sea gull. . . . My heart is full of you. [Looks round.]

TREPLEV. We are alone.

NINA. I fancy there is someone there.

TREPLEV. There's nobody. [They kiss.]

NINA. What tree is this?

TREPLEV. An elm.

NINA. Why is it so dark?

TREPLEV. It's evening; everything is getting dark. Don't go away early, I entreat you!

NINA. I must.

TREPLEV. And if I come to you, Nina, I'll stand in the garden all night, watching your window.

NINA. You can't; the watchman would notice you. Trésor is not used to you, and he would bark.

TREPLEV. I love you!

NINA. Sh-h. . . .

TREPLEV. [*Hearing footsteps.*] Who is there? You, Yakov?

YAKOV. [*Behind the stage.*] Yes, sir.

TREPLEV. Take your places. It's time to begin. Is the moon rising?

YAKOV. Yes, sir.

TREPLEV. Have you got the methylated spirit? Have you got the sulphur? When the red eyes appear there must be a smell of sulphur. [*To* NINA.] Go, it's all ready. Are you nervous?

NINA. Yes, awfully! Your mother is all right—I am not afraid of her—but there's Trigorin . . . I feel frightened and ashamed of acting before him . . . a celebrated author. . . . Is he young?

TREPLEV. Yes.

NINA. How wonderful his stories are.

TREPLEV. [*Coldly.*] I don't know. I haven't read them.

NINA. It is difficult to act in your play. There are no living characters in it.

TREPLEV. Living characters! One must depict life not as it is, and not as it ought to be, but as we see it in our dreams.

NINA. There is very little action in your play—nothing but speeches. And to my mind there ought to be love in a play. [*Both go behind the stage.*]

[*Enter* POLINA ANDREYEVNA *and* DORN.]

POLINA. It is getting damp. Go back and put on your galoshes.

DORN. I am hot.

POLINA. You don't take care of yourself. It's obstinacy. You are a doctor, and you know perfectly well that damp air is bad for you but you want to make me miserable; you sat out on the veranda all yesterday evening on purpose. . . .

DORN. [*Hums.*] "Do not say that youth is ruined."

POLINA. You were so absorbed in conversation with Irina Nikolayevna . . . you did not notice the cold. Own up . . . you are attracted by her.

DORN. I am fifty-five.

POLINA. Nonsense! That's not old for a man. You look very young for your age, and are still attractive to women.

Dorn. Well, what would you have?

Polina. All you men are ready to fall down and worship an actress, all of you!

Dorn. [Hums.] "Before thee once again I stand." If artists are liked in society and treated differently from merchants, for example, that's only in the nature of things. It's idealism.

Polina. Women have always fallen in love with you and thrown themselves on your neck. Is that idealism too?

Dorn. [Shrugs his shoulders.] Well, in the attitude of women to me there has been a great deal that was good. What they principally loved in me was a first-rate doctor. You remember that ten or fifteen years ago I was the only decent accoucheur in the district. Then, too, I have always been an honest man.

Polina. [Seizes him by the hand.] Dearest!

Dorn. Sh-h! They are coming.

[Enter Madame Arkadin arm in arm with Sorin, Trigorin, Shamraev, Medvedenko, and Masha.]

Shamraev. In the year 1873 she acted marvellously at the fair at Poltava. It was a delight! She acted exquisitely! Do you happen to know, madam, where Pavel Semyonitch Tchadin, a comic actor, is now? His Rasplyuev was inimitable, even finer than Sadovsky's, I assure you, honoured lady. Where is he now?

Madame Arkadin. You keep asking me about antediluvians. How should I know? [Sits down.]

Shamraev. [With a sigh.] Pashka Tchadin! There are no such actors now. The stage has gone down, Irina Nikolayevna! In old days there were mighty oaks, but now we see nothing but stumps.

Dorn. There are few actors of brilliant talents nowadays, that's true; but the average level of acting is far higher than it was.

Shamraev. I can't agree with you. But, of course, it's a matter of taste. De gustibus aut bene aut nihil.

[Treplev comes out from behind the stage.]

Madame Arkadin. [To her son.] My dear son, when is it going to begin?

Treplev. In a minute. I beg you to be patient.

Madame Arkadin. [Recites from Hamlet.]
"Oh Hamlet, speak no more!
Thou turn'st mine eyes into my very soul;
And there I see such black and grained spots
As will not leave their tinct."

Treplev. [Paraphrasing from Hamlet].

"Then why do you yield to sin, seek love in the depths of wickedness?"

[*A horn is sounded behind the stage.*]

TREPLEV. Ladies and gentlemen, we begin! I beg you to attend. [*A pause.*]
I begin. [*Taps with a stick and recites aloud.*] Oh, you venerable old
shadows that float at night-time over this lake, lull us to sleep and let us
dream of what will be in two hundred thousand years!

SORIN. There will be nothing in two hundred thousand years.

TREPLEV. Then let them present that nothing to us.

MADAME ARKADIN. Let them. We are asleep.

[*The curtain rises; the view of the lake is revealed; the moon is above the
horizon, its reflection in the water;* NINA ZARETCHNY, *all in white, is sitting
on a big stone.*]

NINA. Men, lions, eagles and partridges, horned deer, geese, spiders, silent
fish that dwell in the water, starfishes and creatures which cannot be seen
by the eye—all living things, all living things, all living things, having
completed their cycle of sorrow, are extinct. . . . For thousands of years
the earth has borne no living creature on its surface, and this poor moon
lights its lamp in vain. On the meadow the cranes no longer waken with
a cry, and there is no sound of the May beetles in the lime trees. It is
cold, cold, cold! Empty, empty, empty! Dreadful, dreadful, dreadful!
[*A pause.*] The bodies of living creatures have vanished into dust, and
eternal matter has transformed them into rocks, into water, into clouds,
while the souls of all have melted into one. That world-soul I am—I. . . .
In me is the soul of Alexander the Great, of Caesar, of Shakespeare, and
of Napoleon, and of the lowest leech. In me the consciousness of men is
blended with the instincts of the animals, and I remember all, all, all!
And I live through every life over again in myself! [*Will-of-the-wisps
appear.*]

MADAME ARKADIN. [*Softly.*] It's something decadent.

TREPLEV. [*In an imploring and reproachful voice.*] Mother!

NINA. I am alone. Once in a hundred years I open my lips to speak, and
my voice echoes mournfully in the void, and no one hears. . . . You
too, pale lights, hear me not. . . . The stagnant marsh begets you before
daybreak and you wander until dawn, but without thought, without will,
without the tremor of life. For fear that life should spring up in you the
father of eternal matter, the devil, keeps the atoms in you, as in the
stones and in the water, in continual flux, and you are changing per-
petually. For in all the universe nothing remains permanent and unchanged but the spirit. [*A pause.*] Like a prisoner cast into a deep, empty
well I know not where I am and what awaits me. All is hidden from me
but that in the cruel, persistent struggle with the devil—the principle of

the forces of matter—I am destined to conquer, and, after that, matter and spirit will be blended in glorious harmony and the Kingdom of the Cosmic Will will come. But that will come only little by little, through long long thousands of years when the moon and the bright Sirius and the earth are changed to dust. . . . Till then—terror, terror . . . [*A pause; two red spots appear upon the background of the lake.*] Here my powerful foe, the devil, is approaching. I see his dreadful crimson eyes. . . .

MADAME ARKADIN. There's a smell of sulphur. Is that as it should be?

TREPLEV. Yes.

MADAME ARKADIN. [*Laughs.*] Oh, it's a stage effect!

TREPLEV. Mother!

NINA. He is dreary without man—

POLINA. [*To* DORN.] You have taken your hat off. Put it on or you will catch cold.

MADAME ARKADIN. The doctor has taken his hat off to the devil, the father of eternal matter.

TREPLEV. [*Firing up, aloud.*] The play is over! Enough! Curtain!

MADAME ARKADIN. What are you cross about?

TREPLEV. Enough! The curtain! Let down the curtain! [*Stamping.*] Curtain! [*The curtain falls.*] I am sorry! I lost sight of the fact that only a few of the elect may write plays and act in them. I have infringed the monopoly. I . . . I . . . [*Tries to say something more, but with a wave of his hand goes out on left.*]

MADAME ARKADIN. What's the matter with him?

SORIN. Irina, you really must have more consideration for youthful vanity, my dear.

MADAME ARKADIN. What did I say to him?

SORIN. You hurt his feelings.

MADAME ARKADIN. He told us beforehand that it was a joke, and I regarded his play as a joke.

SORIN. All the same . . .

MADAME ARKADIN. Now it appears that he has written a great work. What next! So he has got up this performance and smothered us with sulphur not as a joke but as a protest. . . . He wanted to show us how to write and what to act. This is getting tiresome! These continual sallies at my expense—these continual pinpricks would put anyone out of patience, say what you like. He is a vain, whimsical boy!

SORIN. He meant to give you pleasure.

MADAME ARKADIN. Really? He did not choose an ordinary play, however, but made us listen to this decadent delirium. For the sake of a joke I am ready to listen to delirium, but here we have pretensions to new forms and a new view of art. To my thinking it's no question of new forms at all, but simply bad temper.

TRIGORIN. Everyone writes as he likes and as he can.

MADAME ARKADIN. Let him write as he likes and as he can, only let him leave me in peace.

DORN. Jupiter! you are angry. . . .

MADAME ARKADIN. I am not Jupiter—I am a woman. [*Lights a cigarette.*] I am not angry—I am only vexed that a young man should spend his time so drearily. I did not mean to hurt his feelings.

MEDVEDENKO. No one has any grounds to separate spirit from matter, seeing that spirit itself may be a combination of material atoms. [*With animation, to* TRIGORIN.] But you know someone ought to write a play on how we poor teachers live, and get it acted. We have a hard, hard life.

MADAME ARKADIN. That's true, but don't let us talk either of plays or of atoms. It is such a glorious evening! Do you hear? There is singing! [*Listens.*] How nice it is!

POLINA. It's on the other side of the lake. [*A pause.*]

MADAME ARKADIN. [*To* TRIGORIN.] Sit down beside me. Ten or fifteen years ago there were sounds of music and singing on that lake continually almost every night. There are six country houses on the shores of the lake. I remember laughter, noise, shooting, and love affairs without end. . . . The *jeune premier* and the idol of all those six households was in those days our friend here, the doctor [*Motions with her head towards* DORN.] Yevgeny Sergeitch. He is fascinating still, but in those days he was irresistible. But my conscience is beginning to trouble me. Why did I hurt my poor boy's feelings? I feel worried. [*Aloud.*] Kostya! Son! Kostya!

MASHA. I'll go and look for him.

MADAME ARKADIN. Please do, my dear.

MASHA. [*Going to the left.*] Aa-oo! Konstantin Gavrilitch! Aa-oo! [*Goes off.*]

NINA. [*Coming out from behind the stage.*] Apparently there will be no going on, and I may come out. Good evening! [*Kisses* MADAME ARKADIN *and* POLINA ANDREYEVNO.]

SORIN. Bravo! Bravo!

MADAME ARKADIN. Bravo! Bravo! We admired you. With such an appearance, with such a lovely voice, you really cannot stay in the country; it is a sin. You must have talent. Do you hear? It's your duty to go on the stage.

NINA. Oh, that's my dream! [*Sighing.*] But it will never be realized.

MADAME ARKADIN. Who knows? Here, let me introduce Boris Alexeyevitch Trigorin.

NINA. Oh, I am so glad . . . [*Overcome with embarrassment.*] I am always reading your . . .

MADAME ARKADIN. [*Making her sit down beside them.*] Don't be shy, my dear. He is a celebrity, but he has a simple heart. You see, he is shy himself.

Dorn. I suppose we may raise the curtain; it's rather uncanny.

Shamraev. [*Aloud.*] Yakov, pull up the curtain, my lad. [*The curtain goes up.*]

Nina. [*To* Trigorin.] It is a queer play, isn't it?

Trigorin. I did not understand it at all. But I enjoyed it. You acted so genuinely. And the scenery was delightful. [*A pause.*] There must be a lot of fish in that lake.

Nina. Yes.

Trigorin. I love angling. There is nothing I enjoy so much as sitting on the bank of a river in the evening and watching the float.

Nina. But I should have thought that for anyone who has known the enjoyment of creation, no other enjoyment can exist.

Madame Arkadin. [*Laughing.*]. Don't talk like that. When people say nice things to him he is utterly floored.

Shamraev. I remember one evening in the opera theater in Moscow the celebrated Silva took the lower C! As it happened, there was sitting in the gallery the bass of our church choir, and all at once—imagine our intense astonishment—we heard from the gallery "Bravo, Silva!" a whole octave lower—like this: [*In a deep bass.*] "Bravo, Silva!" The audience sat spellbound. [*A pause.*]

Dorn. The angel of silence has flown over us.

Nina. It's time for me to go. Good-bye.

Madame Arkadin. Where are you off to? Why so early? We won't let you go.

Nina. My father expects me.

Madame Arkadin. What a man, really . . . [*Kisses her.*] Well, there is no help for it. I am sorry—I am sorry to let you go.

Nina. If you knew how grieved I am to go.

Madame Arkadin. Someone ought to see you home, my little dear.

Nina. [*Frightened.*] Oh, no, no!

Sorin. [*To her, in an imploring voice.*] Do stay!

Nina. I can't, Pyotr Nikolayevitch.

Sorin. Stay for an hour. What is there in that?

Nina. [*Thinking a minute, tearfully.*] I can't! [*Shakes hands and hurriedly goes off.*]

Madame Arkadin. Unfortunate girl she is, really. They say her mother left her father all her immense property—every farthing of it—and now the girl has got nothing, as her father has already made a will leaving everything to his second wife. It's monstrous!

Dorn. Yes, her father is a pretty thorough scoundrel, one must do him the justice to say so.

Sorin. [*Rubbing his cold hands.*] Let us go too, it's getting damp. My legs ache.

MADAME ARKADIN. They seem like wooden legs, you can hardly walk. Let us go, unlucky old man! [*Takes his arm.*]

SHAMRAEV. [*Offering his arm to his wife.*] Madame?

SORIN. I heard that dog howling again. [*To* SHAMRAEV.] Be so kind, Ilya Afanasyitch, as to tell them to let it off the chain.

SHAMRAEV. It's impossible, Pyotr Nikolayevitch, I am afraid of thieves getting into the barn. Our millet is there. [*To* MEDVEDENKO, *who is walking beside him.*] Yes, a whole octave lower: "Bravo, Silva!" And he not a singer—simply a church chorister!

MEDVEDENKO. And what salary does a chorister get? [*All go out except* DORN.]

DORN. [*Alone.*] I don't know, perhaps I know nothing about it, or have gone off my head, but I liked the play. There is something in it. When that girl talked about loneliness and afterwards when the devil's eyes appeared, I was so excited that my hands trembled. It is fresh, naïve. . . . Here he comes, I believe. I want to say all the nice things I can to him.

TREPLEV. [*Enters.*] They have all gone.

DORN. I am here.

TREPLEV. Mashenka is looking for me all over the park. Insufferable creature she is!

DORN. Konstantin Gavrilitch, I liked your play extremely. It's a strange thing, and I haven't heard the end, and yet it made a strong impression! You are a gifted man—you must persevere.

[TREPLEV *presses his hand warmly and embraces him impulsively.*]

DORN. Fie, what a hysterical fellow! There are tears in his eyes! What I mean is this. You have taken a subject from the realm of abstract ideas. So it should be, for a work of art ought to express a great idea. A thing is only fine when it is serious. How pale you are!

TREPLEV. So you tell me to persevere?

DORN. Yes. . . . But write only of what is important and eternal. You know, I have had varied experiences of life, and have enjoyed it; I am satisfied, but if it had been my lot to know the spiritual heights which artists reach at the moment of creation, I should, I believe, have despised my bodily self and all that appertains to it and left all things earthly as far behind as possible.

TREPLEV. Excuse me, where is Nina?

DORN. And another thing. In a work or art there ought to be a clear definite idea. You ought to know what is your aim in writing, for if you go along that picturesque route without a definite goal you will be lost and your talent will be your ruin.

TREPLEV. [*Impatiently.*] Where is Nina?

DORN. She has gone home.

TREPLEV. [*In despair.*] What am I to do? I want to see her . . . I must see her. . . . I must go. . . .

[*Enter* MASHA.]

DORN. [*To* TREPLEV.] Calm yourself, my boy.

TREPLEV. But I am going all the same. I must go.

MASHA. Come indoors, Konstantin Gavrilitch. Your mother wants you. She is worried.

TREPLEV. Tell her that I have gone away. And I beg you—all of you—leave me in peace! Let me alone! Don't follow me about!

DORN. Come, come, come, dear boy. . . . You can't go on like that. . . . That's not the thing.

TREPLEV. [*In tears.*] Good-bye, doctor. Thank you . . . [*Goes off.*]

DORN. [*With a sigh.*] Youth! youth!

MASHA. When people have nothing better to say, they say, "Youth! youth!" . . . [*Takes a pinch of snuff.*]

DORN. [*Takes her snuffbox from her and flings it into the bushes.*] That's disgusting! [*A pause.*] I believe they are playing the piano indoors. We must go in.

MASHA. Wait a little.

DORN. What is it?

MASHA. I want to tell you once more. I have a longing to talk . . . [*Growing agitated.*] I don't care for my father . . . but I feel drawn to you. For some reason I feel with all my heart that you are very near me. . . . Help me, help me, or I shall do something silly, I shall make a mock of my life and ruin it. . . . I can't go on. . . .

DORN. What is it? Help you in what?

MASHA. I am miserable. No one, no one knows how miserable I am! [*Laying her head on his breast, softly.*] I love Konstantin!

DORN. How hysterical they all are! How hysterical! And what a lot of love. . . . Oh, the sorcery of the lake. [*Tenderly.*] But what can I do, my child? What? What?

[*Curtain*]

ACT II

[*A croquet lawn. The house with a big veranda in the background on the right; on the left is seen the lake with the blazing sun reflected in it.*]

[*Flower beds. Mid-day. Hot.* MADAME ARKADIN, DORN, *and* MASHA *are sitting on a garden seat in the shade of an old lime tree on one side of the croquet lawn.* DORN *has an open book on his knee.*]

MADAME ARKADIN. [*To* MASHA.] Come, let us stand up. [*They both get up.*] Let us stand side by side. You are twenty-two and I am nearly twice as old. Yevgeny Sergeitch, which of us looks the younger?

DORN. You, of course.

MADAME ARKADIN. There! And why is it? Because I work, I feel I am always on the go, while you stay always in the same place and have no life at all. . . . And it is my rule never to look into the future. I never think about old age or death. What is to be, will be.

MASHA. And I feel as though I had been born long, long ago; I trail my life along like an endless train. . . . And often I have not the slightest desire to go on living. [*Sits down.*] Of course, that's all nonsense. I must shake myself and throw it all off.

DORN. [*Hums quietly.*] "Tell her, my flowers."

MADAME ARKADIN. Then I am as particular as an Englishman. I keep myself in hand, as they say, my dear, and am always dressed and have my hair done *comme il faut*. Do I allow myself to go out of the house even into the garden in a dressing gown, or without my hair being done? Never! What has preserved me is that I have never been a dowdy, I have never let myself go, as some women do . . . [*Walks about the lawn with her arms akimbo.*] Here I am, as brisk as a bird. I could take the part of a girl of fifteen.

DORN. Nevertheless, I shall go on. [*Takes up the book.*] "We stopped at the corn merchant and the rats. . . ."

MADAME ARKADIN. And the rats. Read. [*Sits down.*] But give it to me, I'll read. It is my turn. [*Takes the book and looks in it.*] And rats. . . . Here it is. . . . [*Reads.*] "And of course for society people to spoil novelists and to attract them to themselves is as dangerous as for a corn merchant to rear rats in his granaries. And yet they love them. And so, when a woman has picked out an author whom she desires to captivate, she lays siege to him by means of compliments, flattery, and favors . . ." Well, that may be so with the French, but there is nothing like that with us, we have no set rules. Among us, before a woman sets to work to captivate an author, she is generally head over ears in love herself, if you please. To go no further, take Trigorin and me. . . .

[*Enter* SORIN, *leaning on his stick and with him* NINA; MEDVEDENKO *wheels an empty bath chair in after them.*]

SORIN. [*In a caressing tone, as to a child.*] Yes? We are delighted, aren't we? We are happy today at last? [*To his sister.*] We are delighted! Our father and stepmother have gone off to Tver, and we are free now for three whole days.

NINA. [*Sits down beside* MADAME ARKADIN *and embraces her.*] I am happy! Now I belong to you.

SORIN. [*Sits down in his bath chair.*] She looks quite a beauty today.

MADAME ARKADIN. Nicely dressed and interesting. . . . That's a good girl. [*Kisses* NINA.] But we mustn't praise you too much for fear of ill luck. Where is Boris Alexeyevitch?

NINA. He is in the bathing house, fishing.

MADAME ARKADIN. I wonder he doesn't get sick of it! [*Is about to go on reading.*]

NINA. What is that?

MADAME ARKADIN. Maupassant's "Sur l'eau," my dear. [*Reads a few lines to herself.*] Well, the rest isn't interesting or true. [*Shuts the book.*] I feel uneasy. Tell me, what's wrong with my son? Why is he so depressed and ill humored? He spends whole days on the lake and I hardly ever see him.

MASHA. His heart is troubled. [*To* NINA, *timidly.*] Please, do read us something out of his play!

NINA. [*Shrugging her shoulders.*] Would you like it? It's so uninteresting.

MASHA. [*Restraining her enthusiasm.*] When he reads anything himself his eyes glow and his face turns pale. He has a fine mournful voice, and the gestures of a poet.

[*There is a sound of* SORIN *snoring.*]

DORN. Good night!

MADAME ARKADIN. Petrusha!

SORIN. Ah?

MADAME ARKADIN. Are you asleep?

SORIN. Not a bit of it. [*A pause.*]

MADAME ARKADIN. You do nothing for your health, brother, and that's not right.

SORIN. I should like to take something, but the doctor won't give me anything.

DORN. Take medicine at sixty!

SORIN. Even at sixty one wants to live!

DORN. [*With vexation.*] Oh, very well, take valerian drops!

MADAME ARKADIN. It seems to me it would do him good to go to some mineral springs.

DORN. Well, he might go. And he might not.

MADAME ARKADIN. What is one to make of that?

DORN. There's nothing to make of it. It's quite clear. [*A pause.*]

MEDVEDENKO. Pyotr Nikolayevitch ought to give up smoking.

SORIN. Nonsense!

DORN. No, it's not nonsense. Wine and tobacco destroy the personality. After a cigar or a glass of vodka, you are not Pyotr Nikolayevitch any more but Pyotr Nikolayevitch plus somebody else; your ego is diffused and you feel toward yourself as to a third person.

SORIN. [*Laughs.*] It's all very well for you to argue! You've lived your life, but what about me? I have served in the Department of Justice for twenty-eight years, but I haven't lived yet, I've seen and done nothing as a matter of fact, and very naturally I want to live very much. You've had enough and you don't care, and so you are inclined to be philosophical, but I want to live, and so I drink sherry at dinner and smoke cigars and so on. That's all it comes to.

DORN. One must look at life seriously, but to go in for cures at sixty and to regret that one hasn't enjoyed oneself enough in one's youth is frivolous, if you will forgive my saying so.

MASHA. [*Gets up.*] It must be lunch-time. [*Walks with a lazy, lagging step.*] My leg is gone to sleep. [*Goes off.*]

DORN. She will go and have a couple of glasses before lunch.

SORIN. She has no personal happiness, poor thing.

DORN. Nonsense, your Excellency.

SORIN. You argue like a man who has had all he wants.

MADAME ARKADIN. Oh, what can be more boring than this sweet country boredom! Hot, still, no one ever doing anything, everyone airing their theories. . . . It's nice being with you, my friends, charming to listen to you, but . . . to sit in a hotel room somewhere and learn one's part is ever so much better.

NINA. [*Enthusiastically.*] Delightful! I understand you.

SORIN. Of course, it's better in town. You sit in your study, the footman lets no one in unannounced, there's a telephone . . . in the streets there are cabs and everything. . . .

DORN. [*Hums.*] "Tell her, my flowers."

[*Enter* SHAMRAEV, *and after him* POLINA ANDREYEVNA.]

SHAMRAEV. Here they are! Good morning! [*Kisses* MADAME ARKADIN'S *hand and then* NINA'S.] Delighted to see you in good health. [*To* MADAME ARKADIN.] My wife tells me that you are proposing to drive into town with her today. Is that so?

MADAME ARKADIN. Yes, we are thinking of it.

SHAMRAEV. Hm! that's splendid, but how are you going, honoured lady? They are carting the rye today; all the men are at work. What horses are you to have, allow me to ask?

MADAME ARKADIN. What horses? How can I tell which?

SORIN. We've got carriage horses.

SHAMRAEV. [*Growing excited.*] Carriage horses! But where am I to get collars for them? Where am I to get collars? It's a strange thing! It passes my understanding! Honoured lady! forgive me, I am full of reverence for your talent. I would give ten years of my life for you, but I cannot let you have the horses!

MADAME ARKADIN. But if I have to go! It's a queer thing!

SHAMRAEV. Honoured lady! you don't know what farming means.

MADAME ARKADIN. [*Flaring up.*] That's the old story! If that's so, I go back to Moscow today. Give orders for horses to be hired for me at the village, or I'll walk to the station.

SHAMRAEV. [*Flaring up.*] In that case I resign my position! You must look for another steward. [*Goes off.*]

MADAME ARKADIN. It's like this every summer; every summer I am insulted here! I won't set my foot in the place again. [*Goes off at left where the bathing shed is supposed to be; a minute later she can be seen entering the house.* TRIGORIN *follows her, carrying fishing rods and tackle, and a pail.*]

SORIN. [*Flaring up.*] This is insolence! It's beyond everything. I am thoroughly sick of it. Send all the horses here this minute!

NINA. [*To* POLINA ANDREYEVNA.] To refuse Irina Nikolayevna, the famous actress! Any wish of hers, any whim even, is of more consequence than all your farming. It's positively incredible!

POLINA. [*In despair.*] What can I do? Put yourself in my position: what can I do?

SORIN. [*To* NINA.] Let us go to my sister. We will all entreat her not to go away. Won't we? [*Looking in the direction in which* SHAMRAEV *has gone.*] Insufferable man! Despot!

NINA. [*Preventing him from getting up.*] Sit still, sit still. We will wheel you in. [*She and* MEDVEDENKO *push the bath chair.*] Oh, how awful it is!

SORIN. Yes, yes, it's awful. But he won't leave, I'll speak to him directly.

[*They go out;* DORN *and* POLINA ANDREYEVNA *are left alone on the stage.*]

DORN. People are tiresome. Your husband ought to be simply kicked out, but it will end in that old woman Pyotr Nikolayevitch and his sister begging the man's pardon. You will see!

POLINA. He has sent the carriage horses into the fields too! And there are misunderstandings like this every day. If you only knew how it upsets me! It makes me ill; see how I am trembling. . . . I can't endure his rudeness. [*In an imploring voice.*] Yevgeny, dearest, light of my eyes, my darling, let me come to you. . . . Our time is passing, we are no longer young, and if only we could lay aside concealment and lying for the end of our lives, anyway . . . [*A pause.*]

DORN. I am fifty-five; it's too late to change my life.

POLINA. I know you refuse me because there are other women too who are as near to you. You can't take them all to live with you. I understand. Forgive me, you are tired of me.

[NINA *appears near the house; she is picking flowers.*]

DORN. No, it's all right.

POLINA. I am wretched from jealousy. Of course you are a doctor, you can't avoid women. I understand.

DORN. [*To* NINA, *who comes up to them.*] How are things going?

NINA. Irina Nikolayevna is crying and Pyotr Nikolayevitch has an attack of asthma.

DORN. [*Gets up.*] I'd better go and give them both valerian drops.

NINA. [*Gives him the flowers.*] Please take these.

DORN. *Merci bien.* [*Goes toward the house.*]

POLINA. [*Going with him.*] What charming flowers! [*Near the house, in a smothered voice.*] Give me those flowers! Give me those flowers! [*On receiving them tears the flowers to pieces and throws them away; both go into the house.*]

NINA. [*Alone.*] How strange it is to see a famous actress cry, and about such a trivial thing! And isn't it strange? A famous author, adored by the public, written about in all the papers, his photographs for sale, his works translated into foreign languages—and he spends the whole day fishing and is delighted that he has caught two gudgeon. I thought famous people were proud, unapproachable, that they despised the crowd, and by their fame and the glory of their name, as it were, revenged themselves on the vulgar herd for putting rank and wealth above everything. But here they cry and fish, play cards, laugh and get cross like everyone else!

TREPLEV. [*Comes in without a hat on, with a gun and a dead sea gull.*] Are you alone here?

NINA. Yes.

[TREPLEV *lays the sea gull at her feet.*]

NINA. What does that mean?

TREPLEV. I was so mean as to kill this bird today. I lay it at your feet.

NINA. What is the matter with you? [*Picks up the bird and looks at it.*]

TREPLEV. [*After a pause.*] Soon I shall kill myself in the same way.

NINA. You have so changed, I hardly know you.

TREPLEV. Yes, ever since the day when I hardly knew you. You have changed to me, your eyes are cold, you feel me in the way.

NINA. You have become irritable of late, you express yourself so incomprehensibly, as it were in symbols. This bird is a symbol too, I suppose, but forgive me, I don't understand it. [*Lays the sea gull on the seat.*] I am too simple to understand you.

TREPLEV. This began from that evening when my play came to grief so stupidly. Women never forgive failure. I have burnt it all; every scrap of it. If only you knew how miserable I am! Your growing cold to me is awful, incredible, as though I had waked up and found this lake had suddenly dried up or sunk into the earth. You have just said that you are too simple to understand me. Oh, what is there to understand? My play was not liked, you despise my inspiration, you already consider me commonplace, insignificant, like so many others . . . [*Stamping.*] How well I understand it all, how I understand it! I feel as though I had a nail in my brain, damnation take it together with my vanity which is sucking away my life, sucking it like a snake . . . [*Sees* TRIGORIN, *who comes in reading a book.*] Here comes the real genius, walking like Hamlet and with a book too. [*Mimics.*] "Words, words, words." . . . The sun has scarcely reached you and you are smiling already, your eyes are melting in its rays. I won't be in your way. [*Goes off quickly.*]

TRIGORIN. [*Making notes in his book.*] Takes snuff and drinks vodka. Always in black. The schoolmaster is in love with her. . . .

NINA. Good morning, Boris Alexeyevitch!

TRIGORIN. Good morning. Circumstances have turned out so unexpectedly that it seems we are setting off today. We are hardly likely to meet again. I am sorry. I don't often have the chance of meeting young girls, youthful and charming; I have forgotten how one feels at eighteen or nineteen and can't picture it to myself, and so the young girls in my stories and novels are usually false. I should like to be in your shoes just for one hour to find out how you think, and altogether what sort of person you are.

NINA. And I should like to be in your shoes.

TRIGORIN. What for?

NINA. To know what it feels like to be a famous, gifted author. What does it feel like to be famous? How does it affect you, being famous?

TRIGORIN. How? Nohow, I believe. I have never thought about it. [*After a moment's thought.*] It's one of two things: either you exaggerate my fame, or it never is felt at all.

NINA. But if you read about yourself in the newspapers?

TRIGORIN. When they praise me I am pleased, and when they abuse me I feel out of humour for a day or two.

NINA. What a wonderful world! If only you knew how I envy you! How different people's lots in life are! Some can scarcely get through their dull, obscure existence, they are all just like one another, they are all unhappy; while others—you, for instance—you are one out of a million, have an interesting life full of brightness and significance. You are happy.

TRIGORIN. I? [*Shrugging his shoulders.*] Hm. . . . You talk of fame and happiness, of bright interesting life, but to me all those fine words, if you will forgive my saying so, are just like a sweetmeat which I never taste. You are very young and very good natured.

NINA. Your life is splendid!

TRIGORIN. What is there particularly nice in it? [*Looks at his watch.*] I must go and write directly. Excuse me, I mustn't stay . . . [*Laughs.*] You have stepped on my favourite corn, as the saying is, and here I am beginning to get excited and a little cross. Let us talk though. We will talk about my splendid bright life. . . . Well, where shall we begin?

[*After thinking a little.*] There are such things as fixed ideas, when a man thinks day and night, for instance, of nothing but the moon. And I have just such a moon. I am haunted day and night by one persistent thought: I ought to be writing, I ought to be writing, I ought . . . I have scarcely finished one novel when, for some reason, I must begin writing another, then a third, after the third a fourth. I write incessantly, post haste, and I can't write in any other way. What is there splendid and bright in that, I ask you? Oh, it's an absurd life! Here I am with you; I am excited, yet every moment I remember that my unfinished novel is waiting for me. Here I see a cloud that looks like a grand piano. I think that I must put into a story somewhere that a cloud sailed by that looked like a grand piano. There is a scent of heliotrope. I hurriedly make a note: a sickly smell, a widow's flower, to be mentioned in the description of a summer evening. I catch up myself and you at every sentence, every word, and make haste to put those sentences and words away into my literary treasure house—it may come in useful! When I finish work I race off to the theater or to fishing; if only I could rest in that and forget myself. But no, there's a new subject rolling about in my head like a heavy iron cannon ball, and I am drawn to my writing table and must make haste again to go on writing and writing. And it's always like that, always. And I have no rest from myself, and I feel that I am eating up my own life, and that for the sake of the honey I give to someone in space I am stripping the pollen from my best flowers, tearing up the flowers themselves and trampling on their roots. Don't you think I am mad? Do my friends and acquaintances treat me as though I were sane? "What are you writing? What are you giving us?" It's the same thing again and again, and it seems to me as though my friends' notice, their praises, their enthusiasm—that it's all a sham, that they are deceiving me as an invalid and I am somehow afraid that they will steal up to me from behind, snatch me and carry me off and put me in a madhouse. And in those years, the best years of my youth, when I was beginning, my writing was unmixed torture. A small writer, particularly when he is not successful, seems to himself clumsy, awkward, unnecessary; his nerves are strained and overwrought. He can't resist hanging about people connected with literature and art, unrecognized and unnoticed by anyone, afraid to look anyone boldly in the face, like a passionate gambler without any money. I hadn't seen my reader, but for some reason I always imagined him hostile, and mistrustful. I was afraid of the public, it alarmed me, and when I had to produce my first play it always seemed to me that all the dark people felt hostile and all the fair ones were coldly indifferent. Oh, how awful it was! What agony it was!

NINA. But surely inspiration and the very process of creation give you moments of exalted happiness?

TRIGORIN. Yes. While I am writing I enjoy it. And I like reading my proofs, but . . . as soon as it is published I can't endure it, and I see that it is all wrong, a mistake, that it ought not to have been written at all, and I feel vexed and sick about it . . . [*Laughing.*] And the public reads it and says: "Yes, charming, clever. Charming, but very inferior to Tolstoy," or, "It's a fine thing, but Turgenev's *Fathers and Children* is finer." And it will be the same to my dying day, only charming and clever, charming and clever—and nothing more. And when I die my friends, passing by my tomb, will say, "Here lies Trigorin. He was a good writer, but inferior to Turgenev."

NINA. Forgive me, but I refuse to understand you. You are simply spoiled by success.

TRIGORIN. What success? I have never liked myself; I dislike my own work. The worst of it is that I am in a sort of delirium, and often don't understand what I am writing. I love this water here, the trees, the sky. I feel nature, it arouses in me a passionate, irresistible desire to write. But I am not simply a landscape painter; I am also a citizen. I love my native country, my people; I feel that if I am a writer I am in duty bound to write of the people, of their sufferings, of their future, to talk about science and the rights of man and so on, and so on, and I write about everything. I am hurried and flustered, and on all sides they whip me up and are angry with me; I dash about from side to side like a fox beset by hounds. I see life and culture continually getting farther and farther away while I fall farther and farther behind like a peasant too late for the train; and what it comes to is that I feel I can only describe scenes and in everything else I am false to the marrow of my bones.

NINA. You are overworked and have not the leisure nor the desire to appreciate your own significance. You may be dissatisfied with yourself, but for others you are great and splendid! If I were a writer like you, I should give up my whole life to the common herd, but I should know that there could be no greater happiness for them than to rise to my level, and they would harness themselves to my chariot.

TRIGORIN. My chariot, what next! Am I an Agamemnon, or what? [*Both smile.*]

NINA. For such happiness as being a writer or an artist I would be ready to endure poverty, disappointment, the dislike of those around me; I would live in a garret and eat nothing but rye bread, I would suffer from being dissatisfied with myself, from recognizing my own imperfections, but I should ask in return for fame . . . real, resounding fame. . . . [*Covers her face with her hands.*] It makes me dizzy. . . . Ough!

[*The voice of* MADAME ARKADIN *from the house.*]

MADAME ARKADIN. Boris Alexeyevitch!

TRIGORIN. They are calling for me. I suppose it's to pack. But I don't want to leave here. [*Looks round at the lake.*] Just look how glorious it is! It's splendid!

NINA. Do you see the house and garden on the other side of the lake?

TRIGORIN. Yes.

NINA. That house was my dear mother's. I was born there. I have spent all my life beside this lake and I know every little islet on it.

TRIGORIN. It's very delightful here! [*Seeing the sea gull.*] And what's this?

NINA. A sea gull. Konstantin Gavrilitch shot it.

TRIGORIN. A beautiful bird. Really, I don't want to go away. Try and persuade Irina Nikolayevna to stay. [*Makes a note in his book.*]

NINA. What are you writing?

TRIGORIN. Oh, I am only making a note. A subject struck me. [*Putting away the notebook.*] A subject for a short story: a young girl, such as you, has lived all her life beside a lake; she loves the lake like a sea gull, and is as free and happy as a sea gull. But a man comes by chance, sees her, and having nothing better to do, destroys her like that sea gull here. [*A pause.*]

[MADAME ARKADIN *appears at the window.*]

MADAME ARKADIN. Boris Alexeyevitch, where are you?

TRIGORIN. I am coming. [*Goes and looks back at* NINA. *To* MADAME ARKADIN *at the window.*] What is it?

MADAME ARKADIN. We are staying.

[TRIGORIN *goes into the house.*]

NINA. [*Advances to the footlights; after a few moments' meditation.*] It's a dream!

[*Curtain*]

ACT III

[*The dining-room in* SORIN'S *house. Doors on right and on left. A sideboard. A medicine cupboard. A table in the middle of the room. A portmanteau and hatboxes; signs of preparation for departure.* TRIGORIN *is having lunch;* MASHA *stands by the table.*]

MASHA. I tell all this to you as a writer. You may make use of it. I am telling you the truth: if he had hurt himself seriously I would not have gone on living another minute. But I have pluck enough all the same. I just made up my mind that I would tear this love out of my heart, tear it out by the roots.

TRIGORIN. How are you going to do that?

MASHA. I am going to be married. To Medvedenko.

TRIGORIN. That's the schoolmaster?

MASHA. Yes.

TRIGORIN. I don't understand what's the object of it.

MASHA. To love without hope, to spend whole years waiting for something. . . . But when I marry, there will be no time left for love, new cares will smother all the old feelings. And, anyway, it will be a change, you know. Shall we have another?

TRIGORIN. Won't that be too much?

MASHA. Oh, come! [*Fills two glasses.*] Don't look at me like that! Women drink much oftener than you imagine. Only a small proportion drink openly as I do, the majority drink in secret. Yes. And it's always vodka or brandy. [*Clinks glasses.*] My best wishes! You are a good-hearted man; I am sorry to be parting from you. [*They drink.*]

TRIGORIN. I don't want to go myself.

MASHA. You should beg her to stay.

TRIGORIN. No, she won't stay now. Her son is behaving very tactlessly. First, he shoots himself, and now they say he is going to challenge me to a duel. And whatever for? He sulks, and snorts, and preaches new forms of art. . . . But there is room for all—new and old—why quarrel about it?

MASHA. Well, there's jealousy too. But it is nothing to do with me.

[*A pause.* YAKOV *crosses from right to left with a portmanteau.* NINA *enters and stands by the window.*]

MASHA. My schoolmaster is not very brilliant, but he is a good-natured man, and poor, and he is very much in love with me. I am sorry for him. And I am sorry for his old mother. Well, let me wish you all happiness. Don't remember evil against me. [*Shakes hands with him warmly.*] I am very grateful for your friendly interest. Send me your books and be sure to put in an inscription. Only don't write, "To my honored friend," but write simply, "To Marya who belongs nowhere and has no object in life." Good-bye! [*Goes out.*]

NINA. [*Stretching out her arm toward* TRIGORIN, *with her fist clenched.*] Odd or even?

TRIGORIN. Even.

NINA. [*With a sigh.*] Wrong. I had only one pea in my hand. I was trying my fortune whether to go on the stage or not. I wish someone would advise me.

TRIGORIN. It's impossible to advise in such a matter. [*A pause.*]

NINA. We are parting and . . . perhaps we shall never meet again. Won't you please take this little medallion as a parting gift? I had your initials engraved on one side of it . . . and on the other the title of your book, *Days and Nights.*

TRIGORIN. How exquisite! [*Kisses the medallion.*] A charming present!

NINA. Think of me sometimes.

TRIGORIN. I shall think of you. I shall think of you as you were on that sunny day—do you remember?—a week ago, when you were wearing a light dress . . . we were talking . . . there was a white sea gull lying on the seat.

NINA. [*Pensively.*] Yes, a sea gull . . . [*A pause.*] We can't talk any more, there's someone coming. . . . Let me have two minutes before you go, I entreat you . . . [*Goes out on the left.*]

[*At the same instant* MADAME ARKADIN, SORIN *in a dress coat with a star of some order on it, then* YAKOV, *occupied with the luggage, enter on the right.*]

MADAME ARKADIN. Stay at home, old man. With your rheumatism you ought not to go gadding about. [*To* TRIGORIN.] Who was that went out? Nina?

TRIGORIN. Yes.

MADAME ARKADIN. Pardon, we interrupted you. [*Sit down.*] I believe I have packed everything. I am worn out.

TRIGORIN. [*Reads on the medallion.*] "*Days and Nights*, page 121, lines 11 and 12."

YAKOV. [*Clearing the table.*] Am I to pack your fishing things too, sir?

TRIGORIN. Yes, I shall want them again. You can give away the hooks.

YAKOV. Yes, sir.

TRIGORIN. [*To himself.*] Page 121, lines 11 and 12. What is there in those lines? [*To* MADAME ARKADIN.] Are there copies of my books in the house?

MADAME ARKADIN. Yes, in my brother's study, in the corner bookcase.

TRIGORIN. Page 121 . . . [*Goes out.*]

MADAME ARKADIN. Really, Petrusha, you had better stay at home.

SORIN. You are going away; it will be dreary for me at home without you.

MADAME ARKADIN. And what is there in the town?

SORIN. Nothing particular, but still . . . [*Laughs.*] There will be the laying of the foundation stone of the Zemstvohall, and all that sort of thing. One longs to shake oneself free from this stagnant existence, if only for an hour or two. I've been too long on the shelf like some old cigarette holder. I have ordered the horses for one o'clock; we'll set off at the same time.

MADAME ARKADIN. [*After a pause.*] Come, stay here, don't be bored and don't catch cold. Look after my son. Take care of him. Give him good advice. [*A pause.*] Here I am going away and I shall never know why Konstantin tried to shoot himself. I fancy jealousy was the chief cause, and the sooner I get Trigorin away from here, the better.

SORIN. What can I say? There were other reasons too. It's easy to understand; he is young, intelligent, living in the country, in the wilds, with no money, no position and no future. He has nothing to do. He is ashamed of his idleness and afraid of it. I am very fond of him indeed, and he is attached to me, yet in spite of it all he feels he is superfluous in the house, that he is a dependent, a poor relation. It's easy to understand, it's *amour propre*. . . .

MADAME ARKADIN. He is a great anxiety to me! [*Pondering.*] He might go into the service, perhaps.

SORIN. [*Begins to whistle, then irresolutely.*] I think that quite the best thing would be if you were to . . . let him have a little money. In the first place he ought to be able to be dressed like other people and all that. Just look at him, he's been going about in the same wretched jacket for the last three years and he has no overcoat . . . [*Laughs.*] It would do him no harm to have a little fun . . . to go abroad or something. . . . It wouldn't cost much.

MADAME ARKADIN. But all the same . . . I might manage the suit, perhaps, but as for going abroad . . . No, just at the moment I can't even manage the suit. [*Resolutely.*] I have no money!

[SORIN *laughs.*]

MADAME ARKADIN. No!

SORIN. [*Begins to whistle.*] Quite so. Forgive me, my dear, don't be cross. I believe you. . . . You are a generous, noble-hearted woman.

MADAME ARKADIN. [*Weeping.*] I have no money.

SORIN. If I had money, of course I would give him some myself, but I have nothing, not a half-penny. [*Laughs.*] My steward takes all my pension and spends it all on the land and the cattle and the bees, and my money is all wasted. The bees die, and the cows die, they never let me have horses. . . .

MADAME ARKADIN. Yes, I have money, but you see I am an actress; my dresses alone are enough to ruin me.

SORIN. You are a kind, good creature . . . I respect you. . . . Yes . . . but there, I got a touch of it again . . . [*Staggers.*] I feel dizzy. [*Clutches at the table.*] I feel ill and all that.

MADAME ARKADIN. [*Alarmed.*] Petrusha! [*Trying to support him.*] Petrusha, my dear! [*Calling.*] Help! help!

[*Enter* TREPLEV, with a bandage round his head, and MEDVEDENKO.]

MADAME ARKADIN. He feels faint!

SORIN. It's all right, it's all right! [*Smiles and drinks some water.*] It's passed off . . . and all that.

TREPLEV. [*To his mother.*] Don't be frightened, Mother, it's not serious. Uncle often has these attacks now. [*To his uncle.*] You must lie down, Uncle.

SORIN. For a little while, yes. . . . But I am going to the town all the same. . . . I'll lie down a little and then set off. . . . It's quite natural. [*Goes out leaning on his stick.*]

MEDVEDENKO. [*Gives him his arm.*] There's a riddle: in the morning on four legs, at noon on two, in the evening on three. . . .

SORIN. [*Laughs.*] Just so. And at night on the back. Thank you, I can manage alone. . . .

MEDVEDENKO. Oh come, why stand on ceremony! [*Goes out with* SORIN.]

MADAME ARKADIN. How he frightened me!

TREPLEV. It is not good for him to live in the country. He gets depressed. If you would be generous for once, mother, and lend him fifteen hundred or two thousand roubles, he could spend a whole year in town.

MADAME ARKADIN. I have no money. I am an actress, not a banker. [*A pause.*]

TREPLEV. Mother, change my bandage. You do it so well.

MADAME ARKADIN. [*Takes out of the medicine cupboard some iodoform and a box with bandaging material.*] The doctor is late.

TREPLEV. He promised to be here at ten, and it is midday already.

MADAME ARKADIN. Sit down. [*Takes the bandage off his head.*] It's like a turban. Yesterday a stranger asked in the kitchen what nationality you were. But you have almost completely healed. There is the merest trifle left. [*Kisses him on the head.*] You won't do anything naughty again while I am away, will you?

TREPLEV. No, Mother. It was a moment of mad despair when I could not control myself. It won't happen again. [*Kisses her hand.*] You have such clever hands. I remember, long ago, when you were still acting at the Imperial Theater—I was little then—there was a fight in our yard and a washerwoman, one of the tenants, was badly beaten. Do you remember? She was picked up senseless . . . you looked after her, took her remedies and washed her children in a tub. Don't you remember?

MADAME ARKADIN. No. [*Puts on a fresh bandage.*]

TREPLEV. Two ballet dancers lived in the same house as we did at the time. . . . They used to come to you and have coffee. . . .

MADAME ARKADIN. I remember that.

TREPLEV. They were very pious. [*A pause.*] Just lately, these last days, I have loved you as tenderly and completely as when I was a child. I have no one left now but you. Only why, why do you give yourself up to the influence of that man?

MADAME ARKADIN. You don't understand him, Konstantin. He is a very noble character. . . .

TREPLEV. And yet when he was told I was going to challenge him, the nobility of his character did not prevent him from funking it. He is going away. Ignominious flight!

MADAME ARKADIN. What nonsense! It is I who am asking him to go.

TREPLEV. A very noble character! Here you and I are almost quarreling over him, and at this very moment he is somewhere in the drawing room or the garden laughing at us . . . developing Nina, trying to convince her finally that he is a genius.

MADAME ARKADIN. You take a pleasure in saying unpleasant things to me. I respect that man and beg you not to speak ill of him before me.

TREPLEV. And I don't respect him. You want me to think him a genius too, but forgive me, I can't tell lies, his books make me sick.

MADAME ARKADIN. That's envy. There's nothing left for people who have pretension without talent but to attack real talent. Much comfort in that, I must say!

TREPLEV. [Ironically.] Real talent! [Wrathfully.] I have more talent than all of you put together if it comes to that! [Tears the bandage off his head.] You, with your hackneyed conventions, have usurped the supremacy in art and consider nothing real and legitimate but what you do yourselves; everything else you stifle and suppress. I don't believe in you! I don't believe in you or in him!

MADAME ARKADIN. Decadent!

TREPLEV. Get away to your charming theater and act there in your paltry, stupid plays!

MADAME ARKADIN. I have never acted in such plays. Let me alone! You are not capable of writing even a wretched burlesque! You are nothing but a Kiev shopman! Living on other people!

TREPLEV. You miser.

MADAME ARKADIN. You ragged beggar!

[TREPLEV sits down and weeps quietly.]

MADAME ARKADIN. Nonentity! [Walking up and down in agitation.] Don't cry. . . . You mustn't cry. [Weeps.] Don't . . . [Kisses him on the forehead, on the cheeks and on the head.] My dear child, forgive me. . . . Forgive your sinful mother. Forgive me, you know I am wretched.

TREPLEV. [Puts his arms around her.] If only you knew! I have lost everything! She does not love me, and now I cannot write . . . all my hopes are gone. . . .

MADAME ARKADIN. Don't despair . . . Everything will come right. He is going away directly, she will love you again. [Wipes away his tears.] Give over. We have made it up now.

TREPLEV. [Kisses her hands.] Yes, Mother.

MADAME ARKADIN. [Tenderly.] Make it up with him too. You don't want a duel, do you?

TREPLEV. Very well. Only, Mother, do allow me not to meet him. It's painful to me—it's more than I can bear. [Enter TRIGORIN.] Here he is

. . . I am going . . . [*Rapidly puts away the dressings in the cupboard.*] The doctor will do the bandaging now.

TRIGORIN. [*Looking in a book.*] Page 121 . . . lines 11 and 12. Here it is. [*Reads.*] "If ever my life can be of use to you, come and take it."

[TREPLEV *picks up the bandage from the floor and goes out.*]

MADAME ARKADIN. [*Looking at her watch.*] The horses will soon be here.

TRIGORIN. [*To himself.*] "If ever my life can be of use to you, come and take it."

MADAME ARKADIN. I hope all your things are packed?

TRIGORIN. [*Impatiently.*] Yes, yes. [*Musing.*] Why is it that I feel so much sorrow in that appeal from a pure soul and that it wrings my heart so painfully? "If ever my life can be of use to you, come and take it." [*To* MADAME ARKADIN.] Let us stay one day longer.

[MADAME ARKADIN *shakes her head.*]

TRIGORIN. Let us stay!

MADAME ARKADIN. Darling, I know what keeps you here. But have control over yourself. You are a little intoxicated, try to be sober.

TRIGORIN. You be sober too, be sensible and reasonable, I implore you; look at it all as a true friend should. [*Presses her hand.*] You are capable of sacrifice. Be a friend to me, let me be free!

MADAME ARKADIN. [*In violent agitation.*] Are you so enthralled?

TRIGORIN. I am drawn to her! Perhaps it is just what I need.

MADAME ARKADIN. The love of a provincial girl? Oh, how little you know yourself!

TRIGORIN. Sometimes people sleep as they talk—that's how it is with me, I am talking to you and yet I am asleep and dreaming of her. . . . I am possessed by sweet, marvelous dreams. . . . Let me be free. . . .

MADAME ARKADIN. [*Trembling.*] No, no! I am an ordinary woman, you can't talk like that to me. Don't torture me, Boris. It terrifies me.

TRIGORIN. If you cared to, you could be not ordinary. Love—youthful, charming, poetical, lifting one into a world of dreams—that's the only thing in life that can give happiness! I have never yet known a love like that. . . . In my youth I never had time, I was always hanging about the editors' offices, struggling with want. Now it is here, that love, it has come, it beckons to me. What sense is there in running away from it?

MADAME ARKADIN. [*Wrathfully.*] You have gone mad!

TRIGORIN. Well, let me!

MADAME ARKADIN. You are all in a conspiracy together to torment me today! [*Weeps.*]

TRIGORIN. [*Clutching at his heart.*] She does not understand! She won't understand!

Madame Arkadin. Am I so old and ugly that you don't mind talking of other women to me? [*Puts her arms round him and kisses him.*] Oh, you are mad! My wonderful, splendid darling. . . . You are the last page of my life! [*Falls on her knees.*] My joy, my pride, my bliss! . . . [*Embraces his knees.*] If you forsake me even for one hour I shall not survive it, I shall go mad, my marvelous, magnificent one, my master. . . .

Trigorin. Someone may come in. [*Helps her to get up.*]

Madame Arkadin. Let them, I am not ashamed of my love for you. [*Kisses his hands.*] My treasure, you desperate boy, you want to be mad, but I won't have it, I won't let you . . . [*Laughs.*] You are mine . . . mine, . . . This forehead is mine, and these eyes, and this lovely silky hair is mine too . . . you are mine all over. You are so gifted, so clever, the best of all modern writers, you are the one hope of Russia . . . You have so much truthfulness, simplicity, freshness, healthy humor. . . . In one touch you can give all the essential characteristics of a person or a landscape, your characters are living, One can't read you without delight! You think this is exaggerated? That I am flattering you? But look into my eyes . . . look. . . . Do I look like a liar? You see, I am the only one who can appreciate you; I am the only one who tells you the truth, my precious, wonderful darling. . . . Are you coming? Yes? You won't abandon me? . . .

Trigorin. I have no will of my own . . . I have never had a will of my own. . . . Flabby, feeble, always submissive—how can a woman care for such a man? Take me, carry me off, but don't let me move a step away from you. . . .

Madame Arkadin. [*To herself.*] Now he is mine! [*In an easy tone as though nothing had happened.*] But, of course, if you like, you can stay. I'll go by myself and you can come afterwards, a week later. After all, why should you be in a hurry?

Trigorin. No, we may as well go together.

Madame Arkadin. As you please. Let us go together then. [*A pause.*]

[Trigorin *makes a note.*]

Madame Arkadin. What are you writing?

Trigorin. I heard a good name this morning, *The Maiden's Forest.* It may be of use. [*Stretches.*] So we are to go then? Again there will be railway carriages, stations, refreshment bars, mutton chops, conversations. . . .

Shamraev. [*Enters.*] I have the honour to announce, with regret, that the horses are ready. It's time, honoured lady, to set off for the station; the train comes in at five minutes past two. So please do me a favor, Irina Nikolayevna, do not forget to inquire what has become of the actor Suzdaltsev. Is he alive and well? We used to drink together at one time. . . . In *The Plundered Mail* he used to play incomparably . . . I remember the tragedian Izmaïlov, also a remarkable personality, acted with him in Elisavetograd. . . . Don't be in a hurry, honored lady, you need not start for five minutes. Once they were acting conspirators in a melodrama and when they were suddenly discovered Izmaïlov had to say, "We are caught in a trap," but he said, "We are caught in a tap!" [*Laughs.*] A tap!

[*While he is speaking* YAKOV *is busy looking after the luggage. The maid brings* MADAME ARKADIN *her hat, her coat, her umbrella, and her gloves; they all help* MADAME ARKADIN *to put on her things. The man cook looks in at the door on left and after some hesitation comes in. Enter* POLINA ANDREYEVNA, *then* SORIN *and* MEDVEDENKO.]

POLINA. [*With a basket.*] Here are some plums for the journey. . . . Very sweet ones. You may be glad to have something nice. . . .

MADAME ARKADIN. You are very kind, Polina Andreyevna.

POLINA. Good-bye, my dear! If anything has not been to your liking, forgive it. [*Weeps.*]

MADAME ARKADIN. [*Embraces her.*] Everything has been nice, everything! But you mustn't cry.

POLINA. The time flies so fast!

MADAME ARKADIN. There's no help for it.

SORIN. [*In a greatcoat with a cape to it, with his hat on and a stick in his hand, enters from door on left, crossing the stage.*] Sister, it's time to start, or you may be too late after all. I am going to get into the carriage. [*Goes out.*]

MEDVEDENKO. And I shall walk to the station . . . to see you off. I'll be there in no time . . . [*Goes out.*]

MADAME ARKADIN. Good-bye, dear friends. . . . If we are all alive and well, we shall meet again next summer. [THE MAID, THE COOK, *and* YAKOV *kiss her hand.*] Don't forget me. [*Gives* THE COOK *a rouble.*] Here's a rouble for the three of you.

THE COOK. We humbly thank you, madam! Good journey to you! We are very grateful for your kindness!

YAKOV. May God give you good luck!

SHAMRAEV. You might rejoice our hearts with a letter! Good-bye, Boris Alexeyevitch!

MADAME ARKADIN. Where is Konstantin? Tell him that I am starting; I must say good-bye. Well, don't remember evil against me. [*To* YAKOV.] I gave the cook a rouble. It's for the three of you.

[*All go out on right. The stage is empty. Behind the scenes the noise that is usual when people are being seen off.* THE MAID *comes back to fetch the basket of plums from the table and goes out again.*]

TRIGORIN. [*Coming back.*] I have forgotten my stick. I believe it is out there, on the veranda. [*Goes and, at door on left, meets* NINA, *who is coming in.*] Is that you? We are going. . . .

NINA. I felt that we should see each other once more. [*Excitedly.*] Boris Alexeyevitch, I have come to a decision, the die is cast, I am going on the stage. I shall be gone from here tomorrow; I am leaving my father, I am abandoning everything, I am beginning a new life. Like you, I am going . . . to Moscow. We shall meet there.

TRIGORIN. [*Looking round.*] Stay at the "Slavyansky Bazaar". . . Let me know at once . . . Molchanovka, Groholsky House. . . . I am in a hurry . . . [A *pause.*]

NINA. One minute more. . . .

TRIGORIN. [*In an undertone.*] You are so lovely. . . . Oh, what happiness to think that we shall see each other soon! [*She sinks on his breast.*] I shall see again those wonderful eyes, that inexpressibly beautiful tender smile . . . those soft features, the expression of angelic purity. . . . My darling . . . [A *prolonged kiss.*]

[*Curtain*]

ACT IV

[*Between the Third and Fourth Acts there is an interval of two years.*]

[*One of the drawing rooms in* SORIN'S *house, which has been turned into a study for* KONSTANTIN TREPLEV. *On the right and left, doors leading to inner apartments. In the middle, glass door leading on to the veranda. Besides the usual drawing-room furniture there is, in corner on right, a writing table, near door on left, a sofa, a bookcase, and books in windows and on the chairs. Evening. There is a single lamp alight with a shade on it. It is half dark. There is the sound of the trees rustling, and the wind howling in the chimney. A watchman is tapping.*]

[*Enter* MEDVEDENKO *and* MASHA.]

MASHA. [*Calling.*] Konstantin Gavrilitch! Konstantin Gavrilitch! [*Looking round.*] No, there is no one here. The old man keeps asking every minute, where is Kostya, where is Kostya? He cannot live without him. . . .

MEDVEDENKO. He is afraid of being alone. [*Listening.*] What awful weather! This is the second day of it.

MASHA. [*Turns up the lamp.*] There are waves on the lake. Great big ones.

MEDVEDENKO. How dark it is in the garden! We ought to have told them to break up that stage in the garden. It stands as bare and ugly as a skeleton, and the curtain flaps in the wind. When I passed it yesterday evening, it seemed as though someone were crying in it.

MASHA. What next . . . [*A pause.*]

MEDVEDENKO. Let us go home, Masha.

MASHA. [*Shakes her head.*] I shall stay here for the night.

MEDVEDENKO. [*In an imploring voice.*] Masha, do come! Our baby must be hungry.

MASHA. Nonsense. Matryona will feed him. [*A pause.*]

MEDVEDENKO. I am sorry for him. He has been three nights now without his mother.

MASHA. You are a bore. In old days you used at least to discuss general subjects, but now it is only home, baby, home, baby—that's all one can get out of you.

MEDVEDENKO. Come along, Masha!

MASHA. Go by yourself.

MEDVEDENKO. Your father won't let me have a horse.

MASHA. Yes, he will. You ask, and he will.

MEDVEDENKO. Very well, I'll ask. Then you will come tomorrow?

MASHA. [*Taking a pinch of snuff.*] Very well, tomorrow. How you pester me.

[*Enter* TREPLEV *and* POLINA ANDREYEVNA. TREPLEV *brings in pillows and a quilt, and* POLINA ANDREYEVNA *sheets and pillowcases; they lay them on the sofa, then* TREPLEV *goes to his table and sits down.*]

MASHA. What's this for, Mother?

POLINA. Pyotr Nikolayevitch asked us to make a bed for him in Kostya's room.

MASHA. Let me do it. [*Makes the bed.*]

POLINA. [*Sighing.*] Old people are like children. [*Goes up to the writing table and, leaning on her elbow, looks at the manuscript; a pause.*]

MEDVEDENKO. Well, I am going then. Good-bye, Masha. [*Kisses his wife's hand.*] Good-bye, Mother. [*Tries to kiss his mother-in-law's hand.*]

POLINA. [*With vexation.*] Come, if you are going, go.

MEDVEDENKO. Good-bye, Konstantin Gavrilitch.

[TREPLEV *gives him his hand without speaking;* MEDVEDENKO *goes out.*]

POLINA. [*Looking at the manuscript.*] No one would have guessed or thought that you would have become a real author, Kostya. And now, thank God, they send you money from the magazines. [*Passes her hand over his hair.*] And you have grown good-looking too. . . . Dear, good Kostya, do be a little kinder to my Mashenka!

MASHA. [*As she makes the bed.*] Leave him alone, Mother.

POLINA. [*To* TREPLEV.] She is a nice little thing. [*A pause.*] A woman wants nothing, you know, Kostya, so long as you give her a kind look. I know from myself.

[TREPLEV *gets up from the table and walks away without speaking.*]

MASHA. Now you have made him angry. What induced you to pester him?

POLINA. I feel so sorry for you, Mashenka.

MASHA. Much use that is!

POLINA. My heart aches for you. I see it all, you know, I understand it all.

MASHA. It's all foolishness. There is no such thing as hopeless love except in novels. It's of no consequence. The only thing is one mustn't let oneself go and keep expecting something, waiting for the tide to turn. . . . When love gets into the heart there is nothing to be done but to clear it out. Here they promised to transfer my husband to another district. As soon as I am there, I shall forget it all. . . . I shall tear it it out of my heart.

[*Two rooms away a melancholy waltz is played.*]

POLINA. That's Kostya playing. He must be depressed.

MASHA. [*Noiselessly dances a few waltz steps.*] The great thing, Mother, is not to have him before one's eyes. If they only give my Semyon his transfer, trust me, I shall get over it in a month. It's all nonsense.

[*Door on left opens.* DORN *and* MEDVEDENKO *wheel in* SORIN *in his chair.*]

MEDVEDENKO. I have six of them at home now. And flour is two kopeks per pound.

DORN. You've got to look sharp to make both ends meet.

MEDVEDENKO. It's all very well for you to laugh. You've got more money than you know what to do with.

DORN. Money? After thirty years of practice, my boy, troublesome work during which I could not call my soul my own by day or by night, I only succeeded in saving two thousand roubles, and that I spent not long ago abroad. I have nothing.

MASHA. [*To her husband.*] You have not gone?

MEDVEDENKO. [*Guiltily.*] Well, how can I when they won't let me have a horse?

MASHA. [*With bitter vexation in an undertone.*] I can't bear the sight of you.

[*The wheel chair remains in the left half of the room;* POLINA ANDREYEVNA, MASHA, *and* DORN *sit down beside it,* MEDVEDENKO *moves mournfully to one side.*]

DORN. What changes there have been here! The drawing room has been turned into a study.

MASHA. It is more convenient for Konstantin Gavrilitch to work here. Whenever he likes, he can walk out into the garden and think there.

[*A watchman taps.*]

SORIN. Where is my sister?

DORN. She has gone to the station to meet Trigorin. She will be back directly.

SORIN. Since you thought it necessary to send for my sister, I must be dangerously ill. [*After a silence.*] It's a queer thing, I am dangerously ill and here they don't give me any medicines.

DORN. Well, what would you like to have? Valerian drops? Soda? Quinine?

SORIN. Ah, he is at his moralizing again! What an infliction it is! [*With a motion of his head toward the sofa.*] Is that bed for me?

POLINA. Yes, it's for you, Pyotr Nikolayevitch.

SORIN. Thank you.

DORN. [*Hums.*] "The moon is floating in the midnight sky."

SORIN. I want to give Kostya a subject for a story. It ought to be called "The Man Who Wished"—*L'homme qui a voulu.* In my youth I wanted to become a literary man—and didn't; I wanted to speak well—and I spoke horribly badly [*mimicking himself*], "and all the rest of it, and all that, and so on, and so forth". . . and I would go plodding on and on, trying to sum up till I was in a regular perspiration; I wanted to get married—and I didn't; I always wanted to live in town and here I am ending my life in the country—and so on.

DORN. I wanted to become an actual civil councilor—and I have.

SORIN. [*Laughs.*] That I had no hankerings after. That happened of itself.

DORN. To be expressing dissatisfaction with life at sixty-two is really ungracious, you know.

SORIN. What a persistent fellow he is! You might understand that one wants to live!

DORN. That's just frivolity. It's the law of nature that every life must have an end.

SORIN. You argue like a man who has had enough. You are satisfied and so you are indifferent to life, nothing matters to you. But even you will be afraid to die.

DORN. The dread of death is an animal fear. One must overcome it. A rational fear of death is only possible for those who believe in eternal life and are conscious of their sins. And you, in the first place, don't believe, and, in the second, what sins have you to worry about? You have served in the courts of justice for twenty-five years—that's all.

SORIN. [*Laughs.*] Twenty-eight. . . ,

[TREPLEV *comes in and sits down on a stool at* SORIN's *feet.* MASHA *never takes her eyes off him.*]

DORN. We are hindering Konstantin Gavrilitch from working.

TREPLEV. Oh no, it doesn't matter. [*A pause.*]

MEDVEDENKO. Allow me to ask you, doctor, what town did you like best abroad?

DORN. Genoa.

TREPLEV. Why Genoa?

DORN. The life in the streets is so wonderful there. When you go out of the hotel in the evening, the whole street is packed with people. You wander aimlessly zigzagging about among the crowd, backwards and forwards; you live with it, are psychologically at one with it and begin almost to believe that a world-soul is really possible, such as was acted by Nina Zaretchny in your play. And, by the way, where is she now? How is she getting on?

TREPLEV. I expect she is quite well.

DORN. I was told that she was leading a rather peculiar life. How was that?

TREPLEV. That's a long story, doctor.

DORN. Well, tell it to us shortly. [A *pause.*]

TREPLEV. She ran away from home and had an affair with Trigorin. You know that?

DORN. I know.

TREPLEV. She had a child. The child died. Trigorin got tired of her and went back to his old ties, as might have been expected. Though, indeed, he had never abandoned them, but in his weak-willed way contrived to keep both going. As far as I can make out from what I have heard, Nina's private life was a complete failure.

DORN. And the stage?

TREPLEV. I fancy that was worse still. She made her debut at some holiday place near Moscow, then went to the provinces. All that time I did not lose sight of her, and wherever she went I followed her. She always took big parts, but she acted crudely, without taste, screamingly, with violent gestures. There were moments when she uttered a cry successfuly or died successfully, but they were only moments.

DORN. Then she really has some talent?

TREPLEV. It was difficult to make it out. I suppose she has. I saw her but she would not see me, and the servants would not admit me at the hotel. I understood her state of mind and did not insist on seeing her. [A *pause.*] What more can I tell you? Afterwards, when I was back at home, I had some letters from her—warm, intelligent, interesting letters. She did not complain, but I felt that she was profoundly unhappy; every line betrayed sick overstrained nerves. And her imagination is a little unhinged. She signed herself the Sea Gull. In Pushkin's *Mermaid* the miller says that he is a raven, and in the same way in her letters she kept repeating that she was a sea gull. Now she is here.

DORN. Here? How do you mean?

TREPLEV. In the town, staying at an inn. She has been there for five days, I did go to see her, and Marya Ilyinishna here went too, but she won't see anyone. Semyon Semyonitch declares he saw her yesterday afternoon in the fields a mile and a half from here.

MEDVEDENKO. Yes, I saw her. She went in that direction, toward the town. I bowed to her and asked her why she did not come to see us. She said she would come.

TREPLEV. She won't come. [*A pause.*] Her father and stepmother refuse to recognize her. They have put watchmen about so that she may not even go near the house. [*Walks away with the doctor toward the writing table.*] How easy it is to be a philosopher on paper, Doctor, and how difficult it is in life!

SORIN. She was a charming girl.

DORN. What?

SORIN. She was a charming girl, I say. Actual Civil Councilor Sorin was positively in love with her for a time.

DORN. The old Lovelace.

[SHAMRAEV's *laugh is heard.*]

POLINA. I fancy our people have come back from the station. . . .

TREPLEV. Yes, I hear mother.

[*Enter* MADAME ARKADIN, TRIGORIN, *and with them* SHAMRAEV.]

SHAMRAEV. [*As he enters.*] We all grow old and dilapidated under the influence of the elements, while you, honored lady, are still young . . . a light blouse, sprightliness, grace. . . .

MADAME ARKADIN. You want to bring me ill luck again, you tiresome man!

TRIGORIN. How do you do, Pyotr Nikolayevitch! So you are still poorly? That's bad! [*Seeing* MASHA, *joyfully.*] Marya Ilyinishna!

MASHA. You know me, do you? [*Shakes hands.*]

TRIGORIN. Married?

MASHA. Long ago.

TRIGORIN. Are you happy? [*Bows to* DORN *and* MEDVEDENKO, *then hesitatingly approaches* TREPLEV.] Irina Nikolayevna has told me that you have forgotten the past and are no longer angry.

[TREPLEV *holds out his hand.*]

MADAME ARKADIN. [*To her son.*] Boris Alexeyevitch has brought the magazine with your new story in it.

TREPLEV. [*Taking the magazine; to* TRIGORIN.] Thank you, you are very kind. [*They sit down.*]

TRIGORIN. Your admirers send their greetings to you. . . . In Petersburg and Moscow there is great interest in your work and I am continually being asked questions about you. People ask what you are like, how old you are, whether you are dark or fair. Everyone imagines, for some reason, that you are no longer young. And no one knows your real name, as you always publish under a pseudonym. You are as mysterious as the Iron Mask.

TREPLEV. Will you be able to make a long stay?

TRIGORIN. No, I think I must go back to Moscow tomorrow. I am obliged to. I am in a hurry to finish my novel, and besides, I have promised something for a collection of tales that is being published. It's the old story, in fact.

[*While they are talking* MADAME ARKADIN *and* POLINA ANDREYEVNA *put a card table in the middle of the room and open it out.* SHAMRAEV *lights candles and set chairs. A game of lotto is brought out of the cupboard.*]

TRIGORIN. The weather has not given me a friendly welcome. There is a cruel wind. If it has dropped by tomorrow morning I shall go to the lake to fish. And I must have a look at the garden and that place where—you remember?—your play was acted. I've got a subject for a story, I only want to revive my recollections of the scene in which it is laid.

MASHA. [*To her father.*] Father, let my husband have a horse! He must get home.

SHAMRAEV. [*Mimicking.*] Must get home—a horse! [*Sternly.*] You can see for yourself: they have just been to the station. I can't send them out again.

MASHA. But there are other horses. [*Seeing that her father says nothing, waves her hand.*] There's no doing anything with you.

MEDVEDENKO. I can walk, Masha. Really. . . .

POLINA. [*With a sigh.*] Walk in such weather . . . [*Sits down to the card table.*] Come, friends.

MEDVEDENKO. It is only four miles. Good-bye. [*Kisses his wife's hand.*] Good-bye, Mother. [*His mother-in-law reluctantly holds out her hand for him to kiss.*] I wouldn't trouble anyone, but the baby . . . [*Bows to the company.*] Good-bye . . . [*Goes out with a guilty step.*]

SHAMRAEV. He can walk right enough. He's not a general.

POLINA. [*Tapping on the table.*] Come, friends. Don't let us waste time, we shall soon be called to supper.

[SHAMRAEV, MASHA, *and* DORN *sit down at the table.*]

MADAME ARKADIN. [*To* TRIGORIN.] When the long autumn evenings come on they play lotto here. Look, it's the same old lotto that we had when our mother used to play with us, when we were children. Won't you have a game before supper? [*Sits down to the table with* TRIGORIN.] It's a dull game, but it is not so bad when you are used to it. [*Deals three cards to everyone.*]

TREPLEV. [*Turning the pages of the magazine.*] He has read his own story, but he has not even cut mine. [*Puts the magazine down on the writing table, then goes toward door on left; as he passes his mother he kisses her on the head.*]

MADAME ARKADIN. And you, Kostya?

TREPLEV. Excuse me, I would rather not . . . I am going out. [*Goes out.*]

MADAME ARKADIN. The stake is ten kopeks. Put it down for me, Doctor, will you?

DORN. Right.

MASHA. Has everyone put down their stakes? I begin . . . Twenty-two.

MADAME ARKADIN. Yes.

MASHA. Three!

DORN. Right!

MASHA. Did you play three? Eight! Eighty-one! Ten!

SHAMRAEV. Don't be in a hurry!

MADAME ARKADIN. What a reception I had in Harkov! My goodness! I feel dizzy with it still.

MASHA. Thirty-four!

[*A melancholy waltz is played behind the scenes.*]

MADAME ARKADIN. The students gave me an ovation. . . . Three baskets of flowers . . . two wreaths and this, see. [*Unfastens a brooch on her throat and lays it on the table.*]

SHAMRAEV. Yes, that is a thing. . . .

MASHA. Fifty!

DORN. Exactly fifty?

MADAME ARKADIN. I had a wonderful dress. . . . Whatever I don't know, I do know how to dress.

POLINA. Kostya is playing the piano; he is depressed, poor fellow.

SHAMRAEV. He is awfully abused in the newspapers.

MASHA. Seventy-seven!

MADAME ARKADIN. As though that mattered!

TRIGORIN. He never quite comes off. He has not yet hit upon his own medium. There is always something queer and vague, at times almost like delirium. Not a single living character.

MASHA. Eleven!

MADAME ARKADIN. [*Looking round at* SORIN.] Petrusha, are you bored? [*A pause.*] He is asleep.

DORN. The Actual Civil Councilor is asleep.

MASHA. Seven! Ninety!

TRIGORIN. If I lived in such a place, beside a lake, do you suppose I should write? I should overcome this passion and should do nothing but fish.

MASHA. Twenty-eight!

TRIGORIN. Catching perch is so delightful!

DORN. Well, I believe in Konstantin Gavrilitch. There is something in him! There is something in him! He thinks in images; his stories are vivid, full of color, and they affect me strongly. The only pity is that he has not got definite aims. He produces an impression and that's all, but you can't get far with nothing but an impression. Irina Nikolayevna, are you glad that your son is a writer?

MADAME ARKADIN. Only fancy, I have not read anything of his yet. I never have time.

MASHA. Twenty-six!

[TREPLEV *comes in quietly and sits down at his table.*]

SHAMRAEV. [*To* TRIGORIN.] We have still got something here belonging to you, Boris Alexeyevitch.

TRIGORIN. What's this?

SHAMRAEV. Konstantin Gavrilitch shot a sea gull and you asked me to get it stuffed for you.

TRIGORIN. I don't remember! [*Pondering.*] I don't remember!

MASHA. Sixty-six! One!

TREPLEV. [*Flinging open the window, listens.*] How dark it is! I don't know why I feel so uneasy.

MADAME ARKADIN. Kostya, shut the window, there's a draught.

[TREPLEV *shuts the window.*]

MASHA. Eighty-eight!

TRIGORIN. The game is mine!

MADAME ARKADIN. [*Gaily.*] Bravo, bravo!

SHAMRAEV. Bravo!

MADAME ARKADIN. That man always has luck in everything. [*Gets up.*] And now let us go and have something to eat. Our great man has not dined today. We will go on again after supper. [*To her son.*] Kostya, leave your manuscripts and come to supper.

TREPLEV. I don't want any, Mother, I am not hungry.

MADAME ARKADIN. As you like. [*Wakes* SORIN.] Petrushka, supper! [*Takes* SHAMRAEV'S *arm.*] I'll tell you about my reception in Harkov.

[POLINA ANDREYEVNA *puts out the candles on the table. Then she and* DORN *wheel the chair. All go out by door on left; only* TREPLEV, *sitting at the writing table, is left on the stage.*]

TREPLEV. [*Settling himself to write; runs through what he has written already.*] I have talked so much about new forms and now I feel that little by little I am falling into a convention myself. [*Reads.*] "The placard on the wall proclaimed. . . . The pale face in its setting of dark hair." Proclaimed, setting. That's stupid. [*Scratches out.*] I will begin where the hero is awakened by the patter of the rain, and throw out all the rest. The description of the moonlight evening is long and overelaborate. Trigorin has worked out methods for himself, it's easy for him now. . . . With him the broken bottleneck glitters on the dam and the mill wheel casts black shadow—and there you have the moonlight night, while I have the tremulous light, and the soft twinkling of the stars, and the faraway strains of the piano dying away in the still fragrant air. . . . It's agonizing. [*A pause.*] I come more and more to the conviction that it is not a question of new and old forms, but that what matters is that a man should write without thinking about forms at all, write because it springs freely from his soul. [*There is a tap at the window nearest to the table.*] What is that? [*Looks out of window.*] There is nothing to be seen . . . [*Opens the glass door and looks out into the garden.*] Someone ran down the steps. [*Calls.*] Who is there? [*Goes out and can be heard walking rapidly along the veranda; returns half a minute later with* Nina Zaretchny.] Nina, Nina!

[Nina *lays her head on his breast and weeps with subdued sobs.*]

Treplev. [*Moved.*] Nina! Nina! It's you . . . you. . . . It's as though I had foreseen it, all day long my heart has been aching and restless. [*Takes off her hat and cape.*] Oh, my sweet, my precious, she has come at last. Don't let us cry, don't let us!

Nina. There is someone here.

Treplev. No one.

Nina. Lock the doors, someone may come in.

Treplev. No one will come in.

Nina. I know Irina Nikolayevna is here. Lock the doors.

Treplev. [*Locks the door on right, goes to door on left.*] There is no lock on this one. I'll put a chair against it. [*Puts an armchair against the door.*] Don't be afraid, no one will come.

Nina. [*Looking intently into his face.*] Let me look at you. [*Looking round.*] It's warm, it's nice. . . . In old days this was the drawing room. Am I very much changed?

Treplev. Yes . . . You are thinner and your eyes are bigger. Nina, how strange it is that I should be seeing you. Why would not you let me see you? Why haven't you come all this time? I know you have been here almost a week. . . . I have been to you several times every day; I stood under your window like a beggar.

Nina. I was afraid that you might hate me. I dream every night that you look at me and don't know me. If only you knew! Ever since I came I have been walking here . . . by the lake. I have been near your house many times and could not bring myself to enter it. Let us sit down. [*They sit down.*] Let us sit down and talk and talk. It's nice here, it's warm and snug. Do you hear the wind? There's a passage in Turgenev, "Well for the man on such a night who sits under the shelter of home who has a warm corner in safety." I am a sea gull. . . . No, that's not it. [*Rubs her forehead.*] What was I saying? Yes . . . Turgenev . . .

"And the Lord help all homeless wanderers!" . . . It doesn't matter. [*Sobs.*]

TREPLEV. Nina you are crying again. . . . Nina!

NINA. Never mind, it does me good . . . I haven't cried for two years. Yesterday, late in the evening, I came into the garden to see whether our stage was still there. It is still standing. I cried for the first time after two years and it eased the weight on my heart and made it lighter. You see, I am not crying now. [*Takes him by the hand.*] And so now you are an author. . . . You are an author, I am an actress. . . . We too have been drawn into the whirlpool. I lived joyously like a child—I woke up singing in the morning; I loved you and dreamed of fame, and now? Early tomorrow morning I must go to Yelets third-class . . . with peasants, and at Yelets the cultured tradesmen will pester me with attentions. Life is a coarse business!

TREPLEV. Why to Yelets?

NINA. I have taken an engagement for the whole winter. It is time to go.

TREPLEV. Nina, I cursed you, I hated you, I tore up your letters and photographs, but I was conscious every minute that my soul is bound to yours for ever. It's not in my power to leave off loving you, Nina. Ever since I lost you and began to get my work published my life has been unbearable—I am wretched. . . . My youth was, as it were, torn away all at once and it seems to me as though I have lived for ninety years already. I call upon you, I kiss the earth on which you have walked; wherever I look I see your face, that tender smile that lighted up the best days of my life. . . .

NINA. [*Distractedly.*] Why does he talk like this, why does he talk like this?

TREPLEV. I am alone in the world, warmed by no affection. I am as cold as though I were in a cellar, and everything I write is dry, hard, and gloomy. Stay here, Nina, I entreat you, or let me go with you!

[NINA *rapidly puts on her hat and cape.*]

TREPLEV. Nina, why is this? For God's sake, Nina! [*Looks at her as she puts her things on; a pause.*]

NINA. My horses are waiting at the gate. Don't see me off, I'll go alone. . . . [*Through her tears.*] Give me some water. . . .

TREPLEV. [*Gives her some water.*] Where are you going now?

NINA. To the town. [*A pause.*] Is Irina Nikolayevna here?

TREPLEV. Yes. . . . Uncle was taken worse on Thursday and we telegraphed for her.

NINA. Why do you say that you kissed the earth on which I walked? I ought to be killed. [*Bends over table.*] I am so tired! If I could rest . . . if I could rest! [*Raising her head.*] I am a sea gull. . . . No, that's not it. I am an actress. Oh, well! [*Hearing* MADAME ARKADIN *and* TRIGORIN *laughing, she listens, then runs to door on left and looks through the keyhole.*] He is here too. . . . [*Turning back to* TREPLEV.] Oh, well . . . it doesn't matter . . . no. . . . He did not believe in the stage, he always laughed at my dreams and little by little I left off believing in it too, and lost heart. . . . And then I was fretted by love and jealousy, and continually anxious over my little one. . . . I grew petty and trivial, I acted stupidly. . . . I did not know what to do with my arms, I did not know how to stand on the stage, could not control my voice. You can't understand what it feels like when one knows one is acting disgracefully. I am a sea gull. No, that's not it. . . . Do you remember you shot a sea gull? A man came by chance, saw it, and, just to pass the time, destroyed it. . . . A subject for a short story. . . . That's not it, though. [*Rubs her forehead.*] What was I saying? . . . I am talking of the stage. Now I am not like that. I am a real actress, I act with enjoyment, with enthusiasm, I am intoxicated when I am on the stage and feel that I am splendid. And since I have been here, I keep walking about and thinking, thinking and feeling that my soul is getting stronger every day. Now I know, I understand, Kostya, that in our work—in acting or writing—what matters is not fame, not glory, not what I dreamed of, but knowing how to be patient. To bear one's cross and have faith. I have faith and it all doesn't hurt so much, and when I think of my vocation I am not afraid of life.

TREPLEV. [*Mournfully.*] You have found your path, you know which way you are going, but I am still floating in a chaos of dreams and images, not knowing what use it is to anyone. I have no faith and don't know what my vocation is.

NINA. [*Listening.*] Sh-sh . . . I am going. Good-bye. When I become a great actress, come and look at me. Will you promise? But now . . . [*presses his hand*] it's late. I can hardly stand on my feet. . . . I am worn out and hungry. . . .

TREPLEV. Stay, I'll give you some supper.

NINA. No, no. . . . Don't see me off, I will go by myself. My horses are close by. . . . So she brought him with her? Well, it doesn't matter. When you see Trigorin, don't say anything to him. . . . I love him! I love him even more than before. . . . A subject for a short story . . . I love him, I love him passionately, I love him to despair. It was nice in the old days, Kostya! Do you remember? How clear, warm, joyous, and pure life was, what feelings we had—feelings like tender, exquisite flowers. . . . Do you remember? [*Recites.*] "Men, lions, eagles, and partridges, horned deer, geese, spiders, silent fish that dwell in the water, starfishes, and creatures which cannot be seen by the eye—all living things, all living things, all living things, have completed their cycle of sorrow, are extinct. . . . For thousands of years the earth has borne no living creature on its surface, and this poor moon lights its lamp in vain. On the meadow the cranes no longer waken with a cry and there is no sound of the May beetles in the lime trees . . ."

[*Impulsively embraces* TREPLEV *and runs out of the glass door.*]

TREPLEV. [*After a pause.*] It will be a pity if someone meets her in the garden and tells mother. It may upset mother. . . .

[*He spends two minutes in tearing up all his manuscripts and throwing them under the table; then unlocks the door on right and goes out.*]

DORN. [*Trying to open the door on left.*] Strange. The door seems to be locked . . . [*Comes in and puts the armchair in its place.*] An obstacle race.

[*Enter* MADAME ARKADIN *and* POLINA ANDREYEVNA, *behind them* YAKOV *carrying a tray with bottles;* MASHA; *then* SHAMRAEV *and* TRIGORIN.]

MADAME ARKADIN. Put the claret and the beer for Boris Alexeyevitch here on the table. We will play as we drink it. Let us sit down, friends.

POLINA. [*To* YAKOV.] Bring tea too at the same time. [*Lights the candles and sits down to the card table.*]

SHAMRAEV. [*Leads* TRIGORIN *to the cupboard.*] Here's the thing I was speaking about just now. [*Takes the stuffed sea gull from the cupboard.*] This is what you ordered.

TRIGORIN. [*Looking at the sea gull.*] I don't remember it. [*Musing.*] I don't remember.

[*The sound of a shot coming from right of stage; everyone starts.*]

MADAME ARKADIN. [*Frightened.*] What's that?

DORN. That's nothing. It must be something in my medicine chest that has gone off. Don't be anxious. [*Goes out at door on right, comes back in half a minute.*] That's what it is. A bottle of ether has exploded. [*Hums.*] "I stand before thee enchanted again. . . ."

MADAME ARKADIN. [*Sitting down to the table.*] Ough, how frightened I was. It reminded me of how . . . [*Hides her face in her hands.*] It made me quite dizzy. . . .

DORN. [*Turning over the leaves of the magazine, to* TRIGORIN.] There was an article in this two months ago—a letter from America—and I wanted to ask you among other things [*puts his arm round* TRIGORIN's *waist and leads him to the footlights*] as I am very much interested in the question. . . . [*In a lower tone, dropping his voice.*] Get Irina Nikolayevna away somehow. The fact is, Konstantin Gavrilitch has shot himself. . . .

[CURTAIN]

William Butler Yeats 1865–1939

The Words Upon the Window-Pane [1]

PERSONS IN THE PLAY

Dr. Trench	Cornelius Patterson
Miss Mackenna	Abraham Johnson
John Corbet	Mrs. Mallet
	Mrs. Henderson

[*A lodging-house room, an armchair, a little table in front of it, chairs on either side. A fireplace and window. A kettle on the hob and some tea-things on a dresser. A door to back and towards the right. Through the door one can see an entrance hall. The sound of a knocker.* Miss Mackenna *passes through and then she re-enters hall together with* John Corbet, *a man of twenty-two or twenty-three, and* Dr. Trench, *a man of between sixty and seventy.*]

Dr. Trench [*in hall*]. May I introduce John Corbet, one of the Corbets of Ballymoney, but at present a Cambridge student? This is Miss Mackenna, our energetic secretary. [*They come into room, take off their coats.*]

Miss Mackenna. I thought it better to let you in myself. This country is still sufficiently medieval to make spiritualism an undesirable theme for gossip. Give me your coats and hats, I will put them in my own room. It is just across the hall. Better sit down; your watches must be fast. Mrs

---

[1] *Words . . . Pane,* Yeats writes in his poem "Blood and the Moon,"
    Swift beating on his breast in sibylline frenzy blind
    Because the heart in his blood-sodden breast had dragged him down into mankind.
This play explores the familiar Yeatsean antithesis between passion and intellect and also the everyday and the heroic in terms of the relationship between the eighteenth-century novelist, poet, and essayist Jonathan Swift, and two women in his life. Swift knew Esther Johnson (Stella) intimately for many years, though the two seem never to have lived as man and wife. Hester Vanhomrigh (Vanessa) became infatuated with Swift at a later date, pursued him from England to Ireland, and—according to legend—challenged him concerning his relationship with Stella. Her subsequent death has been attributed to grief.

Henderson is lying down, as she always does before a séance. We won't begin for ten minutes yet. [*She goes out with hats and coats.*]

Dr. Trench. Miss Mackenna does all the real work of the Dublin Spiritualists' Association. She did all the correspondence with Mrs. Henderson, and persuaded the landlady to let her this big room and a small room upstairs. We are a poor society and could not guarantee anything in advance. Mrs. Henderson has come from London at her own risk. She was born in Dublin and wants to spread the movement here. She lives very economically and does not expect a great deal. We all give what we can. A poor woman with the soul of an apostle.

John Corbet. Have there been many séances?

Dr. Trench. Only three so far.

John Corbet. I hope she will not mind my scepticism. I have looked into Myers' *Human Personality* and a wild book by Conan Doyle, but am unconvinced.

Dr. Trench. We all have to find the truth for ourselves. Lord Dunraven, then Lord Adare, introduced my father to the famous David Home. My father often told me that he saw David Home floating in the air in broad daylight, but I did not believe a word of it. I had to investigate for myself, and I was very hard to convince. Mrs. Piper, an American trance medium, not unlike Mrs. Henderson, convinced me.

John Corbet. A state of somnambulism and voices coming through her lips that purport to be those of dead persons?

Dr. Trench. Exactly: quite the best kind of mediumship if you want to establish the identity of a spirit. But do not expect too much. There has been a hostile influence.

John Corbet. You mean an evil spirit?

Dr. Trench. The poet Blake said that he never knew a bad man that had not something very good about him. I say a hostile influence, an influence that disturbed the last séance very seriously. I cannot tell you what happened, for I have not been at any of Mrs. Henderson's séances. Trance mediumship has nothing new to show me—I told the young people when they made me their President that I would probably stay at home, that I could get more out of Emanuel Swedenborg than out of any séance. [*A knock.*] That is probably old Cornelius Patterson; he thinks they race horses and whippets in the other world, and is, so they tell me, so anxious to find out if he is right that he is always punctual. Miss Mackenna will keep him to herself for some minutes. He gives her tips for Harold's Cross.

[Miss Mackenna *crosses to hall door and admits* Cornelius Patterson. *She brings him to her room across the hall.*]

John Corbet [*who has been wandering about*]. This is a wonderful room for a lodging-house.

DR. TRENCH. It was a private house until about fifty years ago. It was not so near the town in those days, and there are large stables at the back. Quite a number of notable people lived here. Grattan was born upstairs; no, not Grattan, Curran perhaps—I forget—but I do know that this house in the early part of the eighteenth century belonged to friends of Jonathan Swift, or rather of Stella. Swift chaffed her in the *Journal to Stella* because of certain small sums of money she lost at cards probably in this very room. That was before Vanessa appeared upon the scene. It was a country-house in those days, surrounded by trees and gardens. Somebody cut some lines from a poem of hers upon the window-pane —tradition says Stella herself. [*A knock.*] Here they are, but you will hardly make them out in this light. [*They stand in the window.* CORBET *stoops down to see better.* MISS MACKENNA *and* ABRAHAM JOHNSON *enter and stand near door.*]

ABRAHAM JOHNSON. Where is Mrs. Henderson?

MISS MACKENNA. She is upstairs; she always rests before a séance.

ABRAHAM JOHNSON. I must see her before the séance. I know exactly what to do to get rid of this evil influence.

MISS MACKENNA. If you go up to see her there will be no séance at all. She says it is dangerous even to think, much less to speak, of an evil influence.

ABRAHAM JOHNSON. Then I shall speak to the President.

MISS MACKENNA. Better talk the whole thing over first in my room. Mrs. Henderson says that there must be perfect harmony.

ABRAHAM JOHNSON. Something must be done. The last séance was completely spoiled. [*A knock.*]

MISS MACKENNA. That may be Mrs. Mallet; she is a very experienced spiritualist. Come to my room, old Patterson and some others are there already. [*She brings him to the other room and later crosses to hall door to admit* MRS. MALLET.]

JOHN CORBET. I know those lines well—they are part of a poem Stella wrote for Swift's fifty-fourth birthday. Only three poems of hers—and some lines she added to a poem of Swift's—have come down to us, but they are enough to prove her a better poet than Swift. Even those few words on the window make me think of a seventeenth-century poet, Donne or Crashaw. [*He quotes*]

> 'You taught how I might youth prolong
> By knowing what is right and wrong,
> How from my heart to bring supplies
> Of lustre to my fading eyes.'

How strange that a celibate scholar, well on in life, should keep the love of two such women! He met Vanessa in London at the height of his political power. She followed him to Dublin. She loved him for nine years, perhaps died of love, but Stella loved him all her life.

Dr. Trench. I have shown that writing to several persons, and you are the first who has recognised the lines.

John Corbet. I am writing an essay on Swift and Stella for my doctorate at Cambridge. I hope to prove that in Swift's day men of intellect reached the height of their power—the greatest position they ever attained in society and the State, that everything great in Ireland and in our character, in what remains of our architecture, comes from that day; that we have kept its seal longer than England.

Dr. Trench. A tragic life: Bolingbroke, Harley, Ormonde, all those great Ministers that were his friends, banished and broken.

John Corbet. I do not think you can explain him in that way—his tragedy had deeper foundations. His ideal order was the Roman Senate, his ideal men Brutus and Cato. Such an order and such men had seemed possible once more, but the movement passed and he foresaw the ruin to come, Democracy, Rousseau, the French Revolution; that is why he hated the common run of men,—'I hate lawyers, I hate doctors,' he said, 'though I love Dr. So-and-so and Judge So-and-so'—that is why he wrote *Gulliver*, that is why he wore out his brain, that is why he felt *saeva indignatio*, that is why he sleeps under the greatest epitaph in history. You remember how it goes? It is almost finer in English than in Latin: 'He has gone where fierce indignation can lacerate his heart no more.'

[Abraham Johnson *comes in, followed by* Mrs. Mallet *and* Cornelius Patterson.]

Abraham Johnson. Something must be done, Dr. Trench, to drive away the influence that has destroyed our séances. I have come here week after week at considerable expense. I am from Belfast. I am by profession a minister of the Gospel, I do a great deal of work among the poor and ignorant. I produce considerable effect by singing and preaching, but I know that my effect should be much greater than it is. My hope is that I shall be able to communicate with the great Evangelist Moody. I want to ask him to stand invisible beside me when I speak or sing, and lay his hands upon my head and give me such a portion of his power that my work may be blessed as the work of Moody and Sankey was blessed.

Mrs. Mallet. What Mr. Johnson says about the hostile influence is quite true. The last two séances were completely spoilt. I am thinking of starting a tea-shop in Folkstone. I followed Mrs. Henderson to Dublin to get my husband's advice, but two spirits kept talking and would not let any other spirit say a word.

Dr. Trench. Did the spirits say the same thing and go through the same drama at both séances?

Mrs. Mallet. Yes—just as if they were characters in some kind of horrible play.

DR. TRENCH. That is what I was afraid of.

MRS. MALLET. My husband was drowned at sea ten years ago, but constantly speaks to me through Mrs. Henderson as if he were still alive. He advises me about everything I do, and I am utterly lost if I cannot question him.

CORNELIUS PATTERSON. I never did like the Heaven they talk about in churches: but when somebody told me that Mrs. Mallet's husband ate and drank and went about with his favourite dog, I said to myself, 'That is the place for Corney Patterson.' I came here to find out if it was true, and I declare to God I have not heard one word about it.

ABRAHAM JOHNSON. I ask you, Dr. Trench, as President of the Dublin Spiritualists' Association, to permit me to read the ritual of exorcism appointed for such occasions. After the last séance I copied it out of an old book in the library of Belfast University. I have it here. [*He takes paper out of his pocket.*]

DR. TRENCH. The spirits are people like ourselves, we treat them as our guests and protect them from discourtesy and violence, and every exorcism is a curse or a threatened curse. We do not admit that there are evil spirits. Some spirits are earth-bound—they think they are still living and go over and over some action of their past lives, just as we go over and over some painful thought, except that where they are thought is reality. For instance, when a spirit which has died a violent death comes to a medium for the first time, it re-lives all the pains of death.

MRS. MALLET. When my husband came for the first time the medium gasped and struggled as if she was drowning. It was terrible to watch.

DR. TRENCH. Sometimes a spirit re-lives not the pain of death but some passionate or tragic moment of life. Swedenborg describes this and gives the reason for it. There is an incident of the kind in the *Odyssey*, and many in Eastern literature; the murderer repeats his murder, the robber his robbery, the lover his serenade, the soldier hears the trumpet once again. If I were a Catholic I would say that such spirits were in Purgatory. In vain do we write *requiescat in pace* upon the tomb, for they must suffer, and we in our turn must suffer until God gives peace. Such spirits do not often come to séances unless those séances are held in houses where those spirits lived, or where the event took place. This spirit which speaks those incomprehensible words and does not answer when spoken to is of such a nature. The more patient we are, the more quickly will it pass out of its passion and its remorse.

ABRAHAM JOHNSON. I am still convinced that the spirit which disturbed the last séance is evil. If I may not exorcise it I will certainly pray for protection.

DR. TRENCH. Mrs. Henderson's control, Lulu, is able and experienced and can protect both medium and sitters, but it may help Lulu if you pray that the spirit find rest.

[ABRAHAM JOHNSON *sits down and prays silently, moving his lips.* MRS. HENDERSON *comes in with* MISS MACKENNA *and others.* MISS MACKENNA *shuts the door.*]

DR. TRENCH. Mrs. Henderson, may I introduce to you Mr. Corbet, a young man from Cambridge and a sceptic, who hopes that you will be able to convince him?

MRS. HENDERSON. We were all sceptics once. He must not expect too much from a first séance. He must persevere. [*She sits in the armchair, and the others begin to seat themselves.* MISS MACKENNA *goes to* JOHN CORBET *and they remain standing.*]

MISS MACKENNA. I am glad that you are a sceptic.

JOHN CORBET. I thought you were a spiritualist.

MISS MACKENNA. I have seen a good many séances, and sometimes think it is all coincidence and thought-transference. [*She says this in a low voice.*] Then at other times I think as Dr. Trench does, and then I feel like Job—you know the quotation—the hair of my head stands up. A spirit passes before my face.

MRS. MALLET. Turn the key, Dr. Trench, we don't want anybody blundering in here. [DR. TRENCH *locks door.*] Come and sit here, Miss Mackenna.

MISS MACKENNA. No, I am going to sit beside Mr. Corbet.

[CORBET *and* MISS MACKENNA *sit down.*]

JOHN CORBET. You feel like Job to-night?

MISS MACKENNA. I feel that something is going to happen, that is why I am glad that you are a sceptic.

JOHN CORBET. You feel safer?

MISS MACKENNA. Yes, safer.

MRS. HENDERSON. I am glad to meet all my dear friends again and to welcome Mr. Corbet amongst us. As he is a stranger I must explain that we do not call up spirits, we make the right conditions and they come. I do not know who is going to come; sometimes there are a great many and the guides choose between them. The guides try to send somebody for everybody but do not always succeed. If you want to speak to some dear friend who has passed over, do not be discouraged. If your friend cannot come this time, maybe he can next time. My control is a dear little girl called Lulu who died when she was five or six years old. She describes the spirits present and tells us what spirit wants to speak. Miss Mackenna, a verse of a hymn, please, the same we had last time, and will everyone join in the singing.

[*They sing the following lines from Hymn 564, Irish Church Hymnal.*]

> 'Sun of my soul, Thou Saviour dear,
> It is not night if Thou be near:
> O may no earth-born cloud arise
> To hide Thee from Thy servant's eyes.'

[MRS. HENDERSON *is leaning back in her chair asleep.*]

MISS MACKENNA [*to* JOHN CORBET]. She always snores like that when she is going off.

MRS. HENDERSON [*in a child's voice*]. Lulu so glad to see all her friends.

MRS. MALLET. And we are glad you have come, Lulu.

MRS. HENDERSON [*in a child's voice*]. Lulu glad to see new friend.

MISS MACKENNA [*to* JOHN CORBET]. She is speaking to you.

JOHN CORBET. Thank you, Lulu.

MRS. HENDERSON [*in a child's voice*]. You mustn't laugh at the way I talk.

JOHN CORBET. I am not laughing, Lulu.

MRS. HENDERSON [*in a child's voice*]. Nobody must laugh. Lulu does her best but can't say big long words. Lulu sees a tall man here, lots of hair on face [MRS. HENDERSON *passes her hands over her cheeks and chin*], not much on the top of his head [MRS. HENDERSON *passes her hand over the top of her head*], red necktie, and such a funny sort of pin.

MRS. MALLET. Yes. . . . Yes. . . .

MRS. HENDERSON [*in a child's voice*]. Pin like a horseshoe.

MRS. MALLET. It's my husband.

MRS. HENDERSON [*in a child's voice*]. He has a message.

MRS. MALLET. Yes.

MRS. HENDERSON [*in a child's voice*]. Lulu cannot hear. He is too far off. He has come near. Lulu can hear now. He says . . . he says, 'Drive that man away!' He is pointing to somebody in the corner, that corner over there. He says it is the bad man who spoilt everything last time. If they won't drive him away, Lulu will scream.

MISS MACKENNA. That horrible spirit again.

ABRAHAM JOHNSON. Last time he monopolised the séance.

MRS. MALLET. He would not let anybody speak but himself.

MRS. HENDERSON [*in a child's voice*]. They have driven that bad man away. Lulu sees a young lady.

MRS. MALLET. Is not my husband here?

MRS. HENDERSON [*in a child's voice*]. Man with funny pin gone away. Young lady here—Lulu thinks she must be at a fancy dress party, such funny clothes, hair all in curls—all bent down on floor near that old man with glasses.

DR. TRENCH. No, I do not recognise her.

MRS. HENDERSON [*in a child's voice*]. That bad man, that bad old man in the corner, they have let him come back. Lulu is going to scream. O. . . . O. . . . [*in a man's voice*]. How dare you write to her? How dare you ask if we were married? How dare you question her?

DR. TRENCH. A soul in its agony—it cannot see us or hear us.

MRS. HENDERSON [*upright and rigid, only her lips moving, and still in a man's voice*]. You sit crouching there. Did you not hear what I said? How dared you question her? I found you an ignorant little girl without intellect, without moral ambition. How many times did I not stay away from great men's houses, how many times forsake the Lord Treasurer, how many times neglect the business of the State that we might read Plutarch together!

[ABRAHAM JOHNSON *half rises.* DR. TRENCH *motions him to remain seated.*]

DR. TRENCH. Silence!

ABRAHAM JOHNSON. But, Dr. Trench . . .

DR. TRENCH. Hush—we can do nothing.

MRS. HENDERSON [*speaking as before*]. I taught you to think in every situation of life not as Hester Vanhomrigh would think in that situation, but as Cato or Brutus would, and now you behave like some common slut with her ear against the keyhole.

JOHN CORBET [*to* MISS MACKENNA]. It is Swift, Jonathan Swift, talking to the woman he called Vanessa. She was christened Hester Vanhomrigh.

MRS. HENDERSON [*in* VANESSA's *voice*]. I questioned her, Jonathan, because I love. Why have you let me spend hours in your company if you did not want me to love you? [*In* SWIFT's *voice.*] When I rebuilt Rome in your mind it was as though I walked its streets. [*In* VANESSA's *voice.*] Was that all, Jonathan? Was I nothing but a painter's canvas? [*In* SWIFT's *voice.*] My God, do you think it was easy? I was a man of strong passions and I had sworn never to marry. [*In* VANESSA's *voice.*] If you and she are not married, why should we not marry like other men and women? I loved you from the first moment when you came to my mother's house and began to teach me. I thought it would be enough to look at you, to speak to you, to hear you speak. I followed you to Ireland five years ago and I can bear it no longer. It is not enough to look, to speak, to hear. Jonathan, Jonathan, I am a woman, the women Brutus and Cato loved were not different. [*In* SWIFT's *voice.*] I have something in my blood that no child must inherit. I have constant attacks of dizziness; I pretend they come from a surfeit of fruit when I was a child. I had them in London. . . . There was a great doctor there, Dr. Arbuthnot; I told him of those attacks of dizziness, I told him of worse things. It was he who explained. There is a line of Dryden's. . . . [*In* VANESSA's *voice.*] O, I know—'Great wits are sure to madness near allied.' If you had children, Jonathan, my blood would make them healthy. I will take your hand, I will lay it upon my heart—upon the Vanhomrigh blood that has been healthy for generations. [MRS. HENDERSON *slowly raises her left hand.*] That is the first time you have touched my body, Jonathan. [MRS. HENDERSON *stands up and remains rigid. In* SWIFT'S *voice.*] What do I care if it be healthy? What do I care if it could make mine healthy? Am I to add another to the healthy rascaldom and knavery of the world? [*In* VANESSA'S *voice.*] Look at me, Jonathan. Your arrogant intellect separates us. Give me both your hands. I will put them upon my breast. [MRS. HENDERSON *raises her right hand to the level of her left and then raises both to her breast.*] O, it is white—white as the gambler's dice—white ivory dice. Think of the uncertainty. Perhaps a mad child—perhaps a rascal—perhaps a knave—perhaps not, Jonathan. The dice of the intellect are loaded, but I am the common ivory dice. [*Her hands are stretched out as though drawing somebody towards her.*] It is not my hands that draw you back. My hands are weak, they could not draw you back if you did not love as I love. You said that you have strong passions; that is true, Jonathan—no man in Ireland is so passionate. That is why you need me, that is why you need children, nobody has greater need. You are growing old. An old man without children is very solitary. Even his friends, men as old as he, turn away, they turn towards the young, their children or their children's children. They cannot endure an old man like themselves. [MRS. HENDERSON *moves away from the chair, her movements gradually growing convulsive.*] You are not too old for the dice, Jonathan, but a few years if you turn away will make you an old miserable childless man. [*In* SWIFT'S *voice.*] O God, hear the prayer of Jonathan Swift, that afflicted man, and grant that he may leave to posterity nothing but his intellect that came to him from Heaven. [*In* VANESSA'S *voice.*] Can you face solitude with that mind, Jonathan? [MRS. HENDERSON *goes to the door, finds that it is closed.*] Dice, white ivory dice.] *In* SWIFT'S *voice.*] My God, I am left alone with my enemy. Who locked the door, who locked me in with my enemy? [MRS. HENDERSON *beats upon the door, sinks to the floor and then speaks as* LULU.] Bad old man! Do not let him come back. Bad old man does not know he is dead. Lulu cannot find fathers, mothers, sons that have passed over. Power almost gone. [MRS. MALLET *leads* MRS. HENDERSON, *who seems very exhausted, back to her chair. She is still asleep. She speaks again as* LULU.] Another verse of hymn. Everybody sing. Hymn will bring good influence.

[*They sing*]

> 'If some poor wandering child of Thine
> Have spurned to-day the voice divine
> Now, Lord, the gracious work begin;
> Let him no more lie down in sin.'

[*During the hymn* Mrs. Henderson *has been murmuring* 'Stella,' *but the singing has almost drowned her voice. The singers draw one another's attention to the fact that she is speaking. The singing stops.*]

Dr. Trench. I thought she was speaking.

Mrs. Mallet. I saw her lips move.

Dr. Trench. She would be more comfortable with a cushion, but we might wake her.

Mrs. Mallet. Nothing can wake her out of a trance like that until she wakes up herself. [*She brings a cushion and she and* Dr. Trench *put* Mrs. Henderson *into a more comfortable position.*]

Mrs. Henderson [*in* Swift's *voice*]. Stella.

Miss Mackenna [*to* John Corbet]. Did you hear that? She said 'Stella.'

John Corbet. Vanessa has gone, Stella has taken her place.

Miss Mackenna. Did you notice the change while we were singing? The new influence in the room?

John Corbet. I thought I did, but it must have been fancy.

Mrs. Mallet. Hush!

Mrs. Henderson [*in* Swift's *voice*]. Have I wronged you, beloved Stella? Are you unhappy? You have no children, you have no lover, you have no husband. A cross and aging man for friend—nothing but that. But no, do not answer—you have answered already in that poem you wrote for my last birthday. With what scorn you speak of the common lot of women 'with no endowments but a face—'

> 'Before the thirtieth year of life
> A maid forlorn or hated wife.'

It is the thought of the great Chrysostom who wrote in a famous passage that women loved according to the soul, loved as saints can love, keep their beauty longer, have greater happiness than women loved according to the flesh. That thought has comforted me, but it is a terrible thing to be responsible for another's happiness. There are moments when I doubt, when I think Chrysostom may have been wrong. But now I have your poem to drive doubt away. You have addressed me in these noble words:

> 'You taught how I might youth prolong
> By knowing what is right and wrong;
> How from my heart to bring supplies
> Of lustre to my fading eyes;
> How soon a beauteous mind repairs
> The loss of chang'd or falling hairs;
> How wit and virtue from within
> Can spread a smoothness o'er the skin.'

JOHN CORBET. The words upon the window-pane!

MRS. HENDERSON [*in* SWIFT's *voice*]. Then, because you understand that I am afraid of solitude, afraid of outliving my friends—and myself—you comfort me in that last verse—you overpraise my moral nature when you attribute to it a rich mantle, but O how touching those words which describe your love:

> 'Late dying may you cast a shred
> Of that rich mantle o'er my head;
> To bear with dignity my sorrow,
> One day alone, then die to-morrow.'

Yes, you will close my eyes, Stella. O, you will live long after me, dear Stella, for you are still a young woman, but you will close my eyes. [MRS. HENDERSON *sinks back in chair and speaks as* LULU.] Bad old man gone. Power all used up. Lulu can do no more. Good-bye, friends. [MRS. HENDERSON, *speaking in her own voice*.] Go away, go away! [*She wakes.*] I saw him a moment ago, has he spoilt the séance again?

MRS. MALLET. Yes, Mrs. Henderson, my husband came, but he was driven away.

DR. TRENCH. Mrs. Henderson is very tired. We must leave her to rest. [*To* MRS. HENDERSON.] You did your best and nobody can do more than that. [*He takes out money.*]

MRS. HENDERSON. No. . . . No. . . . I cannot take any money, not after a séance like that.

DR. TRENCH. Of course you must take it, Mrs. Henderson. [*He puts money on table, and* MRS. HENDERSON *gives a furtive glance to see how much it is. She does the same as each sitter lays down his or her money.*]

MRS. MALLET. A bad séance is just as exhausting as a good séance, and you must be paid.

MRS. HENDERSON. No. . . . No. . . . Please don't. It is very wrong to take money for such a failure. [MRS. MALLET *lays down money.*]

CORNELIUS PATTERSON. A jockey is paid whether he wins or not. [*He lays down money.*]

MISS MACKENNA. That spirit rather thrilled me. [*She lays down money.*]

MRS. HENDERSON. If you insist, I must take it.

ABRAHAM JOHNSON. I shall pray for you to-night. I shall ask God to bless and protect your séances. [*He lays down money.*]

[*All go out except* JOHN CORBET *and* MRS. HENDERSON.]

JOHN CORBET. I know you are tired, Mrs. Henderson, but I must speak to you. I have been deeply moved by what I have heard. This is my contribution to prove that I am satisfied, completely satisfied. [*He puts a note on the table.*]

Mrs. Henderson. A pound note—nobody ever gives me more than ten shillings, and yet the séance was a failure.

John Corbet [*sitting down near* Mrs. Henderson]. When I say I am satisfied I do not mean that I am convinced it was the work of spirits. I prefer to think that you created it all, that you are an accomplished actress and scholar. In my essay for my Cambridge doctorate I examine all the explanations of Swift's celibacy offered by his biographers and prove that the explanation you selected was the only plausible one. But there is something I must ask you. Swift was the chief representative of the intellect of his epoch, that arrogant intellect free at last from superstition. He foresaw its collapse. He foresaw Democracy, he must have dreaded the future. Did he refuse to beget children because of that dread? Was Swift mad? Or was it the intellect itself that was mad?

Mrs. Henderson. Who are you talking of, sir?

John Corbet. Swift, of course.

Mrs. Henderson. Swift? I do not know anybody called Swift.

John Corbet. Jonathan Swift, whose spirit seemed to be present to-night.

Mrs. Henderson. What? That dirty old man?

John Corbet. He was neither old nor dirty when Stella and Vanessa loved him.

Mrs. Henderson. I saw him very clearly just as I woke up. His clothes were dirty, his face covered with boils. Some disease had made one of his eyes swell up, it stood out from his face like a hen's egg.

John Corbet. He looked like that in his old age. Stella had been dead a long time. His brain had gone, his friends had deserted him. The man appointed to take care of him beat him to keep him quiet.

Mrs. Henderson. Now they are old, now they are young. They change all in a moment as their thought changes. It is sometimes a terrible thing to be out of the body, God help us all.

Dr. Trench [*at doorway*]. Come along, Corbet, Mrs. Henderson is tired out.

John Corbet. Good-bye, Mrs. Henderson. [*He goes out with* Dr. Trench. *All the sitters except* Miss Mackenna, *who has returned to her room, pass along the passage on their way to the front door.* Mrs. Henderson *counts the money, finds her purse, which is in a vase on the mantelpiece, and puts the money in it.*]

Mrs. Henderson. How tired I am! I'd be the better of a cup of tea. [*She finds the teapot and puts kettle on fire, and then as she crouches down by the hearth suddenly lifts up her hands and counts her fingers, speaking in* Swift's *voice.*] Five great Ministers that were my friends are gone, ten great Ministers that were my friends are gone. I have not fingers enough to count the great Ministers that were my friends and that are gone.

[*She wakes with a start and speaks in her own voice.*]

Where did I put that tea-caddy? Ah! there it is. And there should be a cup and saucer. [*She finds the saucer.*] But where's the cup? [*She moves aimlessly about the stage and then, letting the saucer fall and break, speaks in* SWIFT's *voice.*] Perish the day on which I was born!

Edward Albee 1928–

The Zoo Story

A PLAY IN ONE SCENE

PLAYERS

PETER, *a man in his early forties, neither fat nor gaunt, neither handsome nor homely. He wears tweeds, smokes a pipe, carries horn-rimmed glasses. Although he is moving into middle age, his dress and his manner would suggest a man younger.*

JERRY, *a man in his late thirties, not poorly dressed, but carelessly. What was once a trim and lightly muscled body has begun to go to fat; and while he is no longer handsome, it is evident that he once was. His fall from physical grace should not suggest debauchery; he has, to come closest to it, a great weariness.*

Scene. It is Central Park; a Sunday afternoon in summer; the present. There are two park benches, one toward either side of the stage; they both face the audience. Behind them: foliage, trees, sky. At the beginning, Peter is seated on one of the benches.

[As the curtain rises, PETER *is seated on the bench stage-right. He is reading a book. He stops reading, cleans his glasses, goes back to reading.* JERRY *enters.*]

JERRY. I've been to the zoo. [PETER *doesn't notice.*] I said, I've been to the ZOO. MISTER, I'VE BEEN TO THE ZOO!
PETER. Hm? . . . What? . . . I'm sorry, were you talking to me?
JERRY. I went to the zoo, and then I walked until I came here. Have I been walking north?
PETER [*puzzled*]. North? Why . . . I . . . I think so. Let me see.
JERRY [*pointing past the audience*]. Is that Fifth Avenue?
PETER. Why yes; yes, it is.
JERRY. And what is that cross street there; that one, to the right?
PETER. That? Oh, that's Seventy-fourth Street.
JERRY. And the zoo is around Sixty-fifth Street; so, I've been walking north.
PETER [*anxious to get back to his reading*]. Yes; it would seem so.

520

JERRY. Good old north.

PETER [*lightly, by reflex*]. Ha, ha.

JERRY [*after a slight pause*]. But not due north.

PETER. I . . . well, no, not due north; but, we . . . call it north. It's northerly.

JERRY. [*Watches as* PETER, *anxious to dismiss him, prepares his pipe.*] Well, boy; *you're* not going to get lung cancer, are you?

PETER. [*Looks up, a little annoyed, then smiles.*] No, sir. Not from this.

JERRY. No, sir. What you'll probably get is cancer of the mouth, and then you'll have to wear one of those things Freud wore after they took one whole side of his jaw away. What do they call those things?

PETER [*uncomfortable*]. A prosthesis?

JERRY. The very thing! A prosthesis. You're an educated man, aren't you? Are you a doctor?

PETER. Oh, no; no. I read about it somewhere; *Time* magazine, I think. [*He turns to his book.*]

JERRY. Well, *Time* magazine isn't for blockheads.

PETER. No, I suppose not.

JERRY [*after a pause*]. Boy, I'm glad that's Fifth Avenue there.

PETER [*vaguely*]. Yes.

JERRY. I don't like the west side of the park much.

PETER. Oh? [*Then, slightly wary, but interested.*] Why?

JERRY [*offhand*]. I don't know.

PETER. Oh. [*He returns to his book.*]

JERRY. [*He stands for a few seconds, looking at* PETER, *who finally looks up again, puzzled.*] Do you mind if we talk?

PETER [*obviously minding*]. Why . . . no, no.

JERRY. Yes, you do; you do.

PETER. [*Puts his book down, his pipe out and away, smiling.*] No, really; I don't mind.

JERRY. Yes you do.

PETER [*finally decided*]. No; I don't mind at all, really.

JERRY. It's . . . it's a nice day.

PETER. [*Stares unnecessarily at the sky.*] Yes. Yes, it is; lovely.

JERRY. I've been to the zoo.

PETER. Yes, I think you said so . . . didn't you?

JERRY. You'll read about it in the papers tomorrow, if you don't see it on your TV tonight. You have TV, haven't you?

PETER. Why yes, we have two; one for the children.

JERRY. You're married!

PETER [*with pleased emphasis*]. Why, certainly.

JERRY. It isn't a law, for God's sake.

PETER. No . . . no, of course not.

JERRY. And you have a wife.

PETER [*bewildered by the seeming lack of communication*]. Yes!

JERRY. And you have children.

PETER. Yes; two.

JERRY. Boys?

PETER. No, girls . . . both girls.

JERRY. But you wanted boys.

PETER. Well . . . naturally, every man wants a son, but . . .

JERRY [*lightly mocking*]. But that's the way the cookie crumbles?

PETER [*annoyed*]. I wasn't going to say that.

JERRY. And you're not going to have any more kids, are you?

PETER [*a bit distantly*]. No. No more. [*Then back, and irksome.*] Why did you say that? How would you know about that?

JERRY. The way you cross your legs, perhaps; something in the voice. Or maybe I'm just guessing. Is it your wife?

PETER [*furious*]. That's none of your business! [*A silence.*] Do you understand? [JERRY *nods.* PETER *is quiet now.*] Well, you're right. We'll have no more children.

JERRY [*softly*]. That *is* the way the cookie crumbles.

PETER [*forgiving*]. Yes . . . I guess so.

JERRY. Well, now; what else?

PETER. What were you saying about the zoo . . . that I'd read about it, or see . . . ?

JERRY. I'll tell you about it, soon. Do you mind if I ask you questions?

PETER. Oh, not really.

JERRY. I'll tell you why I do it; I don't talk to many people—except to say like: give me a beer, or where's the john, or what time does the feature go on, or keep your hands to yourself, buddy. You know—things like that . . .

PETER. I must say I don't . . .

JERRY. But every once in a while I like to talk to somebody, really *talk*; like to get to know somebody, know all about him.

PETER [*lightly laughing, still a little uncomfortable*]. And am I the guinea pig for today?

JERRY. On a sun-drenched Sunday afternoon like this? Who better than a nice married man with two daughters and . . . uh . . . a dog? [PETER *shakes his head.*] No? Two dogs. [PETER *shakes his head again.*] Hm. No dogs? [PETER *shakes his head, sadly.*] Oh, that's a shame. But you look like an animal man. CATS? [PETER *nods his head, ruefully.*] Cats! But, that can't be your idea. No, sir. Your wife and daughters? [PETER *nods his head.*] Is there anything else I should know?

PETER. [*He has to clear his throat.*] There are . . . there are two parakeets. One . . . uh . . . one for each of my daughters.

JERRY. Birds.

PETER. My daughters keep them in a cage in their bedroom.

JERRY. Do they carry disease? The birds.

PETER. I don't believe so.

JERRY. That's too bad. If they did you could set them loose in the house and the cats could eat them and die, maybe. [PETER *looks blank for a moment, then laughs.*] And what else? What do you do to support your enormous household?

PETER. I . . . uh . . . I have an executive position with a . . . a small publishing house. We . . . uh . . . we publish textbooks.

JERRY. That sounds nice; very nice. What do you make?

PETER [*still cheerful*]. Now look here!

JERRY. Oh, come on.

PETER. Well, I make around eighteen thousand a year, but I don't carry more than forty dollars at any one time . . . in case you're a . . . a holdup man . . . ha, ha, ha.

JERRY [*ignoring the above*]. Where do you live? [PETER *is reluctant.*] Oh, look; I'm not going to rob you, and I'm not going to kidnap your parakeets, your cats, or your daughters.

PETER [*too loud*]. I live between Lexington and Third Avenue, on Seventy-fourth Street.

JERRY. That wasn't so hard, was it?

PETER. I didn't mean to seem . . . ah . . . it's that you don't really carry on a conversation; you just ask questions. And I'm . . . I'm normally . . . uh . . . reticent. Why do you just stand there?

JERRY. I'll start walking around in a little while, and eventually I'll sit down. [*recalling.*] Wait until you see the expression on his face.

PETER. What? Whose face? Look here; is this something about the zoo?

JERRY [*distantly*]. The what?

PETER. The zoo; the zoo. Something about the zoo.

JERRY. The zoo?

PETER. You've mentioned it several times.

JERRY [*still distant, but returning abruptly*]. The zoo? Oh, yes; the zoo. I was there before I came here. I told you that. Say, what's the dividing line between upper-middle-middle-class and lower-upper-middle-class?

PETER. My dear fellow, I . . .

JERRY. Don't my dear fellow me.

PETER [*unhappily*]. Was I patronizing? I believe I was; I'm sorry. But, you see, your question about the classes bewildered me.

JERRY. And when you're bewildered you become patronizing?

PETER. I . . . I don't express myself too well, sometimes. [*He attempts a joke on himself.*] I'm in publishing, not writing.

JERRY [*amused, but not at the humor*]. So be it. The truth *is:* I was being patronizing.

PETER. Oh, now; you needn't say that. [*It is at this point that* JERRY *may begin to move about the stage with slowly increasing determination and authority, but pacing himself, so that the long speech about the dog comes at the high point of the arc.*]

JERRY. All right. Who are your favorite writers? Baudelaire and J. P. Marquand?

PETER [*wary*]. Well, I like a great many writers; I have a considerable . . . catholicity of taste, if I may say so. Those two men are fine, each in his way. [*Warming up.*] Baudelaire, of course . . . uh . . . is by far the finer of the two, but Marquand has a place . . . in our . . . uh . . . national . . .

JERRY. Skip it.

PETER. I . . . sorry.

JERRY. Do you know what I did before I went to the zoo today? I walked all the way up Fifth Avenue from Washington Square; all the way.

PETER. Oh; you live in the Village! [*This seems to enlighten* PETER.]

JERRY. No, I don't. I took the subway down to the Village so I could walk all the way up Fifth Avenue to the zoo. It's one of those things a person has to do; sometimes a person has to go a very long distance out of his way to come back a short distance correctly.

PETER [*almost pouting*]. Oh, I thought you lived in the Village.

JERRY. What were you trying to do? Make sense out of things? Bring order? The old pigeonhole bit? Well, that's easy; I'll tell you. I live in a four-story brownstone rooming-house on the upper West Side between Columbus Avenue and Central Park West. I live on the top floor; rear; west. It's a laughably small room, and one of my walls is made of beaverboard; this beaverboard separates my room from another laughably small room, so I assume that the two rooms were once one room, a small room, but not necessarily laughable. The room beyond my beaverboard wall is occupied by a colored queen who always keeps his door open; well, not always but *always* when he's plucking his eyebrows, which he does with Buddhist concentration. This colored queen has rotten teeth, which is rare, and he has a Japanese kimono, which is also pretty rare; and he wears this kimono to and from the john in the hall, which is pretty frequent. I mean, he goes to the john a lot. He never bothers me, and he never brings anyone up to his room. All he does is pluck his eyebrows, wear his kimono and go to the john. Now, the two front rooms on my floor are a little larger, I guess; but they're pretty small, too. There's a Puerto Rican family in one of them, a husband, a wife, and some kids; I don't know how many. These people entertain a lot. And in the other front room, there's somebody living there, but I don't know who it is. I've never seen who it is. Never. Never ever.

PETER [*embarrassed*]. Why . . . why do you live there?

JERRY [*from a distance again*]. I don't know.

PETER. It doesn't sound like a very nice place . . . where you live.

JERRY. Well, no; it isn't an apartment in the East Seventies. But, then again, I don't have one wife, two daughters, two cats and two parakeets. What I do have, I have toilet articles, a few clothes, a hot plate that I'm not supposed to have, a can opener, one that works with a key, you know; a knife, two forks, and two spoons, one small, one large; three plates, a cup, a saucer, a drinking glass, two picture frames, both empty, eight or nine books, a pack of pornographic playing cards, regular deck, an old Western Union typewriter that prints nothing but capital letters, and a small strongbox without a lock which has in it . . . what? Rocks! Some rocks . . . sea-rounded rocks I picked up on the beach when I was a kid. Under which . . . weighed down . . . are some letters . . . please letters . . . please why don't you do this, and please when will you do that letters. And when letters, too. When will you write? When will you come? When? These letters are from more recent years.

PETER. [*Stares glumly at his shoes, then*] About those two empty picture frames . . . ?

JERRY. I don't see why they need any explanation at all. Isn't it clear? I don't have pictures of anyone to put in them.

PETER. Your parents . . . perhaps . . . a girl friend . . .

JERRY. You're a very sweet man, and you're possessed of a truly enviable innocence. But good old Mom and good old Pop are dead . . . you know? . . . I'm broken up about it, too . . . I mean really. BUT. That particular vaudeville act is playing the cloud circuit now, so I don't see how I can look at them, all neat and framed. Besides, or, rather, to be pointed about it, good old Mom walked out on good old Pop when I was ten and a half years old; she embarked on an adulterous turn of our southern states . . . a journey of a year's duration . . . and her most constant companion . . . among others, among many others . . . was a Mr. Barleycorn. At least, that's what good old Pop told me after he went down . . . came back . . . brought her body north. We'd received the news between Christmas and New Year's, you see, that good old Mom had parted with the ghost in some dump in Alabama. And, without the ghost . . . she was less welcome. I mean, what was she? A stiff . . . a northern stiff. At any rate, good old Pop celebrated the New Year for an even two weeks and then slapped into the front of a somewhat moving city omnibus, which sort of cleaned things out family-wise. Well no; then there was Mom's sister, who was given neither to sin nor the consolations of the bottle. I moved in on her, and my memory of her is slight excepting I remember still that she did all things dourly: sleeping, eating, working, praying. She dropped dead on the stairs to her apartment, my apartment then, too, on the afternoon of my high school graduation. A terribly middle-European joke, if you ask me.

PETER. Oh, my; oh, my.

JERRY. Oh, your what? But that was a long time ago, and I have no feeling about any of it that I care to admit to myself. Perhaps you can see, though, why good old Mom and good old Pop are frameless. What's your name? Your first name?

Peter. I'm Peter.

Jerry. I'd forgotten to ask you. I'm Jerry.

Peter [*with a slight, nervous laugh*]. Hello, Jerry.

Jerry. [*Nods his hello.*] And let's see now; what's the point of having a girl's picture, especially in two frames? I have two picture frames, you remember. I never see the pretty little ladies more than once, and most of them wouldn't be caught in the same room with a camera. It's odd, and I wonder if it's sad.

Peter. The girls?

Jerry. No. I wonder if it's sad that I never see the little ladies more than once. I've never been able to have sex with, or, how is it put? . . . make love to anybody more than once. Once; that's it. . . . Oh, wait; for a week and a half, when I was fifteen . . . and I hang my head in shame that puberty was late . . . I was a h-o-m-o-s-e-x-u-a-l. I mean, I was queer . . . [*very fast*] . . . queer, queer, queer . . . with bells ringing, banners snapping in the wind. And for those eleven days, I met at least twice a day with the park superintendent's son . . . a Greek boy, whose birthday was the same as mine, except he was a year older. I think I was very much in love . . . maybe just with sex. But that was the jazz of a very special hotel, wasn't it? And now; oh, do I love the little ladies; really, I love them. For about an hour.

Peter. Well, it seems perfectly simple to me. . . .

Jerry [*angry*]. Look! Are you going to tell me to get married and have parakeets?

Peter [*angry himself*]. Forget the parakeets! And stay single if you want to. It's no business of mine. I didn't start this conversation in the . . .

Jerry. All right, all right. I'm sorry. All right? You're not angry?

Peter [*laughing*]. No, I'm not angry.

Jerry [*relieved*]. Good. [*Now back to his previous tone.*] Interesting that you asked me about the picture frames. I would have thought that you would have asked me about the pornographic playing cards.

Peter [*with a knowing smile*]. Oh, I've seen those cards.

Jerry. That's not the point. [*Laughs.*] I suppose when you were a kid you and your pals passed them around, or you had a pack of your own.

Peter. Well, I guess a lot of us did.

Jerry. And you threw them away just before you got married.

Peter. Oh, now; look here. I didn't *need* anything like that when I got older.

Jerry. No?

Peter [*embarrassed*]. I'd rather not talk about these things.

JERRY. So? Don't. Besides, I wasn't trying to plumb your post-adolescent sexual life and hard times; what I wanted to get at is the value difference between pornographic playing cards when you're a kid, and pornographic playing cards when you're older. It's that when you're a kid you use the cards as a substitute for a real experience, and when you're older you use real experience as a substitute for the fantasy. But I imagine you'd rather hear about what happened at the zoo.

PETER [*enthusiastic*]. Oh, yes; the zoo. [*Then, awkward.*] That is . . . if you. . . .

JERRY. Let me tell you about why I went . . . well, let me tell you some things. I've told you about the fourth floor of the rooming-house where I live. I think the rooms are better as you go down, floor by floor. I guess they are; I don't know. I don't know any of the people on the third and second floors. Oh, wait! I do know that there's a lady living on the third floor, in the front. I know because she cries all the time. Whenever I go out or come back in, whenever I pass her door, I always hear her crying, muffled, but . . . very determined. Very determined indeed. But the one I'm getting to, and all about the dog, is the landlady. I don't like to use words that are too harsh in describing people. I don't like to. But the landlady is a fat, ugly, mean, stupid, unwashed, misanthropic, cheap, drunken bag of garbage. And you may have noticed that I very seldom use profanity, so I can't describe her as well as I might.

PETER. You describe her . . . vividly.

JERRY. Well, thanks. Anyway, she has a dog, and I will tell you about the dog, and she and her dog are the gatekeepers of my dwelling. The woman is bad enough; she leans around in the entrance hall, spying to see that I don't bring in things or people, and when she's had her mid-afternoon pint of lemon-flavored gin she always stops me in the hall, and grabs ahold of my coat or my arm, and she presses her disgusting body up against me to keep me in a corner so she can talk to me. The smell of her body and her breath . . . you can't imagine it . . . and somewhere, somewhere in the back of that pea-sized brain of hers, an organ developed just enough to let her eat, drink, and emit, she has some foul parody of sexual desire. And, I Peter, I am the object of her sweaty lust.

PETER. That's disgusting. That's . . . horrible.

JERRY. But I have found a way to keep her off. When she talks to me, when she presses herself to my body and mumbles about her room and how I should come there, I merely say: but, Love; wasn't yesterday enough for you, and the day before? Then she puzzles, she makes slits of her tiny eyes, she sways a little, and then, Peter . . . and it is at this moment that I think I might be doing some good in that tormented house . . . a simple-minded smile begins to form on her unthinkable face, and she giggles and groans as she thinks about yesterday and the day before; as she believes and relives what never happened. Then, she motions to that black monster of a dog she has, and she goes back to her room. And I am safe until our next meeting.

PETER. It's so . . . unthinkable. I find it hard to believe that people such as that really *are*.

JERRY [*lightly mocking*]. It's for reading about, isn't it?

PETER [*seriously*]. Yes.

JERRY. And fact is better left to fiction. You're right, Peter. Well, what I have been meaning to tell you about is the dog; I shall, now.

PETER [*nervously*]. Oh, yes; the dog.

JERRY. Don't go. You're not thinking of going, are you?

PETER. Well . . . no, I don't think so.

JERRY [*as if to a child*]. Because after I tell you about the dog, do you know what then? Then . . . then I'll tell you about what happened at the zoo.

PETER [*laughing faintly*]. You're . . . you're full of stories, aren't you?

JERRY. You don't *have* to listen. Nobody is holding you here; remember that. Keep that in your mind.

PETER [*irritably*]. I know that.

JERRY. You do? Good. [*The following long speech, it seems to me, should be done with a great deal of action, to achieve a hypnotic effect on* PETER, *and on the audience, too. Some specific actions have been suggested, but the director and the actor playing* JERRY *might best work it out for themselves.*] ALL RIGHT. [*As if reading from a huge billboard.*] THE STORY OF JERRY AND THE DOG! [*Natural again.*] What I am going to tell you has something to do with how sometimes it's necessary to go a long distance out of the way in order to come back a short distance correctly; or, maybe I only think that it has something to do with that. But, it's why I went to the zoo today, and why I walked north . . . northerly, rather . . . until I came here. All right. The dog, I think I told you, is a black monster of a beast: an oversized head, tiny, tiny ears, and eyes . . . bloodshot, infected, maybe; and a body you can see the ribs through the skin. The dog is black, all black; all black except for the bloodshot eyes, and . . . yes . . . and an open sore on its . . . *right* forepaw; that is red, too. And, oh yes; the poor monster, and I do believe it's an old dog . . . it's certainly a misused one . . . almost always has an erection . . . of sorts. That's red, too. And . . . what else? . . . oh, yes; there's a gray-yellow-white color, too, when he bares his fangs. Like this: Grrrrrr! Which is what he did when he saw me for the first time . . . the day I moved in. I worried about that animal the very first minute I met him. Now, animals don't take to me like Saint Francis had birds hanging off him all the time. What I mean is: animals are indifferent to me . . . like people [*He smiles slightly.*] . . . most of the time. But this dog wasn't indifferent. From the very beginning he'd snarl and then go for me, to get one of my legs. Not like he was rabid, you know; he was sort of a stumbly dog, but he wasn't half-assed, either. It was a good, stumbly run; but I always got away. He got a piece of my trouser leg, look, you can see right here, where it's mended; he got that the second day I lived there; but, I kicked free and got upstairs fast, so that was that. [*Puzzles.*] I still don't know to this day how the other roomers manage it, but you know what I *think*: I think it had to do only with me. Cozy. So. Anyway, this went on for over a week, whenever I came in; but never when I went out. That's funny. Or, it *was* funny. I could pack up and live in the street for all the dog cared. Well, I thought about it up in my room one day, one of the times after I'd bolted upstairs, and I made up my mind. I decided: First, I'll kill the dog with kindness, and if that doesn't work . . . I'll just kill him. [PETER *winces.*] Don't react, Peter; just listen. So, the next day I went out and bought a bag of hamburgers, medium rare, no catsup, no onion; and on the way home I threw away all the rolls and kept just the meat. [*Action for the following, perhaps.*] When I got back to the roominghouse the dog was waiting for me. I half opened the door that led into the entrance hall, and there he was; waiting for me. It figured. I went in, very cautiously, and I had the hamburgers, you remember; I opened the bag, and I set the meat down about twelve feet from where the dog was snarling at me. Like so! He snarled; stopped snarling; sniffed; moved slowly; then faster; then faster toward the meat. Well, when he got to it he stopped, and he looked at me. I smiled; but tentatively, you understand. He turned his face back to the hamburgers, smelled, sniffed some more, and then . . . RRRAAAAGGGGGHHHH, like that . . . he tore into them. It was as if he had never eaten anything in his life before, except like garbage. Which might very well have been the truth. I don't think the landlady ever eats anything but garbage. But. He ate all the hamburgers, almost all at once, making sounds in his throat like a woman. *Then*, when he'd finished the meat, the hamburger, and tried to eat the paper, too, he sat down and smiled. I think he smiled; I know cats do. It was a very gratifying few moments. Then, BAM, he snarled and made for me again. He didn't get me this time, either. So, I got upstairs, and I lay down on my bed and started to think about the dog again. To be truthful, I was offended, and I was damn mad, too. It was six perfectly good hamburgers with not enough pork in them to make it disgusting. I was offended. But, after a while, I decided to try it for a few more days. If you think about it, this dog had what amounted to an antipathy toward me; really. And, I wondered if I mightn't overcome this antipathy. So, I tried it for five more days, but it was always the same: snarl, sniff; move; faster; stare; gobble; RAAGGGHHH; smile; snarl; BAM. Well, now; by this time Columbus Avenue was strewn with hamburger rolls and I was less offended than disgusted. So, I decided to kill the dog. [PETER *raises a hand in protest.*] Oh, don't be so alarmed, Peter; I didn't succeed. The day I tried to kill the dog I bought only one hamburger and what I thought was a murderous portion of rat poison. When I bought the hamburger I asked the man not to bother with the roll, all I wanted was the meat. I expected some reaction from him, like: we don't sell no hamburgers without rolls; or, wha' d'ya wanna do, eat it out'a ya han's? But no; he smiled benignly, wrapped up the hamburger in waxed paper, and said: A bite for ya pussy-cat? I wanted to say: No, not really; it's part of a plan to poison a dog I know. But, you can't say "a dog I know" without sounding funny; so I said, a little too loud, I'm afraid, and too formally: YES, A BITE FOR MY PUSSY-CAT. People looked up. It always happens when I try to simplify things; people look up. But that's neither hither nor thither. So. On my way back to the roominghouse, I kneaded the hamburger and the rat poison together between my hands, at that point feeling as much sadness as disgust. I opened the door to the entrance hall, and there the monster was, waiting to take the offering and then jump me. Poor bastard; he never learned that the moment he took to smile before he went for me gave me time enough to get out of range. BUT, there he was; malevolence with an erection, waiting. I put the poison patty down, moved toward the stairs and watched. The poor animal gobbled the food down as usual, smiled, which made me almost sick, and then, BAM. But, I sprinted up the stairs, as usual, and the dog didn't get me, as usual. AND IT CAME TO PASS THAT THE BEAST WAS DEATHLY ILL. I knew this because he no longer attended me, and because the landlady sobered up. She stopped me in the hall the same evening of the attempted murder and confided the information that God had struck her puppy-dog a surely fatal blow. She had forgotten her bewildered lust, and her eyes were wide open for the first time. They looked like the dog's eyes. She sniveled and implored me to pray for the animal. I wanted to say to her: Madam, I have myself to pray for, the colored queen, the Puerto Rican family, the person in the front room whom I've never seen, the woman who cries deliberately behind her closed door, and the rest of the people in all roominghouses, everywhere; besides, Madam, I don't understand how to pray. But . . . to simplify things . . . I told her I would pray. She looked up. She said that I was a liar, and that I probably wanted the dog to die. I told her, and there was so much truth here, that I didn't want the dog to die. I didn't, and not just because I'd poisoned him. I'm afraid that I must tell you I wanted the dog to live so that I could see what our new relationship might come to. [PETER *indicates his increasing displeasure and slowly growing antagonism.*] Please understand, Peter; that sort of thing is important. You must believe me; it *is* important. We have to know the effect of our actions. [*Another deep sigh.*] Well, anyway; the dog recovered. I have no idea why, unless he was a descendant of the puppy that guarded the gates of hell or some such resort. I'm not up on my mythology. [*He pronounces the word myth-o-logy.*] Are you? [PETER *sets to thinking, but* JERRY *goes on.*] At any rate, and you've missed the eight-thousand-dollar question, Peter; at any rate, the dog recovered his health and the landlady recovered her thirst, in no way altered by the bow-wow's deliverance. When I came home from a movie that was playing on Forty-second Street, a movie I'd seen, or one that was very much like one or several I'd seen, after the landlady told me puppykins was better, I was so hoping for the dog to be waiting for me. I was . . . well, how would you put it . . . enticed? . . . fascinated? . . . no, I don't think so . . . heart-shatteringly anxious, that's it; I was heart-shatteringly anxious to confront my friend again. [PETER *reacts scoffingly.*] Yes, Peter; friend. That's the only word for it. I was heart-shatteringly et cetera to confront my doggy friend again. I came in the door and advanced, unafraid, to the center of the entrance hall. The beast was there . . . looking at me. And, you know, he looked better for his scrape with the nevermind. I stopped; I looked at him; he looked at me. I think . . . I think we stayed a long time that way . . . still, stone-statue . . . just looking at one another. I looked more into his face than he looked into mine. I mean, I can concentrate longer at looking into a dog's face than a dog can concentrate at looking into mine, or into anybody else's face, for that matter. But during that twenty seconds or two hours that we looked into each other's face, we made contact. Now, here is what I had wanted to happen: I loved the dog now, and I wanted him to love me. I had tried to love, and I had tried to kill, and both had been unsuccessful by themselves. I hoped . . . and I don't really know why I expected the dog to understand anything, much less my motivations . . . I hoped that the dog would understand. [PETER *seems to be hypnotized.*] It's just . . . it's just that . . . [JERRY *is abnormally tense, now.*] . . . it's just that if you can't deal with people, you have to make a start somewhere. WITH ANIMALS! [*Much faster now, and like a conspirator.*] Don't you see? A person has to have some way of dealing with SOMETHING. If not with people . . . if not with people . . . SOMETHING. With a bed, with a cockroach, with a mirror . . . no, that's too hard, that's one of the last steps. With a cockroach, with a . . . with a . . . with a carpet, a roll of toilet paper . . . no, not that, either . . . that's a mirror, too; always check bleeding. You see how hard it is to find things? With a street corner, and too many lights, all colors reflecting on the oily-wet streets . . . with a wisp of smoke, a wisp . . . of smoke . . . with . . . with pornographic playing cards, with a strongbox . . . WITHOUT A LOCK . . . with love, with vomiting, with crying, with fury because the pretty little ladies aren't pretty little ladies, with making money with your body which is an act of love and I could prove it, with howling because you're alive; with God. How about that? WITH GOD WHO IS A COLORED QUEEN WHO WEARS A KIMONO AND PLUCKS HIS EYEBROWS, WHO IS A WOMAN WHO CRIES WITH DETERMINATION BEHIND HER CLOSED DOOR . . . with God who, I'm told, turned his back on the whole thing some time ago . . . with . . . some day, with people. [JERRY *sighs the next word heavily.*] People. With an idea; a concept. And where better, where ever better in this humiliating excuse for a jail, where better to communicate one single, simple-minded idea than in an entrance hall? Where? It would be A START! Where better to make a beginning . . . to understand and just possibly be understood . . . a beginning of an understanding, than with . . . [*Here* JERRY *seems to fall into almost grotesque fatigue.*] . . . than with A DOG. Just that; a dog. [*Here there is a silence that might be prolonged for a moment or so; then* JERRY *wearily finishes his story.*] A dog. It seemed like a perfectly sensible idea. Man is a dog's best friend, remember. So: the dog and I looked at each other. I longer than the dog. And what I saw then has been the same ever since. Whenever the dog and I see each other we both stop where we are. We regard each other with a mixture of sadness and suspicion, and then we feign indifference. We walk past each other safely; we have an understanding. It's very sad, but you'll have to admit that it is an understanding. We had made many attempts at contact, and we had failed. The dog has returned to garbage, and I to solitary but free passage. I have not returned. I mean to say, I have *gained* solitary free passage, if that much further loss can be said to be gain. I have learned that neither kindness nor cruelty by themselves, independent of each other, creates any effect beyond themselves; and I have learned that the two combined, together, at the same time, are the teaching emotion. And what is gained is loss. And what has been the result: the dog and I have attained a compromise; more of a bargain, really. We neither love nor hurt because we do not try to reach each other. And, *was* trying to feed the dog an act of love? And, perhaps, was the dog's attempt to bite me *not* an act of love? If we can so misunderstand, well then, why have we invented the word love in the first place? [*There is silence.* JERRY *moves to* PETER's *bench and sits down beside him. This is the first time* JERRY *has sat down during the play.*] The Story of Jerry and the Dog: the end. [PETER *is silent.*] Well, Peter? [JERRY *is suddenly cheerful.*] Well, Peter? Do you think I could sell that story to the *Reader's Digest* and make a couple of hundred bucks for *The Most Unforgettable Characer I've Ever Met?* Huh? [JERRY *is animated, but* PETER *is disturbed.*] Oh, come on now, Peter; tell me what you think.

PETER [*numb*]. I . . . I don't understand what . . . I don't think I . . . [*Now, almost tearfully.*] Why did you tell me all of this?

JERRY. Why not?

PETER. I DON'T UNDERSTAND!

JERRY [*furious, but whispering*]. That's a lie.

PETER. No. No, it's not.

JERRY [*quietly*]. I tried to explain it to you as I went along. I went slowly; it all has to do with . . .

PETER. I DON'T WANT TO HEAR ANY MORE. I don't understand you, or your landlady, or her dog. . . .

JERRY. *Her* dog! I thought it was my . . . No. No, you're right. It *is* her dog. [*Looks at* PETER *intently, shaking his head.*] I don't know what I was thinking about; of course you don't understand. [*In a monotone, wearily.*] I don't live in your block; I'm not married to two parakeets, or whatever your setup is. I am a *permanent transient*, and my home is the sickening roominghouses on the West Side of New York City, which is the greatest city in the world. Amen.

PETER. I'm . . . I'm sorry; I didn't mean to . . .

JERRY. Forget it. I suppose you don't quite know what to make of me, eh?

PETER [*a joke*]. We get all kinds in publishing. [*Chuckles.*]

JERRY. You're a funny man. [*He forces a laugh.*] You know that? You're a very . . . a richly comic person.

PETER [*modestly, but amused*]. Oh, now, not really [*still chuckling*].

JERRY. Peter, do I annoy you, or confuse you?

PETER [*lightly*]. Well, I must confess that this wasn't the kind of afternoon I'd anticipated.

JERRY. You mean, I'm not the gentleman you were expecting.

PETER. I wasn't expecting anybody.

JERRY. No, I don't imagine you were. But I'm here, and I'm not leaving.

PETER [*consulting his watch*]. Well, you may not be, but I must be getting home soon.

JERRY. Oh, come on; stay a while longer.

PETER. I really should get home; you see . . .

JERRY. [*Tickles* PETER's *ribs with his fingers.*] Oh, come on.

PETER. [*He is very ticklish; as* JERRY *continues to tickle him his voice becomes falsetto.*] No, I . . . OHHHHH! Don't do that. Stop, Stop. Ohhh, no, no.

JERRY. Oh, come on.

PETER [*as* JERRY *tickles*]. Oh, hee, hee, hee. I must go. I . . . hee, hee, hee. After all, stop, stop, hee, hee, hee, after all, the parakeets will be getting dinner ready soon. Hee, hee. And the cats are setting the table. Stop, stop, and, and . . . [PETER *is beside himself now.*] . . . and we're having . . . hee, hee . . . uh . . . ho, ho, ho. [JERRY *stops tickling* PETER, *but the combination of the tickling and his own mad whimsy has* PETER *laughing almost hysterically. As his laughter continues, then subsides,* JERRY *watches him, with a curious fixed smile.*]

JERRY. Peter?

Peter. Oh, ha, ha, ha, ha, ha. What? What?

Jerry. Listen, now.

Peter. Oh, ho, ho. What . . . what is it, Jerry? Oh, my.

Jerry [*mysteriously*]. Peter, do you want to know what happened at the zoo?

Peter. Ah, ha, ha. The what? Oh, yes; the zoo. Oh, ho, ho. Well, I had my own zoo there for a moment with . . . hee, hee, the parakeets getting dinner ready, and the . . . ha, ha, whatever it was, the . . .

Jerry [*calmly*]. Yes, that was very funny, Peter. I wouldn't have expected it. But do you want to hear about what happened at the zoo, or not?

Peter. Yes. Yes, by all means; tell me what happened at the zoo. Oh, my. I don't know what happened to me.

Jerry. Now I'll let you in on what happened at the zoo; but first, I should tell you why I went to the zoo. I went to the zoo to find out more about the way people exist with animals, and the way animals exist with each other, and with people too. It probably wasn't a fair test, what with everyone separated by bars from everyone else, the animals for the most part from each other, and always the people from the animals. But, if it's a zoo, that's the way it is. [*He pokes* Peter *on the arm.*] Move over.

Peter [*friendly*]. I'm sorry, haven't you enough room? [*He shifts a little.*]

Jerry [*smiling slightly*]. Well, all the animals are there, and all the people are there, and it's Sunday and all the children are there. [*He pokes* Peter *again.*] Move over.

Peter [*patiently, still friendly*]. All right. [*He moves some more, and* Jerry *has all the room he might need.*]

Jerry. And it's a hot day, so all the stench is there, too, and all the balloon sellers, and all the ice cream sellers, and all the seals are barking, and all the birds are screaming. [*Pokes* Peter *harder.*] Move over!

Peter [*beginning to be annoyed*]. Look here, you have more than enough room! [*But he moves more, and is now fairly cramped at one end of the bench.*]

Jerry. And I am there, and it's feeding time at the lions' house, and the lion keeper comes into the lion cage, one of the lion cages, to feed one of the lions. [*Punches* Peter *on the arm, hard.*] MOVE OVER!

Peter [*very annoyed*]. I can't move over any more, and stop hitting me. What's the matter with you?

Jerry. Do you want to hear the story? [*Punches* Peter's *arm again.*]

Peter [*flabbergasted*]. I'm not so sure! I certainly don't want to be punched in the arm.

Jerry. [*Punches* Peter's *arm again.*] Like that?

Peter. Stop it! What's the matter with you?

Jerry. I'm crazy, you bastard.

PETER. That isn't funny.

JERRY. Listen to me, Peter. I want this bench. You go sit on the bench over there, and if you're good I'll tell you the rest of the story.

PETER [*flustered*]. But . . . whatever for? What *is* the matter with you? Besides, I see no reason why I should give up this bench. I sit on this bench almost every Sunday afternoon, in good weather. It's secluded here, there's never anyone sitting here, so I have it all to myself.

JERRY [*softly*]. Get off this bench, Peter; I want it.

PETER [*almost whining*]. No.

JERRY. I said I want this bench, and I'm going to have it. Now get over there.

PETER. People can't have everything they want. You should know that; it's a rule; people can have some of the things they want, but they can't have everything.

JERRY. [*Laughs.*] Imbecile! You're slow-witted!

PETER. Stop that!

JERRY. You're a vegetable! Go lie down on the ground.

PETER [*intense*]. Now *you* listen to me. I've put up with you all afternoon.

JERRY. Not really.

PETER. LONG ENOUGH. I've put up with you long enough. I've listened to you because you seemed . . . well, because I thought you wanted to talk to somebody.

JERRY. You put things well; economically, and, yet . . . oh, what is the word I want to put justice to your . . . JESUS, you make me sick . . . get off here and give me my bench.

PETER. MY BENCH!

JERRY. [*Pushes* PETER *almost, but not quite, off the bench.*] Get out of my sight.

PETER [*regaining his position*]. God da . . . mn you. That's enough! I've had enough of you. I will not give up this bench; you can't have it, and that's that. Now, go away. [JERRY *snorts but does not move.*] Go away, I said. [JERRY *does not move.*] Get away from here. If you don't move on . . . you're a bum . . . that's what you are. . . . If you don't move on, I'll get a policeman here and make you go. [JERRY *laughs, stays.*] I warn you, I'll call a policeman.

JERRY [*softly*]. You won't find a policeman around here; they're all over on the west side of the park chasing fairies down from trees or out of the bushes. That's all they do. That's their function. So scream your head off; it won't do you any good.

PETER. POLICE! I warn you, I'll have you arrested. POLICE! [*Pause.*] I said POLICE! [*Pause.*] I feel ridiculous.

JERRY. You look ridiculous: a grown man screaming for the police on a bright Sunday afternoon in the park with nobody harming you. If a

policeman *did* fill his quota and come sludging over this way he'd probably take you in as a nut.

Peter [*with disgust and impotence*]. Great God, I just came here to read,
and now you want me to give up the bench. You're mad.

Jerry. Hey, I got news for you, as they say. I'm on your precious bench,
and you're never going to have it for yourself again.

Peter [*furious*]. Look, you; get off my bench. I don't care if it makes any
sense or not. I want this bench to myself; I want you off it!

Jerry [*mocking*]. Aw . . . look who's mad.

Peter. get out!

Jerry. No.

Peter. I warn you!

Jerry. Do you know how ridiculous you look *now?*

Peter. [*His fury and self-consciousness have possessed him.*] It doesn't
matter. [*He is almost crying.*] get away from my bench!

Jerry. Why? You have everything in the world you want; you've told me
about your home, and your family, and *your own* little zoo. You have
everything, and now you want this bench. Are these the things men fight
for? Tell me, Peter, is this bench, this iron and this wood, is this your
honor? Is this the thing in the world you'd fight for? Can you think of
anything more absurd?

Peter. Absurd? Look, I'm not going to talk to you about honor, or even
try to explain it to you. Besides, it isn't a question of honor; but even if
it were, you wouldn't understand.

Jerry [*contemptuously*]. You don't even know what you're saying, do you?
This is probably the first time in your life you've had anything more
trying to face than changing your cats' toilet box. Stupid! Don't you
have any idea, not even the slightest, what other people *need?*

Peter. Oh, boy, listen to you; well, you don't need this bench. That's for
sure.

Jerry. Yes; yes, I do.

Peter [*quivering*]. I've come here for years; I have hours of great pleasure,
great satisfaction, right here. And that's important to a man. I'm a responsible person, and I'm a grownup. This is my bench, and you have
no right to take it away from me.

Jerry. Fight for it, then. Defend yourself; defend your bench.

Peter. You've *pushed* me to it. Get up and fight.

Jerry. Like a man?

Peter [*still angry*]. Yes, like a man, if you insist on mocking me even
further.

Jerry. I'll have to give you credit for one thing: you *are* a vegetable, and a
slightly nearsighted one, I think . . .

Peter. that's enough. . . .

JERRY. . . . . but, you know, as they say on TV all the time—you know—
and I mean this, Peter, you have a certain dignity; it surprises me. . . .

PETER. STOP!

JERRY. [*Rises lazily.*] Very well, Peter, we'll battle for the bench, but we're
not evenly matched. [*He takes out and clicks open an ugly-looking
knife.*]

PETER [*suddenly awakening to the reality of the situation*]. You *are* mad!
You're stark raving mad! YOU'RE GOING TO KILL ME! [*But before* PETER
has time to think what to do, JERRY *tosses the knife at* PETER'*s feet.*]

JERRY. There you go. Pick it up. You have the knife and we'll be more
evenly matched.

PETER [*horrified*]. No!

JERRY. [*Rushes over to* PETER, *grabs him by the collar;* PETER *rises; their
faces almost touch.*] Now you pick up that knife and you fight with me.
You fight for your self-respect; you fight for that goddamned bench.

PETER [*struggling*]. No! Let . . . let go of me! He . . . Help!

JERRY. [*Slaps* PETER *on each "fight."*] You fight, you miserable bastard;
fight for that bench; fight for your parakeets; fight for your cats; fight for
your two daughters; fight for your wife; fight for your manhood, you
pathetic little vegetable. [*Spits in* PETER'*s face.*] You couldn't even get
your wife with a male child.

PETER. [*Breaks away, enraged.*] It's a matter of genetics, not manhood, you
. . . you monster. [*He darts down, picks up the knife and backs off a
little; he is breathing heavily.*] I'll give you one last chance; get out of
here and leave me alone! [*He holds the knife with a firm arm, but far in
front of him, not to attack, but to defend.*]

JERRY. [*Sighs heavily.*] So be it! [*With a rush he charges* PETER *and impales
himself on the knife. Tableau: For just a moment, complete silence,*
JERRY *impaled on the knife at the end of* PETER'*s still firm arm. Then*
PETER *screams, pulls away, leaving the knife in* JERRY. JERRY *is motionless, on point. Then he, too, screams, and it must be the sound of an
infuriated and fatally wounded animal. With the knife in him, he
stumbles back to the bench that* PETER *had vacated. He crumbles there,
sitting, facing* PETER, *his eyes wide in agony, his mouth open.*]

PETER [*whispering*]. Oh my God, oh my God, oh my God. . . . [*He repeats these words many times, very rapidly.*]

JERRY. [JERRY *is dying; but now his expression seems to change. His features relax, and while his voice varies, sometimes wrenched with pain, for
the most part he seems removed from his dying. He smiles.*] Thank you,
Peter. I mean that, now; thank you very much. [PETER'*s mouth drops
open. He cannot move; he is transfixed.*] Oh, Peter, I was so afraid I'd
drive you away. [*He laughs as best he can.*] You don't know how afraid I
was you'd go away and leave me. And now I'll tell you what happened at

the zoo. I think . . . I think this is what happened at the zoo . . . I think. I think that while I was at the zoo I decided that I would walk north . . . northerly, rather . . . until I found you . . . or somebody . . . and I decided that I would talk to you . . . I would tell you things . . . and things that I would tell you would . . . Well, here we are. You see? Here we *are*. But . . . I don't know . . . could I have planned all this? No . . . no, I couldn't have. But I think I did. And now I've told you what you wanted to know, haven't I? And now you know all about what happened at the zoo. And now you know what you'll see in your TV, and the face I told you about . . . you remember . . . the face I told you about . . . my face, the face you see right now. Peter . . . Peter? . . . Peter . . . thank you. I came unto you [*He laughs, so faintly.*] and you have comforted me. Dear Peter.

PETER [*almost fainting*]. Oh my God!

JERRY. You'd better go now. Somebody might come by, and you don't want to be here when anyone comes.

PETER. [*Does not move, but begins to weep.*] Oh my God, oh my God.

JERRY [*most faintly, now; he is very near death*]. You won't be coming back here any more, Peter; you've been dispossessed. You've lost your bench, but you've defended your honor. And Peter, I'll tell you something now; you're not really a vegetable; it's all right, you're an animal. You're an animal, too. But you'd better hurry now, Peter. Hurry, you'd better go . . . see? [JERRY *takes a handkerchief and with great effort and pain wipes the knife handle clean of fingerprints.*] Hurry away, Peter. [PETER *begins to stagger away.*] Wait . . . wait, Peter. Take your book . . . book. Right here . . . beside me . . . on your bench . . . my bench, rather. Come . . . take your book. [PETER *starts for the book, but retreats.*] Hurry . . . Peter. [PETER *rushes to the bench, grabs the book, retreats.*] Very good, Peter . . . very good. Now . . . hurry away. [PETER *hesitates for a moment, then flees, stage-left.*] Hurry away. . . . [*His eyes are closed now.*] Hurry away, your parakeets are making the dinner . . . the cats . . . are setting the table . . .

PETER. [*Off stage, a pitiful howl*]. OH MY GOD!

JERRY. [*His eyes still closed, he shakes his head and speaks; a combination of scornful mimicry and supplication.*] Oh . . . my . . . God. [*He is dead.*]

[*Curtain*]

Poetry

Sir Thomas Wyatt 1503–1542

Whoso List to Hunt

Whoso list to hunt, I know where is an hind,
But as for me, alas, I may no more;
The vain travail hath wearied me so sore,
I am of them that farthest cometh behind.
Yet may I by no means my wearied mind   5
Draw from the deer; but as she fleeth afore,
Fainting I follow. I leave off therefore,
Since in a net I seek to hold the wind.
Who list her hunt, I put him out of doubt,
As well as I may spend his time in vain;   10
And, graven with diamonds, in letters plain
There is written her fair neck round about:
"*Noli me tangere*, for Caesar's I am,
And wild for to hold, though I seem tame."

1. *list* wishes. 13. *Noli me tangere* touch me not (Latin motto, supposedly engraved on the collars of Caesar's hounds).

My Galley Chargéd with Forgetfulness

My galley chargéd with forgetfulness
Thorough sharp seas, in winter nights doth pass
'Tween rock and rock; and eke mine enemy, alas,
That is my lord, steereth with cruelness;
And every oar a thought in readiness,   5
As though that death were light in such a case.
An endless wind doth tear the sail apace
Of forcéd sighs and trusty fearfulness.
A rain of tears, a cloud of dark disdain,
Hath done the wearied cords great hinderance,   10
Wreathéd with error and eke with ignorance.
The stars be hid that led me to this pain;
Drownéd is reason that should me consort,
And I remain despairing of the port.

3. *eke* also; *enemy* Cupid. 13. *consort* accompany.

541

They Flee from Me

They flee from me that sometime did me seek
With naked foot stalking in my chamber.
I have seen them gentle, tame, and meek
That now are wild and do not remember
5   That sometime they put themselves in danger
To take bread at my hand; and now they range,
Busily seeking with a continual change.

Thankéd be Fortune, it hath been otherwise
Twenty times better; but once in special,
10   In thin array after a pleasant guise,
When her loose gown from her shoulders did fall,
And she me caught in her arms long and small;
And therewith all sweetly did me kiss,
And softly said, "Dear heart, how like you this?"

15   It was no dream; I lay broad waking.
But all is turned thorough my gentleness
Into a strange fashion of forsaking;
And I have leave to go of her goodness,
And she also to use newfangleness.
20   But since that I so kindely am served,
I fain would know what she hath deserved.

19. *newfangleness* fickleness.   20. *kindely* according to nature; also a pun.

Sir Philip Sidney 1554–1586

From *Astrophel and Stella*

1

Loving in truth, and fain in verse my love to show,
That she, dear she, might take some pleasure of my pain,
Pleasure might cause her read, reading might make her know,
Knowledge might pity win, and pity grace obtain,

I sought fit words to paint the blackest face of woe,   5
Studying inventions fine, her wits to entertain,
Oft turning others' leaves, to see if thence would flow
Some fresh and fruitful showers upon my sunburnt brain.
But words came halting forth, wanting Invention's stay;
Invention, Nature's child, fled stepdame Study's blows;   10
And others' feet still seemed but strangers in my way.
Thus, great with child to speak, and helpless in my throes,
Biting my truant pen, beating myself for spite,
"Fool," said my Muse to me, "look in thy heart and write."

9. *stay* support.

31

With how sad steps, O Moon, thou climb'st the skies,
How silently, and with how wan a face!
What, may it be that even in heavenly place
That busy archer his sharp arrows tries?
Sure, if that long-with-love-acquainted eyes   5
Can judge of love, thou feel'st a lover's case;
I read it in thy looks, thy languished grace,
To me, that feel the like, thy state descries.
Then, even of fellowship, O Moon, tell me
Is constant love deemed there but want of wit?   10
Are beauties there as proud as here they be?
Do they above love to be loved, and yet
Those lovers scorn whom that love doth possess?
Do they call virtue there ungratefulness?

4. *archer* Cupid.

Leave Me, O Love

Leave me, O Love, which reachest but to dust,
And thou my mind aspire to higher things;
Grow rich in that which never taketh rust;
Whatever fades, but fading pleasure brings.
Draw in thy beams, and humble all thy might   5
To that sweet yoke where lasting freedoms be;
Which breaks the clouds and opens forth the light,
That doth both shine and give us sight to see.
O take fast hold; let that light be thy guide,
In this small course which birth draws out to death,   10

And think how evil becometh him to slide,
Who seeketh heaven, and comes of heavenly breath.
Then farewell, world, thy uttermost I see;
Eternal Love, maintain thy life in me.

Edmund Spenser 1552–1599

From *Amoretti*

70

Fresh spring, the herald of love's mighty king,
In whose coat armor richly are displayed
All sorts of flowers the which on earth do spring
In goodly colors gloriously arrayed.
5   Go to my love, where she is careless laid,
Yet in her winter's bower not well awake;
Tell her the joyous time will not be stayed
Unless she do him by the forelock take.
Bid her therefore herself soon ready make,
10   To wait on Love amongst his lovely crew;
Where every one that misseth then her make
Shall be by him amerced with penance due.
Make haste therefore, sweet love, whilst it is prime,
For none can call again the passéd time.

11. *make* mate.   12. *amerced* punished.   13. *prime* spring; also the first hour in the
morning.

75

One day I wrote her name upon the strand,
But came the waves and washéd it away;
Again I wrote it with a second hand,
But came the tide, and made my pains his prey.
5   "Vain man," said she, "that dost in vain essay
A mortal thing so to immortalize,
For I myself shall like to this decay,
And eke my name be wipéd out likewise."
"Not so," quoth I; "let baser things devise

8. *eke* also.

To die in dust, but you shall live by fame;   10
My verse your virtues rare shall eternize,
And in the heavens write your glorious name:
Where, whenas death shall all the world subdue,
Our love shall live, and later life renew."

William Shakespeare 1564–1616

From *Sonnets*

18

Shall I compare thee to a summer's day?
Thou art more lovely and more temperate;
Rough winds do shake the darling buds of May,
And summer's lease hath all too short a date;
Sometime too hot the eye of heaven shines,   5
And often is his gold complexion dimmed,
And every fair from fair sometime declines,
By chance or nature's changing course untrimmed;
But thy eternal summer shall not fade,
Nor lose possession of that fair thou ow'st,   10
Nor shall death brag thou wander'st in his shade,
When in eternal lines to time thou grow'st;
So long as men can breathe or eyes can see,
So long lives this, and this gives life to thee.

7. *fair* beauty.   8. *untrimmed* stripped of adornment.   10. *ow'st* ownest.

29

When in disgrace with fortune and men's eyes
I all alone beweep my outcast state,
And trouble deaf heaven with my bootless cries,
And look upon myself and curse my fate;
Wishing me like to one more rich in hope,   5
Featured like him, like him with friends possessed,
Desiring this man's art and that man's scope,
With what I most enjoy contented least;
Yet in these thoughts myself almost despising,
Haply I think on thee, and then my state,   10
Like to the lark at break of day arising

From sullen earth, sings hymns at heaven's gate;
For thy sweet love remembered such wealth brings
That then I scorn to change my state with kings.

35

No more be grieved at that which thou hast done:
Roses have thorns, and silver fountains mud,
Clouds and eclipses stain both moon and sun,
And loathsome canker lives in sweetest bud.
5 All men make faults, and even I in this,
Authorizing thy trespass with compare,
Myself corrupting, salving thy amiss,
Excusing thy sins more than thy sins are;
For to thy sensual fault I bring in sense—
10 Thy adverse party is thy advocate—
And 'gainst myself a lawful plea commence.
Such civil war is in my love and hate,
That I an accessáry needs must be
To that sweet thief which sourly robs from me.

4. *canker* cankerworm. 6. *compare* i.e., the comparisons of lines 2–4. 9. *sense* reason.

73

That time of year thou mayst in me behold
When yellow leaves, or none, or few, do hang
Upon those boughs which shake against the cold,
Bare ruined choirs, where late the sweet birds sang.
5 In me thou see'st the twilight of such day
As after sunset fadeth in the west,
Which by and by black night doth take away,
Death's second self that seals up all in rest.
In me thou see'st the glowing of such fire
10 That on the ashes of his youth doth lie,
As the deathbed whereon it must expire,
Consumed with that which it was nourished by.
This thou perceiv'st, which makes thy love more strong,
To love that well which thou must leave ere long.

87

Farewell, thou art too dear for my possessing,
And like enough thou know'st thy estimate;
The charter of thy worth gives thee releasing;
My bonds in thee are all determinate.

4. *determinate* ended.

For how do I hold thee but by thy granting, 5
And for that riches where is my deserving?
The cause of this fair gift in me is wanting,
And so my patent back again is swerving.
Thyself thou gavest, thy own worth then not knowing,
Or me to whom thou gavest it, else mistaking; 10
So thy great gift, upon misprision growing,
Comes home again, on better judgment making.
Thus have I had thee as a dream doth flatter,
In sleep a king, but waking no such matter.

11. *misprision* misunderstanding.

94

They that have power to hurt and will do none,
That do not do the thing they most do show,
Who, moving others, are themselves as stone,
Unmovéd, cold, and to temptation slow;
They rightly do inherit heaven's graces, 5
And husband nature's riches from expense;
They are the lords and owners of their faces,
Others but stewards of their excellence.
The summer's flower is to the summer sweet,
Though to itself it only live and die, 10
But if that flower with base infection meet,
The basest weed outbraves his dignity,
For sweetest things turn sourest by their deeds,
Lilies that fester smell far worse than weeds.

2. *show* seem to do.   6. *expense* expenditure.

107

Not mine own fears, nor the prophetic soul
Of the wide world dreaming on things to come,
Can yet the lease of my true love control,
Supposed as forfeit to a cónfined doom.
The mortal moon hath her eclipse endured, 5
And the sad augurs mock their own presage;
Incertainties now crown themselves assured,
And peace proclaims olives of endless age.
Now with the drops of this most balmy time
My love looks fresh, and death to me subscribes, 10

4. *Supposed . . . doom* supposed doomed to a limited length of life.   6. *mock . . . presage* are mocked by their prophecies.   10. *subscribes* submits.

Since, spite of him, I'll live in this poor rhyme,
While he insults o'er dull and speechless tribes:
And thou in this shalt find thy monument,
When tyrants' crests and tombs of brass are spent.

116

Let me not to the marriage of true minds
Admit impediments. Love is not love
Which alters when it alteration finds,
Or bends with the remover to remove.
5   O no, it is an ever-fixéd mark
That looks on tempests and is never shaken;
It is the star to every wandering bark,
Whose worth's unknown, although his height be taken.
Love's not Time's fool, though rosy lips and cheeks
10   Within his bending sickle's compass come.
Love alters not with his brief hours and weeks,
But bears it out even to the edge of doom.
If this be error and upon me proved,
I never writ, nor no man ever loved.

8. *worth's . . . taken* The position of a star may be known even though its influence is not.

129

Th' expense of spirit in a waste of shame
Is lust in action, and till action, lust
Is perjured, murderous, bloody, full of blame,
Savage, extreme, rude, cruel, not to trust;
5   Enjoyed no sooner but despiséd straight,
Past reason hunted, and no sooner had,
Past reason hated as a swallowed bait,
On purpose laid to make the taker mad:
Mad in pursuit and in possession so,
10   Had, having, and in quest, to have extreme;
A bliss in proof, and proved, a very woe,
Before, a joy proposed, behind, a dream;
All this the world well knows, yet none knows well,
To shun the heaven that leads men to this hell.

11. *in proof* during the experience.

146

Poor soul, the center of my sinful earth,
[Thrall to] these rebel powers that thee array,

Why dost thou pine within and suffer dearth
Painting thy outward walls so costly gay?
Why so large cost, having so short a lease,   5
Dost thou upon thy fading mansion spend?
Shall worms, inheritors of this excess,
Eat up thy charge? Is this thy body's end?
Then, soul, live thou upon thy servant's loss,
And let that pine to aggravate thy store;   10
Buy terms divine in selling hours of dross;
Within be fed, without be rich no more;
So shalt thou feed on death, that feeds on men,
And death once dead, there's no more dying then.

10. *let . . . store* Let the body deteriorate to increase the soul's riches.

Michael Drayton 1563–1631

From *Idea's Mirror*

61

Since there's no help, come let us kiss and part;
Nay, I have done; you get no more of me,
And I am glad, yea, glad with all my heart,
That thus so cleanly I myself can free;
Shake hands forever, cancel all our vows,   5
And when we meet at any time again,
Be it not seen in either of our brows
That we one jot of former love retain;
Now at the last gasp of Love's latest breath,
When, his pulse failing, Passion speechless lies,   10
When Faith is kneeling by his bed of death,
And Innocence is closing up his eyes,
Now if thou wouldst, when all have given him over,
From death to life thou mightst him yet recover.

John Donne 1572–1631

The Sun Rising

     Busy old fool, unruly sun,
     Why dost thou thus
Through windows and through curtains call on us?
Must to thy motions lovers' seasons run?
5   Saucy, pedantic wretch, go chide
      Late schoolboys and sour prentices,
  Go tell court huntsmen that the king will ride,
  Call country ants to harvest offices;
Love, all alike, no season knows nor clime,
10 Nor hours, days, months, which are the rags of time.

     Thy beams, so reverend and strong
     Why shouldst thou think?
I could eclipse and cloud them with a wink,
But that I would not lose her sight so long;
15   If her eyes have not blinded thine,
      Look, and tomorrow late, tell me
  Whether both the Indias of spice and mine
  Be where thou left'st them, or lie here with me.
Ask for those kings whom thou saw'st yesterday,
20 And thou shalt hear, All here in one bed lay,

     She is all states, and all princes, I;
     Nothing else is.
Princes do but play us; compared to this,
All honor's mimic, all wealth alchemy.
25   Thou, sun, art half as happy as we,
      In that the world's contracted thus;
  Thine age asks ease, and since thy duties be
  To warm the world, that's done in warming us.
Shine here to us, and thou art everywhere;
30 This bed thy center is, these walls thy sphere.

9. *all alike* to which all times are alike. 17. *both* . . . *mine* the East and the West
Indies (which exported spice and metals).

The Canonization

For God's sake hold your tongue, and let me love,
   Or chide my palsy, or my gout,
My five gray hairs, or ruined fortune, flout,
   With wealth your state, your mind with arts improve,
      Take you a course, get you a place,
      Observe his honor, or his grace,
   Or the king's real, or his stampéd face;
   Contemplate, what you will, approve,
      So you will let me love.

Alas, alas, who's injured by my love?
   What merchant's ships have my sighs drowned?
Who says my tears have overflowed his ground?
   When did my colds a forward spring remove?
      When did the heats which my veins fill
      Add one more to the plaguey bill?
   Soldiers find wars, and lawyers find out still
   Litigious men, which quarrels move,
      Though she and I do love.

Call us what you will, we are made such by love;
   Call her one, me another fly,
We are tapers too, and at our own cost die,
   And we in us find the eagle and the dove.
      The phoenix riddle hath more wit
      By us: we two being one, are it.
   So to one neutral thing both sexes fit,
   We die and rise the same, and prove
      Mysterious by this love.

We can die by it, if not live by love,
   And if unfit for tombs and hearse
Our legend be, it will be fit for verse;
   And if no piece of chronicle we prove,
      We'll build in sonnets pretty rooms;
      As well a well-wrought urn becomes

5

10

15

20

25

30

4. *arts* studies.   7. *stampéd face* i.e., on coins.   8. *approve* find by experience.
13. *forward* early.   15. *plaguey bill* weekly list of deaths from the plague.   20. *fly*
moth.   22–23. *eagle . . . phoenix* The eagle and dove are symbols of strength (earthly
wisdom) and purity (heavenly meekness). The phoenix was a unique mythological bird
that rose from its own ashes.

The greatest ashes, as half-acre tombs,
And by these hymns, all shall approve
Us canonized for love;

35

And thus invoke us: You whom reverend love
Made one another's hermitage;
You, to whom love was peace, that now is rage;
Who did the whole world's soul contract, and drove
Into the glasses of your eyes
(So made such mirrors, and such spies,
That they did all to you epitomize)
Countries, towns, courts: beg from above
A pattern of your love!

40

45

44. *Countries . . . courts* These are objects of the verb "drove."

A Valediction: Forbidding Mourning

As virtuous men pass mildly away,
And whisper to their souls to go,
Whilst some of their sad friends do say,
The breath goes now, and some say, No;

So let us melt, and make no noise,
No tear-floods nor sigh-tempests move,
'Twere profanation of our joys
To tell the laity our love.

5

Moving of th' earth brings harms and fears,
Men reckon what it did and meant,
But trepidation of the spheres,
Though greater far, is innocent.

10

Dull sublunary lovers' love
(Whose soul is sense) cannot admit
Absence, because it doth remove
Those things which elemented it.

15

11. *trepidation . . . spheres* The movement of one of the concentric spheres surrounding the earth (in Ptolemaic astronomy) was thought to change the date of the equinoxes. Though greater than earthquakes, this movement is harmless. 16. *elemented* composed.

But we by a love so much refined
   That our selves know not what it is,
Inter-assuréd of the mind,
   Care less eyes, lips, and hands to miss.   20

Our two souls therefore, which are one,
   Though I must go, endure not yet
A breach, but an expansion,
   Like gold to airy thinness beat.

If they be two, they are two so   25
   As stiff twin compasses are two;
Thy soul, the fixed foot, makes no show
   To move, but doth if the other do.

And though it in the center sit,
   Yet when the other far doth roam,   30
It leans and hearkens after it,
   And grows erect, as that comes home.

Such wilt thou be to me, who must
   Like th' other foot obliquely run,
Thy firmness makes my circle just,
   And makes me end where I begun.   35

35. *just* perfect. The circle is an emblem of perfection.

From *Holy Sonnets*

10

Death, be not proud, though some have calléd thee
Mighty and dreadful, for thou art not so;
For those whom thou think'st thou dost overthrow
Die not, poor death, nor yet canst thou kill me.
From rest and sleep, which but thy pictures be,   5
Much pleasure; then from thee much more must flow,
And soonest our best men with thee do go,
Rest of their bones, and soul's delivery.
Thou art slave to fate, chance, kings, and desperate men,
And dost with poison, war, and sickness dwell,   10
And poppy or charms can make us sleep as well
And better than thy stroke; why swell'st thou then?

12. *swell'st* puff up with pride.

One short sleep past, we wake eternally,
And death shall be no more; death, thou shalt die.

14

Batter my heart, three-personed God; for you
As yet but knock, breathe, shine, and seek to mend;
That I may rise and stand, o'erthrow me, and bend
Your force to break, blow, burn, and make me new.
5   I, like an usurped town, to another due,
Labor to admit you, but O, to no end;
Reason, your viceroy in me, me should defend,
But is captived, and proves weak or untrue.
Yet dearly I love you, and would be lovéd fain,
10   But am betrothed unto your enemy.
Divorce me, untie or break that knot again;
Take me to you, imprison me, for I,
Except you enthrall me, never shall be free,
Nor ever chaste, except you ravish me.

George Herbert 1593–1633

The Collar

I struck the board, and cried, "No more;
    I will abroad!
What? shall I ever sigh and pine?
My lines and life are free; free as the road,
5   Loose as the wind, as large as store,
      Shall I be still in suit?
Have I no harvest but a thorn
To let me blood, and not restore
What I have lost with cordial fruit?
10   Sure there was wine
Before my sighs did dry it: there was corn
Before my tears did drown it.

5. *store* abundance. 6. *be . . . suit* always be forced to beg.

Is the year only lost to me?
   Have I no bays to crown it?
No flowers, no garlands gay? all blasted?   15
    All wasted?
Not so, my heart: but there is fruit,
   And thou hast hands.
Recover all thy sigh-blown age
On double pleasures: leave thy cold dispute   20
Of what is fit, and not; forsake thy cage,
   Thy rope of sands,
Which petty thoughts have made, and made to thee
   Good cable, to enforce and draw,
    And be thy law,   25
   While thou didst wink and wouldst not see.
    Away; take heed:
    I will abroad.
Call in thy death's head there: tie up thy fears.
    He that forbears   30
  To suit and serve his need,
    Deserves his load."
But as I raved and grew more fierce and wild
   At every word,
Me thought I heard one calling, *Child:*   35
   And I replied, *My Lord.*

14. *bays* the poet's wreath.   26. *wink* keep the eyes closed.

The Flower

   How fresh, oh Lord, how sweet and clean
Are thy returns! even as the flowers in spring;
   To which, besides their own demesne,
The late-past frosts tributes of pleasure bring.
      Grief melts away   5
      Like snow in May,
   As if there were no such cold thing.

   Who would have thought my shriveled heart
Could have recovered greenness? It was gone
   Quite underground; as flowers depart   10
To see their mother-root, when they have blown,

11. *blown* bloomed.

Where they together
All the hard weather,
Dead to the world, keep house unknown.

15   These are thy wonders, Lord of power,
Killing and quickening, bringing down to hell
And up to heaven in an hour,
Making a chiming of a passing-bell.
            We say amiss
20   This or that is;
Thy word is all, if we could spell.

Oh that I once past changing were,
Fast in thy Paradise, where no flower can wither!
Many a spring I shoot up fair,
25 Offering at heaven, growing and groaning thither;
            Nor doth my flower
            Want a spring shower,
My sins and I joining together.

But while I grow in a straight line,
30 Still upwards bent, as if heaven were mine own,
Thy anger comes, and I decline;
What frost to that? what pole is not the zone
            Where all things burn,
            When thou dost turn,
35   And the least frown of thine is shown?

And now in age I bud again,
After so many deaths I live and write;
I once more smell the dew and rain,
And relish versing: Oh my only light,
40   It cannot be
            That I am he
On whom thy tempests fell all night.

These are thy wonders, Lord of love,
To make us see we are but flowers that glide;
45   Which when we once can find and prove,
Thou hast a garden for us where to bide;

27. *spring* shower i.e., the tears of contrition.   32. *what . . . zone* i.e., what polar cold would not seem like the heat of the equator?   44. *glide* slip away imperceptibly. 45. *prove* experience.

Who would be more,
Swelling through store,
Forfeit their Paradise by their pride.

Love (III)

Love bade me welcome; yet my soul·drew back,
 Guilty of dust and sin.
But quick-eyed Love, observing me grow slack
 From my first entrance in,
Drew nearer to me, sweetly questioning   5
 If I lacked anything.

"A guest," I answered, "worthy to be here".
 Love said, "You shall be he."
"I, the unkind, ungrateful? Ah, my dear,
 I cannot look on thee."   10
Love took my hand, and smiling did reply,
 "Who made the eyes but I?"

"Truth, Lord, but I have marred them; let my shame
 Go where it doth deserve."
"And know you not," says Love, "who bore the blame?" 15
 "My dear, then I will serve."
"You must sit down," says Love, "and taste my meat."
 So I did sit and eat.

Andrew Marvell 1621–1678

To His Coy Mistress

Had we but world enough, and time,
This coyness, lady, were no crime.
We would sit down, and think which way
To walk and pass our long love's day.
Thou by the Indian Ganges' side   5

Shouldst rubies find; I by the tide
Of Humber would complain. I would
Love you ten years before the flood,
And you should, if you please, refuse
10   Till the conversion of the Jews.
My vegetable love should grow
Vaster than empires and more slow.
An hundred years should go to praise
Thine eyes, and on thy forehead gaze.
15   Two hundred to adore each breast,
But thirty thousand to the rest.
An age at least to every part,
And the last age should show your heart.
For, lady, you deserve this state,
20   Nor would I love at lower rate.
   But at my back I always hear
Time's wingéd chariot hurrying near;
And yonder all before us lie
Deserts of vast eternity.
25   Thy beauty shall no more be found;
Nor, in thy marble vault, shall sound
My echoing song; then worms shall try
That long-preserved virginity;
And your quaint honor turn to dust,
30   And into ashes all my lust.
The grave's a fine and private place,
But none, I think, do there embrace.
   Now therefore, while the youthful hue
Sits on thy skin like morning dew,
35   And while thy willing soul transpires
At every pore with instant fires,
Now let us sport us while we may;
And now, like amorous birds of prey,
Rather at once our time devour,
40   Than languish in his slow-chapped power.
Let us roll all our strength and all
Our sweetness up into one ball;
And tear our pleasures with rough strife
Thorough the iron gates of life.
45   Thus, though we cannot make our sun
Stand still, yet we will make him run.

35. *transpires* breathes forth.   40. *slow-chapped* slowly crushing.

The Definition of Love

My love is of a birth as rare
As 'tis for object strange and high;
It was begotten by despair
Upon impossibility.

Magnanimous despair alone   5
Could show me so divine a thing,
Where feeble hope could ne'er have flown
But vainly flapped its tinsel wing.

And yet I quickly might arrive
Where my extended soul is fixed,   10
But Fate does iron wedges drive,
And always crowds itself betwixt.

For Fate with jealous eye does see
Two perfect loves, nor lets them close;
Their union would her ruin be,   15
And her tyrannic power depose.

And therefore her decrees of steel
Us as the distant poles have placed,
(Though love's whole world on us doth wheel)
Not by themselves to be embraced.   20

Unless the giddy heaven fall,
And earth some new convulsion tear,
And, us to join, the world should all
Be cramped into a planisphere.

As lines, so loves oblique may well   25
Themselves in every angle greet;
But ours, so truly parallel,
Though infinite can never meet.

Therefore the love which us doth bind,
But fate so enviously debars,   30

14. *close* unite. 24. *planisphere* a flat sphere with united poles.

Is the conjunction of the mind,
And opposition of the stars.

31–32. *conjunction* . . . *opposition* These terms in astrology refer to stars or planets which are (1) close to one another (uniting their influences) or (2) in opposite parts of the sky (with opposing influences).

The Garden

How vainly men themselves amaze
To win the palm, the oak, or bays;
And their incessant labors see
Crowned from some single herb or tree,
5   Whose short and narrow-vergéd shade
Does prudently their toils upbraid;
While all flowers and all trees do close
To weave the garlands of repose.

Fair Quiet, have I found thee here,
10   And Innocence, thy sister dear!
Mistaken long, I sought you then
In busy companies of men.
Your sacred plants, if here below,
Only among the plants will grow.
15   Society is all but rude
To this delicious solitude.

No white nor red was ever seen
So amorous as this lovely green.
Fond lovers, cruel as their flame,
20   Cut in these trees their mistress' name.
Little, alas, they know or heed
How far these beauties hers exceed!
Fair trees! wheresoe'er your barks I wound
No name shall but your own be found.

25   When we have run our passion's heat,
Love hither makes his best retreat.
The gods, that mortal beauty chase,
Still in a tree did end their race:
Apollo hunted Daphne so,

2. *palm* . . . *bays* crowns for athletics, civic accomplishment, and poetry. 7. *close* unite.

Only that she might laurel grow. 30
And Pan did after Syrinx speed,
Not as a nymph, but for a reed.

What wondrous life is this I lead!
Ripe apples drop about my head;
The luscious clusters of the vine 35
Upon my mouth do crush their wine;
The nectarine and curious peach
Into my hands themselves do reach;
Stumbling on melons, as I pass,
Insnared with flowers, I fall on grass. 40

Meanwhile the mind, from pleasure less,
Withdraws into its happiness;
The mind, that ocean where each kind
Does straight its own resemblance find;
Yet it creates, transcending these, 45
Far other worlds and other seas;
Annihilating all that's made
To a green thought in a green shade.

Here at the fountain's sliding foot,
Or at some fruit tree's mossy root, 50
Casting the body's vest aside,
My soul into the boughs does glide;
There like a bird it sits and sings,
Then whets and combs its silver wings;
And, till prepared for longer flight, 55
Waves in its plumes the various light.

Such was that happy garden-state,
While man there walked without a mate;
After a place so pure and sweet,
What other help could yet be meet! 60
But 'twas beyond a mortal's share
To wander solitary there;
Two paradises 'twere in one
To live in paradise alone.

How well the skillful gardener drew 65
Of flowers and herbs this dial new;

37. *curious* exquisite. 54. *whets* preens. 66. *dial* clock.

Where, from above, the milder sun
Does through a fragrant zodiac run;
And, as it works, th' industrious bee
70   Computes its time as well as we.
How could such sweet and wholesome hours
Be reckoned but with herbs and flowers!

John Milton 1608–1674

Lycidas

*In this monody the author bewails a learned friend, unfortunately
drowned in his passage from Chester on the Irish Seas, 1637; and by
occasion, foretells the ruin of our corrupted clergy, then in their height.*

Yet once more, O ye laurels, and once more
Ye myrtles brown, with ivy never sere,
I come to pluck your berries harsh and crude,
And with forced fingers rude,
5   Shatter your leaves before the mellowing year.
Bitter constraint, and sad occasion dear,
Compels me to disturb your season due;
For Lycidas is dead, dead ere his prime,
Young Lycidas, and hath not left his peer.
10   Who would not sing for Lycidas? he knew
Himself to sing, and build the lofty rhyme.
He must not float upon his watery bier
Unwept, and welter to the parching wind,
Without the meed of some melodious tear.
15   Begin, then, Sisters of the sacred well,
That from beneath the seat of Jove doth spring,
Begin, and somewhat loudly sweep the string.
Hence with denial vain, and coy excuse;
So may some gentle Muse
20   With lucky words favor my destined urn,
And as he passes turn,

1–2. *laurels . . . ivy* classical emblems of poetic achievement. 3. *crude* unripe.
6. *dear* costly. 15. *Sisters* the Muses.

And bid fair peace be to my sable shroud.
For we were nursed upon the self-same hill,
Fed the same flock, by fountain, shade, and rill.
   Together both, ere the high lawns appeared   25
Under the opening eyelids of the morn,
We drove a-field, and both together heard
What time the grey-fly winds her sultry horn,
Battening our flocks with the fresh dews of night,
Oft till the star that rose at evening bright   30
Toward heaven's descent had sloped his westering wheel.
Meanwhile the rural ditties were not mute,
Tempered to th' oaten flute,
Rough Satyrs danced, and Fauns with cloven heel
From the glad sound would not be absent long,   35
And old Damaetas loved to hear our song.
   But O the heavy change, now thou art gone,
Now thou art gone and never must return!
Thee, Shepherd, thee the woods and desert caves,
With wild thyme and the gadding vine o'ergrown,   40
And all their echoes mourn.
The willows and the hazel copses green
Shall now no more be seen,
Fanning their joyous leaves to thy soft lays.
As killing as the canker to the rose,   45
Or taint-worm to the weanling herds that graze,
Or frost to flowers that their gay wardrobe wear,
When first the white-thorn blows;
Such, Lycidas, thy loss to shepherd's ear.
   Where were ye, Nymphs, when the remorseless deep   50
Closed o'er the head of your loved Lycidas?
For neither were ye playing on the steep
Where your old bards, the famous Druids, lie,
Nor on the shaggy top of Mona lie,
Nor yet where Deva spreads her wizard stream.   55
Ay me, I fondly dream!
Had ye been there—for what could that have done?
What could the Muse herself that Orpheus bore,
The Muse herself, for her enchanting son,
Whom universal nature did lament,   60

25. *lawns* upland pastures. 48. *blows* blossoms. 52–53. *steep . . . Druids* a mountain in Wales where old bardic priests were buried. 54–55. *Mona . . . Deva* the Isle of Man off Wales; the river Dee. 56. *fondly* foolishly. 58–63. *Muse . . . shore* The Thracian poet, son of the Muse Calliope, was torn to pieces by the Bacchantes, and his head was thrown into the river Hebrus and floated to Lesbos.

When by the rout that made the hideous roar,
His gory visage down the stream was sent,
Down the swift Hebrus to the Lesbian shore?
    Alas! what boots it with uncessant care
65 To tend the homely, slighted, shepherd's trade,
And strictly meditate the thankless Muse?
Were it not better done as others use,
To sport with Amaryllis in the shade,
Or with the tangles of Neaera's hair?
70 Fame is the spur that the clear spirit doth raise
(That last infirmity of noble mind)
To scorn delights, and live laborious days;
But the fair guerdon when we hope to find,
And think to burst out into sudden blaze,
75 Comes the blind Fury with th' abhorréd shears,
And slits the thin-spun life. "But not the praise,"
Phoebus replied, and touched my trembling ears:
"Fame is no plant that grows on mortal soil,
Nor in the glistering foil
80 Set off to the world, nor in broad rumor lies,
But lives and spreads aloft by those pure eyes
And perfect witness of all-judging Jove;
As he pronounces lastly on each deed,
Of so much fame in Heaven expect thy meed."
85   O fountain Arethuse, and thou honored flood,
Smooth-sliding Mincius, crowned with vocal reeds,
That strain I heard was of a higher mood;
But now my oat proceeds,
And listens to the Herald of the Sea
90 That came in Neptune's plea.
He asked the waves, and asked the felon winds,
What hard mishap hath doomed this gentle swain?
And questioned every gust of rugged wings
That blows from off each beakéd promontory;
95 They knew not of his story,
And sage Hippotades their answer brings
That not a blast was from his dungeon strayed;
The air was calm, and on the level brinc,
Sleek Panopé with all her sisters played.

---

61. *rout* noisy band.   79. *glistering foil* glittering setting (of a jewel).   85–86. *Arethuse . . . Mincius* a fountain and a river associated with pastoral poetry.   88. *oat*
oaten pipe.   89. *Herald of the Sea* Triton, Neptune's representative.   96. *Hippotades*
Aeolus, god of the winds.   99. *Panopé* a sea nymph.

It was that fatal and perfidious bark,   100
Built in th' eclipse, and rigged with curses dark,
That sunk so low that sacred head of thine.
    Next, Camus, reverend sire, went footing slow,
His mantle hairy, and his bonnet sedge,
Inwrought with figures dim, and on the edge   105
Like to that sanguine flower inscribed with woe.
"Ah! who hath reft," quoth he, "my dearest pledge?"
Last came and last did go
The Pilot of the Galilean Lake;
Two massy keys he bore of metals twain   110
(The golden opes, the iron shuts amain).
He shook his mitred locks, and stern bespake,
"How well could I have spared for thee, young swain,
Enow of such as for their bellies' sake
Creep and intrude and climb into the fold!   115
Of other care they little reckoning make
Than how to scramble at the shearers' feast,
And shove away the worthy bidden guest.
Blind mouths! that scarce themselves know how to hold
A sheep-hook, or have learnt aught else the least   120
That to the faithful herdman's art belongs!
What recks it them? What need they? They are sped;
And when they list, their lean and flashy songs
Grate on their scrannel pipes of wretched straw.
The hungry sheep look up, and are not fed,   125
But swoln with wind, and the rank mist they draw,
Rot inwardly, and foul contagion spread;
Besides what the grim wolf with privy paw
Daily devours apace, and nothing said,
But that two-handed engine at the door   130
Stands ready to smite once, and smite no more."
    Return, Alpheus, the dread voice is past
That shrunk thy streams; return, Sicilian Muse,
And call the vales, and bid them hither cast
Their bells and flowerets of a thousand hues.   135
Ye valleys low where the mild whispers use
Of shades and wanton winds, and gushing brooks,

101. *eclipse* suggesting evil omens.   103. *Camus* god of the river Cam in Cambridge.
106. *sanguine . . . woe* the hyacinth, said to be marked with the Greek word *ai* (alas).
109. *Pilot* St. Peter.   122. *recks it* does it concern; *sped* well-established.   123. *list*
wish.   124. *scrannel* harsh, thin.   128. *wolf* the Roman Catholic Church.   130. *en-*
gine probably the sword of God's justice.   132. *Alpheus* river associated with pastoral
poetry; lover of Arethusa.

On whose fresh lap the swart star sparely looks,
Throw hither all your quaint enameled eyes,
140 That on the green turf suck the honeyed showers,
And purple all the ground with vernal flowers.
Bring the rathe primrose that forsaken dies,
The tufted crow-toe, and pale jessamine,
The white pink, and the pansy freaked with jet,
145 The glowing violet,
The musk rose, and the well-attired woodbine,
With cowslips wan that hang the pensive head,
And every flower that sad embroidery wears;
Bid amaranthus all his beauty shed,
150 And daffodillies fill their cups with tears,
To strew the laureate hearse where Lycid lies.
For so to interpose a little ease,
Let our frail thoughts dally with false surmise.
Ay me! whilst thee the shores and sounding seas
155 Wash far away, where'er thy bones are hurled,
Whether beyond the stormy Hebrides,
Where thou perhaps under the whelming tide
Visit'st the bottom of the monstrous world;
Or whether thou to our moist vows denied,
160 Sleep'st by the fable of Bellerus old,
Where the great vision of the guarded mount
Looks toward Namancos and Bayona's hold;
Look homeward, Angel, now, and melt with ruth.
And, O ye dolphins, waft the hapless youth.
165 Weep no more, woeful shepherds, weep no more,
For Lycidas, your sorrow, is not dead,
Sunk though he be beneath the watery floor,
So sinks the day-star in the ocean bed,
And yet anon repairs his drooping head,
170 And tricks his beams, and with new-spangled ore
Flames in the forehead of the morning sky:
So Lycidas sunk low, but mounted high,
Through the dear might of him that walked the waves,
Where other groves and other streams along,

138. *swart star* Sirius, associated with late summer. 139. *quaint* intricately designed. 142. *rathe* early. 144. *freaked* spotted. 149. *amaranthus* a real flower; also an imaginary unfading flower. 151. *hearse* bier. 160. *Bellerus* a fabulous giant. 161. *mount* off the Cornish coast. 162. *Namancos, Bayona* on the Spanish coast. 163. *Angel* St. Michael, who is asked to turn from Spain to England. 164. *hapless youth* Arion was carried to shore by dolphins who had been charmed by his song. 170. *tricks* dresses; *ore* gold.

With nectar pure his oozy locks he laves,   175
And hears the unexpressive nuptial song,
In the blest kingdoms meek of joy and love.
There entertain him all the saints above,
In solemn troops and sweet societies
That sing, and singing in their glory move,   180
And wipe the tears for ever from his eyes.
Now, Lycidas, the shepherds weep no more;
Henceforth thou art the genius of the shore,
In thy large recompense, and shalt be good
To all that wander in that perilous flood.   185
    Thus sang the uncouth swain to th' oaks and rills,
While the still morn went out with sandals grey;
He touched the tender stops of various quills,
With eager thought warbling his Doric lay;
And now the sun had stretched out all the hills,   190
And now was dropped into the western bay;
At last he rose, and twitched his mantle blue:
Tomorrow to fresh woods, and pastures new.

183. *genius* local divinity.   186. *uncouth* rustic.   188. *quills* the hollow reeds of pastoral
pipes.   189. *Doric* pastoral.   192. *twitched* pulled up.

On His Having Arrived at the Age of Twenty-three

    How soon hath Time, the subtle thief of youth,
Stoln on his wing my three and twentieth year!
My hasting days fly on with full career,
But my late spring no bud or blossom show'th.
Perhaps my semblance might deceive the truth,   5
That I to manhood am arrived so near,
And inward ripeness doth much less appear,
That some more timely-happy spirits endu'th.
Yet be it less or more, or soon or slow,
It shall be still in strictest measure even   10
To that same lot, however mean, or high,
Toward which Time leads me, and the will of Heaven;
All is, if I have grace to use it so,
As ever in my great taskmaster's eye.

8. *endu'th* endoweth.

On the Late Massacre in Piedmont

Avenge, O Lord, thy slaughtered saints, whose bones
Lie scattered on the Alpine mountains cold;
Even them who kept thy truth so pure of old
When all our fathers worshiped stocks and stones,
5   Forget not; in thy book record their groans
Who were thy sheep and in their ancient fold
Slain by the bloody Piedmontese that rolled
Mother with infant down the rocks. Their moans
The vales redoubled to the hills, and they
10   To Heaven. Their martyred blood and ashes sow
O'er all th' Italian fields where still doth sway
The triple tyrant; that from these may grow
A hundredfold, who having learnt thy way
Early may fly the Babylonian woe.

On . . . Piedmont In 1655 the freedom of worship of the Waldenses, a sect akin to Protestantism (in its avoidance of images—"stocks and stones"), was terminated with this massacre.   12. *triple tyrant* the Pope (i.e., his triple crown).   14. *Babylonian woe* The Roman Church was frequently identified with the "whore of Babylon" (Revelation xvii–xviii).

On His Blindness

When I consider how my light is spent,
Ere half my days, in this dark world and wide,
And that one talent which is death to hide,
Lodged with me useless, though my soul more bent
5   To serve therewith my Maker, and present
My true account, lest he returning chide;
"Doth God exact day-labor, light denied?"
I fondly ask; but Patience, to prevent
That murmur, soon replies, "God doth not need
10   Either man's work or his own gifts; who best
Bear his mild yoke, they serve him best. His state
Is kingly; thousands at his bidding speed
And post o'er land and ocean without rest:
They also serve who only stand and wait."

8. *fondly* foolishly; *prevent* forestall.

Jonathan Swift 1667–1745

Stella's Birthday

WRITTEN IN THE YEAR 1718
Stella this day is thirty-four
(We shan't dispute a year or more),
However, Stella, be not troubled,
Although thy size and years are doubled,
Since first I saw thee at sixteen,   5
The brightest virgin of the green.
So little is thy form declin'd,
Made up so largely in thy mind.

Oh, would it please the gods to split
Thy beauty, size, and years, and wit,   10
No age could furnish out a pair
Of nymphs so graceful, wise, and fair
With half the luster of your eyes,
With half your wit, your years, and size:
And then, before it grew too late,   15
How should I beg of gentle fate
(That either nymph might have her swain)
To split my Worship too in twain.

Stella's Birthday Cf. Yeats's "The Words upon the Window-Pane."

569

Alexander Pope 1688–1744

The Rape of the Lock

AN HEROI-COMICAL POEM

Nolueram, Belinda, tuos violare capillos;
sed juvat hoc precibus me tribuisse tuis.
—MARTIAL

To Mrs. Arabella Fermor

Canto I

What dire offense from am'rous causes springs,
What mighty contests rise from trivial things,
I sing—This verse to Caryll, Muse! is due:
This, even Belinda may vouchsafe to view:
5   Slight is the subject, but not so the praise,
If she inspire, and he approve my lays.
    Say what strange motive, Goddess! could compel
A well-bred lord to assault a gentle belle?
Oh, say what stranger cause, yet unexplored,
10   Could make a gentle belle reject a lord?
In tasks so bold can little men engage,
And in soft bosoms dwells such mighty rage?
    Sol through white curtains shot a tim'rous ray,
And oped those eyes that must eclipse the day;
15   Now lapdogs give themselves the rousing shake,
And sleepless lovers just at twelve awake.
Thrice rung the bell, the slipper knocked the ground,
And the pressed watch returned a silver sound.
Belinda still her downy pillow pressed,
20   Her guardian Sylph prolonged the balmy rest.
'Twas he had summoned to her silent bed
The Morning Dream that hovered o'er her head.
A youth more glitt'ring than a birthnight beau

Nolueram . . . tuis I was sorry, Belinda, to injure your locks, but I am pleased to have made this offering in answer to your prayers. *Mrs. Arabella Fermor* the "Belinda" of the poem; "Mrs." for our "Miss."   3. *Caryll* a friend of Pope who suggested that the poet "write a poem to make a jest of" the "stealing of Miss Belle Fermor's hair" (Pope).

(That even in slumber caused her cheek to glow)
Seemed to her ear his winning lips to lay,   25
And thus in whispers said, or seemed to say:
  "Fairest of mortals, thou distinguished care
Of thousand bright inhabitants of air!
If e'er one vision touched thy infant thought,
Of all the nurse and all the priest have taught,   30
Of airy elves by moonlight shadows seen,
The silver token, and the circled green,
Or virgins visited by angel powers,
With golden crowns and wreaths of heavenly flowers,
Hear and believe! thy own importance know,   35
Nor bound thy narrow views to things below.
Some secret truths, from learned pride concealed,
To maids alone and children are revealed:
What though no credit doubting wits may give?
The fair and innocent shall still believe.   40
Know, then, unnumbered spirits round thee fly,
The light militia of the lower sky:
These, though unseen, are ever on the wing,
Hang o'er the box, and hover round the Ring.
Think what an equipage thou hast in air,   45
And view with scorn two pages and a chair.
As now your own, our beings were of old,
And once enclosed in woman's beauteous mold;
Thence, by a soft transition, we repair
From earthly vehicles to these of air.   50
Think not, when woman's transient breath is fled,
That all her vanities at once are dead:
Succeeding vanities she still regards,
And though she plays no more, o'erlooks the cards.
Her joy in gilded chariots, when alive,   55
And love of ombre, after death survive.
For when the Fair in all their pride expire,
To their first elements their souls retire:
The sprites of fiery termagants in flame
Mount up, and take a Salamander's name.   60
Soft yielding minds to water glide away,
And sip, with Nymphs, their elemental tea.

---

44. *box . . . Ring* the box in the theater and the fashionable drive in Hyde Park.
46. *chair* sedan chair. 58. *elements* Of the four elements—earth, air, water, and fire
—one was supposed to predominate in every temperament. The salamander (l. 60)
was thought to live in fire.

The graver prude sinks downward to a Gnome,
In search of mischief still on earth to roam.
65 The light coquettes in Sylphs aloft repair,
And sport and flutter in the fields of air.
"Know further yet; whoever fair and chaste
Rejects mankind, is by some Sylph embraced:
For spirits, freed from mortal laws, with ease
70 Assume what sexes and what shapes they please.
What guards the purity of melting maids,
In courtly balls, and midnight masquerades,
Safe from the treacherous friend, the daring spark,
The glance by day, the whisper in the dark,
75 When kind occasion prompts their warm desires,
When music softens, and when dancing fires?
'Tis but their Sylph, the wise Celestials know,
Though Honor is the word with men below.
"Some nymphs there are, too conscious of their face,
80 For life predestined to the Gnomes' embrace.
These swell their prospects and exalt their pride,
When offers are disdained, and love denied.
Then gay ideas crowd the vacant brain,
While peers, and dukes, and all their sweeping train,
85 And garters, stars, and coronets appear,
And in soft sounds, 'your Grace' salutes their ear.
'Tis these that early taint the female soul,
Instruct the eyes of young coquettes to roll,
Teach infant cheeks a bidden blush to know,
90 And little hearts to flutter at a beau.
"Oft, when the world imagine women stray,
The Sylphs through mystic mazes guide their way,
Through all the giddy circle they pursue,
And old impertinence expel by new.
95 What tender maid but must a victim fall
To one man's treat, but for another's ball?
When Florio speaks what virgin could withstand,
If gentle Damon did not squeeze her hand?
With varying vanities, from every part,
100 They shift the moving toyshop of their heart;
Where wigs with wigs, with sword-knots sword-knots strive,
Beaux banish beaux, and coaches coaches drive.
This erring mortals levity may call;
Oh, blind to truth! the Sylphs contrive it all.

101. *sword-knots* tassels tied to the hilts of swords.

"Of these am I, who thy protection claim, 105
A watchful sprite, and Ariel is my name.
Late, as I ranged the crystal wilds of air,
In the clear mirror of thy ruling star
I saw, alas! some dread event impend,
Ere to the main this morning sun descend, 110
But Heaven reveals not what, or how, or where:
Warned by the Sylph, O pious maid, beware!
This to disclose is all thy guardian can.
Beware of all, but most beware of Man!"
He said; when Shock, who thought she slept too long, 115
Leaped up, and waked his mistress with his tongue.
'Twas then, Belinda! if report say true,
Thy eyes first opened on a billet-doux;
Wounds, charms, and ardors were no sooner read,
But all the vision vanished from thy head. 120
And now, unveiled, the toilet stands displayed,
Each silver vase in mystic order laid.
First, robed in white, the nymph intent adores,
With head uncovered, the cosmetic powers.
A heavenly image in the glass appears; 125
To that she bends, to that her eyes she rears.
Th' inferior priestess, at her altar's side,
Trembling begins the sacred rites of Pride.
Unnumbered treasures ope at once, and here
The various off'rings of the world appear; 130
From each she nicely culls with curious toil,
And decks the goddess with the glitt'ring spoil.
This casket India's glowing gems unlocks,
And all Arabia breathes from yonder box.
The tortoise here and elephant unite, 135
Transformed to combs, the speckled and the white.
Here files of pins extend their shining rows,
Puffs, powders, patches, Bibles, billet-doux.
Now awful Beauty puts on all its arms;
The fair each moment rises in her charms, 140
Repairs her smiles, awakens every grace,
And calls forth all the wonders of her face;
Sees by degrees a purer blush arise,
And keener lightnings quicken in her eyes.
The busy Sylphs surround their darling care, 145
These set the head, and those divide the hair,

115. *Shock* Belinda's lapdog. 138. *patches* beauty patches.

Some fold the sleeve, whilst others plait the gown;
And Betty's praised for labors not her own.

148. *Betty* Belinda's maid, the "inferior priestess" of line 127.

Canto II

Not with more glories, in th' ethereal plain,
The sun first rises o'er the purpled main,
Than, issuing forth, the rival of his beams
Launched on the bosom of the silver Thames.
5   Fair nymphs and well-dressed youths around her shone,
But ev'ry eye was fixed on her alone.
On her white breast a sparkling cross she wore,
Which Jews might kiss, and infidels adore.
Her lively looks a sprightly mind disclose,
10   Quick as her eyes, and as unfixed as those:
Favors to none, to all she smiles extends;
Oft she rejects, but never once offends.
Bright as the sun, her eyes the gazers strike,
And, like the sun, they shine on all alike.
15   Yet graceful ease, and sweetness void of pride,
Might hide her faults, if belles had faults to hide:
If to her share some female errors fall,
Look on her face, and you'll forget 'em all.
This nymph, to the destruction of mankind,
20   Nourished two locks which graceful hung behind
In equal curls, and well conspired to deck
With shining ringlets the smooth iv'ry neck.
Love in these labyrinths his slaves detains,
And mighty hearts are held in slender chains.
25   With hairy springes we the birds betray,
Slight lines of hair surprise the finny prey,
Fair tresses man's imperial race ensnare,
And beauty draws us with a single hair.
The adventurous Baron the bright locks admired,
30   He saw, he wished, and to the prize aspired.
Resolved to win, he meditates the way,
By force to ravish, or by fraud betray;
For when success a lover's toil attends,
Few ask if fraud or force attained his ends.
35   For this, ere Phoebus rose, he had implored
Propitious Heaven, and ev'ry power adored,
But chiefly Love—to Love an altar built,

25. *springes* snares.

Of twelve vast French romances, neatly gilt.
There lay three garters, half a pair of gloves,
And all the trophies of his former loves.   40
With tender billet-doux he lights the pyre,
And breathes three am'rous sighs to raise the fire.
Then prostrate falls, and begs with ardent eyes
Soon to obtain, and long possess the prize:
The powers gave ear, and granted half his prayer,   45
The rest the winds dispersed in empty air.
　But now secure the painted vessel glides,
The sunbeams trembling on the floating tides,
While melting music steals upon the sky,
And softened sounds along the waters die.   50
Smooth flow the waves, the zephyrs gently play,
Belinda smiled, and all the world was gay.
All but the Sylph—with careful thoughts oppressed,
The impending woe sat heavy on his breast.
He summons straight his denizens of air;   55
The lucid squadrons round the sails repair:
Soft o'er the shrouds aërial whispers breathe
That seemed but zephyrs to the train beneath.
Some to the sun their insect-wings unfold,
Waft on the breeze, or sink in clouds of gold.   60
Transparent forms too fine for mortal sight,
Their fluid bodies half dissolved in light,
Loose to the wind their airy garments flew,
Then glitt'ring textures of the filmy dew,
Dipped in the richest tincture of the skies,   65
Where light disports in ever-mingling dyes,
While ev'ry beam new transient colors flings,
Colors that change whene'er they wave their wings.
Amid the circle, on the gilded mast,
Superior by the head, was Ariel placed;   70
His purple pinions opening to the sun,
He raised his azure wand, and thus begun:
　"Ye Sylphs and Sylphids, to your chief give ear!
Fays, Fairies, Genii, Elves, and Daemons, hear!
Ye know the spheres and various tasks assigned   75
By laws eternal to the aërial kind.

45–46. *powers . . . air* a common response to prayers in epic poetry.　47. *painted vessel*
the boat of the Thames waterman conveying the company to Hampton Court.　70. *Su-*
perior . . . head Like other epic heroes, taller than the rest.　73–74. *Ye . . . hear* Cf.
the angelic invocations in *Paradise Lost*.

Some in the fields of purest ether play,
And bask and whiten in the blaze of day.
Some guide the course of wandering orbs on high,
80   Or roll the planets through the boundless sky.
Some less refined, beneath the moon's pale light
Pursue the stars that shoot athwart the night,
Or suck the mists in grosser air below,
Or dip their pinions in the painted bow,
85   Or brew fierce tempests on the wintry main,
Or o'er the glebe distill the kindly rain.
Others on earth o'er human race preside,
Watch all their ways, and all their actions guide:
Of these the chief the care of nations own,
90   And guard with arms divine the British Throne.
    "Our humbler province is to tend the Fair,
Not a less pleasing, though less glorious care:
To save the powder from too rude a gale,
Nor let the imprisoned essences exhale,
95   To draw fresh colors from the vernal flowers,
To steal from rainbows e'er they drop in showers
A brighter wash; to curl their waving hairs,
Assist their blushes, and inspire their airs;
Nay oft, in dreams invention we bestow,
100   To change a flounce, or add a furbelow.
    "This day black omens threat the brightest fair,
That e'er deserved a watchful spirit's care;
Some dire disaster, or by force or slight,
But what, or where, the Fates have wrapped in night:
105   Whether the nymph shall break Diana's law,
Or some frail china jar receive a flaw,
Or stain her honor or her new brocade,
Forget her prayers, or miss a masquerade,
Or lose her heart, or necklace, at a ball;
110   Or whether Heaven has doomed that Shock must fall.
Haste, then, ye spirits! to your charge repair:
The flutt'ring fan be Zephyretta's care;
The drops to thee, Brillante, we consign;
And, Momentilla, let the watch be thine;
115   Do thou, Crispissa, tend her favorite Lock;
Ariel himself shall be the guard of Shock.
    "To fifty chosen Sylphs, of special note,

105. *Diana's law* chastity.   112–116. The sylphs' names are adapted to their functions.
113. *drops* diamond ear rings.

We trust th' important charge, the petticoat;
Oft have we known that sevenfold fence to fail,
Though stiff with hoops, and armed with ribs of whale.   120
Form a strong line about the silver bound,
And guard the wide circumference around.
    "Whatever spirit, careless of his charge,
His post neglects, or leaves the Fair at large,
Shall feel sharp vengeance soon o'ertake his sins,   125
Be stopped in vials, or transfixed with pins,
Or plunged in lakes of bitter washes lie,
Or wedged whole ages in a bodkin's eye;
Gums and pomatums shall his flight restrain,
While clogged he beats his silken wings in vain,   130
Or alum styptics with contracting power
Shrink his thin essence like a riveled flower:
Or, as Ixion fixed, the wretch shall feel
The giddy motion of the whirling mill,
In fumes of burning chocolate shall glow,   135
And tremble at the sea that froths below!"
    He spoke; the spirits from the sails descend;
Some, orb in orb, around the nymph extend;
Some thread the mazy ringlets of her hair;
Some hang upon the pendants of her ear;   140
With beating hearts the dire event they wait,
Anxious, and trembling for the birth of Fate.

119. *sevenfold fence* like the sevenfold shield of a Homeric hero.   128. *bodkin's eye* a blunt needle with a large eye.   132. *riveled* shriveled.   134. *mill* the beater for stirring the chocolate.

Canto III

    Close by those meads, forever crowned with flowers,
Where Thames with pride surveys his rising towers,
There stands a structure of majestic frame,
Which from the neighboring Hampton takes its name.
- Here Britain's statesmen oft the fall foredoom   5
Of foreign tyrants and of nymphs at home;
Here thou, great Anna! whom three realms obey,
Dost sometimes counsel take—and sometimes tea.
    Hither the heroes and the nymphs resort,
To taste awhile the pleasures of a court;   10
In various talk the instructive hours they passed,
Who gave the ball, or paid the visit last;

3. *structure* Hampton Court Palace.

One speaks the glory of the British Queen,
And one describes a charming Indian screen;
15 A third interprets motions, looks, and eyes;
At every word a reputation dies.
Snuff, or the fan, supply each pause of chat,
With singing, laughing, ogling, and all that.
Meanwhile, declining from the noon of day,
20 The sun obliquely shoots his burning ray;
The hungry judges soon the sentence sign,
And wretches hang that jurymen may dine;
The merchant from th' Exchange returns in peace,
And the long labors of the toilet cease.
25 Belinda now, whom thirst of fame invites,
Burns to encounter two adventurous knights,
At ombre singly to decide their doom,
And swells her breast with conquests yet to come.
Straight the three bands prepare in arms to join,
30 Each band the number of the sacred nine.
Soon as she spreads her hand, the aërial guard
Descend, and sit on each important card:
First Ariel perched upon a Matadore,
Then each, according to the rank they bore;
35 For Sylphs, yet mindful of their ancient race,
Are, as when women, wondrous fond of place.
Behold, four Kings in majesty revered,
With hoary whiskers and a forky beard;
And four fair Queens whose hands sustain a flower,
40 Th' expressive emblem of their softer power;
Four Knaves in garbs succinct, a trusty band,
Caps on their heads, and halberts in their hand;
And parti-colored troops, a shining train,
Draw forth to combat on the velvet plain.
45 The skillful nymph reviews her force with care;
"Let Spades be trumps!" she said, and trumps they were.
Now move to war her sable Matodores,
In show like leaders of the swarthy Moors.
Spadillio first, unconquerable lord!
50 Led off two captive trumps, and swept the board.

27. *ombre* This game is played with an ordinary deck of cards (though the 10's, 9's, and 8's are removed). Forty cards are dealt to three players (9 apiece) and a stock (13), and the high bidder (*ombre*) names the trumps and has to win more tricks than his combined opponents. 46. *Let . . . were* Cf. Genesis 1.3. 49. *Spadillio* Belinda holds the ace of spades ("Spadillio"), the two of spades ("Manillio"), and the ace of clubs ("Basto")—her "sable Matadores."

As many more Manillio forced to yield,
And marched a victor from the verdant field.
Him Basto followed, but his fate more hard
Gained but one trump and one plebeian card.
With his broad saber next, a chief in years,   55
The hoary Majesty of Spades appears,
Puts forth one manly leg, to sight revealed,
The rest his many-colored robe concealed.
The rebel Knave, who dares his prince engage,
Proves the just victim of his royal rage.   60
Even mighty Pam, that kings and queens o'erthrew
And mowed down armies in the fights of loo,
Sad chance of war! now destitute of aid,
Falls undistinguished by the victor Spade.
    Thus far both armies to Belinda yield;   65
Now to the Baron fate inclines the field.
His warlike amazon her host invades,
The imperial consort of the crown of Spades.
The Club's black tyrant first her victim died,
Spite of his haughty mien and barbarous pride.   70
What boots the regal circle on his head,
His giant limbs, in state unwieldy spread?
That long behind he trails his pompous robe,
And of all monarchs only grasps the globe?
    The Baron now his Diamonds pours apace;   75
Th' embroidered King who shows but half his face,
And his refulgent Queen, with powers combined
Of broken troops an easy conquest find.
Clubs, Diamonds, Hearts, in wild disorder seen,
With throngs promiscuous strew the level green.   80
Thus when dispersed a routed army runs,
Of Asia's troops, and Afric's sable sons,
With like confusion different nations fly,
Of various habit, and of various dye,
The pierced battalions disunited fall   85
In heaps on heaps; one fate o'erwhelms them all.
    The Knave of Diamonds tries his wily arts,
And wins (oh shameful chance!) the Queen of Hearts.
At this, the blood the virgin's cheek forsook,
A livid paleness spreads o'er all her look;   90
She sees, and trembles at the approaching ill,

61. *Pam* the highest trump in the game of loo, the knave of clubs.

Just in the jaws of ruin, and Codille,
And now (as oft in some distempered state)
On one nice trick depends the gen'ral fate.
95   An Ace of Hearts steps forth: the King unseen
Lurked in her hand, and mourned his captive Queen.
He springs to vengeance with an eager pace,
And falls like thunder on the prostrate Ace.
The nymph exulting fills with shouts the sky,
100   The walls, the woods, and long canals reply.
    O thoughtless mortals! ever blind to fate,
Too soon dejected, and too soon elate:
Sudden these honors shall be snatched away,
And cursed forever this victorious day.
105   For lo! the board with cups and spoons is crowned,
The berries crackle, and the mill turns round;
On shining altars of Japan they raise
The silver lamp; the fiery spirits blaze:
From silver spouts the grateful liquors glide,
110   While China's earth receives the smoking tide.
At once they gratify their scent and taste,
And frequent cups prolong the rich repast.
Straight hover round the fair her airy band;
Some, as she sipped, the fuming liquor fanned,
115   Some o'er her lap their careful plumes displayed,
Trembling, and conscious of the rich brocade.
Coffee (which makes the politician wise,
And see through all things with his half-shut eyes)
Sent up in vapors to the Baron's brain
120   New stratagems, the radiant Lock to gain.
Ah, cease, rash youth! desist ere 'tis too late,
Fear the just Gods, and think of Scylla's fate!
Changed to a bird, and sent to flit in air,
She dearly pays for Nisus' injured hair!
125   But when to mischief mortals bend their will,
How soon they find fit instruments of ill!
Just then, Clarissa drew with tempting grace
A two-edged weapon from her shining case;
So ladies in romance assist their knight,
130   Present the spear, and arm him for the fight.

___

92. *Codille* the loss of a hand at cards.   106. *berries . . . round* i.e., the roasting and grinding of coffee.   107. *altars of Japan* lacquered tables. Cf. the sacrifices in epic poems. 122. *Scylla's fate* Scylla betrayed her father, Nisus, by plucking the purple hair on which his life depended.

He takes the gift with rev'rence, and extends
The little engine on his fingers' ends;
This just behind Belinda's neck he spread,
As o'er the fragrant steams she bends her head.
Swift to the Lock a thousand sprites repair,   135
A thousand wings, by turns, blow back the hair,
And thrice they twitched the diamond in her ear,
Thrice she looked back, and thrice the foe drew near.
Just in that instant, anxious Ariel sought
The close recesses of the virgin's thought;   140
As on the nosegay in her breast reclined,
He watched th' ideas rising in her mind,
Sudden he viewed, in spite of all her art,
An earthly lover lurking at her heart.
Amazed, confused, he found his power expired,   145
  The Peer now spreads the glitt'ring forfex wide,
Resigned to fate, and with a sigh retired.
T'inclose the Lock; now joins it, to divide.
Ev'n then, before the fatal engine closed,
A wretched Sylph too fondly interposed;   150
Fate urged the shears, and cut the Sylph in twain
(But airy substance soon unites again);
The meeting points the sacred hair dissever
From the fair head, forever, and forever!
  Then flashed the living lightning from her eyes,   155
And screams of horror rend th' affrighted skies.
Not louder shrieks to pitying Heav'n are cast,
When husbands or when lapdogs breathe their last;
Or when rich china vessels fall'n from high,
In glitt'ring dust and painted fragments lie!   160
  "Let wreaths of triumph now my temples twine,"
The victor cried, "the glorious prize is mine!
While fish in streams, or birds delight in air,
Or in a coach and six the British Fair,
As long as *Atalantis* shall be read,   165
Or the small pillow grace a lady's bed,
While visits shall be paid on solemn days,
When num'rous wax-lights in bright order blaze,
While nymphs take treats, or assignations give,
So long my honor, name, and praise shall live!   170
What Time would spare, from Steel receives its date,

147. *forfex* scissors. 165. *Atalantis* a scandalous novel of the period.

And monuments, like men, submit to fate!
Steel could the labor of the Gods destroy,
And strike to dust th' imperial towers of Troy;
175   Steel could the works of mortal pride confound,
And hew triumphal arches to the ground.
What wonder then, fair nymph! thy hairs should feel,
The conqu'ring force of unresisted Steel?"

Canto IV

But anxious cares the pensive nymph oppressed,
And secret passions labored in her breast.
Not youthful kings in battle seized alive,
Not scornful virgins who their charms survive,
5   Not ardent lovers robbed of all their bliss,
Not ancient ladies when refused a kiss,
Not tyrants fierce that unrepenting die,
Not Cynthia when her manteau's pinned awry,
E'er felt such rage, resentment, and despair,
10   As thou, sad virgin! for thy ravished hair.
    For, that sad moment, when the Sylphs withdrew
And Ariel weeping from Belinda flew,
Umbriel, a dusky, melancholy sprite
As ever sullied the fair face of light,
15   Down to the central earth, his proper scene,
Repaired to search the gloomy Cave of Spleen.
    Swift on his sooty pinions flits the Gnome,
And in a vapor reached the dismal dome.
No cheerful breeze this sullen region knows,
20   The dreaded east is all the wind that blows.
Here in a grotto, sheltered close from air,
And screened in shades from day's detested glare,
She sighs forever on her pensive bed,
Pain at her side, and Megrim at her head.
25   Two handmaids wait the throne: alike in place,
But differing far in figure and in face.
Here stood Ill-Nature like an ancient maid,
Her wrinkled form in black and white arrayed;
With store of prayers for mornings, nights, and noons,
30   Her hand is filled; her bosom with lampoons.
    There Affectation, with a sickly mien,
Shows in her cheek the roses of eighteen,

16. *Spleen* or often "the vapors," usually a neurotic illness. 17. *Gnome* Belinda is now guarded by former prudes instead of former coquettes. 24. *Megrim* migraine headache.

Practiced to lisp, and hang the head aside,
Faints into airs, and languishes with pride,
On the rich quilt sinks with becoming woe, 35
Wrapped in a gown, for sickness and for show.
The fair ones feel such maladies as these,
When each new nightdress gives a new disease.
　A constant vapor o'er the palace flies,
Strange phantoms rising as the mists arise; 40
Dreadful as hermit's dreams in haunted shades,
Or bright as visions of expiring maids.
Now glaring fiends, and snakes on rolling spires,
Pale specters, gaping tombs, and purple fires;
Now lakes of liquid gold, Elysian scenes, 45
And crystal domes, and angels in machines.
　Unnumbered throngs on every side are seen
Of bodies changed to various forms by Spleen.
Here living teapots stand, one arm held out,
One bent; the handle this, and that the spout: 50
A pipkin there, like Homer's tripod, walks;
Here sighs a jar, and there a goose pie talks;
Men prove with child, as powerful fancy works,
And maids, turned bottles, call aloud for corks.
　Safe passed the Gnome through this fantastic band, 55
A branch of healing spleenwort in his hand.
Then thus addressed the Power: "Hail, wayward Queen!
Who rule the sex to fifty from fifteen,
Parent of vapors and of female wit,
Who give the hysteric or poetic fit, 60
On various tempers act by various ways,
Make some take physic, others scribble plays;
Who cause the proud their visits to delay,
And send the godly in a pet to pray.
A nymph there is that all your power disdains, 65
And thousands more in equal mirth maintains.
But oh! if e'er thy Gnome could spoil a grace,
Or raise a pimple on a beauteous face,
Like citron-waters matrons' cheeks inflame,
Or change complexions at a losing game; 70
If e'er with airy horns I planted heads,
Or rumpled petticoats, or tumbled beds,
Or caused suspicion when no soul was rude,

69. *citron-waters* brandy flavored with lemon peel.　71. *heads* i.e., of those thought to
be cuckolds.

Or discomposed the headdress of a prude,
75   Or e'er to costive lapdog gave disease,
Which not the tears of brightest eyes could ease,
Hear me, and touch Belinda with chagrin:
That single act gives half the world the spleen."
    The Goddess with a discontented air
80   Seems to reject him, though she grants his prayer.
A wondrous bag with both her hands she binds,
Like that where once Ulysses held the winds;
There she collects the force of female lungs,
Sighs, sobs, and passions, and the war of tongues.
85   A vial next she fills with fainting fears,
Soft sorrows, melting griefs, and flowing tears.
The Gnome rejoicing bears her gifts away,
Spreads his black wings, and slowly mounts to day.
    Sunk in Thalestris' arms the nymph he found,
90   Her eyes dejected and her hair unbound.
Full o'er their heads the swelling bag he rent,
And all the Furies issued at the vent.
Belinda burns with more than mortal ire,
And fierce Thalestris fans the rising fire.
95   "O wretched maid!" she spread her hands, and cried
(While Hampton's echoes, "Wretched maid!" replied),
"Was it for this you took such constant care
The bodkin, comb, and essence to prepare?
For this your locks in paper durance bound,
100   For this with torturing irons wreathed around?
For this with fillets strained your tender head,
And bravely bore the double loads of lead?
Gods! shall the ravisher display your hair,
While the fops envy, and the ladies stare!
105   Honor forbid! at whose unrivaled shrine
Ease, pleasure, virtue, all our sex resign.
Methinks already I your tears survey,
Already hear the horrid things they say,
Already see you a degraded toast,
110   And all your honor in a whisper lost!
How shall I, then, your helpless fame defend?
'Twill then be infamy to seem your friend!
And shall this prize, th' inestimable prize,
Exposed through crystal to the gazing eyes,

98. *bodkin* hairpin.   114–115. *Exposed . . . rays* The baron will wear the lock as a ring.

And heightened by the diamond's circling rays,   115
On that rapacious hand forever blaze?
Sooner shall grass in Hyde Park Circus grow,
And wits take lodgings in the sound of Bow;
Sooner let earth, air, sea, to chaos fall,
Men, monkeys, lapdogs, parrots, perish all!"   120
    She said; then raging to Sir Plume repairs,
And bids her beau demand the precious hairs
(Sir Plume of amber snuffbox justly vain,
And the nice conduct of a clouded cane).
With earnest eyes, and round unthinking face,   125
He first the snuffbox opened, then the case,
And thus broke out—"My Lord, why, what the devil!
Z——ds! damn the lock! 'fore Gad, you must be civil!
Plague on't! 'tis past a jest—nay prithee, pox!
Give her the hair"—he spoke, and rapped his box.   130
    "It grieves me much," replied the Peer again,
"Who speaks so well should ever speak in vain.
But by this Lock, this sacred Lock I swear
(Which never more shall join its parted hair;
Which never more its honors shall renew,   135
Clipped from the lovely head where late it grew),
That while my nostrils draw the vital air,
This hand, which won it, shall forever wear."
He spoke, and speaking, in proud triumph spread
The long-contended honors of her head.   140
    But Umbriel, hateful Gnome, forbears not so;
He breaks the vial whence the sorrows flow.
Then see! the nymph in beauteous grief appears,
Her eyes half languishing, half drowned in tears;
On her heaved bosom hung her drooping head,   145
Which, with a sigh, she raised, and thus she said:
    "Forever cursed be this detested day,
Which snatched my best, my fav'rite curl away!
Happy! ah, ten times happy had I been,
If Hampton Court these eyes had never seen!   150
Yet am not I the first mistaken maid,
By love of courts to num'rous ills betrayed.
Oh, had I rather unadmired remained
In some lone isle, or distant northern land;
Where the gilt chariot never marks the way,   155

117. *Circus* the Ring of I.44.   118. *Bow* St. Mary-le-Bow, a church in London's mercantile quarter.

Where none learn ombre, none e'er taste bohea!
There kept my charms concealed from mortal eye,
Like roses that in deserts bloom and die.
What moved my mind with youthful lords to roam?
160   Oh, had I stayed, and said my prayers at home!
'Twas this the morning omens seemed to tell;
Thrice from my trembling hand the patch box fell;
The tottering china shook without a wind,
Nay, Poll sat mute, and Shock was most unkind!
165   A Sylph too warned me of the threats of fate,
In mystic visions, now believed too late!
See the poor remnants of these slighted hairs!
My hands shall rend what ev'n thy rapine spares.
These in two sable ringlets taught to break,
170   Once gave new beauties to the snowy neck.
The sister lock now sits uncouth, alone,
And in its fellow's fate foresees its own;
Uncurled it hangs, the fatal shears demands,
And tempts once more thy sacrilegious hands.
175   Oh, hadst thou, cruel! been content to seize
Hairs less in sight, or any hairs but these!"

156. *bohea* tea, pronounced tăy.

Canto V

She said: the pitying audience melt in tears.
But Fate and Jove had stopped the Baron's ears.
In vain Thalestris with reproach assails,
For who can move when fair Belinda fails?
5   Not half so fixed the Trojan could remain,
While Anna begged and Dido raged in vain.
Then grave Clarissa graceful waved her fan;
Silence ensued, and thus the nymph began:
"Say why are beauties praised and honored most,
10   The wise man's passion, and the vain man's toast?
Why decked with all that land and sea afford,
Why angels called, and angel-like adored?
Why round our coaches crowd the white-gloved beaux,
Why bows the side box from its inmost rows?
15   How vain are all these glories, all our pains,
Unless good sense preserve what beauty gains;
That men may say, when we the front box grace,

5-6. *Not . . . vain* Dido and her sister Anna beg Aeneas to remain in Carthage (in *Aeneid*, IV).   9-34. Cf. Sarpedon's address to Glaucus in *Iliad*, XII.

'Behold the first in virtue as in face!'
Oh! if to dance all night, and dress all day,
Charmed the smallpox, or chased old age away,   20
Who would not scorn what housewife's cares produce,
Or who would learn one earthly thing of use?
To patch, nay ogle, might become a saint,
Nor could it sure be such a sin to paint.
But since, alas! frail beauty must decay,   25
Curled or uncurled, since locks will turn to gray;
Since painted, or not painted, all shall fade,
And she who scorns a man must die a maid;
What then remains but well our power to use,
And keep good humor still whate'er we lose?   30
And trust me, dear! good humor can prevail
When airs, and flights, and screams, and scolding fail.
Beauties in vain their pretty eyes may roll;
Charms strike the sight, but merit wins the soul."
    So spoke the dame, but no applause ensued;   35
Belinda frowned, Thalestris called her prude.
"To arms, to arms!" the fierce virago cries,
And swift as lightning to the combat flies.
All side in parties, and begin the attack;
Fans clap, silks rustle, and tough whalebones crack;   40
Heroes' and heroines' shouts confus'dly rise,
And bass and treble voices strike the skies.
No common weapons in their hands are found,
Like Gods they fight, nor dread a mortal wound.
    So when bold Homer makes the Gods engage,   45
And heavenly breasts with human passions rage;
'Gainst Pallas, Mars; Latona, Hermes arms;
And all Olympus rings with loud alarms:
Jove's thunder roars, heav'n trembles all around,
Blue Neptune storms, the bellowing deeps resound: 50
Earth shakes her nodding towers, the ground gives way,
And the pale ghosts start at the flash of day!
    Triumphant Umbriel on a sconce's height
Clapped his glad wings, and sat to view the fight:
Propped on their bodkin spears, the sprites survey   55
The growing combat, or assist the fray.
    While through the press enraged Thalestris flies,
And scatters death around from both her eyes,
A beau and witling perished in the throng,
One died in metaphor, and one in song.   60

"O cruel nymph! a living death I bear,"
Cried Dapperwit, and sunk beside his chair.
A mournful glance Sir Fopling upwards cast,
"Those eyes are made so killing"—was his last.
65 Thus on Mæander's flowery margin lies
Th' expiring swan, and as he sings he dies.
　　When bold Sir Plume had drawn Clarissa down,
Chloe stepped in, and killed him with a frown;
She smiled to see the doughty hero slain,
70 But, at her smile, the beau revived again.
　　Now Jove suspends his golden scales in air,
Weighs the men's wits against the lady's hair;
The doubtful beam long nods from side to side;
At length the wits mount up, the hairs subside.
75 　　See, fierce Belinda on the Baron flies,
With more than usual lightning in her eyes;
Nor feared the chief the unequal fight to try,
Who sought no more than on his foe to die.
But this bold lord with manly strength endued,
80 She with one finger and a thumb subdued:
Just where the breath of life his nostrils drew,
A charge of snuff the wily virgin threw;
The Gnomes direct, to every atom just,
The pungent grains of titillating dust.
85 Sudden, with starting tears each eye o'erflows,
And the high dome re-echoes to his nose.
　　"Now meet thy fate," incensed Belinda cried,
And drew a deadly bodkin from her side.
(The same, his ancient personage to deck,
90 Her great-great-grandsire wore about his neck,
In three seal rings; which after, melted down,
Formed a vast buckle for his widow's gown:
Her infant grandame's whistle next it grew,
The bells she jingled, and the whistle blew;
95 Then in a bodkin graced her mother's hairs,
Which long she wore, and now Belinda wears.)
　　"Boast not my fall," he cried, "insulting foe!
Thou by some other shalt be laid as low.
Nor think to die dejects my lofty mind:
100 All that I dread is leaving you behind!
Rather than so, ah, let me still survive,

71–74. Now . . . subside Cf. the Iliad and Paradise Lost, IV. 996ff.

And burn in Cupid's flames—but burn alive."
"Restore the Lock!" she cries, and all around
"Restore the Lock!" the vaulted roofs rebound.
Not fierce Othello in so loud a strain   105
Roared for the handkerchief that caused his pain.
But see how oft ambitious aims are crossed,
And chiefs contend till all the prize is lost!
The lock, obtained with guilt, and kept with pain,
In every place is sought, but sought in vain: 110
With such a prize no mortal must be blessed,
So Heaven decrees! with Heaven who can contest?
    Some thought it mounted to the lunar sphere,
Since all things lost on earth are treasured there.
There heroes' wits are kept in ponderous vases,   115
And beaux' in snuffboxes and tweezer cases.
There broken vows and deathbed alms are found,
And lovers' hearts with ends of riband bound,
The courtier's promises, and sick man's prayers,
The smiles of harlots, and the tears of heirs,   120
Cages for gnats, and chains to yoke a flea,
Dried butterflies, and tomes of casuistry.
    But trust the Muse—she saw it upward rise,
Though marked by none but quick, poetic eyes
(So Rome's great founder to the heavens withdrew,   125
To Proculus alone confessed in view);
A sudden star, it shot through liquid air,
And drew behind a radiant trail of hair.
Not Berenice's locks first rose so bright,
The heavens bespangling with disheveled light.   130
The Sylphs behold it kindling as it flies,
And pleased pursue its progress through the skies.
    This the beau monde shall from the Mall survey,
And hail with music its propitious ray.
This the blest lover shall for Venus take,   135
And send up vows from Rosamonda's Lake.
This Partridge soon shall view in cloudless skies,
When next he looks through Galileo's eyes;
And hence the egregious wizard shall foredoom

105–106. *Othello . . . pain* Cf. *Othello*, IV. i. 125–126. *So . . . view* The Roman
senator Proculus saw Romulus carried up to heaven. 129–130. *Not . . . light* Berenice
dedicated this hair (which became a constellation) to insure her husband's return from
battle. 133. *Mall* promenade in St. James' Park. 136. *Lake* pond in the Park named
for the supposed mistress of Henry II. 137. *Partridge* "a ridiculous star-gazer" (Pope),
who annually gave out false prophecies.

140   The fate of Louis, and the fall of Rome.
            Then cease, bright nymph! to mourn thy ravished hair,
        Which adds new glory to the shining sphere!
        Not all the tresses that fair head can boast,
        Shall draw such envy as the Lock you lost.
145   For, after all the murders of your eye,
        When, after millions slain, yourself shall die:
        When those fair suns shall set, as set they must,
        And all those tresses shall be laid in dust,
        This Lock the Muse shall consecrate to fame,
150   And 'midst the stars inscribe Belinda's name.

140. *Louis* England had long been at war with Louis XIV.

William Blake 1757–1827

From SONGS OF EXPERIENCE

The Sick Rose

        O Rose, thou art sick!
        The invisible worm
        That flies in the night,
        In the howling storm,

5   Has found out thy bed
        Of crimson joy,
        And his dark secret love
        Does thy life destroy.

The Tiger

        Tiger! tiger! burning bright
        In the forests of the night,
        What immortal hand or eye
        Could frame thy fearful symmetry?

In what distant deeps or skies   5
Burnt the fire of thine eyes?
On what wings dare he aspire?
What the hand dare seize the fire?

And what shoulder, and what art,
Could twist the sinews of thy heart?   10
And when thy heart began to beat,
What dread hands? and what dread feet?

What the hammer? what the chain?
In what furnace was thy brain?
What the anvil? what dread grasp   15
Dare its deadly terrors clasp?

When the stars threw down their spears,
And watered heaven with their tears,
Did he smile his work to see?
Did he who made the Lamb make thee?   20

Tiger, tiger burning bright
In the forests of the night,
What immortal hand or eye
Dare frame thy fearful symmetry?

London

I wander through each chartered street,
Near where the chartered Thames does flow,
And mark in every face I meet
Marks of weakness, marks of woe.

In every cry of every man,   5
In every infant's cry of fear,
In every voice, in every ban,
The mind-forged manacles I hear.

How the chimney-sweeper's cry
Every blackening church appalls;   10

1. *chartered* i.e., pre-empted, rented out. 7. *ban* prohibition; curse; marriage proclamation.

And the hapless Soldier's sigh
Runs in blood down palace walls.

But most through midnight streets I hear
How the youthful harlot's curse
15   Blasts the new born infant's tear,
And blights with plagues the marriage hearse

16. *hearse* bier.

A Poison Tree

I was angry with my friend:
I told my wrath, my wrath did end.
I was angry with my foe:
I told it not, my wrath did grow.

5   And I watered it in fears,
Night and morning with my tears;
And I sunnéd it with smiles,
And with soft deceitful wiles.

And it grew both day and night,
10   Till it bore an apple bright;
And my foe beheld it shine,
And he knew that it was mine,

And into my garden stole
When the night had veiled the pole:
15   In the morning glad I see
My foe outstretched beneath the tree.

Mock on, Mock on, Voltaire, Rousseau

Mock on, mock on, Voltaire, Rousseau:
Mock on, mock on: 'tis all in vain!
You throw the sand against the wind,
And the wind blows it back again.

5   And every sand becomes a gem
Reflected in the beams divine;

Blown back they blind the mocking eye,
But still in Israel's paths they shine.

The atoms of Democritus
And Newton's particles of light   10
Are sands upon the Red Sea shore,
Where Israel's tents do shine so bright.

From *Preface to Milton*

And did those feet in ancient time
Walk upon England's mountains green?
And was the holy Lamb of God
On England's pleasant pastures seen?

And did the Countenance Divine   5
Shine forth upon our clouded hills?
And was Jerusalem builded here
Among these dark satanic mills?

Bring me my bow of burning gold:
Bring me my arrows of desire: 10
Bring me my spear: O clouds unfold!
Bring me my chariot of fire.

I will not cease from mental fight,
Nor shall my sword sleep in my hand
Till we have built Jerusalem   15
In England's green and pleasant land.

Milton In Blake's prophetic poem, the events of the Bible (and a kind of spiritual Israel)
are as relevant to England as to Palestine. 15. *Jerusalem* Cf. Revelation xxi–xxii: the
New Jerusalem, the Bride of Christ, when the fallen world will become the new heaven
and earth.

William Wordsworth 1770–1850

Lines

COMPOSED A FEW MILES ABOVE TINTERN ABBEY ON REVISITING THE
BANKS OF THE WYE DURING A TOUR. JULY 13, 1798.

    Five years have passed; five summers, with the length
Of five long winters! and again I hear
These waters, rolling from their mountain-springs
With a soft inland murmur.—Once again
5 Do I behold these steep and lofty cliffs,
That on a wild secluded scene impress
Thoughts of more deep seclusion; and connect
The landscape with the quiet of the sky.
The day is come when I again repose
10 Here, under this dark sycamore, and view
These plots of cottage-ground, these orchard-tufts,
Which at this season, with their unripe fruits,
Are clad in one green hue, and lose themselves
'Mid groves and copses. Once again I see
15 These hedgerows, hardly hedgerows, little lines
Of sportive wood run wild: these pastoral farms,
Green to the very door; and wreaths of smoke
Sent up, in silence, from among the trees!
With some uncertain notice, as might seem
20 Of vagrant dwellers in the houseless woods,
Or of some hermit's cave, where by his fire
The hermit sits alone.

              These beauteous forms,
Through a long absence, have not been to me
As is a landscape to a blind man's eye;
25 But oft, in lonely rooms, and 'mid the din
Of towns and cities, I have owed to them
In hours of weariness, sensations sweet,
Felt in the blood, and felt along the heart;

Tintern Abbey a picturesque ruin in Monmouthshire. 14. *copses* thickets.

594

And passing even into my purer mind,
With tranquil restoration—feelings too   30
Of unremembered pleasure: such, perhaps,
As have no slight or trivial influence
On that best portion of a good man's life,
His little, nameless, unremembered acts
Of kindness and of love. Nor less, I trust,   35
To them I may have owed another gift,
Of aspect more sublime; that blessèd mood
In which the burthen of the mystery,
In which the heavy and the weary weight
Of all this unintelligible world,   40
Is lightened—that serene and blessèd mood,
In which the affections gently lead us on—
Until, the breath of this corporeal frame
And even the motion of our human blood
Almost suspended, we are laid asleep   45
In body, and become a living soul;
While with an eye made quiet by the power
Of harmony, and the deep power of joy,
We see into the life of things.

                        If this
Be but a vain belief, yet, oh! how oft—   50
In darkness and amid the many shapes
Of joyless daylight; when the fretful stir
Unprofitable, and the fever of the world,
Have hung upon the beatings of my heart—
How oft, in spirit, have I turned to thee,   55
O sylvan Wye! thou wanderer through the woods,
How often has my spirit turned to thee!

    And now, with gleams of half-extinguished thought,
With many recognitions dim and faint,
And somewhat of a sad perplexity,   60
The picture of the mind revives again;
While here I stand, not only with the sense
Of present pleasure, but with pleasing thoughts
That in this moment there is life and food
For future years. And so I dare to hope,   65
Though changed, no doubt, from what I was when first
I came among these hills; when like a roe
I bounded o'er the mountains, by the sides

Of the deep rivers, and the lonely streams,
70   Wherever nature led: more like a man
Flying from something that he dreads than one
Who sought the thing he loved. For nature then
('The coarser pleasures of my boyish days,
And their glad animal movements all gone by)
75   To me was all in all.—I cannot paint
What then I was. The sounding cataract
Haunted me like a passion; the tall rock,
The mountain, and the deep and gloomy wood,
Their colors and their forms, were then to me
80   An appetite; a feeling and a love,
That had no need of a remoter charm,
By thought supplied, nor any interest
Unborrowed from the eye.—That time is past,
And all its aching joys are now no more,
85   And all its dizzy raptures. Not for this
Faint I, nor mourn nor murmur; other gifts
Have followed; for such loss, I would believe,
Abundant recompense. For I have learned
To look on nature, not as in the hour
90   Of thoughtless youth; but hearing oftentimes
The still, sad music of humanity,
Nor harsh nor grating, though of ample power
To chasten and subdue. And I have felt
A presence that disturbs me with the joy
95   Of elevated thoughts; a sense sublime
Of something far more deeply interfused,
Whose dwelling is the light of setting suns,
And the round ocean and the living air,
And the blue sky, and in the mind of man:
100   A motion and a spirit, that impels
All thinking things, all objects of all thought,
And rolls through all things. Therefore am I still
A lover of the meadows and the woods
And mountains; and of all that we behold
105   From this green earth; of all the mighty world
Of eye, and ear—both what they half create,
And what perceive; well pleased to recognize
In nature and the language of the sense
The anchor of my purest thoughts, the nurse,
110   The guide, the guardian of my heart, and soul
Of all my moral being.

Nor perchance,

If I were not thus taught, should I the more
Suffer my genial spirits to decay:
For thou art with me here upon the banks
Of this fair river; thou my dearest friend,   115
My dear, dear friend; and in thy voice I catch
The language of my former heart, and read
My former pleasures in the shooting lights
Of thy wild eyes. Oh! yet a little while
May I behold in thee what I was once,   120
My dear, dear sister! and this prayer I make,
Knowing that Nature never did betray
The heart that loved her; 'tis her privilege,
Through all the years of this our life, to lead
From joy to joy: for she can so inform   125
The mind that is within us, so impress
With quietness and beauty, and so feed
With lofty thoughts, that neither evil tongues,
Rash judgments, nor the sneers of selfish men,
Nor greetings where no kindness is, nor all   130
The dreary intercourse of daily life,
Shall e'er prevail against us, or disturb
Our cheerful faith, that all which we behold
Is full of blessings. Therefore let the moon
Shine on thee in thy solitary walk;   135
And let the misty mountain winds be free
To blow against thee: and, in after years,
When these wild ecstasies shall be matured
Into a sober pleasure; when thy mind
Shall be a mansion for all lovely forms,   140
Thy memory be as a dwelling place
For all sweet sounds and harmonies; oh! then,
If solitude, or fear, or pain, or grief
Should be thy portion, with what healing thoughts
Of tender joy wilt thou remember me,   145
And these my exhortations! Nor, perchance—
If I should be where I no more can hear
Thy voice, nor catch from thy wild eyes these gleams
Of past existence—wilt thou then forget
That on the banks of this delightful stream   150
We stood together; and that I, so long

115. *friend* Wordsworth's sister, Dorothy.

A worshiper of Nature, hither came
Unwearied in that service; rather say
With warmer love—oh! with far deeper zeal
155   Of holier love. Nor wilt thou then forget,
That after many wanderings, many years
Of absence, these steep woods and lofty cliffs,
And this green pastoral landscape, were to me
More dear, both for themselves and for thy sake!

Composed upon Westminster Bridge, September 3, 1802

Earth has not anything to show more fair:
Dull would he be of soul who could pass by
A sight so touching in its majesty:
This city now doth, like a garment, wear
5   The beauty of the morning; silent, bare,
Ships, towers, domes, theaters, and temples lie
Open unto the fields, and to the sky;
All bright and glittering in the smokeless air.
Never did sun more beautifully steep
10   In his first splendor, valley, rock, or hill;
Ne'er saw I, never felt, a calm so deep!
The river glideth at his own sweet will:
Dear God! the very houses seem asleep;
And all that mighty heart is lving still!

It Is a Beauteous Evening

It is a beauteous evening, calm and free,
The holy time is quiet as a nun
Breathless with adoration; the broad sun
Is sinking down in its tranquility;
5   The gentleness of heaven broods o'er the sea:
Listen! the mighty Being is awake,
And doth with his eternal motion make
A sound like thunder—everlastingly.
Dear child! dear girl! that walkest with me here,
10   If thou appear untouched by solemn thought,
Thy nature is not therefore less divine:

9. *child* the natural daughter of Wordsworth and Annette Vallon.

Thou liest in Abraham's bosom all the year,
And worship'st at the Temple's inner shrine,
God being with thee when we know it not.

12. *Abraham's bosom* God's grace and care; a place where departed souls prepare for heaven. Cf. Luke xvi. 19–31.

The World Is Too Much with Us

The world is too much with us; late and soon,
Getting and spending, we lay waste our powers:
Little we see in Nature that is ours;
We have given our hearts away, a sordid boon!
The sea that bares her bosom to the moon;   5
The winds that will be howling at all hours,
And are up-gathered now like sleeping flowers;
For this, for everything, we are out of tune;
It moves us not.—Great God! I'd rather be
A pagan suckled in a creed outworn;   10
So might I, standing on this pleasant lea,
Have glimpses that would make me less forlorn;
Have sight of Proteus rising from the sea;
Or hear old Triton blow his wreathéd horn.

London, 1802

Milton! thou should'st be living at this hour:
England hath need of thee: she is a fen
Of stagnant waters: altar, sword, and pen,
Fireside, the heroic wealth of hall and bower,
Have forfeited their ancient English dower   5
Of inward happiness. We are selfish men;
Oh! raise us up, return to us again;
And give us manners, virtue, freedom, power.
Thy soul was like a star, and dwelt apart:
Thou hadst a voice whose sound was like the sea: 10
Pure as the naked heavens, majestic, free,
So didst thou travel on life's common way,
In cheerful godliness; and yet thy heart
The lowliest duties on herself did lay.

London, 1802 The poet wrote that he was impressed by the "vanity and parade" in England after returning from the "desolation" in post-revolutionary France.

Samuel Taylor Coleridge 1772–1834

Kubla Khan

In Xanadu did Kubla Khan
A stately pleasure-dome decree:
Where Alph, the sacred river, ran
Through caverns measureless to man
5   Down to a sunless sea.
So twice five miles of fertile ground
With walls and towers were girdled round:
And there were gardens bright with sinuous rills,
Where blossomed many an incense-bearing tree;
10   And here were forests ancient as the hills,
Enfolding sunny spots of greenery.

But oh, that deep romantic chasm which slanted
Down the green hill athwart a cedarn cover!
A savage place! as holy and enchanted
15   As e'er beneath a waning moon was haunted
By woman wailing for her demon-lover!
And from this chasm, with ceaseless turmoil seething,
As if this earth in fast thick pants were breathing,
A mighty fountain momently was forced:
20   Amid whose swift half-intermitted burst
Huge fragments vaulted like rebounding hail,
Or chaffy grain beneath the thresher's flail:
And 'mid these dancing rocks at once and ever
It flung up momently the sacred river.
25   Five miles meandering with a mazy motion
Through wood and dale the sacred river ran,
Then reached the caverns measureless to man,
And sank in tumult to a lifeless ocean:
And 'mid this tumult Kubla heard from far
30   Ancestral voices prophesying war!
    The shadow of the dome of pleasure
    Floated midway on the waves;

1. *Kubla Khan* 13th-century Mongol Emperor of China.

600

Where was heard the mingled measure
From the fountain and the caves.
It was a miracle of rare device,   35
A sunny pleasure-dome with caves of ice!

A damsel with a dulcimer
In a vision once I saw:
It was an Abyssinian maid,
And on her dulcimer she played,   40
Singing of Mount Abora.
Could I revive within me
Her symphony and song,
To such a deep delight 'twould win me,
That with music loud and long,   •   45
I would build that dome in air,
That sunny dome! those caves of ice!
And all who heard should see them there,
And all should cry, Beware! Beware!
His flashing eyes, his floating hair!   50
Weave a circle round him thrice,
And close your eyes with holy dread,
For he on honey-dew hath fed,
And drunk the milk of Paradise.

John Keats 1795–1821

On First Looking into Chapman's Homer

Much have I traveled in the realms of gold,
And many goodly states and kingdoms seen;
Round many western islands have I been
Which bards in fealty to Apollo hold.
Oft of one wide expanse had I been told   5
That deep-browed Homer ruled as his demesne;
Yet did I never breathe its pure serene
Till I heard Chapman speak out loud and bold:

4. *in fealty* by oath of fidelity.   8. *Chapman* George; Elizabethan dramatic poet, translator.

Then felt I like some watcher of the skies
10   When a new planet swims into his ken;
Or like stout Cortez when with eagle eyes
He stared at the Pacific—and all his men
Looked at each other with a wild surmise—
Silent, upon a peak in Darien.

11. *Cortez* mistaken for Balboa.

When I Have Fears

When I have fears that I may cease to be
Before my pen has gleaned my teeming brain,
Before high-piléd books, in charactery,
Hold like rich garners the full ripened grain;
5   When I behold, upon the night's starred face,
Huge cloudy symbols of a high romance,
And think that I may never live to trace
Their shadows, with the magic hand of chance;
And when I feel, fair creature of an hour,
10   That I shall never look upon thee more,
Never have relish in the faery power
Of unreflecting love;—then on the shore
Of the wide world I stand alone, and think
Till love and fame to nothingness do sink.

3. *charactery* letters, words, symbols.   4. *garners* granaries.

Bright Star

Bright star, would I were steadfast as thou art—
Not in lone splendor hung aloft the night
And watching, with eternal lids apart,
Like nature's patient, sleepless Eremite,
5   The moving waters at their priestlike task
Of pure ablution round earth's human shores,
Or gazing on the new soft fallen mask
Of snow upon the mountains and the moors—
No—yet still steadfast, still unchangeable,
10   Pillowed upon my fair love's ripening breast,
To feel forever its soft fall and swell,

Awake forever in a sweet unrest,
Still, still to hear her tender-taken breath,
And so live ever—or else swoon to death.

Bright Star (an earlier version)

Bright Star! would I were steadfast as thou art!
Not in lone splendor hung amid the night;
Not watching, with eternal lids apart
Like Nature's devout sleepless Eremite
The morning waters at their priestlike task   5
Of pure ablution round earth's human shores;
Or gazing on the new soft fallen mask
Of snow upon the mountains and the moors:—
No;—yet still steadfast, still unchangeable
Cheek-pillow'd on my Love's white ripening breast,   10
To touch, for ever, its warm sink and swell,
Awake, for ever, in a sweet unrest;
. To hear, to feel her tender-taken breath,
Half-passionless, and so swoon on to death.

La Belle Dame sans Merci

O what can ail thee, Knight at arms,
  Alone and palely loitering?
The sedge has withered from the Lake
  And no birds sing!

O what can ail thee, Knight at arms,   5
  So haggard, and so woebegone?
The squirrel's granary is full
  And the harvest's done.

I see a lily on thy brow
  With anguish moist and fever dew,   10
And on thy cheeks a fading rose
  Fast withereth too.

"I met a Lady in the Meads,
  Full beautiful, a faery's child
Her hair was long, her foot was light,   15
  And her eyes were wild.

"I made a Garland for her head,
　And bracelets too, and fragrant Zone;
She looked at me as she did love
20　　And made sweet moan.

"I set her on my pacing steed
　And nothing else saw all day long
For sidelong would she bend and sing
　A faery's song.

25　"She found me roots of relish sweet
　And honey wild, and manna dew,
And sure in language strange she said
　I love thee true.

"She took me to her elfin grot
30　　And there she wept and sighed full sore,
And there I shut her wild wild eyes
　With kisses four.

"And there she lulléd me asleep
　And there I dreamed, Ah woe betide!
35　The latest dream I ever dreamt
　On the cold hill side.

"I saw pale Kings, and Princes too,
　Pale warriors, death-pale were they all;
They cried, La belle dame sans merci
40　　Thee hath in thrall.

"I saw their starved lips in the gloam
　With horrid warning gapéd wide,
And I awoke, and found me here
　On the cold hill's side.

18. *Zone* girdle.　21. This is the first version of the poem. The revised version for this stanza and for the second below reads as follows:

I set her on my pacing steed,
　And nothing else saw all day long;
For sideways would she lean, and sing
　A faery's song. . . .

She took me to her elfin grot,
　And there she gazed and sighéd deep,
And there I shut her wild sad eyes—
　So kissed to sleep.

"And this is why I sojourn here,   45
     Alone and palely loitering;
Though the sedge is withered from the Lake
     And no birds sing."

Ode to a Nightingale

1

My heart aches, and a drowsy numbness pains
     My sense, as though of hemlock I had drunk,
Or emptied some dull opiate to the drains
     One minute past, and Lethe-wards had sunk:
'Tis not through envy of thy happy lot,   5
     But being too happy in thine happiness,—
          That thou, light-wingéd Dryad of the trees,
               In some melodious plot
     Of beechen green, and shadows numberless,
          Singest of summer in full-throated ease.   10

2

O, for a draught of vintage! that hath been
     Cool'd a long age in the deep-delvéd earth,
Tasting of Flora and the country green,
     Dance, and Provençal song, and sunburnt mirth!
O for a beaker full of the warm South,   15
     Full of the true, the blushful Hippocrene,
          With beaded bubbles winking at the brim,
               And purple-stainéd mouth;
     That I might drink, and leave the world unseen,
          And with thee fade away into the forest dim: 20

3

Fade far away, dissolve, and quite forget
     What thou among the leaves hast never known,
The weariness, the fever, and the fret
     Here, where men sit and hear each other groan;
Where palsy shakes a few, sad, last gray hairs,   25
     Where youth grows pale, and specter-thin, and dies;
          Where but to think is to be full of sorrow

---

13. *Flora* flowers or the goddess of flowers.   14. *Provençal song* lyrics by medieval troubadours of Provence.   16. *Hippocrene* fountain of the Muses on Mt. Helicon, whose waters inspired poets.

And leaden-eyed despairs,
Where Beauty cannot keep her lustrous eyes,
30   Or new Love pine at them beyond to-morrow.

4

Away! away! for I will fly to thee,
Not charioted by Bacchus and his pards,
But on the viewless wings of Poesy,
Though the dull brain perplexes and retards:
35   Already with thee! tender is the night,
And haply the Queen-Moon is on her throne,
Clustered around by all her starry Fays;
But here there is no light,
Save what from heaven is with the breezes blown
40   Through verdurous glooms and winding mossy ways.

5

I cannot see what flowers are at my feet,
Nor what soft incense hangs upon the boughs,
But, in embalmèd darkness, guess each sweet
Wherewith the seasonable month endows
45   The grass, the thicket, and the fruit tree wild;
White hawthorn, and the pastoral eglantine;
Fast fading violets covered up in leaves;
And mid-May's eldest child,
The coming musk-rose, full of dewy wine,
50   The murmurous haunt of flies on summer eves.

6

Darkling I listen; and for many a time
I have been half in love with easeful Death,
Called him soft names in many a musèd rhyme,
To take into the air my quiet breath;
55   Now more than ever seems it rich to die,
To cease upon the midnight with no pain,
While thou art pouring forth thy soul abroad
In such an ecstasy!
Still wouldst thou sing, and I have ears in vain—
60   To thy high requiem become a sod.

---

32. *Bacchus* the god of wine whose chariot was drawn by leopards. 33. *viewless* invisible. 37. *Fays* fairies. 43. *embalmèd* perfumed. 46. *eglantine* sweetbriar, honeysuckle. 51. *Darkling* in darkness.

7

Thou was not born for death, immortal Bird!
  No hungry generations tread thee down;
The voice I hear this passing night was heard
  In ancient days by emperor and clown:
Perhaps the selfsame song that found a path   65
    Through the sad heart of Ruth, when, sick for home,
      She stood in tears amid the alien corn;
        The same that ofttimes hath
Charmed magic casements, opening on the foam
Of perilous seas, in faery lands forlorn.   70

8

Forlorn! the very word is like a bell
  To toll me back from thee to my sole self!
Adieu! the fancy cannot cheat so well
  As she is famed to do, deceiving elf.
Adieu! adieu! thy plaintive anthem fades   75
    Past the near meadows, over the still stream,
      Up the hill side; and now 'tis buried deep
        In the next valley-glades:
Was it a vision, or a waking dream?
Fled is that music:—Do I wake or sleep?   80

66. *Ruth* Cf. Ruth ii.

Ode on a Grecian Urn

1

Thou still unravished bride of quietness,
  Thou foster-child of silence and slow time,
Sylvan historian, who canst thus express
  A flowery tale more sweetly than our rhyme:
What leaf-fringed legend haunts about thy shape   5
  Of deities or mortals, or of both,
    In Tempe or the dales of Arcady?
What men or gods are these? What maidens loth?
  What mad pursuit? What struggle to escape?
    What pipes and timbrels? What wild ecstasy?   10

2

Heard melodies are sweet, but those unheard
  Are sweeter; therefore, ye soft pipes, play on;

Not to the sensual ear, but, more endeared,
Pipe to the spirit ditties of no tone:
15   Fair youth, beneath the trees, thou canst not leave
Thy song, nor ever can those trees be bare;
Bold Lover, never, never canst thou kiss,
Though winning near the goal—yet, do not grieve;
She cannot fade, though thou hast not thy bliss,
20   For ever wilt thou love, and she be fair!

3

Ah, happy, happy boughs! that cannot shed
Your leaves, nor ever bid the spring adieu;
And, happy melodist, unwearièd,
For ever piping songs for ever new;
25   More happy love! more happy, happy love!
For ever warm and still to be enjoyed,
For ever panting, and for ever young;
All breathing human passion far above,
That leaves a heart high-sorrowful and cloyed,
30   A burning forehead, and a parching tongue.

4

Who are these coming to the sacrifice?
To what green altar, O mysterious priest,
Lead'st thou that heifer lowing at the skies,
And all her silken flanks with garlands drest?
35   What little town by river or sea shore,
Or mountain-built with peaceful citadel,
Is emptied of this folk, this pious morn?
And, little town, thy streets for evermore
Will silent be; and not a soul to tell
40   Why thou art desolate, can e'er return.

5

O Attic shape! Fair attitude! with brede
Of marble men and maidens overwrought,
With forest branches and the trodden weed;
Thou, silent form, dost tease us out of thought
45   As doth eternity: Cold Pastoral!
When old age shall this generation waste,
Thou shalt remain, in midst of other woe
Than ours, a friend to man, to whom thou say'st,

41–42. *brede . . . overwrought* ornamented with a pattern.

Beauty is truth, truth beauty,—that is all
Ye know on earth, and all ye need to know.   50

Percy Bysshe Shelley 1792–1822

Ozymandias

I met a traveller from an antique land
Who said: Two vast and trunkless legs of stone
Stand in the desert . . . Near them, on the sand,
Half sunk, a shattered visage lies, whose frown,
And wrinkled lip, and sneer of cold command,   5
Tell that its sculptor well those passions read
Which yet survive, stamped on these lifeless things,
The hand that mocked them, and the heart that fed:
And on the pedestal these words appear:
"My name is Ozymandias, king of kings: 10
Look on my works, ye Mighty, and despair!"
Nothing beside remains. Round the decay
Of that colossal wreck, boundless and bare
The lone and level sands stretch far away.

Ozymandias Rameses II of Egypt, 13th century B.C. A Greek historian wrote that Egypt's largest statue had the inscription: "I am Ozymandias, king of kings; if anyone wishes to know what I am and where I lie, let him surpass me in some of my exploits."

Ode to the West Wind

I

O wild West Wind, thou breath of Autumn's being,
Thou, from whose unseen presence the leaves dead
Are driven, like ghosts from an enchanter fleeing,

Yellow, and black, and pale, and hectic red,
Pestilence-stricken multitudes: O thou,   5
Who chariotest to their dark wintry bed

Wind The word often carries associated meanings of breath, soul, and spirit. **4.** *hectic* feverish.

The wingéd seeds, where they lie cold and low,
Each like a corpse within its grave, until
Thine azure sister of the Spring shall blow

10   Her clarion o'er the dreaming earth, and fill
(Driving sweet buds like flocks to feed in air)
With living hues and odors plain and hill:

Wild Spirit, which art moving everywhere;
Destroyer and preserver; hear, oh, hear!

II

15   Thou on whose stream, mid the steep sky's commotion,
Loose clouds like earth's decaying leaves are shed,
Shook from the tangled boughs of Heaven and Ocean,

Angels of rain and lightning: there are spread
On the blue surface of thine aëry surge,
20   Like the bright hair uplifted from the head

Of some fierce Maenad, even from the dim verge
Of the horizon to the zenith's height,
The locks of the approaching storm. Thou dirge

Of the dying year, to which this closing night
25   Will be the dome of a vast sepulchre,
Vaulted with all thy congregated might

Of vapors, from whose solid atmosphere
Black rain, and fire, and hail will burst: oh, hear!

III

Thou who didst waken from his summer dreams
30   The blue Mediterranean, where he lay,
Lulled by the coil of his crystálline streams,

Beside a pumice isle in Baiae's bay,
And saw in sleep old palaces and towers
Quivering within the wave's intenser day,

35   All overgrown with azure moss and flowers
So sweet, the sense faints picturing them! Thou
For whose path the Atlantic's level powers

Cleave themselves into chasms, while far below
The sea-blooms and the oozy woods which wear
The sapless foliage of the ocean, know   40

Thy voice, and suddenly grow gray with fear,
And tremble and despoil themselves: oh, hear!

IV

If I were a dead leaf thou mightest bear,
If I were a swift cloud to fly with thee;
A wave to pant beneath thy power, and share   45

The impulse of thy strength, only less free
Than thou, O uncontrollable! If even
I were as in my boyhood, and could be

The comrade of thy wanderings over Heaven,
As then, when to outstrip thy skyey speed   50
Scarce seemed a vision; I would ne'er have striven

As thus with thee in prayer in my sore need.
Oh, lift me as a wave, a leaf, a cloud!
I fall upon the thorns of life! I bleed!

A heavy weight of hours has chained and bowed   55
One too like thee; tameless, and swift, and proud.

V

Make me thy lyre, even as the forest is:
What if my leaves are falling like its own!
The tumult of thy mighty harmonies

Will take from both a deep, autumnal tone,   60
Sweet though in sadness. Be thou, Spirit fierce,
My spirit! Be thou me, impetuous one!

Drive my dead thoughts over the universe
Like withered leaves to quicken a new birth!
And, by the incantation of this verse,   65

39–42. *sea . . . themselves* "The vegetation at the bottom of the sea . . . sympathizes with that of the land in the change of season" (Shelley).   57. *lyre* The wind harp or Aeolian lyre responds to the wind with a musical chord.

Scatter, as from an unextinguished hearth
Ashes and sparks, my words among mankind!
Be through my lips to unawakened earth

The trumpet of a prophecy! O Wind,
70   If Winter comes, can Spring be far behind?

Alfred, Lord Tennyson 1809–1892

The Kraken

Below the thunders of the upper deep,
Far, far beneath in the abysmal sea,
His ancient, dreamless, uninvaded sleep
The Kraken sleepeth: faintest sunlights flee
5   About his shadowy sides; above him swell
Huge sponges of millennial growth and height;
And far away into the sickly light,
From many a wondrous grot and secret cell
Unnumber'd and enormous polypi
10   Winnow with giant arms the slumbering green.
There hath he lain for ages, and will lie
Battening upon huge sea-worms in his sleep,
Until the latter fire shall heat the deep;
Then once by man and angels to be seen,
15   In roaring he shall rise and on the surface die.

The Kraken a gigantic mythical sea beast.   9. *polypi* octopuses.   13. *fire* Cf. Revelation xvi. 3–9.

Ulysses

It little profits that an idle king,
By this still hearth, among these barren crags,
Matched with an aged wife, I mete and dole
Unequal laws unto a savage race,

Ulysses Homer's *Odyssey* celebrates the famous ten-year homeward voyage of Ulysses (Odysseus), king of Ithaca and hero of the Trojan wars.

That hoard, and sleep, and feed, and know not me. 5
I cannot rest from travel; I will drink
Life to the lees; all times I have enjoyed
Greatly, have suffered greatly, both with those
That loved me, and alone; on shore, and when
Through scudding drifts the rainy Hyades 10
Vexed the dim sea: I am become a name;
For always roaming with a hungry heart
Much have I seen and known; cities of men
And manners, climates, councils, governments,
Myself not least, but honored of them all; 15
And drunk delight of battle with my peers,
Far on the ringing plains of windy Troy.
I am a part of all that I have met;
Yet all experience is an arch wherethrough
Gleams that untraveled world, whose margin fades 20
Forever and forever when I move.
How dull it is to pause, to make an end,
To rust unburnished, not to shine in use!
As though to breathe were life. Life piled on life
Were all too little, and of one to me 25
Little remains; but every hour is saved
From that eternal silence, something more,
A bringer of new things; and vile it were
For some three suns to store and hoard myself,
And this gray spirit yearning in desire 30
To follow knowledge like a sinking star,
Beyond the utmost bound of human thought.
    This is my son, mine own Telemachus
To whom I leave the scepter and the isle—
Well-loved of me, discerning to fulfill 35
This labor, by slow prudence to make mild
A rugged people, and through soft degrees
Subdue them to the useful and the good.
Most blameless is he, centered in the sphere
Of common duties, decent not to fail 40
In offices of tenderness, and pay
Meet adoration to my household gods,
When I am gone. He works his work, I mine.
    There lies the port; the vessel puffs her sail;
There gloom the dark broad seas. My mariners, 45
Souls that have toiled, and wrought, and thought with me—
That ever with a frolic welcome took

The thunder and the sunshine, and opposed
Free hearts, free foreheads—you and I are old;
50   Old age hath yet his honor and his toil;
Death closes all; but something ere the end,
Some work of noble note, may yet be done,
Not unbecoming men that strove with gods.
The lights begin to twinkle from the rocks;
55   The long day wanes; the slow moon climbs; the deep
Moans round with many voices. Come, my friends,
'Tis not too late to seek a newer world.
Push off, and sitting well in order smite
The sounding furrows; for my purpose holds
60   To sail beyond the sunset, and the baths
Of all the western stars, until I die.
It may be that the gulfs will wash us down;
It may be we shall touch the Happy Isles,
And see the great Achilles, whom we knew.
65   Though much is taken, much abides; and though
We are not now that strength which in old days
Moved earth and heaven, that which we are, we are;
One equal temper of heroic hearts,
Made weak by time and fate, but strong in will
70   To strive, to seek, to find, and not to yield.

61. *stars* In Greek mythology, the stars descended into an outer ocean which surrounded the flat circle of the earth.   63. *Happy Isles* Elysium, reserved for heroes after death.

Robert Browning 1812–1889

My Last Duchess

FERRARA

That's my last Duchess painted on the wall,
Looking as if she were alive. I call
That piece a wonder, now: Frà Pandolf's hands
Worked busily a day, and there she stands.
5   Will't please you sit and look at her? I said

My Last Duchess The model for the duke in the poem is probably Alfonso II, Duke of Ferrara in the 16th century.   3. *Frà Pandolf* an imaginary friar and artist.

"Frà Pandolf" by design, for never read
Strangers like you that pictured countenance,
The depth and passion of its earnest glance,
But to myself they turned (since none puts by
The curtain I have drawn for you, but I)   10
And seemed as they would ask me, if they durst,
How such a glance came there; so, not the first
Are you to turn and ask thus. Sir, 'twas not
Her husband's presence only, called that spot
Of joy into the Duchess' cheek: perhaps   15
Frà Pandolf chanced to say "Her mantle laps
Over my Lady's wrist too much," or "Paint
Must never hope to reproduce the faint
Half-flush that dies along her throat,": such stuff
Was courtesy, she thought, and cause enough   20
For calling up that spot of joy. She had
A heart—how shall I say?—too soon made glad,
Too easily impressed; she liked whate'er
She looked on, and her looks went everywhere.
Sir, 'twas all one! My favour at her breast,   25
The dropping of the daylight in the West.
The bough of cherries some officious fool
Broke in the orchard for her, the white mule
She rode with round the terrace—all and each
Would draw from her alike the approving speech,   30
Or blush, at least. She thanked men,—good; but thanked
Somehow—I know not how—as if she ranked
My gift of a nine-hundred-years-old name
With anybody's gift. Who'd stoop to blame
This sort of trifling? Even had you skill   35
In speech—(which I have not)—to make your will
Quite clear to such an one, and say, "Just this
Or that in you disgusts me; here you miss,
Or there exceed the mark"—and if she let
Herself be lessoned so, nor plainly set   40
Her wits to yours, forsooth, and made excuse,
—E'en then would be some stooping, and I choose
Never to stoop. Oh, Sir, she smiled, no doubt,
Whene'er I passed her; but who passed without
Much the same smile? This grew; I gave commands;   45

13. *Sir* the ambassador of Ferdinand II, Count of Tyrol, whose sister Barbara the Duke
wishes to marry. 45–46. Browning once explained that she might have been placed in a
convent or killed.

Then all smiles stopped together. There she stands
As if alive. Will't please you rise? We'll meet
The company below, then. I repeat,
The Count your Master's known munificence
50   Is ample warrant that no just pretence
Of mine for dowry will be disallowed;
Though his fair daughter's self, as I avowed
At starting, is my object. Nay, we'll go
Together down, Sir! Notice Neptune, though,
55   Taming a sea-horse, thought a rarity,
Which Claus of Innsbruck cast in bronze for me.

56. *Claus* an imaginary artist.

The Bishop Orders His Tomb at Saint Praxed's Church

ROME, 15—

Vanity, saith the preacher, vanity!
Draw round my bed: is Anselm keeping back?
Nephews—sons mine . . . ah God, I know not! Well—
She, men would have to be your mother once,
5   Old Gandolf envied me, so fair she was!
What's done is done, and she is dead beside,
Dead long ago, and I am Bishop since,
And as she died so must we die ourselves,
And thence ye may perceive the world's a dream.
10   Life, how and what is it? As here I lie
In this state chamber, dying by degrees,
Hours and long hours in the dead night, I ask
"Do I live, am I dead?" Peace, peace seems all.
Saint Praxed's ever was the church for peace;
15   And so, about this tomb of mine. I fought
With tooth and nail to save my niche, ye know:
—Old Gandolf cozened mė, despite my care;
Shrewd was that snatch from out the corner south
He graced his carrion with, God curse the same!
20   Yet still my niche is not so cramped but thence
One sees the pulpit o' the epistle side,
And somewhat of the choir, those silent seats,
And up into the aery dome where live

Church Church of S. Prassede in Rome, remarkable for its mosaics. 1. V*anity* C
Ecclesiastes i.2: "All is vanity." 3. *Nephews* common euphemism for sons of Renai
sance churchmen. 21. *epistle side* to the right of the altar.

The angels, and a sunbeam's sure to lurk:
And I shall fill my slab of basalt there,   25
And 'neath my tabernacle take my rest,
With those nine columns round me, two and two,
The odd one at my feet where Anselm stands:
Peach-blossom marble all, the rare, the ripe
As fresh-poured red wine of a mighty pulse.   30
—Old Gandolf with his paltry onion-stone,
Put me where I may look at him! True peach,
Rosy and flawless: how I earned the prize!
Draw close: that conflagration of my church
—What then? So much was saved if aught were missed!   35
My sons, ye would not be my death? Go dig
The white-grape vineyard where the oil-press stood,
Drop water gently till the surface sink,
And if ye find . . . Ah God, I know not, I! . . .
Bedded in store of rotten fig leaves soft,   40
And corded up in a tight olive-frail,
Some lump, ah God, of *lapis lazuli*,
Big as a Jew's head cut off at the nape,
Blue as a vein o'er the Madonna's breast . . .
Sons, all have I bequeathed you, villas, all,   45
That brave Frascati villa with its bath,
So, let the blue lump poise between my knees,
Like God the Father's globe on both his hands
Ye worship in the Jesu Church so gay,
For Gandolf shall not choose but see and burst!   50
Swift as a weaver's shuttle fleet our years:
Man goeth to the grave, and where is he?
Did I say basalt for my slab, sons? Black—
'Twas ever antique-black I meant! How else
Shall ye contrast my frieze to come beneath?   55
The bas-relief in bronze ye promised me,
Those Pans and Nymphs ye wot of, and perchance
Some tripod, thyrsus, with a vase or so,
The Saviour at his sermon on the mount,
Saint Praxed in a glory, and one Pan   60
Ready to twitch the Nymph's last garment off,
And Moses with the tables . . . but I know

26. *tabernacle* canopy.   30. *pulse* strength.   31. *onion-stone* marble made of thin layers.
41. *olive-frail* olive basket.   46. *Frascati* hill town near Rome with splendid villas.
49. *Jesu* Il Jesu, Jesuit church in Rome.   51. *Swift . . . years* Cf. Job vii. 6.   58. *tripod*
a Greek three-legged vessel; *thyrsus* a staff carried by followers of Bacchus.   62. *Moses
. . . tables* Cf. Exodus xxiv.

Ye mark me not! What do they whisper thee,
Child of my bowels, Anselm? Ah, ye hope
65   To revel down my villas while I gasp
Bricked o'er with beggar's moldy travertine
Which Gandolf from his tomb-top chuckles at!
Nay, boys, ye love me—all of jasper, then!
'Tis jasper ye stand pledged to, lest I grieve
70   My bath must needs be left behind, alas!
One block, pure green as a pistachio nut,
There's plenty jasper somewhere in the world—
And have I not Saint Praxed's ear to pray
Horses for ye, and brown Greek manuscripts,
75   And mistresses with great smooth marbly limbs?
—That's if ye carve my epitaph aright,
Choice Latin, picked phrase, Tully's every word,
No gaudy ware like Gandolf's second line—
Tully, my masters? Ulpian serves his need!
80   And then how I shall lie through centuries,
And hear the blessed mutter of the mass,
And see God made and eaten all day long,
And feel the steady candle flame, and taste
Good strong thick stupefying incense-smoke!
85   For as I lie here, hours of the dead night,
Dying in state and by such slow degrees,
I fold my arms as if they clasped a crook,
And stretch my feet forth straight as stone can point,
And let the bedclothes, for a mortcloth, drop
90   Into great laps and folds of sculptor's-work:
And as yon tapers dwindle, and strange thoughts
Grow, with a certain humming in my ears,
About the life before I lived this life,
And this life too, popes, cardinals, and priests,
95   Saint Praxed at his sermon on the mount,
Your tall pale mother with her talking eyes,
And new-found agate urns as fresh as day,
And marble's language, Latin pure, discreet
—Aha, ELUCESCEBAT quoth our friend?
100   No Tully, said I, Ulpian at the best!
Evil and brief hath been my pilgrimage.

77. *Tully* Marcus Tullius Cicero, master of the best Latin style.   79. *Ulpian* Dominius Ulpianus, whose style was regarded as degenerate.   82. *God . . . eaten* reference to the conversion of the bread into the body of Christ in the Mass.   87. *crook* a crozier, symbol of episcopal rank.   89. *mortcloth* cloth to cover the dead.   99. *Elucescebat* "he was famous."

All *lapis*, all, sons! Else I give the Pope
My villas! Will ye ever eat my heart?
Ever your eyes were as a lizard's quick,
They glitter like your mother's for my soul,   105
Or ye would heighten my impoverished frieze,
Piece out its starved design, and fill my vase
With grapes, and add a vizor and a Term,
And to the tripod ye would tie a lynx
That in his struggle throws the thyrsus down,   110
To comfort me on my entablature
Whereon I am to lie till I must ask
"Do I live, am I dead?" There, leave me, there!
For ye have stabbed me with ingratitude
To death—ye wish it—God, ye wish it! Stone—   115
Gritstone, a-crumble! Clammy squares which sweat
As if the corpse they keep were oozing through—
And no more *lapis* to delight the world!
Well go! I bless ye. Fewer tapers there,
But in a row: and, going, turn your backs   120
—Aye, like departing altar-ministrants,
And leave me in my church, the church for peace,
That I may watch at leisure if he leers—
Old Gandolf, at me, from his onion-stone,
As still he envied me, so fair she was!   125

108. *vizor* mask; *Term* a pillar adorned with a head or bust.

Matthew Arnold 1822–1888

Shakespeare

Others abide our question. Thou art free.
We ask and ask—Thou smilest and art still,
Out-topping knowledge. For the loftiest hill,
Who to the stars uncrowns his majesty,

Planting his steadfast footsteps in the sea,   5
Making the heaven of heavens his dwelling place,

Spares but the cloudy border of his base
To the foiled searching of mortality;

And thou, who didst the stars and sunbeams know,
10   Self-schooled, self-scanned, self-honored, self-secure,
Didst tread on earth unguessed at.—Better so!

All pains the immortal spirit must endure,
All weakness which impairs, all griefs which bow,
Find their sole speech in that victorious brow.

Dover Beach

The sea is calm tonight.
The tide is full, the moon lies fair
Upon the straits—on the French coast the light
Gleams and is gone; the cliffs of England stand,
5   Glimmering and vast, out in the tranquil bay.
Come to the window, sweet is the night air!
Only, from the long line of spray
Where the sea meets the moon-blanched land,
Listen! you hear the grating roar
10   Of pebbles which the waves draw back, and fling,
At their return, up the high strand,
Begin, and cease, and then again begin,
With tremulous cadence slow, and bring
The eternal note of sadness in.

15   Sophocles long ago
Heard it on the Aegean, and it brought
Into his mind the turbid ebb and flow
Of human misery; we
Find also in the sound a thought,
20   Hearing it by this distant northern sea.

The Sea of Faith
Was once, too, at the full, and round earth's shore
Lay like the folds of a bright girdle furled.
But now I only hear
25   Its melancholy, long, withdrawing roar,

15. *Sophocles* In his tragedy *Antigone* (lines 583ff.) the Greek dramatist recounts the
fate of the house of Oedipus.

Retreating, to the breath
Of the night wind, down the vast edges drear
And naked shingles of the world.

Ah, love, let us be true
To one another! for the world, which seems   30
To lie before us like a land of dreams,
So various, so beautiful, so new,
Hath really neither joy, nor love, nor light,
Nor certitude, nor peace, nor help for pain;
And we are here as on a darkling plain   35
Swept with confused alarms of struggle and flight,
Where ignorant armies clash by night.

28. *shingles* pebbly beaches.

George Meredith 1828–1909

From *Modern Love*

XLIII

Mark where the pressing wind shoots javelin-like,
Its skeleton shadow on the broad-backed wave!
Here is a fitting spot to dig Love's grave;
Here where the ponderous breakers plunge and strike,
And dart their hissing tongues high up the sand: 5
In hearing of the ocean, and in sight
Of those ribbed wind-streaks running into white.
If I the death of Love had deeply planned,
I never could have made it half so sure,
As by the unblest kisses which upbraid   10
The full-waked senses; or failing that, degrade!
'Tis morning: but no morning can restore
What we have forfeited. I see no sin:
The wrong is mixed. In tragic life, God wot,
No villain need be! Passions spin the plot: 15
We are betrayed by what is false within.

Lucifer in Starlight

On a starred night Prince Lucifer uprose.
Tired of his dark dominion swung the fiend
Above the rolling ball in cloud part screened,
Where sinners hugged their spectre of repose.
5   Poor prey to his hot fit of pride were those.
And now upon his western wing he leaned,
Now his huge bulk o'er Afric's sands careened,
Now the black planet shadowed Arctic snows.
Soaring through wider zones that pricked his scars
10   With memory of the old revolt from Awe,
He reached a middle height, and at the stars,
Which are the brain of heaven, he looked, and sank.
Around the ancient track marched, rank on rank,
The army of unalterable law.

Walt Whitman 1819–1892

A Sight in Camp in the Daybreak Gray and Dim

A sight in camp in the daybreak gray and dim,
As from my tent I emerge so early sleepless,
As slow I walk in the cool fresh air the path near by the hospital tent,
Three forms I see on stretchers lying, brought out there untended lying,
5   Over each the blanket spread, ample brownish woolen blanket,
Gray and heavy blanket, folding, covering all.

Curious I halt and silent stand,
Then with light fingers I from the face of the nearest the first just
   lift the blanket;
Who are you elderly man so gaunt and grim, with well-gray'd hair,
   and flesh all sunken about the eyes?
10   Who are you my dear comrade?

A *Sight in Camp* The poem refers to an experience in the Civil War.

Then to the second I step—and who are you my child and darling?
Who are you sweet boy with cheeks yet blooming?

Then to the third—a face nor child nor old, very calm, as of beautiful
yellow-white ivory;
Young man I think I know you—I think this face is the face of the
Christ himself,
Dead and divine and brother of all, and here again he lies.   15

A Noiseless Patient Spider

A noiseless patient spider,
I mark'd where on a little promontory it stood isolated,
Mark'd how to explore the vacant vast surrounding,
It launch'd forth filament, filament, filament, out of itself,
Ever unreeling them, ever tirelessly speeding them.   5

And you O my soul where you stand,
Surrounded, detached, in measureless oceans of space,
Ceaselessly musing, venturing, throwing, seeking the spheres to con-
nect them,
Till the bridge you will need be form'd, till the ductile anchor hold,
Till the gossamer thread you fling catch somewhere, O my soul.   10

Emily Dickinson   1830–1886

I taste a liquor never brewed

I taste a liquor never brewed—
From Tankards scooped in Pearl—
Not all the Frankfort Berries
Yield such an Alcohol!
Inebriate of Air—am I—   5
And Debauchee of Dew—
Reeling—thro endless summer days—
From inns of Molten Blue—
When "Landlords" turn the drunken Bee

10 Out of the Foxglove's door—
When Butterflies—renounce their "drams"—
I shall but drink the more!
Till Seraphs swing their snowy Hats—
And Saints—to windows run—
15 To see the little Tippler
From Manzanilla come!

16. *Manzanilla* a flower of the camomile family; also a sherry. Another version of the line reads "Leaning against the sun!"

The Soul selects her own Society

The Soul selects her own Society—
Then—shuts the Door—
To her divine Majority—
Present no more—
5 Unmoved—she notes the Chariots—pausing—
At her low Gate—
Unmoved—an Emperor be kneeling
Upon her Mat—
I've known her—from an ample nation—
10 Choose One—
Then—close the Valves of her attention—
Like Stone—

3–4. *To . . . more* These lines are usually printed in another version: "On her divine majority/Obtrude no more."

———

I heard a Fly buzz—when I died

I heard a Fly buzz—when I died—
The Stillness in the Room
Was like the Stillness in the Air—
Between the Heaves of Storm—
5 The Eyes around—had wrung them dry—
And Breaths were gathering firm
For that last Onset—when the King
Be witnessed—in the Room—
I willed my Keepsakes—Signed away
10 What portion of me be
Assignable—and then it was
There interposed a Fly—

With Blue—uncertain stumbling Buzz—
Between the light—and me—
And then the Windows failed—and then   15
I could not see to see—

●

I like to see it lap the Miles

I like to see it lap the Miles—
And lick the Valleys up—
And stop to feed itself at Tauks—
And then—prodigious step
Around a Pile of Mountains—   5
And supercilious peer
In Shanties—by the sides of Roads—
And then a Quarry pare
To fit its sides
And crawl between   10
Complaining all the while
In horrid—hooting stanza—
Then chase itself down Hill—
And neigh like Boanerges—
Then—prompter than a Star   15
Stop—docile and omnipotent
At its own stable door—

14. *Boanerges* A surname meaning "sons of thunder," given by Christ to James and John (Mark iii.17). 15. *prompter . . . Star* Another version reads "punctual as a Star."

Gerard Manley Hopkins 1844–1889

God's Grandeur

The world is charged with the grandeur of God.
    It will flame out, like shining from shook foil;
    It gathers to a greatness, like the ooze of oil

2. *foil* "I mean foil in its sense of leaf or tinsel . . . Shaken goldfoil gives off broad glows like sheet lightning . . ." (Hopkins).

Crushed. Why do men then now not reck his rod?
5 Generations have trod, have trod, have trod;
    And all is seared with trade; bleared, smeared with toil;
    And wears man's smudge and shares man's smell: the soil
Is bare now, nor can foot feel, being shod.

And for all this, nature is never spent;
10   There lives the dearest freshness deep down things;
And though the last lights off the black West went
    Oh, morning, at the brown brink eastward, springs—
Because the Holy Ghost over the bent
    World broods with warm breast and with ah! bright wings.

Pied Beauty

Glory be to God for dappled things—
    For skies of couple-color as a brinded cow;
        For rose-moles all in stipple upon trout that swim;
Fresh-firecoal chestnut-falls; finches' wings;
5   Landscape plotted and pieced—fold, fallow, and plough;
        And áll trádes, their gear and tackle and trim.

All things counter, original, spare, strange;
    Whatever is fickle, freckled (who knows how?)
        With swift, slow; sweet, sour; adazzle, dim;
10   He fathers-forth whose beauty is past change:
            Praise him.

2. *brinded* brindled, streaked. 3. *stipple* dots or spots. 4. *chestnut-falls* roasted chestnuts stripped of their husks. 5. *fold* enclosure for animals; *fallow* field plowed but not seeded. 6. *trim* equipment.

The Windhover

TO CHRIST OUR LORD
        I caught this morning morning's minion, kingdom of daylight's
            dauphin, dapple-dawn-drawn Falcon, in his riding
        Of the rolling level underneath him steady air, and striding
        High there, how he rung upon the rein of a wimpling wing

Windhover the kestril, called "windhover" because it hovers in the air facing the wind. 4. *rung upon the rein* the curving flight of the bird is compared to the motion of a horse at the end of the trainer's rein; *wimpling* beautifully curved; swinging, fluttering.

In his ecstasy! then off, off forth on swing,   5
  As a skate's heel sweeps smooth on a bow-bend: the hurl and
    gliding
Rebuffed the big wind. My heart in hiding
Stirred for a bird,—the achieve of, the mastery of the thing!

Brute beauty and valor and act, oh, air, pride, plume, here
  Buckle! AND the fire that breaks from thee then, a billion   10
Times told lovelier, more dangerous, O my chevalier!

  No wonder of it: shéer plód makes plough down sillion
Shine, and blue-bleak embers, ah my dear,
  Fall, gall themselves, and gash gold-vermilion.

12. *sillion* furrow.

Spring and Fall

TO A YOUNG CHILD
  Márgarét, are you gríeving
  Over Goldengrove unleaving?
  Leáves, líke the things of man, you
  With your fresh thoughts care for, can you?
  Áh! ás the heart grows older   5
  It will come to such sights colder
  By and by, nor spare a sigh
  Though worlds of wanwood leafmeal lie;
  And yet you wíll weep and know why.
  Now no matter, child, the name: 10
  Sórrow's spríngs áre the same.
  Nor mouth had, no nor mind, expressed
  What heart heard of, ghost guessed:
  It ís the blight man was born for,
  It is Margaret you mourn for.   15

8. *leafmeal* Cf. "inchmeal." The line suggests leaves falling one by one, then rotting
to form pale fragments.   13. *ghost guessed* spirit foreknowing its state after death.
Cf. Genesis iii. 18.

[Carrion Comfort]

  Not, I'll not, carrion comfort, Despair, not feast on thee;
  Not untwist—slack they may be—these last strands of man

In me ór, most weary, cry *I can no more.* I can;
Can something, hope, wish day come, not choose not to be.
5   But ah, but O thou terrible, why wouldst thou rude on me
Thy wring-world right foot rock? lay a lionlimb against me? scan
With darksome devouring eyes my bruisèd bones? and fan,
O in turns of tempest, me heaped there; me frantic to avoid thee
and flee?

Why? That my chaff might fly; my grain lie, sheer and clear.
10   Nay in all that toil, that coil, since (seems) I kissed the rod,
Hand rather, my heart lo! lapped strength, stole joy, would laugh,
chéer.
Cheer whom though? the hero whose heaven-handling flung me,
fóot tród
Me? or me that fought him? O which one? is it each one? That night,
that year
Of now done darkness I wretch lay wrestling with (my God!) my
God.

10. *coil* disturbance.

No Worst, There Is None

No worst, there is none. Pitched past pitch of grief,
More pangs will, schooled at forepangs, wilder wring.
Comforter, where, where is your comforting?
Mary, mother of us, where is your relief?
5   My cries heave, herds-long, huddle in a main, a chief
Woe, world-sorrow; on an age-old anvil wince and sing—
Then lull, then leave off. Fury had shrieked "No lingering!
Let me be fell: force I must be brief."

O the mind, mind has mountains; cliffs of fall
10   Frightful, sheer, no-man-fathomed. Hold them cheap
May who ne'er hung there. Nor does long our small
Durance deal with that steep or deep. Here! creep,
Wretch, under a comfort serves in a whirlwind: all
Life death does end and each day dies with sleep.

5. *main . . . chief* adjectives modifying "Woe."   8. *fell: force* fierce: perforce.

Thomas Hardy 1840–1928

Neutral Tones

We stood by a pond that winter day,
And the sun was white, as though chidden of God,
And a few leaves lay on the starving sod;
    —They had fallen from an ash, and were gray.

Your eyes on me were as eyes that rove   5
Over tedious riddles of years ago;
And some words played between us to and fro
    On which lost the more by our love.

The smile on your mouth was the deadest thing
Alive enough to have strength to die;   10
And a grin of bitterness swept thereby
    Like an ominous bird a-wing. . . .

Since then, keen lessons that love deceives,
And wrings with wrong, have shaped to me
Your face, and the God-cursed sun, and a tree,   15
    And a pond edged with grayish leaves.

The Darkling Thrush

I leant upon a coppice gate
    When Frost was specter-gray,
And Winter's dregs made desolate
    The weakening eye of day.
The tangled bine-stems scored the sky   5
    Like strings of broken lyres,
And all mankind that haunted nigh
    Had sought their household fires.

Darkling in the dark. 1. *coppice* small wood or thicket. 5. *bine-stems* twining stems
of shrubs.

The land's sharp features seemed to be
    The Century's corpse outleant,
His crypt the cloudy canopy,
    The wind his death-lament.
The ancient pulse of germ and birth
    Was shrunken hard and dry,
And every spirit upon earth
    Seemed fervorless as I.

At once a voice arose among
    The bleak twigs overhead
In a full-hearted evensong
    Of joy illimited;
An aged thrush, frail, gaunt, and small,
    In blast-beruffled plume,
Had chosen thus to fling his soul
    Upon the growing gloom.

So little cause for carolings
    Of such ecstatic sound
Was written on terrestrial things
    Afar or nigh around,
That I could think there trembled through
    His happy good-night air
Some blessed Hope, whereof he knew
    And I was unaware.

10. *Century's corpse* This poem was written on the last day of the 19th century.

In Time of "The Breaking of Nations"

(Jeremiah li. 20)

Only a man harrowing clods
    In a slow silent walk
With an old horse that stumbles and nods
    Half asleep as they stalk.

Only thin smoke without flame
    From the heaps of couch-grass;
Yet this will go onward the same
    Though Dynasties pass.

In . . . Nations The poem was written during World War I.

Yonder a maid and her wight
  Come whispering by: 10
War's annals will fade into night
  Ere their story die.

William Butler Yeats 1865–1939

Two Songs from a Play

I

I saw a staring virgin stand
Where holy Dionysus died,
And tear the heart out of his side,
And lay the heart upon her hand
And bear that beating heart away;   5
And then did all the Muses sing
Of Magnus Annus at the spring,
As though God's death were but a play.

Another Troy must rise and set,
Another lineage feed the crow,   10
Another Argo's painted prow
Drive to a flashier bauble yet.
The Roman Empire stood appalled:
It dropped the reigns of peace and war
When that fierce virgin and her Star   15
Out of the fabulous darkness called.

II

In pity for man's darkening thought
He walked that room and issued thence
In Galilean turbulence;
The Babylonian starlight brought   20
A fabulous, formless darkness in;

7. *Magnus Annus* The Great Year refers to an astronomical cycle which is completed in 2000 years or more and marks the span of an historical, cultural, and religious epoch. 9. *Troy* Rome. Virgil's fourth *Eclogue*, once considered a prophecy of the birth of Christ, foresees another heroic voyage like that of Jason for the Golden Fleece. 13. *Roman Empire* during the balanced reign of Augustus (27 B.C.–A.D. 14).

Odour of blood when Christ was slain
Made all Platonic tolerance vain
And vain all Doric discipline.

25   Everything that man esteems
Endures a moment or a day.
Love's pleasure drives his love away,
The painter's brush consumes his dreams;
The herald's cry, the soldier's tread
30   Exhaust his glory and his might:
Whatever flames upon the night
Man's own resinous heart has fed.

32. *resinous* as in the pine torches which were carried by the women who worshiped Dionysus. The words of this stanza are echoed in Yeats's *Autobiography:* "Our love letters wear out our love; no school of painting outlasts its founders, every stroke of the brush exhausts the impulse. . . . Why should we believe that religion can never bring round its antithesis?"

The Magi

Now as at all times I can see in the mind's eye,
In their stiff, painted clothes, the pale unsatisfied ones
Appear and disappear in the blue depth of the sky
With all their ancient faces like rain-beaten stones,
5   And all their helms of silver hovering side by side,
And all their eyes still fixed, hoping to find once more,
Being by Calvary's turbulence unsatisfied,
The uncontrollable mystery on the bestial floor.

7. *Calvary's turbulence* Cf. "The Second Coming" and "Two Songs from a Play."

The Dolls

A doll in the doll-maker's house
Looks at the cradle and bawls:
"That is an insult to us."
But the oldest of all the dolls,
5   Who had seen, being kept for show,
Generations of his sort,

The Dolls Yeats writes of this and the previous poem: "I had noticed once again how all thought among us is frozen into 'something other than human life.' After I had made the poem, I looked up one day into the blue of the sky, and suddenly imagined, as if lost in the blue of the sky, stiff figures in procession." "The Magi" became "complementary forms of those enraged dolls."

Out-screams the whole shelf: "Although
There's not a man can report
Evil of this place,
The man and the woman bring   10
Hither, to our disgrace,
A noisy and filthy thing."
Hearing him groan and stretch
The doll-maker's wife is aware
Her husband has heard the wretch,   15
And crouched by the arm of his chair,
She murmurs into his ear,
Head upon shoulder leant:
"My dear, my dear, O dear,
It was an accident."   20

The Second Coming

Turning and turning in the widening gyre
The falcon cannot hear the falconer;
Things fall apart; the center cannot hold;
Mere anarchy is loosed upon the world,
The blood-dimmed tide is loosed, and everywhere   5
The ceremony of innocence is drowned;
The best lack all conviction, while the worst
Are full of passionate intensity.

Surely some revelation is at hand;
Surely the Second Coming is at hand.   10
The Second Coming! Hardly are those words out
When a vast image out of *Spiritus Mundi*
Troubles my sight: somewhere in sands of the desert
A shape with lion body and the head of a man,
A gaze blank and pitiless as the sun,   15
Is moving its slow thighs, while all about it
Reel shadows of the indignant desert birds.
The darkness drops again; but now I know
That twenty centuries of stony sleep
Were vexed to nightmare by a rocking cradle,   20
And what rough beast, its hour come round at last,
Slouches towards Bethlehem to be born?

1. *gyre* (pronounced with a hard *g*) a spiraling turn; a cone.   12. *Spiritus Mundi* spirit
of the world or universe.

Sailing to Byzantium

1

That is no country for old men. The young
In one another's arms, birds in the trees
—Those dying generations—at their song,
The salmon-falls, the mackerel-crowded seas,
5   Fish, flesh, or fowl, commend all summer long
Whatever is begotten, born, and dies.
Caught in that sensual music all neglect
Monuments of unaging intellect.

2

An aged man is but a paltry thing,
10   A tattered coat upon a stick, unless
Soul clap its hands and sing, and louder sing
For every tatter in its mortal dress,
Nor is there singing school but studying
Monuments of its own magnificence;
15   And therefore I have sailed the seas and come
To the holy city of Byzantium.

3

O sages standing in God's holy fire
As in the gold mosaic of a wall,
Come from the holy fire, perne in a gyre,
20   And be the singing-masters of my soul.
Consume my heart away; sick with desire
And fastened to a dying animal
It knows not what it is; and gather me
Into the artifice of eternity.

4

25   Once out of nature I shall never take
My bodily form from any natural thing,
But such a form as Grecian goldsmiths make
Of hammered gold and gold enameling

Byzantium capital of the Eastern Roman Empire, the "holy city" of the Greek Orthodox Church, and the chief example for Yeats of a world in which intellect, art, and life were unified. 17. *sages* holy men, like figures in the mosaics of Hagia Sophia ("Holy Wisdom") in Byzantium. 19. *perne in a gyre* i.e., whirl round in a spiral motion. 27. *form* Yeats writes that in the Emperor's palace in Byzantium there "was a tree made of gold and silver, and artificial birds that sang."

To keep a drowsy Emperor awake;
Or set upon a golden bough to sing   30
To lords and ladies of Byzantium
Of what is past, or passing, or to come.

Byzantium

The unpurged images of day recede;
The Emperor's drunken soldiery are abed;
Night resonance recedes, night-walkers' song
After great cathedral gong;
A starlit or a moonlit dome disdains   5
All that man is,
All mere complexities,
The fury and the mire of human veins.

Before me floats an image, man or shade,
Shade more than man, more image than a shade;   10
For Hades' bobbin bound in mummy-cloth
May unwind the winding path;
A mouth that has no moisture and no breath
Breathless mouths may summon;
I hail the superhuman;   15
I call it death-in-life and life-in-death.

Miracle, bird or golden handiwork,
More miracle than bird or handiwork,
Planted on the star-lit golden bough,
Can like the cocks of Hades crow,   20
Or, by the moon embittered, scorn aloud
In glory of changeless metal
Common bird or petal
And all complexities of mire or blood.

Byzantium In *A Vision*, Yeats writes that in Byzantium (later Constantinople, now Istanbul) "religious, aesthetic and practical life were one . . . architect and artificers . . . spoke to the multitude and the few alike." He refers to "the work of many that seemed the work of one, that made building, picture, pattern, metal-work . . . seem but a single image." 5. *starlit . . . moonlit* images in Yeats's system of states of being rather than of becoming or change. 9. *image* the guide who will lead the spirits to a state of purification. 11. *Hades' bobbin* Associated with the wrappings around a mummy, the unwinding spool of man's fate may lead him to the realm of spirit. 20. *cocks of Hades* the eternal birds who proclaim the cycles of rebirth, to whom the golden birds of art are compared.

25   At midnight on the Emperor's pavement flit
Flames that no faggot feeds, nor steel has lit,
Nor storm disturbs, flames begotten of flame,
Where blood-begotten spirits come
And all complexities of fury leave,
30   Dying into a dance,
An agony of trance,
An agony of flame that cannot singe a sleeve.

Astraddle on the dophin's mire and blood,
Spirit after spirit! The smithies break the flood,
35   The golden smithies of the Emperor!
Marbles of the dancing floor
Break bitter furies of complexity,
Those images that yet
Fresh images beget,
40   That dolphin-torn, that gong-tormented sea.

32. *cannot . . . sleeve* i.e., because these flames are not earthly.

A Dialogue of Self and Soul

1

My Soul. I summon to the winding ancient stair;
Set all your mind upon the steep ascent,
Upon the broken, crumbling battlement,
Upon the breathless starlit air,
5   Upon the star that marks the hidden pole;
Fix every wandering thought upon
That quarter where all thought is done:
Who can distinguish darkness from the soul?

My Self. The consecrated blade upon my knees
10   Is Sato's ancient blade, still as it was,
Still razor-keen, still like a looking-glass
Unspotted by the centuries;
That flowering, silken, old embroidery, torn
From some court-lady's dress and round
15   The wooden scabbard bound and wound,
Can, tattered, still protect, faded adorn.

10. *Sato's . . . blade* This sword was given to Yeats by a Japanese named Sato. It and its embroidered scabbard are seen as "Emblematical" in l. 19.

My Soul. Why should the imagination of a man
    Long past his prime remember things that are
    Emblematical of love and war?
    Think of ancestral night that can,   20
    If but imagination scorn the earth
    And intellect its wandering
    To this and that and t'other thing,
    Deliver from the crime of death and birth.

My Self. Montashigi, third of his family, fashioned it   25
    Five hundred years ago, about it lie
    Flowers from I know not what embroidery—
    Heart's purple—and all these I set
    For emblems of the day against the tower
    Emblematical of the night,   30
    And claim as by a soldier's right
    A charter to commit the crime once more.

My Soul. Such fullness in that quarter overflows
    And falls into the basin of the mind
    That man is stricken deaf and dumb and blind,   35
    For intellect no longer knows
    Is from the *Ought,* or *Knower* from the *Known*—
    That is to say, ascends to Heaven;
    Only the dead can be forgiven;
    But when I think of that my tongue's a stone.   40

    2
My Self.   A living man is blind and drinks his drop.
    What matter if the ditches are impure?
    What matter if I live it all once more?
    Endure that toil of growing up;
    The ignominy of boyhood; the distress   45
    Of boyhood changing into man;
    The unfinished man and his pain
    Brought face to face with his own clumsiness;

    The finished man among his enemies?—
    How in the name of Heaven can he escape   50
    That defiling and disfigured shape
    The mirror of malicious eyes
    Casts upon his eyes until at last
    He thinks that shape must be his shape?

55   And what's the good of an escape
        If honour find him in the wintry blast?

        I am content to live it all again
        And yet again, if it be life to pitch
        Into the frog-spawn of a blind man's ditch,
60   A blind man battering blind men;
        Or into that most fecund ditch of all,
        The folly that man does
        Or must suffer, if he woos
        A proud woman not kindred of his soul.

65   I am content to follow to its source,
        Every event in action or in thought;
        Measure the lot; forgive myself the lot!
        When such as I cast out remorse
        So great a sweetness flows into the breast
70   We must laugh and we must sing,
        We are blest by everything,
        Everything we look upon is blest.

A Prayer for My Daughter

        Once more the storm is howling, and half hid
        Under this cradle-hood and coverlid
        My child sleeps on. There is no obstacle
        But Gregory's wood and one bare hill
5   Whereby the haystack- and roof-leveling wind,
        Bred on the Atlantic, can be stayed;
        And for an hour I have walked and prayed
        Because of the great gloom that is in my mind.

        I have walked and prayed for this young child an hour
10   And heard the sea-wind scream upon the tower,
        And under the arches of the bridge, and scream
        In the elms above the flooded stream;
        Imagining in excited reverie
        That the future years had come,
15   Dancing to a frenzied drum,
        Out of the murderous innocence of the sea.

Daughter Yeats's daughter was born in Ballylee Castle (near Coole Park) where Yeats lived in Galway.

May she be granted beauty and yet not
Beauty to make a stranger's eye distraught,
Or hers before a looking-glass, for such,
Being made beautiful overmuch,   20
Consider beauty a sufficient end,
Lose natural kindness and maybe
The heart-revealing intimacy
That chooses right, and never find a friend.

Helen being chosen found life flat and dull   25
And later had much trouble from a fool,
While that great Queen, that rose out of the spray,
Being fatherless could have her way
Yet chose a bandy-leggèd smith for man.
It's certain that fine women eat   30
A crazy salad with their meat
Whereby the Horn of Plenty is undone.

In courtesy I'd have her chiefly learned;
Hearts are not had as a gift but hearts are earned
By those that are not entirely beautiful;
Yet many, that have played the fool   35
For beauty's very self, has charm made wise,
And many a poor man that has roved,
Loved and thought himself beloved,
From a glad kindness cannot take his eyes.   40

May she become a flourishing hidden tree
That all her thoughts may like the linnet be,
And have no business but dispensing round
Their magnanimities of sound,
Nor but in merriment begin a chase,   45
Nor but in merriment a quarrel.
O may she live like some green laurel
Rooted in one dear perpetual place.

My mind, because the minds that I have loved,
The sort of beauty that I have approved,   50
Prosper but little, has dried up of late,
Yet knows that to be choked with hate
May well be of all evil chances chief.

26. *fool* Paris, who stole Helen from her husband. 27. *Queen* Aphrodite, goddess of
love and wife of Hephaestus, the lame god of the forge.

If there's no hatred in a mind
55   Assault and battery of the wind
Can never tear the linnet from the leaf.

An intellectual hatred is the worst,
So let her think opinions are accursed.
Have I not seen the loveliest woman born
60   Out of the mouth of Plenty's horn,
Because of her opinionated mind
Barter that horn and every good
By quiet natures understood
For an old bellows full of angry wind?

65   Considering that, all hatred driven hence,
The soul recovers radical innocence
And learns at last that it is self-delighting,
Self-appeasing, self-affrighting,
And that its own sweet will is Heaven's will;
70   She can, though every face should scowl
And every windy quarter howl
Or every bellows burst, be happy still.

And may her bridegroom bring her to a house
75   Where all's accustomed, ceremonious;
For arrogance and hatred are the wares
Peddled in the thoroughfares.
How but in custom and in ceremony
Are innocence and beauty born?
80   Ceremony's a name for the rich horn,
And custom for the spreading laurel tree.

Leda and the Swan

A sudden blow: the great wings beating still
Above the staggering girl, her thighs caressed
By the dark webs, her nape caught in his bill,
He holds her helpless breast upon his breast.

Leda . . . Swan When ravished by Zeus in the form of a swan, Leda gave birth to Helen of Troy and (according to one tradition) Clytemnestra, wife of Agamemnon, leader of the Greek expedition against Troy. Helen's elopement with the Trojan Paris initiated the war. Agamemnon was murdered by his wife after his glorious return from the destruction of Troy ("broken wall . . . tower").

How can those terrified vague fingers push   5
The feathered glory from her loosening thighs?
And how can body, laid in that white rush,
But feel the strange heart beating where it lies?
A shudder in the loins engenders there
The broken wall, the burning roof and tower   10
And Agamemnon dead.
                  Being so caught up,
So mastered by the brute blood of the air,
Did she put on his knowledge with his power
Before the indifferent beak could let her drop?   15

Leda and the Swan

(THREE EARLIER VERSIONS)

I

Now can the swooping godhead have his will
Yet hovers, though her helpless thighs are pressed
By the webbed toes; and that all powerful bill
Has suddenly bowed her face upon his breast.

How can those terrified vague fingers push   5
The feathered glory from her loosening thighs?
All the stretched body's laid in that white rush
And feels the strange heart beating where it lies.
A shudder in the loins engenders there
The broken wall, the burning roof and Tower   10
And Agamemnon dead. . . .
                 Being so caught up
Did nothing pass before her in the air?
Did she put on his knowledge with his power
Before the indifferent beak could let her drop?   15

II

The swooping godhead is half hovering still
Yet climbs upon her trembling body pressed
By the webbed toes; and that all powerful bill
Has suddenly bowed her face upon his breast.

The swooping godhead is half hovering still   20
But mounts, until her trembling thighs are pressed
By the webbed toes, and that all powerful bill

Can hold her helpless body on his breast.
How can those terrified vague fingers push
25   The feathered glory from her loosening thighs?
All the stretched body's laid on that white rush
And feels the strange heart beating where it lies.
A shudder in the loins engenders there
The broken wall, the burning roof and tower
30   And Agamemnon dead.
                   Being mounted so
So mastered by the brute blood of the air,
Did she put on his knowledge with his power
Before the indifferent beak could her her go?

III

35   A rush, a sudden wheel, and hovering still
The bird descends, and her frail thighs are pressed
By the webbed toes, and that all-powerful bill
Has laid her helpless face upon his breast.
How can those terrified vague fingers push
40   The feathered glory from her loosening thighs!
All the stretched body's laid on the white rush
And feels the strange heart beating where it lies;
A shudder in the loins engenders there
The broken wall, the burning roof and tower
45   And Agamemnon dead.
                   Being so caught up,
So mastered by the brute blood of the air,
Did she put on his knowledge with his power
Before the indifferent beak could let her drop?

Among School Children

1

I walk through the long schoolroom questioning;
A kind old nun in a white hood replies;
The children learn to cipher and to sing,
To study reading-books and history,
5   To cut and sew, be neat in everything
In the best modern way—the children's eyes
In momentary wonder stare upon
A sixty year old smiling public man.

2

I dream of a Ledaean body; bent
Above a sinking fire, a tale that she   10
Told of a harsh reproof, or trivial event
That changed some childish day to tragedy—
Told, and it seemed that our two natures blent
Into a sphere from youthful sympathy,
Or else, to alter Plato's parable,   15
Into the yolk and white of the one shell.

3

And thinking of that fit of grief or rage
I look upon one child or t'other there
And wonder if she stood so at that age—
For even daughters of the swan can share   20
Something of every paddler's heritage—
And had that colour upon cheek or hair,
And thereupon my heart is driven wild:
She stands before me as a living child.

4

Her present image floats into the mind—   25
Did Quattrocento finger fashion it
Hollow of cheek as though it drank the wind
And took a mess of shadows for its meat?
And I though never of Ledaean kind
Had pretty plumage once—enough of that,   30
Better to smile on all that smile, and show
There is a comfortable kind of old scarecrow.

5

What youthful mother, a shape upon her lap
Honey of generation had betrayed,
And that must sleep, shriek, struggle to escape   35
As recollection or the drug decide,

9. *Ledaean* like that of the beautiful Leda and of her daughter, Helen of Troy.   15.
Plato's parable Aristophanes accounts for love in Plato's *Symposium* by suggesting that
primeval man, forming a circle, was divided into two, and ever afterward the two
parts yearned to reunite with one another. As the daughter of Zeus (when disguised
as a swan), Helen was born from an egg.   26. *Quattrocento finger* referring to the style
of Italian painters of the 15th century.   34. *Honey of generation* spermatic fluid; also
a phrase used by Yeats to refer to the drug taken by the mother which destroys the
child's recollection of prenatal freedom and thus (despite his "struggle to escape")
betrays an infant (the "shape upon her lap") into birth.

Would think her son, did she but see that shape
With sixty or more winters on its head,
A compensation for the pang of his birth,
40 Or the uncertainty of his setting forth?

6

Plato thought nature but a spume that plays
Upon a ghostly paradigm of things;
Solider Aristotle played the taws
Upon the bottom of a king of kings;
45 World-famous golden-thighed Pythagoras
Fingered upon a fiddle stick or strings
What a star sang and careless Muses heard:
Old clothes upon old sticks to scare a bird.

7

Both nuns and mothers worship images,
50 But those the candles light are not as those
That animate a mother's reveries,
But keep a marble or a bronze repose.
And yet they too break hearts—O Presences
That passion, piety or affection knows,
55 And that all heavenly glory symbolize—
O self-born mockers of man's enterprise;

8

Labour is blossoming or dancing where
The body is not bruised to pleasure soul,
Nor beauty born out of its own despair,
60 Nor blear-eyed wisdom out of midnight oil.
O chestnut-tree, great-rooted blossomer,
Are you the leaf, the blossom or the bole?
O body swayed to music, O brightening glance,
How can we know the dancer from the dance?

41, 43. *Plato, Aristotle* Reality for Plato lay in the "ghostly paradigm," the forms lying behind nature ("spume"), whereas "Solider Aristotle" attributed a degree of reality to nature itself, seeing form as immanent in matter. He spanked his famous pupil, Alexander the Great ("king of kings"), with a strap ("taws"). 45. *Pythagoras* Called "golden-thighed" by his followers, this early Greek philosopher initiated a system of thought in which mathematics, music, and astronomy (the music of the spheres: "What a star sang") were related to one another. 49. *images* the idealized objects of religious worship (e.g., statues) and of a mother's love (her children). 56. *mockers* the "Presences" often invented by man and suggesting for him "all heavenly glory."

Coole Park and Ballylee, 1931

Under my window-ledge the waters race,
Otters below and moor-hens on the top,
Run for a mile undimmed in Heaven's face
Then darkening through "dark" Raftery's "cellar" drop,
Run underground, rise in a rocky place   5
In Coole demesne, and there to finish up
Spread to a lake and drop into a hole.
What's water but the generated soul?

Upon the border of that lake's a wood
Now all dry sticks under a wintry sun,   10
And in a copse of beeches there I stood,
For Nature's pulled her tragic buskin on
And all the rant's a mirror of my mood:
At sudden thunder of the mounting swan
I turned about and looked where branches break   15
The glittering reaches of the flooded lake.

Another emblem there! That stormy white
But seems a concentration of the sky;
And, like the soul, it sails into the sight
And in the morning's gone, no man knows why;   20
And is so lovely that it sets to right
What knowledge or its lack had set awry,
So arrogantly pure, a child might think
It can be murdered with a spot of ink.

Sound of a stick upon the floor, a sound   25
From somebody that toils from chair to chair;
Beloved books that famous hands have bound,
Old marble heads, old pictures everywhere;
Great rooms where travelled men and children found
Content or joy; a last inheritor   30
Where none has reigned that lacked a name and fame
Or out of folly into folly came.

Coole Park the home of Lady Gregory in Galway, where Yeats spent most of his
summers after 1896. Great houses such as hers and Yeats's tower at Ballylee serve a
symbolic function in several of his poems.   4. *Raftery* the blind Irish poet.

A spot whereon the founders lived and died
Seemed once more dear than life; ancestral trees,
35   Or gardens rich in memory glorified
Marriages, alliances, and families,
And every bride's ambition satisfied.
Where fashion or mere fantasy decrees
We shift about—all that great glory spent—
40   Like some poor Arab tribesman and his tent.

We were the last romantics—chose for theme
Traditional sanctity and loveliness;
Whatever's written in what poets name
The book of the people; whatever most can bless
45   The mind of man or elevate a rhyme;
But all is changed, that high horse riderless,
Though mounted in that saddle Homer rode
Where the swan drifts upon a darkening flood.

For Anne Gregory

"Never shall a young man,
Thrown into despair
By those great honey-coloured
Ramparts at your ear,
5   Love you for yourself alone
And not your yellow hair."

"But I can get a hair-dye
And set such colour there,
Brown, or black, or carrot,
10   That young men in despair
May love me for myself alone
And not my yellow hair."

"I heard an old religious man
But yesternight declare
15   That he had found a text to prove
That only God, my dear,
Could love you for yourself alone
And not your yellow hair."

Crazy Jane and the Bishop

Bring me to the blasted oak
That I, midnight upon the stroke,
(*All find safety in the tomb.*)
May call down curses on his head
Because of my dear Jack that's dead.   5
Coxcomb was the least he said:
The solid man and the coxcomb.

Nor was he Bishop when his ban
Banished Jack the Journeyman,
(*All find safety in the tomb.*)   10
Nor so much as parish priest,
Yet he, an old book in his fist,
Cried that we lived like beast and beast:
The solid man and the coxcomb.

The Bishop has a skin, God knows,   15
Wrinkled like the foot of a goose,
(*All find safety in the tomb.*)
Nor can he hide in holy black
The heron's hunch upon his back,
But a birch-tree stood my Jack: 20
The solid man and the coxcomb.

Jack had my virginity,
And bids me to the oak, for he
(*All find safety in the tomb.*)
Wanders out into the night   25
And there is shelter under it,
But should that other come, I spit:
The solid man and the coxcomb.

Crazy Jane Talks with the Bishop

I met the Bishop on the road
And much said he and I.
"Those breasts are flat and fallen now
Those veins must soon be dry;
Live in a heavenly mansion,   5
Not in some foul sty."

"Fair and foul are near of kin,
And fair needs foul," I cried.
"My friends are gone, but that's a truth
10   Nor grave nor bed denied,
Learned in bodily lowliness
And in the heart's pride.

"A woman can be proud and stiff
When on love intent;
15   But Love has pitched his mansion in
The place of excrement;
For nothing can be sole or whole
That has not been rent."

Meru

Civilisation is hooped together, brought
Under a rule, under the semblance of peace
By manifold illusion; but man's life is thought,
And he, despite his terror, cannot cease
5   Ravening through century after century,
Ravening, raging, and uprooting that he may come
Into the desolation of reality:
Egypt and Greece, good-bye, and good-bye, Rome!
Hermits upon Mount Meru or Everest,
10   Caverned in night under the drifted snow,
Or where that snow and winter's dreadful blast
Beat down upon their naked bodies, know
That day brings round the night, that before dawn
His glory and his monuments are gone.

Lapis Lazuli

(FOR HARRY CLIFTON)

I have heard that hysterical women say
They are sick of the palette and fiddle-bow,

Lapis Lazuli Yeats once received a present of a piece of this blue stone, "carved by some Chinese sculptor into the semblance of a mountain with temple, trees, paths, and an ascetic and pupil about to climb the mountain. Ascetic, pupil, hard stone, eternal theme of the sensual east. The heroic cry in the midst of despair. But no, I am wrong, the east has its solutions always and therefore knows nothing of tragedy. It is we, not the east, that must raise the heroic cry."

Of poets that are always gay,
For everybody knows or else should know
That if nothing drastic is done   5
Aeroplane and Zeppelin will come out,
Pitch like King Billy bomb-balls in
Until the town lie beaten flat.

All perform their tragic play,
There struts Hamlet, there is Lear,   10
That's Ophelia, that Cordelia;
Yet they, should the last scene be there,
The great stage curtain about to drop,
If worthy their prominent part in the play,
Do not break up their lines to weep.   15
They know that Hamlet and Lear are gay;
Gaiety transfiguring all that dread.
All men have aimed at, found and lost;
Black out; Heaven blazing into the head:
Tragedy wrought to its uttermost.   20
Though Hamlet rambles and Lear rages,
And all the drop-scenes drop at once
Upon a hundred thousand stages,
It cannot grow by an inch or an ounce.

On their own feet they come, or on shipboard,   25
Camel-back, horse-back, ass-back, mule-back,
Old civilisations put to the sword.
Then they and their wisdom went to rack:
No handiwork of Callimachus,
Who handled marble as if it were bronze,   30
Made draperies that seemed to rise
When sea-wind swept the corner, stands;
His long lamp-chimney shaped like the stem
Of a slender palm, stood but a day;
All things fall and are built again,   35
And those that build them again are gay.

Two Chinamen, behind them a third,
Are carved in lapis lazuli,
Over them flies a long-legged bird,
A symbol of longevity;   40

7. *Billy* probably William III, then of Orange, who bombed Irish towns in 1690 in a
war against King James II.   29. *Callimachus* Greek sculptor (5th century B.C.).

The third, doubtless a serving-man,
Carries a musical instrument.

Every discoloration of the stone,
Every accidental crack or dent,
45   Seems a water-course or an avalanche,
Or lofty slope where it still snows
Though doubtless plum or cherry-branch
Sweetens the little half-way house
Those Chinamen climb towards, and I
50   Delight to imagine them seated there;
There, on the mountain and the sky,
On all the tragic scene they stare.
One asks for mournful melodies;
Accomplished fingers begin to play.
55   Their eyes mid many wrinkles, their eyes,
Their ancient, glittering eyes, are gay.

An Acre of Grass

Picture and book remain,
An acre of green grass
For air and exercise,
Now strength of body goes;
5   Midnight, an old house
Where nothing stirs but a mouse.

My temptation is quiet.
Here at life's end
Neither loose imagination,
10   Nor the mill of the mind
Consuming its rag and bone,
Can make the truth known.

Grant me an old man's frenzy,
Myself must I remake
15   Till I am Timon and Lear
Or that William Blake
Who beat upon the wall
Till Truth obeyed his call;

15. *Timon* heroic and misanthropic protagonist of Shakespeare's *Timon of Athens*.

A mind Michael Angelo knew
That can pierce the clouds,   20
Or inspired by frenzy
Shake the dead in their shrouds;
Forgotten else by mankind,
An old man's eagle mind.

20–22. *That can . . . shrouds* perhaps a reference to Michelangelo's fresco of *The Last Judgment* in Rome's Sistine Chapel.

Long-Legged Fly

That civilisation may not sink,
Its great battle lost,
Quiet the dog, tether the pony
To a distant post;
Our master Caesar is in the tent   5
Where the maps are spread,
His eyes fixed upon nothing,
A hand under his head.
Like a long-legged fly upon the stream
His mind moves upon silence.   10

That the topless towers be burnt
And men recall that face,
Move most gently if move you must
In this lonely place.
She thinks, part woman, three parts a child,   15
That nobody looks; her feet
Practise a tinker shuffle
Picked up on a street.
Like a long-legged fly upon the stream
Her mind moves upon silence.   20

That girls at puberty may find
The first Adam in their thought,
Shut the door of the Pope's chapel,
Keep those children out.
There on that scaffolding reclines   25
Michael Angelo.
With no more sound than the mice make
His hand moves to and fro.
Like a long-legged fly upon the stream
His mind moves upon silence.   30

The Circus Animals' Desertion

I

I sought a theme and sought for it in vain,
I sought it daily for six weeks or so.
Maybe at last, being but a broken man,
I must be satisfied with my heart, although
5   Winter and summer till old age began
My circus animals were all on show,
Those stilted boys, that burnished chariot,
Lion and woman and the Lord knows what.

II

What can I but enumerate old themes?
10   First that sea-rider Oisin led by the nose
Through three enchanted islands, allegorical dreams,
Vain gaiety, vain battle, vain repose,
Themes of the embittered heart, or so it seems,
That might adorn old songs or courtly shows;
15   But what cared I that set him on to ride,
I, starved for the bosom of his faery bride?

And then a counter-truth filled out its play,
The Countess Cathleen was the name I gave it;
She, pity-crazed, had given her soul away,
20   But masterful Heaven had intervened to save it.
I thought my dear must her own soul destroy,
So did fanaticism and hate enslave it,
And this brought forth a dream and soon enough
This dream itself had all my thought and love.

25   And when the Fool and Blind Man stole the bread
Cuchulain fought the ungovernable sea;
Heart-mysteries there, and yet when all is said
It was the dream itself enchanted me:
Character isolated by a deed
30   To engross the present and dominate memory.
Players and painted stage took all my love,
And not those things that they were emblems of.

Circus Animals characters and themes in the poems and plays of a lifetime. 10. *Oisin* hero of Irish legend and subject of an early long poem by Yeats (1889). 18. *The Countess Cathleen* title of a play by Yeats (1892). 25–26. *And . . . sea* cf. Yeats's play *On Baile's Strand* (1904).

III
Those masterful images because complete
Grew in pure mind, but out of what began?
A mound of refuse or the sweepings of a street, 35
Old kettles, old bottles, and a broken can,
Old iron, old bones, old rags, that raving slut
Who keeps the till. Now that my ladder's gone,
I must lie down where all the ladders start,
In the foul rag-and-bone shop of the heart. 40

Edwin Arlington Robinson 1869–1935

Karma

Christmas was in the air and all was well
With him, but for a few confusing flaws
In divers of God's images. Because
A friend of his would neither buy nor sell,
Was he to answer for the axe that fell? 5
He pondered; and the reason for it was,
Partly, a slowly freezing Santa Claus
Upon the corner, with his beard and bell.

Acknowledging an improvident surprise,
He magnified a fancy that he wished 10
The friend whom he had wrecked were here again.
Not sure of that, he found a compromise;
And from the fulness of his heart he fished
A dime for Jesus who had died for men.

Robert Frost 1874–1963

Reluctance

Out through the fields and the woods
    And over the walls I have wended;
I have climbed the hills of view
    And looked at the world, and descended;
5   I have come by the highways home,
      And lo, it is ended.

The leaves are all dead on the ground,
    Save those that the oak is keeping
To ravel them one by one
10   And let them go scraping and creeping
Out over the crusted snow,
      When others are sleeping.

And the dead leaves lie huddled and still,
    No longer blown hither and thither;
15   The last lone aster is gone;
    The flowers of the witch-hazel wither;
The heart is still aching to seek,
      But the feet question 'Whither?'

Ah, when to the heart of man
20   Was it ever less than a treason
To go with the drift of things,
    To yield with a grace to reason,
And bow and accept the end
      Of a love or a season?

After Apple-Picking

My long two-pointed ladder's sticking through a tree
Toward heaven still,
And there's a barrel that I didn't fill
Beside it, and there may be two or three

Apples I didn't pick upon some bough. 5
But I am done with apple-picking now.
Essence of winter sleep is on the night,
The scent of apples: I am drowsing off.
I cannot rub the strangeness from my sight
I got from looking through a pane of glass 10
I skimmed this morning from the drinking trough
And held against the world of hoary grass.
.It melted, and I let it fall and break.
But I was well
Upon my way to sleep before it fell, 15
And I could tell
What form my dreaming was about to take.
Magnified apples appear and disappear,
Stem end and blossom end,
And every fleck of russet showing clear. 20
My instep arch not only keeps the ache,
It keeps the pressure of a ladder-round.
I feel the ladder sway as the boughs bend.
And I keep hearing from the cellar bin
The rumbling sound 25
Of load on load of apples coming in.
For I have had too much
Of apple-picking: I am overtired
Of the great harvest I myself desired.
There were ten thousand thousand fruit to touch, 30
Cherish in hand, lift down, and not let fall.
For all
That struck the earth,
No matter if not bruised or spiked with stubble,
Went surely to the cider-apple heap 35
As of no worth.
One can see what will trouble
This sleep of mine, whatever sleep it is.
Were he not gone,
The woodchuck could say whether it's like his 40
Long sleep, as I describe its coming on,
Or just some human sleep.

Once by the Pacific

The shattered water made a misty din.
Great waves looked over others coming in,

And thought of doing something to the shore
That water never did to land before.
5   The clouds were low and hairy in the skies
Like locks blown forward in the gleam of eyes.
You could not tell, and yet it looked as if
The shore was lucky in being backed by cliff,
The cliff in being backed by continent.
10   It looked as if a night of dark intent
Was coming, and not only a night, an age.
Someone had better be prepared for rage.
There would be more than ocean water broken
Before God's last *Put out the light* was spoken.

Bereft

Where had I heard this wind before
Change like this to a deeper roar?
What would it take my standing there for,
Holding open a restive door,
5   Looking down hill to a frothy shore?
Summer was past and day was past.
Somber clouds in the west were massed.
Out in the porch's sagging floor,
Leaves got up in a coil and hissed,
10   Blindly struck at my knee and missed.
Something sinister in the tone
Told me my secret must be known:
Word I was in the house alone
Somehow must have gotten abroad,
15   Word I was in my life alone,
Word I had no one left but God.

Desert Places

Snow falling and night falling fast, oh, fast
In a field I looked into going past,
And the ground almost covered smooth in snow,
But a few weeds and stubble showing last.

5   The woods around it have it—it is theirs.
All animals are smothered in their lairs.

I am too absent-spirited to count;
The loneliness includes me unawares.

And lonely as it is that loneliness
Will be more lonely ere it will be less—   10
A blanker whiteness of benighted snow
With no expression, nothing to express.

They cannot scare me with their empty spaces
Between stars—on stars where no human race is.
I have it in me so much nearer home   15
To scare myself with my own desert places.

14. *on . . . is* An earlier version reads, "on stars void of human races."

Design

I found a dimpled spider, fat and white,
On a white heal-all, holding up a moth
Like a white piece of rigid satin cloth—
Assorted characters of death and blight
Mixed ready to begin the morning right,   5
Like the ingredients of a witch's broth—
A snow-drop spider, a flower like froth,
And dead wings carried like a paper kite.
What had that flower to do with being white,
The wayside blue and innocent heal-all?   10
What brought the kindred spider to that height,
Then steered the white moth thither in the night?
What but design of darkness to appall?—
If design govern in a thing so small.

2. *heal-all,* a perennial herb with violet or purple flowers.

Directive

Back out of all this now too much for us,
Back in a time made simple by the loss
Of detail, burned, dissolved, and broken off
Like graveyard marble sculpture in the weather,
There is a house that is no more a house   5
Upon a farm that is no more a farm
And in a town that is no more a town.

The road there, if you'll let a guide direct you
Who only has at heart your getting lost,

10 May seem as if it should have been a quarry—
Great monolithic knees the former town
Long since gave up pretence of keeping covered.
And there's a story in a book about it:
Besides the wear of iron wagon wheels

15 The ledges show lines ruled southeast northwest,
The chisel work of an enormous Glacier
That braced his feet against the Arctic Pole.
You must not mind a certain coolness from him
Still said to haunt this side of Panther Mountain.

20 Nor need you mind the serial ordeal
Of being watched from forty cellar holes
As if by eye pairs out of forty firkins.
As for the woods' excitement over you
That sends light rustle rushes to their leaves,

25 Charge that to upstart inexperience.
Where were they all not twenty years ago?
They think too much of having shaded out
A few old pecker-fretted apple trees.
Make yourself up a cheering song of how

30 Someone's road home from work this once was,
Who may be just ahead of you on foot
Or creaking with a buggy load of grain.
The height of the adventure is the height
Of country where two village cultures faded

35 Into each other. Both of them are lost.
And if you're lost enough to find yourself
By now, pull in your ladder road behind you
And put a sign up CLOSED to all but me.
Then make yourself at home. The only field

40 Now left's no bigger than a harness gall.
First there's the children's house of make believe,
Some shattered dishes underneath a pine,
The playthings in the playhouse of the children.
Weep for what little things could make them glad.

45 Then for the house that is no more a house,
But only a belilaced cellar hole,
Now slowly closing like a dent in dough.
This was no playhouse but a house in earnest.
Your destination and your destiny's

22. *firkins* small wooden casks.

A brook that was the water of the house,   50
Cold as a spring as yet so near its source,
Too lofty and original to rage.
(We know the valley streams that when aroused
Will leave their tatters hung on barb and thorn.)
I have kept hidden in the instep arch   55
Of an old cedar at the waterside
A broken drinking goblet like the Grail
Under a spell so the wrong ones can't find it,
So can't get saved, as Saint Mark says they mustn't.
(I stole the goblet from the children's playhouse.)   60
Here are your waters and your watering place.
Drink and be whole again beyond confusion.

59. *Saint Mark* Cf. Mark iv. 11–12 or viii. 35.

Thomas Stearns Eliot 1888–1965

The Love Song of J. Alfred Prufrock

> *S'io credesse che mia risposta fosse*
> *A persona che mai tornasse al mondo,*
> *Questa fiamma staria senza piu scosse.*
> *Ma perciocche giammai di questo fondo*
> *Non torno vivo alcun, s'i'odo il vero,*
> *Senza tema d'infamia ti rispondo.**

Let us go then, you and I,
When the evening is spread out against the sky
Like a patient etherized upon a table;
Let us go, through certain half-deserted streets,
The muttering retreats   5
Of restless nights in one-night cheap hotels
And sawdust restaurants with oyster shells:

> * If I believed my answer were for one
> Who ever should return into the world,
> Then this my flame would stop its quivering.
> But since out of this deep henceforth no one
> Ever returns alive—if I hear truly—
> I answer you without fear of infamy.
> —Dante's *Inferno*, Canto XXVII, ll. 60–65.

Streets that follow like a tedious argument
Of insidious intent
10 To lead you to an overwhelming question . . .
Oh, do not ask, "What is it?"
Let us go and make our visit.

In the room the women come and go
Talking of Michelangelo.

15 The yellow fog that rubs its back upon the windowpanes,
The yellow smoke that rubs its muzzle on the windowpanes
Licked its tongue into the corners of the evening,
Lingered upon the pools that stand in drains,
Let fall upon its back the soot that falls from chimneys,
20 Slipped by the terrace, made a sudden leap,
And seeing that it was a soft October night,
Curled once about the house, and fell asleep.

And indeed there will be time
For the yellow smoke that slides along the street,
25 Rubbing its back upon the windowpanes;
There will be time, there will be time
To prepare a face to meet the faces that you meet;
There will be time to murder and create,
And time for all the works and days of hands
30 That lift and drop a question on your plate;
Time for you and time for me,
And time yet for a hundred indecisions,
And for a hundred visions and revisions,
Before the taking of a toast and tea.

35 In the room the women come and go
Talking of Michelangelo.

And indeed there will be time
To wonder, "Do I dare?" and, "Do I dare?"
Time to turn back and descend the stair,
40 With a bald spot in the middle of my hair—
(They will say: "How his hair is growing thin!")
My morning coat, my collar mounting firmly to the chin,

23. *there . . . time* Cf. the opening of Marvell's "To His Coy Mistress." 29. *works and days* the title of a poem in praise of harsh agricultural toil written by the ancient Greek poet Hesiod.

My necktie rich and modest, but asserted by a simple pin—
(They will say: "But how his arms and legs are thin!")
Do I dare   45
Disturb the universe?
In a minute there is time
For decisions and revisions which a minute will reverse.

For I have known them all already, known them all—
Have known the evenings, mornings, afternoons,   50
I have measured out my life with coffee spoons;
I know the voices dying with a dying fall
Beneath the music from a farther room.
  So how should I presume?

And I have known the eyes already, known them all—   55
The eyes that fix you in a formulated phrase,
And when I am formulated, sprawling on a pin,
When I am pinned and wriggling on the wall,
Then how should I begin
To spit out all the butt-ends of my days and ways?   60
  And how should I presume?

And I have known the arms already, known them all—
Arms that are braceleted and white and bare
(But in the lamplight, downed with light brown hair!)
Is it perfume from a dress   65
That makes me so digress?
Arms that lie along a table, or wrap about a shawl.
  And should I then presume?
  And how should I begin?

    . . .

Shall I say, I have gone at dusk through narrow streets   70
And watched the smoke that rises from the pipes
Of lonely men in shirt-sleeves, leaning out of windows? . . .

I should have been a pair of ragged claws
Scuttling across the floors of silent seas.

    . . .

And the afternoon, the evening, sleeps so peacefully!   75
Smoothed by long fingers,
Asleep . . . tired . . . or it malingers,
Stretched on the floor, here beside you and me.

52. *dying fall* Cf. the opening of Shakespeare's *Twelfth Night.*

Should I, after tea and cakes and ices,
80   Have the strength to force the moment to its crisis?
But though I have wept and fasted, wept and prayed,
Though I have seen my head (grown slightly bald) brought in upon
      a platter,
I am no prophet—and here's no great matter;
I have seen the moment of my greatness flicker,
85   And I have seen the eternal Footman hold my coat, and snicker,
And in short, I was afraid.

And would it have been worth it, after all,
After the cups, the marmalade, the tea,
Among the porcelain, among some talk of you and me,
90   Would it have been worth while,
To have bitten off the matter with a smile,
To have squeezed the universe into a ball
To roll it toward some overwhelming question,
To say: "I am Lazarus, come from the dead,
95   Come back to tell you all, I shall tell you all"—
If one, settling a pillow by her head,
    Should say: "That is not what I meant at all.
    That is not it, at all."

And would it have been worth it, after all,
100   Would it have been worth while,
After the sunsets and the dooryards and the sprinkled streets,
After the novels, after the teacups, after the skirts that trail along
      the floor—
And this, and so much more?—
It is impossible to say just what I mean!
105   But as if a magic lantern threw the nerves in patterns on a screen:
Would it have been worth while
If one, settling a pillow or throwing off a shawl,
And turning toward the window, should say:
    "That is not it at all,
110   That is not what I meant, at all."
               . . .

No! I am not Prince Hamlet, nor was meant to be;
Am an attendant lord, one that will do

---

83. *prophet* John the Baptist's head, at the request of Salome, was "brought in upon a platter." 92. *squeezed . . . ball* Cf. the ending of Marvell's poem. 94. *Lazarus* raised from the dead by Christ (John xi.1–44). 112. *attendant lord* Cf. Polonius, a kind of "Fool" in *Hamlet*.

To swell a progress, start a scene or two,
Advise the prince; no doubt, an easy tool,
Deferential, glad to be of use,   115
Politic, cautious, and meticulous;
Full of high sentence, but a bit obtuse;
At times, indeed, almost ridiculous—
Almost, at times, the Fool.

I grow old . . . I grow old . . .   120
I shall wear the bottoms of my trousers rolled.

Shall I part my hair behind? Do I dare to eat a peach?
I shall wear white flannel trousers, and walk upon the beach.
I have heard the mermaids singing, each to each.

I do not think that they will sing to me.   125

I have seen them riding seaward on the waves
Combing the white hair of the waves blown back
When the wind blows the water white and black.

We have lingered in the chambers of the sea
By sea-girls wreathed with seaweed red and brown   130
Till human voices wake us, and we drown.

The Hollow Men

MISTAH KURTZ—HE DEAD.

A PENNY FOR THE OLD GUY

I

We are the hollow men
We are the stuffed men
Leaning together
Headpiece filled with straw. Alas!
Our dried voices, when   5
We whisper together

Mistah . . . dead In Conrad's *Heart of Darkness,* this is spoken by the cabin boy to announce the death of Mr. Kurtz, a great European trader, who had been barbarized by the African jungle.   A . . . *Guy* Guy Fawkes attempted unsuccessfully to blow up the House of Commons in 1605. On the day marking this event, children collect pennies for fireworks.

Are quiet and meaningless
As wind in dry grass
Or rat's feet over broken glass
10 In our dry cellar

Shape without form, shade without color,
Paralyzed force, gesture without motion;

Those who have crossed
With direct eyes, to death's other Kingdom
15 Remember us—if at all—not as lost
Violent souls, but only
As the hollow men
The stuffed men.

II
Eyes I dare not meet in dreams
20 In death's dream kingdom
These do not appear:
There, the eyes are
Sunlight on a broken column
There, is a tree swinging
25 And voices are
In the wind's singing
More distant and more solemn
Than a fading star.

Let me be no nearer
30 In death's dream kingdom
Let me also wear
Such deliberate disguises
Rat's skin, crowskin, crossed staves
In a field
35 Behaving as the wind behaves
No nearer—

Not that final meeting
In the twilight kingdom

11–12. *Shape . . . motion* Cf. *Hamlet* III.iv.78ff. 13–14. *Those . . . Kingdom* Cf.
Inferno, III, in which Dante tells of those who have crossed the river Acheron to hell
(cf. l. 60). 20. *death's . . . kingdom* apparently a state marked by illusion and mean-
inglessness and the avoidance of moral choices. 33. *crossed staves* e.g., scarecrows.

III

This is the dead land
This is cactus land   40
Here the stone images
Are raised, here they receive
The supplication of a dead man's hand
Under the twinkle of a fading star.
Is it like this   45
In death's other kingdom
Waking alone
At the hour when we are
Trembling with tenderness
Lips that would kiss   50
Form prayers to broken stone.

IV

The eyes are not here
There are no eyes here
In this valley of dying stars
In this hollow valley   55
This broken jaw of our lost kingdoms

In this last of meeting places
We grope together
And avoid speech
Gathered on this beach of the tumid river   60

Sightless, unless
The eyes reappear
As the perpetual star
Multifoliate rose   65
Of death's twilight kingdom
The hope only
Of empty men.

V

Here we go round the prickly pear

37–38. *Not . . . kingdom* perhaps the purgation which the "I" of the poem fears. The "Eyes" of 1.19 may be compared with the severe eyes of Beatrice when she rebukes Dante (*Purgatorio*, XXX) for his weakness.   64. *Multifoliate rose* traditionally an emblem of Christ and the Virgin. In *Paradiso*, XXVIII–XXX, Dante, conducted by Beatrice, sees Paradise form itself into a rose with petals which are the souls of the blessed. 68. *Hear . . . pear* The mulberry bush of the nursery rhyme has become the prickly pear. Cf. the "cactus land" of 1. 40.

Prickly pear prickly pear
Here we go round the prickly pear
At five o'clock in the morning.

Between the idea
And the reality
Between the motion
And the act
Falls the Shadow
            For Thine is the Kingdom

Between the conception
And the creation
Between the emotion
And the response
Falls the Shadow
                    Life is very long

Between the desire
And the spasm
Between the potency
And the existence
Between the essence
And the descent
Falls the Shadow
            For Thine is the Kingdom

For Thine is
Life is
For Thine is the

This is the way the world ends
This is the way the world ends
This is the way the world ends
Not with a bang but a whimper.

70
75
80
85
90
95

74–75. *motion . . . act* Cf. *Julius Caesar* (II.1.63ff):

                Between the acting of a dreadful thing
                And the first motion, all the interim is
                Like a phantasma or a hideous dream.

98. *bang . . . whimper* Fawkes was capable of action, even if violent; the hollow men are capable of nothing.

Wystan Hugh Auden 1907–

Lay Your Sleeping Head, My Love

Lay your sleeping head, my love,
Human on my faithless arm;
Time and fevers burn away
Individual beauty from
Thoughtful children, and the grave   5
Proves the child ephemeral:
But in my arms till break of day
Let the living creature lie,
Mortal, guilty, but to me
The entirely beautiful.   10

Soul and body have no bounds:
To lovers as they lie upon
Her tolerant enchanted slope
In their ordinary swoon,
Grave the vision Venus sends   15
Of supernatural sympathy,
Universal love and hope;
While an abstract insight wakes
Among the glaciers and the rocks
The hermit's sensual ecstasy.   20

Certainty, fidelity
On the stroke of midnight pass
Like vibrations of a bell,
And fashionable madmen raise
Their pedantic boring cry: 25
Every farthing of the cost,
All the dreaded cards foretell,
Shall be paid, but from this night
Not a whisper, not a thought,
Not a kiss nor look be lost.   30

Beauty, midnight, vision dies:
Let the winds of dawn that blow

Softly round your dreaming head
Such a day of sweetness show
35 Eye and knocking heart may bless,
Find the mortal world enough;
Noons of dryness see you fed
By the involuntary powers,
Nights of insult let you pass
40 Watched by every human love.

From *In Time of War*

1

So from the years the gifts were showered; each
Ran off with his at once into his life:
Bee took the politics that make a hive,
Fish swam as fish, peach settled into peach.

5 And were successful at the first endeavour;
The hour of birth their only time at college,
They were content with their precocious knowledge,
And knew their station and were good for ever.

Till finally there came a childish creature
10 On whom the years could model any feature,
And fake with ease a leopard or a dove;

Who by the lightest wind was changed and shaken,
And looked for truth and was continually mistaken,
And envied his few friends and chose his love.

XXVII

Wandering lost upon the mountains of our choice,
Again and again we sigh for an ancient South,
For the warm nude ages of instinctive poise,
For the taste of joy in the innocent mouth.

5 Asleep in our huts, how we dream of a part
In the glorious balls of the future; each intricate maze
Has a plan, and the disciplined movements of the heart
Can follow for ever and ever its harmless ways.

We envy streams and houses that are sure:
But we are articled to error; we   10
Were never nude and calm like a great door,

And never will be perfect like the fountains;
We live in freedom by necessity,
A mountain people dwelling among mountains.

In Memory of W. B. *Yeats*

1

He disappeared in the dead of winter:
The brooks were frozen, the airports almost deserted,
And snow disfigured the public statues;
The mercury sank in the mouth of the dying day.
O all the instruments agree   5
The day of his death was a dark cold day.

Far from his illness
The wolves ran on through the evergreen forests,
The peasant river was untempted by the fashionable quays;
By mourning tongues   10
The death of the poet was kept from his poems.

But for him it was his last afternoon as himself,
An afternoon of nurses and rumors;
The provinces of his body revolted.
The squares of his mind were empty,   15
Silence invaded the suburbs,
The current of his feeling failed: he became his admirers.

Now he is scattered among a hundred cities
And wholly given over to unfamiliar affections;
To find his happiness in another kind of wood   20
And be punished under a foreign code of conscience.
The words of a dead man
Are modified in the guts of the living.

But in the importance and noise of tomorrow
When the brokers are roaring like beasts on the floor of the Bourse, 25
And the poor have the sufferings to which they are fairly accustomed,

25. *Bourse* the French stock exchange.

And each in the cell of himself is almost convinced of his freedom;
A few thousand will think of this day
As one thinks of a day when one did something slightly unusual.
30   O all the instruments agree
The day of his death was a dark cold day.

2

You were silly like us: your gift survived it all;
The parish of rich women, physical decay,
Yourself; mad Ireland hurt you into poetry.
35   Now Ireland has her madness and her weather still,
For poetry makes nothing happen: it survives
In the valley of its saying where executives
Would never want to tamper; it flows south
From ranches of isolation and the busy griefs,
40   Raw towns that we believe and die in; it survives,
A way of happening, a mouth.

3

Earth, receive an honored guest;
William Yeats is laid to rest:
Let the Irish vessel lie
45   Emptied of its poetry.

Time that is intolerant
Of the brave and innocent,
And indifferent in a week
To a beautiful physique,

50   Worships language and forgives
Everyone by whom it lives;
Pardons cowardice, conceit,
Lays its honors at their feet.

Time that with this strange excuse
55   Pardoned Kipling and his views,
And will pardon Paul Claudel,
Pardons him for writing well.

In the nightmare of the dark
All the dogs of Europe bark,

55. *Kipling . . . views* alluding to Kipling's imperialism. 56. *Claudel* violently anti-Protestant French Catholic poet.

And the living nations wait,   60
Each sequestered in its hate;

Intellectual disgrace
Stares from every human face,
And the seas of pity lie
Locked and frozen in each eye.   65

Follow, poet, follow right
To the bottom of the night,
With your unconstraining voice
Still persuade us to rejoice;

With the farming of a verse   70
Make a vineyard of the curse,
Sing of human unsuccess
In a rapture of distress;

In the deserts of the heart
Let the healing fountain start,   75
In the prison of his days
Teach the free man how to praise.

Wallace Stevens   1879–1955

The Emperor of Ice-Cream

Call the roller of big cigars,
The muscular one, and bid him whip
In kitchen cups concupiscent curds.
Let the wenches dawdle in such dress
As they are used to wear, and let the boys   5
Bring flowers in last month's newspapers.
Let be be finale of seem.
The only emperor is the emperor of ice-cream.

Take from the dresser of deal,
Lacking the three glass knobs, that sheet   10

9. *deal* fir or pine.

On which she embroidered fantails once
And spread it so as to cover her face.
If her horny feet protrude, they come
To show how cold she is, and dumb.
15   Let the lamp affix its beam.
The only emperor is the emperor of ice-cream.

Sunday Morning

1

Complacencies of the peignoir, and late
Coffee and oranges in a sunny chair,
And the green freedom of a cockatoo
Upon a rug mingle to dissipate
5   The holy hush of ancient sacrifice.
She dreams a little, and she feels the dark
Encroachment of that old catastrophe,
As a calm darkens among water-lights.
The pungent oranges and bright, green wings
10   Seem things in some procession of the dead,
Winding across wide water, without sound.
The day is like wide water, without sound,
Stilled for the passing of her dreaming feet
Over the seas, to silent Palestine,
15   Dominion of the blood and sepulchre.

2

Why should she give her bounty to the dead?
What is divinity if it can come
Only in silent shadows and in dreams?
Shall she not find in comforts of the sun,
20   In pungent fruit and bright, green wings, or else
In any balm or beauty of the earth,
Things to be cherished like the thought of heaven?
Divinity must live within herself:
Passions of rain, or moods in falling snow;
25   Grievings in loneliness, or unsubdued
Elations when the forest blooms; gusty
Emotions on wet roads on autumn nights;
All pleasures and all pains, remembering

1. *peignoir* a loose dressing-gown.

The bough of summer and the winter branch.
These are the measures destined for her soul. 30

3

Jove in the clouds had his inhuman birth.
No mother suckled him, no sweet land gave
Large-mannered motions to his mythy mind.
He moved among us, as a muttering king,
Magnificent, would move among his hinds, 35
Until our blood, commingling, virginal,
With heaven, brought such requital to desire
The very hinds discerned it, in a star.
Shall our blood fail? Or shall it come to be
The blood of paradise? And shall the earth 40
Seem all of paradise that we shall know?
The sky will be much friendlier then than now,
A part of labor and a part of pain,
And next in glory to enduring love,
Not this dividing and indifferent blue. 45

4

She says, "I am content when wakened birds,
Before they fly, test the reality
Of misty fields, by their sweet questionings;
But when the birds are gone, and their warm fields
Return no more, where, then, is paradise?" 50
There is not any haunt of prophecy,
Nor any old chimera of the grave,
Neither the golden underground, nor isle
Melodious, where spirits gat them home,
Nor visionary south, nor cloudy palm 55
Remote on heaven's hill, that has endured
As April's green endures; or will endure
Like her remembrance of awakened birds,
Or her desire for June and evening, tipped
By the consummation of the swallow's wings. 60

5

She says, "But in contentment I still feel
The need of some imperishable bliss."
Death is the mother of beauty; hence from her,

38. *hinds . . . star* shepherds seeing the star of Bethlehem. 54. *gat* (archaic) got.

Alone, shall come fulfillment to our dreams
65   And our desires. Although she strews the leaves
Of sure obliteration on our paths,
The path sick sorrow took, the many paths
Where triumph rang its brassy phrase, or love
Whispered a little out of tenderness,
70   She makes the willow shiver in the sun
For maidens who were wont to sit and gaze
Upon the grass, relinquished to their feet.
She causes boys to pile new plums and pears
On disregarded plate. The maidens taste
75   And stray impassioned in the littering leaves.

6

Is there no change of death in paradise?
Does ripe fruit never fall? Or do the boughs
Hang always heavy in that perfect sky,
Unchanging, yet so like our perishing earth,
80   With rivers like our own that seek for seas
They never find, the same receding shores
That never touch with inarticulate pang?
Why set the pear upon those river-banks
Or spice the shores with odors of the plum?
85   Alas, that they should wear our colors there,
The silken weavings of our afternoons,
And pick the strings of our insipid lutes!
Death is the mother of beauty, mystical,
Within whose burning bosom we devise
90   Our earthly mothers waiting, sleeplessly.

7

Supple and turbulent, a ring of men
Shall chant in orgy on a summer morn
Their boisterous devotion to the sun,
Not as a god, but as a god might be,
95   Naked among them, like a savage source.
Their chant shall be a chant of paradise,
Out of their blood, returning to the sky;
And in their chant shall enter, voice by voice,
The windy lake wherein their lord delights,
100   The trees, like serafin, and echoing hills,

100. *serafin* (seraphim) the highest order of angels.

That choir among themselves long afterward.
They shall know well the heavenly fellowship
Of men that perish and of summer morn.
And whence they came and whither they shall go
The dew upon their feet shall manifest.   105

8

She hears, upon that water without sound,
A voice that cries, "The tomb in Palestine
Is not the porch of spirits lingering.
It is the grave of Jesus, where he lay."
We live in an old chaos of the sun,   110
Or old dependency of day and night,
Or island solitude, unsponsored, free,
Of that wide water, inescapable.
Deer walk upon our mountains, and the quail
Whistle about us their spontaneous cries;   115
Sweet berries ripen in the wilderness;
And, in the isolation of the sky,
At evening, casual flocks of pigeons make
Ambiguous undulations as they sink,
Downward to darkness, on extended wings.   120

William Carlos Williams   1883–1963

The Yachts

contend in a sea which the land partly encloses
shielding them from the too heavy blows
of an ungoverned ocean which when it chooses

tortures the biggest hulls, the best man knows
to pit against its beating, and sinks them pitilessly.   5
Mothlike in mists, scintillant in the minute

brilliance of cloudless days, with broad bellying sails
they glide to the wind tossing green water
from their sharp prows while over them the crew crawls

10   ant-like, solicitously grooming them, releasing,
      making fast as they turn, lean far over and having
      caught the wind again, side by side, head for the mark.

      In a well guarded arena of open water surrounded by
      lesser and greater craft which, sycophant, lumbering
15   and flittering follow them, they appear youthful, rare

      as the light of a happy eye, live with the grace
      of all that in the mind is feckless, free and
      naturally to be desired. Now the sea which holds them

      is moody, lapping their glossy sides, as if feeling
20   for some slightest flaw but fails completely.
      Today no race. Then the wind comes again. The yachts

      move, jockeying for a start, the signal is set and they
      are off. Now the waves strike at them but they are too
      well made, they slip through, though they take in canvas.

25   Arms with hands grasping seek to clutch at the prows.
      Bodies thrown recklessly in the way are cut aside.
      It is a sea of faces about them in agony, in despair

      until the horror of the race dawns staggering the mind,
      the whole sea become an entanglement of watery bodies
30   lost to the world bearing what they cannot hold. Broken,

      beaten, desolate, reaching from the dead to be taken up
      they cry out, failing, failing! their cries rising
      in waves still as the skillful yachts pass over.

Ezra Pound 1885–

A Virginal

      No, no! Go from me. I have left her lately.
      I will not spoil my sheath with lesser brightness,

For my surrounding air hath a new lightness;
Slight are her arms, yet they have bound me straitly
And left me cloaked as with a gauze of ether;   5
As with sweet leaves: as with a subtle clearness.
Oh, I have picked up magic in her nearness
To sheathe me half in half the things that sheathe her.
No, no! Go from me. I have still the flavor,
Soft as spring wind that's come from birchen bowers.   10
Green come the shoots, aye April in the branches,
As winter's wound with her sleight hand she staunches,
Hath of the trees a likeness of the savor:
As white their bark, so white this lady's hours.

Portrait d'une Femme

Your mind and you are our Sargasso Sea,
London has swept about you this score years
And bright ships left you this or that in fee:
Ideas, old gossip, oddments of all things,
Strange spars of knowledge and dimmed wares of price.   5
Great minds have sought you—lacking someone else.
You have been second always. Tragical?
No. You preferred it to the usual thing:
One dull man, dulling and uxorious,
One average mind—with one thought less, each year.   10
Oh, you are patient, I have seen you sit
Hours, where something might have floated up.
And now you pay one. Yes, you richly pay.
You are a person of some interest, one comes to you
And takes strange gain away: 15
Trophies fished up; some curious suggestion;
Fact that leads nowhere; and a tale or two,
Pregnant with mandrakes, or with something else
That might prove useful and yet never proves,
That never fits a corner or shows use,   20
Or finds its hour upon the loom of days:
The tarnished, gaudy, wonderful old work;
Idols and ambergris and rare inlays,
These are your riches, your great store; and yet
For all this sea-hoard of deciduous things   25

Portrait . . . Femme Portrait of a Lady. 1. *Sargasso Sea* part of the Atlantic between
the Azores and the West Indies, named for the seaweed which accumulates there.

Strange woods half sodden, and new brighter stuff:
In the slow float of differing light and deep,
No! there is nothing! In the whole and all,
Nothing that's quite your own.
30   Yet this is you.

Marianne Moore 1887–

What Are Years?

  What is our innocence,
what is our guilt? All are
  naked, none is safe. And whence
is courage: the unanswered question,
5 the resolute doubt,—
dumbly calling, deafly listening—that
in misfortune, even death,
  encourages others
  and in its defeat, stirs

10 the soul to be strong? He
sees deep and is glad, who
  accedes to mortality
and in his imprisonment rises
upon himself as
15 the sea in a chasm, struggling to be
free and unable to be,
  in its surrendering
  finds its continuing.

  So he who strongly feels,
20 behaves. The very bird,
  grown taller as he sings, steels
his form straight up. Though he is captive,
his mighty singing
says, satisfaction is a lowly
25 thing, how pure a thing is joy.
  This is mortality,
  this is eternity.

Poetry

I, too, dislike it; there are things that are important beyond all this fiddle.
  Reading it, however, with a perfect contempt for it, one discovers in
  it after all, a place for the genuine.
    Hands that can grasp, eyes
      that can dilate, hair that can rise   5
         if it must, these things are important not because a

high-sounding interpretation can be put upon them but because they are
  useful. When they become so derivative as to become unintelligible,
  the same thing may be said for all of us, that we
    do not admire what   10
    we cannot understand: the bat
        holding on upside down or in quest of something to

eat, elephants pushing, a wild horse taking a roll, a tireless wolf under
  a tree, the immovable critic twitching his skin like a horse that feels a
  flea, the base-
ball fan, the statistician—   15
    nor is it valid
        to discriminate against 'business documents and

school-books'; all these phenomena are important. One must make a
    distinction
    however: when dragged into prominence by half poets, the result is
    not poetry,
nor till the poets among us can be   20
    'literalists of
    the imagination'—above
        insolence and triviality and can present

for inspection, 'imaginary gardens with real toads in them,' shall we have
    it. In the meantime, if you demand on the one hand,   25
    the raw material of poetry in
        all its rawness and
        that which is on the other hand
            genuine, then you are interested in poetry.

John Crowe Ransom 1888–

Piazza Piece

    —I am a gentleman in a dustcoat trying
To make you hear. Your ears are soft and small
And listen to an old man not at all,
They want the young men's whispering and sighing.
5   But see the roses on your trellis dying
And hear the spectral singing of the moon;
For I must have my lovely lady soon,
I am a gentleman in a dustcoat trying.

    —I am a lady young in beauty waiting
10   Until my truelove comes, and then we kiss.
But what grey man among the vines is this
Whose words are dry and faint as in a dream?
Back from my trellis, Sir, before I scream!
I am a lady young in beauty waiting.

The Equilibrists

    Full of her long white arms and milky skin
He had a thousand times remembered sin.
Alone in the press of people travelled he,
Minding her jacinth and myrrh and ivory.

5   Mouth he remembered: the quaint orifice
From which came heat that flamed upon the kiss,
Till cold words came down spiral from the head,
Grey doves from the officious tower illsped.

    Body: it was a white field ready for love.
10   On her body's field, with the gaunt tower above,
The lilies grew, beseeching him to take,
If he would pluck and wear them, bruise and break.

Equilibrists usually associated with acrobats and their feats of balancing.

Eyes talking: Never mind the cruel words,
Embrace my flowers but not embrace the swords.
But what they said, the doves came straightway flying   15
And unsaid: Honor, Honor, they came crying.

Importunate her doves. Too pure, too wise,
Clambering on his shoulder, saying, Arise,
Leave me now, and never let us meet,
Eternal distance now command thy feet.   20

Predicament indeed, which thus discovers
Honor among thieves, Honor between lovers.
O such a little word is Honor, they feel!
But the grey word is between them cold as steel.

At length I saw these lovers fully were come   25
Into their torture of equilibrium:
Dreadfully had forsworn each other, and yet
They were bound each to each, and they did not forget.

And rigid as two painful stars, and twirled
About the clustered night their prison world,   30
They burned with fierce love always to come near,
But Honor beat them back and kept them clear.

Ah, the strict lovers, they are ruined now!
I cried in anger. But with puddled brow
Devising for those gibbeted and brave   35
Came I descanting: Man, who would you have?

For spin your period out, and draw your breath,
A kinder saeculum begins with Death.
Would you ascend to Heaven and bodiless dwell?
Or take your bodies honorless to Hell?   40

In Heaven you have heard no marriage is,
No white flesh tinder to your lecheries,
Your male and female tissue sweetly shaped
Sublimed away, and furious blood escaped.

Great lovers lie in Hell, the stubborn ones   45
Infatuate of the flesh upon the bones;

24. *cold as steel* as with the swords frequently separating medieval lovers. Cf. Marvell's
"The Definition of Love."   38. *saeculum* cycle, age, period of time (Latin).

Stuprate, they rend each other when they kiss;
The pieces kiss again—no end to this.

But still I watched them spinning, orbited nice.
50   Their flames were not more radiant than their ice.
I dug in the quiet earth and wrought the tomb
And made these lines to memorize their doom:—

Equilibrists lie here; stranger, tread light;
Close, but untouching in each other's sight;
55   *Mouldered the lips and ashy the tall skull,*
Let them lie perilous and beautiful.

47. *Stuprate* from Latin *Stuprare*, "to ravish." The stanza suggests the tortures of t
damned in Dante's *Inferno*, Canto V.

Archibald MacLeish 1892–

The End of the World

Quite unexpectedly as Vasserot
The armless ambidextrian was lighting
A match between his great and second toe
And Ralph the lion was engaged in biting
5   The neck of Madame Sossman while the drum
Pointed, and Teeny was about to cough
In waltz-time swinging Jocko by the thumb—
Quite unexpectedly the top blew off:

And there, there overhead, there, there, hung over
Those thousands of white faces, those dazed eyes,
There in the starless dark the poise, the hover,
10   There with vast wings across the canceled skies,
There in the sudden blackness the black pall
Of nothing, nothing, nothing—nothing at all.

Theodore Roethke 1908–1963

Moss-Gathering

To loosen with all ten fingers held wide and limber
And lift up a patch, dark-green, the kind for lining cemetery baskets,
Thick and cushiony, like an old-fashioned door-mat,
The crumbling small hollow sticks on the underside mixed with roots,
And wintergreen berries and leaves still stuck to the top,—   5
That was moss-gathering.
But something always went out of me when I dug loose those carpets
Of green, or plunged to my elbows in the spongy yellowish moss of
   the marshes:
And afterwards I always felt mean, jogging back over the logging road,
As if I had broken the natural order of thing in that swampland;   10
Disturbed some rhythm, old and of vast importance,
By pulling off flesh from the living planet;
As if I had committed, against the whole scheme of life, a desecration.

I Knew a Woman

I knew a woman, lovely in her bones,
When small birds sighed, she would sigh back at them;
Ah, when she moved, she moved more ways than one:
The shapes a bright container can contain!
Of her choice virtues only gods should speak,   5
Or English poets who grew up on Greek
(I'd have them sing in chorus, cheek to cheek).

How well her wishes went! She stroked my chin,
She taught me Turn, and Counter-turn, and Stand;
She taught me Touch, that undulant white skin;   10
I nibbled meekly from her proffered hand;
She was the sickle; I, poor I, the rake,
Coming behind her for her pretty sake
(But what prodigious mowing we did make).

Love likes a gander, and adores a goose: 15
Her full lips pursed, the errant note to seize;

She played it quick, she played it light and loose;
My eyes, they dazzled at her flowing knees;
Her several parts could keep a pure repose,
20   Or one hip quiver with a mobile nose
(She moved in circles, and those circles moved).

Let seed be grass, and grass turn into hay:
I'm martyr to a motion not my own;
What's freedom for? To know eternity.
25   I swear she cast a shadow white as stone.
But who would count eternity in days?
These old bones live to learn her wanton ways:
(I measure time by how a body sways).

In a Dark Time

In a dark time, the eye begins to see.
I meet my shadow in the deepening shade;
I hear my echo in the echoing wood—
A lord of nature weeping to a tree.
5   I live between the heron and the wren,
Beasts of the hill and serpents of the den.

What's madness but nobility of soul
At odds with circumstance? The day's on fire!
I know the purity of pure despair,
10   My shadow pinned against a sweating wall.
That place among the rocks—is it a cave,
Or winding path? The edge is what I have.

A steady storm of correspondences!
A night flowing with birds, a ragged moon,
15   And in broad day the midnight comes again!
A man goes far to find out what he is—
Death of the self in a long, tearless night,
All natural shapes blazing unnatural light.

Dark, dark my light, and darker my desire.
20   My soul, like some heat-maddened summer fly,
Keeps buzzing at the sill. Which I is I?
A fallen man, I climb out of my fear.
The mind enters itself, and God the mind,
And one is One, free in the tearing wind.

Dylan Thomas 1914–1953

The Force That Through the Green Fuse Drives the Flower

The force that through the green fuse drives the flower
Drives my green age; that blasts the roots of trees
Is my destroyer.
And I am dumb to tell the crooked rose
My youth is bent by the same wintry fever. 5

The force that drives the water through the rocks
Drives my red blood; that dries the mouthing streams
Turns mine to wax.
And I am dumb to mouth unto my veins
How at the mountain spring the same mouth sucks. 10

The hand that whirls the water in the pool
Stirs the quicksand; that ropes the blowing wind
Hauls my shroud sail.
And I am dumb to tell the hanging man
How of my clay is made the hangman's lime. 15

The lips of time leech to the fountain head;
Love drips and gathers, but the fallen blood
Shall calm her sores.
And I am dumb to tell a weather's wind
How time has ticked a heaven round the stars. 20

And I am dumb to tell the lover's tomb
How at my sheet goes the same crooked worm.

A Refusal to Mourn the Death, by Fire, of a Child in London

Never until the mankind making
Bird beast and flower
Fathering and all humbling darkness
Tells with silence the last light breaking

5 And the still hour
Is come of the sea tumbling in harness

And I must enter again the round
Zion of the water bead
And the synagogue of the ear of corn
10 Shall I let pray the shadow of a sound
Or sow my salt seed
In the least valley of sackcloth to mourn

The majesty and burning of the child's death.
I shall not murder
15 The mankind of her going with a grave truth
Nor blaspheme down the stations of the breath
With any further
Elegy of innocence and youth.

Deep with the first dead lies London's daughter,
20 Robed in the long friends,
The grains beyond age, the dark veins of her mother,
Secret by the unmourning water
Of the riding Thames.
After the first death, there is no other.

Randall Jarrell 1914–1965

2nd Air Force

Far off, above the plain the summer dries,
The great loops of the hangars sway like hills.
Buses and weariness and loss, the nodding soldiers
Are wire, the bare frame building, and a pass
5 To what was hers; her head hides his square patch
And she thinks heavily: My son is grown.
She sees a world: sand roads, tar-paper barracks,
The bubbling asphalt of the runways, sage,
The dunes rising to the interminable ranges,
10 The dim flights moving over clouds like clouds.

The armorers in their patched faded green,
Sweat-stiffened, banded with brass cartridges,
Walk to the line; their Fortresses, all tail,
Stand wrong and flimsy on their skinny legs,
And the crews climb to them clumsily as bears.   15
The head withdraws into its hatch (a boy's),
The engines rise to their blind laboring roar,
And the green, made beasts run home to air.
Now in each aspect death is pure.
(At twilight they wink over men like stars   20
And hour by hour, through the night, some see
The great lights floating in—from Mars, from Mars.)
How emptily the watchers see them gone.

They go, there is silence; the woman and her son
Stand in the forest of the shadows, and the light   25
Washes them like water. In the long-sunken city
Of evening, the sunlight stills like sleep
The faint wonder of the drowned; in the evening,
In the last dreaming light, so fresh, so old,
The soldiers pass like beasts, unquestioning,   30
And the watcher for an instant understands
What there is then no need to understand;
But she wakes from her knowledge, and her stare,
A shadow now, moves emptily among
The shadows learning in their shadowy fields   35
The empty missions.
                    Remembering,
She hears the bomber calling, *Little Friend!*
To the fighter hanging in the hostile sky,
And sees the ragged flame eat, rib by rib,   40
Along the metal of the wing into her heart:
The lives stream out, blossom, and float steadily
To the flames of the earth, the flames
That burn like stars above the lands of men.

She saves from the twilight that takes everything   45
A squadron shipping, in its last parade—
Its dogs run by it, barking at the band—
A gunner walking to his barracks, half-asleep,
Starting at something, stumbling (above, invisible,
The crews in the steady winter of the sky   50
Tremble in their wired fur); and feels for them

The love of life for life. The hopeful cells
Heavy with someone else's death, cold carriers
Of someone else's victory, grope past their lives
55   Into her own bewilderment: The years meant *this?*

But for them the bombers answer everything.

Robert Lowell   1917–

After the Surprising Conversions

September twenty-second, Sir: today
I answer. In the latter part of May,
Hard on our Lord's Ascension, it began
To be more sensible. A gentleman
5   Of more than common understanding, strict
In morals, pious in behavior, kicked
Against our goad. A man of some renown,
An useful, honored person in the town,
He came of melancholy parents; prone
10   To secret spells, for years they kept alone—
His uncle, I believe, was killed of it:
Good people, but of too much or little wit.
I preached one Sabbath on a text from Kings;
He showed concernment for his soul. Some things
15   In his experience were hopeful. He
Would sit and watch the wind knocking a tree
And praise this countryside our Lord has made.
Once when a poor man's heifer died, he laid
A shilling on the doorsill; though a thirst
20   For loving shook him like a snake, he durst
Not entertain much hope of his estate

Surprising Conversions This poem is based on a letter written by Jonathan Edwards (1703–1758), American theologian and preacher, to a clergyman who had asked about the religious revival, marked by many "conversions," which Edwards had inspired in western Massachusetts. The letter is dated May 30, 1735, and is followed by a note telling of the suicide of Edwards' uncle Hawley (the "man" of 1.7), who was depressed by one of Edwards' sermons. In a later account of the reason for these conversions, Edwards writes that "it began to be very sensible that the spirit of God was gradually withdrawing from us." Lines 42–43 are taken from this later account.

In heaven. Once we saw him sitting late
Behind his attic window by a light
That guttered on his Bible; through that night
He meditated terror, and he seemed 25
Beyond advice or reason, for he dreamed
That he was called to trumpet Judgment Day
To Concord. In the latter part of May
He cut his throat. And though the coroner
Judged him delirious, soon a noisome stir 30
Palsied our village. At Jehovah's nod
Satan seemed more let loose amongst us: God
Abandoned us to Satan, and he pressed
Us hard, until we thought we could not rest
Till we had done with life. Content was gone. 35
All the good work was quashed. We were undone.
The breath of God had carried out a planned
And sensible withdrawal from this land;
The multitude, once unconcerned with doubt,
Once neither callous, curious nor devout, 40
Jumped at broad noon, as though some peddler groaned
At it in its familiar twang: "My friend,
Cut your own throat. Cut your own throat. Now! Now!"
September twenty-second, Sir, the bough
Cracks with the unpicked apples, and at dawn 45
The small-mouth bass breaks water, gorged with spawn.

Richard Wilbur 1921–

Still, Citizen Sparrow

Still, citizen sparrow, this vulture which you call
Unnatural, let him but lumber again to air
Over the rotten office, let him bear
The carrion ballast up, and at the tall

Tip of the sky lie cruising. Then you'll see 5
That no more beautiful bird is in heaven's height,
No wider more placid wings, no watchfuller flight;
He shoulders nature there, the frightfully free,

The naked-headed one. Pardon him, you
10 Who dart in the orchard aisles, for it is he
Devours death, mocks mutability,
Has heart to make an end, keeps nature new.

Thinking of Noah, childheart, try to forget
How for so many bedlam hours his saw
15 Soured the song of birds with its wheezy gnaw,
And the slam of his hammer all the day beset

The people's ears. Forget that he could bear
To see the towns like coral under the keel,
And the fields so dismal deep. Try rather to feel
20 How high and weary it was, on the waters where

He rocked his only world, and everyone's.
Forgive the hero, you who would have died
Gladly with all you knew; he rode that tide
To Ararat; all men are Noah's sons.

Museum Piece

The good gray guardians of art
Patrol the halls on spongy shoes,
Impartially protective, though
Perhaps suspicious of Toulouse.

5 Here dozes one against the wall,
Disposed upon a funeral chair.
A Degas dancer pirouettes
Upon the parting of his hair.

See how she spins! The grace is there,
10 But strain as well is plain to see.
Degas loved the two together:
Beauty joined to energy.

Edgar Degas purchased once
A fine El Greco, which he kept
15 Against the wall beside his bed
To hang his pants on while he slept.

Philip Larkin 1922–

Church Going

Once I am sure there's nothing going on
I step inside, letting the door thud shut.
Another church: matting, seats, and stone,
And little books; sprawlings of flowers, cut
For Sunday, brownish now; some brass and stuff   5
Up at the holy end; the small neat organ;
And a tense, musty, unignorable silence,
Brewed God knows how long. Hatless, I take off
My cycle-clips in awkward reverence,

Move forward, run my hand around the font.   10
From where I stand, the roof looks almost new—
Cleaned, or restored? Someone would know: I don't.
Mounting the lectern, I peruse a few
Hectoring large-scale verses, and pronounce
'Here endeth' much more loudly than I'd meant.   15
The echoes snigger briefly. Back at the door
I sign the book, donate an Irish sixpence,
Reflect the place was not worth stopping for.

Yet stop I did: in fact I often do,
And always end much at a loss like this,   20
Wondering what to look for; wondering, too,
When churches fall completely out of use
What we shall turn them into, if we shall keep
A few cathedrals chronically on show,
Their parchment, plate and pyx in locked cases,   25
And let the rest rent-free to rain and sheep.
Shall we avoid them as unlucky places?

Or, after dark, will dubious women come
To make their children touch a particular stone;
Pick simples for a cancer; or on some   30
Advised night see walking a dead one?
Power of some sort or other will go on

In games, in riddles, seemingly at random;
But superstition, like belief, must die,
35 And what remains when disbelief has gone?
Grass, weedy pavement, brambles, buttress, sky,

A shape less recognisable each week,
A purpose more obscure. I wonder who
Will be the last, the very last, to seek
40 This place for what it was; one of the crew
That tap and jot and know what rood-lofts were?
Some ruin-bibber, randy for antique,
Or Christmas-addict, counting on a whiff
Of gown-and-bands and organ-pipes and myrrh?
45 Or will he be my representative,

Bored, uninformed, knowing the ghostly silt
Dispersed, yet tending to this cross of ground
Through suburb scrub because it held unspilt
So long and equably what since is found
50 Only in separation—marriage, and birth,
And death, and thoughts of these—for which was built
This special shell? For, though I've no idea
What this accoutred frowsty barn is worth,
It pleases me to stand in silence here;

55 A serious house on serious earth it is,
In whose blent air all our compulsions meet,
Are recognised, and robed as destinies.
And that much never can be obsolete,
Since someone will forever be surprising
60 A hunger in himself to be more serious,
And gravitating with it to this ground,
Which, he once heard, was proper to grow wise in,
If only that so many dead lie round.

Thom Gunn 1929–

The Unsettled Motorcyclist's Vision of His Death

Across the open countryside,
Into the walls of rain I ride.
It beats my cheek, drenches my knees,
But I am being what I please.

The firm heath stops, and marsh begins. 5
Now we're at war: whichever wins
My human will cannot submit
To nature, though brought out of it.
The wheels sink deep; the clear sound blurs:
Still, bent on the handle-bars, 10
I urge my chosen instrument
Against the mere embodiment.
The front wheel wedges fast between
Two shrubs of glazed insensate green
—Gigantic order in the rim 15
Of each flat leaf. Black eddies brim
Around my heel which, pressing deep,
Accelerates the waiting sleep.

I used to live in sound, and lacked
Knowledge of still or creeping fact. 20
But now the stagnant strips my breath,
Leant on my cheek in weight of death.
Though so oppressed I find I may
Through substance move. I pick my way,
Where death and life in one combine, 25
Through the dark earth that is not mine,
Crowded with fragments, blunt, unformed;
While past my ear where noises swarmed
The marsh plant's white extremities,
Slow without patience, spread at ease 30
Invulnerable and soft, extend
With a quiet grasping toward their end.

And though the tubers, once I rot,
Reflesh my bones with pallid knot,
35   Till swelling out my clothes they feign
This dummy is a man again,
It is as servants they insist,
Without volition that they twist;
And habit does not leave them tired,
40   By men laboriously acquired.
Cell after cell the plants convert
My special richness in the dirt:
All that they get, they get by chance.

And multiply in ignorance.

Modes of Pleasure

New face, strange face, for my unrest.
I hunt your look, and lust marks time
Dark in his doubtful uniform,
Preparing once more for the test.

5   You do not know you are observed:
Apart, contained, you wait on chance,
Or seem to, till your callous glance
Meets mine, as callous and reserved.

And as it does we recognize
10   That sharing an anticipation
Amounts to a collaboration—
A warm game for a warmer prize.

Yet when I've had you once or twice
I may not want you any more:
15   A single night is plenty for
Every magnanimous device.

Why should that matter? Why pretend
Love must accompany erection?
This is a momentary affection,
20   A curiosity bound to end,

Which as good-humored muscle may
Against the muscle try its strength

—Exhausted into sleep at length—
And will not last long into day.

Sylvia Plath 1932–1963

Daddy

You do not do, you do not do
Any more, black shoe
In which I have lived like a foot
For thirty years, poor and white,
Barely daring to breathe or Achoo.   5

Daddy, I have had to kill you.
You died before I had time—
Marble-heavy, a bag full of God,
Ghastly statue with one grey toe
Big as a Frisco seal   10

And a head in the freakish Atlantic
Where it pours bean green over blue
In the waters off beautiful Nauset.
I used to pray to recover you.
Ach, du.   15

In the German tongue, in the Polish town
Scraped flat by the roller
Of wars, wars, wars.
But the name of the town is common.
My Polack friend   20

Says there are a dozen or two.
So I never could tell where you
Put your foot, your root,
I never could talk to you.
The tongue stuck in my jaw.   25

15, 27. *Ach, du* . . . *Ich* Oh, you; I.

It stuck in a barb wire snare.
Ich, ich, ich, ich,
I could hardly speak.
I thought every German was you.
30   And the language obscene

An engine, an engine
Chuffing me off like a Jew.
A Jew to Dachau, Auschwitz, Belsen.
I began to talk like a Jew.
35   I think I may well be a Jew.

The snows of the Tyrol, the clear beer of Vienna
Are not very pure or true.
With my gypsy ancestress and my weird luck
And my Taroc pack and my Taroc pack
40   I may be a bit of a Jew.

I have always been scared of *you*,
With your Luftwaffe, your gobbledygoo.
And your neat moustache
And your Aryan eye, bright blue.
45   Panzer-man, panzer-man, O You—

Not God but a swastika
So black no sky could squeak through.
Every woman adores a Fascist,
The boot in the face, the brute
50   Brute heart of a brute like you.

You stand at the blackboard, daddy,
In the picture I have of you,
A cleft in your chin instead of your foot
But no less a devil for that, no not
55   Any less the black man who

Bit my pretty red heart in two.
I was ten when they buried you.
At twenty I tried to die
And get back, back, back to you.
60   I thought even the bones would do.

39. *Taroc* i.e., the Tarot or playing-card deck, often used in fortune-telling.   45. *Panzer-man* i.e., belonging to German mechanized troop⁻ in World War II.

But they pulled me out of the sack,
And they stuck me together with glue.
And then I knew what to do.
I made a model of you,
A man in black with a Meinkampf look   65

And a love of the rack and the screw.
And I said I do, I do.
So daddy, I'm finally through.
The black telephone's off at the root,
The voices just can't worm through.   70

If I've killed one man, I've killed two—
The vampire who said he was you
And drank my blood for a year,
Seven years, if you want to know.
Daddy, you can lie back now.   75

There's a stake in your fat black heart
And the villagers never liked you.
They are dancing and stamping on you.
They always *knew* it was you.
Daddy, daddy, you bastard, I'm through.   80

Biographical Notes

Edward Albee (1928–   ) is an American playwright whose theatrical career began with the off-Broadway productions of *The Zoo Story* (1958), *The Sandbox*, and *The Death of Bessie Smith* (1959), and *The American Dream* (1960). *Who's Afraid of Virginia Woolf* (1961–62), his first full length play, was followed by *Tiny Alice* (1964), *Ballad of the Sad Café* (1965), *A Delicate Balance* (1966), *Everything in the Garden* (1967).

Matthew Arnold (1822–1888), son of the famous Headmaster of Rugby, Thomas Arnold, was first a poet but later abandoned poetry to become a lecturer, a critic of life and literature, and an inspector of schools. His *Collected Poems* appeared in 1869, *Essays in Criticism* in 1865 and 1888, *Culture and Anarchy* in 1869, *Friendship's Garland* in 1879, and *Mixed Essays* in 1879.

W. H. Auden (1907–   ) was, during the 1930's, one of a group of left-wing British poets that included Stephen Spender and Louis MacNeice. Since World War II Auden has concentrated on literary and philosophical themes rather than on political topics. His *Collected Poetry* appeared in 1945. Other works include *The Age of Anxiety* (1947), which won a Pulitzer Prize, *Nones* (1951), *The Shield of Achilles* (1955), *Homage to Clio* (1960), and *The Dyer's Hand* (1962). He has taught at a number of American colleges and is now an American citizen.

William Blake (1757–1827), poet and artist, illustrated his poems with his own engravings. His works include *Songs of Innocence* (1789), *Songs of Experience* (1794), *The Marriage of Heaven and Hell* (1790), *The Gates of Paradise* (1793), and *Visions of the Daughters of Albion* (1793).

Robert Browning (1812–1889), English poet, whose work covers a wide range from lyric poetry to drama, is best known today for his dramatic monologues, published under the titles *Men and Women* (1855), *Dramatis Personae* (1864), and *Dramatic Idyls* (1879–1880). In 1846 he eloped with Elizabeth Barrett and went to Italy to live. After her death in 1861 he returned to England and began work on his long poem, *The Ring and the Book* (1868–1869).

Albert Camus (1913–1960), a French colonial born in Algiers, was a journalist and social critic before he turned to the writing of fiction, essays, and drama.

In 1940 he left Algeria for France and became active in the resistance movement. Among his works are the novels, *The Stranger* (1942), *The Plague* (1947), and *The Fall* (1956); existential essays, *The Myth of Sisyphus* (1942), and *The Rebel* (1951); and a play, *Caligula* (1944). In 1957 he received a Nobel prize for literature.

Anton Chekhov (1860–1904), Russian story writer and playwright, practiced medicine briefly before devoting himself to literature. Among his plays are *The Sea Gull* (1896), *Uncle Vanya* (1900), *The Three Sisters* (1901), and *The Cherry Orchard* (1904). His stories, translated by Constance Garnett, were published as *The Tales of Chekhov* (1916–1923).

Samuel Taylor Coleridge (1772–1834), poet and critic of the Romantic movement, was a friend of Wordsworth and contributed "The Rime of the Ancient Mariner" to *Lyrical Ballads* (1798). Later he turned from poetry to literary criticism and philosophy. His *Biographia Literaria* (1817) is a seminal work in English literary criticism.

Joseph Conrad (1857–1924), was born in the Ukraine of an aristocratic Polish family. Orphaned at an early age, he left Poland to make a career as a seaman. From 1878 to 1894 he was an officer on British merchant ships. His novels include *The Nigger of the Narcissus* (1897), *Lord Jim* (1900), *Nostromo* (1904), and *Victory* (1915).

Emily Dickinson (1830–1886), lived and wrote in Amherst, Massachusetts. The definitive edition of her poems appeared in 1955. She published only anonymously during her lifetime, living as a virtual recluse in the home of her father.

John Donne (1572–1631), metaphysical poet and sermon writer, was born into a family of strong Roman Catholic traditions. After his years at Cambridge, his expedition to Cadiz with Essex in 1596, and his life as secretary to Lord Keeper Egerton, he entered the Anglican Church in 1615, where he rose to the position of Dean of Saint Paul's. His early songs and sonnets, widely known in London literary cliques, were followed by religious poems and powerful sermons.

Michael Drayton (1563–1631), wrote the historical *England's Heroical Epistles* (1597), a long geographical descriptive poem, *Poly-Olbion* (1622), a number of odes, satires, and a sonnet sequence, *Idea's Mirror* (1594).

T. S. Eliot (1888–1965) was born in St. Louis, educated at Harvard, and studied in Paris and Oxford. He settled in England in 1914 and became a British subject in 1927. His most influential poem, *The Wasteland*, was published in 1922, followed by *The Hollow Men* (1925), *Poems: 1909–1925* (1925), and *Poems: 1909–1935* (1936). His criticism includes *The Use of Poetry and the Use of Criticism* (1933), *Essays Ancient and Modern* (1936), *Notes Toward the Definition of Culture* (1948), and *To Criticize the Critic* (1965). His best-known poetic dramas are *Murder in the Cathedral* (1935), *The Family Reunion* (1939), and *The Cocktail Party* (1950).

William Faulkner (1897–1962) lived most of his life in Oxford, Mississippi. After a year at the University of Mississippi, he joined the Royal Canadian Air Force. His novels, set in his imaginary Yoknapatawpha County, include *The Sound and the Fury* (1929), *Light in August* (1932), *Absalom, Ab-*

salom! (1936), and *The Hamlet* (1940). In 1950 he received a Nobel prize for literature.

Robert Frost (1874–1963) was born in San Francisco but spent most of his life in New England as farmer, teacher, and poet. His first volume, *A Boy's Will* (1913), was published in England where he was then living. It was followed by *North of Boston* (1914). Subsequent volumes include *West Running Brook* (1928), *A Further Range* (1936), *A Witness Tree* (1942), *Collected Poems* (1939, 1949), and *In the Clearing* (1962).

Thom Gunn (1929–   ), born and educated in England, came to the United States as a Fulbright scholar and now lives here. He has taught at the University of California. His works include *Fighting Terms* (1954), *The Sense of Movement* (1957), *My Sad Captains and Other Poems* (1961), and *Positives* (1966).

Thomas Hardy (1840–1928), unable to gain recognition as a poet, for years supported himself as architect and prolific novelist. Among his best-known novels are *The Return of the Native* (1878) and *The Mayor of Casterbridge* 1886). After the bitter critical attacks on *Tess of the D'Urbervilles* (1891) and *Jude the Obscure* (1895), he returned to poetry. *The Dynasts,* a long poetic drama of the Napoleonic Wars, was published between 1904 and 1908. *Collected Poems* appeared in 1919 and 1925.

Nathaniel Hawthorne (1804–1864) was born of New England Puritan stock in Salem, Massachusetts. His first publication, *Twice Told Tales* (1837), was followed by the novels, *The Scarlet Letter* (1850), *The House of Seven Gables* (1851), and *The Marble Faun* (1860). Other short fiction includes a second series of *Twice Told Tales* (1842), *Mosses from an Old Manse* (1846), and *The Snow Image and Other Twice Told Tales* (1851).

Ernest Hemingway (1898–1961), novelist and short-story writer, began his career as a reporter and during World War I served with an ambulance unit in France and Italy. After the war he lived in Paris as a correspondent for the Hearst papers. During the Spanish Civil War he went to Spain as a war correspondent. His works include the collections of short stories, *In Our Time* (1925), *Men Without Women* (1927), *The Fifth Column and the First 49 Stories* (1938), and the novels, *The Sun Also Rises* (1926), *A Farewell to Arms* (1929), *For Whom the Bell Tolls* (1940), and *The Old Man and the Sea* (1952), which was awarded a Pulitzer Prize. In 1954 he received a Nobel Prize.

George Herbert (1593–1633), received an M.A. from Cambridge (1616) and was appointed Public Orator (1619). He gave up the political advancement that his family connections would have afforded him to become a parish priest at Bemerton. His poems, collected in one volume, *The Temple* (1633), appeared after his death.

Gerard Manley Hopkins (1844–1889), whose poetry, edited by Robert Bridges, was published posthumously in 1918, became an important influence on modern poets. An Oxford scholar, he was converted to Catholicism and became a Jesuit priest in 1866. At this time he burned all his poems, but later returned to writing religious poetry and experimenting with Anglo-Saxon and medieval verse forms. A second edition of his poetry, edited by

Charles Williams, was published in 1930, and a third edition was edited by W. H. Gardner in 1948. His letters were published in 1935, the *Notebooks and Papers* in 1937.

Henrik Ibsen (1828–1906), Norwegian dramatist, served as director of theaters in Bergen and Oslo. Among his plays are a poetic drama, *Peer Gynt* (1867), *A Doll's House* (1879), *The Wild Duck* (1884), *Hedda Gabler* (1890), and *The Master Builder* (1892).

Henry James (1843–1916) was born in New York City. He traveled frequently with his family in England, Switzerland, France, and Germany. He began his literary career after leaving Harvard Law School in 1862. In 1875 he emigrated to Europe and became a British citizen in 1915. His fiction includes *Daisy Miller* (1879), *The Portrait of a Lady* (1881), *The Princess Cassamassima* (1886), *The Wings of the Dove* (1902), and *The Ambassadors* (1903). His prefaces to his novels have been collected in *The Art of the Novel* (1934). His *Notebooks* (1947) provide additional commentary upon his creative processes.

Randall Jarrell (1914–1965), poet and critic, taught at Kenyon College and the University of South Carolina. He published several volumes of poetry, *Little Friend, Little Friend* (1945), *Seven League Crutches* (1951), and *The Woman at the Washington Zoo* (1960). He also published a volume of criticism, *Poetry and the Age* (1953), and a satiric novel of college life, *Pictures from an Institution* (1954). He won the National Book Award for poetry in 1960 and for fiction in 1962.

James Joyce (1882–1941) was born in Dublin, Ireland, and educated at University College, Dublin. He left Ireland in 1902 and spent most of his life on the continent where he taught languages to support his family. His major works include a collection of short stories, *Dubliners* (1914), *A Portrait of the Artist As a Young Man* (1916), *Ulysses* (1922), and *Finnegan's Wake* (1939).

Franz Kafka (1883–1924), born in Prague, Czechoslovakia, received a doctor's degree in jurisprudence, but supported himself by working in the Government Bureau of Insurance. Among his works translated into English are *The Castle* (1930), *The Great Wall of China* (1933), *The Trial* (1937), *The Metamorphosis* (1937), and *Amerika* (1938).

John Keats (1795–1821), English Romantic poet, is best known for his odes published in the volume *Lamia, Isabella, The Eve of St. Agnes*, and *Other Poems* (1820). His letters contain significant statements of his aesthetic theory. He died in Italy of tuberculosis at the age of twenty-six. Shelley wrote the elegy, "Adonais," in memory of Keats.

Philip Larkin (1922–   ), English poet and novelist, is librarian at the University of Hull, Yorkshire. His novels are *Jill* (1946) and *A Girl in Winter* (1947); his volumes of verse are entitled *The North Ship* (1945), *The Less Deceived* (1955), and *The Whitsun Weddings* (1964).

D. H. Lawrence (1885–1930), English poet, short-story writer, and novelist, was born in Nottinghamshire, England, the son of a coal miner father and a mother who had been a schoolteacher. He lived for a time in Italy, France, Mexico, and the United States. His first published work was *The White Pea-*

cock (1911), followed by *Sons and Lovers* (1913), *The Rainbow* (1915), *Women in Love* (1920), and *Lady Chatterley's Lover* (1928). Other works include *Studies in Classical American Literature* (1923) and *Collected Poems* (1928). A complete edition of his poems was published in 1964.

Robert Lowell (1917–), of a Boston "Brahmin" background, is a graduate of Kenyon College, where he studied with John Crowe Ransom. He has taught at various colleges and universities. His volumes of poetry include *Lord Weary's Castle* (1946), for which he received a Pulitzer Prize, and *Life Studies* (1959). He has written a translation of Racine's *Phèdre*, a collection of poems adapted from several languages, *Imitations* (1961), and a dramatic adaptation of tales of Hawthorne and Melville, *The Old Glory* (1965). *For the Union Dead* was published in 1964 and *Near the Ocean* in 1967.

Archibald MacLeish (1892–), American poet, began his literary career in the 1920's as an expatriate in Paris. He was Librarian of Congress from 1939 to 1944 and was Boylston Professor of Rhetoric at Harvard from 1949 to 1962. He received the Pulitzer Prize for his *Conquistador* (1932). His *Collected Poems, 1917–1952* was followed by *Songs for Eve* (1955), a verse play, *J. B.* (1958), and criticism, *Poetry and Experience* (1960).

Katherine Mansfield (1888–1923), short-story writer and critic, was born in New Zealand. With her husband, John Middleton Murry, she edited a number of literary magazines. Her journals recount aspects of her inner life, her long bout with tuberculosis, and reflections on the creative process. Her short stories include *In a German Pension* (1911), *Bliss* (1920), *The Garden Party* (1922), and *The Dove's Nest* (1923). *Novels and Novelists* (1930) is a selection of her criticism.

Andrew Marvell (1621–1678), lyric and metaphysical poet, was educated at Cambridge, served in the Commonwealth government as assistant to Milton, and in 1659 was elected to Cromwell's Parliament. Though he is best known for his lyric poetry, he also wrote satirical verse.

George Meredith (1828–1909), son of a Portsmouth tailor, was largely self-educated, after one year at a German school. Widely read and a brilliant conversationalist, he turned to journalism and reading for publishers to make a living. His first novel, *The Ordeal of Richard Feverel* (1859), was followed by his sonnet sequence, *Modern Love* (1862), based on the breakup of his marriage to Mary Peacock. During his lifetime his novels, especially *The Egoist* (1879) and *Diana of the Crossways* (1885), won greater recognition than his poetry, published as *Poems and Lyrics in the Joy of Earth* (1883) and *A Reading of Earth* (1888).

John Milton (1608–1674), whose early poems, "L'Allegro" and "Il Penseroso," were written during a tour of Europe that followed his years at Cambridge, became Cromwell's Latin Secretary. During the period of the English civil war he wrote various political tracts, among them the famous defense of freedom of the press, *Areopagitica* (1645). He lost his eyesight in 1652 and retired from public life to write his great epic, *Paradise Lost* (1667), and its sequel, *Paradise Regained* (1671). Other important works include the poetic drama *Samson Agonistes* (1671).

Marianne Moore (1887–   ) was born in Missouri, graduated from Bryn Mawr, taught at an Indian school, worked in the New York Public Library, and edited *The Dial* (1925–1929). Her early poems were published in 1921, her *Collected Poems* in 1951. She is also the author of *Predilections* (1955), a volume of critical essays, a poetic translation of La Fontaine's *Fables* (1954), and a collection of poetry, *Tell Me, Tell Me* (1967).

Vladimir Nabokov (1899–   ) was born in Russia but educated at Trinity College, Cambridge. After writing fiction in Russian for fifteen years, he began to write in English and settled in the United States in 1940. He has been a professor at Cornell University and a regular contributor to many popular magazines such as *The New Yorker*. Among his works in English are *The Real Life of Sebastian Knight* (1941), *Pnin* (1957), *Lolita* (1958), *Pale Fire* (1962), and two collections of short stories, *Nabokov's Dozen* (1958), and *Nabokov's Quartet* (1966).

Flannery O'Connor (1925–1965), born in Georgia, was educated in Georgia schools and the University of Iowa. She received the O. Henry Award (1957) and a Ford Foundation grant in 1959. Her books include the novels, *Wise Blood* (1952) and *The Violent Bear It Away* (1960). Her collection of short stories, *Everything That Rises Must Converge*, was published post-humously in 1965.

Sylvia Plath (1932–1963) was born in Boston of Austrian and German parent-age and was educated at Smith College. While living in England she married the British poet, Ted Hughes. Her volume of poetry, *The Colossus*, was published in 1962. *Ariel* was edited by her husband in 1965. In 1963 she wrote an autobiographical novel, *The Bell Jar*, which was published under the name of Victoria Lucas.

Alexander Pope (1688–1744), neoclassical satirical poet, is distinguished for his skill in the use of the closed or heroic couplet, and for his invective wit. His *Pastorals*, written when he was seventeen, were published in 1709. Other works include *An Essay on Criticism* (1711), *An Essay on Man* (1733), *The Dunciad* (1728), translations of Virgil and Homer, and *Moral Essays* (1721 and 1735), and the *Epistle to Dr. Arbuthnot* (1735).

Katherine Anne Porter (1890–   ), American short-story writer, novelist, and critic, was born in Texas and educated in convent schools in Texas and New Orleans. She has been a visiting lecturer at numerous colleges and universities and has lived and traveled in Mexico, Germany, and France. Her books include *Flowering Judas* (1930), *Noon-Wine* (1937), *Pale Horse, Pale Rider* (1939), critical essays, *The Days Before* (1952), and a novel, *Ship of Fools* (1962).

Ezra Pound (1885–   ) was born and educated in the United States. While living in London (1908–1920) he became a leading literary figure of the avant-garde and closely associated with the Imagists. He moved to Italy in 1924, and during World War II he broadcast criticism of the United States. In 1945, following the war, he was indicted for treason, was found mentally incompetent, and committed to St. Elizabeth's Hospital. In 1958 he was released and returned to Italy. His first poems, *Personae*, were published in 1909; *Hugh Selwyn Mauberley* in 1920; his *Cantos* in 1919; *Selected Poems* in 1957; *The Translations of Ezra Pound* in 1953, and *Literary Essays of Ezra Pound* in 1954.

John Crowe Ransom (1888–   ), poet, critic, and professor at Vanderbilt University, has been a leading figure among the New Critics, and has served as editor of *The Kenyon Review*. His criticism includes *God Without Thunder* (1930), *The World's Body* (1938), and *The New Criticism* (1941). His *Selected Poems* was published in 1945 and revised in 1963.

Edwin Arlington Robinson (1869–1935) was reared in Gardiner, Maine, the "Tilbury Town" of his poems. After two years at Harvard he was forced to take jobs as subway laborer and advertising copy writer to earn a living. His first poems were published in 1896 at his own expense, but subsequently he won recognition for *The Town down the River* (1910) and *The Three Taverns* (1920). He won Pulitzer Prizes in 1922, 1925, and 1927.

Theodore Roethke (1908–1963), American poet, taught in the last years of his life at the University of Washington. *The Waking: Poems, 1933–1953* was the winner of the Pulitzer Prize for poetry in 1953. He received the Bollingen Award for poetry in 1958. A collected volume, *Words for the Wind,* appeared in 1958, and *The Far Field* was published posthumously in 1964.

Delmore Schwartz (1913–1966), American poet and critic, was a teacher of English at Harvard from 1940 to 1947. He is best known for *In Dreams Begin Responsibilities* (1938), which consists of a story, poems, and verse-drama, and for a collection of poems, *Summer Knowledge: New and Selected Poems 1938–1958* (1959). He was an editor of *Partisan Review* and poetry editor of *The New Republic*.

Percy Bysshe Shelley (1792–1822) was an English Romantic poet. After leaving his first wife, Harriet, to elope with Mary Godwin, he moved to Italy. He was drowned at sea off the bay of Lerici in Italy. In addition to odes and shorter lyrics, his longer poetic works include the verse plays, *Prometheus Unbound* (1820) and *The Cenci* (1819).

William Shakespeare (1564–1616) was a playwright, poet, actor, and theater manager in London for most of his working life. In the last decade of the 16th century he wrote primarily history plays and comedies, at least three tragedies, two long narrative poems, and all or most of his sonnets. By 1611, he had written the problem plays, the great tragedies, and the last romances. In twenty years he completed about thirty-six plays.

Sir Philip Sidney (1554–1586), poet and literary critic, was also a soldier, courtier, and diplomat. Sidney is often referred to as the ideal example of the Renaissance man. His works include the sonnet sequence, *Astrophel and Stella* (1591), pastoral prose romance, *Arcadia* (1590), and the *Defence of Poesie* (1595), literary criticism.

Sophocles (495–406 B.C.), one of the three great tragic dramatists of ancient Greece, was born at Colonus, but later became a citizen of Athens. In 468 B.C. he entered the annual drama contest, winning first prize over Aeschylus. He wrote 123 plays, of which only seven are extant—*Oedipus Rex, Oedipus at Colonus, Antigone, Electra, The Trachiniae, Ajax,* and *Philoctetes.*

Edmund Spenser (1552–1599) is known chiefly for his long allegorical epic romance, *The Faerie Queene* (1590–1596). Among his other works are the sonnet sequence, *Amoretti*, a pastoral, *The Shepherd's Calendar* (1579), and two poems, *Prothalamion* and *Epithalamion*. The verse form he used in *The Faerie Queene*, called the Spenserian stanza (rhyming *a, b, a, b, b, c, b, c, c,* with its concluding six foot line), was an important contribution to later English poetry.

John Steinbeck (1902–   ) has written novels, short stories, travel sketches, and essays. Born in Salinas, California, he studied at Stanford University. Before he achieved success as a writer, he worked as ranch hand, laborer, and newspaperman. Among his novels are *Tortilla Flat* (1935), *Of Mice and Men* (1937), *The Grapes of Wrath* (1939), which was awarded a Pulitzer Prize, and *East of Eden* (1952). In 1962 he was awarded a Nobel Prize for literature.

Wallace Stevens (1879–1955) was born in Pennsylvania, educated at Harvard and New York University Law School. He practiced law until 1916 and then worked for the Hartford Accident and Indemnity Company, becoming a vice-president in 1934. His early poems, *Harmonium*, were published in 1923, his *Collected Poems* in 1954. He won the Bollingen Award for poetry in 1949, the Pulitzer Prize and the National Book Award in 1955.

Jonathan Swift (1667–1745), born in Dublin and educated at Trinity College, entered the household of Sir William Temple as secretary in 1689. He defended Temple's position in *The Battle of the Books*, which was published with *A Tale of a Tub* in 1704. He was a friend of Addison, Steele, and Pope, and played a prominent—if ambiguous—role in politics, shifting from Whig to Tory. The *Journal to Stella* records his close friendship with Esther Johnson, whom he tutored in the home of Sir William Temple. He was made Dean of St. Patrick's, Dublin, in 1713. Known largely for his satires, *Gulliver's Travels* (1726), *Drapier's Letters* (1724), *A Modest Proposal* (1729), he also wrote occasional poems. After 1738 he suffered from increasing ill health and loss of his mental powers.

Alfred, Lord Tennyson (1809–1892) was son of an English clergyman. He came under the influence of the early Romantic poets during his Cambridge years. His long poem, *In Memoriam* (1850), is a series of elegies commemorating his friend, Arthur Henry Hallam. In 1850 he succeeded Wordsworth as Poet Laureate. In addition to many volumes of poems he wrote poetic dramas, *Queen Mary* (1875), *Harold* (1876) and *Becket* (1884). His work on Arthurian material, published over a period of years, was collected as *Idylls of the King* (1885).

Dylan Thomas (1914–1953) was born in Wales. He was a newspaper reporter for a time and worked for the B.B.C. during World War II. He gained recognition as a lyric poet in his twenties and grew in popularity until his death while on a lecture tour in the United States. His *Collected Poems* appeared in 1953. A collection of his stories, sketches, and essays, *Quite Early One Morning*, was published in 1954; a group of stories and essays, *A Prospect of the Sea*, in 1955, and a verse play, *Under Milk Wood*, in 1954.

James Thurber (1894–1961), American humorist, cartoonist, and writer, was born in Columbus, Ohio. After working for several newspapers, Thurber joined the staff of *The New Yorker*, to which he contributed numerous satirical drawings and prose sketches. *The Thurber Carnival* and *The Thurber Album* represent his own selection of his best work. His books include *Is Sex Necessary?* (1929), *The Owl in the Attic, and Other Perplexities* (1931), *My Life and Hard Times* (1933), *Let Your Mind Alone* (1937), and a play, *The Male Animal* (1940).

Lionel Trilling (1905–   ) was born in New York City and received his doctorate from Columbia University, where he is a professor of literature. His works include two critical biographies, *Matthew Arnold* (1939) and *E. M. Forster* (1943); a novel, *The Middle of the Journey* (1949); and literary criticism and social commentary in his collections of essays, *The Liberal Imagination* (1950), *The Opposing Self* (1955), and *Beyond Culture* (1965).

Eudora Welty (1909–   ) was born in Jackson, Mississippi. After graduating from the University of Wisconsin, she returned to Mississippi and worked for a time as a newspaper reporter and radio writer. Her collections of short stories include *A Curtain of Green* (1941), *The Wide Net* (1943), *The Golden Apples* (1949), and *The Ponder Heart* (1954). Her stories have been awarded two O. Henry Memorial Awards.

Walt Whitman (1819–1892), American poet, served as Civil War nurse and journalist. Many of his poems appeared in various editions of *Leaves of Grass*. *Drum-taps* (1865) grew out of his Civil War experience. A volume of prose, *Democratic Vistas*, was published in 1871.

Richard Wilbur (1921–   ) teaches at Wesleyan University. He has received two Guggenheim awards, the Prix de Rome (1954), and a Pulitzer Prize (1957). *The Poems of Richard Wilbur* appeared in 1963. He has also translated Molière and edited the poems of Poe.

William Carlos Williams (1883–1963), American poet, practiced medicine in Rutherford, New Jersey, the factory town in which he was born. *Selected Poems* appeared in 1949, *Collected Later Poetry* (1950), and *Collected Poems 1951*). His long epic poem, *Paterson*, won the National Book Award for Poetry in 1950. *Desert Music* appeared in 1954, *Journey to Love* in 1955. He has also written novels, *White Mule* (1937) and *In the Money* (1940), short stories, *Life Along the Passaic* (1938), *Selected Essays* (1954), and an *Autobiography* (1951). He received the Bollingen Award for poetry in 1953.

William Wordsworth (1770–1850) lived for most of his life in the English Lake district of Cumberland where he was born. He attended St. John's College, Cambridge, and in 1791 went to France because of his enthusiasm for the cause of the French Revolution, with which he later became disillusioned. In 1798 he and Coleridge collaborated on *Lyrical Ballads*—most of them written by Wordsworth. The second edition in 1800 contains the famous *Preface*. His long poem, *The Prelude* (1850), is an autobiographical account of the growth of the poet's mind. *The Excursion* appeared in 1814. From 1843 to his death he was Poet Laureate.

Sir Thomas Wyatt (1503–1542) took an M.A. degree at Cambridge and was sent on diplomatic missions to France and Italy. Through his "imitations" (translations) of Petrarch, he is credited with introducing the Italian sonnet into English. He also wrote many lyrics, satires, and epistles. Ninety-seven of his poems appeared in *Tottel's Miscellany* in 1557.

William Butler Yeats (1865–1939), the leading poet of the Irish literary revival and a playwright, was born near Dublin and educated in London and Dublin. He wrote plays for the Irish National Theatre Society (later called The Abbey Theatre). For a number of years he served as a senator of the Irish Free State. His volumes of poetry range from *The Wanderings of Oisin* (1889) to *The Last Poems* (1939). *The Collected Poems of W. B. Yeats* appeared in 1933, 1950, and 1956; *The Collected Plays of W. B. Yeats* were published in 1934 and 1952.

Index by Authors, Titles, and First Lines